PRACTICAL COOKERY

14TH EDITION

FOR LEVEL 2 COMMIS CHEF APPRENTICES AND NVQS

DAVID FOSKETT
PATRICIA PASKINS
NEIL RIPPINGTON
STEVE THORPE

Every effort has been made to trace all copyright holders, but if any have been inadvertently overlooked, the Publishers will be pleased to make the necessary arrangements at the first opportunity.

Although every effort has been made to ensure that website addresses are correct at time of going to press, Hodder Education cannot be held responsible for the content of any website mentioned in this book. It is sometimes possible to find a relocated web page by typing in the address of the home page for a website in the URL window of your browser.

Hachette UK's policy is to use papers that are natural, renewable and recyclable products and made from wood grown in well-managed forests and other controlled sources. The logging and manufacturing processes are expected to conform to the environmental regulations of the country of origin.

Orders: please contact Bookpoint Ltd, 130 Park Drive, Milton Park, Abingdon, Oxon OX14 4SE. Telephone: +44 (0)1235 827827. Fax: +44 (0)1235 400401. Email education@bookpoint.co.uk Lines are open from 9 a.m. to 5 p.m., Monday to Saturday, with a 24-hour message answering service. You can also order through our website: www.hoddereducation.co.uk

ISBN: 9781510461710

ISBN (Low-Priced Edition): 9781510461802

© David Foskett, Patricia Paskins, Neil Rippington and Steve Thorpe 2019

First published 1962
Second edition 1967
Third edition 1972
Fourth edition 1974
Fifth edition 1981
Sixth edition 1987
Seventh edition 1990
Eighth edition 1995
Ninth edition 2000
Tenth edition 2004
Eleventh edition 2008
Twelfth edition 2012
Thirteenth edition published 2015

This edition published in 2019 by
Hodder Education,
An Hachette UK Company
Carmelite House
50 Victoria Embankment
London EC4Y 0DZ

www.hoddereducation.co.uk

Impression number   10 9 8 7 6 5 4 3 2

Year   2023 2022 2021 2020

All rights reserved. Apart from any use permitted under UK copyright law, no part of this publication may be reproduced or transmitted in any form or by any means, electronic or mechanical, including photocopying and recording, or held within any information storage and retrieval system, without permission in writing from the publisher or under licence from the Copyright Licensing Agency Limited. Further details of such licences (for reprographic reproduction) may be obtained from the Copyright Licensing Agency Limited, www.cla.co.uk

Cover photo © Andrew Callaghan Photography Ltd

City & Guilds and the City & Guilds logo are trade marks of The City and Guilds of London Institute.
City & Guilds Logo © City & Guilds 2019

Illustrations by Aptara Inc.

Typeset in India by Aptara Inc.

Printed in India

A catalogue record for this title is available from the British Library.

Contents

How to use this book ... vi

Acknowledgements ... vii

Conversion tables ... viii

1 Culinary knowledge, skills and behaviours — 1

The seasonal calendar of food ... 1
Modern technology in the kitchen ... 1
The importance of *mise-en-place* ... 2
Food safety ... 2
Taste – basic flavour profile ... 3
Common food groups and basic requirements for a balanced diet ... 3
Special diets ... 8
Food allergies and intolerances ... 9
Knives ... 9
Commonly used kitchen equipment for cooking, processing and finishing dishes ... 16
Operational control ... 24
Standard operating procedures and standards of performance: setting brand standards ... 25
Portion control ... 25
Responding to feedback ... 26
Key influences, trends and fashions ... 26

2 Food safety — 29

What is food safety and why does it matter? ... 29
What the law says ... 29
Keeping yourself clean and hygienic to comply with legislation ... 30
Keeping work areas clean and hygienic ... 33
Preparing, cooking and holding food safely ... 34
Storing food safely ... 41
Food safety management systems ... 48

3 People — 54

Basic team roles in the professional kitchen ... 54
Developing your skills ... 60

Practical Cookery 14th edition

4 Business — 63

- General costs for hospitality and catering 63
- The food supply chain 66
- Sourcing and purchasing of food commodities 66
- Food waste management and recycling 67
- Risks and hazards within food preparation areas 70
- Identifying and mitigating risks 71
- Legal requirements for reporting incidents and accidents 76

5 Stocks, soups and sauces — 78

- Stocks 79
- Soups 80
- Sauces 83

6 Eggs — 134

- The structure of eggs 134
- Types of eggs 135
- Purchasing and quality points 135
- Preparing and cooking eggs 136
- Storing eggs 136

7 Rice, pulses and grains — 150

- Rice 150
- Pulses 152
- Grains 154

8 Pasta and noodles — 173

- Pasta 173
- Noodles 177

9 Fish and shellfish — 192

- Fish 192
- Shellfish 204

10 Meat and offal — 255

- Meat 256
- Lamb and mutton 260
- Beef 264
- Veal 269
- Pork 271
- Bacon 274
- Offal and other edible parts of the carcass 275
- Other meat preparations 277

11 Poultry and game — 340

- Poultry 340
- Chicken 341
- Turkey 346
- Duck and geese 348
- Game 348

12 Vegetables and vegetable protein — 387

- Vegetables 388
- Vegetable protein 396

13 Bread and dough products — 472

- Ingredients 472
- Dough 472
- Bread 474
- Finishing and presentation 475
- Allergies 475

14 Basic pastry products — 498

- Ingredients for pastry work 498
- Storage and food safety 504
- Preparation and cooking techniques in pastry work ... 505
- Finishing and presentation 506

15 Cakes, sponges, biscuits and scones — 546

- Cakes 546
- Batters and whisked sponges 548
- Biscuits 550
- Convenience cake, biscuit and sponge mixes ... 550
- Decorating and finishing for presentation ... 551
- Storing cakes, sponges, biscuits and scones ... 551

16 Cold and hot desserts — 573

- Ingredients commonly used in desserts 574
- Egg custard-based desserts 575
- Ice creams and sorbets 576
- Fruit-based and other desserts 579
- Finishing and presentation 579
- Healthy eating and desserts 579

Glossary — 625

Index — 630

Practical Cookery 14th edition

How to use this book

This book has been designed to help you develop the knowledge, understanding and skills you will need as you train to become a professional chef. You may be completing a Level 2 NVQ Diploma in Food Production and Cooking or a Level 2 NVQ Diploma in Professional Cookery; or you may be an apprentice following the Commis Chef apprenticeship standard.

Each chapter includes some underpinning knowledge and theory. If the chapter topic is a food commodity, there is also a list of the recipes on the first page of the chapter. A complete index of recipes can be found at the back of the book.

The Level 2 NVQ qualifications are assessed by a portfolio of evidence completed for each unit throughout the qualification. The main source of evidence will be direct observation of your performance in the work environment by an assessor, but questioning, witness testimonies, simulations and other documentary evidence may also be used to assess some aspects of the course.

If you are an apprentice Commis Chef, you will be working in a kitchen and learning how to carry out the basic functions in every section under the supervision of a more senior chef. Although your assessor will likely record your progress throughout your apprenticeship, you will be assessed at the end of the apprenticeship (when your employer thinks you have developed the skills, knowledge and behaviours set out in the apprenticeship standard) by an End Point Assessment (EPA). The EPA will be include the following assessment methods:
- multiple choice test
- practical observation in the work environment
- culinary challenge observation in a controlled environment
- professional discussion.

The following features in this book may help you throughout your NVQ course or apprenticeship:

Know it features, which incorporate Test yourself questions, summarise and test the knowledge and understanding you will need when preparing for professional discussions or knowledge tests.

Show it features help you to consider how to showcase your practical skills.

Live it features encourage you to reflect on how you have demonstrated professional behaviours.

In the recipes, the main methods of cookery are shown by icons. So if you want to practise shallow frying for example, look for the relevant icon. They look like this:

- Baking
- Boiling
- Stewing
- Deep frying
- Shallow frying
- Grilling
- Poaching
- Roasting
- Steaming
- Braising

Recipes also include the following features:
- **Ingredients lists** are provided for making smaller and larger quantities.
- **Nutritional data** is included for most recipes to help you make informed choices about what to cook and eat.
- **Professional tips** help you to understand the dish and produce it successfully.
- **Healthy eating tips** provide suggestions on how recipes can be adapted to make them healthier.
- **Variation boxes** suggest alternative ingredients, cooking methods or presentation, finishing and serving styles that could be used.

Acknowledgements

Photography

Most of the photos in this book are by Andrew Callaghan of Callaghan Studios. The photography work could not have been completed without the generous help of the authors and their colleagues and students at the University of West London (UWL) and University College Birmingham (UCB). The publishers would particularly like to acknowledge the following for their work.

Gary Farrelly and Ketharanathan Vasanthan organised the cookery at UWL. They were assisted in the kitchen by:

- Josephine Barone
- Khloe Best
- Jonathon Bowers
- Livio Capillera
- James Cher
- Tia-Louise Hudson Halsey
- Freya Massingham
- Violeta Saninta
- Grimaldy Cassidy Dos Santos
- Rachel Shelly
- Amilda Venancio.

Neil Rippington organised the photography at UCB. He was assisted in the kitchen by:

- Richard Taylor
- Mathew Shropshall
- Lewis Walker
- Kristiana Kaudzite
- Smit Patel
- Milton de Sousa
- Michael Harrison-Morgan
- João Narciso
- Howard David W.

The authors and publishers are grateful to everyone involved for their hard work.

We are also very grateful to Watts Farms for providing much of the fruit and vegetables shown in the photographs. Watts Farms is a family-run fresh produce business specialising in the growing, packing and supply of a wide range of seasonal produce from spinach, baby leaf salads, herbs and legumes to fruit, chillies, asparagus, brassicas and specialist interest crops.

Picture credits

Every effort has been made to trace the copyright holders of material reproduced here. The authors and publishers would like to thank the following for permission to reproduce copyright illustrations:

Page 5 Crown copyright; pages 10 & 11 © Russums; page 16 1st, 5th, 7th, 8th, 9th & 11th © Russums, 2nd © Eugen Wais – Fotolia, 4th © Joe Gough – Fotolia, 6th © Coprid – Fotolia, 10th © Rigamondis/Shutterstock.com; page 17 2nd, 4th–6th, 9th & 10th © Russums, 8th © vich – Fotolia, 11th © shutswis – Fotolia; page 18 1st–6th & 8th © Russums, 9th © pioneer – Fotolia; page 19 1st, 6th, 7th, 9th & 10th © Russums, 2nd © Schlierner – Fotolia, 4th © Shawn Hempel/stock.adobe.com; page 20 t © Lincat Ltd, m © chaoss – Fotolia, b © Enodis; page 22 t & m © Enodis, b © RH Hall; page 23 l © Enodis; page 46 © Russums; page 73 © WoGi/stock.adobe.com; page 155 © woyzzeck – Fotolia; page 175 tl © Constantinos – Fotolia, tm © Denisa V – Fotolia, tr © spinetta – Fotolia; pages 261, 262 t, 263 b, 265–6, 270, 272, 273 t, 274 b, 275 t, 276–7 © AHDB; pages 289 b & 359 t © Sarah Bailey/Hodder Education; page 395 © AHDB.

The photos on pages 6 b, 140, 165–8, 191, 197 b, 199, 207, 212, 241, 252, 262 b, 263 t, 271, 298 t, 316 t, 347, 357, 363, 370, 373, 391, 414, 421, 433 t, 438, 452 t, 461, 470, 484 t, 490, 530 b, 536, 581 are © Sam Bailey/Hodder Education.

Except where stated above, photographs are by Andrew Callaghan.

Nutritional analysis

New nutritional analysis for this book was carried out by Annemarie Aburrow (Expert Dietitian – Nutrition & Dietetic Consultancy).

Some of the nutritional analysis was created for earlier editions by Annemarie Aburrow, Jane Krause (JK Health & Nutrition), Joanne Tucker (University of West London), Jenny Arthur, Dr Jenny Poulter, Jane Cliff and Pat Bacon.

Conversion tables

In this book, metric weights and measures are used. All temperatures are given in degrees Celsius.

Weights and measures

Imperial	Approximate metric equivalent
¼ oz	5 g
½ oz	10 g
1 oz	25 g
2 oz	50 g
3 oz	75 g
4 oz	100 g
5 oz	125 g
6 oz	150 g
7 oz	175 g
8 oz	200 g
9 oz	225 g
10 oz	250 g
11 oz	275 g
12 oz	300 g
13 oz	325 g
14 oz	350 g
15 oz	375 g
16 oz	400 g
2 lb	1 kg
¼ pt	125 ml
½ pt	250 ml
¾ pt	375 ml
1 pt	500 ml
1½ pt	750 ml
2 pt (1 qt)	1 litre
2 qt	2 litres
1 gal	4.5 litres
¼ in	0.5 cm
½ in	1 cm
1 in	2 cm
1½ in	4 cm
2 in	5 cm

Imperial	Approximate metric equivalent
2½ in	6 cm
3 in	8 cm
4 in	10 cm
5 in	12 cm
6 in	15 cm
6½ in	16 cm
7 in	18 cm
12 in	30 cm
18 in	45 cm

Spoons and cups

Imperial	Approximate metric equivalent
1 teaspoon (tsp)	5 ml
1 dessertspoon (dsp)	10 ml
1 tablespoon (tbsp)	15 ml
¼ cup	60 ml
⅓ cup	80 ml
½ cup	125 ml
1 cup	250 ml

Oven temperatures

	°C	Gas regulo	°F
slow (cool)	110	¼	225
	130	½	250
	140	1	275
	150	2	300
	160	3	325
moderate	180	4	350
	190	5	375
	200	6	400
hot	220	7	425
	230	8	450
very hot	250	9	475

1 Culinary knowledge, skills and behaviours

There are some basic culinary principles and skills that it is important for all chefs to know about and be able to apply in the professional kitchen. Some of these basic principles are explored in this chapter.

The seasonal calendar of food

Seasonality is about the time of year when a particular food is available and is at its optimum flavour; this is usually around the time when the food is harvested. While many foods are now available all year round because they can be imported from different countries when they are not in season, there is a growing trend towards using more seasonal and locally sourced food and beverage items. Seasonal and local ingredients are generally less expensive and more sustainable than food that has travelled a long way. The quality, taste, freshness and nutritional value are all at their peak, and supplies are more plentiful and cheaper.

Food operators can make cost savings by using regional food. The benefits can include:
- improved menu planning, as suppliers can give information in advance on what they are able to provide
- more reliable products and service, with greater flexibility to respond to customer needs
- increased marketing opportunities through making a feature of using locally sourced food and beverage items, and through special promotions related to local seasons and food and beverage specialities
- support for training of staff from local suppliers.

Using seasonal and local ingredients also addresses customers' increasing awareness of ethical issues, such as:
- ensuring the sustainability of foods consumed
- fair trade
- the acceptability, or otherwise, of genetically modified (GM) foods or irradiated foods
- reducing food packaging and food waste
- reducing the effects of food production and food transportation on the environment.

See Chapters 9–12 for further information on the seasonal calendar for fish, meat, game and vegetables, and how seasonality has an impact on the cost, quality and flavour of these commodities.

Food provenance is also increasingly important to customers. They are now far more interested in where and how food is grown, raised or reared, processed and transported. This has resulted in:
- greater availability of fresh foods (as opposed to processed foods)
- certified foods such as Red Tractor and RSPCA Assured (formerly Freedom Foods), which guarantee food safety, and higher standards of environmental performance and animal welfare.

Modern technology in the kitchen

Technology can bring many benefits to professional kitchens.
- **Mobile app ordering service:** customers use an app to enter an order, which is sent directly to the kitchen, and printed out or displayed on a monitor for the kitchen staff. The app helps improve the speed of service, enabling more people to be served quickly. This automates and improves the management processes.
- **Smart meters to reduce food costs:** food wastage tracking systems provide a way to monitor and track the food waste of a professional kitchen and reduce costs.
- **Vacuum packaging machine:** vacuum packaging helps minimise waste and costs. Purchasing food in bulk cuts food costs and, with a vacuum packaging machine, portion sizes can be packed according to demand and need. This makes work practices more efficient by spreading the workload: food can be prepared and kept in prime condition until needed for service.

- **Programmable cookers:** these can perform a wide variety of cooking processes. They allow chefs to easily program cooking requirements such as times, temperatures and loads, which can be stored and transferred to different ovens. This helps to ensure precise consistent results and saves time. Some also record HACCP information.
- **Thermomix:** this is a food processor with an integrated heating system. It is able to steam, chop, whip, mix, emulsify, blend, knead and cook, replacing the need for multiple appliances. Processes are much quicker to perform and cooking times are reduced, which can help to save energy. The machine also 'washes itself'.
- **Labelling software:** food labels in many kitchens are often written by hand, including data such as product name, ingredients, best before dates and other compliance details. Labelling food by hand is time consuming, prone to error and not always legible. Using software to generate labels can ensure consistency, save time and improve operating efficiency.
- **Kitchen management:** software packages are available to help with kitchen management and can transform working practices (Kitchen CUT – www.kitchencut.com – is an example). Features of this type of software usually include:
  - supplier management
  - allergen tracking
  - nutritional analysis
  - recipe costing and menu planning
  - stock control and wastage tracking
  - sales and profit reporting information and analytics.

The software allows kitchen staff to create recipes, menus and dish standard operating procedures (SOPs) that are linked to suppliers' pricing, so that costs and gross profit margins are provided instantly. Such systems can also be used to procure, receive and manage supplier orders, so that costs, invoices and credit notes are controlled. (See page 25, later in this chapter, for more information on SOPs.)

Social media

Social media can be a useful tool to allow restaurants and other hospitality businesses to promote their food to customers, and engaging with it is an increasingly key factor in ensuring a business's success. Many people use social media as a way to discover new establishments, find recommendations for restaurants and read reviews. Reviews on sites such as Facebook, Twitter and TripAdvisor, and photos of dishes posted on Instagram, can have a significant influence on whether people choose to eat somewhere, with customers more likely to visit those restaurants that have positive reviews. Good reviews act as free word-of-mouth advertising for a business, providing cost savings on expensive advertising such as newspaper adverts, flyers and listings in business directories.

Social media can allow a restaurant to engage directly with its customers – to provide information about its menu and to create interest in its dishes and the dining experience. Posting photos of dishes or videos of chefs at work in the kitchen can give customers a good insight into your brand and what they can expect before they even visit your restaurant.

Social media is also a useful tool for gaining feedback. It provides the opportunity to hear what customers are saying, take feedback on board, and make changes to improve your menu or service. It allows you to react quickly to negative reviews – and hopefully win back unhappy customers.

Training

It is essential that all members of staff fully understand their responsibilities and duties, that they have been trained to carry out their duties and also know the standards of performance that are expected of them. Technology can have an important role to play in the effective and efficient training of staff. For example, many establishments use videos and online training packages to train staff, especially for food safety and health and safety training

The importance of *mise-en-place*

Translated literally from French, *mise-en-place* means 'put in place'. This is general practice for all professional chefs. *Mise-en-place* is simple: it means being organised and prepared in the kitchen.

However, in the professional kitchen, *mise-en-place* is not just about assembling all the ingredients, equipment, plates and serving dishes needed for a particular service. It is also about state of mind. The *mise-en-place* concept means that the chef is able to keep many tasks in mind simultaneously, weighing and assigning each its proper value and priority. This ensures that the chef is prepared and ready for every situation that could logically occur during a service period. Being organised and prepared in the kitchen saves time and money.

Food safety

A knowledge and understanding of food safety and ensuring you demonstrate high standards of personal and kitchen hygiene are essential when working in a professional kitchen. Information on the food safety and conditions for storage, the consequences of poor food safety, the principles of safe handling of food, and maintaining a clean and hygienic kitchen environment is provided in Chapter 2.

See Chapter 4 for guidance on Control of Substances Hazardous to Health (COSHH) Regulations.

Taste – basic flavour profile

We detect the flavour of food through the senses of taste and smell. There are five primary tastes of food:

1 sweet (sweet fruits such as mango and passion fruit, sugar, carrots, coconut)
2 sour (citrus fruits, yoghurt, fermented foods, vinegar)
3 salt (natural salt, sea salt, sea vegetables, seaweed)
4 bitter (coffee, citrus peel, beer, unsweetened cocoa, kale)
5 umami (tomato, mushroom, Parmesan cheese, soy sauce, yeast extract, anchovy).

The sensation of taste is detected by taste buds in the mouth, mostly on the upper surface of the tongue. Different parts of the tongue are particularly sensitive to different primary tastes. Our sensitivity to different primary tastes varies greatly.

The temperature of food affects our sensitivity to its taste: the lower the temperature, the weaker the taste. Maximum taste sensitivity ranges from 22 to 44°C.

Sweet and sour are enhanced at the upper end, salt and bitter at the lower end. At any given temperature, however, we are much more sensitive to bitter substances than we are to sweet, sour or salty ones, by a factor of about 10,000. Synthetic sweeteners are effective at concentrations nearer to bitter substances than to table sugar.

Because the nose shares an airway – the pharynx – with the mouth, we smell and taste our food simultaneously, and what we call the flavour, or the 'taste', of the food is really a combination of these two sensations.

Our sensitivity to the flavour of food in our mouth is greatest when we breathe out with the mouth closed; air from the lungs passes along the back of the mouth on its way to the nose and brings some food vapours with it.

The colour of food is extremely important to our enjoyment of it. People are sensitive to the colour of the food they eat, and will reject food that is not considered to have the accepted colour. The depth of colour in food also affects our sense of taste. We associate strong colours with strong flavours.

Asian cuisine is based on umami-rich ingredients. Chinese cuisine has referenced umami for more than 1,200 years. Umami is found naturally in many foods, both animal and vegetable. It is a combination of proteins, amino acids and nucleotides. When the proteins break down through cooking, fermenting, ageing or ripening, the umami flavours intensify.

It is important when assessing food to remember that taste, smell and colour are closely linked and contribute to the overall assessment of the dish. Training and knowledge are therefore essential if one is to develop a discriminating palate and to acquire the ability to identify individual flavours.

Seasoning

To add flavour and to season try always to use the minimum amount of salt. Instead season using a range of different herbs and spices, to enhance the flavour of dishes. Spices add a range of taste sensations, a pungent aroma, colour and flavour. Like herbs, they bring unique chemical compounds to the food to create sensual qualities.

Common food groups and basic requirements for a balanced diet

Nutrients from food

Healthy eating is about selecting certain foods that provide the nutrients that are needed by the body in different amounts. If people choose foods in the advised proportions, they should obtain all the nutrients they need in the quantities that promote good health.

Nutrients perform different functions in the body. Table 1.1 summarises some of the key nutritional terms you will encounter, plus the current guidance for health.

Why healthy eating is important

Obesity and its related health problems have increased dramatically in recent years. In the UK, for example, an estimated 24 million adults are classed as obese. Worldwide, it is estimated that half a billion adults are obese. There is also concern about the rising numbers of obese children.

Healthy eating is not just about reducing obesity, however. Research suggests that a third of all cancers are caused by poor diet. Diet can also be linked to high blood pressure, heart disease, diabetes, osteoporosis and tooth decay. Eating a balanced nutritious diet can help to protect us from these illnesses.

Increasing numbers of people now eat away from their own homes so those providing the food have a responsibility to be mindful of good nutrition.

Table 1.1 Key nutritional terms and current guidance for health

Nutrient	Recommendations for a healthy diet
Fat is a very concentrated source of energy. The same weight of pure fat has more than twice as much energy as sugar or starch. Fat is present in foods in two main types: saturated fat in foods from animal sources such as butter, cheese, meat and milk; unsaturated fat in foods from plants (e.g. oils, nuts and seeds) and oily fish (e.g. tuna, salmon, mackerel).	Cut down on fat intake, particularly the saturated types (usually from animal sources) that push up blood cholesterol. Switch to foods containing unsaturated fats. For example, use oils instead of butter and incorporate more oily fish, such as salmon, in menu planning.
Carbohydrate may be one of two types: sugars, which occur naturally in certain foods such as fruit and honey (but are added to many manufactured foods, particularly confectionery, cakes and biscuits); and starches, found naturally in satisfying foods such as bread, breakfast cereals, rice, pasta and potatoes.	We should aim for 50 per cent of our energy from starch, preferably unrefined starches, and cut back on sugars.
Fibre is found in plant foods and aids a healthy digestive system. Good sources include all wholegrain cereals, pulses, fruits, vegetables and nuts.	On current estimates we eat around 20 g dietary fibre per day – the healthy goal is around 30 g per day.
Protein is the 'body building' nutrient found in meat, fish, cheese and eggs, but also in vegetable sources such as cereals (e.g. pasta, breakfast cereals, bread), pulses and nuts.	Protein requirements are often overestimated. For example, adults need only between 35 g and 50 g of protein per day. This can be provided by a 100 g portion of chicken plus a carton of yoghurt and 200 g of baked beans.
Vitamins and minerals are needed in minute amounts for many bodily processes. Since the body cannot make these essential micronutrients, they have to be provided by the diet.	Recommended daily amounts for nine vitamins and 11 minerals are given in the government's report on Dietary Reference Values (see www.nutrition.org.uk/nutritionscience/nutrients-food-and-ingredients/nutrient-requirements).
Salt is sodium chloride, which is involved in maintaining the body's water balance. Sodium is a type of mineral; sodium chloride is added to many manufactured foods, and in particularly high amounts in cured and snack foods.	There is now stronger evidence that our salt intakes are too high (estimated at about 8 g per day) and can lead to high blood pressure. The aim should be about 4 g of salt per day.
Energy comes from carbohydrates, fats, protein and alcohol. It is measured in calories, or joules, which are so tiny they are usually expressed in kilocalories (kcals) or kilojoules (kJ).	We need to balance energy intake through food with energy output through activity; this is needed for good health and control of body weight.

Culinary knowledge, skills and behaviours

Food, nutrition and exercise are crucial to our health and well-being. There is no doubt that making the right choices about what we eat and drink, combined with taking regular exercise, can protect against many diseases and poor health. There are also many immediate health and lifestyle benefits to be gained from healthy eating.

A balanced diet and good health

Foods are not 'good' or 'bad' – it is the overall balance of the diet that matters. This means having a variety of foods, basing meals on starchy foods and eating at least five portions of fruit and vegetables a day. The balance to strive for is illustrated in nationally agreed advice, the Eatwell Guide (see image).

The Eatwell Guide focuses on the food groups that provide the basic nutrients. The advice given is that the diet should consist of:

- **more starchy foods** – such as cereals, breads, pasta, potatoes and rice; these provide energy and enable the body to function
- **more fruit and vegetables** – aim for five portions per day; fruit and vegetables provide vitamins and fibre across the diet, as well as antioxidants, which are thought to help prevent some cancers
- **moderate amounts of food from the milk and dairy, and meat, fish and alternative proteins groups** – as a guideline, two to three portions from each group per day; these provide protein and minerals that enable the body to maintain itself
- **very small amounts of foods containing fats and sugars, and drinks containing sugars** – selecting lower-fat options where possible; in addition, foods that are high in salt should be restricted. These foods are linked to heart disease, stroke, high blood pressure and obesity; by reducing our intake, we help to reduce the risk of these diseases.

Information on the portions of different types of foods that make up a healthy diet is given in the Eatwell Guide from the UK government. For more information visit: www.gov.uk/government/publications/the-eatwell-guide.

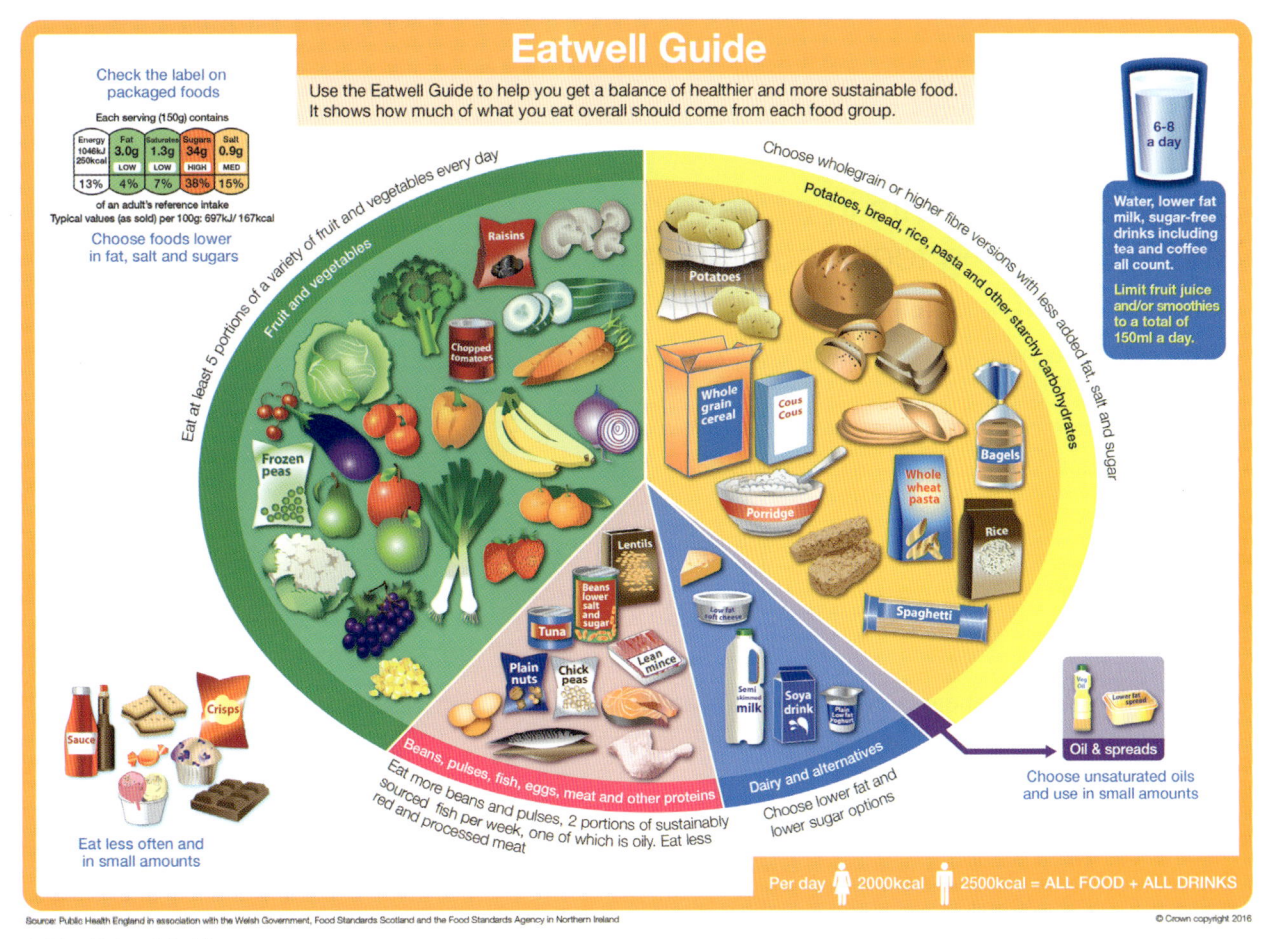

▲ The Eatwell Guide

Media coverage and advice on nutrition can seem confusing, but the most reliable advice remains the same and is outlined in Table 1.2.

Table 1.2 Healthy eating

What it is about	What it is not about	Immediate benefits
The bulk of the diet needs to come from starchy foods, preferably wholemeal bread, brown rice and pasta, and potatoes	Drastically cutting down on food	Better weight control
	Going hungry	Improved self-esteem
	Depriving yourself of treats	Looking and feeling better
Eating more fruit and vegetables	Spending more money on food	Feeling fitter, with more energy
Eating a little less of some food items	Not enjoying food	Enjoying a wide variety of foods
Enjoying good food and making wise food choices	'Brown and boring food'	Not buying expensive 'diet' products
Making small, gradual changes	Just salads	Knowing that changes made today will have long-term benefits
Feeling satisfied and good about food	Making major changes	
	Going on a 'special diet'	

Preparing ingredients in a healthy way, and cooking techniques to maximise nutritional value

Chefs have a vital role in making healthy eating an exciting reality for us all. Customer trends show that many people are looking for healthier eating options, particularly if they eat away from home every day. Interest in healthy eating is one of the major consumer trends to emerge in the past 20 years, and represents an important and lasting commercial opportunity for chefs.

As well as escalating consumer demand, in some sectors, such as school catering, there are strict requirements relating to nutritional standards. Healthy options and nutritional information are now regularly included on contract catering menus.

Chefs can be highly influential in healthy eating. The ingredients and the proportions in which they are used, plus the cooking and service methods chosen, can all influence the nutritional content of a dish or meal. The most effective approach to healthy catering is to make small changes to popular dishes, which may involve:

- small changes in portion sizes – for example, adding a bread roll or jacket potato to a meal; this yields more starch in proportion to fat (effectively diluting the fat)
- subtle modifications to recipes – for example, pizzas could be made with a thicker base, topped with mushrooms and roasted peppers, and with less mozzarella than usual but a sprinkling of Parmesan for flavour; omit the salt and rely on Parmesan, black pepper and chopped oregano to add flavour.

▲ A healthy portion size: baked hake with vegetables and mashed potato

▲ A traditional dish made healthier: Mexican bean pot and salad

Chefs are vital in developing healthier recipes that work. The skill is in deciding how dishes can be modified without losing quality. Some highly traditional dishes are best left alone, while subtle changes can be made to others with no loss of texture, appearance or flavour. See the 'Healthy eating tips' throughout the recipe sections for ideas on how to prepare and cook food in a way that maximises nutritional values and how to present healthier dishes that are attractive to customers.

The key to healthier catering is to:
- **substitute healthier ingredients** – for example, use low-fat yoghurt or crème fraîche instead of cream; use wholemeal breadcrumbs
- **add extra vegetables** – for example, add a garnish to a dish; this could increase fibre, vitamins and minerals
- **reduce added fat** – for example, use olive oil or sunflower oil in place of butter or animal fats; trim fat from meats
- **change cooking method** – grill instead of frying, or steam vegetables instead of boiling, to preserve vitamins
- **reduce sugar** – replace with a natural sweetener or alternative
- **reduce salt** – use herbs or spices in place of salt, to enhance flavour; use low-salt products.

Reading and interpreting food labelling

A number of outlets, such as restaurants, pubs, leisure attractions and cafés, have introduced nutritional information on their menus. This may include the use of recognised symbols that indicate a healthy choice or vegetarian choice, or where a specific item is included in the dish.

When using prepared commodities in the kitchen it is important to read the labels correctly. As well as the use of symbols, it is now common for any items from a list of common allergens to be written in bold.

Many establishments have agreed to:
- display calorie information for most food and drink they serve
- print calorie information on menus
- provide recipe cards or information for each dish on the menu
- ensure the information is clear and easily visible at the point where people choose their food.

Information to consumers

In December 2014, the EU Food Information for Consumers (EU FIC) Regulation came in to force in the UK and changed the way allergen information must be displayed on packaged food, non-packaged food, and in restaurants and other food outlets outside the home.

It is a legal requirement for food providers to give details on request of specific allergens that are present within the food on offer (European Directives 2003/89/EC and 2006/142/EC). The EU identified 14 specific allergens and, where these are used, the food server or someone else in the establishment must be able to provide details. The details may appear on the menu, a separate leaflet, a notice in the restaurant or may be given verbally. Where the food is packaged, the allergen information must be printed or written on the packaging; most food producers do this by highlighting the allergenic ingredients in bold.

As well as providing accurate information to customers about possible allergens in the food being supplied, it is essential to ensure that all staff dealing with food are well informed about possible allergens in food and where they may be on the menu.

Trade descriptions

The Trade Descriptions Act 1968 makes it a criminal offence to mis-describe goods or services. The chef or manager must be very careful when wording menus, and especially when describing menu items to customers. To describe a duck as Aylesbury duck when in fact the duck was imported would be an offence under the Act. The menu must clearly state the conditions covering service charges, cover charges and any extras. Under the Trade Descriptions Act 1968 there are required declarations, as follows.
- You must state if a food ingredient (e.g. soya) is genetically modified; if so, the food or ingredients must be labelled genetically modified. Alternatively, a general notice clearly displayed at the point of food selection may state words to the effect that some of the food contains genetically modified material and that further information is available from staff.
- Staff must be well trained, and know the menu and the ingredients so that they can advise customers effectively and accurately.

> **Health and safety**
>
> Take care when providing nutritional information on menus as there may be a danger of making misleading claims, which could break the law. If unsure, take advice.

Sauces, dressings, toppings and condiments

Where a variety of sauces, dressings and condiments are offered this will give the customer flexibility to make an informed decision with regard to healthier options. For example, offer a choice of butter, crème fraîche or cheese to accompany a baked potato.

Special diets

There will be occasions when caterers are asked to provide dishes or information on dishes to meet specific customer dietary requirements. Reasons for special diets generally fall into three categories:

1. belief or ethical choice (for example, vegetarianism)
2. religious choice
3. medical reasons (for example, food intolerance or allergy).

Vegetarian/vegan and other ethical diets

Many people do not eat meat or fish for a variety of reasons, and some people do not eat any type of dish made with or containing the products of animals. You should be aware of the following diets:

- **semi-vegetarian or demi-vegetarian** – occasionally eat fish and/or meat
- **ovo-vegetarian** – do not eat milk and dairy products
- **lacto-vegetarian** – do not eat eggs
- **vegan** – do not eat any food of animal origin (including honey, dairy products and eggs); acceptable foods are vegetables, fruits, grains, legumes, pasta made without eggs, soya products and other products of plants
- **fruitarian or fructarian** – eat only fruit, nuts and berries.

Religious diets

People who follow the religions listed below have strict dietary requirements.

- **Hindu:** do not eat meat, fish or eggs. Orthodox Hindus are usually strict vegetarians; less strict Hindus may eat lamb, poultry and fish, but definitely not beef as cattle have a deep religious meaning – milk, however, is highly regarded.
- **Jewish:** do not eat pork, pork products, shellfish and eels, meat and milk served at the same time or cooked together. Strict Jews eat only Kosher meat; milk and milk products are usually avoided at lunch and dinner (but are acceptable at breakfast).
- **Muslim:** do not eat pork, meat that is not halal (slaughtered according to custom), and shellfish, and do not drink alcohol (even when used in cooking).
- **Rastafarian:** do not eat processed food, pork, fish without fins (e.g. eels), or drink alcohol, coffee or tea.
- **Sikh:** beef, pork, lamb, poultry and fish may be acceptable to Sikh men, but Sikh women tend to avoid all meat.

Medical diets

For medical reasons, people following the special diets below do not eat the foods listed.

- **Dairy/milk free:** milk, butter, cheese, yoghurt and any prepared foods that include milk products (check label).
- **Diabetics:** dishes that are high in sugar and/or fat (low-calorie sweeteners can be used to sweeten desserts).
- **Gluten-free:** wheat, wholemeal, whole-wheat and wheatmeal flour, wheat bran, rye, barley and oats (some doctors say oats are permitted; the Coeliac Society advises against); and any dishes made with these, including pasta, noodles, semolina, bread, pastries, some yoghurts, some cheese spreads, barley-based drinks, malted drinks, beer, some brands of mustard, and proprietary sauces made with flour (use cornflour to thicken; rice, potato, corn and sago are also acceptable).

Culinary knowledge, skills and behaviours

- **Low-cholesterol and saturated fat:** liver, egg yolks and shellfish (which are high in cholesterol), beef, pork and lamb (which contain saturated fats), butter, cream, groundnut oil and margarine (use oils and margarines labelled high in polyunsaturated fats).
- **Low fat:** any food that contains fat or has been fried or roasted.
- **Low residue:** wholemeal bread, brown rice and pasta, fried and fatty foods.
- **Low salt:** foods and dishes that have had salt added during cooking or processing (including smoked and cured fishes and meats, and hard cheeses) or contain monosodium glutamate.
- **Nut allergy:** nuts, blended cooking oils and margarine (since these may include nut oil; use pure oils or butter) and any dishes containing these (check label).

The five Cs

Listed below are some of the safeguards (known as the 'five Cs') that can be set in place in kitchens when providing dishes to meet specific allergen requirements.

1. **Content:** read the ingredients lists for potential allergens; for example, malt vinegar contains barley and therefore should not be in dishes for coeliac (gluten-free) diets.
2. **Contact:** even small traces of ingredients can cause an issue; wash hands after handling nuts or wear gloves. Segregate foods containing major allergens from other foods. If possible, keep certain preparation areas nut free.
3. **Contamination:** assess work practices to avoid cross-contamination of products. For example, if making dairy-free ice cream, make it first and then store it separately; avoid frying with oils that have been used to cook other foods, such as fish or nut cutlets.
4. **Cleaning:** ensure that equipment is cleaned correctly; even better, use separate equipment. Detergent and hot water followed by thorough rinsing have been shown to be effective in removing allergen traces.
5. **Communication:** this should be into and out of the kitchen, to ensure customers have sufficient confidence in the organisation to meet their requirements. Service staff should be able to pass information to customers about the contents of each dish, as well as explain to the kitchen staff the needs of each customer, ensuring that it is clear and recorded to enable it to be checked and confirmed as each dish is served.

There could also be a sixth C: common sense. If you are not clear about the ingredients or dishes being offered, then say so.

Food allergies and intolerances

For customers who have an intolerance or allergy to certain foods, these foods can be life threatening. Chapter 2 has full information and legal guidelines on allergens, the symptoms of allergic reactions, minimising the risk of allergen reactions and preventing contamination.

Knives

Common knives and their correct use

Knives are essential pieces of equipment in kitchens, and have different styles and characteristics to deal with a wide range of culinary tasks. To achieve the best possible results from knives they must be well cared for, cleaned well after use and kept sharp. All chefs need to be trained in the best, safest and most efficient ways to use a range of knives, as well as cleavers, scissors and secateurs.

The types, availability and styles of professional knives have developed considerably in recent years. Quality knives are a good investment for a chef and should be chosen carefully.

You will need to consider:
- the tasks you are completing – for example, if you work in a fish restaurant a good quality filleting knife would be a good investment
- how the knife feels to hold – they do vary in style, weight and balance
- ease of sharpening
- the cost and what you are prepared to spend
- preferences in style and the materials used to make the knife
- how you are going to clean and store the knife safely.

Practical Cookery 14th edition

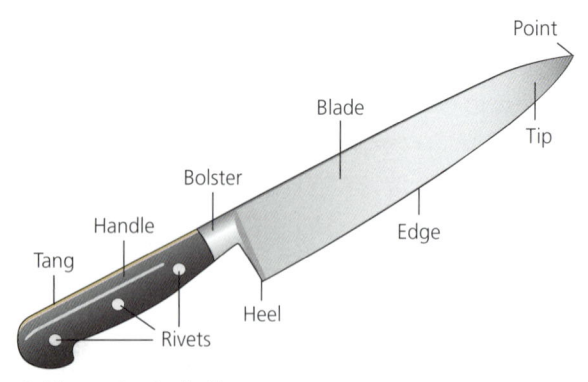

▲ The parts of a knife

Types of knives

The professional chef will use a range of knives in the kitchen and a very wide choice is available. The most commonly used knives are straight bladed or serrated.

Straight-bladed knives

- **Chopping knife (cook's knife or chef's knife):** this will have a broad, rigid blade between 15 and 30 cm long, and a 'heel'. This is probably the chef's most useful knife and is used for a variety of tasks, including chopping, cutting, slicing vegetables, meat, poultry, fish and fruit, as well as tasks such as shredding of salads and vegetables.
- **Paring knife:** a small, multi-purpose knife used mainly for topping, tailing and trimming vegetables, and peeling fruits and vegetables. It may also be used on smaller vegetable cuts and for garnish preparation.
- **Filleting knife:** used for filleting fish. This knife often has a flexible blade, which allows the chef to move the knife easily around the bone structure, and between the flesh and bone of the fish.
- **Boning knife:** a short-bladed knife with a pointed end used for boning meat. The blade is strong and rigid (not flexible) in order to get close to the bones, cut away the meat and manoeuvre between bones safely.
- **Palette knife:** a flat knife with a blunt, rounded end blade. It is used for lifting and turning food, scraping and spreading. It probably has most use in the pastry section but is also used in other kitchen areas.
- **Vegetable and fruit peeler:** these usually have a sharp rounded blade for peeling vegetables and fruit. They come in various sizes.

- **Turning knife:** a small curve-bladed knife used for shaping vegetables in a variety of ways.
- **Carving knife and fork:** a French carving knife has a long, thin blade and is also known as a tranchard. Long strokes with the blade enable neat and efficient carving of meat. A carving fork is two pronged, strong enough to support meats for carving and also for lifting them once carved.

Serrated knives

Serrated knives are used for slicing or for foods that are softer on the inside than the outside, such as crusty bread or tomatoes. A serrated knife allows you to cut neat slices, so is good for slicing bread and pastry items. The serrated blade is used in long strokes with a light sawing action, which does not compress the food. It can also be used to slice foods such as meat or terrines into neat slices. Special palette knives are also available with a serrated edge for slicing cakes, sponges and other pastry goods. Small serrated knives can be used for cutting tomatoes and soft fruits, and a small, pointed serrated table knife may also be a cutlery item when serving steaks.

Serrated knifes are not usually sharpened in the kitchen but are sent to a specialist company for sharpening.

▲ A palette knife

▲ A turning knife

▲ A carving fork

Other cutting equipment

Other tools used for cutting in the kitchen include the following.

- **Butchers' saws:** commonly used in butchery to saw through meat bones; they have serrated blades.
- **Meat cleavers (choppers):** usually used for heavy chopping tasks, such as bones in meat. The heavy, flat blade allows this to be done more easily.

Culinary knowledge, skills and behaviours

- **Secateurs:** similar to scissors, with two long, pointed blades. Some secateurs have the handles set at an angle to the blades to allow for easy and efficient use. Secateurs have a variety of uses including cutting through chicken joints and trimming whole fish.
- **Kitchen scissors:** a wide range of uses including trimming fish, snipping herbs, cutting lengths from filo pastry, cutting paper to line tins and moulds, and opening bags and packets safely.

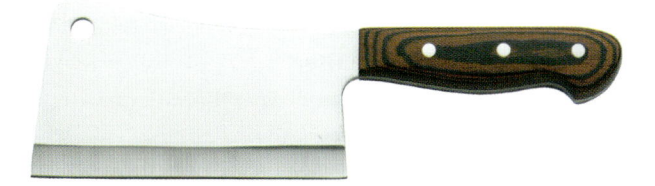

▲ A butcher's saw

▲ A meat cleaver

Materials used for knives

The materials used for knife blades include the following.

- **Carbon steel:** easy to sharpen and get a good edge, but can rust and stain easily.
- **Stainless steel:** now very popular for chefs' knives. It is softer than carbon steel so will need sharpening more frequently but is resistant to rust stains.
- **High-carbon stainless steel:** a higher-grade stainless steel with a high carbon content. These knives resist rust and staining, and maintain their sharp edge for longer than standard stainless steel.
- **Laminated** blades are made with a hard steel and a more brittle steel sandwiched together to combine the advantages of a tougher blade that stays sharp for longer.
- **Ceramic** is the hardest material available for knife blades and will hold a sharp edge for the longest time. However, the blade can chip and may break if the knife is dropped. It also needs specialist sharpening. Ceramic knives tend to be lighter than steel and usually have plastic handles.
- **Folded steel** knives are of Japanese origin, and have a strong and very sharp blade. The blade is made from numerous layers of soft and hard steel with a central layer of very hard steel forming the cutting edge. The layers are heated, folded and hammered to create soft layers that act as shock absorbers for the hard steel, which tends to be brittle. The techniques used are labour intensive so these knives tend to be relatively expensive.

Knife handles were traditionally made from wood with the blade 'tang' – the metal piece at the end of the blade that goes into the handle – secured by rivets. Although wooden-handled knives are still manufactured, plastics have generally replaced wooden handles.

Knives made in one piece, with a stainless steel handle and blade, have become increasingly popular. They are forged with hard molybdenum/vanadium stainless steel, which retains a good edge, and are considered to be more hygienic because of the lack of joints. The handles are often of a hollow construction, which may be filled with sand for weight and balance purposes.

Using knives

Knives are essential tools for all chefs but they can cause serious injury to the user or to someone else if they are used wrongly or carelessly. Always use the correct knife for the task you are about to complete. This will make the work easier and you are more likely to achieve a professional finish. Make sure the knife is undamaged, sharpened, and that the blade and handle are completely clean and grease free; this will help to avoid accidents. Quality knives that are looked after and treated with care will give good service and will be less likely to cause injury.

Most chefs have their own set of knives that they will clean, sharpen and replace as necessary. However, where knives are provided for you, it is essential to look after them as required by the employer and report any damaged knives to them immediately.

All knives can potentially be dangerous if not used properly. If wrongly used, serious injury can be the result, as well as more minor injuries. By following a few simple rules and treating knives with respect, injuries and accidental cuts should be kept to a minimum. Use knives correctly at all times and encourage others around you to do the same.

Any accidents/injuries that do occur when using knives must be reported to the supervisor, senior chef or first-aid person, then properly recorded according to the establishment's operational procedure. This means that there is a record of all accidents and incidents, and when they happened, which is a legal requirement for all workplaces.

Holding a knife

Generally, you should grasp a knife with your fingers around the handle (thumb and index fingers on opposite sides) and well clear of the blade edge. The exact way that you hold the knife will vary depending on the size and design of the knife and the task being carried out. Grasp the knife firmly to give full control. Make sure that the fingers and thumb of the hand not holding the knife are well tucked in, away from the blade edge, to avoid cutting them.

The cutting surface

Most of the cutting and chopping you do will be on a suitable chopping board placed on a working surface. First, make sure that the work surface is free from items other than those you actually need for the task, and that it is thoroughly cleaned and sanitised.

Select the correct board for the task you are completing, and make sure it is clean and disinfected/sanitised too. This will help to avoid cross-contamination from bacteria, physical items or chemicals and allergens (see the information on colour-coded chopping boards on page 46). Make sure the board is firmly secured before starting to cut or chop. This is important because, if the board moves as you use it, you will lose full control of the knife and injury can result. The board can be secured by placing non-slip rubber matting between the board and surface, or using damp kitchen paper/a damp cloth to do the same thing.

Safety with knives

- When carrying a knife in the kitchen hold it down by the side of your body, with the blade pointing down and backwards.
- Never run holding a knife, and take care not to trip or slip.
- When handing a knife to someone else, offer them the handle while you hold the top (blunt edge) of the blade.
- Keep the sharp edge of the blade away from you when cleaning or drying knives, and do not run your fingers along the blade edge.
- Do not have more than one knife at a time on the chopping board. When not actually using the knife, place it alongside the board with the blade edge facing inwards.
- Never carry knives around on top of a chopping board; they could slide off and cause injury.
- Do not allow knives to overhang the edge of the work surface; they could be knocked off or fall and cause injury. Never try to catch a falling knife – step back and wait until it reaches the floor.
- Never leave a knife with the blade pointing upwards. You or someone else could put a hand down on the blade. (Many knives are now designed so that it is impossible for them to be placed 'blade upwards'.)
- Keep the knife handle clean, grease free and dry. If the handle is wet or greasy it can slip in use and could cause cuts to the user.
- Keep knives visible – do not leave them under vegetable peelings, packaging or a cloth.
- Store knives carefully, preferably in a box or carrying case with compartments to keep the knives separate and easy to find. Do not place knives loosely into a drawer or locker because you or someone else could grasp the blade by accident.
- Any knives that have become damaged, badly worn or dangerous in any way should be removed from use immediately to avoid injury. Damaged workplace-owned knives must be removed from use and reported to a head chef or supervisor.

Sharpening knives

Sharp knives are safer than blunt knives, provided that they are handled with care. This is because a sharp blade will cut cleanly and efficiently through the food without the need for excessive pressure. A blunt knife is less easy to control. It will need more pressure and force, and is likely to slip sideways, possibly causing injury as well as badly prepared food.

Knives need to be kept sharp by sharpening them frequently with a steel, whetstone or other sharpening tool. Take time to learn how to do this properly and safely.

Steels are used for sharpening knives. The metal shaft may be circular or oval; diamond steels embedded with abrasive diamond particles are considered to be the easiest and best to use. Steels usually have a guard to protect the hands and a handle similar to a knife handle. To sharpen a knife, run the knife at an angle (usually 45 degrees) along the steel edge.

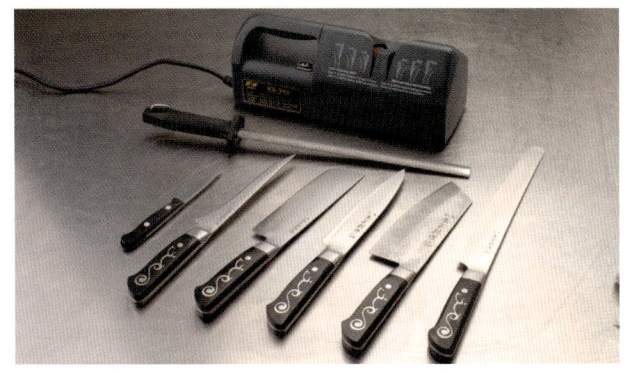

▲ A selection of knives, a steel and an electric sharpener

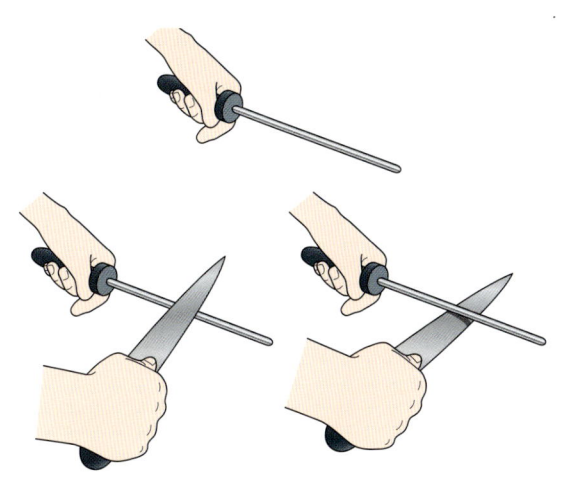

▲ Sharpening a knife with a steel

Once a blade becomes really blunt it may need to be 'reground' by a specialist. An electric or manually operated grinding wheel is used to replace the lost 'edge' on the knife blade. Arrangements can be made for mobile units to visit your premises to regrind knives, or they can be sent away to be reground.

Cleaning knives

Taking care to clean knives well will avoid cross-contamination and make them safer to use (greasy knife handles can cause them to slip and cause injury). Good care and cleaning tends to make knives last for longer.

- Clean knives in hot water with detergent, but keep hold of them and take care not to run fingers along the edge of the blade. Remember to clean the handle too.
- Do not leave knives in washing-up water where they are not visible – the blade could be grasped, resulting in cuts to the hand.
- Rinse and dry thoroughly, and store in an appropriate safe place.
- Generally it is not recommended to clean knives in a dishwasher (the blade edge can be damaged).

Food safety and knives

A knife can very easily transfer harmful bacteria from one place to another or from one food to another, making it a vehicle of contamination. It is also very important to remember that an unwashed knife could cause allergen contamination. For example, if a knife is used to chop nuts, then – without thorough cleaning – is used to slice cooked chicken, the chicken will have traces of nuts, which could cause a severe allergic reaction in someone with a nut allergy.

- Always make sure that knives and the cutting surface (such as chopping boards) are clean and sanitised before use, to avoid possible cross-contamination.
- Wash and dry knives thoroughly between use on different food types to avoid cross-contamination. Some kitchens have knives with colour-coded handles (along with chopping boards and other equipment) to use on foods for allergy sufferers. The equipment intended for use in this way is usually purple. This separate equipment will help to avoid cross-contamination with allergens, which could make an allergy sufferer seriously ill, but also remember that these items need to be cleaned and disinfected.
- Do not use the same cloth to clean knives between tasks when you are preparing raw, high-risk or allergen-related foods.
- When knives have been used on raw meat and poultry, make sure the knife is cleaned and disinfected before using on other tasks. Detergents used in cleaning will remove the grease but disinfectants or very high temperatures are needed to kill bacteria.
- When cleaning knives it is important to clean both the handle and blade well. A dirty handle could contaminate the hands.
- When you have finished working with knives, clean and dry them thoroughly before storing them safely. Bacteria will multiply on wet or dirty knives.

The knife is probably the most important utensil for a chef in the kitchen as it is essential for virtually all food preparation. A good sharp knife will help get the job done more effectively and with greater ease – and is certainly safer and easier to use than a knife with a blunt blade.

Practical Cookery 14th edition

Using knife skills and cutting equipment

▲ Example of boning

▲ Crushing

▲ Carving

▲ Dicing

▲ Chopping, e.g. finely, coarsely, mirepoix

▲ Filleting

▲ Coring

▲ Jointing

Culinary knowledge, skills and behaviours

▲ Marking and scoring

▲ Skinning 2

▲ Peeling

▲ Slicing

▲ Segmenting

▲ Trimming

▲ Shredding

▲ Turning/shaping

▲ Skinning 1

15

Commonly used kitchen equipment for cooking, processing and finishing dishes

Kitchen equipment can be divided into two categories, as follows.

1. **Small equipment and utensils** – for example, spoons, whisks and ladles. This also includes small mechanical equipment such as peelers, mincers and mixers.
2. **Large equipment** – for example, ovens, hobs, grills, steamers and fryers. This also includes large mechanical equipment such as refrigerators and dishwashers.

Types and characteristics of tools and small equipment

Each piece of small equipment has a specific use in the kitchen. Small equipment and utensils are made from a variety of materials, including non-stick coated metal, iron, steel and heatproof plastic. Small equipment must be looked after, cleaned and stored safely and hygienically.

Cooking pans and trays

Equipment	Description	
Baking sheet	Made in various sizes from black wrought steel. They are used for baking and pastry work.	
Baking tin	Sometimes called **cake tins**, they are used for baking cakes, bread and sponges. The mixture is placed in the tin before cooking.	
Gastronome tray	A modular storing and serving system; they come in a variety of sizes that can be moved from refrigerator to oven.	
Griddle pan	Have raised ribs to mark the food. The griddle lines (quadrillage) give the food a chargrilled effect. Modern griddle pans have a non-stick surface.	
Non-stick frying pan	Coated with a material such as Teflon, which prevents the food from sticking to them. They are usually used for shallow frying.	
Roasting tray	Metal trays, usually made of stainless steel. They have deep sides and are used for roasting food such as meat and vegetables.	
Saucepan	Come in various sizes and are made in a variety of materials. Some are made solely of stainless steel; others contain a mixture of metals, such as stainless steel with an aluminium layer and a thick copper coil. Saucepans are used for a variety of cooking methods, including boiling, poaching and stewing.	
Sauté pan	Shallow, straight-sided pans made from stainless steel or a mixture of metals. They are used for shallow frying when a sauce is made after the food is fried. They may also be used for poaching, especially for shallow-poached fish.	
Sauteuse	A type of sauté pan with sloping sides, often used for reducing sauces and poaching.	
Stainless steel tray	Used to store food in the refrigerator.	
Wok	Shallow, rounded frying pans used for stir frying and oriental cookery. They are made from material that can conduct heat quickly. Thick copper-core stainless steel is the most effective.	

Culinary knowledge, skills and behaviours

Tools and small equipment

Equipment	Description
Blow torches	Used, for example, to caramelise sugar on a crème brûlée or flans, or to remove skin from peppers, etc.
Bowls	Come in various sizes and can be stainless steel or plastic. They are used for a variety of purposes, including mixing, blending and storing food.
Can openers	Can be hand held, table top or electric.
Chinois	A very fine mesh conical strainer.
Colanders	Available in a variety of sizes and usually made from stainless steel. They are used for draining liquids.
Conical strainers	Usually stainless steel with large mesh. They are used for general straining and passing of liquids, soups and sauces.
Cooling racks	Made from stainless steel mesh and usually rectangular. Baked items are placed on cooling racks to cool. The mesh allows air to circulate, enabling the items to cool quickly.
Cutlet bats	Made from metal and used to bat out meat, making it thinner.
Flan rings	Used to make flan cases and flans. The flan ring is lined with pastry to make the pastry case, and then filled with the flan mixture or tart filling.
Fish slices	Made from stainless steel. They are used for lifting and sliding food on and off trays to serving dishes.
Food mixers	Labour-saving electrical devices used for many different tasks in the kitchen. They have a range of attachments for different jobs, such as mincing, cutting, blending and mixing.
Food processors	Electrical machines used for many jobs in the kitchen. They usually come with a range of blades for cutting, puréeing, slicing, grating and mixing. They come in a variety of sizes. • A **thermomix** is a type of food processor with an integrated heating system. It is able to steam, chop, whip, mix, emulsify, blend, knead and cook. • A **pacojet** is a piece of equipment that micro-purées deep-frozen foods into ultra-fine textures such as mousses, sauces and sorbets.

→

17

Equipment	Description
Graters	Made from stainless steel. They come in various sizes and are used to shred and grate food such as cheese, the zest of citrus fruits, and vegetables. Graters usually have a choice of grating edges: fine, medium or large.
Gravity-feed slicers	Have very sharp cutting blades and must be operated with a safety guard. They are used for slicing meat so that every slice is the same thickness.
Ladles	Come in various sizes. They are large, scoop-shaped spoons used to add liquids to cooking pots, and to serve sauces and stews.
Liquidisers and blenders	Pieces of mechanical equipment used to blend solid food into liquids. They can be made from glass, plastic or stainless steel.
Mandolins	Specialist pieces of equipment used for slicing vegetables. The blade is made from stainless steel and is adjustable to different widths, for thick or thin slices of food. They are usually used to slice vegetables such as potatoes, courgettes, cucumbers and carrots. The blade is particularly sharp, so you should be very careful when using one. Modern mandolins have an in-built safety guard.
Mashers/ricers	Can be manual or electric, and are used for mashing vegetables.
Measuring jugs	Available in a variety of sizes. They can be made from stainless steel, glass or plastic. They are used for measuring liquids.
Mincers	Standalone or attachments that fit to a mixer. They have a circular cutting blade that forces the food through a plate with different-sized holes depending on the requirements of the size of mince required.
Moulds	Come in many shapes and sizes. They are used for shaping and moulding food for presentation – for example, tartlets, mousses, custards and blancmange. Moulds can be very difficult to clean – you must make sure that all food debris is removed and that the mould is cleaned properly to prevent cross-contamination.
Mushrooms	Usually made of wood and, as their name suggests, shaped like a mushroom. They are used for passing food through a sieve.
Pastry brushes	Used to brush pastry with egg wash or milk, to glaze and to brush excess flour from raw pastry.
Piping bags and nozzles	Used to decorate food for presentation, to fill moulds for cleanliness and accuracy. Piping bags are usually disposable for hygiene purposes. Nozzles are plastic and come in a variety of sizes; plain and star nozzles are the most common.

Culinary knowledge, skills and behaviours

Equipment	Description
Pokers	Used to remove the centre bull's eye from the centre of the stove; also used for marking fish and meat with a criss-cross effect known as quadrillage.
Rolling pins	Used for rolling pastry manually. Today they are usually made from plastic.
Scales	Used to weigh ingredients.
Sieves	Made from plastic with a nylon or metal mesh. They are available in various sizes. They are a type of strainer and can be used to sieve dry ingredients such as flour or for purées.
Skimming spoons	Made from stainless steel and have holes in them. They are used for skimming and draining. Skimming is removing fat and other unwanted substances from the top of liquids, such as stocks and soups.
Spatulas	Flat spoons used for stirring and scraping.
Spiders	Made from stainless steel. They are used for removing food from containers, saucepans, water, etc. They are also used to remove food from a deep fat fryer.
Spoons	Come in a variety of sizes for serving and moving food to and from containers. They are made from stainless steel.
Temperature probes	An essential piece of equipment used in the kitchen to check temperatures of food on arrival in the kitchen from suppliers, and to take the core temperature of food before serving to make sure it has reached a safe temperature.
Trussing needles	Used to truss poultry and game. These are not in common use today as most poultry and game is purchased already tied.
Whisks	Wired and used for whisking and beating air into products – for example, whisking egg whites. Heavier wired whisks are available for whisking sauces; these are known as sauce whisks. A sauce whisk is stronger than a balloon whisk, which is lighter and has an end shaped like a balloon. A balloon whisk is used for whisking ingredients such as egg whites and cream.

Cutting boards

These are used for chopping and slicing food on. The most popular boards are made from polyethylene or plastic. Different boards should be used for different foods, to avoid cross-contamination. See Chapter 2 (page 46) for the UK system of colour coding.

Cutting boards must be stored correctly in a safe and hygienic way, preferably on a rack allowing circulation of air so that after they have been thoroughly cleaned they are allowed to dry and other types of boards or equipment cannot contaminate them. Incorrect storage of boards may lead to cross-contamination and food poisoning.

Types and characteristics of large equipment

Ovens

Conventional ovens come in a wide range of types; they can be fuelled by either gas or electricity. Some have grills built in.

19

Types of oven	Description and cleaning guidelines
Convection (fan-assisted) ovens	Have a built-in fan, which circulates hot air around the oven. This increases the temperature in all parts of the oven, making it more efficient and meaning that cooking temperatures can be lowered. For example, something that would have to be cooked at 200 °C in a conventional oven might cook at 180 °C in a convection oven. Convection ovens are very good for baking and roasting. To clean conventional and convection ovens, allow the equipment to cool before scrubbing it down and wiping it clean. Apply a little oil to the surface of solid tops to keep the surface in good condition.
Combination ovens	Can be used as an oven or steamer or both. Steam is injected into the oven when you are baking and roasting, to increase the moisture content (humidity) of the oven. These ovens are fuelled by gas or electricity. They are fully automatic, having built-in computers that can be pre-programmed to cook food for exactly the right amount of time, and are also able to keep food at the correct temperature. The latest versions monitor the internal temperatures of the food, allowing the chef to achieve the exact core temperature required and to deliver precise cooking textures. A computer system also records how often the oven is used and the temperatures used. Many modern models are self-cleaning, but they need to be checked regularly to make sure the cleaning programme is efficient.

Hobs

Types of hob	Description and cleaning guidelines
Solid hob tops or solid-top hobs	Made of solid metal with a burner. They have a single flat surface, meaning saucepans can be moved around easily during cooking. The middle of the hob has intense heat; the side is not so hot and is used to simmer. Solid-top hobs may be gas or electric. Gas-operated hobs have removable rings in the centre, which can be removed to expose the flame and allow the chef to place the saucepan directly on to the flame. This intense heat allows the food to cook faster or liquid to reduce quickly. To clean solid top hobs, remove all food debris, clean with hot detergent water, dry and oil lightly.
Open range hobs	Stoves where the flame is exposed; the saucepans are placed on metal bars over the flame. It is more difficult to move the saucepans around on this type of hob than on solid-top hobs. To simmer, the flame has to be reduced using a switch that controls each flame. To clean open range hobs, remove the metal bars, wash in hot detergent water and dry. Clean the stove surface with hot detergent water after removing any food debris; a light abrasive may be required for any baked-on food. Dry and replace metal bars.
Induction hobs	Have burners called induction coils. A coil will heat up only when a pan with a metal base (such as a stainless steel pan) is in direct contact with the hob. When the pan is removed from the hob it turns off straight away and cools down quickly. The hob will feel slightly warm after it is turned off. Water boils rapidly on an induction hob and, overall, food cooks more quickly than on other types of hob. Induction hobs are very easy to clean and usually require only a wipe down with mild detergent water.

Culinary knowledge, skills and behaviours

Steamers

All steamers are available in a variety of sizes.

In addition, combination ovens can be used to combine steaming and conventional oven cooking to get the benefits of both.

Cleaning steamers

Steamers have to be cleaned regularly. The inside of the steamer, trays and runners should be washed in hot detergent water, then rinsed and dried. Door controls should occasionally be greased lightly and the door left slightly open to allow air to circulate when the steamer is not in use. If water is held in the steamer then it must be changed regularly. The water chamber should be drained and cleaned before fresh water is added.

Types of steamer	Description
Atmospheric steamer	Operates at normal atmospheric pressure (the same pressure as outside the steamer), creating steam at just above 100 °C. These are often normal saucepans with a metal basket in them.
Pressure steamer	A good way to cook delicate food and foods cooked in a pouch. Some pressure steamers cook at high pressure and some at low pressure. In low-pressure steamers the temperature of the steam is 70 °C and so food is cooked slowly. In high-pressure steamers the temperature of the steam is 120 °C and so food is cooked faster.
Dual steamer	This can switch between low and high pressure. At low pressure they cook in the same way as pressure steamers. At high pressure the food is cooked more quickly than in atmospheric steamers and pressure steamers.

Pans

Types of pan	Description and cleaning guidelines
Boiling pans	Can be powered by gas or electricity, and can be supplied with indirect heat by using a water jacket or by direct heat. For delicate sauces/custards etc. indirect heat would be used. Boiling pans come in sizes from 60 litres up to 540 litres and are ideal for small restaurants for large-volume production cooking. These boiling pans can be supplied with easy-to-use mechanical controls or electronic digital controls for precise cooking control. These days they are tilted for ease of operation and safety. To clean boiling pans, remove all food debris and clean with hot detergent water. Rinse with clean water.
Bratt pans	Heavy-duty commercial cooking appliances that can perform up to eight cooking functions: braising, boiling, steaming, poaching, stewing, roasting, deep fat frying and shallow frying. Because they are so versatile they can replace numerous other pieces of heavy kitchen equipment. Bratt pans are deep, rectangular cooking pots with a counterbalanced pull-down lid. The heat source to the base of the pan is either gas or electric. They all have a tilting feature, operated electrically or by a hand-driven mechanism. Bratt pans are typically used in mass catering establishments such as schools, hospitals, hotels or large staff restaurants for producing large volumes of food. Although bratt pans are generally large appliances, they can save vast amounts of space in comparison to individual appliances that can do limited kitchen tasks. Cleaning is easy in comparison to similar-sized machines. As all the cooking is done in the large pan, you can simply tilt the pan using either a hand crank or electric motor, depending on the model. As bratt pans usually have a central spout, any remaining food is easily removed ready for cleaning. Use hot water and detergent. Rinse thoroughly.

Deep fat fryers

A deep fat fryer has a container with enough oil in it to cover the food. The oil is heated to very hot temperatures. A cool zone, which is a chamber at the base of the cooking pan, collects odd bits of food such as breadcrumbs or batter from fish when it is being fried. Some fryers are computerised; these can be programmed to heat the oil to the correct temperature and cook the food for the right amount of time.

Cleaning a deep fat fryer

When frying, remove all the food debris immediately and keep the oil as clean as possible. You will need to remove the oil to clean the fryer. Make sure the fryer is switched off and the oil is cool before removing it, and put suitable containers in place to drain the oil into. Replace with clean oil.

Bains-marie

Bain-marie means 'water bath'. These are open wells of water for keeping food hot. They are available in many designs, some of which are built into hot cupboards and some into serving controls. They are heated by steam, gas or electricity. Water baths are also used for the gentle cooking of foods in a vacuum bag.

Cleaning bains-marie

Turn off the heat after use. Drain the water away and clean the bain-marie inside and out with hot detergent water. Then rinse and dry it. If it has a drain-off tap, this should be closed.

Grills

Types of grill	Description and cleaning guidelines	
Salamander (also known as an overhead grill)	Heated from above by gas or electricity. Most salamanders have more than one set of heating elements or jets, and it is not always necessary to have them all fully turned on. Salamanders have a tray to catch grease and food debris. This needs to be emptied and cleaned thoroughly with hot detergent water. Soda is very useful for removing grease.	
Under-fired or under-heated grills	The heat source is underneath the grill. Under-fired grills are used to cook food quickly, so they need to reach a high temperature. This type of grill makes criss-cross marks on the food, known as **quadrillage**. When the bars are cool, they should be removed and washed in hot water containing a grease solvent (detergent). They should then be rinsed, dried and replaced in the grill. If fire bricks are used for lining the grill, take care with these as they break easily.	
Contact grills, sometimes called double-sided grills or infragrills	These have two heating surfaces, which face each other. The food is placed on one surface and is then covered by the second. These grills are electrically heated and cook certain foods, such a toast in a toaster, very quickly. Turn off the electricity when cleaning and avoid using water. Lightly scrape clean.	

Culinary knowledge, skills and behaviours

Hot cupboards

Commonly referred to as a hotplate, a hot cupboard is used for heating plates and serving dishes, and for keeping food hot. You must make sure that the temperature in the hot cupboard is kept at around 63–70 °C so that the food is not too hot or too cold. Hot cupboards may be heated by gas, steam or electricity.

Cleaning hot cupboards

Hot cupboards must be emptied and cleaned after each service.

Proving cabinets

Proving cabinets are used for proving yeast products, such as bread dough. They provide a warm and moist atmosphere that allows the yeast to grow, causing the dough to rise (prove). The most suitable temperature for this is 37 °C. Proving cabinets have a drain to collect the excess water as the moist air cools.

Refrigerators and chill rooms

Refrigerators and chill rooms keep food chilled at between 1 and 5 °C. These cold conditions slow down the growth of bacteria and spoilage enzymes that make food 'go off'. They are used to store a whole range of products.

Cleaning refrigerators and chill rooms

Chill rooms and refrigerators must be tidied once a day and cleaned out once a week. Clean with hot water and suitable cleaning chemicals – diluted bicarbonate of soda is most suitable.

▲ Refrigerators and chill rooms

Vacuum packaging machine

These are used in the sous vide process, and for packaging and storing food, to prolong shelf life and prevent discoloration. Sous vide is a combination of vacuum sealing food in plastic pouches, tightly controlled cooking using steam or hot water, and rapid chilling. It is a form of cook/chill food production that can be used by almost any type of catering operation.

▲ Vacuum packing machines

Vacuum pressures are as important as cooking temperatures with regard to weight loss and heat absorption. The highest temperature used in sous vide cooking is 100 °C, and 1,000 millibars is the minimum amount of vacuum pressure used.

As there is no oxidation or discoloration involved, this method is ideal for conserving fruits, such as apples and pears (e.g. pears in red wine, fruits in syrup). When preparing meats in sauces, the meat is pre-blanched then added to the completed sauce.

Cleaning vacuum packaging machines

Vacuum packaging machines must be cleaned carefully, removing all debris, and sanitised. It is advisable to have separate vacuum packing machines for raw and cooked food.

Water baths

Water baths are used to cook delicate foods at lower temperatures for longer periods of time, to improve yields and texture. They are used in conjunction with the sous vide process.

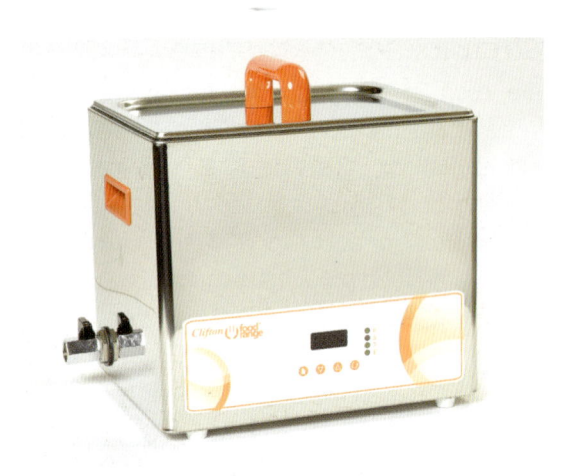

▲ Water baths

Freezers

Freezers are used to store food at between −18 and −20°C. Food in the freezer does not last indefinitely, but the low temperature slows down the growth of bacteria and means that the food will last longer.

Cleaning freezers

Most freezers today are frost-free, which means that they do not need to be defrosted. Tidy the freezer at least once a week. Clean it out every three to six months using a mild cleaning fluid, mild detergent or diluted bicarbonate of soda.

Operational control

Food is expensive and efficient control is essential to help the profitability of the business. The process for food production control can be summarised into the four stages shown in the diagram below.

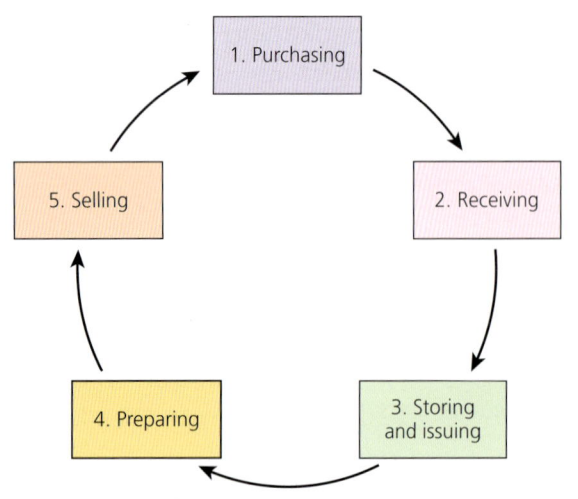

▲ The food production control cycle of daily operation

1. **Purchasing:** amounts are calculated and a specification is written. Orders are placed through a purchase order that is sent to the supplier. The purchase order states the items required, amount, size, weight and other pertinent information.
2. **Receiving:** receiving practices vary in different organisations, but the general principles of control are as follows:
   - Check delivery note to see if the products delivered agree with it.
   - Inspect products/raw materials to determine if they match the purchase order and specification.
   - Tag all meats with date of receipt, weight and other information needed to identify the delivery properly.
   - List all items received on the daily receiving report.
   - Accept the products by signing the delivery note and returning the copy to the driver/delivery person.
   - Store or deliver to the correct place.
3. **Storing and issuing:** raw materials should be stored correctly under the right conditions – temperature, etc.
4. **Preparing:** the ingredients before cooking.
5. **Selling:** to the guest or customer.

Food stocks are affected by a range of factors, including food price fluctuations, customer demand and the influence of the media. Establishments need to devise their own systems and ensure they have an efficient control system. Factors that assist with this include:
- a constant menu, with very little change over time
- standardised recipes and purchasing specifications
- a menu with a limited number of dishes.

These factors can make stock control easier and costing more accurate.

Stock checking and stock control

Checking, reporting and carrying out stock checks, and recording these activities on appropriate documentation are other important aspects of ensuring an efficient stock control system.

Holding too much stock is wasteful of space and ties up money unnecessarily. Accurate holding levels are important; if there is a risk of running out of a commodity or ingredient, this could endanger the levels of sales. A record-keeping system must be developed to monitor the daily operation.

Communication must be given to the person responsible for ordering. Many computer stock control systems automatically order when stocks drop below a certain level.

Documentation for stock control

A large catering operation needs two levels of stock control:
1. a stock card for each item stocked, showing the stock level, purchases and issues
2. a stock summary sheet, which records the total holding at trading period end, along with item cost prices and total value.

Where a formal store system is in use, an accurate note must be kept of all transfers out of the stores to work areas. This transfer note should contain the signatures of both the giver and receiver to ensure full responsibility and to reduce errors. The target for most types of catering operation should be that sufficient stock is held for not less than one week and not more than three weeks' trading.

See Chapter 2 for information on stock rotation, including the 'first in, first out' system.

Standard operating procedures and standards of performance: setting brand standards

Essential to any food service business is the setting and maintenance of standards of performance or standard operating procedures. These are often referred to as 'SOPs' – a term that is often used to refer to the standards themselves, or to the manuals that contain the details of them. Standards of performance set out the standards for all aspects of the operation, including:
- professional service
- preparation for service
- service of food
- stores management
- clearing down duties.

As individual standards are agreed, under each of the aspects above, a 'standards of performance manual' can be created. Many organisations have standards of performance manuals – these can be very bulky and highly detailed, and are designed to ensure brand standards are documented so that dishes and menus can be produced consistently and on time.

Large restaurant brand chains have set standards for each dish on the menu. There will be detailed recipe specifications, including ingredients and quantities, tools and equipment to use, with photographs of each dish. Staff will be trained to follow these standard operating procedures.

Portion control

Recipe specifications will also include set portion control standards. Being consistent with the amount of food served to every customer – or portion control – is essential in order to achieve profit margins. Sound portion control can save a restaurant hundreds, or even thousands, of pounds every year.

The amount of food allowed per portion depends upon the following criteria.

- **The type of customer, restaurant and establishment:** There will be a difference in the size of portions served in different types of restaurant. There is also likely to be a difference in portion size of, for instance, meat being served as part of a three-course menu for £30, and when the same meat dish alone costs £30 on an à la carte menu. Restaurants will focus on a certain customer profile, which will include age range, lifestyle, income and buying patterns.
- **The quality of the food:** Better quality food usually yields a greater number of portions than poor quality food. For example, low quality fatty meat is likely to require so much trimming that it may be difficult to work out the number of portions required per kilo. The time and labour involved in preparing lower quality meat is often a false economy.
- **The buying price of the food:** An experienced chef will ensure that the price paid for the food matches its quality. A fair price, providing good quality, should in turn mean a good yield, resulting in high levels of quality control.

Setting standards of performance, and training staff to achieve the standards, needs to be supported by regular reviews of the extent to which the standards are being met. In addition, there needs to be a continuous process for the review and development of the standards.

Responding to feedback

Feedback from your line manager

See Chapter 3, page 60, for advice on responding to feedback from your line manager.

Feedback from customers

In your work, you will probably need to respond to both positive and negative feedback from customers. Doing so will help you expand sales opportunities in the case of positive feedback, and act on any problems in the case of negative feedback. This will help the restaurant and business to move forward.

Responding to positive feedback

- Reinforce the customer's positive response. Agree with them and let them know they are making a good decision.
- Explain other aspects of the food and menu offer, highlighting the positive benefits.

Responding to negative feedback

When feedback is negative, you need to be careful in handling the response. Avoid being defensive or arguing with the customer. Instead, take the following steps.

- **Take note and recognise:** The first thing when an objection arises is to recognise the customer's concern. Empathise, not sympathise.
- **Understand:** The next stage is to understand the concern and find out what the problem really is.
- **Act:** Once the problem is thoroughly understood, then – and only then – should you directly attempt to sort out the problem.
- **Establish:** The last stage is to establish that the problem or complaint has been answered and dealt with.

Professional development

See Chapter 3 for advice and recommendations on professional development and improving your skills in food preparation, cooking and service.

Key influences, trends and fashions

To create new operations, or renovate existing ones, the business must be aware of current trends and fashions. These can have an impact on the design of the restaurant, the dishes and menus, approaches to production and service, and kitchen equipment and tableware such as crockery, glassware and cutlery.

Trends in the international market have an increasingly rapid impact on food, restaurants and customers. One example is nouvelle cuisine, which in the 1970s initiated a new movement in terms of understanding food and ingredients. From this, other food production styles have since developed, offering new and exciting modes of food delivery, such as eclectic or fusion cuisine (where different culinary styles and traditions are combined) and molecular gastronomy (applying scientific principles to the preparation of food).

Other trends in restaurant design include:
- the opening up of the kitchen to be viewed by the customer as part of the total dining experience; some fine dining restaurants offer the opportunity to sit at the chef's table as part of the meal experience
- minimalistic New York loft-style restaurants
- traditional plates have been replaced by food presentation on wooden boards, glass plates, marble squares and slate, which can offer new and novel service concepts and, for some, a unique and exciting customer experience
- street food and pop-up restaurants have now become popular
- chef's tables, where customers eat in the kitchen and the chefs serve the food as part of the experience
- themed and branded restaurants, which continue to be developed, aiming at providing a consistent product
- more focus on local produce and seasonal food.

Culinary knowledge, skills and behaviours

Know it

- Identify the factors that influence the types of dishes and menus offered by the business.
- Recognise how technology supports the development and production of dishes.
- Recognise the importance of checking food stocks and keeping the storage areas in good order, know the procedures to carry out, and how to deal with identified shortages and food close to expiry date.
- Know how to undertake set-up, preparation and cleaning tasks to standard while working in a challenging, timebound environment.
- Identify correct ingredients and portion sizes for each dish in line with recipe specifications.
- Identify the principles of basic food preparation and cooking; taste; allergens; diet and nutrition.
- Identify commonly used knives and kitchen equipment, and their specific functions.
- Recognise and understand sources and quality points of common food groups and commodities.
- Identify traditional cuts of, and basic preparation methods for, meat, poultry, fish and vegetables.
- Recognise the impact of seasonality on the availability, quality and price of ingredients.

Test yourself

1. The components of food are divided into six main nutrient groups. What are they?
2. How could you increase dietary fibre in recipes with which you are familiar?
3. Which cooking methods do not require the addition of fat?
4. Give three reasons why too much fat should be avoided.
5. List three groups that may request specific foods for dietary requirements.
6. Which food item should not be included in a dish for diabetic customers?
7. How many portions of fruit/vegetables is it recommended that we eat each day? Suggest what these could be; include portion sizes.
8. What is meant by an 'allergy'?
9. Which religious/cultural diets forbid the eating of pork and pork products?
10. Suggest three ways that chefs could make the food that they cook healthier.
11. List a selection of knives that you would need to work using a range of foods.
12. Describe three straight-bladed knives and say what they are used for.
13. What is the best way to clean a knife after use? Why should knives be clean and grease free?
14. Describe the safest way to carry a knife in the kitchen. How should it be stored after use?
15. Why is it essential to clean a knife thoroughly between use on different foods?
16. Why is a sharp knife safer to use than a blunter knife?
17. What action can be taken with knives and other equipment to prevent allergic reactions in customers?
18. What are the main uses for scissors and secateurs in the kitchen?
19. If you were preparing, cutting and filleting a selection of fish, which knives would you need?
20. Suggest three pieces of equipment you could use to sharpen knives.
21. Name the basic elements of taste.
22. How does temperature affect our taste sensitivity?
23. Why is it important for chefs to introduce seasonal food on their menus?
24. What is the meaning of *mise-en-place*, and why is it important?
25. What is meant by the term 'customer profile'?

26. Chain restaurants have brand specifications. How do these support the business?
27. How should a chef respond to customer feedback?
28. How do the latest developments in technology assist the chef in large-scale food production?
29. Suggest ways in which social media can help promote a restaurant.
30. Consider the latest trends in food and restaurants in your area. Suggest other types of restaurants that you think could be attractive in the local market.

Show it

- Contribute to reviewing and refreshing menus in line with business and customer requirements.
- Use available technology in line with business procedures and guidelines to achieve the best result.
- Check food stocks, report on shortages, prioritise food that is close to expiry and keep the storage areas in good order.
- Work methodically to prioritise tasks, ensuring they are completed at the right moment and to the required standard.
- Measure dish ingredients and portion sizes accurately.
- Demonstrate a range of craft preparation and basic cooking skills and techniques to prepare, produce and present dishes and menu items in line with business requirements.
- Use correct knives and knife skills when preparing food, and use the correct equipment when preparing, cooking and presenting food.
- Correctly store and use food commodities when preparing dishes.
- Apply correct preparation and selection methods when using meat, poultry, fish and vegetables in dishes.
- Complete preparation and cooking tasks to a high standard, delivered on time and presented as described within the recipe specification.
- Maintain a clean and hygienic kitchen environment at all times, completing kitchen documentation as required.

Live it

- Show enthusiasm for keeping up to date with business and industry trends.
- Use technology and equipment in line with training.
- Deal promptly with sub-standard ingredients, or those nearing their use-by date.
- Demonstrate the ability to identify when tasks are not going to plan, and have the confidence to request support when needed.
- Pay attention to detail and work consistently to achieve standards.
- Show commitment to developing skills and knowledge; trying out new ingredients and dishes; practising and reflecting on different preparation and cooking techniques.
- Demonstrate care and attention when using knives and equipment.
- Consistently use the correct volume and quality of commodities in each dish, maintaining attention to detail.
- Utilise the correct cuts and preparation methods to produce high quality, technically sound dishes.
- Have an appreciation of ingredients.
- Demonstrate high personal hygiene standards.

2 Food safety

This chapter provides the necessary information to enable you to prepare and cook food safely. It focuses on the key food safety control areas outlined by the Food Standards Agency: cooking, cleaning, chilling and prevention of cross-contamination. It also discusses food safety hazards and the measures necessary to control them, from delivery of food up until the time it is served to the customer, and how to comply with food safety legislation.

What is food safety and why does it matter?

Everyone eating food prepared and cooked for them should reasonably expect to be served safe food that will not cause them illness or harm them in any way. Food poisoning is still a significant problem and it can be serious; food handlers must take great care to prevent it.

Food safety means putting in place all of the measures needed to make sure that food and drinks are suitable, safe and wholesome through all the processes of food provision, from selecting suppliers and delivery of food right through to serving the food to the customer.

Eating 'contaminated' food can result in food poisoning, causing harm, illness and, in some cases, even death.

The number of reported cases of food poisoning in the UK each year remains unacceptably high: between 70,000 and 94,000 cases. However, as a large number of food poisoning cases are never reported, no one really knows the actual number.

The term 'food poisoning' covers a range of illnesses of the digestive system and is usually caused by eating food that has become contaminated with bacteria and/or the toxins they may produce. However, there are a number of ways that food can become contaminated and cause harm, and all must be avoided.

This chapter covers the various ways that food businesses and food handlers can keep food safe to eat and avoid causing food poisoning.

Although the main reason for adopting high standards of food safety is to prevent the possibility of food poisoning, there are many more benefits a food business can gain by keeping food safety standards high. These include:

- being compliant with food safety law
- reducing food wastage and improving efficiency
- return business from satisfied customers
- building a good reputation and receiving fewer complaints.

What the law says

The most important and relevant regulations for all food businesses in the United Kingdom are the Food Hygiene (England/Wales/Scotland/Northern Ireland, as applicable) Regulations 2006. This legislation strengthened the existing Food Safety Act 1990 and related regulations, although most of the requirements remained the same. The laws provide a framework for EU Regulation (EC) No. 852/2004 to be enforced in the UK.

Under this legislation it is a legal requirement for food businesses to have a system based on the seven principles of HACCP. See page 49 later in this chapter for more information on HACCP.

Legislation concerning food safety covers a wide range of topics, including:

- controlling and reducing outbreaks of food poisoning
- registration of premises/vehicles
- content and labelling of food, including allergen information
- preventing the manufacture and sale of injurious food
- food imports
- prevention of contamination of food, equipment and premises
- training of food handlers
- provision of clean water, sanitary facilities and washing facilities.

For further information on food safety legislation, visit www.food.gov.uk.

Keeping yourself clean and hygienic to comply with legislation

All food handlers are a potential source of contamination from food poisoning bacteria and other hazards, so it is very important that they are aware of the importance of high standards of appearance and personal hygiene. This reflects the professionalism of the individual as well as the establishment they work for, giving a positive impression of the food business.

All food handlers need to ensure that they have a daily bath or shower, wear clean clothes every day and use a suitable underarm deodorant.

Protective clothing

Protective clothing is worn to protect food from contamination by food handlers and to protect the wearer from potential hazards such as excessive heat, burns and sharp objects.

It is very important that food handlers wear suitable clothing that protects their body; protective footwear should also be worn.

Clothing worn in the kitchen must be strong to make it 'protective' and withstand the hard wear and frequent washing needed. Clothing will also need to be lightweight, comfortable and absorbent to deal with perspiration caused by a hot kitchen.

Kitchen clothing must be clean and changed at least once a day – more frequently if it becomes soiled – to avoid contamination of food, surfaces and equipment. It should cover any other clothing and only be worn in the kitchen area. Outdoor clothing, and other clothing that has been taken off before wearing whites, should be kept in a suitable locker.

According to the **Personal Protective Equipment (PPE) at Work Regulations 1992**, employees must wear personal protective clothing/equipment suitable for the work they are involved in. For example, chefs need to wear protective chefs' whites, but they may also need gauntlet gloves and eye goggles if cleaning an oven.

Jackets and trousers

Chefs' jackets are usually made of cotton or a cotton mixture, are double-breasted and ideally have long sleeves; these protect the chest and arms from the heat of the stove, and prevent hot foods or liquids from burning or scalding the body.

Trousers worn as part of a chef's uniform are usually made from a lightweight cotton or coated cotton. They should be loose fitting for both safety and comfort.

White coats

It is good practice to keep these available in kitchen areas to wear over standard kitchen clothing when completing other tasks such as unloading a delivery or unpacking raw meat. A white coat should be worn over other clothing when leaving the kitchen to complete another job or go for a break. It is also good practice to offer white coats to anyone visiting the kitchen to cover their own clothing, which could cause contamination.

Aprons

Aprons are designed to provide extra protection to the body from being scalded or burned, and particularly to protect the legs from any liquids that may be spilled. For this reason the apron should be of sufficient length with long ties, allowing it to be wrapped around the body and tied at the front, so that it can be removed quickly if a hot spillage occurs.

Hats

The main purpose of a hat is to prevent loose hairs from falling into food and to absorb perspiration on the forehead. As well as the traditional chef's toque (tall white hat), a variety of designs are now available, some with a net incorporated to contain the hair completely. Lightweight disposable hats are now used by many establishments.

Footwear

This should be strong and in good repair so as to protect and support the feet. As kitchen staff are on their feet for many hours at a time, care of the feet is essential. Suitable, clean, comfortable kitchen footwear and socks need to be worn. Open-toed shoes and trainers are unsuitable as they would not offer protection from spillage of hot liquids, falling knives or heavy items.

Disposable gloves

These are now available for use in most kitchens. They provide a barrier between the food handler and the food, helping to prevent cross-contamination, for example, when handling raw meat or handling high-risk food. Gloves are also useful for the food handler to wear when completing first-aid tasks or to avoid a blue plaster falling off from the hand. It is important that gloves are changed frequently.

Hair

Hair can be a source of food poisoning bacteria, and contamination from this source must be avoided. Hair falling into food can also be a physical hazard. Hair must be washed regularly, long hair tied back, and kept covered with a suitable kitchen hat and/or net to prevent loose hair falling into food. The hair/head should never be scratched, combed or touched in the kitchen as bacteria and loose hair could be transferred to the food or food preparation equipment.

Jewellery, rings and watches

The wearing of jewellery is not acceptable when handling food. Jewellery can trap particles of food and provide a warm, damp environment for bacteria to grow, which can then be transferred to food being prepared. This is particularly relevant to items worn on the hands such as rings and watches. Jewellery or parts of jewellery can also fall into food, especially as some food preparation involves plunging hands into water. (Body piercing items can also be a breeding ground for bacteria, so remove them or cover them completely before handling food.)

Fingernails

These should always be kept clean and short as dirt can easily lodge under the nails and be transferred to food, introducing harmful bacteria. Nails must be kept neatly trimmed and nail varnish must never be worn in food areas.

Hand washing

Hands are frequently in contact with food and numerous other items; if they are not kept clean they can very easily transfer harmful bacteria to food, surfaces and equipment. To avoid contamination from hands they must be washed thoroughly and frequently, particularly after using the toilet, before commencing work, during the handling of food, and especially between different tasks and after dealing with waste. Hand washing must be completed using a basin just for this purpose. It must have hot and cold running water, suitable soap (preferably in a dispenser) and paper towels for drying hands. Some establishments also provide an anti-bacterial gel to apply after hand washing.

To ensure that hands are washed thoroughly follow the steps listed below.

1. Use a basin provided just for hand washing, with hot and cold running water (preferably with a mixer tap).
2. Wet hands under warm running water.
3. Apply liquid soap.
4. Rub hands together thoroughly, remembering to clean between fingers and thumbs.
5. Remember fingertips, nails and wrists.
6. Rinse off under running water.
7. Dry hands on a paper towel and use the paper towel to turn off the tap before disposing of it.

A nail brush may also be used to aid thorough hand washing but always ensure this is clean and disinfected (for example, keep it in a sanitising solution or consider using disposable brushes).

You must wash your hands:
- when you enter the kitchen, before starting work and handling any food
- after a break (especially after using the toilet)
- between different tasks, but especially after handling raw food and before handling ready-to-eat food
- after touching hair, nose or mouth, or using a tissue for sneezing or coughing
- after you apply or change a dressing on a cut or burn
- after cleaning preparation areas, equipment or contaminated surfaces
- after handling kitchen waste, external food packaging, money or flowers.

This will help to reduce the risk of cross-contamination from contact between food and hands.

You can also avoid excessive hand contact with food by using slices, ladles, tongs and spoons where possible, and by using disposable plastic gloves when appropriate (change these frequently, especially between tasks).

Unsafe behaviour

Touching your face, nose or mouth

When working with food it is of great importance not to touch your face, nose or mouth, blow your nose or scratch any skin areas. If you do need to do any of these things, wash your hands very thoroughly afterwards.

The nose should not be touched when food is being handled. If a handkerchief/tissue is used, the hands should be washed thoroughly afterwards. The nose is an area where there can be vast numbers of harmful bacteria; it is therefore very important not to sneeze on food, other people, working surfaces or equipment. If a sneeze or cough is unavoidable, turn away and sneeze into the shoulder area.

The mouth also harbours large numbers of bacteria, therefore the mouth or lips should not be touched when working with food.

Ears too are a source of bacteria and should not be touched when handling food.

Chewing gum

Chewing gum is not acceptable when preparing food. It produces more saliva, and may involve touching the lips and mouth, which can transfer bacteria to food. It also looks unprofessional.

Eating in the kitchen

As a chef you will frequently need to taste the food you cook, to assess the flavour, texture and seasonings. This should be done in a controlled and hygienic way, using a clean teaspoon. Use the spoon only once then clean and disinfect it before using again. Do not use cooking utensils such as wooden spoons for tasting food, nor should fingers be used for this purpose as bacteria may be transferred to the food.

Eating would refer to consuming a meal or a snack while working or in your working area, or picking at the food being prepared. This is a hazard because you are likely to touch your face or mouth, which can then transfer harmful bacteria to the food.

Smoking

Smoking is now illegal in all buildings and certainly where there is food. If food handlers smoke at break times, hands must be washed thoroughly afterwards because, when a cigarette is taken from the mouth, bacteria from the mouth can be transferred via the fingers on to food.

Cuts, burns, infections and grazes

It is particularly important to keep all cuts, burns, boils, scratches, grazes and similar abrasions covered with a waterproof dressing (blue plaster) to avoid contaminating food with bacteria. If these become infected there are large numbers of harmful bacteria that must not be allowed to come in to contact with food. In most cases people suffering in this way should not handle food. Report any infected skin problems or injuries to your supervisor before starting work.

Minor cuts, grazes and burns do occur occasionally in kitchens because of the nature of the work. Most minor cuts can usually be treated using the contents of the first-aid box, maybe with the assistance of an appointed first aider. For more serious cuts and burns it is important to seek advice from the first aider and get medical help as soon as possible. It is important to cover any open cuts or burns immediately to prevent bacteria from the wound getting in to and contaminating food.

- **Minor cuts and grazes:** place the cut/graze under cold running water, dry it thoroughly and apply a blue waterproof dressing of suitable size. If necessary, also wear a disposable glove. If the cut continues to bleed and is not being contained by the dressing, seek further help.
- **Minor burns:** place the injury under cold running water and keep it there for a minimum of ten minutes (an ice pack could also be used). If the burn is more serious and/or the skin is broken, cover lightly with a sterile dressing and seek medical help. Do not let adhesive items, creams, antiseptics or kitchen cloths come into contact with the wound.

See Chapter 4 for information on the legal requirements relating to reporting illness and infections.

Keeping work areas clean and hygienic

Suitable buildings with well-planned fittings, layout and equipment allow for good food safety practices to take place. All surfaces and equipment must be in good condition and kept clean. Certain basics need to be available if a building is to be used for food production:

- there must be an electricity supply and preferably a gas supply
- drinking water and good drainage
- suitable road access for deliveries and refuse collection
- no risk of contamination from the surrounding area and buildings, such as chemicals, smoke, odours or dust.

It is important to keep your own work area clean, tidy and well organised as you work. Completing tasks hygienically and protecting food from contamination are legal food safety requirements, as well as allowing you to work efficiently and professionally.

Ensure that food contact surfaces, such as chopping boards, are clean and sanitised before use. Clean well and sanitise areas between tasks. Organise the equipment you will need for the work you are completing and consider the best way to complete each task with maximum efficiency.

Store equipment and ingredients in the proper places once you have finished using them. Make sure that food items being put away into fridges, freezers and other storage areas are correctly covered or wrapped, and labelled and dated according to the establishment's policy.

Working efficiently means that tasks are completed within the time allowed, in a well-organised, clean and tidy way, without causing undue stress or tiredness.

Layout

When planning food premises, a linear workflow should be in place. This means there will be no crossover of activities that could result in cross-contamination. Clean and dirty – and raw and cooked – processes should be well segregated.

There must be adequate storage areas; proper refrigerated storage is especially important. Cleaning and disinfection should be planned with separate storage areas for cleaning materials and chemicals.

Sufficient, suitable staff hand-washing/drying facilities must be provided, as well as personal hygiene facilities for staff, including changing and storage areas for personal clothing and belongings.

All areas should allow for efficient cleaning, disinfection and pest control.

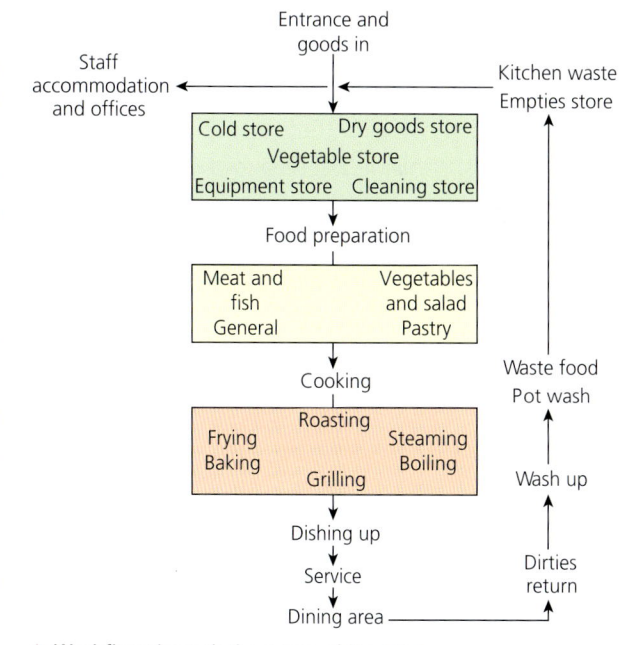

▲ Workflow through the areas of the kitchen

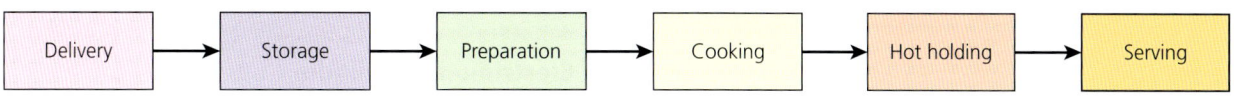

▲ Linear workflow

Preparing, cooking and holding food safely

Food safety hazards: food poisoning and vehicles of contamination

There are a number of ways that food could be exposed to hazards that could result in it becoming contaminated. Contaminated food can cause illness or even be fatal to those eating it. It is important to be aware of this, and to check food frequently and follow the required procedures from delivery right through until the time it is served.

Contamination of food from pathogenic bacteria (biological contamination) is considered to be the most dangerous hazard of all because food can be dangerously contaminated with bacteria but still look, smell and taste fine. There is increasing concern about allergenic hazards too, especially as these can be hidden ingredients in food but can still cause dangerous reactions.

Biological contamination

Biological contamination can occur from **pathogenic bacteria** and the toxins they may produce. Viruses, yeasts, moulds, spoilage bacteria and enzymes are all around us: in the environment, on raw food, and on humans, animals, birds and insects. Pathogenic bacteria are harmful as they can multiply to dangerous levels but still not be visible except with a microscope. When pathogenic bacteria multiply in food or use food to get into the human body, illness can result.

Bacteria and food poisoning

Not all bacteria are harmful: some are very useful and are used to good effect in the manufacture of foods and medicines. Making milk into yoghurt and making cheese may use bacteria in the process.

Pathogenic bacteria can cause food poisoning. Bacteria are very small – so small that you would need to use a microscope to see them; you would not be able to taste them or smell them on food. This is why pathogenic bacteria are so dangerous: you can't tell if they are in food or not.

Symptoms of food poisoning include headache, fever, stomach pain, diarrhoea and vomiting.

Common food-poisoning bacteria include the following:

- **Salmonella** used to be the most common cause of food poisoning in the UK but since measures were put in place to reduce salmonella in chickens and in eggs, food poisoning from this source has reduced. The main source of salmonella now is the human and animal gut and excreta, but it is also found on pests such as rodents, insects and birds, and in raw meat and poultry, eggs and shellfish. Salmonella poisoning can also be passed on through human carriers (someone carrying salmonella but not showing any signs of illness).
- **Staphylococcus aureus** is found mainly on the human body and can be present on the skin, hair and scalp, nose and throat. Cuts, spots, burns and boils will also be a source of this organism. When it multiplies in food, a toxin (poison) is produced that is very difficult to kill, even with boiling temperatures. To avoid food poisoning from this organism, food handlers need to maintain very high standards of personal hygiene and report any illness they may have to their supervisor before handling food.
- **Clostridium perfringens** can be present in human and animal faeces, and raw meat, poultry and vegetables (as well as insects, soil, dust and sewage). A number of food-poisoning incidents from this organism have occurred when large amounts of meat are brought up to cooking temperatures slowly and then allowed to cool slowly. Clostridium perfringens can produce spores during this heating/cooling process. Spores are very resistant to any further cooking and allow bacteria to survive in conditions that would usually kill them.
- **Bacillus cereus** is another organism that can produce spores, and it can also produce two different toxins, so it is a very dangerous pathogen. It is often associated with cooking rice in large quantities, cooling it too slowly and then reheating. The reheating temperatures are not enough to destroy the spores and toxins. It has also been linked with other cereal crops, spices, soil and vegetables.
- **Clostridium botulinum**, fortunately, is rare; the symptoms can be very serious, even fatal. Sources tend to be the intestines of fish, as well as soil and vegetables.

Toxins

Toxins (poisons) can be produced by some bacteria as they multiply in food. They are heat resistant and may not be killed by the normal cooking processes that kill bacteria, so they remain in the food and can cause illness. Other bacteria produce toxins as they die, usually in the intestines of the person who has eaten the food.

Spores

Some bacteria are able to form spores when the conditions surrounding them become hostile, such as when temperatures rise or in the presence of chemicals such as disinfectant. A spore forms a protective 'shell' inside the bacteria, protecting the essential parts from the high temperatures of normal cooking, disinfection and dehydration.

Prolonged cooking times and/or very high temperatures are needed to kill spores. Time is very important in preventing the formation of spores. When large pieces of food such as meat are brought slowly to cooking temperature, this allows time for spores to form, which are then very difficult to kill. Always bring food up to cooking temperature quickly and cool food quickly.

Food-borne illness

Some different organisms from the ones named above are said to cause food-borne illness. These pathogens do not multiply in food but use food to get into the human gut, where they then multiply and cause a range of illnesses (some of them serious), including severe abdominal pain, diarrhoea, vomiting, headaches, blurred vision, flu symptoms, septicaemia and miscarriage. These organisms may be transmitted from person to person, in water or be airborne, as well as through food.

Food-borne pathogens include those listed below.

- **Campylobacter:** causes more food-related illness than any other organism. It is found in raw poultry and meat, sewage, animals, insects and birds.
- **E. coli 0157:** present in the intestines and excreta of animals and humans, raw meat, and can be present on raw vegetables.
- **Listeria:** dangerous because it can multiply (slowly) at fridge temperatures, that is, below 5 °C. It has been linked with chilled products such as unpasteurised cheeses, pâté and prepared salads, as well as cook/chill meals.
- **Norovirus:** like all viruses, norovirus will not multiply on food but it may live for a short time on surfaces, utensils and food, and thereby get into the body. The usual way this is spread is airborne, person to person, water or sewage.

Chemical contamination

Chemical contamination can occur when chemical items get into food accidentally; these can then make the consumer suffer discomfort or become ill. The kinds of chemical that can get into food could be cleaning fluids, disinfectants, machine oil, degreasers and pesticides. Problems can also occur when there are chemical reactions between things such as metal containers and acidic foods.

Physical contamination

Physical contamination is caused when something gets into foods that should not be there, such as glass; nuts, bolts and oil from machinery; mercury from thermometers; flaking paint; pen tops; threads and buttons from clothing; blue plasters; hair and insects.

Poisoning from other items

Some foods can be naturally poisonous, such as some types of mushroom and undercooked red kidney beans. Some oily fish can develop toxins if stored at too high a temperature, and occasionally some shellfish can cause illness when they have fed on poisonous plankton.

Some moulds can produce toxins as they grow; these are called **mycotoxins**. Mycotoxins can cause serious illness and have been linked with cancers. Do not use mouldy food (controlled moulds, such as in blue cheeses, are fine).

Allergen and intolerance contamination

Allergens are different types of foods to which individuals may have an allergic reaction.

Symptoms of allergic reaction

When someone has a food allergy, their immune system mistakes certain foods for a harmful substance and a reaction takes place. This could be:

- itching and/or swelling of the lips, mouth, tongue and throat
- skin reactions such as swelling, itching and eczema

- diarrhoea, nausea, vomiting and bloating
- coughing and runny nose
- breathlessness and wheezing
- sore, itchy eyes.

There may also be symptoms such as extreme fatigue or arthritis symptoms.

Some food allergies result in an immediate, severe allergic reaction called **anaphylactic shock**, which is potentially fatal. This is often linked to peanuts and other nut or seed products. Symptoms can include:
- dizziness
- rapid pulse
- a drop in blood pressure
- swelling of the airways and throat, making it difficult to breathe.

These symptoms could result in loss of consciousness, and can be fatal if left untreated.

Other food allergies cause symptoms that may take longer to develop – for example, gluten intolerance (coeliac disease).

Some establishments that provide foods for vulnerable groups (for example, young children) completely remove certain allergenic foods, such as nuts, from their menus.

Food intolerance

This is different from an allergy and does not involve the immune system. However, people suffering from a food intolerance may still suffer illness or discomfort after eating certain foods.

Protecting against allergenic food poisoning

It is important to provide completely accurate information to customers about ingredients and allergens in food. Allergenic food poisoning can be avoided by the following means.

1 **Providing information**
   - There is a legal requirement to provide verbal information to customers and a menu listing possible allergens.
   - Ensure that everyone involved in producing and serving the food is well informed of the allergens in each product/menu item (including in frying oils, sauces and garnishes).
   - Records of dishes containing allergens must be kept up to date.
   - Service staff must be able to check easily if a menu item contains specific allergens. Displaying a list of the allergens (shown below) in the kitchen would enable staff to provide the correct information to customers.

2 **Training for all staff**
   - Kitchen staff must understand the importance of thorough hand washing before preparing food for an allergic customer.
   - Service staff should be trained in dealing with specific customer requests for allergen information and in knowing where to find this information.
   - They may also raise the topic of possible allergies with their customers: when the food server greets their customer/guest, this is a good time to ask if anyone in the party has an allergy to certain items, and whether they would like allergy advice relating to the menu.

3 **Communication in the food production chain**
   - Communication from suppliers through to the customer must be excellent. For example, any change of ingredient in a product or dish must be communicated to everyone in the production and service chain.

Allergen rules

Allergenic ingredients must be clearly indicated in a list of the ingredients in a substance or product. The 14 allergens are:

1 cereals containing gluten, such as wheat (including spelt and khorasan wheat), rye, barley, oats
2 crustaceans, such as prawns, crabs, lobster and crayfish
3 eggs
4 fish
5 peanuts
6 soybeans
7 milk (including lactose)
8 nuts – almonds, hazelnuts, walnuts, cashews, pecans, brazil nuts, pistachio nuts, macadamia (or Queensland) nuts
9 celery (including celeriac)
10 mustard
11 sesame
12 sulphur dioxide/sulphites, where added and at a level above 10 mg/kg or 10 mg/l in the finished product (sometimes used as a preservative in dried fruit)
13 lupin, which includes lupin seeds and flour; can be found in types of bread, pastries and pasta
14 molluscs, such as mussels, whelks, oysters, snails and squid.

All food that may cause an allergic reaction must be checked when delivered. The packaging should be intact and not damaged, food should be stored carefully and all labels of prepared items should be checked for allergens

Handling procedures

When handling food with allergenic ingredients, or any other food to which customers may be intolerant, you can avoid allergen cross-contamination by:
- cleaning areas thoroughly between different food types
- using specific equipment for allergic customers
- taking care that items such as sauces and garnishes do not contain allergens
- retaining food packaging for allergen information.

The organisation's procedures for items causing reactions

All staff will be trained in allergens and food intolerances. Many restaurants have a separate area of the kitchen for preparing allergenic ingredients, separate equipment such as knives and serving equipment for handling allergen dishes, to prevent allergen contamination. Some establishments use purple-coloured boards as a precaution to avoid cross-contamination.

Surfaces and equipment

Lighting and ventilation

Lighting (natural and artificial) must be sufficient for the tasks being completed, to allow for safe working and so that cleaning can be carried out efficiently.

Good ventilation is also essential in food premises to prevent excessive heat, condensation, circulation of airborne contaminants, grease vapours and odours.

Drainage

Drainage must be adequate for the work being completed, without causing flooding. If channels, grease traps and gullies are used they should allow for frequent and easy cleaning.

Floors

These need to be durable and in good condition; they must be non-porous, non-slip and easy to clean. Suitable materials are: non-slip quarry tiles, epoxy resins, industrial vinyl sheeting and granolithic flooring. Where the materials allow, edges between floor and walls should be coved (curved) to prevent debris collecting in corners.

Walls

Walls need to be non-porous, smooth, easy to clean and preferably light in colour. Suitable wall coverings are: plastic cladding, stainless steel sheeting, ceramic tiles, epoxy resin, or rubberised painted plaster or brickwork. Walls should be coved where they join the floor. Lagging and ducting around pipes should be sealed and gaps sealed where pipes enter the building, to stop pests getting in.

Ceilings

Ceiling finishes must resist the build-up of condensation, which could encourage mould. They should be washable and of a non-flaking material. Non-porous ceiling panels and tiles are frequently used and may incorporate lighting.

Windows and doors

Windows and doors provide possibilities for pests to enter the building, so they should be fitted with suitable screening, strip curtains, metal kick plates, and so on. Doors and windows should also fit well into their frames to stop pests gaining access.

Damaged surfaces and equipment

Damaged surfaces can contaminate food by allowing waste and bacteria to build up in cracks and crevasses. Loose parts, chipped or broken fittings and pieces of broken equipment can also fall into food, causing physical contamination.

If you notice that a piece of equipment is damaged, broken, cracked, has loose parts or is not working properly, either remove it from use or – if it's too large to do that – put up a sign warning others not to use it. Report the problem with the equipment immediately to a supervisor or whoever is in charge of food safety. These measures must be taken to prevent injury to the person using the equipment, but also to prevent contamination of food and illness or injury to the consumer.

The same applies to damaged surfaces or fittings, such as work surfaces, walls, ceilings, floors and furniture.

Make sure that serving and display equipment is undamaged and in good working order. Cracks and crevices can hold food debris and bacteria, which can then be transferred to food. Loose parts from broken equipment, cracked tiles or flaking paint can fall into food as it is being prepared. These could cause illness and injury to the person eating the food, so damaged surfaces and equipment must be reported to the responsible person immediately.

Cleaning

Clean food areas are essential in the production of safe food, and it is a requirement to plan, record and check all cleaning as part of a **cleaning schedule**. In general, you should **clean as you go**, thoroughly clean down after each service and deep clean the kitchen once a month.

Clean premises, work areas and equipment are important to:
- control the bacteria that cause food poisoning
- discourage growth of moulds
- reduce the possibility of physical and chemical contamination
- make accidents less likely – for example, slips on a greasy floor
- create a positive image for customers, visitors and employees
- comply with the law
- avoid attracting pests to the kitchen.

The cleaning schedule needs to include the following information:
- **what** is to be cleaned
- **who** should do it (name if possible)
- **how** it is to be done and how long it should take
- **when** it should be done (for example, the time of day)
- **materials** to be used, including chemicals, dilution, cleaning equipment and protective clothing to be worn
- **safety** precautions necessary
- **signatures** of cleaner and supervisor checking the work, as well as the date and time.

As a food handler it is important to clean as you go and not allow waste to accumulate in the area where you are working; this is because it is very difficult to keep untidy areas clean.

Cleaning products

Different cleaning products are designed for different tasks, as described in Table 2.1.

Table 2.1 Different cleaning products and their uses

Product	Use of product
Detergent	Designed to remove grease and dirt, and hold them in suspension in water.
	May be in the form of liquid, powder, gel or foam, and usually needs to be added to water.
	Detergent will not kill pathogens (although the hot water it is mixed with may help to do this), but it will clean and degrease so that disinfectant can work properly.
	Detergents work best with hot water.
Disinfectant	Designed to destroy bacteria if used properly; make sure you use only a disinfectant intended for kitchen use.
	Disinfectants must be left on a clean, grease-free surface for the required amount of time (contact time) to be effective.
	Heat may also be used to disinfect – for example, the use of steam cleaners or the hot rinse cycle of a dishwasher.
Sanitiser	Cleans and disinfects, and usually comes in spray form.
	Sanitiser is very useful for work surfaces and equipment, especially between tasks.
	It is usual to clean surfaces with hot water and detergent before spraying with sanitiser.

Items that should be both cleaned and disinfected include:
- all items that come into contact with food, such as preparation surfaces, chopping boards, bowls, trays, knives, serving equipment and utensils, and food display items
- all hand-contact surfaces, such as door and refrigerator handles, telephones and switches.
- all equipment used for cleaning, such as cloths, mops, buckets, brooms, dustpans and hand brushes.

Cleaning cloths

Take great care with kitchen cloths – they are a breeding area for bacteria. Different cloths for different areas will help to reduce cross-contamination and it is certainly good practice to use different cloths for raw food and high-risk food areas. Use of disposable kitchen towel is the most hygienic way to dry utensils and food preparation areas.

If a tea towel is used, treat it with great care: remember that it can easily spread bacteria so don't use it as an 'all-purpose cloth' and don't keep it on your shoulder (the cloth touches neck and hair, picking up bacteria).

Cleaning procedures

Cleaning kitchen surfaces should be planned and all staff need to be trained in a suitable cleaning method, such as one of the following:

Six-stage process for cleaning a surface
1 Remove debris and loose particles.
2 Main clean to remove soiling grease.
3 Rinse using clean hot water and cloth to remove the detergent.
4 Apply disinfectant and leave for the contact time recommended on the container.
5 Rinse off the disinfectant (if recommended).
6 Allow to air dry or use kitchen paper.

Four-stage process for cleaning a surface
1 Remove debris and loose particles.
2 Main clean using hot water and sanitiser.
3 Rinse using clean hot water and cloth, if recommended on instructions.
4 Allow to air dry or use kitchen paper.

Cleaning is essential to prevent hazards but, if not managed properly, can become a hazard in itself. Do not store cleaning chemicals in food preparation and cooking areas, and take care with their use to avoid chemical contamination. Make sure that items such as cloths, paper towels and fibres from mops do not get into open food (physical contamination). Bacterial contamination could occur by using the same cleaning cloths and equipment in raw food areas and in high-risk food areas, or by using dirty cloths and equipment.

Dishwashing

Automatic dishwashing
The most efficient and hygienic method of cleaning dishes and crockery is the use of a dishwashing machine as this will clean and disinfect items that will then air dry, removing the need for cloths. The dishwasher can also be used to clean/disinfect small equipment such as chopping boards. The stages in machine dishwashing are as follows.
1 Remove waste food.
2 Pre-rinse or spray.
3 Load on to the appropriate racks with a space between each item.
4 The wash cycle runs at 50 to 60 °C using a detergent.
5 The rinse cycle runs at 82 to 88 °C, which will disinfect items ready for air drying.

Dishwashing by hand
If items need to be washed by hand the recommended way to do this is as follows.
1 Scrape/rinse off residue food.
2 Wash items in a sink of hot water (the temperature should be 50 to 60 °C, which means that rubber gloves need to be worn). Use a dishwashing brush rather than a cloth.
3 Rinse in very hot water – if rinsing can be done at 82 °C for 30 seconds it will disinfect the dishes.
4 Allow to air dry; do not use tea towels.

Waste disposal

It is important to deal with kitchen waste quickly, hygienically and appropriately. If waste is allowed to build up in kitchen areas, it can encourage pests, allow for multiplication of bacteria, produce unpleasant odours, and items such as food trimmings and packaging materials could fall into food that is being prepared. Some guidelines are listed below.
- All food handlers should keep areas clear, clean and with a minimum of waste.
- Kitchen waste should be placed in waste bins with lids. These should preferably be foot operated to reduce contamination to the hands.
- Food waste is stored in clearly identified bins and, in many establishments, is sent for composting. There will be separate bins for paper and cardboard, glass and plastic.
- In 1991 the Water Industry Act made it a legal requirement for the hospitality industry to ensure that waste oil is stored and disposed of correctly.
- Bins should be made of a strong material, usually a thick plastic, with a strong plastic liner bag placed inside, and should be easy to clean and pest proof.

- To deal with waste hygienically, bins should be emptied regularly to avoid waste build-up; the task of keeping kitchen waste bins emptied and cleaned/disinfected should be listed on the cleaning schedule, with a specific person responsible for doing this. An over-full, heavy bin is much more difficult to handle and empty than a bin that is emptied regularly.
- Outside waste should be in strong containers with lids to prevent pests getting in. They should preferably be raised off the floor (usually by wheels) and on a hard surface, such as concrete, which can be hosed down and kept clean. Outside waste bins should be emptied regularly.

Pests

When there are reports of food premises being heavily fined or forcibly closed down, an infestation of pests is often the reason. As pests can be a serious source of contamination and disease, they must be eliminated for food safety reasons and to comply with the law. Pests can carry food-poisoning bacteria into food premises from their fur/feathers, feet/paws, saliva, urine and droppings. Other problems caused by pests include damage to food stock and packaging; damage to buildings, equipment and wiring; and blockages in equipment and piping.

Pests are attracted to food premises because there may be food, warmth, shelter, water and possible nesting materials; all reasonable measures must be put in place to keep them out. Any possible signs that pests may be present must be reported to the supervisor or manager immediately.

Common pests that may cause problems in food areas are: rats, mice, cockroaches, wasps, flies, ants (including pharaoh ants), birds and domestic pets. Pest management needs to be planned as part of the food safety management system. Regular visits from a recognised pest control company are advisable because it will offer advice as well as deal with problems arising. Companies conducting a regular audit will provide a pest audit report, which should be kept and could be used as part of the food safety management system.

Table 2.2 Signs of pest presence

Pest	Signs that they are present
Rats and mice	Sightings of rodents, droppings, unpleasant smell, gnawed wires, etc. Greasy marks on lower walls, damaged food stock, paw prints.
Flies and wasps	Sighting of flies and wasps, hearing them, dead insects, maggots.
Cockroaches	Sightings (dead or alive) usually at night, unpleasant smell.
Ants	Sightings and present in food; the tiny, pale-coloured pharaoh ants are difficult to spot, but can still be the source of a variety of pathogens.
Weevils	Sightings of weevils in stored products, e.g. flour or cornflour; very difficult to see – tiny black insects moving in flour.
Birds	Sightings, droppings, in outside storage areas and around refuse.
Domestic pets	These must be kept out of food areas as they carry pathogens on fur, whiskers, saliva, urine, etc.

Measures to keep pests out of the building are of great importance and need to be planned. Pest control contractors can offer advice on keeping pests out, as well as organise eradication systems for any pests that do get in. Some basic guidelines are:

- block entry – for example, no holes around pipe work, avoid all gaps and cavities where they could get in, sealed drain covers
- damage to the building or fixtures and fittings should be repaired quickly
- window/door screening/netting should be in place
- check deliveries/packaging for pests
- baits and traps used as appropriate
- electronic fly killer (EFK) in place to deal with flying insects
- use of sealed containers so no open food left out
- not allowing a build-up of waste in the kitchen
- outside waste not kept too close to the kitchen
- planned pest management control, surveys and reports.

Flying insects cause problems as they can find their way in through very small spaces or from other parts of the building. They can then spread bacteria around the

Food safety

kitchen and on to open food. To eliminate insects such as flies, bluebottles and wasps, an EFK is recommended. These use ultraviolet light to attract the insects, which are then electrocuted on charged wires and fall into catch trays. Do not position an EFK directly above food preparation areas, and make sure the catch trays are emptied regularly.

Pest control measures can also introduce food safety hazards. The bodies of dead insects, or even rodents, may remain in the kitchen (physical and bacterial contamination). Pesticides, insecticides and baits could cause chemical contamination if not managed properly. Pest control is best managed by professionals.

Storing food safely

Checking food on delivery

For food to remain in top condition and be safe to eat, it is essential that food deliveries are checked carefully, that correct storage is in place and that procedures are fully understood by all kitchen staff. Only approved suppliers should be used, which can ensure that food is delivered in the best condition in suitable, undamaged packaging, properly date coded and at the correct temperature. Food suppliers need to be able to provide information on the product from source through to the time it is delivered to you (traceability). Packaged or processed food of any kind will have a list of ingredients on the pack. If the food is removed from this packaging for storage, retain the ingredient lists because they will give essential allergy advice.

- All deliveries should be checked then moved to the appropriate storage area as soon as possible and chilled/frozen food within 15 minutes of delivery.
- Use a food probe to check the temperature of food deliveries; record these temperatures and keep as part of the food safety management system:
  - chilled food should be below 5°C (reject it if above 8°C)
  - frozen food should be at or below −18°C (reject it if above −15°C).
- Many suppliers now provide a printout of the temperatures at which food was delivered (save these printouts in kitchen records).
- Dry goods should be in undamaged packaging, well within best-before dates, be completely dry and in perfect condition on delivery.

When receiving a delivery of food, check:
- the items are the quantity, size and quality ordered
- packaging and food are undamaged
- food is at the required temperature (see above)
- food is within use-by dates or has a suitable best-before date
- there are no signs of deterioration or spoilage of the food
- there are no signs of pests present in the food or packaging
- no cross-contamination is evident in the delivery – for example, raw and cooked food packaged together.

Preparing food for storage

It is important to prepare food for storage to ensure there is no risk of cross-contamination, and that food is labelled and maintained at correct temperatures. Remove food items from their outer packaging – being careful to check for any possible pests that may have found their way in – before placing the products in a refrigerator, freezer or dry store.

Fresh food, such as meat or fish on trays, should be covered well with cling film, dated and labelled, and placed in the appropriate refrigerated area.

Segregate any unfit food from other food until it is thrown away or collected by the supplier. This is to avoid any possible contamination to other foods.

The storage area

Once a food delivery has been accepted it must be placed in the correct storage area. This will reduce the possibility of cross-contamination, and help to ensure that the food remains fresh and in best condition. All storage areas (refrigerators, freezers, cold rooms, dry store areas) must be kept clean and tidy, and this needs to be planned as part of the cleaning schedule. If you notice that these areas are not clean and tidy, report this to a supervisor who can deal with the matter properly.

The multi-use refrigerator

The following guidelines apply if a refrigerator is used to store various types of food.
- It is best practice to keep the refrigerator running at between 1 and 4°C (the legal requirement is 8°C).

41

- Food must be covered, and labelled with name of item and date.
- Always store raw food at the bottom of the refrigerator, with other items above.
- Keep high-risk foods well away from raw foods.
- Never overload a refrigerator – to operate properly, cold air must be allowed to circulate between items.
- Wrap strong-smelling foods very well as their smell (and taste) can transfer to other foods – for example, milk.
- Record the temperature at which the refrigerator is operating at least once a day. Keep the fridge temperatures with other kitchen records.

Refrigerators must be cleaned regularly. Take the following steps.
- Remove food to another refrigerator.
- Clean according to the cleaning schedule using a recommended sanitiser (a solution of bicarbonate of soda and water is also good for cleaning refrigerators).
- Remember to empty and clean any drip trays, and clean door seals thoroughly.
- Rinse, then dry with kitchen paper.
- Make sure the refrigerator front and handle are cleaned and disinfected to avoid cross-contamination.
- Make sure the refrigerator is back down to a temperature between 1 and 4°C before replacing the food in the proper positions. Check the dates and condition of all food before replacing.

Correct food storage

Storing raw meat and poultry
Raw meat and poultry should be stored in a separate refrigerator running at temperatures between 1 and 4°C where possible. If not already packaged, place on trays, cover well with cling film and label. If it is necessary to store meat or poultry in a multi-use refrigerator, make sure it is covered, labelled and placed at the bottom of the refrigerator, well away from other items.

Storing fish
A separate fish refrigerator running at between 1 and 4°C is best. Remove fresh fish from ice containers and place on trays, cover well with cling film and label. If it is necessary to store fish in a multi-use refrigerator, make sure it is well covered, labelled and placed at the bottom of the refrigerator, well away from other items. Remember that odours from fish can permeate other items, such as milk or eggs.

Storing dairy products and eggs
Pasteurised milk and cream, eggs and cheese should be stored in their original containers between 1 and 4°C. Sterilised or UHT milk can be kept in the dry store following the storage instructions on the label.

After delivery, eggs should be stored at a constant temperature – a refrigerator is the best place.

Storing and defrosting frozen foods
Store frozen food in a freezer running at −18°C or below. Separate raw foods from ready-to-eat foods. (For information on defrosting see the section on 'Defrosting frozen foods before cooking', page 47.)

Storing fruit, vegetables and salad items
Storage conditions will vary according to type. For example, sacks of potatoes, root vegetables and some fruit can be stored in a cool, well-ventilated store room, but salad items, green vegetables, soft fruit and tropical fruit would be better in refrigerated storage. If possible, a specific refrigerator running at around 8°C would be ideal to avoid any chill damage.

Storing dry goods
Dry goods, such as rice, dried pasta, sugar, flour and grains, should be stored at ambient temperatures (room temperature). They should be kept in clean, covered containers on wheels or in smaller sealed containers on shelves to stop pests getting in to them. Storage should be in a cool, well-ventilated dry store area and well-managed stock rotation is essential. Remember to keep packaging information as this may include essential **allergy advice**.

Storing and handling canned products
Cans are usually stored in the dry store area and, once again, rotation of stock is essential. Canned food will carry best-before dates and it is not advisable to use it after this date. 'Blown' cans must never be used, and

do not use badly dented or rusty cans. Once opened, transfer any unused canned food to a clean bowl, cover and label it, and store it in the refrigerator for up to two days.

Storing cooked, ready-to-eat and finished foods

Foods that are purchased ready-cooked or cooked and then stored include a wide range of items, such as cooked meats and fish, pies and other pastry items, pâté, cream cakes, desserts and savoury flans. They will usually be 'high-risk foods' so correct storage is essential. Check the labelling on individual items for specific storage instructions, but generally keep them refrigerated between 1 and 4 °C. Store carefully, wrapped and labelled, and well away from and above raw foods, to avoid any cross-contamination.

Food being held for service must be kept above **63 °C (or below 5 °C)**. If food is being cooled to serve cold or for reheating at a later time, it must be protected from contamination and cooled quickly – that is, to **8 °C within 90 minutes**. The best way to do this is in a blast-chiller. Any food that has been above 8 °C (but below 63 °C) for more than two hours must be thrown away.

Any food that is to be chilled or frozen must be well wrapped or placed in a suitable container with a lid (items may also be vacuum packed). Make sure that all food is labelled and dated before chilling or freezing.

Stock rotation

First in – first out

This term is used to describe stock rotation and is applied to all categories of food. It simply means that foods already in storage must be used before that from new deliveries (provided that stock is still within recommended dates and in sound condition). Food deliveries should be labelled with their delivery date and preferably the date by which they should be used (see 'Food labelling codes', below). Written stock records should form a part of a food safety management system.

Food labelling codes

- **Use-by dates** appear on perishable foods with a short life. Legally, the food must be used by this date and should not stored or used after it. Food past its use-by date must be thrown away and disposed of. The best way to dispose of food safely is to remove any packaging and place in the food waste bin for composting.
- **Best-before dates** apply to foods that are expected to have a longer life, such as dry products or canned food. A best-before date advises that food is at its best before this date; using it after this date is still legal but not advised.

Food spoilage and food preservation

Most foods have a limited life and will eventually deteriorate due to moulds, yeasts, enzymes or bacteria. Spoilage of food also occurs due to exposure to oxygen, moisture or chemicals; damage by pests; or by poor handling and bad storage.

Unlike bacterial contamination, which is impossible to detect in a normal kitchen situation, food spoilage can usually be observed by sight, smell, taste and touch. Spoilage could include mouldy, slimy, dried-up or over-wet fresh foods. Blown cans and vac packs, and food with freezer burn, are also a sign of food spoilage.

Different methods have been developed to prolong the natural life of various foods and keep them fresh. These include:

- **use of heat** – cooking, canning, sterilisation, UHT, pasteurisation
- **use of heat and sealing** – canning, bottling, cooking then vacuum packaging
- **use of low temperatures** – chilling, freezing
- **exclusion of air** – vacuum packaging
- **changing gases surrounding food** – modified atmosphere packaging
- **removal of moisture** – dehydrated foods
- **use of acids, sugar or salt concentrations**
- **food preservatives** – for example, nitrates.

Food preservation will often combine methods to ensure effective preservation – for example, vacuum-packed fish will also be refrigerated, as would pasteurised milk.

Factors that enable the growth of food poisoning organisms

Some bacteria cause food poisoning by very large numbers multiplying in food then being eaten, entering the digestive system and infecting the body. Others can form spores or toxins (see page 35).

Food

Most foods can easily be contaminated by bacteria; those less likely to cause food poisoning are dry, have a high concentration of vinegar, sugar or salt, or are preserved in some way.

Some foods support the multiplication of bacteria more than others when given the right conditions; these are referred to as high-risk foods. They are usually foods that:

- are ready to eat
- have a protein and moisture content
- will not always go through a cooking process that will destroy bacteria.

High-risk foods include:
- stock, sauces, gravies, soups
- eggs and egg products
- meat and meat products (sausages, pâté/parfait, pies, cold meats, sandwiches)
- milk and milk products
- cooked rice
- all foods that are handled then have no further cooking
- all foods that are reheated.

Extra care must be taken to prevent these foods from being contaminated and being left in conditions where bacteria can multiply.

Moisture

Bacteria need water to support their life cycle and processes. The amount of water in food is referred to as 'a_w' (water activity).

Most food contains some moisture, and a wide variety of foods contain enough water to support bacterial multiplication. Even dry foods such as dried pasta or rice will have water added to them in the cooking process, so once again will become vulnerable to bacterial growth.

Some food preservation methods remove enough moisture to make the food safe for long periods – for example, sundried tomatoes or food preserved with salt or sugar (osmosis).

Temperature

Food poisoning bacteria multiply most rapidly at human body temperature (37 °C), but can multiply anywhere between temperatures of 5 °C and 63 °C. This is referred to as the **danger zone**.

Warm kitchen temperatures provide ideal conditions for bacterial growth, and food should be kept refrigerated wherever possible. Chilled and frozen food deliveries should be put into temperature-controlled storage within 15 minutes of delivery. Cold foods need to be stored at temperatures below 5 °C.

Bacteria are not killed by cold, although they multiply only slowly at very low temperatures; at freezer temperatures they will lie dormant for long periods. Once food is removed from cold storage, bacteria will start to multiply again as the temperature rises.

- Foods that have been taken out of the refrigerator, kept in a warm kitchen and returned to the refrigerator for later use could be contaminated with a higher level of pathogenic bacteria.
- Foods that have been taken from the freezer and defrosted will be susceptible to bacterial growth as the temperature rises, so food should never be re-frozen once it has defrosted.
- When cooking, food must be heated to a sufficiently high temperature and for the required amount of time, to be sure of safe food; any reheating of food must be done very thoroughly, to a minimum of 75 °C.

Water temperature is important.
- Warm water is not suitable for washing crockery, cutlery or equipment as bacteria will not be destroyed.
- Hot water must be used for washing-up or cleaning equipment, and, where possible, use a dishwasher that will clean items thoroughly and disinfect them.
- Boiling water will kill bacteria in a few seconds, but to destroy toxins, prolonged boiling is needed.

Spores are almost impossible to kill with normal cooking temperatures: long cooking times and/or very high temperatures are needed.

Food canning processes use 'botulinum cook', which is high-heat cooking at 121 °C for three minutes, or a tested alternative time/temperature combination, to kill any spores that may be present.

Different organisms prefer slightly different temperature ranges for growth (multiplication) – for example, Clostridium perfringens grows best at 45 °C, while Listeria monocytogenes grows most efficiently at 30 °C but can still multiply right down at refrigerator temperatures.

Time

Under ideal conditions, bacteria can multiply by dividing into two every 20 minutes; in this way, a single bacterium could increase to 2,097,152 within seven hours.

Time	Bacteria
12:00	1
12:20	2
12:40	4
13:00	8
14:00	64
15:00	512
16:00	4096
17:00	32,768
18:00	262,144
19:00	2,097,152

▲ How bacteria reproduce over time

Therefore, foods left at ambient temperatures could contain large numbers of harmful bacteria within a few hours.

Time is the element of bacterial growth that the food handler is most able to control, by:
- making sure that food spends as little time as possible at kitchen temperatures – keep it cold in a refrigerator or hot, not in between
- when heating or cooking food, taking it through 'danger zone temperatures' as quickly as possible; this may mean cooking in smaller pans or in smaller batches
- not holding food on display for too long.

In addition to the requirements described above, two further conditions are needed for bacteria to multiply.

Oxygen requirement
- Some bacteria need oxygen to multiply; this group of bacteria is referred to as **aerobes**.
- Some can multiply only where there is no oxygen; these are called **anaerobes**.
- Most bacteria can multiply with or without oxygen; these are called **facultative anaerobes**.

pH

This is a measure of how acid or alkaline a food or liquid may be. The scale runs from 1.0 to 14.0. Acid foods are below 7.0 on the scale, 7.0 is neutral, and above 7.0 up to 14.0 is alkaline. Bacteria multiply best around a neutral pH. Most bacteria cannot multiply at a pH below 4.0 or above 8.0, so foods such as citrus fruits do not support bacterial multiplication.

Controlling hazards and risks

As a food handler it is your responsibility, along with those working with you, to assist in the control of food hazards and risks. There are a number of ways that the range of hazards described above can be controlled. These include:
- strict and careful standards of personal hygiene
- reporting of illness to the appropriate person
- keeping work areas clean and hygienic
- storing food correctly and at the appropriate temperatures
- cooking food to the required temperature
- taking care to avoid cross-contamination.

The food handler is also in a good position to spot any possible hazards that could be a risk to food safety. Corrective action should be taken if a hazard is spotted. This has to be reported to the appropriate person, which will usually be the supervisor. For example, if the food has gone out of temperature then the supervisor may order the food to be discarded. Hazards should be reported immediately to a supervisor, head chef or senior chef, or anyone else with responsibility for food safety in the area.

Cross-contamination

Cross-contamination occurs when bacteria are transferred from one place to another. This is usually from contaminated food (mostly raw food), equipment or surfaces to ready-to-eat food. It is the cause of significant amounts of food poisoning and care must be taken to avoid it. Cross-contamination could be caused by:

- foods touching – for example, raw and cooked meat
- raw meat or poultry dripping onto high-risk foods
- soil from dirty vegetables coming into contact with high-risk foods
- dirty cloths, dirty staff uniforms or dirty equipment
- equipment used for raw then cooked food – for example, chopping boards or knives
- hands touching raw then cooked food, not washing hands between tasks, and so on
- pests spreading bacteria around the kitchen.

Controlling cross-contamination

Completely separate working areas and storage areas for raw and high-risk foods are strongly recommended. If this is not possible, keep them well away from each other and make sure that working areas are thoroughly cleaned and disinfected between tasks.

Vegetables should be washed before preparation and again afterwards. Leafy vegetables may need to be washed in several changes of cold water to remove all of the soil present.

Good personal hygiene practices by staff, in particular frequent and effective hand washing, are very important in controlling cross-contamination and will avoid the significant amounts of contamination caused by faecal/oral routes (this is when pathogens normally found in faeces are transferred to ready-to-eat foods resulting in cross-contamination and illness). See page 30 for more advice on personal hygiene.

Colour-coded chopping boards are a good way to keep different types of food separate. Worktops and chopping boards come into contact with the food being prepared so need special attention. Make sure that chopping boards are in good condition: cracks and splits could trap bacteria and this could be transferred to food.

As well as colour-coded chopping boards, some kitchens also provide colour-coded knives, cloths, cleaning equipment, storage trays, bowls and even staff uniforms, to help prevent cross-contamination.

▲ The colour-coding system

Clean and sanitise worktops and chopping boards before working on them and do this again after use, paying particular attention when they have been used for raw foods.

Chopping boards can be disinfected after use by putting them through a dishwasher with a high rinse temperature of 82 °C (high temperatures will kill bacteria).

Small equipment, such as knives, bowls, spoons and tongs, could also be the cause of cross-contamination; it is important to wash them thoroughly (once again a dishwasher does it well). This is especially important when they are used for a variety of cooked and raw food.

Methods, times, temperatures and checks for keeping food safe

Defrosting frozen foods before cooking

Most frozen foods will need to be defrosted before use. This is because if the food is still frozen or partly frozen, it is unlikely to reach the temperatures required in the centre to kill any bacteria present. The exceptions to this are small or thin foods such as pizza, vegetables, and small items of prepared fish or chicken that would defrost fully in the cooking process.

If you need to defrost frozen food, such as a whole chicken, place it in a deep tray, cover it with film and label it, stating what the item is and the date when defrosting was started. Place at the bottom of the refrigerator where thawing liquid can't drip onto anything else. Thaw food completely (no ice crystals on any part), then cook thoroughly within 12 hours. Make sure that you allow enough time for the thawing process – it may take longer than you think! (A 2 kg chicken will take about 24 hours to defrost at 3 °C.)

Cooking and reheating

Thorough cooking is one of the best methods available to control bacteria.

Cooking to **75 °C** and holding that temperature for at least **two minutes** will kill most pathogens (but not spores and toxins). These temperatures are important, especially where large amounts are being cooked or the consumers are in high-risk categories. However, some popular dishes on hotel and restaurant menus are cooked to a lower temperature than this, according to individual dish and customer requirements.

Keep food being held for service **above 63 °C**, or cool it rapidly and keep **below 5 °C**. Never put hot or warm food into a refrigerator or freezer – this will raise the temperature and put food into the **danger zone**.

Checking food is thoroughly cooked/reheated

Electronic temperature probes are very useful to measure the temperature in the centre of both hot and cold food. They are also very useful for recording the temperature of deliveries and checking food temperatures in refrigerators. Make sure that the probe is clean and disinfected before use (disposable disinfectant wipes are useful for this). Place the probe into the centre of the food, making sure it is not touching bone or the cooking container.

Check regularly that probes are working correctly (calibration). This can be done electronically, but a simple and low-cost check is to place the probe in icy water – the reading should be 0 °C. Next, place the probe in boiling water and the temperature reading should be 100 °C. In both cases one degree higher or lower is acceptable. If probes read outside of these temperatures they need to be repaired or replaced. When calibration of probes has been completed, record these temperatures and keep as part of the food safety management system.

Cooling/chilling cooked food

See page 43 for advice on cooling and storing cooked food.

The running temperature of refrigerators, freezers and chill cabinets should be checked and recorded at least once a day. Refrigerators and chill cabinets should be below 5 °C and freezers below −18 °C.

Systems are now available to automatically log temperatures of all fridges, freezers and display cabinets in a business. Temperatures are recorded and sent to a central computer several times a day. These can then be printed or stored electronically as part of due diligence record keeping. Units not running at correct temperatures will be highlighted by the system.

Holding food for service

Wherever possible, food on display should be kept under refrigeration and the temperature should be checked to ensure that it is being maintained at a safe level. Where customers are close to displayed food it should be behind a clear sneeze screen.

Dishes prepared in advance should be covered with cling film and refrigerated at between 1 and 3 °C to keep them safe and stop them drying out.

Table 2.3 Important temperatures when dealing with food

Food	Important temperature
Food stored in a freezer (no bacterial growth but does not kill bacteria, toxins or spores)	Store at −18 to −23 °C
Refrigerated food: • raw meat/poultry • raw fish and shellfish • cooked meats/meat products • cooked fish/fish products • dairy products/fats • eggs • salad items, herbs, leafy vegetables • cooked foods/high-risk items	Store at 1 to 4 °C
Ambient stored food: • canned food • dry goods • grains • general grocery items	Store at 10 to 15 °C in a cool, well-ventilated place
Cooked hot food (a temperature that will kill bacteria but not spores and probably not toxins)	Core (centre) temperature must reach 75 °C
Cooked fish (Environmental Health Officers may advise a higher temperature)	Core (centre) temperature must reach 63 °C
Reheated food	Core (centre) temperature must reach 75 °C (82 °C in Scotland)
Hot food being held for service	Keep above 63 °C; if below this temperature for more than two hours it must be thrown away

Note: Although the law says that 'foods which support growth of pathogens or formation of toxins must not be stored above 8 °C' it is recognised best practice to store below 5 °C.

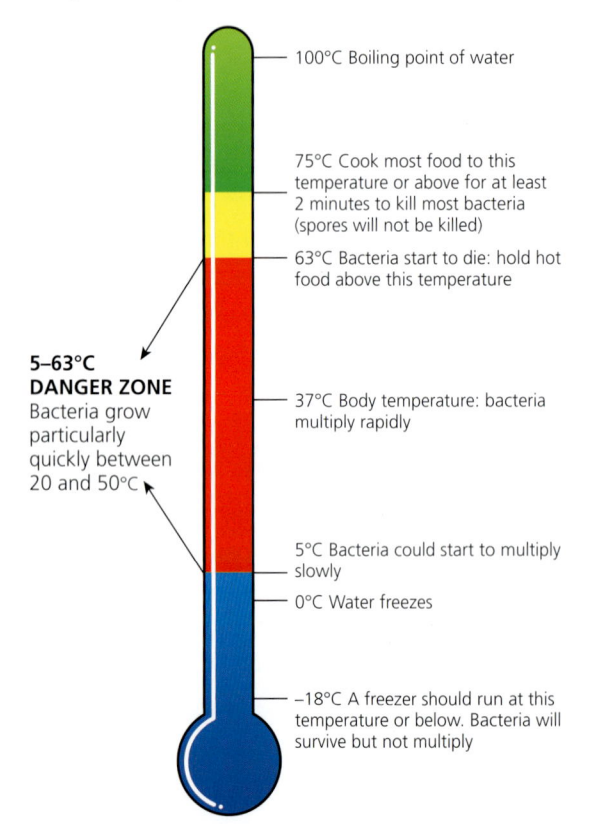

5–63°C DANGER ZONE Bacteria grow particularly quickly between 20 and 50°C

- 100°C Boiling point of water
- 75°C Cook most food to this temperature or above for at least 2 minutes to kill most bacteria (spores will not be killed)
- 63°C Bacteria start to die: hold hot food above this temperature
- 37°C Body temperature: bacteria multiply rapidly
- 5°C Bacteria could start to multiply slowly
- 0°C Water freezes
- −18°C A freezer should run at this temperature or below. Bacteria will survive but not multiply

▲ Important food safety temperatures

Food safety management systems

In line with the Food Standards Agency's commitment to reduce food poisoning, all food businesses are required by law to have a food safety management system and this will be checked by Environmental Health Officers (EHOs) when they inspect premises.

Managing food safety with a good recording system will help to control hazards and keep them at a safe level. If hazards are not controlled, contamination could occur and outbreaks of food poisoning could be the result. All food handlers must be well trained to make them aware of possible hazards and that, in terms of food safety, some hazards are more important than others. They must remain aware of the procedures in their workplace for what to do when things go wrong and how to report potential hazards. As discussed earlier in this chapter, hazards are controlled by: cooking, chilling, cleaning and avoiding cross-contamination.

Hazard Analysis Critical Control Points

The importance of risk assessment

It is a legal requirement for all food businesses to have a food safety management system in place. Article 5 of the Food Hygiene (England) Regulations 2006 gave effect to the EU Regulations and states that:

'Food business operators shall put into place, implement and maintain a permanent procedure based on the principles of hazard analysis critical control points (HACCP).'

All food safety management systems must be based on **Hazard Analysis Critical Control Points (HACCP)**. This is a recognised system that looks at identifying the critical points for stages in any process, the hazards that may occur and how these will be controlled. Controls and checks are then put in place to assess and deal with the risks, making the possible risks safe.

The HACCP system

Before setting up a new HACCP system, certain processes need to be in place first.

- **Suppliers:** these should be approved suppliers and, where possible, should provide written specifications.
- **Traceability:** systems in place to trace the source of all foods.
- **Premises, structure and equipment:** records that premises are properly maintained; a flow diagram showing the process from delivery to service, avoiding any cross-over of procedures that could result in cross-contamination.
- **Storage and stock control:** effective stock control, stock rotation and temperature-controlled storage must be in place.
- **Staff hygiene:** protective clothing, hand-washing facilities, toilets and changing facilities need to be provided; policies for personal hygiene and illness reporting need to be established, with appropriate training.
- **Pest control:** a written policy, ideally as part of a pest management system and involving a recognised contractor.
- **Cleaning/disinfection/waste:** a documented system that includes cleaning schedules and how waste removal will be managed.
- **Staff training:** records of all staff training, with dates, levels completed and topics covered.

Processes to monitor

For the HACCP system to work, all processes in the kitchen must be monitored so it is easier to identify if the procedure is not working properly. Where there are problems, such as food not reaching the required temperature to kill bacteria, systems must be in place for staff to report this so that correct procedures are put in place immediately. The system needs to provide a documented record of the stages all food will go through, right up to the time it is eaten, and may include:

- purchase and delivery
- receipt of food
- storage
- preparation
- cooking
- cooling
- hot holding
- reheating
- chilled storage
- freezing and defrosting
- serving.

Once the hazards have been identified, corrective measures are put in place to control the hazards and keep the food safe.

The system must be updated regularly, especially when new items are introduced to the menu or systems change – specific new controls must be put in place to include them (for example, if a new piece of cooking equipment has been installed).

Stages of the HACCP system

There are seven stages, as follows.
1. Identify hazards – what could go wrong?
2. Identify the CCPs (critical control points), i.e. the important points where things could go wrong.
3. Set critical limits for each CCP, e.g. temperature requirements on delivery of fresh chicken.
4. Monitor CCPs, put checks in place to stop problems happening.
5. Corrective action, what will be done if something goes wrong?
6. Verification, check that the HACCP plan is working.
7. Documentation, record all of the above.

For example, when dealing with a fresh chicken it is necessary to recognise the possible hazards at all of the identified stages.

- **Hazard** – pathogenic bacteria are likely to be present in raw chicken.
- **Control** – the chicken needs to be cooked thoroughly to 75 °C to ensure pathogens are killed.
- **Monitor** – check the temperature where the thigh joins the body with a calibrated temperature probe, making sure no parts of the flesh are pink and juices are running clear, not red or pink.
- **Hot holding** – the chicken must be kept above **63 °C** before service; this can be checked with a temperature probe.
- **Or chill and refrigerate** – chill to below 10 °C within 90 minutes. Cover, label and refrigerate below 5 °C.
- **Documentation** – temperatures must be measured and recorded. Hot-holding equipment should be checked and the temperature recorded. Record any corrective measures necessary.

Safer Food, Better Business

The HACCP system may seem complicated and difficult to set up for a small or fairly limited business. With this in mind, the Food Standards Agency launched its **Safer Food, Better Business** system for England and Wales.

This is based on the principles of HACCP but in an easy-to-understand format, with pre-printed pages and charts to enter the relevant information, such as temperatures of individual dishes. It is divided into two parts.

1. The first part is about safe methods – for example, avoiding cross-contamination, personal hygiene, cleaning, chilling and cooking.
2. The second part covers opening and closing checks, proving methods are safe, recording safe methods, training records, supervision, stock control, and the selection of suppliers and contractors.

Safer Food, Better Business is available to download from www.food.gov.uk.

Similar systems have been developed in Scotland (CookSafe) and Northern Ireland (Safe Catering).

Due diligence

'Due diligence' can be used as defence under food safety legislation when something relating to food safety goes wrong. It involves providing proof that a business took all reasonable care and precautions, and did everything it could to prevent food safety problems – that is, it exercised all due diligence. To prove due diligence, accurate and up-to-date written documents are essential. These should include:

- staff training records
- staff sickness records
- temperature records (cooking and cold storage)
- pest control policy and audits
- cleaning schedules and deep-clean reports
- equipment maintenance records
- CCP monitoring activities – changes made, corrective actions and recalls
- modifications to the HACCP system
- customer complaints/investigation results
- calibration of instruments
- lists of suppliers (traceability of food).

Training

Food businesses must ensure that all staff who handle food are supervised and instructed and/or trained in food hygiene appropriate to the work they do. The person responsible for the food safety management of a business must also be responsible for staff training.

Appropriate training can take place in-house or with a training provider. Records of staff training must include the date, level of the training and topics covered. All records of staff training must be kept for possible inspection.

Environmental Health Officers

Food safety standards and legislation are enforced in the UK by Environmental Health Officers (EHOs) and Environmental Health Practitioners (EHPs).

Enforcement officers may visit food premises as a matter of routine, as a follow-up when problems have been identified, or after a complaint. The frequency of visits depends on the type of business and food being handled, possible hazards within the business, the risk rating and any previous problems or convictions. Generally, businesses posing a higher risk will be visited more frequently than those considered low risk.

EHOs/EHPs can enter a food business at any reasonable time without previous notice or appointment, usually when the business is open. The main purpose of these inspections is to identify any possible risks from the food business and to assess the effectiveness of the business's own food safety management systems, and also to identify any non-compliance of regulations so this can be monitored and corrected.

The role of the EHO/EHP is to:
- offer professional food safety advice to food businesses on routine visits, and provide useful information such as leaflets and posters
- advise on new food safety legislation
- investigate complaints about the business
- ensure that food offered for sale is safe and fit for consumption
- monitor food operations within a business and identify possible sources of contamination
- ensure food safety law compliance
- observe the effectiveness of the food safety management system
- deal with food-poisoning outbreaks
- advise on food safety training
- deal with non-compliance by formal action/serving notices. They have the power to:
  - close the business
  - seize/remove food
  - instigate prosecution
  - seize records.

Notices and orders for non-compliance

- A **Hygiene Improvement Notice** will be served if the EHO/EHP believes that a food business does not comply with regulations. The notice is served in writing and states the name and address of the business, what is wrong, why it is wrong, what needs to be done to put it right and the time in which this must be completed (usually not less than 14 days).
- A **Hygiene Emergency Prohibition Notice** is served if the EHO/EHP believes that there is an imminent risk to health from the business. This would include serious issues such as sewage contamination, lack of water supply, rodent infestation, and so on. Serving this Notice means immediate closure of the business for three days, during which time the EHO/EHP must apply to magistrates for a **Hygiene Emergency Prohibition Order** to keep the premises closed. Notices/orders must be displayed in a visible place on the premises. The owner of the business must apply for a **Certificate of Satisfaction** before they can reopen.
- A **Hygiene Prohibition Order** prohibits a person (the owner/manager) from working in a food business.

Magistrates' courts can impose fines of up to £5,000, a six-month prison sentence or both. For serious offences, such as knowingly selling food dangerous to health, magistrates could impose fines of up to £20,000. In a Crown Court, unlimited fines and/or two years' imprisonment can be imposed.

The Food Standards Agency

The Food Standards Agency was established in 2000 'to protect public health from risks which may arise in connection with the consumption. of food and otherwise to protect the interest of customers in relation to food'. The Agency is committed to putting customers first, to being open and accessible, and to being an independent voice on food-related matters.

Scores on the Doors

Scores on the Doors is a strategy introduced by the Food Standards Agency to raise food safety standards and reduce the incidence of food poisoning. When an EHO/EHP inspection has been carried out, a star rating will be awarded ranging from 0 to 5 stars, as shown in Table 2.4.

Table 2.4 Scores on the Doors star ratings

Number of stars	Rating
*****	Excellent
****	Very good
***	Good
**	Broadly compliant
*	Poor
None	Very poor

The intention is that the given star rating will be placed in a prominent position on the door or window of premises, but it is not mandatory to do so.

It is hoped that the Scores on the Doors scheme will have a lasting, positive impact on food safety standards.

Know it

- Identify the personal hygiene standards, food safety practices and procedures required, understand the importance of following them and consequences of failing to meet them.
- Know how to store, prepare and cook ingredients to maintain quality, in line with food safety legislation.

Test yourself

1. Why should long hair be tied back and covered in the kitchen?
2. Describe how to wash your hands safely, and give three examples of when your hands must be washed when working with food.
3. There are certain illnesses that a food handler must report to their supervisor before being involved with food. What are they?
4. When cleaning, what do each of the following do:
   a. detergent
   b. sanitiser
   c. disinfectant?
5. Pest control is important.
   a. Why must you keep pests out of food premises?
   b. Suggest three types of pests that could be found in food premises and describe ways that you could keep each of them out.
6. Give four examples of foods that could cause an allergic reaction in some people.
7. Give four examples of how you can avoid cross-contamination in a kitchen.
8. It is essential to keep food above 63 °C or below 5 °C when holding food for service.
   a. Why is this important?
   b. What is the name given to this range of temperatures?
9. What are the temperatures at which you would recommend storing:
   a. dairy foods
   b. frozen fish
   c. fresh meat
   d. soft fruit
   e. flour?
10. All food businesses are required by law to have a food safety management system.
    a. Why is it important to monitor hazards to food safety in a kitchen?
    b. State the key stages in the monitoring process when cooking a fresh chicken for later reheating.

Food safety

Show it

- Maintain a clean and hygienic kitchen environment at all times, and complete kitchen documentation as required.
- Store, prepare and cook ingredients correctly to deliver a quality product that is safe for the consumer.

Live it

- Demonstrate high personal hygiene standards at all times.
- Follow safe working practices when storing, preparing and cooking ingredients, to maintain their quality and safety.

3 People

When working in a kitchen, or in any hospitality role, you will be working as part of a team. This may include:
- completing tasks on your own but as part of a wider team
- completing tasks with one or two other people as part of a wider team
- working as part of a large team that may be subdivided into sections.

Kitchen teams vary in size and type depending on the establishment – a large hotel may have an extensive kitchen brigade with a formal structure, but a small restaurant will have a smaller and less formal team.

Basic team roles in the professional kitchen

The organisation of the staffing hierarchy depends on the establishment.

Many establishments operate a system of kitchen organisation called the partie system, created in the 1890s. This divides the professional kitchen into sections based on the way food is cooked and processed. Over the years this system has been streamlined due to labour costs and skill shortages.

Kitchen porters will also be employed, and in large establishments a kitchen clerk or personal assistant to the chef will be employed to assist with paperwork.

In some operations, such as hospitals and centralised kitchens, a kitchen manager will take charge of the kitchen and have a number of cooks and kitchen assistants working under them. A centralised kitchen is one that serves a number of different outlets; the food is transported to these outlets, usually chilled or frozen. Each outlet will have a satellite or finishing kitchen where the food is finished and made ready to serve to the customer.

Responsibilities and requirements of specific job roles

Modern kitchens are organised in many different ways, but in each case a senior member of staff will be responsible for the smooth operation of the kitchen. This person must have leadership skills, human resource management skills and detailed product knowledge.

- **Executive head chef:** some very large establishments, such as a large five-star hotel, will have an executive head chef. This position is mainly administrative, as he or she will have a head chef that looks after the day-to-day running of the kitchen. There may be other responsibilities, such as duty management in a large hotel at weekends.
- **Head chef:** has overall responsibility for the organisation and management of the kitchen, including staffing, training, menus, budget control and sourcing of food. The head chef is also responsible for implementing food safety, and health and safety legislation and practices.
- **Sous chef:** the deputy to the head chef, he or she will take overall responsibility in the head chef's absence. The sous chef may also have specific areas of responsibility, such as food safety, health and safety, quality control or staff training.
- **Chef de partie:** in charge of a specific section within the kitchen, such as meat, vegetables or fish, and responsible for setting tasks within their section. There may be a demi chef de partie working on an opposite shift, covering the chef de partie's days off. Commis chefs and apprentices usually work with these chefs in different sections.
- **Commis chef:** the junior chef in the kitchen, who works under overall supervision of the chef de partie and sous chef. A commis chef will work around the various kitchen sections.
- **Apprentice:** similar to a commis chef, an apprentice will complete the same tasks but is usually on a planned programme of learning, often managed by a college or training provider.

People 3

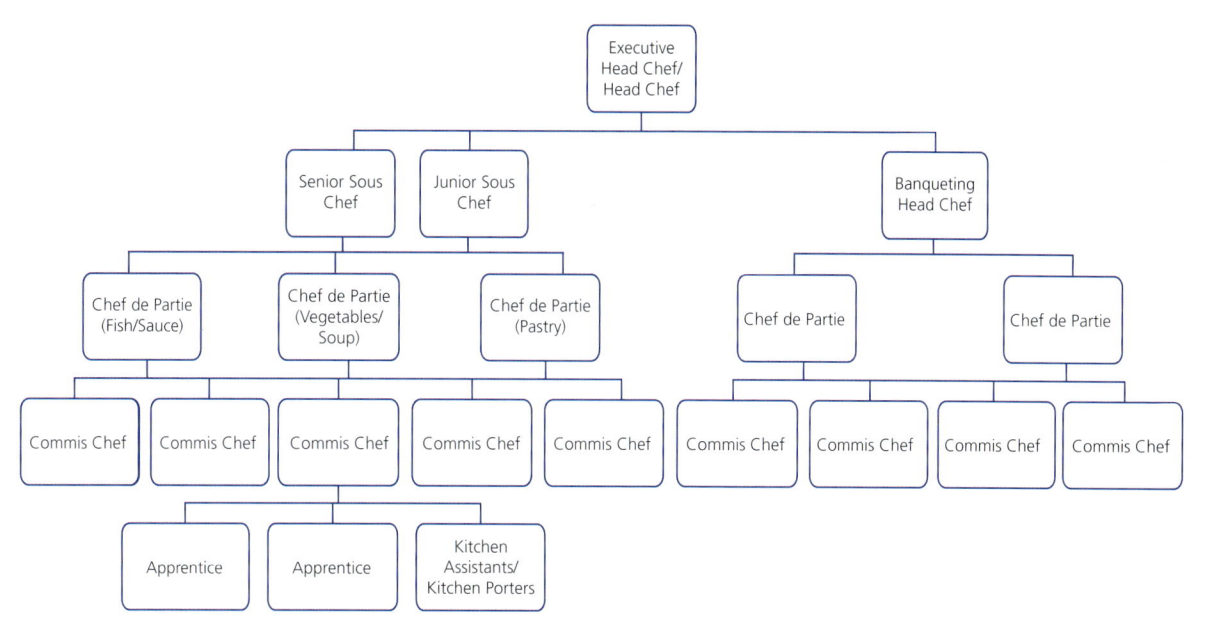

▲ Staffing structure for a medium-sized hotel kitchen

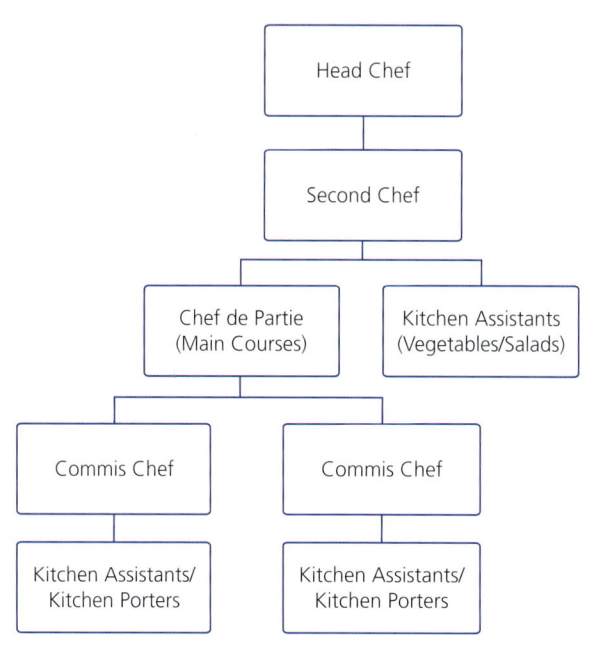

▲ Kitchen organisation structure for a brasserie

The relationship to other departments

All restaurants must have a direct and good working relationship with the kitchen and food production areas.
- The executive chef and the head chef generally report to the general manager of the establishment or organisation.
- Some executive chefs also assume the role of food and beverage manager, and are responsible for the staffing and profitability of the restaurant and bar areas.

Good communication is essential between departments, to deliver the required quality and level of service the customer is paying for, and to match their expectations. It is important that each department respects the others and works to achieve the main objectives of the organisation. Teamwork is crucial in the hospitality industry and team briefings are essential before each service period.

To be successful as part of a kitchen team you will need to develop the skills to communicate and work with others. You need to make sure that the instructions and allocated tasks given to you are clearly understood so that mistakes are not made, and time and food are not wasted. If there is something you do not understand, ask for a further explanation or to be shown the procedure again.

The tasks to be completed by each kitchen section and each member of staff need to be planned and organised so that all work is completed efficiently, to the required standards and on time.

Following instructions

You will be given a number of instructions during your working day; it is important to complete these tasks to the best of your ability and with accuracy. These may be written down as a task list for you to complete or you may receive verbal instruction. Whichever way you are given the instructions, read and/or listen carefully; if possible, confirm back what is required of you, and ask for further instruction if you don't understand what you are being asked to do.

With a list of tasks it will be necessary to prioritise which are most important or need to be done first. For example, some vegetables required for lunch service in an hour's time will need to be dealt with before the preparation of items for dinner or tomorrow's menu.

Also, you need to organise your time efficiently: while something is cooking in the oven you could be working on something else. If you need help or advice on how to prioritise tasks, or if you are unsure that you have got it right, ask for guidance. As the day's work progresses it may be necessary to change the order and priority of tasks as some things may become more urgent. Writing down the instructions given to you will help you to work efficiently and professionally.

Types of instructions

- **The recipe:** one of the most important sets of instructions you will use; it is important to follow it accurately. You will frequently need to scale the recipe up or down (multiplying or dividing the amounts) to match the quantities you will need; take care to do this accurately. It is advisable to write down and double check the amended recipe amounts. Read the whole recipe through at least once before starting the task and ask about anything you are unsure of. Assemble the ingredients you will need before starting preparation or cooking, and also assemble all of the tools and equipment you will need.
- **Use of equipment and machinery:** always make sure you have been shown how to prepare and use equipment for specific tasks. For example, does a dessert mould need lining with silicone film? Does a loaf tin need to be greased and floured? You must receive full instructions and training before using new equipment or machinery.
- **Health and safety/food safety instructions:** follow the guidelines or training given by your employer and any training courses you may have completed. Some of these instructions will be legal requirements and it is your legal responsibility to comply with them. Apart from following the necessary instructions, it is essential that you report anything that may cause problems in maintaining the required standards of health and safety or food safety. For example, it would be essential to report a refrigerator not maintaining the required temperature (as food at the wrong temperature can cause food poisoning) or an electrical appliance with a damaged flex (which could cause an electric shock or fire).
- **Uniform and personal hygiene:** instructions on the required standards of kitchen uniform and the standards of personal hygiene required must be followed precisely. This will give you pride in your own appearance and professionalism, and will also maintain the standards and reputation of the establishment you work for. You will have been given instructions about reporting any sickness or infection you may have before you start work. It is of the utmost importance, and a legal requirement, that you follow these instructions fully.
- **Emergency procedure instructions:** you will have been told the procedure to follow in an emergency such as a fire. Be aware of the procedures and follow evacuation instructions correctly.
- **Standard operational procedure:** some instructions you are given about the way that you work and complete tasks will be specific to the individual workplace or a group of establishments. It means that all employees will be completing tasks in the same way and will be maintaining the same standards. This is called the 'standard operational procedure' (SOP), and will detail the steps and activities of a process and the required quality and presentation of the finished product. An example would be the way a specific dish is produced, presented, garnished and served at a banqueting event so each plate looks exactly the same.

Efficient use of time

Organising and managing your time well is important because kitchen work is generally more time-specific than many other areas of work. For example, if some office-based data entry was completed an hour later than planned it may not be too much of a problem, but if someone ordered lunch that was an hour late, the customer would rightly have cause for complaint and would probably not come back again. To meet the time constraints of a busy kitchen, careful planning and organisation are essential.

The impact of individual and team performance

Good teamwork is essential in all working environments. Whether the kitchen is large or small, the kitchen staff all have to work as a cohesive team, working together and supporting one another. Working as part of a team can allow people to feel valued and learn from one another's skills and expertise.

- A high-performing team is able to deliver to customer expectations and create an excellent and memorable food experience. People feel supported in their role and there is a positive and creative working environment. Such a team also creates great job satisfaction for its members and a real sense of true professionalism.
- Poor individual performance can have a negative effect on the team and reduce team morale. It is the role of the manager to motivate the team.
- A disjointed team or a team whose members are not supporting one another will not be able to function effectively, and can have a negative impact on food production, the business and the customer experience. The product and service can suffer as standards are lowered; this can result in dissatisfied customers, an increase in complaints, and therefore a decrease in sales and profits.

Standards of performance

Essential to any food service business is the setting and maintenance of standards of performance. Many organisations have standards of performance manuals. These are often referred to as SOPs. This term is often used to refer to the standards themselves or to the manuals that contain the details of them.

Setting standards of performance, and training staff to achieve the standards, needs to be supported by regular reviews of the extent to which the standards are being met. In addition, there needs to be a continuous process for the review and development of the standards. An approach to developing and maintaining standards of performance relies on four key elements:
1 standards of performance
2 supporting reference materials
3 regular standards audit, and
4 continuous review and action planning.

Asking for help

Working as part of a team means that you will be working together with others to reach the desired goals within a specific time. The requirements and pressures of work in different areas can vary, and you may need to ask for help from others to reach your targets on time.

You may also need to ask for help or further instruction if you don't understand what you are being asked to do. If you need advice on how to prioritise tasks, or if you are unsure that you have got a task right, you should speak to your supervisor or line manager.

Supporting others

On occasion you may need to offer help and assistance to others so that the team reaches its targets on time. However, do this only when:
- you have sufficient time and your own work will not suffer by helping others
- the help you offer is within your capabilities
- it does not contradict what a supervisor or senior chef has asked you to do.

If you are not sure about any of this, ask your section chef, head chef or line manager.

Remember that it is the outcome and product of the team that define a successful business or operation. It is less likely that those working in isolation will achieve the same goals.

Behaviour that helps teams to work effectively

Employers value good team members. They will look for employees with the personal qualities to work as part of a successful and productive team, and who are able to develop good working relationships and act as role models to others. A good team member:
- is reliable, dependable and always punctual
- takes pride in their personal appearance, is clean, smart, tidy and well groomed, and is proud to wear a chef's or company uniform
- is committed to company training programmes
- is flexible, responds well to shift requests and regularly attends team meetings
- is a good communicator, listening to instructions and passing on relevant information clearly and promptly

- is someone who completes work on time, asks for help when needed and offers help to others when appropriate
- is well organised, with the ability to think ahead and prioritise tasks as appropriate
- is open to feedback, always willing to learn new skills and techniques, and learns from experience
- is someone who has empathy with others, listening to and respecting the points of view of other team members, and responding politely
- is confident and assertive within the specific job role.

Negative behaviour

Sometimes, however, negative behaviour occurs in a workplace. This must be discouraged and dealt with promptly and effectively by someone managing or supervising the area. Negative behaviour can include:

- poor timekeeping and being unreliable
- poor standards of dress and personal appearance
- being inconsiderate to others and unhelpful
- laziness; not completing tasks properly
- use of inappropriate language, swearing
- producing work that is not of the required standard or not produced on time.

Working relationship problems

Occasionally in busy kitchens, pressure, workload and personality differences can have negative effects on good working relationships within a team. It is important that you bring any concerns about such problems to the attention of your line manager or supervisor. You will need to discuss what the problem is and why you are concerned, giving specific examples where possible. You should also say when the problems occur and the frequency. Try to remain constructive in your discussion of relationship problems so that a solution can be planned in the most amicable way.

Signs of damaging behaviour within the workplace must be taken very seriously and reported immediately. Examples of this kind of behaviour may include:

- intimidation – deliberately making someone feel frightened or nervous in certain situations
- harassment – annoying or unpleasant behaviour that takes place regularly, for example, threats, offensive remarks or even physical attacks
- victimisation – to single someone out and treat them unfairly
- bullying – hurting, frightening, threatening, persecuting or tormenting others; it could also be forcing someone to do something they do not want to do.

The above may take the form of:

- racist comments or gestures
- remarks about religion, belief, gender or sexuality
- remarks about personal characteristics or disabilities
- physical or sexual abuse
- belittling and undermining an individual's achievements
- ignoring individuals and making them feel isolated
- excluding individuals from information and what is going on
- threatening behaviour
- humiliating individuals in front of others
- setting of unrealistic or unachievable targets.

No employee should suffer any of the above and a solution to the problem must be found as soon as possible. Discuss any concerns that you may have with your line manager, supervisor or head chef.

Equality and diversity in the workplace

The hospitality industry embraces equality and diversity, and celebrates different cultures and customs. This means that all employees should be treated equally, without discrimination, and have equal opportunities in the workplace. Celebrating diversity in the workplace means that the company actively welcomes people from a variety of backgrounds, and reflects this attitude in its hiring policies and workplace culture.

It is important to respect people from different cultures and backgrounds, and to understand how to communicate with them.

Hospitality is a very diverse industry, employing people from many different cultural backgrounds; many companies do offer diversity training for employees, as well as guidance on how to deal with customers and guests from many different backgrounds.

Communicating clearly and effectively

Good communication is essential to a successful kitchen team to ensure the dishes produced are of high quality, delivered on time and to the standard required. There

will be many different communication methods used between:
- individuals working together
- other kitchen sections and service staff
- other departments and management
- suppliers and contractors
- customers/guests.

Speaking and listening are the most widely used forms of communication in a kitchen, so it is important that they are carried out effectively.
- Speak clearly and listen carefully so the message is understood. This is especially important in a noisy kitchen.
- Non-verbal gestures, such as facial expressions and hand gestures, may help to reinforce the message and will confirm understanding.
- Take time to communicate properly; avoid speaking from a distance or speaking while walking past the other person.
- Avoid interrupting and avoid distractions; listen to what is being said then respond.
- Do not shout, swear or use inappropriate language.
- When receiving verbal instruction, ask questions where necessary and summarise the instruction at the end.

However, there are many other ways that communication takes place in kitchens, including the following.
- **Non-verbal gestures:** such as a nod, a raised hand or 'thumbs up' can be useful, but make sure they are not misunderstood, especially when communicating between different nationalities and cultures.
- **Written communication:** this is very widely used, from formal letters through task lists and brief notes. Make sure they are clearly written so that the recipient will fully understand the meaning.
- **Pictorial communication:** pictures or diagrams are often used in instructions and signs around the kitchen (especially for health and safety instruction). These are often standardised and are recognised internationally. A picture, diagram or sketch could also be used to convey meaning where there is a language barrier.
- **Telephone:** this remains a very widely used method of communication and there may be specific systems used in an establishment (for example, land line phones or mobile/smartphones).
- **Fax messaging:** this older technology still has numerous uses, especially when exact copies, signed copies, drawings or diagrams need to be sent elsewhere.
- **Electronic systems:** these have become increasingly sophisticated and are very popular. Frequently used systems include email, text messaging, QR codes, electronic ordering systems, data-logging systems and systems designed for specific company use, such as Vocera, Maytas or Opera.
- **Social media:** increasingly, communication takes place through social media such as Twitter, Facebook, LinkedIn and Rehoba.

It is extremely important to learn how to communicate with colleagues, customers and guests who come from a variety of diverse backgrounds.

Passing on information

At some time in the day you may be left a message or given information that needs to be passed on to others in the team. It is essential that such information is passed on quickly and accurately. Make sure that the person you are giving the information to fully hears and understands what you are telling them. If a written note has been left or an email sent, make sure it has been seen and read by the relevant person.

Such information may include:
- a message from a member of staff saying they will not be in to work or will be late – record and pass on details such as the time of the call, how late they will be or the reason for absence, and how long they expect to be away from work (a contact number may also be useful)
- a late delivery from a supplier or items that could not be supplied
- bookings or cancellations
- arrival of visitors such as maintenance contractors, inspectors or company representatives
- faulty equipment or supplies running low
- changes in the menu
- information about special dietary requirements or allergies
- changes in timing – for example, a buffet lunch required one hour earlier.

Use the most appropriate communication method to pass on the information.

Potential challenges in the workplace

There are always potential challenges in a busy professional kitchen. It is important to know how to deal with them. Executive chefs and head chefs are usually very experienced in dealing with unexpected situations and challenges. For example:

- if food supplies do not arrive on time or there are shortages, there is always a contingency plan
- if equipment breaks down, a 24-hour maintenance plan is in place.

If you are unsure how to deal with a challenge or unexpected situation, you should seek advice from your line manager.

Developing your skills

Good employees will be keen to learn as much as they can about the job they are employed to do, as well as improving and refining their own knowledge and skills. Professional development within the job role will lead to progression and promotion, and will also provide interesting challenges.

Improving your knowledge and skills

Improving your knowledge and skills through training and personal development is not only beneficial for you and your career progression, but will help to raise the skills within the team, and provide variety and diversity within the workplace. The advantages of well-produced training programmes include:

- clearly identified and specified responsibilities
- following rules and instructions linked with required standards of performance
- improved competence ability and confidence of staff, and
- more efficient, safe and hygienic working practices.

You may also encourage others working with you to develop their skills and knowledge too.

The ways that you can develop and progress within your job role include:

- attending training provided by your employer or asking about courses that interest you
- attending a full-time or part-time college course
- completing a work-based qualification managed by a training provider or college
- asking questions of others, as well as finding things out for yourself
- working with skilled and experienced colleagues
- asking for feedback and progression advice
- discussing your progress with your managers, supervisors and mentors
- actively participating in formal appraisals, discussing your performance targets and progression
- producing or working to a development plan (see below).

Seeking feedback on performance and progression

Asking for feedback on your work and progression from your peers, supervisors or senior chefs is a good way of evaluating your performance. Listen to what is said and maybe take notes. When receiving feedback, you may like to ask questions and discuss which parts of your work are up to standard and where improvements could be made. Agreements can be made, and targets set for future improvement and progression. Recording your progress and achievements in a learning or progression plan is an excellent way to check your progress, and allows you to refer to your initial targets and work towards the final outcome.

Development plans

A development plan allows learning and development to be organised, and your progress and achievement can be monitored. The plan needs to state the long-term aims of what you ultimately want to achieve, as well as short-term aims that are the steps to get you there. Producing, developing and taking interest in your development plan will show your employer that you are ambitious, proactive and well organised. Planning future progress is a good skill in itself and will help you to focus on planning your career.

Having a personal development plan will help you to identify targets and time-scales to improve your skills and advance your career for personal and professional success.

A development plan could be put in place by:

- your employer, human resources department or training department
- your head chef, supervisor or mentor

- a training provider or college managing your learning
- you – you can produce your own development plan or simply keep a notebook or chart of your goals and achievements; these can then be discussed at appraisal or progress meetings.

Reviewing and updating plans

The progress you are making may be monitored and updated by:
- keeping your own record with dates in a suitable notebook or file, or electronically on a laptop or tablet
- regular progress meetings with a tutor, head chef or mentor
- verbal and written feedback
- formal appraisals
- letters or emails
- logbooks, charts and electronic tracking systems.

Performance appraisals

Appraisal is a method by which the job performance of an employee is reviewed and evaluated, usually by a manager, supervisor or head chef. An appraisal is a part of guiding and managing career development, and is a good opportunity for uninterrupted discussion between an employee and their line manager.

Performance appraisals are a time to discuss your recent successes, achievements, personal strengths and weaknesses, and suitability for promotion or further education/training. It is an excellent opportunity to identify areas for development to address skills and knowledge gaps, and discuss ways to enhance your career prospects. Your development plan may help you to contribute positively to your appraisal.

Know it

- Understand how personal and team performance impact on the successful production of dishes and menu items.
- Know how to communicate with colleagues and team members from a diverse range of backgrounds and cultures.
- Understand the importance of training and development to maximise own performance.
- Know how to support team members when the need arises.
- Have an understanding of professional behaviours and organisational culture.
- Recognise how all teams are dependent on one another, and understand the importance of teamwork both back and front of house.

Test yourself

1. Give three reasons why good, effective teamwork is essential in a kitchen.
2. Why is it important to understand exactly what you are required to do in order to complete the jobs allocated to you? What will be the likely consequences if you do not understand fully what is required?
3. Suggest two occasions when you may offer help to someone else in your team. Also, suggest two occasions when you should not give help to someone else.
4. When might you ask for help from someone else?
5. Describe four pieces of information you may need to pass on to someone else. What are the ways you could use to pass on the information clearly?
6. Give three examples of positive behaviour in a team and three examples of negative behaviour.
7. If you were concerned about poor working relationships in your kitchen, what could you do about it?

8 What are the benefits to you of continuing to improve your work knowledge and skills?

9 How can you get feedback on how you are progressing with your learning and skills?

10 Suggest a good way to keep a record of your targets and achievements.

Show it

- Work effectively with others to ensure dishes produced are of high quality, delivered on time and to the standard required.
- Use suitable methods of communication, and operate in a fair and equal manner that demonstrates effective team working.
- Develop your own skills and knowledge through training and experiences.
- Support your team members to produce dishes and menu items on time, to quality standards set by your establishment.
- Perform your job role to the best of own ability in line with the business values and culture.
- Develop good working relationships across the team and with colleagues in other parts of the organisation, and deal with challenges and problems constructively to drive a positive outcome.

Live it

- Take pride in your role through an enthusiastic and professional approach to tasks.
- Listen to and respect other people's point of view, and respond politely.
- Welcome and act on feedback to improve personal methods of working, recognising the impact that personal performance has on the team. Recognise your own personal growth and achievement.
- Respond positively to instruction and be aware of team members who may need support to get menu items out on time without compromising quality.
- Behave in a manner that is in line with the values and culture of the business.
- Communicate and behave effectively to help team members achieve the best result for the customers and the business.

4 Business

Hospitality is a business and, like any other business, it involves finance. Chefs are required to cost all the dishes on the menu, procure the food and other materials, control waste and comply with legislation. Operational control is essential in order to obtain a return on investment.

General costs for hospitality and catering

Costing menu items

Food costs and dish costing are important because it is essential to know the exact cost of each process and every item produced. Understanding these costs is important because:

- they tell you the gross and net profit made by each section of the organisation and show the cost of each meal produced
- they will reveal possible ways to economise, and can result in a more effective use of stores, labour and materials
- costing provides the information necessary to develop a good pricing policy
- cost records help to provide speedy quotations for special functions, such as parties and wedding receptions
- they enable the caterer to keep to a budget; if food costing is controlled accurately, the cost of particular items on the menu and the total expenditure on food over a given period can be worked out.

Understanding food costs helps to control costs, prices and profits. An efficient food cost system will show up any bad buying and inefficient storage, and should help to prevent waste and pilfering. This can help the chef to run an efficient business and give the customer value for money.

Example of dish costing

Name of dish: Navarin of lamb

Number of portions: 20

Ingredients	Amount	Cost per unit	Total cost £ p
Stewing lamb (shoulder)	2.5 kg	£6.50 per kg	£16.25
Carrots	500 g	60p per kg	£0.30
Onions	500 g	65p per kg	£0.32
Oil	75 ml	£1 per litre	£0.75
Garlic clove	5 cloves	30p per bulb	£0.30
Flour (white)	120 g	£1.50 per kg	£0.18
Tomato paste	70 g	50p per 100 g	£0.35
Brown stock	2.5 litres	50p per litre	£2.50
Bouquet garni			£0.30
		Total	£21.25

Cost of 1 portion = £21.25 ÷ 20 = £1.06 per portion.

Elements of cost

Costing dishes is a very important process for a chef and allows the selling price to be established. To calculate the total cost of any one item or meal provided, it is necessary to analyse the total expenditure under several headings. The total cost of each item consists of the three main elements described in Table 4.1.

Table 4.1 The three main elements that make up total cost

Type of cost	Impact on the costing menu items
Food and materials	These costs can change on a daily or weekly basis, according to the volume of business. This is called a **variable cost**. Having excess stock in storage is a cost, and can result in food wastage.
Labour	Wages paid to part-time or extra staff are variable costs, but salaries and wages paid regularly to permanent staff are **fixed costs**.
Overheads	These consist of rent, rates, cleaning materials, heating, lighting and equipment, maintenance, gas, electricity and sundry expenses, insurance and marketing costs.

63

Labour costs in the majority of operations fall into two categories, as follows.

1 Direct labour costs: the salaries and wages paid to staff such as chefs, waiters, bar staff, housekeepers and room service assistants, which can be allocated to income from food, drink and accommodation sales.
2 Indirect labour costs: includes salaries and wages paid, for example, to managers, office staff and maintenance staff who work for all departments in the establishment (so their labour cost should be charged to all departments).

Gross profit

Gross profit (or kitchen profit) is the difference between the cost of an item and the price it is sold at.

Gross profit = selling price − food cost

For example, if food costs are £2 and the selling price is £4:

Gross profit = £4 − £2 = £2

It is important for the kitchen staff to operate within budget and to achieve the required gross profit margin. To do this an establishment needs:

- a system of operational control, checking incoming goods for the correct price, quality and weight
- to follow the standardised recipe to achieve the exact yield and portion control to match customer expectations
- to achieve the desired gross profit return.

Net profit

Net profit is the difference between the selling price of the food (sales) and total cost of the product (this includes food, labour and overheads).

Net profit = selling price − total cost

For example, if the selling price is £5 and the total cost is £4:

Net profit = £5 − £4 = £1

Worked example

Costs and sales:
Food sales for 1 week = £25,000
Food costs for 1 week = £12,000
Labour and overheads for 1 week = £9,000
Total costs for 1 week = food costs + labour and overheads = £12,000 + £9,000 = £21,000

To work out the gross profit:
Gross profit = food sales − food cost
= £25,000 − £12,000 = £13,000

To work out the net profit:
Net profit = food sales − total costs
= £25,000 − £21,000 = £4,000

Profit is always expressed as a percentage:

$$\% \text{ net profit} = \frac{\text{net profit}}{\text{sales}} \times 100$$

Using the same example as above, the percentage net profit for the week is:

$$\frac{4,000}{25,000} \times 100 = 16\%$$

Implications of not achieving gross profit targets

A failure to meet gross profit targets is likely to provide insufficient funds to contribute to net costs, leading to a reduced net profit or even a potential net loss. Such losses can lead to trading difficulties, where a business has to make decisions in an attempt to reverse the situation.

In simple terms, the business has to either increase sales, and the margin between costs and selling prices, or reduce costs. In terms of achieving gross profit targets, this can be achieved by reducing expenditure on foods by actions such as purchasing cheaper items or ensuring that wastage is reduced to a minimum. Portion control and yield are also essential. To achieve net profit targets in such a situation, staffing is likely to be examined in the first instance, with the option of reducing labour costs to improve net profit target achievement.

A business that is in a loss-making scenario can quickly find itself in trading difficulty. Insufficient funds lead to issues with obtaining supplies, as suppliers will lose confidence in the business's ability to settle its bills/debts. Without supplies, it is impossible to produce dishes for customers and therefore trading will cease.

Activity

Food costs for one week at the restaurant you work in are £15,000. In the same week, the restaurant spends £12,000 on labour and overheads. Food sales for the week total £30,000.
1 Calculate the **gross profit** the restaurant makes for the week.
2 Calculate the **net profit** the restaurant makes for the week.

Each element of cost is usually expressed as a percentage of the selling price. This enables the caterer to see how to control profits. Table 4.2 shows how each element of cost can be shown as a percentage of sales.

Table 4.1 Elements of cost shown as percentage of sales

	Costs	Percentage of sales
Food cost	£12,000	$\frac{12,000}{25,000} \times 100 = 48\%$
Labour	£6,000	$\frac{6,000}{25,000} \times 100 = 24\%$
Overheads	£3,000	$\frac{3,000}{25,000} \times 100 = 12\%$
Total costs	£21,000	$\frac{21,000}{25,000} \times 100 = 84\%$
Sales	£25,000	
Net profit (sales – total costs)	£4,000	$\frac{4,000}{25,000} \times 100 = 16\%$

Calculating the selling price

If the selling price of a dish is expressed as 100 per cent (the total amount received from its sale), it can be broken down into the amount of money spent on food items and the gross profit. This can be expressed in percentages. Often, caterers need to ensure that an agreed gross profit is achieved. The selling price needed to achieve a specific gross profit percentage can be calculated by dividing the total food cost by the food cost as a percentage of the sale and multiplying by 100.

Food costs as a percentage of the sale =
100 − gross profit %

Worked example

If food costs are £3.50, to calculate the selling price and make sure a 65 per cent gross profit is achieved, the following calculations can be used.

First, calculate food costs as a percentage of the sale:

100 − gross profit % = 100 − 65 = 35%

This is shown in the pie chart below.

■ Food cost ■ Gross profit

35%

65%

The selling price of the dish is 100 per cent: therefore, if gross profit is 65 per cent, the food cost as a percentage of the sale is 35 per cent.

To calculate the selling price:

This can also be presented in monetary terms, as shown in the following diagram.

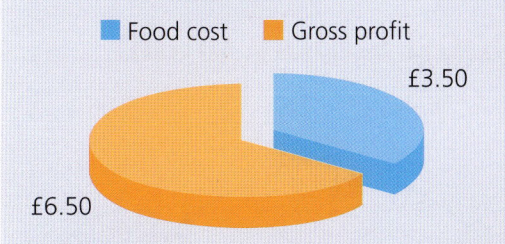

■ Food cost ■ Gross profit

£3.50

£6.50

Here, the total food cost is £3.50 and the selling price is £10; the gross profit is therefore £6.50.

Worked example

Raising the required gross profit reduces the food cost as a percentage of the selling price. For example, if the gross profit requirement were raised to 75 per cent, this would reduce the food cost as a percentage of the selling price to 25 per cent (100% − 75%).

If the food cost is £3.50 and the required gross profit is 75 per cent:

To achieve a 75 per cent gross profit, with a £3.50 food cost, the selling price would need to be £14.00.

The percentages still add up to 100 per cent, but the proportion spent on food is now smaller in terms of the selling price (food costs are now 25 per cent of the selling price) because the percentage gross profit is higher.

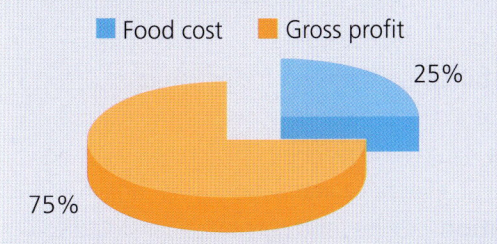

■ Food cost ■ Gross profit

25%

75%

To check that this is correct, the following calculation can be applied:

(brings up to 25%)

… and

(brings up to 75%)

£10.50 (75%) + £3.50 (25%) = £14.00 (100%)

> **Activity**
>
> If a dish costs £3.00 to produce, what should the selling price be to achieve a 70 per cent profit on sales?

The food supply chain

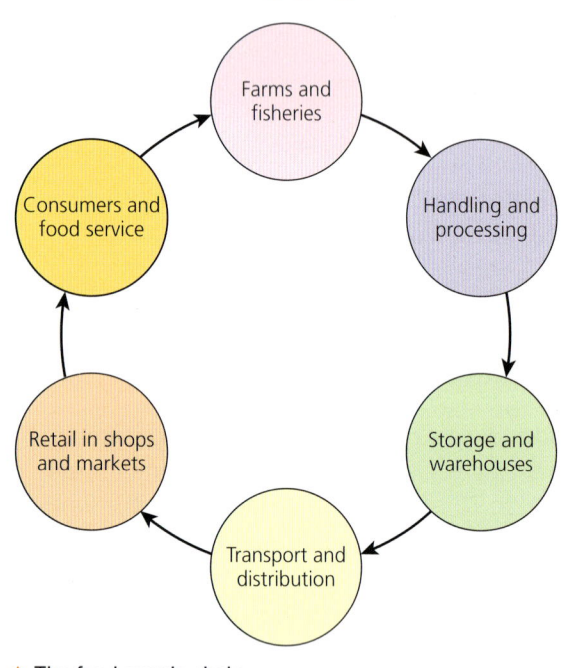

▲ The food supply chain

The food supply chain is about securing the access to food that an establishment needs. Food security has been defined by the United Nations Food and Agriculture Organization as follows: 'when all people at all times, have physical and economic access to sufficient, safe and nutritious food to meet their dietary needs and food preferences for an active and healthy life'.

This includes the following.
- **Availability** – Is there a sufficient amount of food available all the time?
- **Access** – Can it be reached efficiently? Can it be bought at a fair price and is it of a high quality?
- **Utilisation** – Is the food part of a balanced diet?

Therefore food security and the food supply chain are about having continuous access to affordable, safe and nutritious food. Food availability is about how much food is available, as well as the reliability of the supply.

Food miles

The term **food miles** refers to the distance food travels from farm to plate. Approximately 54 per cent of vegetables and 90 per cent of fruit eaten in the UK is imported. Food is transported across the world because people want to eat food all year round that is out of season in the UK – for example, strawberries and asparagus.

Planes are powered by fossil fuel oil. When the oil is burned it gives off carbon dioxide gas emissions, which contribute to global warming. Trees can be planted to absorb the carbon dioxide. This is called **carbon offsetting**. To reduce food miles, some hospitality companies are sourcing their ingredients in the UK and more locally. However many ingredients are transported around the country to distribution centres that are part of the food chain before they get to restaurants.

Food sustainability

We must think where food comes from.
- Has it been produced locally?
- How was it produced – for example, were organic and sustainable methods of farming used?
- Is the food sustainable – for example, is the fish purchased from a sustainable source? Has the meat been purchased from a source that maintains high welfare standards?
- How much energy was used in its production? Were the energy sources used sustainable? What impact has the food production had on the environment, for example, pollution and carbon emissions?

Sourcing and purchasing of food commodities

The menu dictates what a food operation needs to purchase and, based on this, the buyer searches for a market that can supply these requirements. Once the right market is found, the buyer must investigate the various products available. The buyer makes decisions regarding quality, amounts, price, and what will satisfy the customers but also make a profit. A buyer must have knowledge of the internal organisation of the company and be able to obtain the products needed at a competitive price. They must understand how these items are going to be used in the production operations (i.e. how they are going to be prepared and cooked), to make sure that the right item is purchased. Sometimes the item required may not have to be of prime quality – tomatoes for use in soups and sauces, for instance.

It is important to accurately cost dishes, so you should know the cost of all of the ingredients you are using in your dishes.

Purchase tendering and nominated suppliers

Many large hospitality companies use specialist contractors to procure their food suppliers. Asking suppliers to tender is now very common in large organisations as there are many benefits: suppliers often bid for the business based on price, availability of supply and the ability to negotiate with local producers.

Working with a consortium of establishments and organisations means that the business has a great deal of buying power and can negotiate the best possible price with nominated suppliers. Consumers today are interested in provenance and traceability: they want to know where the ingredients come from – the country of origin, whether the farm is local, and the name of the farm and the grower. The tendering process often covers traceability, and will also report on food safety aspects, animal welfare and husbandry, and food sustainability.

The tendering process covers all aspects of due diligence from beginning to end, carefully monitoring quality and prices. Nominated suppliers understand that if there is a problem with quality then products will be returned and a credit note issued.

Contingency planning

It is important for all hospitality companies to make sure there is a constant supply chain for all ingredients. The following contingency plans should be in place.
- Have several nominated suppliers as a contingency if there is a problem with a supplier.
- Have a contingency plan if there are unforeseen shortages of any ingredient.
- Be prepared if necessary to use substitute ingredients.
- It is useful to have a security stock of frozen items in case of severe problems with transport or extreme weather conditions.
- In case of equipment and machinery breaking down, it is advisable to have a 24-hour service contract.

Food waste management and recycling

Waste should be avoided for a number of reasons.
- Wastage means the calculated yield from ingredients will not be achieved.
- Waste is expensive and will affect the overall cost of what is being produced.
- Disposal of excessive waste needs to be paid for.
- Unnecessary waste is now also considered to be ecologically unacceptable, placing strain on the planet's resources.

Be aware of the quantities required before starting preparation. Take care to avoid unnecessary waste, which can be caused by:
- over-production
- incorrect information or lack of information
- careless preparation, such as peeling vegetables too thickly
- poor cooking procedures, such as over-cooking causing excessive shrinkage or food to be completely spoiled.

Effective working practices for waste management

- **Avoid over-buying stock:** purchase only those ingredients that you know your business will use. It can be tempting to 'stock up' or buy in bulk if your supplier is offering a good deal, but doing so can leave you with more food than you need. This will be wasted if it's left to spoil in storage.
- **Store food correctly:** this is vital for preserving its quality and preventing pathogenic bacterial growth – both of which can quickly lead to food waste. See Chapter 2 for guidelines on food storage.
- **Practise stock rotation regularly:** use the 'first in, first out' rule when storing food and displaying food for sale (see Chapter 2, page 43).

- **Temperature control:** good temperature control means that food waste is less likely as the food is unable to spoil (see Chapter 2, page 44).
- **Label food correctly:** keeping stock organised makes it much easier to keep track of what you have and what needs using, preventing unlabelled containers from being thrown away in error or because you don't know what's in them.
- **Keep a stock inventory:** to prevent waste, you should always know exactly which foods you have in stock at all times. This means keeping a detailed list of the foods in all of your storage areas, including their use-by/best-before dates, which you can easily refer to. This avoids foods getting forgotten and going to waste.
- **Pay attention to use-by dates:** use-by dates should be checked on a daily basis (see Chapter 2, page 43).
- **Inspect all deliveries against the order specification:** when a food delivery arrives at your restaurant, accept only those items that you ordered, to prevent excess, wasted food. You should also reject food with visible spoilage or damage, or delivered at the incorrect storage temperature – these foods will only spoil further and be thrown away later in the day.
- **Keep a close eye on portion control:** be wary of oversized food portions and jumbo side dishes. Monitor plate waste carefully – if excessive amounts of food are being left on the plates, cut down the portion sizes.
- **Anticipate the demand with care:** think carefully about how much food your restaurant needs to prepare in advance – can any of this be made to order instead? Large batch cooking means that food may not get used before it goes out of date. Although batch cooking can save time, it can also be a waste of both money and food.
- **Give customers more menu options:** for example, do all your main meals need to come with chips or salad? Give customers more choice over what to include or leave out of their meal, to prevent food from going to waste. Customers might prefer to be given a choice between fries, vegetables or salad, or include these items on the 'side dishes' part of the menu for customers to purchase if they really want them.
- **Incorporate leftovers and use food efficiently:** don't automatically throw away leftover food, as you might be able to make use of it somewhere else. For example, vegetable peelings and animal bones can be used to make stocks and soups, while day-old bread can be made into croutons or breadcrumbs.
- **Compost food waste:** rather than sending it to landfill, put any waste food into a compost bin, such as fruit and vegetable peelings, old bread products, grains, coffee grounds and tea bags – almost any food except for meat, fish and dairy products.
- **Ask if customers want to take leftovers home:** around 30 per cent of waste is food left on customers' plates, so why not offer your customers the option of a 'doggy bag' to take their leftover food home with them? Not every food can be packaged up for eating later, but some can easily be put into a takeaway box, such as pastries and cakes.
- **If you have a buffet or self-service counter, don't provide trays:** food waste is often created by people serving themselves too much food at self-service counters. If people are given only plates, they are less likely to pile on excess food and carry side dishes containing extra food.
- **Train employees in how to reduce waste:** by law, all food handlers must be trained in food safety, but this should also extend to being taught how to reduce waste. Poor food production and preparation contribute to a high level of food waste. Therefore, it is crucial for staff to learn how to store and cook food correctly, keep the premises clean and avoid cross-contamination.

Food waste is created in a number of different ways:
- food that is spoiled or cannot be used because it is past its use-by date
- parts of food that are not eaten – for example, skins of fruits and vegetables or trimmings of meat and bones that are inedible
- food that cannot be eaten due to an error during preparation or cooking
- waste food left on the plate by the customer.

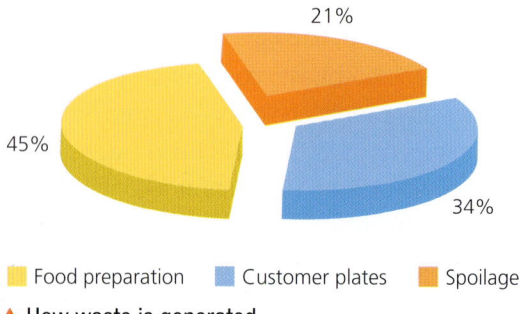

21%
34%
45%

■ Food preparation   ■ Customer plates   ■ Spoilage

▲ How waste is generated

Source: 'Overview of waste in the UK hospitality and food service sector', November 2013, WRAP (www.wrap.org.uk)

Calculating wastage

Today, many chefs use computer software to work out the cost of dishes, the gross profit and the selling price. One such system commonly in use is Kitchen CUT, which is able to assist the chef in many aspects of financial control.

In order to control food wastage it is crucial to pay particular attention to the following:
- purchasing – use detailed purchasing specifications, with no over-ordering
- operate correct storage procedures and stock control
- design the menu taking into account customer requirements and sales mix
- adhere to correct preparation and cooking methods; use standardised recipes that give the exact yields required
- use accurate, consistent portion control in order to ensure dishes are the right size and avoid wastage
- where possible, use accurate forecasting systems and procedures; use accurate and reliable data – for example, sales histories.

Chefs must monitor waste, check storage systems, stock rotation and use-by dates. They need to know how much is thrown away at the end of each day, each week and each month, and set targets to reduce waste. There are examples of chefs/restaurants utilising pretty much everything and avoiding all waste. Others use clear bin liners to make waste very visible, with the intention that this helps to focus the minds of the chefs responsible for preparing foods. Check preparation methods and that the exact yields are being obtained. Incorrect preparation and cooking and presentation methods can result in a waste of ingredients. Standard purchasing specifications and standardised recipes help to reduce waste, if written and followed correctly.

Check the plate waste (how much customers are leaving on their plates). If this is excessive then reduce the portion sizes. Every aspect of the control cycle must address waste and the cost of waste must be calculated.

Waste has to be carefully calculated, and accurate forecasting is essential to avoid over-production and over-ordering. Both of these factors can seriously affect the profit and loss account, and reduce profitability.

- Monitor plate waste as this can be the result of large portions, so it may become necessary to reduce portion sizes.
- Remember, try to economise and use every part of the produce – for example, vegetable peelings can be used for stock; if there is lobster salad on the menu use the shells to make a bisque.

Sustainability

When designing or refurbishing premises, and when selecting equipment, careful evaluation of potential energy and water saving should be a part of each business's cost-saving, sustainability and corporate social responsibility (CSR) strategy. This should also consider the longer-term use of the premises and the equipment. Apart from improved environmental credentials and a positive perception of the business, there is potential for increased energy savings. Food service operations can use two to five times more energy per square metre than other commercial buildings. As costs continue to rise, investing in energy efficiency is therefore one of the most effective ways to protect the business from rising energy costs. Any sustainability programme has to be aimed at encouraging reduction, reuse and recycling, sometimes known as R^3.

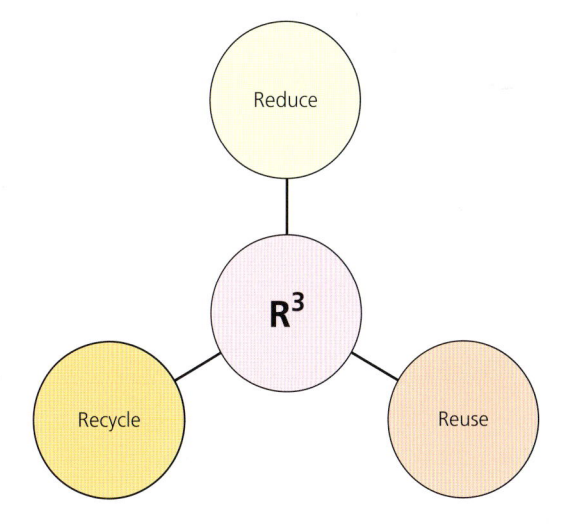

▲ R^3 – Reduce, Reuse, Recycle

Source: developed from CESA, 2009

To back up the corporate social responsibility strategy, it is valuable to have an environmental policy. This can help to reinforce the responsibility of the team so that they are aware that, from arriving at the beginning of their shift to leaving the workplace, their actions will have a direct impact on the environment, the social responsibility charter and the profit of the organisation.

Sustainability in the professional kitchen

Operating the kitchen more responsibly and committing to sustainable practices are both imperative for competitiveness. These practices can not only reduce the carbon footprint but increase the operational profitability of a business. Sustainability and ethical practice are factors that are now considered by many customers when deciding where to eat out.

Conduct energy audits

Energy efficiency is an important step to achieve sustainability. Commercial kitchens are often among the biggest energy consumers per metre of all commercial buildings. Conducting an energy audit can help you to identify where your energy consumption is inefficient and optimise it around the kitchen. This will be able to provide operational, equipment, energy and water saving recommendations to reduce your consumption costs and protect the environment.

Recycle

An important factor in sustainability is the commitment to recycle. It makes both environmental and economic sense. With a recycling programme, a professional kitchen can help divert many tons of material away from landfill and save the cost of waste disposal. WRAP is an organisation looking at ways in which businesses can use resources more efficiently. Read more at its website: www.wrap.org.uk.

Risks and hazards within food preparation areas

There can be a number of inherent hazards when working in kitchen areas. For this reason, it is important to work in a safe and systematic way in order to avoid accidents or injury to yourself or anyone else.

The following are some common causes of accidents in the kitchen:
- slipping on a wet or greasy floor
- tripping over objects or walking into objects
- lifting objects wrongly or lifting loads that are too heavy
- being exposed to hazards such as hot or dangerous substances – for example, steam or oven-cleaning chemicals
- being hit or hurt by moving objects, such as being cut by a knife when chopping
- injury from machines such as vegetable-cutting machines, liquidisers and mincing machines
- fires and explosions
- electric shocks
- not wearing suitable protective clothing or not wearing it properly
- incidents due to poor lighting
- ignoring or abusing the rules put in place for health and safety.

See Chapter 2 for information on keeping yourself safe and hygienic in the workplace, and the correct protective clothing to wear.

Health and safety legal requirements

It is now a legal requirement for all employers to carry out risk assessments for all of the procedures completed in the workplace. The risk assessment must also record the measures in place to keep employees safe and to avoid risk of injury, ill health or harm.

Health and safety legislation covers everyone in the premises, including full- and part-time employees, agency staff, contractors, voluntary workers and those on work placement, as well as customers and guests.

The **Health and Safety Executive (HSE)** is responsible for enforcing health and safety in the workplace. It has the power to investigate premises, to check, dismantle and remove equipment, inspect the records, ask questions, and seize and destroy items.

Everyone working in a kitchen needs to know the laws on health and safety, and how they are affected by these laws.

The **Health and Safety at Work Act 1974** gives employees and employers certain responsibilities that they must adhere to within their working environment.
- All employees and employers must take reasonable care of their own safety and the safety of others they work with.
- Employees must inform their line manager/supervisor if they see anything they think is unsafe and could cause an accident.

- Any procedure, equipment or protective clothing put in place for safety must be used correctly and never be modified or tampered with.
- Employees must co-operate with their employer on health and safety matters and procedures put in place to keep the working environment safe.

Employers must also ensure that all staff are safe at work, and not put staff in dangerous situations where they could injure themselves or others. They must provide safe methods of work for their employees. This includes:
- producing a workplace policy document on health and safety
- completing risk assessments for all equipment and procedures in the workplace
- providing safe equipment and utensils
- training and supervising staff in safe practices
- providing first-aid equipment
- keeping an accurate record of all accidents.

The **Health and Safety Information for Employees Regulations 1989** also require that employers provide health and safety information for their employees. This could be in the form of leaflets, posters, DVDs and information packs. A selection of these is available from the HSE.

Health and safety
Remember! Kitchens can be dangerous places. Remain aware of hazards and potential hazards at all times.

Identifying and mitigating risks

If you become aware of a hazard or potential hazard in your working area, it is important to assess the situation and decide if it is something that you can deal with yourself or if it needs to be reported to someone else, or maybe both (see below). Do not ignore hazards: they may have the potential to cause serious injury. It is essential that you do one or more of the following to minimise risk.
- Deal with the hazard yourself where it is safe to do so; an example of this would be dealing with a wet floor and putting up the appropriate signs (see below).
- Warn others of the hazard verbally – for example, warning of the wet floor before you have dealt with it. Make sure others working around you are aware of hot surfaces and hot equipment, such as trays you have just taken from the oven.
- Report the problem to another colleague – for example, your mentor or someone with responsibility for health and safety.
- Report the problem to a supervisor, head chef or manager.
- Remove dangerous pieces of equipment – for example, a hand-held blender with a damaged electrical cord, or place a 'do not use' sign on larger equipment and inform a supervisor, head chef or manager.

Slips, trips and falls

The majority of accidents in kitchens are slips, trips and falls. Therefore, floor surfaces must be of a suitable construction to reduce this risk. A major cause of this kind of accident is spilt water and grease, which can make the floor surface slippery. For this reason any spillage must be cleaned immediately and warning notices put in place, where appropriate, highlighting the danger. Verbal warnings should also be given.

Falls can also be caused when items are left on floors and in passageways or between stoves and tables. People carrying trays and containers may have a restricted view and may not see hazards and so can trip over them. They may fall on to a hot stove, on to a sharp item, or the item they are carrying may be hot. These falls can have severe consequences. Ensure that nothing is left on the floor that may cause an obstruction and be a hazard. If it is necessary to have articles on the floor temporarily, they should be guarded to prevent accidents.

Kitchen personnel should be trained to think and act in a safe manner so as to avoid this kind of accident.

Hazard warning signs

Safety signs are used to control a hazard. They should not replace other methods of controlling risks.

Yellow signs – warning signs
These are to warn of various dangers, such as slippery floors, hot oil or hot water. They also warn about hazards such as corrosive material.

Blue signs – mandatory signs

These signs inform about precautions that must be taken, such as how to progress safely through a certain area. They are also used when special precautions need to be taken, such as wearing protective clothing.

Red signs – prohibition or fire-fighting signs

Red signs tell people that they should not enter and are to stop people from doing certain tasks in a hazardous area. Red signs are also used for fire-fighting equipment.

Green signs – safe signs

These are route signs designed to show where fire exits and emergency exits are. Green also tends to be used for first-aid equipment.

Electricity and gas

The majority of kitchens will have a range of electrical equipment and great care must be taken when dealing with electricity. Electrical equipment is covered by the **Electricity at Work Regulations 1989**; under these regulations all electrical equipment must be tested each year by a qualified electrician.

If a person comes into direct contact with electricity an electric shock can occur, which can be very serious and sometimes fatal. If a person receives an electric shock, switch off the current. If this is not possible, free the person using something that is dry and that will insulate you from the electricity, such as a thick cloth or something made of wood or rubber. You must take care not to use your bare hands otherwise the electric shock may be transmitted to you.

In the case of electric shock:
- switch off the current
- raise the alarm
- call for medical/first-aid help.

You can give artificial respiration where necessary if you are trained in the procedure.

Gas is often the preferred fuel for industrial stoves and can potentially be hazardous. On leaving the kitchen, make sure that you turn off all gas appliances. It is important to report any gas leaks, faulty equipment or gas smell immediately to a supervisor or line manager.

In some kitchens there are central gas cut-off points where one switch cuts off the gas supply to the whole kitchen. These are used in emergency situations such as a fire.

Hazardous substances

The **Control of Substances Hazardous to Health (COSHH) Regulations (2002)** state that an employer must not carry out work that might expose employees to substances that are hazardous to their health, unless the employer has assessed the risks and put relevant controls in place. These risk assessments must be recorded and available for inspection. All potentially harmful chemicals must be stored, used and then disposed of properly according to COSHH Regulations. The hazardous nature of the chemical must be identified on the packaging with the use of recognisable symbols or pictograms.

The nine pictograms convey the following types of hazard: explosive, flammable, oxidising, corrosive, acute toxicity, hazardous to the environment, health hazard, serious health hazard and gas under pressure.

Chemicals commonly used in kitchens include detergents, disinfectants, sanitisers, degreasers, descalers, oven cleaners and pest-control chemicals. These substances could cause injury if not used correctly by getting them on to the skin, in the eyes or mouth, or breathing in through the nose or mouth.

People using chemical substances must be trained to use them properly and safely. This will include:
- wearing the relevant protective clothing, such as aprons, goggles, gloves and face masks
- following the manufacturer's instructions correctly
- always storing chemicals in their original containers, away from heat and with the lids tightly closed
- not allowing exposure to heat or to naked flames
- never mixing chemicals
- knowing first-aid procedures
- disposing of used chemicals and empty containers correctly.

Emergencies in the workplace

Emergencies that might happen in the workplace include:
- serious accidents involving injury
- outbreak of fire or explosion
- threats such as terrorism or riots
- a bomb scare
- failure of a major system – for example, water or electricity.

An organisation will have systems in place to deal with emergencies. Key staff are usually trained to lead the procedure in cases of emergency, and most organisations will have fire marshals and first aiders. These people will attend regular update meetings. Evacuation procedures will also be in place, which employees will need to practise (for example, fire drills), and fire alarms will be tested regularly.

First aid

When people are injured or fall ill at work, it is important that immediate help is available and, in serious cases, medical assistance is called.

The arrangements for providing first aid in the workplace are set out in the **Health and Safety (First Aid) Regulations 1981**. Since 1982 it has been a legal requirement that adequate first-aid equipment, facilities and personnel are provided at work.

All kitchen staff need to know who they should call or inform if there is an accident, where the first-aid equipment is located and the procedures they should follow when there is an injury or incident, no matter how small.

First-aid equipment needs to be checked regularly, replenished and maintained; making this procedure part of a job role will ensure that the required items are always available.

All injuries, including minor injuries, must be recorded. This is usually done on individual recording forms, which are then kept. Some organisations now record accidents on computer systems – these must also be kept for information and/or inspection.

Dealing with minor cuts and burns

Minor cuts, grazes and burns occur occasionally in kitchens because of the nature of the work. Most minor cuts can usually be treated using the contents of the first-aid box, maybe with the assistance of an appointed first aider. For more serious cuts and burns it is important to seek advice from the first aider and get medical help as soon as possible.

Practical Cookery 14th edition

Safe lifting and handling

Working in a kitchen often includes the need to move heavy or awkwardly shaped objects. This could include deliveries of food and other items that need to be moved to another area, lifting heavy trays from ovens, manoeuvring large pieces of equipment and using heavy cleaning equipment.

Picking up and carrying heavy or difficult loads can lead to accidents, injury and long-term sickness if it is not done properly. Incorrect lifting or lifting something too heavy is a common cause of back injury. The **Manual Handling Operations Regulations 1992** cover safe lifting and handling at work. An employer must carry out a risk assessment on all tasks that involve lifting, and put procedures in place to make them safe. Staff must then be trained in these procedures.

When lifting, the general rules include:
- assessing the load and not attempting to lift anything that is too heavy
- breaking the load into smaller units if appropriate
- using lifting equipment or moving equipment, such as trolleys, where available
- requesting help with lifting.

When lifting, it is essential to use a safe lifting technique:
- assess the load and plan how you are going to lift it
- position yourself with your feet apart, back straight and knees bent
- grip the item firmly at the base or lifting handles
- lift in a smooth movement, keeping the load close to the body
- walk carefully, making sure there are no trip hazards
- lower or place the load, still keeping the back straight and bending the knees if necessary.

Health and safety

Take extra care when lifting hot items. This includes large trays from ovens, roasting trays, large pans of liquids, oven or salamander shelves, and a variety of other kitchen items that could be hot and cause burns. When moving a hot item be sure that you can do it safely and that there is a clear space to put it down. Give others working around you spoken warnings. Wrap an oven cloth around hot pan handles and do not allow hot trays to stick out over the edge of surfaces.

Fire safety

Everyone working in a kitchen needs to be aware of the potential risk of fire. It is important to work safely to prevent fire, especially around open gas jets, and when using fats and oils with cooking appliances. Deep fat fryers should be thermostatically controlled to prevent overheating and should only be used after training has been completed.

All employers have a duty of care for the safety of employees in the event of a fire. The **Regulatory Reform (Fire Safety) Order 2005** emphasises that measures must be taken to prevent fires. All staff must be trained in emergency evacuation, with fire action plans clearly displayed to show the correct evacuation routes for staff, customers and visitors. The fire evacuation procedures should be practised at least once a year, the procedure recorded and reviewed regularly to take into account staff changes and any changes to the premises.

Fire precautions

Effective measures in the prevention of fire include:
- removing all hazards or reducing them as much as possible

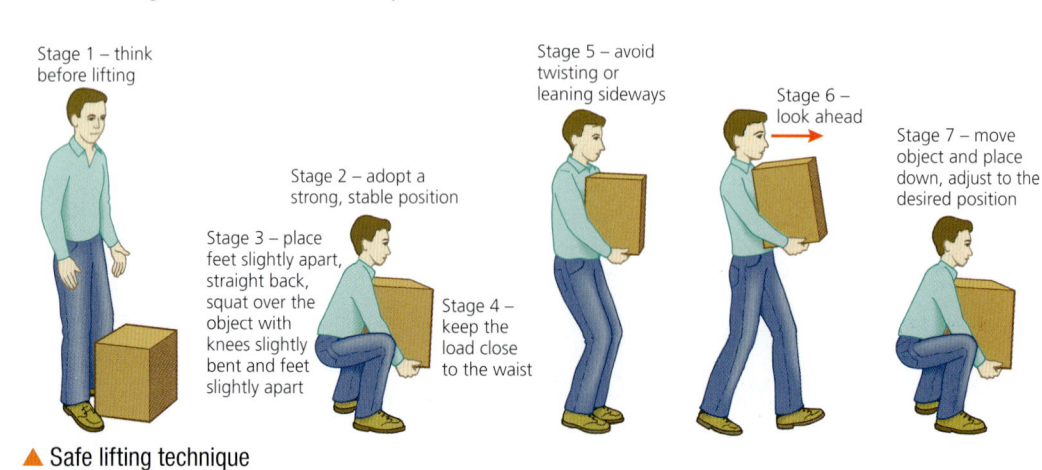

▲ Safe lifting technique

Stage 1 – think before lifting
Stage 2 – adopt a strong, stable position
Stage 3 – place feet slightly apart, straight back, squat over the object with knees slightly bent and feet slightly apart
Stage 4 – keep the load close to the waist
Stage 5 – avoid twisting or leaning sideways
Stage 6 – look ahead
Stage 7 – move object and place down, adjust to the desired position

- making sure that measures have been taken to protect from the risk of fire and the likelihood of a fire spreading
- ensuring that all escape routes are safe and used effectively, and that they are well signed and easy to access
- provision of suitable fire-fighting equipment and staff well trained in its use
- providing suitable ways of detecting a fire (for example, smoke alarms) and instructions on what to do in case of fire
- arrangements in place for what to do if a fire breaks out – employees must be trained in what to do in the event of a fire
- all precautions provided must be installed and maintained by a competent person.

Fires are classified in accordance with British Standard EN2 as follows.

- **Class A:** fires involving solid materials where burning normally forms glowing embers – for example, wood.
- **Class B:** fires involving liquids, such as methylated spirit or any kind of flammable gel used under a burner.
- **Class C:** fires involving gases.
- **Class D:** fires involving metals.
- **Class F:** fires involving cooking oils or fats.

Different types of fire extinguisher are suitable for different types of fire. Generally, portable fire extinguishers contain one of the following five substances:
1. water
2. foam
3. powder
4. carbon dioxide
5. vaporising liquids.

The most useful form of general-purpose fire-fighting equipment is the water-type extinguisher or hose reel. Areas of special risk, such as kitchens where oil, fats and electrical equipment are used, may need other types of extinguisher, such as carbon dioxide, wet chemical or dry powder.

Ensure that you know exactly where the fire alarms are in your working area and how they are operated. Also be well aware of the evacuation procedures in your establishment and follow the procedure shown to you. If you need to leave the premises because of fire, the usual steps include the following.

- Raise the alarm and warn others verbally.
- Turn off gas supplies using a central cut-off point if possible.
- Do not put yourself and others in danger; tackle only the smallest of fires, and only if you know how to do this and you are certain that it is safe to do so.
- Leave by the appointed exits, checking that others are also vacating the building. Guests, visitors and customers may need assisting and directing.
- Go to the appointed assembly point and await further instruction.
- Do not re-enter the building until you are told you can do so.

Security procedures

Security in hospitality premises always remains a high priority. In many hospitality establishments large numbers of people can be present in the building at any one time. These may include staff, guests, customers, contractors, visitors and others.

As well as providing security and protection for all these people, consideration needs to be given to the buildings and grounds; fixtures, fittings and furniture; decor and decorative items; equipment; clothing and linen; and stock.

The **Management of Health and Safety at Work Regulations 1999** require employers to conduct a risk assessment regarding the safety of staff in the business. Preventing crime is more efficient and less damaging than having to deal with it once it has happened.

Dealing with security

Everyone entering the premises should be monitored. Reception staff should be trained to spot suspicious individuals and those likely to cause problems. Everyone who comes in to the building should be asked to sign in at reception and, if they are a legitimate visitor, be given a security badge. It is also essential to make sure that any suspicious person does not re-enter the building.

Some companies put the 'right to search' into employee contracts – this means that, from time to time, the employer can carry out searches of employees' lockers, bags and other belongings.

Most establishments will have set procedures in place with regards to **risks, threats and security**. Make sure that you are aware of these policies and carry them out correctly and in line with the establishment's operational procedures. Most employers provide regular training and update sessions for their staff, making sure that everyone is well aware of requirements and that their knowledge is up to date.

Legal requirements for reporting incidents and accidents

If an accident or near-accident occurs in your working area, it is important that it is reported to the appropriate person so it can be recorded and measures put in place to prevent it occurring again.

Health and safety must be monitored regularly in the workplace by the designated health and safety manager/officer. Any accident or near-accident must be recorded, even if no one was injured.

As an employee all accidents and potential accidents must be reported to your line manager or supervisor. Each accident is recorded in an accident book/file, which must be provided in every business.

RIDDOR (Reporting of Injuries, Diseases and Dangerous Occurrences Regulations) 2013

The law says that all serious work-related accidents, diseases and dangerous occurrences must be recorded and reported to the HSE online (www.hse.gov.uk).

There is also a telephone contact number, but this is only for very serious incidents and fatalities (Incident Contact Centre: 0345 300 9923).

The following injuries must be reported:
- bone fractures (except fingers, thumbs or toes)
- amputation (cutting off) of limbs
- dislocation of a hip, knee or spine
- temporary or permanent loss of sight (blindness)
- eye injuries from chemicals getting into the eye, a hot metal burn to the eye or any penetration of the eye
- any injury from electric shock or burning that leads to unconsciousness or the need to resuscitate the person or send them to hospital for more than 24 hours
- any injury resulting in hypothermia (when someone gets too cold), or illness due to heat, that leads to unconsciousness or the need to resuscitate the person or send them to hospital for more than 24 hours (such as an electric shock, or a gas flame blown back and causing burns)
- unconsciousness caused by exposure to a harmful substance or biological agents (such as cleaning products and solvents)
- unconsciousness or illness requiring medical treatment caused by inhaling a harmful substance or absorbing it through the skin (such as breathing in poisonous carbon monoxide leaking from a gas appliance)
- illness requiring medical treatment caused by a biological agent or its toxins or infected material (such as harmful bacteria used in laboratories).

Examples of reportable diseases include:
- dermatitis
- skin cancer
- asthma
- hepatitis
- tuberculosis
- tetanus
- anthrax.

Reporting illnesses and infections

Good levels of health and fitness are required to work in a kitchen, so attention must be paid to maintaining your health with a good diet, adequate exercise, and enough sleep and rest. Many employers now have an occupational health department to support and advise employees in health matters.

It is now a **legal requirement** for all food handlers to report certain illnesses or infections they may have to their line manager/supervisor before starting work as they may be excluded from handling food. This is because, with certain conditions, especially stomach-related illnesses, organisms can easily be transferred from the food handler to the food and this could make the person eating the food unwell. Illnesses that must be reported include:
- diarrhoea, vomiting or other symptoms of a food-borne illness – the food handler must not return to food-handling duties until they have been free from symptoms for 48 hours or more
- any skin infections or infected cuts, boils, grazes or burns
- heavy colds and coughs, eye or ear discharges.

Business 4

Know it

- Understand basic costing and yield of dishes and the meaning of gross profit.
- Understand the principles of supply chain and waste management.
- Recognise potential risks in the working environment, how to address them and the potential consequences of those risks.

Test yourself

1. Suggest three places that you could find out about health and safety.
2. Suggest three hazards that you may come across in your kitchen that you think may cause an injury or accident. Who would you report these to, and how could you warn others working around you?
3. Describe four signs that you may see around the kitchen to warn or inform you of health and safety issues.
4. Why is it important that everyone in the kitchen knows where to find the first-aid equipment, and that first-aid supplies are kept topped up?
5. If you were asked to move some large boxes that had been delivered, how could you do this safely?
6. Suggest three possible causes of fire in a kitchen. Which type of fire-fighting equipment could be used on a deep-fat fryer?
7. Suggest three ways that you could reduce the risk of accidental fire when working in the kitchen.
8. If you see an accident or near-accident in your workplace who should you report it to? Why is reporting it important?
9. Describe three of the security procedures you are aware of in your workplace.
10. If a visitor to your kitchen or a customer left some of their property behind, what is the procedure that should be followed?
11. Why should the hospitality industry recycle and reduce waste?
12. Suggest ways in which waste can be reduced in the professional kitchen.
13. What is the difference between gross profit and net profit?
14. Why is yield important in relation to gross profit?
15. What is the difference between variable costs and fixed costs?

Show it

- Follow instruction to meet targets and effectively control resources.
- Follow procedures regarding usage and waste of resources.
- Undertake all tasks with due care and attention, reporting risks in the appropriate manner.

Live it

- Be financially aware in approaches to all aspects of work.
- Set an example to others by working in ways that minimise waste.
- Be vigilant and aware of potential risks within the kitchen environment and take action to prevent them.

5 Stocks, soups and sauces

Recipes included in this chapter

No.	Recipe	Page
	Stocks	
1	White stock	86
2	Brown stock	86
3	White chicken stock	87
4	White vegetable stock	88
5	Fish stock	88
6	Brown vegetable stock	89
7	Lamb jus	89
8	Reduced veal stock	90
	Broths	
9	Brown onion soup	91
10	Minestrone	92
11	Scotch broth	93
	Cream soups	
12	Cream of green pea soup (*crème St Germain*)	94
13	Cream of tomato soup (*crème de tomates fraiches*)	95
14	Mushroom soup (*crème de champignons*)	96
15	Pulse soup with croutons	97
16	Chicken soup (*crème de volaille* or *crème reine*)	98
17	Asparagus soup (*crème d'asperges*)	99
18	Cream of spinach and celery soup	100
19	Cream of vegetable soup	100
	Purée soups	
20	Vegetable purée soup	101
21	Red lentil soup	102
22	Potato soup (*purée parmentier*)	102
23	Roasted butternut squash soup	103
24	Potato and watercress soup	104
25	Chilled leek and potato soup (vichyssoise)	104
26	Gazpacho	105
27	Tomato soup	106
28	Roasted red pepper and tomato soup	107
29	Carrot and butter bean soup	108
	Velouté soups	
30	Pea velouté	109
31	Pumpkin velouté	109
	Clear soups	
32	Clear soup (*consommé*)	110
	Bisques	
33	Prawn bisque	113

No.	Recipe	Page
	Béchamel sauces	
34	Béchamel sauce (white sauce)	112
35	Reduced-fat béchamel sauce	112
36	Parsley sauce	113
37	Cheese sauce (mornay)	113
38	Soubise	114
	Velouté sauces	
39	Suprême sauce	114
40	Mushroom sauce	115
41	Ivory sauce	116
42	Aurora sauce	116
	Demi-glace sauces	
43	Chasseur sauce	117
44	Devilled sauce (*sauce diable*)	118
45	Robert sauce	118
46	Piquant sauce	119
47	Madeira sauce	120
48	Brown onion sauce (*sauce lyonnaise*)	120
49	Italian sauce	121
50	Pepper sauce (*sauce poivrade*)	122
	Gravies	
51	Beef jus	122
52	Roast chicken jus	123
53	Red wine jus	124
54	Roast gravy (*jus rôti*)	124
55	Thickened gravy (*jus-lié*)	126
56	Curry gravy	127
	Purée-based sauces	
57	Apple sauce	127
58	Tomato sauce (*sauce tomate*)	128
59	Cranberry sauce	128
	Hollandaise sauces	
60	Hollandaise sauce	129
61	Béarnaise sauce	130
	Salsa	
62	Salsa verde	131
	Butter sauces	
63	Melted butter sauce (*beurre fondu*)	131
	Miscellaneous sauces	
64	Horseradish sauce (*sauce raifort*)	132
65	Sweet and sour sauce	132
66	Gribiche sauce	133

Stocks

Stock is the basis of all meat sauces, gravies, soups and purées. It is really just the flavour of meat extracted by long and gentle simmering, or the infusion/transfer of flavour from ingredients such as fish, vegetables or shellfish. In making stock, it should be remembered that the object is to draw the goodness out of the materials and into the liquor, imparting the desired level of flavour and other elements that are important to the end product, whether it be a soup, sauce or reduction.

Stocks are the foundation of many important kitchen preparations; for this reason, the greatest possible care should be taken in their production, and stocks, bouillons and nages should only be made with high-quality ingredients. A good, well-flavoured stock cannot be made with inferior ingredients.

- A **bouillon** is another name for meat, fish or vegetable stock. In some cases a bouillon can be distinguished from stock by being meatier and by being seasoned (whereas stock is not seasoned).
- A **nage** is a light but well-flavoured stock, often used for cooking fish and other seafood. The nage will enhance the flavours.

Preparing and cooking stocks

Quality points for ingredients

It is important to choose high-quality ingredients, bones, carcass and vegetables. Do not use ingredients that are past their best as this will affect both the colour and flavour.

- Unsound meat or bones and decaying vegetables will give stock an unpleasant flavour and cause it to deteriorate quickly.
- Scum should be removed, otherwise it will boil into the stock and spoil the colour and flavour.
- Fat should be skimmed off, otherwise the stock will taste greasy.
- Salt should not be added to stock.
- When making chicken stock the bones will need to be soaked first to remove the blood that is in the cavity.

> **Food safety**
>
> If stocks are not given the correct care and attention, particularly with regard to the soundness of the ingredients used, they can easily become contaminated and a risk to health.

Browning, roasting and boiling

The basic preparation of brown stock involves browning vegetables and bones, usually in the oven. Once browned, they are covered with water, boiled and simmered to give a rich brown colour. White stocks are blanched but not browned, to give a clear white stock.

Simmering

Stock should always simmer gently; if it is allowed to boil quickly, it will evaporate and go cloudy/milky.

Skimming

It is important to skim off the excess fat and impurities with a ladle or perforated spoon to produce a clear and flavoursome stock. If fat is not skimmed off the stock will taste greasy. Stock that is left unattended and not skimmed will become cloudy and may have a bitter taste.

Another way of skimming stock is to use pieces of dish paper dragged across the top of the liquid.

All stock can be chilled down, allowing the fat to settle on the top so that it can be easily removed.

Straining
Stock is poured through a strainer, usually a chinois or muslin, to remove all sediment. This is usually done after the fat has been removed.

Reducing
Stock is placed over a fierce heat and is allowed to evaporate until the volume is reduced to give a more intense flavour.

When cooking predominantly meat stocks, remember that they will contain collagen. This is the main fibrous component of skin, tendons, connective tissue and bones. If you have cooked at a higher heat (e.g. boiling), the collagen content of the sauce will be high, giving you a viscous sauce earlier in the reduction process; due to the thickness of such a sauce, it is impossible to reduce it further without burning.

Glazes
A glaze is a reduced stock that is used to enhance the flavour of soups and sauces. To achieve a glaze, the stock is evaporated on the stove until it is the consistency of treacle or a thick jelly. This thicker consistency is caused by the collagen (which is found in the bones, tendons and connective tissue) breaking down into gelatine as the stock reduces. The result is a more concentrated flavour. Care must be taken not to over reduce the stock otherwise it will become too concentrated and may result in burning. When making a glaze ensure that the base stock used at the start has a medium extraction of collagen. This will give a more flavoursome result and the glaze will be less 'claggy'.

Holding and storing stocks
Once the stock has reached its desired flavour and clarity, strain and chill immediately. Stocks are susceptible to bacterial growth due to their high protein content so special care must be taken in the handling and storage of stocks. Chill the stock rapidly to 5°C in a shallow tray (approximately 3 cm to 5 cm deep) in a blast chiller before storing in a refrigerator.

If stocks are to be frozen they should be labelled and dated, and stored below −18°C.

When taken from storage, stocks must be boiled for at least two minutes before being used. They must not be reheated more than once.

Ideally, stocks should be made fresh daily and discarded at the end of the day.

Convenience stocks
Today many establishments use prepared stocks to save time and labour, but also to reduce the food safety risks associated with the preparation, production and storage of stocks. These stocks are purchased as a chilled stock, frozen or in a paste or a dry powder. Many of the fresh-chilled products are of a very high quality.

Soups
There are many ways to classify soup – a classic velouté thickened with a liaison, a purée of lentils with ham hock stock, a broth with a clear liquid, or even the crystal clarity of consommé. Up until 15 or 20 years ago, most soups were thickened by either purée or by roux. While hearty soups are still with us today – for example, Scotch broth, minestrone, bouillabaisse, chowder and many more – the foundation of modern dining is a lighter approach, with a reduction in flour and fat, offering a more sophisticated dish.

Types of soup
- **Broth**: a soup in which in which bones, meat, fish, grains or vegetables have been simmered in water or stock. Minestrone, an Italian vegetable-based soup, is an example of a broth.
- **Cream**: a soup finished with cream. These soups can be made from a velouté base, such as cream of chicken and cream of mushroom, but they can also be made from a purée base and finished with cream, for example cream of vegetable soup and cream of green pea soup (crème St Germain).
- **Purée**: a soup with a vegetable base that has been puréed in a food mill or blender; it is typically altered after milling with the addition of broth, cream, butter, sour cream or coconut milk.

Stocks, soups and sauces

- **Velouté**: a velvety French soup made with stock and thickened with a liaison (see thickenings below).
- **Clear (consommé)**: clear, unthickened soups that derive their intense flavour from a stock base. They are clarified by a process of careful straining, resulting in a clear soup. Consommé is a clear soup with an intense flavour derived from meat bones and a good stock. Dashi is the Japanese equivalent of consommé and is made from giant seaweed (*kombu*), dried bonito and water.

Other types of soup include:

- **Vichyssoise**: a simple, flavourful puréed potato and leek soup, thickened with the potato itself. Traditionally this is called leek and potato soup if served hot, and a little cream or crème fraiche may be added to give it richness; however, when served cold it is classified as vichyssoise – if fat is added to this preparation the dish would leave a fatty residue on the palate and offer a less-than-clear mouth feel.
- **Bisque**: a very rich soup with a creamy consistency, usually made of lobster or shellfish (crab, shrimp, etc.).
- **Bouillabaisse**: a Mediterranean fish soup/stew made of multiple types of seafood, olive oil, water and seasonings such as garlic, onions, tomato and parsley.
- **Chowder**: a hearty North American soup, usually with a seafood base.
- **Gazpacho**: a Spanish tomato and vegetable soup served ice cold.
- **Potage**: a French term referring to a thick soup.

Preparing and cooking soups

Though the perfection of soups can take experience, the basic principles of soup making are quite simple to follow.

Most soup making begins by preparing a stock. The underlying flavours of the foundation ingredients are then enhanced by the herbs and seasonings added. In many cases, this flavour base begins by preparing a mixture of flavouring elements, cooked in a little fat or oil. Because of their aromatic properties and flavours, most soups begin this phase with a combination of onion, garlic, leeks and carrots (this is called a **mirepoix** or **aromats**). The resulting broth is the foundation of all soups.

Quality points for ingredients

When making soups it is important to use fresh, quality ingredients that have been peeled, prepared and weighed as part of the *mise-en-place*.

If you experience any problems with ingredients it is important to inform the supplier. Only use fresh, good-quality ingredients, otherwise the overall flavour of the finished soup will be impaired.

Weighing and measuring

It is important to weigh every ingredient to determine the exact flavour and consistency, but more importantly to determine the exact nutritional content per portion. Measuring the ingredients accurately will also result in the correct yield and less wastage.

Table 5.1 Guide to soups, their preparation and presentation

Soup type	Base	Passed or unpassed	Finish	Example
Broth	Stock	Unpassed	Chopped herbs	Scotch broth (recipe 11)
	Cut vegetables			Minestrone (recipe 10)
Cream	Stock and vegetables	Passed	Cream, milk or yoghurt	Cream of vegetable (recipe 19)
	Vegetable purée and béchamel velouté			Cream of green pea (recipe 12)
				Cream of tomato (recipe 13)
Purée	Stock	Passed	Croutons	Potato soup (recipe 22)
	Fresh vegetables			Red lentil soup (recipe 21)
	Pulses			
Velouté	Blond roux	Passed	Liaison of yolk and cream	Pea velouté (recipe 30)
	Vegetables			
	Stock			
Clear	Stock	Strained	Usually garnished	Consommé (recipe 32)
Bisque	Shellfish	Passed	Cream	Prawn bisque (recipe 33)
	Fish stock			

Preparing a purée soup

1 Slowly simmer vegetables and seasonings with stock to develop flavours.

2 Purée using a stick blender, liquidiser or food processor.

3 To ensure a smooth consistency, pass the soup through a conical strainer.

4 Use a ladle to carefully pump the soup through.

Blending/liquidising and chopping

Soups can be prepared using stick blenders, liquidisers and food processors. These produce excellent purée soups with a smooth consistency.

For soups that require small cuts of vegetables, such as *paysanne* for minestrone and *gros brunoise* for Scotch broth, the vegetable cutting is usually done by hand, but there are also machines that cut vegetables to the required size available in the market. (For more information on vegetable cuts, see Chapter 12.)

Always use strong, thick-bottomed pans to cook soup to avoid scalding and browning.

Passing and straining

Conical strainers are used to pass soups to obtain a fine consistency. Conical strainers came in a range of sizes, from fine (chinois) to medium. When passing the soup through a chinois, use a ladle to carefully pump the soup through.

Finishing soups

Soups may be served for lunch, dinner, supper and snack meals. Depending on their function and purpose, soups are usually served in portions of 250 ml maximum. Sometimes a speciality soup is served as an **amuse-bouche** and the portion size is reduced to approximately 50 ml.

For food safety, serve hot soups at 63 °C or above to control the growth of pathogenic organisms, and discard if not sold after two hours. Cold soups should be served at 5 °C or below. Chill the soups in a blast chiller to below 8 °C within 90 minutes to slow down bacterial growth.

Soups can be served with the following garnishes:
- Croutons: slices of white or brown bread cut into 1 cm dice then carefully shallow fried in vegetable oil or clarified butter.
- Sippets: corners of bread cut from a flat-tin loaf, finely sliced and toasted in the oven. Both croutons and sippets may be flavoured by rubbing chopped garlic on to the bread.
- Toasted flutes (*croûtes de flute*): very small, thin baguette slices, toasted or sprinkled with olive oil or melted butter and baked in the oven until crisp.

Accompaniments that can be served with soup include:
- *brunoise*, *julienne* or *paysanne* of vegetables
- *concassé*
- fine noodles
- rice
- chopped herbs
- finely diced cooked chicken.

Some soups are finished with cream, crème fraiche, full-cream milk, yoghurt or evaporated milk.

Healthy eating options

With the move towards healthier options, soup offers a very good alternative to other products. Broths and soups containing vegetables, beans and lean protein such as chicken, fish or lean beef, are healthy options that are both light and filling. Minestrone, bouillabaisse and gazpacho are excellent choices. Cream-based soups can often be adapted by using yoghurt or low-fat crème fraiche or fromage frais instead of cream to produce a soup that is lower in fat.

Sauces

A sauce is a liquid that has been thickened by either:
- *beurre manié* (kneaded butter)
- egg yolks
- roux
- cornflour, arrowroot or starch
- cream and/or butter added to reduced stock
- rice (in the case of some shellfish bisques)
- reducing cooking liquor or stock.

Types of sauce

White (béchamel)
Béchamel is a basic white sauce made using butter, flour and milk. Many sauces are derived from a basic béchamel sauce by the addition of appropriate ingredients or garnishes. Parsley, egg, cheese (mornay), soubise, onion, cream, mustard and anchovy are all examples of white sauces.

Velouté
A basic velouté sauce is a blond roux, to which a white stock and chicken, veal, fish, etc. are added. Examples of velouté sauces are caper, suprême, mushroom, ivory and aurora.

Brown (espagnole)
Espagnole is a traditional brown sauce made from brown roux and brown stock, simmered for several hours and skimmed frequently to produce a refined sauce. Because of the lengthy, time-consuming process and a move away from heavy flour-based sauces, in many kitchens a reduced veal stock (see recipe 8) is used as a base for most brown sauces.

Examples of brown sauces include chasseur, devilled, bordelaise, charcutière, Robert, piquant sauce, sherry sauce, Madeira, brown onion, lyonnaise, Italian and pepper sauces.

Demi-glace
Demi-glace is used as the base for a number of derivative sauces. Current practice in most kitchens is to use either stock-reduced sauce, *jus-lié* or a commercially produced powder or granule-based product.

Gravies
Examples of gravies include roast gravy (*jus rôti*) and thickened gravy (*jus-lié*).

A *jus-lié* is a lightly thickened brown stock – traditionally veal – which is flavour-enhanced with tomato and mushroom trimmings and thickened with arrowroot.

Spice-based
Some sauces contain a number of spices used to enhance dishes and to accompany products. Examples include chilli sauce, spicy tomato sauce, curry sauce and Chinese Szechwan sauce.

Purée-based
Purée-based sauces can be fruit based (for example, apple sauce or cranberry sauce), vegetable based (for example, tomato sauce) or herb based (for example, green sauce).

Salsa
Salsa is the Spanish word for a sauce. A wide variety of ingredients can be used and chunky mixtures made to serve with grilled or fried fish, meat and poultry dishes. Recipe 62 is for a salsa.

Butter as a sauce
- **Clarified butter**: clarified butter is butter that has been melted and skimmed. After that, the fat element of the butter is carefully poured off, leaving the milky residue behind. This gives a clear fat that can reach higher temperatures than normal butter without burning, but which can also be used to nap over steamed vegetables or poached or grilled fish.
- **Beurre noisette**: this basically translates to 'nut butter' and its flavour comes from the caramelisation of the milk element in the butter solids. It is achieved by placing diced hard butter into a moderately hot pan and bringing it to a foam (a good indication that it is ready). Like clarified butter, this can be served with poached or steamed vegetables and fish, but the classic use is with shallow-fried fish. If you take the butter a little further, however, and almost burn the sediment, then add a little vinegar, it is called black butter (*beurre noir*) and is traditionally served with skate.

- ***Beurre fondu***: this is basically an emulsion between fat and liquid – for example, melted butter emulsified with any nage described above will give you a slightly thicker sauce that can be used to coat vegetables or fish. To intensify the flavour, however, if you were to add a *beurre noisette* to the pan, or your cooking medium was clarified butter, you could start cooking the product in the pan with the fat. Once it is half cooked, arrest the cooking by adding a nage and then bring quickly to the boil. Through this boiling process the fat and the stock will become emulsified, which gives an emulsified sauce made in the pan, but with the cooking juices also added.
- **Compound butter sauces**: these are made by mixing the flavouring ingredients (for example, herbs) into softened butter, which can then be shaped into a roll 2 cm in diameter, placed in wet greaseproof paper, foil or cling film, hardened in a refrigerator and cut into 0.5 cm slices when required. Examples include parsley butter (chopped parsley and lemon juice), herb butter (mixed herbs – chives, tarragon, fennel, dill – and lemon juice) and garlic butter (mashed to a paste). Compound butters are served with grilled and some fried fish, and with grilled meats.

Using alcohol in sauces

Take great care when using alcohol in sauces. Alcohol must be used sparingly; it should not dominate the overall flavour, but must blend in with the other ingredients. The alcohol must be cooked out and must not have a raw, harsh taste. Alcohol used correctly will enhance the flavour of the sauce and create pleasant combinations to the dishes.

Quality points for sauces

All sauces should be smooth and glossy in appearance, definite in taste and light in texture; the thickening medium should be used in moderation.

It is important that the ingredients for preparing and cooking sauces are of the best quality, otherwise flavours will be compromised. Wine or alcohol that is used must also be of good quality otherwise the finished products will be impaired.

Thickening sauces

Roux

A roux is a combination of fat and flour that is cooked together. There are three degrees to which a roux may be cooked:

- **White roux**: this is used for white (béchamel) sauce and soups. Equal quantities of butter and flour are cooked together without colouring for a few minutes, to a sandy texture. Alternatively polyunsaturated vegetable margarine or vegetable oil can be used to make a roux, using equal quantities of oil and flour. This does give a slack roux but enables the liquid to be incorporated easily.
- **Blond roux**: this is used for veloutés, tomato sauce and soups. Equal quantities of butter or vegetable oil and flour are cooked for a little longer than a white roux, but without colouring, to a sandy texture.
- **Brown roux**: this is traditionally used for brown (espagnole) sauce and soups, and is slightly browned in the roux-making process.

A boiling liquid should never be added to a hot roux as the result may be lumpy and the person making the sauce may be scalded by the steam produced. If allowed to stand for a time over a moderate heat, a sauce made with a roux may become thin due to a chemical change (dextrinisation) in the flour.

Continental roux is a very easy and straightforward thickening agent that can be frozen and used as a quick thickener during service or à la minute. Mix equal quantities of flour and vegetable oil together to a paste and place in the oven at 140 °C. Cook the mixture, mixing it in on itself continually, until a biscuit texture is achieved. Remove and allow to cool to room temperature. When it is cool enough to handle, form into a sausage shape using a double layer of cling film. Chill, then freeze. To use, remove from the freezer and shave a little off the end of the log. Whisk it into the boiling sauce (it is not necessary to add it slowly to prevent lumping – this will not occur the flour is already cooked). Once the desired thickness has been achieved, pass and serve.

Beurre manié

Beurre manié is a paste made from equal quantities of soft butter and flour, which is then added to a simmering liquid while whisking continuously to prevent lumping.

Egg yolks

This is commonly known as a liaison and is traditionally used to thicken a classic velouté. Both egg yolks and cream are mixed together and added to the sauce/velouté off the boil; this mixture is intended to thicken, however it is essential to keep stirring it, otherwise the eggs will curdle. Once thickening is achieved the sauce/velouté must be served immediately. The liquid must not be allowed to boil or simmer.

Egg yolks are used in mayonnaise, hollandaise sauce (recipe 60) and custard sauces (page 620). Refer to the appropriate recipe, though, as the yolks are used in a different manner for each sauce. When making mayonnaise (where the yolks are not cooked) or hollandaise (where temperatures remain low), it is advisable to use pasteurised eggs for safety.

Sabayon

A sabayon is a mixture of egg yolks and a little water whisked to the ribbon stage over a gentle heat. The mixture should be the consistency of thick cream. It is added to sauces to assist their glazing.

Cornflour, arrowroot or starch

Cornflour, arrowroot or starch (such as potato starch) is used for thickening gravy and sauces. These are diluted with water, stock or milk, then stirred into the boiling liquid, allowed to reboil for a few minutes and then strained.

Sauce flour

Sauce flour is a specially milled flour that does not require the addition of fat to prevent it from going lumpy. Sauces may be thickened using this flour. It is useful when making sauces for those on a low-fat diet.

Other thickening agents

- Vegetable or fruit purées are known as a coulis. No other thickening agent is used.
- Blood was traditionally used in recipes such as jugged hare, but is used rarely today.
- Cooking liquor from certain dishes and/or stock can be reduced to give a light sauce.

Finishing sauces

When finishing sauces, it is important to check the seasoning and consistency of the finished product. Some hot sauces are finished with cream or crème fraîche. Some are mounted with butter to give them a good shine and smooth consistency: this is known as *monte au beurre*.

Test yourself

1. List the ingredients and describe the cooking methods for brown beef stock.
2. State four quality points you should look for in a white vegetable stock.
3. Give two examples of each of the following soups:
   a. purée
   b. cream
   c. clear
   d. broth.
5. Name two alternatives to cream when finishing a soup.
6. At what temperature should hot soup be served?
7. Describe how you would cook lobster bisque.
8. Describe how you would prepare and cook espagnole sauce.
9. Give an example of a dish with which chasseur sauce is traditionally served.
10. Describe how you should store stocks and sauces.

Stock recipes

1 White stock

1. Chop the bones into small pieces, and remove any fat or marrow.
2. Place the bones in a large stock pot, cover with cold water and bring to the boil.
3. Wash off the bones under cold water, then clean the pot.
4. Return the bones to the cleaned pot, add the water and reboil.
5. Skim as and when required, wipe round inside the pot and simmer gently.
6. After 2 hours, add the washed, peeled whole vegetables, bouquet garni and peppercorns.
7. Simmer for 6–8 hours. Skim, strain and, if to be kept, cool quickly and refrigerate.

Ingredient	4.5 litres	10 litres
Raw, meaty bones	1 kg	2.5 kg
Water	5 litres	10.5 litres
Onion, carrot, celery, leek	400 g	1.5 kg
Bouquet garni	½	1½
Peppercorns	8	16

2 Brown stock

Ingredient	4½ litres	10 litres
Raw, meaty bones	1 kg	2.5 kg
Water	5 litres	10.5 litres
Onion, carrot, celery, leek	400 g	1.5 kg
Bouquet garni	½	1½
Peppercorns	8	16

Energy	Cals	Fat	Sat fat	Carb	Sugar	Protein	Fibre
4 kJ	1 kcal	0.0 g	0.0 g	0.2 g	0.0 g	0.0 g	0.0 g

Stocks, soups and sauces

1. Chop the beef bones and brown well on all sides either by placing in a roasting tin in the oven or carefully browning in a little fat in a frying pan.
2. Drain off any fat and place the bones in a stock pot.
3. Brown any sediment that may be in the bottom of the tray, deglaze (swill out) with half a litre of boiling water, simmer for a few minutes and add to the bones.
4. Add the cold water, bring to the boil and skim. Simmer for 2 hours.
5. Wash, peel and roughly cut the vegetables, fry in a little fat until brown, strain and add to the bones.
6. Add the bouquet garni and peppercorns.
7. Simmer for 6–8 hours. Skim and strain.

> **Professional tip**
> A few squashed tomatoes and washed mushroom trimmings can be added to brown stocks to improve flavour, as can a calf's foot and/or a knuckle of bacon. Dishes made with the stock will not be suitable for some religious diets if bacon is used.

3 White chicken stock

Ingredient	3 litres
Chicken carcass/wings	5 kg
Onions, peeled	1½
Carrots, peeled	2
Cloves of garlic, crushed	2
Leeks, washed and blemishes removed	1
Celery sticks	2
Bay leaf	1
Sprigs of thyme, small	1
Whole white peppercorns	5 g
Water, cold	7 litres

1. Remove any excess fat from the chicken carcasses and wash off under cold water.
2. Place all the bones into a pot that will hold all the ingredients, leaving 5 cm at the top to skim.
3. Add all the other ingredients and cold water, and bring to a simmer; immediately skim all the fat that rises to the surface.
4. Turn the heat off and allow the bones and vegetables to sink. Once this has happened, turn the heat back on, skim and bring to just under a simmer, making as little movement as possible to create more of an infusion than a stock. Skim continuously.
5. Leave to simmer (infuse) for 12 hours then pass through a fine sieve into a clean pan; reduce down rapidly until you have about 3 litres remaining.

4 White vegetable stock

Ingredient	4 portions	10 portions
Onions	100 g	250 g
Carrots	100 g	250 g
Celery	100 g	250 g
Leeks	100 g	250 g
Water	1.5 litres	3.75 litres

1. Roughly chop all the vegetables.
2. Place all the ingredients into a saucepan, add the water, bring to the boil.
3. Allow to simmer for approximately 1 hour.
4. Skim if necessary. Strain and use.

Variation

White fungi stock: add 200–400 g white mushrooms, stalks and trimmings (all well washed) to the recipe.

Energy	Cals	Fat	Sat fat	Carb	Sugar	Protein	Fibre	Sodium
105 kJ	25 kcal	0.3 g	0.1 g	4.9 g	4.0 g	1.0 g	2.4 g	0.0 g

5 Fish stock

Ingredient	2 litres
Fish bones, no heads, gills or roe (turbot, sole or brill bones are best)	5 kg
Olive oil	100 ml
Onions, finely chopped	3
Leeks, finely chopped	3
Celery sticks, finely chopped	3
Fennel bulb, finely chopped	1
Dry white wine	350 ml
Parsley stalks	10
Thyme	3 sprigs
White peppercorns	15
Lemons, finely sliced	2

1. Wash off the bones in cold water for 1 hour.
2. Heat the olive oil in a pan that will hold all the ingredients and still have a 1 cm gap at the top for skimming. Add all the vegetables and sweat without colour for 3 minutes.
3. Add the fish bones and sweat for a further 3 minutes.
4. Add the white wine and enough water to cover. Bring to a simmer, skim off the impurities and add the herbs, peppercorns and lemon. Turn off the heat.
5. Leave to infuse in the refrigerator for 25 minutes, then pass into another pan and reduce by half. The stock is now ready for use.

6 Brown vegetable stock

Ingredient	4 litres approximately
Onions	300 g
Carrots	300 g
Celery	300 g
Leeks	300 g
Sunflower oil	180 ml
Tomatoes	150 g
Mushroom trimmings	150 g
Peppercorns	18
Water	4 litres
Yeast extract	15 g

1. Cut the vegetables into mirepoix. Fry the mirepoix in the oil until golden brown.
2. Drain and place in a suitable saucepan. Add all the other ingredients except the yeast extract and water.
3. Cover with the water and bring to the boil.
4. Add the yeast extract and simmer gently for approximately 1 hour. Then skim if necessary and use.

Variation

Brown fungi stock: add 200–400 g open or field mushrooms, stalks and trimmings (all well washed) to the recipe.

7 Lamb jus

Ingredient	2 litres
Thyme	bunch
Bay leaves, fresh	4
Garlic	2 bulbs
Red wine	1 litre
Lamb bones	2 kg
Veal bones	1 kg
White onions, peeled	6
Large carrots, peeled	8
Celery sticks	7
Leeks, chopped	4
Tomato purée	6 tbsp

1. Preheat the oven to 175 °C. Place the herbs, garlic and wine in a large, deep container. Place all the bones on to a roasting rack on top of the container of herbs and wine, and roast in the oven for 50–60 minutes. When the bones are completely roasted and have taken on a dark golden-brown appearance, remove from oven.
2. Place all the ingredients in a large pot and cover with cold water. Put the pot on to the heat and bring to the simmer; immediately skim all fat that rises to the surface.
3. Turn the heat off and allow the bones and vegetables to sink. Once this has happened, turn the heat back on and bring to just under a simmer, making as little movement as possible to create more of an infusion than a stock.
4. Skim continuously. Leave to infuse in the refrigerator for 12 hours, then pass through a fine sieve, place in the blast chiller until cold and then in the refrigerator overnight. Next day, reduce down rapidly, until you have about 2 litres remaining.

8 Reduced veal stock

1. Brown the bones and calves' feet in a roasting tray in the oven.
2. Place the browned bones in a stock pot, cover with cold water and bring to simmering point.
3. Using the same roasting tray and the fat from the bones, brown off the carrots, onions and celery.
4. Drain off the fat, add the vegetables to the stock and deglaze the tray.
5. Add the remainder of the ingredients; simmer gently for 4–5 hours. Skim frequently.
6. Strain the stock into a clean pan and reduce until a light consistency is achieved.

Ingredient	4 litres
Veal bones, chopped	4 kg
Calves' feet, split lengthways (optional)	2
Water	4 litres
Carrots, roughly chopped	400 g
Onions, roughly chopped	200 g
Celery, roughly chopped	100 g
Tomatoes, blanched, skinned, quartered	1 kg
Mushrooms, chopped	200 g
Large bouquet garni	1
Unpeeled cloves of garlic (optional)	4

Stocks, soups and sauces | **5**

Soup recipes

9 Brown onion soup

Ingredient	4 portions	10 portions
Onions	600 g	1.5 kg
Butter or margarine	25 g	60 g
Clove of garlic, chopped (optional)	1	2–3
Flour, white or wholemeal	10 g	25 g
Brown stock	1 litre	2.5 litres
Salt and pepper		
Flute (thin French stick, 2 cm in diameter)	¼	¾
Grated cheese	50 g	125 g

Energy	Cals	Fat	Sat fat	Carb	Sugar	Protein	Fibre
827 kJ	197 kcal	9.7 g	5.8 g	20.4 g	8.1 g	8.3 g	3.1 g

1. Peel the onions, halve and slice finely.
2. Melt the butter in a thick-bottomed pan, add the onions and garlic, and cook steadily over a good heat until cooked and well browned.
3. Mix in the flour and cook over a gentle heat, browning slightly.
4. Gradually mix in the stock, bring to the boil, skim and season.
5. Simmer for approximately 10 minutes until the onion is soft. Correct the seasoning.
6. Pour into an earthenware tureen or casserole, or individual dishes.
7. Cut the flute (French loaf) into slices and toast on both sides.
8. Sprinkle the toasted slices of bread liberally on the soup.
9. Sprinkle with grated cheese and brown under the salamander.
10. Place on a dish and serve.

During cooking, the finely sliced onions first become translucent

As the onions continue to cook, they begin to brown without becoming crisp

When the onions are ready, they are well browned

Cook in the flour, and finally the stock

10 Minestrone

Energy	Cals	Fat	Sat fat	Carb	Sugar	Protein	Fibre
1,115 kJ	260 kcal	22.9g	5.8g	11.9g	4.2g	3.8g	4.1g

Using sunflower oil.

1. Cut the peeled and washed mixed vegetables into paysanne.
2. Cook slowly without colour in the oil or butter in the pan with a lid on.
3. Add the stock, bouquet garni and seasoning; simmer for approximately 20 minutes.
4. Add the peas and the beans cut into diamonds and simmer for 10 minutes.
5. Add the spaghetti in 2 cm lengths, the potatoes cut into paysanne, the tomato purée and the tomatoes, and simmer gently until all the vegetables are cooked.
6. Meanwhile finely chop the fat bacon, parsley and garlic, if using, and form into a paste.
7. Mould the paste into pellets the size of a pea and drop into the boiling soup.
8. Remove the bouquet garni, correct the seasoning.
9. Serve grated Parmesan cheese and croutons of bread or slices of French bread (flutes) separately.

Ingredient	4 portions	10 portions
Mixed vegetables (onion, leek, celery, carrot, turnip, cabbage), peeled	300g	750g
Butter or oil	50g	125g
White stock or water	0.5 litres	1.25 litres
Bouquet garni	1	2
Salt, pepper		
Peas	25g	60g
French beans	25g	60g
Spaghetti	25g	60g
Potatoes, peeled	50g	125g
Tomato purée	1 tsp	2½ tsp
Tomatoes, skinned, deseeded, diced	100g	250g
Fat bacon (optional)	50g	125g
Parsley (optional)	50g	125g
Clove of garlic (optional)	1	2½

Healthy eating tips

- Use an unsaturated oil (sunflower or vegetable) to lightly oil the pan. Drain off any excess after the frying is complete and skim the fat from the finished dish.
- Season with the minimum amount of salt as the bacon and cheese are high in salt.

Vegetables chopped into paysanne

Fry or sweat the vegetables

Simmer the ingredients in the stock

Add the pellets of paste to the soup

11 Scotch broth

Ingredient	4 portions	10 portions
Lean beef (skirt)	200 g	500 g
Beef stock	1 litre	2.5 litres
Barley	25 g	60 g
Vegetables (carrot, turnip, leek, celery, onion), cut into paysanne	200 g	500 g
Bouquet garni	1	2
Salt, pepper		
Chopped parsley		

Energy	Cals	Fat	Sat fat	Carb	Sugar	Protein	Fibre	Sodium
655 kJ	157 kcal	7.8g	3.1g	4.9g	2.7g	16.6g	1.6g	0.2g

1 Place the beef, free from fat, in a saucepan and cover with cold water.
2 Bring to the boil, then immediately wash off under running water.
3 Clean the pan, replace the meat, cover with cold stock, bring to the boil and skim.
4 Add the washed barley, simmer for 1 hour.
5 Add the vegetables, bouquet garni and seasoning.
6 Skim when necessary; simmer for approximately 30 minutes, until tender.
7 Remove the meat, allow to cool and cut from the bone, remove all fat and cut the meat into neat dice the same size as the vegetables; return to the broth.
8 Correct the seasoning, skim off all the fat, add the chopped parsley and serve.

Healthy eating tips
- Remove all fat from the meat.
- Use only a small amount of salt.
- There are lots of healthy vegetables in this dish and the addition of a large bread roll will increase the starchy carbohydrate.

12 Cream of green pea soup (crème St Germain)

Ingredient	4 portions	10 portions
Onion, chopped	25 g	60 g
Leek, chopped	25 g	60 g
Celery, chopped	25 g	60 g
Butter or oil	25 g	60 g
Water or white stock	500 ml	1.25 litres
Peas, fresh (shelled) or frozen	250 ml	625 ml
Sprig of mint		
Bouquet garni	1	2
Thin béchamel	500 ml	1.25 litres
Cream, natural yoghurt or fromage frais	60 ml	150 ml

Energy	Cals	Fat	Sat fat	Carb	Sugar	Protein	Fibre
1,356 kJ	323 kcal	23.6 g	12.8 g	19.6 g	8.0 g	9.3 g	8.3 g

1 Sweat the onion, leek and celery in the butter or oil.
2 Moisten with water or stock and bring to the boil.
3 Add the peas, mint and bouquet garni, and allow to boil for approximately 5 minutes.
4 Remove the bouquet garni, add the béchamel and bring to the boil.
5 Remove from the heat and liquidise or pass through a sieve. Skim off any fat.
6 Correct the seasoning and pass through medium strainer.
7 Finish with cream, natural yoghurt or fromage frais.

Healthy eating tips
- Use an unsaturated oil (sunflower or vegetable). Lightly oil the pan and drain off any excess after the frying is complete.
- Season with the minimum amount of salt.

Variation
Variations can be made with the addition of:
- a garnish of 25 g cooked and washed tapioca, added at the same time as the cream
- a garnish of 25 g cooked and washed vermicelli and *julienne* of sorrel cooked in butter
- natural yoghurt, skimmed milk or non-dairy cream may be used in place of cream.

See also the variations listed under pulse soup (recipe 15).

13 Cream of tomato soup (crème de tomates fraiches)

Ingredient	4 portions	10 portions
Butter or oil	50 g	125 g
Bacon trimmings, optional	25 g	60 g
Onion, diced	100 g	250 g
Carrot, diced	100 g	250 g
Flour	50 g	125 g
Tomatoes, fresh, fully ripe	1 kg	2.5 kg
Stock	1 litre	2.5 litres
Bouquet garni	1	2
Salt, pepper		
Croutons – sliced stale bread	1	3
Butter	50 g	125 g

Energy	Cals	Fat	Sat fat	Carb	Sugar	Protein	Fibre	Sodium
1159 kJ	277 kcal	16.2 g	4.8 g	28.5 g	13.6 g	6.3 g	6.6 g	0.3 g

1. Melt the butter or heat the oil in a thick-bottomed pan.
2. Add the bacon, onion and carrot (mirepoix) and brown lightly.
3. Mix in the flour and cook to a sandy texture.
4. Gradually add the hot stock.
5. Stir to the boil.
6. Remove the eyes from the tomatoes, wash them well, and squeeze them into the soup after it has come to the boil.
7. If colour is lacking, add a little tomato purée soon after the soup comes to the boil.
8. Add the bouquet garni and season lightly.
9. Simmer for approximately 1 hour. Skim when required.
10. Remove the bouquet garni and mirepoix.
11. Liquidise or pass firmly through a sieve, then through a conical strainer.
12. Return to a clean pan, correct the seasoning and consistency. Bring to the boil.
13. Serve fried or toasted croutons separately.

Professional tip
- Flour may be omitted from the recipe if a thinner soup is required.
- A slightly sweet/sharp flavour can be added to the soup by preparing what is known as a gastric (gastrique). In a thick-bottomed pan, reduce 100 ml of malt vinegar and 35 g caster sugar until it is a light caramel colour. Mix this into the completed soup.
- Some tomato purée can be stronger than others, so you may have to add a little more or less when making this soup.

Healthy eating tips
- Use soft margarine or sunflower/vegetable oil in place of the butter.
- Toast the croutons rather than frying them.
- Use the minimum amount of salt – there is plenty in the bacon.

Variation
Without fresh tomatoes: substitute 150 g of tomato purée for the fresh tomatoes (375 g for 10 portions). When reboiling the soup (step 12), add 500 ml of milk or 125 ml of cream, yoghurt or fromage frais.

Try adding the juice and lightly grated peel of 1–2 oranges, cooked rice or a chopped fresh herb, such as chives.

14 Mushroom soup (crème de champignons)

1. Gently cook the sliced onions, leek and celery in the butter or oil in a thick-bottomed pan, without colouring.
2. Mix in the flour and cook over a gentle heat to a sandy texture without colouring.
3. Remove from the heat and cool slightly.
4. Gradually mix in the hot stock. Stir to the boil.
5. Add the well-washed, chopped mushrooms, the bouquet garni and season.
6. Simmer for 30–45 minutes. Skim when needed.
7. Remove the bouquet garni. Pass through a sieve or liquidise.
8. Pass through a medium strainer. Return to a clean saucepan.
9. Reboil, correct the seasoning and consistency; add the milk or cream.

Ingredient	4 portions	10 portions
Onion, leek and celery, sliced	100 g	250 g
Butter or oil	50 g	125 g
Flour	50 g	125 g
White stock (preferably chicken)	1 litre	2.5 litres
White mushrooms, washed and chopped	200 g	500 g
Bouquet garni	1	2
Salt, pepper		
Milk (or cream)	125 ml (or 60 ml)	300 ml (or 150 ml)

Energy	Cals	Fat	Sat fat	Carb	Sugar	Protein	Fibre
712 kJ	170 kcal	11.8 g	5.2 g	12.6 g	3.0 g	3.8 g	1.6 g

Using hard margarine.

Variation

Natural yoghurt, skimmed milk or non-dairy cream may be used in place of dairy cream.

A garnish of thinly sliced mushrooms may be added. Wild mushrooms may also be used.

Healthy eating tips

- Use soft margarine or sunflower/vegetable oil in place of the butter.
- Use the minimum amount of salt.
- The least fatty option is to use a combination of semi-skimmed milk and yoghurt or fromage frais – not cream.

15 Pulse soup with croutons

1. Pick and wash the pulses (if pre-soaked, change the water).
2. Place in a thick-bottomed pan; add the stock or water and bring to the boil and skim.
3. Add the remaining ingredients and season lightly.
4. Simmer until tender; skim when necessary.
5. Remove the bouquet garni and ham knuckle (if using).
6. Liquidise and pass through a conical strainer.
7. Return to a clean pan and reboil; correct the seasoning and consistency.
8. Serve accompanied by 0.5 cm-diced bread croutons shallow-fried in butter or olive oil.

Note

Pulses are the dried seeds of plants that form pods. Any type of pulse can be made into soup, for example split green and yellow peas, haricot beans and lentils.

Healthy eating tips

- The fat and salt are reduced if the ham is omitted.
- Try lightly brushing the stale bread with olive oil and oven-baking it with garlic and herbs. Alternatively, serve with sippets.

Variation

Variations can be made with the addition of:
- chopped fresh herbs (parsley, chervil, tarragon, coriander, chives, etc.)
- spices (e.g. garam masala)
- crisp lardons of bacon
- sippets (small, thin pieces of bread, toasted or oven-baked).

Ingredient	4 portions	10 portions
Pulses (soaked overnight if necessary)	200 g	500 g
White stock or water	1.5 litres	3.75 litres
Onions, chopped	50 g	125 g
Carrots, chopped	50 g	125 g
Bouquet garni	1	2
Knuckle of ham or bacon (optional)	50 g	125 g
Salt and pepper		
Croutons		
Stale bread	1 slice	2½ slices
Butter or olive oil	50 g	125 g

Energy	Cals	Fat	Sat fat	Carb	Sugar	Protein	Fibre
728 kJ	177 kcal	1.3 g	0.2 g	32.0 g	3.3 g	11.3 g	3.6 g

One portion (no croutons); one portion (with croutons) provides: 1,223 kJ/291 kcal energy; 111.7 g fat; 6.8 g saturated fat; 36.5 g carbohydrates; 3.6 g sugar; 12.1 g protein; 3.8 g fibre.

16 Chicken soup (*crème de volaille* or *crème reine*)

1. Gently cook the sliced onions, leek and celery in a thick-bottomed pan, in the butter or oil, without colouring.
2. Mix in the flour; cook over a gentle heat to a sandy texture without colouring.
3. Cool slightly; gradually mix in the hot stock. Stir to the boil.
4. Add the bouquet garni and season.
5. Simmer for 30–45 minutes; skim when necessary. Remove the bouquet garni.
6. Liquidise or pass firmly through a fine strainer.
7. Return to a clean pan, reboil and finish with milk or cream; correct the seasoning.
8. Add the chicken garnish and serve.

Ingredient	4 portions	10 portions
Onion, leek and celery, sliced	100 g	250 g
Butter or oil	50 g	125 g
Flour	50 g	125 g
Chicken stock	1 litre	2.5 litres
Bouquet garni	1	2
Salt, pepper		
Milk or cream	250 ml or 125 ml	625 ml or 300 ml
Cooked dice of chicken (garnish)	25 g	60 g

Energy	Cals	Fat	Sat fat	Carb	Sugar	Protein	Fibre	Sodium
900 kJ	217 kcal	16.7 g	10.4 g	12.6 g	2.6 g	4.8 g	1.6 g	0.1 g

Using butter and cream.

Variation

Natural yoghurt, skimmed milk or non-dairy cream may be used in place of dairy cream.

Add cooked small pasta or sliced mushrooms.

Healthy eating tips

- Use soft margarine or sunflower/vegetable oil in place of the butter.
- Use the minimum amount of salt.
- The least fatty option is to use a combination of semi-skimmed milk and yoghurt or fromage frais – not cream.

Stocks, soups and sauces

17 Asparagus soup (*crème d'asperges*)

Ingredient	4 portions	10 portions
Onion, sliced	50 g	125 g
Celery, sliced	50 g	125 g
Butter or oil	50 g	125 g
Flour	50 g	125 g
White stock (preferably chicken)	1 litre	2.5 litres
Asparagus stalk trimmings	200 g	500 g
or		
Tin of asparagus	150 g	325 g
Bouquet garni	1	2
Salt, pepper		
Milk or cream	250 ml or 125 ml	625 ml or 300 ml

Energy	Cals	Fat	Sat fat	Carb	Sugar	Protein	Fibre
919 kJ	223 kcal	13.1 g	8.0 g	18.9 g	8.8 g	8.4 g	2.5 g

Using butter.

1. Gently sweat the onions and celery, without colouring, in the butter or oil.
2. Remove from the heat, mix in the flour, return to a low heat and cook out, without colouring, for a few minutes. Cool.
3. Gradually add the hot stock. Stir to the boil.
4. Add the well-washed asparagus trimmings, or the tin of asparagus, and bouquet garni. Season.
5. Simmer for 30–40 minutes, then remove bouquet garni.
6. Liquidise and pass through a strainer.
7. Return to a clean pan, reboil, correct seasoning and consistency. (Milk with a little cornflour can be added to adjust the consistency.)
8. Add the milk or cream and serve.

Healthy eating tips
- Use an unsaturated oil (sunflower/vegetable) to lightly oil the pan. Drain off any excess after the frying is complete and skim the fat from the finished dish.
- Season with the minimum amount of salt.

Practical Cookery 14th edition

18 Cream of spinach and celery soup

Ingredient	4 portions	10 portions
Shallots, peeled and chopped (small mirepoix)	2	5
Leeks, washed and chopped (small mirepoix)	1	2½
Cloves of garlic, peeled and chopped	2	5
Corn oil	2 tbsp	5 tbsp
Celery sticks, washed and chopped (small mirepoix)	4	10
Flour	15 g	35 g
Fresh spinach, well washed	500 g	1.25 kg
Milk	600 ml	1.5 litres
Vegetable stock	600 ml	1.5 litres
Salt, to taste		

Energy	Cals	Fat	Sat fat	Carb	Sugar	Protein	Fibre	Sodium
886 kJ	214 kcal	12.7 g	4.7 g	15.1 g	11.3 g	10.1 g	6.1 g	0.3 g

1 Cook the shallots, leeks and garlic in the oil for a few minutes, without colour.
2 Add the celery and cook for another few minutes until starting to soften.
3 Add the flour and mix well, then throw in the spinach and mix around. Add the milk and vegetable stock slowly, ensuring there are no lumps.
4 Stir continuously, bring to a simmer, then switch off and remove from heat. Cover and leave for a few minutes.
5 Blend until smooth in a food processor. Check seasoning and serve.

19 Cream of vegetable soup

Ingredient	4 portions	10 portions
Onions, leeks and celery, sliced	100 g	250 g
Other suitable vegetables*, sliced	200 g	500 g
Butter or oil	50 g	125 g
Flour	50 g	125 g
White stock or water	0.5 litres	1.5 litres
Thin béchamel	0.5 litres	1 litre
Bouquet garni	1	2
Salt and pepper		

*Suitable vegetables include Jerusalem artichokes, cauliflower, celery, leeks, onions, parsnips, turnips and fennel.

Analysis based on using butter, cauliflower, turnip and parsnip. 50% stock, 50% semi-skimmed milk used in place of béchamel.

Energy	Cals	Fat	Sat fat	Carb	Sugar	Protein	Fibre	Sodium
862 kJ	206 kcal	12.1 g	7.3 g	20.0 g	8.7 g	5.3 g	3.4 g	0.9 g

Stocks, soups and sauces

1. Gently cook all the sliced vegetables in the fat under a lid, without colour.
2. Mix in the flour and cook slowly for a few minutes without colour. Cool slightly.
3. Gradually mix in the hot stock. Stir and bring to the boil.
4. Add the bouquet garni and season.
5. Simmer for approximately 45 minutes; skim when necessary.
6. Remove the bouquet garni and add the béchamel; liquidise, blend or pass firmly through a sieve and then through a medium strainer.
7. Return to a clean pan, reheat and correct the seasoning and consistency.

Variation

- Instead of using the béchamel, use an additional 250 ml of stock and then finish the soup with 250 ml milk.
- Alternatively, do this with an additional 375 ml of stock and finish with 125 ml of cream.

20 Vegetable purée soup

Ingredient	4 portions	10 portions
Onions, leek and celery, sliced	100 g	250 g
Other suitable vegetables, *sliced	200 g	500 g
Butter or oil	50 g	125 g
Flour	50 g	125 g
White stock or water	1 litre	2.5 litres
Bouquet garni	1	2
Salt, pepper		

*Suitable vegetables include Jerusalem artichokes, cauliflower, celery, leeks, onions, parsnips, turnips and fennel.

Energy	Cals	Fat	Sat fat	Carb	Sugar	Protein	Fibre
601 kJ	143 kcal	10.3 g	4.4 g	11.4 g	1.8 g	1.9 g	1.9 g

Using hard margarine.

1. Gently cook all the sliced vegetables in the fat under a lid, without colour.
2. Mix in the flour and cook slowly for a few minutes without colour. Cool slightly.
3. Gradually mix in the hot stock. Stir to the boil.
4. Add the bouquet garni and season.
5. Simmer for approximately 45 minutes; skim when necessary.
6. Remove the bouquet garni; liquidise or pass firmly through a sieve and then through a medium strainer.
7. Return to a clean pan, reboil, and correct the seasoning and consistency.

Variation

Add a little spice, sufficient to give a subtle background flavour, e.g. garam masala with parsnip soup.

Just before serving add a little freshly chopped herb(s), e.g. parsley, chervil, tarragon, coriander.

Healthy eating tips

- Use an unsaturated oil (sunflower or vegetable) to lightly oil the pan. Drain off any excess after the frying is complete and skim the fat from the finished dish.
- Season with the minimum amount of salt.
- Try using more vegetables to thicken the soup in place of the flour.

Practical Cookery 14th edition

21 Red lentil soup

Ingredient	4 portions	10 portions
Ham hock	320 g	800 g
Onion, peeled	25 g	60 g
Whole carrot, peeled	½	1¼
Baby shallots	1	2½
Leeks	50 g	125 g
Celery	50 g	125 g
Oil	40 ml	100 ml
Red lentils	200 g	500 g
Cooking liquid from the hock	1 litre	2.5 litres
Milk, cream or crème fraiche	120 ml	300 ml

Energy	Cals	Fat	Sat fat	Carb	Sugar	Protein	Fibre
1,807 kJ	432 kcal	71.4g	43.9g	6.7g	1.5g	5.3g	1.5g

1. Place the ham hock, onion and carrot in a pan and cover with about 3 litres of water.
2. Bring to the boil and then turn down to a slow simmer. (When the hock is cooked, the centre bone will slide out in one smooth motion.)
3. Slice the shallots, leek and celery into 1 cm dice.
4. Heat a pan with the oil, add the vegetables and cook until they are slightly coloured; add the lentils and cover them with the ham stock.
5. Bring to the boil, then turn the heat down to a very slow simmer.
6. Cook until all the lentils have broken down.
7. Allow to cool for 10 minutes and then purée until smooth.
8. Correct the consistency as necessary, and finish with boiled milk, cream or crème fraiche.

Variation

Meat-free version: omit the ham hock and use a vegetable stock or water instead of the cooking liquid.

22 Potato soup (*purée parmentier*)

Ingredient	4 portions	10 portions
Butter or oil	25 g	60 g
Onion, peeled and sliced	50 g	125 g
White of leek, washed and sliced	50 g	125 g
White stock or water	1 litre	2.5 litres
Potatoes, peeled and sliced	400 g	1.25 kg
Bouquet garni	1	2
Salt and pepper		
Parsley, chopped		
Croutons		
Stale bread	1 slice	2½ slices
Butter, margarine or oil	50 g	125 g

Energy	Cals	Fat	Sat fat	Carb	Sugar	Protein	Fibre
1,063 kJ	253 kcal	15.7g	9.8g	26.1g	2.1g	3.6g	2.9g

1. Melt the butter or heat the oil in a thick-bottomed pan.
2. Add the onion and leek; cook for a few minutes without colour with the lid on.
3. Add the stock or water, the potatoes and the bouquet garni. Season.
4. Simmer for approximately 30 minutes. Remove the bouquet garni and skim off all fat.
5. Liquidise or pass the soup firmly through a sieve then pass it through a medium conical strainer.
6. Return to a clean pan and reboil. Correct the seasoning and consistency.
7. Serve sprinkled with chopped parsley.
8. Serve fried or toasted croutons separately.

Healthy eating tips

- Use an unsaturated oil (sunflower or vegetable). Lightly oil the pan and drain off any excess after the frying is complete.
- Season with the minimum amount of salt.
- Toast the croutons instead of frying them.

23 Roasted butternut squash soup

Ingredient	4 portions	10 portions
Butternut squash, peeled and de-seeded	600 g	2 kg
Onion	100 g	250 g
Olive oil	2 tbsp	5 tbsp
Garlic (optional), finely chopped	1 clove	2 cloves
Bacon (back rashers), in small pieces	4	10
Chicken or vegetable stock	625 ml	1.5 litres
Salt and pepper		
Cream or thick natural yoghurt	6 tbsp	15 tbsp

Energy	Cals	Fat	Sat fat	Carb	Sugar	Protein	Fibre
923 kJ	220 kcal	12.0g	3.5g	19.6g	13.1g	9.9g	2.8g

1. Cut the squash into thick pieces, place on a lightly oiled baking sheet and roast for 20–25 minutes in a hot oven until the flesh is soft and golden brown.
2. Sweat the onions and garlic in the olive oil without colouring, for approximately 5 minutes.
3. Add the bacon and lightly brown.
4. Add the roasted squash, pour in the stock, and bring to boil. Simmer for 20 minutes.
5. Allow to cool before liquidising or blending until smooth.
6. Season lightly, add yoghurt or cream, then reheat gently and serve.

Variation

Add three to four saffron strands soaked in one tablespoon hot water at step 4.

Healthy eating tips

- Use unsaturated oil (sunflower or olive); lightly oil the pan to sweat the garlic and onions. Drain off any excess fat after cooking the bacon.
- Use low-fat yoghurt to reduce the fat content. Add a little cornflour to stabilise the yoghurt before adding to the soup.

24 Potato and watercress soup

Ingredient	4 portions	10 portions
Butter or oil	25 g	60 g
Onion, peeled and sliced	50 g	125 g
White of leek, sliced	50 g	125 g
White stock or water	1 litre	2.5 litres
Potatoes, peeled and sliced	400 g	1 kg
Watercress	small bunch	small bunch
Bouquet garni		
Salt, pepper		
Parsley, chopped		
Croutons		
Stale bread	1 slice	2½ slices
Butter, margarine or oil	50 g	125 g

Energy	Cals	Fat	Sat fat	Carb	Sugar	Protein	Fibre	Sodium
583 kJ	139 kcal	5.5 g	3.3 g	21.0 g	3.8 g	2.7 g	3.4 g	0.1 g

Using butter.

1. Pick off 12 neat leaves of watercress and plunge into a small pan of boiling water for 1–2 seconds. Refresh under cold water immediately; these leaves are to garnish the finished soup.
2. Melt the butter or heat the oil in a thick-bottomed pan.
3. Add the peeled and washed sliced onion and leek, cook for a few minutes without colour with the lid on.
4. Add the stock, the peeled, washed and sliced potatoes, the rest of the watercress, including the stalks, and the bouquet garni. Season.
5. Simmer for approximately 30 minutes. Remove the bouquet garni, skim off all fat.
6. Liquidise or pass the soup firmly through a sieve then pass through a medium conical strainer.
7. Return to a clean pan, reboil, correct the seasoning and consistency, and serve.
8. Garnish with watercress.
9. Serve fried or toasted croutons separately.

25 Chilled leek and potato soup (vichyssoise)

Ingredient	4 portions	10 portions
Onions, finely sliced	160 g	400 g
Leeks, finely sliced	175 g	430 g
Butter	125 g	300 g
Potatoes, diced small	750 g	1.8 kg
Water/vegetable stock	1.8 litres	4.5 litres
Salt	15 g	30 g
Pepper to taste		
Garnish		
Whipped cream		
Chives, chopped		

Energy	Cals	Fat	Sat fat	Carb	Sugar	Protein	Fibre
1,653 kJ	397 kcal	26.4 g	16.3 g	36.9 g	4.5 g	5.3 g	4.0 g

Stocks, soups and sauces

1. Sweat the sliced onion and leek without colour in the butter. Cook until very tender.
2. Add the potatoes and bring quickly to the boil with the water or vegetable stock.
3. Liquidise in food processor and allow to cool.
4. Check seasoning. Note that seasoning needs to reflect the serving temperature.
5. Serve cold with whipped cream and chopped chives.

26 Gazpacho

Ingredient	4 portions	10 portions
Tomato juice	500 ml	1.25 litres
Tomatoes, skinned, deseeded and diced	100 g	250 g
Cucumber, peeled and diced	100 g	250 g
Green pepper, diced	50 g	125 g
Onion, chopped	50 g	125 g
Mayonnaise	1 tbsp	2–3 tbsp
Vinegar	1 tbsp	2–3 tbsp
Seasoning		
Clove of garlic	1	2–3

Energy	Cals	Fat	Sat fat	Carb	Sugar	Protein	Fibre	Sodium
861 kJ	203 kcal	2.7 g	0.8 g	40.5 g	38.7 g	6.7 g	12.5 g	3.2 g

This soup has many regional variations. It is served chilled and has a predominant flavour of cucumber, tomato and garlic.

1. Mix all the ingredients together.
2. Season and add crushed chopped garlic to taste.
3. Stand in a cool place for an hour.
4. Correct the consistency with iced water and serve chilled.

Variation

Instead of serving with all the ingredients finely chopped, the soup can be liquidised and garnished with chopped tomato, cucumber and pepper.

The soup may also be finished with chopped herbs.

A tray of garnishes may accompany the soup, e.g. chopped red and green pepper, chopped onion, tomato, cucumber and croutons.

27 Tomato soup

Ingredient	4 portions	10 portions
Butter or oil	50 g	125 g
Bacon trimmings, optional	25 g	60 g
Onion, diced	100 g	250 g
Carrot, diced	100 g	250 g
Flour	50 g	125 g
Tomato purée	150 g	375 g
Stock	1.25 litres	3.5 litres
Bouquet garni	1	2
Salt, pepper		
Croutons		
Slice stale bread	1	3
Butter	50 g	125 g

Energy	Cals	Fat	Sat fat	Carb	Sugar	Protein	Fibre
1,150 kJ	274 kcal	21.3g	11.2g	17.1g	3.7g	4.6g	1.0g

Using hard margarine.

1. Melt the butter or heat the oil in a thick-bottomed pan.
2. Add the bacon, onion and carrot (mirepoix) and brown lightly.
3. Mix in the flour and cook to a sandy texture.
4. Remove from the heat, mix in the tomato purée.
5. Return to heat and gradually add the hot stock.
6. Stir to the boil. Add the bouquet garni, season lightly.
7. Simmer for approximately 1 hour. Skim when required.
8. Remove the bouquet garni and mirepoix.
9. Liquidise or pass firmly through a sieve, then through a conical strainer.
10. Return to a clean pan, correct the seasoning and consistency. Bring to the boil.
11. Serve fried or toasted croutons separately.

Professional tip

If a slightly sweet/sour flavour is required, reduce 100 ml vinegar and 35 g caster sugar to a light caramel and mix into the completed soup.

Healthy eating tips

- Use soft margarine or sunflower/vegetable oil in place of the butter.
- Toast the croutons rather than frying them.
- Use the minimum amount of salt – there is plenty in the bacon.

Variation

Variations can be made with the addition of:
- juice and lightly grated zest of 1–2 oranges
- tomato concassé
- cooked rice
- chopped fresh coriander, basil or chives
- 200 g peeled, sliced potatoes with the stock.

28 Roasted red pepper and tomato soup

Energy	Cals	Fat	Sat fat	Carb	Sugar	Protein	Fibre
983 kJ	235 kcal	16.8 g	7.1 g	18.3 g	16.4 g	3.6 g	4.5 g

Ingredient	4 portions	10 portions
Red peppers	4	10
Plum tomatoes	400 g	1.25 kg
Butter or oil	50 g	125 g
Onion, chopped	100 g	250 g
Carrot, chopped	100 g	250 g
Stock	500 ml	1.5 litres
Crème fraiche	2 tbsp	5 tbsp
Basil	25 g	75 g
Croutons		
Slice stale bread	1	3
Butter	50 g	125 g

1. Core and deseed the peppers and halve the tomatoes.
2. Lightly sprinkle with oil and place on a tray into a hot oven or under a grill until the pepper skins are blackened.
3. Allow the peppers to cool in a plastic bag.
4. Remove the skins and slice the flesh.
5. Place the butter or oil in a pan, add the onions and carrots and fry gently for 5 minutes.
6. Add the stock, peppers and tomatoes and bring to the boil.
7. Simmer for 30 minutes, correct the seasoning and blend in a food processor until smooth.
8. Add crème fraiche and basil leaves torn into pieces, and serve with croutons.

29 Carrot and butter bean soup

Ingredient	4 portions	10 portions
Onions, peeled and chopped	1	2½
Cloves of garlic, chopped	2	5
Sunflower oil	15 ml	35 ml
Carrots, large to medium, brunoise	250 g	750 g
Vegetable stock	500 ml	1.25 litres
Butter beans, cooked	400 g	1 kg
Seasoning		

Energy	Cals	Fat	Sat fat	Carb	Sugar	Protein	Fibre	Sodium
638 kJ	152 kcal	4.6g	0.6g	21.9g	8.5g	7.0g	9.4g	0.5g

1 Cook the onion and garlic in the oil for a few minutes, without colour, then add the carrots and stir well.
2 Add the vegetable stock. Bring to the boil, turn down to a simmer and cook for about 15 minutes until the carrot is cooked through.
3 Add the beans and cook for a further 5 minutes or so until they are heated through.
4 Liquidise in a food processor until smooth; check seasoning.

Professional tip
With any soup recipe, it is important to simmer the soup gently. Do not let it boil vigorously, because too much water will evaporate. If the soup has boiled, add more stock or water to make up for this.

Stocks, soups and sauces

30 Pea velouté

Ingredient	4 portions	10 portions
Frozen peas	400 g	1 kg
Vegetable oil	10 ml	25 ml
Shallots, chopped	1	2
Milk	200 ml	500 ml
Double cream	40 ml	100 ml
Butter or margarine	40 g	100 g

Energy	Cals	Fat	Sat fat	Carb	Sugar	Protein	Fibre	Sodium
984 kJ	237 kcal	17.8 g	9.6 g	12.2 g	5.5 g	7.7 g	6.9 g	0.1 g

1 Blanch the peas in a small pan of boiling water for 3 minutes, then drain.
2 Heat the oil in a large saucepan and cook the shallots without letting them colour.
3 Add the peas to this pan, and cook for a further 2–3 minutes, again without colouring.
4 Add the milk, bring to a simmer and cook until the peas are tender.
5 Cool the mixture slightly, then transfer to a food processor and liquidise until very smooth – this may take a while. At this point, the soup can be cooled completely and stored in an airtight container in the refrigerator until ready to serve.
6 Add the cream and butter just before serving.

31 Pumpkin velouté

Ingredient	4 portions	10 portions
Shallots, sliced	1	2½
Butter	320 g	800 g
Clove of garlic, sliced (optional)	½	1¼
Large squash or pumpkin (300 g), flesh diced	1	2½
Parmesan, grated	30 g	75 g
Truffle oil	1 tbsp	2½ tbsp
Salt, pepper		
Chicken stock	400–600 ml	1–1.5 litres

Energy	Cals	Fat	Sat fat	Carb	Sugar	Protein	Fibre	Sodium
2,883 kJ	689 kcal	71.4 g	43.9 g	6.7 g	1.5 g	5.3 g	1.5 g	3.0 g

Using acorn squash and olive oil.

1 Sweat the shallots in the butter, without colour, until cooked and soft.
2 Add the garlic, pumpkin, Parmesan and truffle oil. Correct the seasoning and cook for 5 minutes.
3 Add the chicken stock, bring to the boil, simmer for 5 minutes.
4 Liquidise, pass, correct the seasoning and serve hot. Blast chill if to be stored.

109

32 Clear soup (*consommé*)

Ingredient	4 portions	10 portions
Chopped or minced beef	200 g	500 g
Salt, to taste		
Egg whites	1–2	3–5
White or brown beef stock, cold	1 litre	2.5 litres
Mixed vegetables (onion, carrot, celery, leek)	100 g	250 g
Bouquet garni	1	2
Peppercorns	3–4	8–10

Energy	Cals	Fat	Sat fat	Carb	Sugar	Protein	Fibre
126 kJ	30 kcal	0.0g	0.0g	1.8g	0.0g	5.6g	0.0g

1. Thoroughly mix the beef, salt, egg white and a quarter of the cold stock in a thick-bottomed pan.
2. Peel, wash and finely chop the vegetables.
3. Add to the beef with the remainder of the stock, the bouquet garni and the peppercorns.
4. Place over a gentle heat and bring slowly to the boil, stirring occasionally.
5. Allow to boil rapidly for 5–10 seconds. Give a final stir.
6. Lower the heat so that the consommé is simmering very gently.
7. Cook for 1½–2 hours without stirring.
8. Strain carefully through a double muslin.
9. Remove all fat, using both sides of 8 cm square pieces of kitchen paper.
10. Correct the seasoning and colour, which should be a delicate amber.
11. Degrease again, if necessary. Bring to the boil and serve.

Stocks, soups and sauces

> **Professional tip**
>
> A consommé should be crystal clear. The clarification process is caused by the albumen of the egg white and meat coagulating, rising to the top of the liquid and carrying other solid ingredients. The remaining liquid beneath the coagulated surface should be gently simmering. Cloudiness is due to some or all of the following:
> - poor quality stock
> - greasy stock
> - unstrained stock
> - imperfect coagulation of the clearing agent
> - whisking after boiling point is reached, whereby the impurities mix with the liquid
> - not allowing the soup to settle before straining
> - lack of cleanliness of the pan or cloth
> - any trace of grease or starch.

> **Healthy eating tips**
> - This soup is fat free!
> - Keep the salt to a minimum and serve as a low-calorie starter for anyone wishing to reduce the fat in their diet.

> **Variation**
>
> Consommés are varied in many ways by altering the flavour of the stock (chicken, chicken and beef, game, etc.), also by the addition of numerous garnishes (julienne or brunoise of vegetables, shredded savoury pancakes or pea-sized profiteroles) added at the last moment before serving, or small pasta.
>
> Cold, lightly jellied consommés, served in cups, with or without garnish (diced tomato), may be served in hot weather.

33 Prawn bisque

Energy	Cals	Fat	Sat fat	Carb	Sugar	Protein	Fibre	Sodium
1,578 kJ	381 kcal	31.2g	13.0g	8.2g	4.0g	12.9g	0.8g	1.0g

Ingredient	4 portions	10 portions
Oil	50 ml	125 ml
Butter	30 g	75 g
Unshelled prawns	250 g	625 g
Flour	20 g	50 g
Tomato purée	1 tbsp	2 tbsp
Shellfish nage	1 litre	2.5 litres
Fish stock	150 ml	375 ml
Whipping cream	120 ml	300 ml
Dry sherry	75 ml	180 ml
Paprika, pinch		
Seasoning		
Chives, chopped		

1. Heat the oil and the butter. Add the prawns and cook for 3–4 minutes on a moderately high heat.
2. Sprinkle in the flour and cook for a further 2–3 minutes.
3. Add the tomato purée and cook for a further 2 minutes.
4. Meanwhile, bring the nage up to a simmer and, once the tomato purée has been cooked in, slowly add to the prawn mix, being mindful that you have formed a roux; stir in the fish stock to prevent lumping.
5. Once all the stock has been added, bring to the boil and simmer for 3–4 minutes.
6. Pass through a fine sieve, return the shells to the pan and pound to extract more flavour and more colour.
7. Pour over the fish stock, bring to the boil, then pass this back on to the already passed soup.
8. Bring to the boil, add the cream and sherry, correct the seasoning and served with chopped chives.

111

Sauce recipes

34 Béchamel sauce (white sauce)

Ingredient	1 litre	4.5 litres
Butter or oil	100 g	400 g
Flour	100 g	400 g
Milk, warmed	1 litre	4.5 litres
Onion, studded with cloves	1	2–3

1. Melt the butter or heat the oil in a thick-bottomed pan.
2. Mix in the flour with a heat-proof plastic or wooden spoon.
3. Cook for a few minutes, stirring frequently. As you are making a white roux, do not allow the mixture to colour.
4. Remove the pan from the heat to allow the roux to cool.
5. Return the pan to the stove and, over a low heat, gradually mix the milk into the roux.
6. Add the studded onion.
7. Allow the mixture to simmer gently for 30 minutes, stirring frequently to make sure the sauce does not burn on the bottom.
8. Remove the onion and pass the sauce through a conical strainer.

Variation
For cream sauce, finish with 125 ml single cream per litre of béchamel sauce.

Professional tip
To prevent a skin from forming, brush the surface with melted butter. When ready to use, stir this into the sauce. Alternatively, cover the sauce with cling film or greaseproof paper.

35 Reduced-fat béchamel sauce

Ingredient	
Milk	500 ml
Sauce flour	40 g
Seasoning	

Energy	Cals	Fat	Sat fat	Carb	Sugar	Protein	Fibre
302 kJ	73 kcal	1.8g	1.1g	10.9g	4.8g	4.2g	0.3g

1. The milk may be first infused with an onion clouté (an onion studded with cloves and a bay leaf), carrot and a bouquet garni. Allow to cool.
2. Place the milk in a suitable saucepan and gradually whisk in the sauce flour. Bring slowly to the boil until the sauce has thickened.
3. Season and simmer for approximately 5–10 minutes. Use as required.

Professional tip
Add a little blended cornflour prior to heating to stabilise the sauce.

36 Parsley sauce

Ingredient	Makes 500 ml
Milk	500 ml
Sauce flour	40 g
Parsley, chopped	1 tbsp
Seasoning	

1. The milk may be first infused with a studded onion clouté, carrot and a bouquet garni. Allow to cool.
2. Place the milk in a suitable saucepan, gradually whisk in the sauce flour. Bring slowly to the boil until the sauce has thickened.
3. Season, simmer for approximately 5–10 minutes. Add the parsley. Use as required.

Note

This recipe, like mornay sauce and soubise (recipes 37 and 38) can be made using béchamel as the base.

37 Cheese sauce (mornay)

Ingredient	Makes 500 ml
Milk	500 ml
Grated cheese	50 g
Egg yolk	1
Sauce flour	40 g

1. The milk may be first infused with a studded onion clouté, carrot and a bouquet garni. Allow to cool.
2. Place the milk in a suitable saucepan, gradually whisk in the sauce flour. Bring slowly to the boil until the sauce has thickened.
3. Mix in the cheese and egg yolk when the sauce is boiling.
4. Remove from the heat. Strain if necessary.
5. Do not allow the sauce to reboil at any time.

38 Soubise

Ingredient	Makes 500 ml
Onion, chopped or diced	100 g
Milk	500 ml
Sauce flour	40 g
Seasoning	

Note

This recipe, like mornay sauce and parsley sauce (recipes 36 and 37) uses sauce flour to thicken the sauce, rather than a traditional roux base. This is a simpler method and produces a lower fat content.

1. Cook the onions without colouring them, either by boiling or sweating in butter.
2. The milk may be first infused with a studded onion clouté, carrot and a bouquet garni. Allow to cool.
3. Place the milk in a suitable saucepan, gradually whisk in the sauce flour. Bring slowly to the boil until the sauce has thickened.
4. Add the onions, season, simmer for approximately 5–10 minutes.
5. Blitz well. Pass through a strainer.

39 Suprême sauce

Ingredient	4 portions	10 portions
Margarine, butter or oil	100 g	250 g
Flour	100 g	250 g
Stock (chicken, veal, fish or mutton)	1 litre	2.5 litres
Mushroom trimmings	25 g	60 g
Egg yolk	1	2½
Cream	60 ml	150 ml
Lemon juice	2–3 drops	5–6 drops

Energy	Cals	Fat	Sat fat	Carb	Sugar	Protein	Fibre	Sodium
1339 kJ	322 kcal	25.2 g	15.3 g	21.1 g	1.8 g	4.1 g	1.6 g	0.2 g

Using butter.

1. Melt the fat or oil in a thick-bottomed pan.
2. Add the flour and mix in. Cook to a sandy texture over a gentle heat, without colouring.
3. Allow the roux to cool, then gradually add the boiling stock. Stir until smooth and boiling.
4. Add the mushroom trimmings. Simmer for approximately 1 hour.
5. Pass through a final conical strainer.
6. Finish with a liaison of the egg yolk, cream and lemon juice. Serve immediately.

This sauce can be served hot with boiled chicken, vol-au-vonts, etc., and can also be used for white chaud-froid sauce. The traditional stock base is a good chicken stock.

> **Professional tip**
> Once the liaison has been added, do not reboil this sauce.

40 Mushroom sauce

Ingredient	1 litre	4.5 litres
Butter or oil	100 g	400 g
Flour	100 g	400 g
Stock (chicken, veal, fish, mutton) as required	1 litre	4.5 litres
White button mushrooms, well-washed, sliced, sweated	200 g	900 g
Mushroom trimmings	50 g	225 g
Egg yolk	2	9
Cream	120 ml	540 ml
Lemon, juice of	½	1

1. Melt the butter or heat the oil in a thick-bottomed pan.
2. Add the flour and mix in.
3. Cook out to a sandy texture over gentle heat without colouring.
4. Allow the roux to cool.
5. Gradually add the boiling stock.
6. Stir until smooth and boiling.
7. Add the mushrooms and trimmings. Allow to simmer for approximately 1 hour.
8. Pass it through a fine conical strainer.
9. Simmer for 10 minutes, then add the egg yolk, cream and lemon juice.

41 Ivory sauce

Ingredient	4 portions	10 portions
Chicken or veal velouté	250 ml	625 ml
Mushroom trimmings, washed and dried	50 g	125 g
Cream, single or double	50 ml	125 ml
Lemon, juice of	½	1½
Chicken or beef meat glaze	1 tbsp	2½ tbsp
Seasoning		

1 Place the velouté into a suitable saucepan and bring to the boil.
2 Add the mushroom trimmings; simmer for 10 minutes.
3 Pass the sauce through a fine chinois.
4 Add the meat glaze; stir well to achieve an ivory colour.
5 Add the lemon juice and finish with cream. Correct the seasoning.

Serve with grilled veal or pork chops, grilled or poached chicken.

Energy	Cals	Fat	Sat fat	Carb	Sugar	Protein	Fibre	Sodium
351 kJ	85 kcal	6.8g	4.3g	4.9g	0.8g	1.3g	0.6g	0.0g

Using butter and single cream.

42 Aurora sauce

Ingredient	4 portions	10 portions
Chicken or veal velouté	250 ml	625 ml
Mushroom trimmings, washed and dried	50 g	125 g
Fresh cream, double or single	50 ml	125 mls
Egg yolks	1	3
Lemon, juice of	½	1½
Tomato purée	1 tbsp	1½ tbsp
Seasoning		

Energy	Cals	Fat	Sat fat	Carb	Sugar	Protein	Fibre	Sodium
247 kJ	59 kcal	4.0g	1.9g	3.0g	2.7g	3.1g	0.4g	0.0g

Using single cream, and chicken soup in place of velouté.

Stocks, soups and sauces

1. Place the velouté in a suitable saucepan and bring to the boil.
2. Add the mushroom trimmings. Allow to simmer for 10 minutes.
3. Add the tomato purée; mix well.
4. Strain through a fine chinois.
5. In a basin mix the egg yolks and cream.
6. Add a little of the hot sauce to this mix; whisk well.
7. Return to the main sauce and stir. Do NOT allow to re-boil.
8. Finish with lemon juice.

Serve with poached chicken or poached eggs. If serving with poached or steamed fish use fish velouté.

43 Chasseur sauce

Ingredient	4 portions	10 portions
Butter or oil	25 g	60 g
Shallots, chopped	10 g	25 g
Clove of garlic, chopped (optional)	1	1
Button mushrooms, sliced	50 g	125 g
White wine, dry	60 ml	150 ml
Tomatoes, skinned, deseeded, diced	100 g	250 g
Demi-glace, *jus-lié* or reduced stock	250 ml	625 ml
Parsley and tarragon, chopped		

Energy	Cals	Fat	Sat fat	Carb	Sugar	Protein	Fibre
227 kJ	55 kcal	5.3 g	2.5 g	1.4 g	1.2 g	0.5 g	0.5 g

1. Melt the butter or heat the oil in a small sauteuse.
2. Add the shallots and cook gently for 2–3 minutes without colour.
3. Add the garlic and the mushrooms, cover and cook gently for 2–3 minutes.
4. Strain off the fat.
5. Add the wine and reduce by half. Add the tomatoes.
6. Add the demi-glace; simmer for 5–10 minutes.
7. Correct the seasoning. Add the tarragon and parsley.

May be served with fried steaks, chops, chicken, etc.

Healthy eating tips
- Use an unsaturated oil (sunflower or vegetable). Lightly oil the pan.
- Skim the fat from the finished dish.
- Season with the minimum amount of salt.

44 Devilled sauce (*sauce diable*)

Ingredient	Makes 250 g
Butter	25 g
Shallots, finely chopped	25 g
Dry white wine	150 ml
Reduced brown stock or *jus-lié*	250 ml
Cayenne pepper	2 grams

1. In a suitable pan, add the butter and gently sweat the shallots without colour.
2. Add the white wine; reduce by half.
3. Add the brown stock or *jus-lié*; bring to the boil and simmer for 2 minutes.
4. Season with cayenne pepper. Correct the seasoning and consistency.

Serve with grilled chicken and steaks.

> **Professional tip**
> The sauce should have a background flavour of white wine, with a sharp after taste from the cayenne pepper. The sauce may also be improved with the addition of 15 g of soft butter before serving.

45 Robert sauce

Ingredient	4 portions	10 portions
Oil or butter	20 g	50 g
Onions, finely chipped	10 g	25 g
Vinegar	60 ml	150 g
Demi-glace, *jus-lié* or reduced stock	250 ml	625 ml
English or continental mustard	1 level tbsp	2½ level tbsp
Caster sugar	1 level tbsp	2½ level tbsp

Energy	Cals	Fat	Sat fat	Carb	Sugar	Protein	Fibre	Sodium
401 kJ	96 kcal	5.7 g	3.1 g	8.3 g	6.5 g	2.5 g	0.4 g	0.2 g

Using butter.

1. Melt the fat or oil in a small sauteuse.
2. Add the onions. Cook gently without colour.
3. Add the vinegar and reduce completely.
4. Add the demi-glace; simmer for 5–10 minutes.
5. Remove from the heat and add the mustard, diluted with a little water and the sugar; do not boil.
6. Skim and correct the seasoning.

May be served with fried sausages and burgers or grilled pork chops.

Healthy eating tips
- Use unsaturated oil (sunflower or olive). Lightly oil the pan and drain off any excess after the frying is complete. Skim the fat from the finished dish.
- Season with the minimum amount of salt.

46 Piquant sauce

Ingredient	4 portions	10 portions
Vinegar	60 ml	150 ml
Shallots, chopped	50 g	125 g
Demi-glace, *jus-lié* or reduced stock	250 ml	625 ml
Gherkins, chopped	25 g	60 g
Capers, chopped	10 g	25 g
Chervil, tarragon and parsley, chopped	½ tbsp	1½ tbsp

Energy	Cals	Fat	Sat fat	Carb	Sugar	Protein	Fibre	Sodium
151 kJ	36 kcal	1.3 g	0.5 g	3.0 g	1.3 g	2.4 g	0.7 g	0.0 g

1. Place the vinegar and shallots in a small sauteuse and reduce by half.
2. Add the demi-glace; simmer for 15–20 minutes.
3. Add the rest of the ingredients.
4. Skim and correct the seasoning.

May be served with made-up dishes, sausages and grilled meats.

Practical Cookery 14th edition

47 Madeira sauce

Ingredient	4 portions	10 portions
Demi-glace, *jus-lié* or reduced stock	250 ml	625 ml
Madeira wine	2 tbsp	5 tbsp
Butter	25 g	60 g

Energy	Cals	Fat	Sat fat	Carb	Sugar	Protein	Fibre	Sodium
365 kJ	88 kcal	6.4 g	3.7 g	3.5 g	1.4 g	2.1 g	0.3 g	0.1 g

1. Boil the demi-glace in a small sauteuse.
2. Add the Madeira and reboil.
3. Correct the seasoning.
4. Pass through a fine conical strainer.
5. Gradually mix in the butter.

May be served with braised ox tongue or ham.

Variation

Dry sherry or port wine may be substituted for Madeira (and the sauce renamed accordingly).

48 Brown onion sauce (*sauce lyonnaise*)

Ingredient	4 portions	10 portions
Margarine, oil or butter	25 g	60 g
Onions, sliced	100 g	250 g
Vinegar	2 tbsp	5 tbsp
Demi-glace, *jus-lié* or reduced stock	250 ml	625 ml

1. Melt the fat or oil in a sauteuse.
2. Add the onions; cover with a lid and cook gently until tender and golden in colour.
3. Remove the lid and colour lightly.
4. Add the vinegar and completely reduce.
5. Add the demi-glace; simmer for 5–10 minutes.
6. Skim and correct the seasoning.

May be served with burgers, fried liver or sausages.

Energy	Cals	Fat	Sat fat	Carb	Sugar	Protein	Fibre	Sodium
374 kJ	90 kcal	6.8 g	3.9 g	3.5 g	1.8 g	3.7 g	1.0 g	0.1 g

Using butter.

Healthy eating tips

- Use unsaturated oil (sunflower or olive). Lightly oil the pan and drain off any excess after the frying is complete. Skim the fat from the finished dish.
- Season with the minimum amount of salt.

49 Italian sauce

Ingredient	4 portions	10 portions
Margarine, oil or butter	25 g	60 g
Shallots, chopped	10 g	25 g
Mushrooms, chopped	50 g	125 g
Demi-glace, *jus-lié* or reduced stock	250 ml	625 ml
Lean ham, chopped	25 g	60 g
Tomatoes, skinned, deseeded	100 g	250 g
Diced parsley, chervil and tarragon, chopped		

Energy	Cals	Fat	Sat fat	Carb	Sugar	Protein	Fibre	Sodium
359 kJ	86 kcal	6.5 g	3.7 g	4.4 g	2.2 g	2.4 g	0.8 g	0.1 g

Using butter.

Healthy eating tips
- Use unsaturated oil (sunflower or olive). Lightly oil the pan and drain off any excess after the frying is complete.
- Trim as much fat as possible from the ham.
- The ham is salty, so do not add more salt; flavour will come from the herbs.
- Skim all fat from the finished sauce.

1 Melt the fat or oil in a small sauteuse.
2 To make a duxelle, add the shallots and cook gently for 2–3 minutes.
3 Add the mushrooms and cook gently for a further 2–3 minutes.
4 Add the demi-glace, ham and tomatoes. Simmer for 5–10 minutes.
5 Correct the seasoning; add the chopped herbs.

50 Pepper sauce (sauce poivrade)

Ingredient	4 portions	10 portions
Butter, margarine or oil	25 g	60 g
Onions, chopped into mirepoix	50 g	125 g
Carrots, chopped into mirepoix	50 g	125 g
Celery, chopped into mirepoix	50 g	125 g
Bay leaf	1	1
Sprig of thyme		
White wine	2 tbsp	5 tbsp
Vinegar	2 tbsp	5 tbsp
Mignonette pepper	5 g	12 g
Demi-glace, *jus-lié* or reduced stock	250 ml	625 ml
Cream (optional, to finish)	25 ml	65 ml

Energy	Cals	Fat	Sat fat	Carb	Sugar	Protein	Fibre
247 kJ	60 kcal	5.3 g	2.5 g	2.6 g	2.0 g	0.5 g	0.6 g

1. Melt the fat or heat the oil in a small sauteuse.
2. Add the vegetables (mirepoix) and herbs, and allow to brown.
3. Add the wine, vinegar and pepper. Reduce by half.
4. Add the demi-glace and simmer for 20–30 minutes.
5. Pass through a fine conical strainer.
6. Correct the seasoning.
7. Finish with cream if desired.

Note
Mignonette pepper is coarsely ground black pepper. Softer green or pink peppercorns may be used instead. This sauce is usually served with joints or cuts of venison.

Healthy eating tips
- Use an unsaturated oil (sunflower or vegetable). Lightly oil the pan.
- Skim the fat from the finished dish.
- Season with the minimum amount of salt.

51 Beef jus

Ingredient	1 litre
Mushrooms, finely sliced	750 g
Butter	100 g
Shallots, finely sliced	350 g
Beef trim, diced	350 g
Sherry vinegar	100 ml
Red wine	700 ml
Chicken stock	500 ml
Beef stock	1 litre

1. Caramelise the mushrooms in foaming butter, strain, then put aside in pan.
2. Caramelise the shallots in foaming butter, strain, then put aside in pan.
3. In another pan, caramelise the beef trim until golden brown.
4. Place the mushrooms, shallots and beef trim in one of the pans. Deglaze the other two pans with the vinegar, then add to the pan with the beef, shallots and mushrooms in it.
5. In a separate pan, reduce the wine by half and add to the main pan.
6. Add the stock, then reduce to sauce consistency.
7. Pass through a sieve, then chill and store until needed.

52 Roast chicken jus

Ingredient	1 litre
Chicken stock	600 ml
Lamb jus	600 ml
Chicken wings, chopped small	300 g
Vegetable oil	60 ml
Shallots, sliced	100 g
Butter	50 g
Tomatoes, chopped	200 g
White wine vinegar	40 ml
Red wine vinegar	75 ml
Tarragon	1 tsp
Chervil	1 tsp

1. Put the jus and stock in a pan and reduce to 1 litre.
2. Roast the chicken wings in oil until slightly golden.
3. Add the shallots and butter, and cook until lightly browned (do not allow the butter to burn).
4. Strain off the butter and return the bones to the pan; deglaze with the vinegar and add tomatoes.
5. Ensure the bottom of the pan is clean. Add the reduced stock/jus and simmer for 15 minutes.
6. Pass through a sieve, then reduce to sauce consistency.
7. Remove from the heat and infuse with the aromats for 5 minutes.
8. Pass through a chinois and then muslin cloth.

53 Red wine jus

Ingredient	1 litre
Shallots, sliced	150 g
Butter	50 g
Garlic, halved	10 g
Red wine vinegar	100 ml
Red wine	250 ml
Chicken stock	350 ml
Lamb or beef jus	250 ml
Bay leaves	2
Sprig of thyme	1

1. Caramelise the shallots in foaming butter until golden, adding the garlic at the end.
2. Strain through a colander and then put back into the pan and deglaze with the vinegar.
3. Reduce the red wine by half along with the stock and jus, at the same time as colouring the shallots.
4. When everything is done, combine and simmer for 20 minutes.
5. Pass through a sieve and reduce to sauce consistency.
6. Infuse the aromats for 5 minutes.
7. Pass through muslin cloth and store until needed.

Stocks, soups and sauces

54 Roast gravy (*jus rôti*)

Ingredient	4 portions	10 portions
Raw veal bones or beef and veal trimmings	200 g	500 g
Stock or water	500 ml	1.25 litres
Onions, chopped	50 g	125 g
Celery, chopped	25 g	60 g
Carrots, chopped	50 g	125 g

Energy	Cals	Fat	Sat fat	Carb	Sugar	Protein	Fibre	Sodium
309 kJ	74 kcal	3.9 g	1.5 g	3.3 g	2.7 g	6.2 g	1.3 g	0.1 g

1 Chop the bones and brown in the oven, or brown in a little oil on top of the stove in a frying pan. Drain off all the fat.
2 Place the bones in a saucepan with the stock or water.
3 Bring to the boil, skim and allow to simmer.
4 Add the lightly browned vegetables, which may be fried in a little fat in a frying pan or added to the bones when partly browned.
5 Simmer for 1½–2 hours.
6 Remove the joint from the roasting tin when cooked.
7 Return the tray to a low heat to allow the sediment to settle.
8 Carefully strain off the fat, leaving the sediment in the tin.
9 Return the joint to the stove and brown carefully; deglaze with the brown stock.
10 Allow to simmer for a few minutes.
11 Correct the colour and seasoning. Strain and skim off all fat.
12 Serve with roast meat.

Professional tip
For preference, use beef bones for roast beef gravy and the appropriate bones for lamb, veal, mutton and pork.

Healthy eating tips
- Use an unsaturated oil (sunflower or vegetable). Lightly oil the pan.
- Season with the minimum amount of salt.

125

55 Thickened gravy (*jus-lié*)

1. Start with roast gravy (recipe 54) or reduced veal stock (recipe 8). Add a little tomato purée, a few mushroom trimmings and a pinch of thyme and simmer for 10–15 minutes.
2. Stir some arrowroot diluted in cold water into the simmering gravy.
3. Reboil, simmer for 5–10 minutes and pass through a strainer.

Energy	Cals	Fat	Sat fat	Carb	Sugar	Protein	Fibre	Sodium
247 kJ	59 kcal	2.6g	1.0g	4.7g	1.4g	4.1g	0.7g	0.1g

Variation

Add a little rosemary, thyme or lavender.

56 Curry gravy

Ingredient	4 portions	10 portions
Onions, finely chopped	50 g	125 g
Carrot, finely diced	50 g	125 g
Green pepper	1	2
Tomatoes, peeled, deseeded and diced, concassé	50 g	125 g
Ground coriander	1 tsp	2 ½ tsp
Garlic cloves, crushed and chopped	3	7
Fresh ginger, grated	½ tsp	1 ½ tsp
Curry paste	1 tsp	2 ½ tsp
Vegetable stock, brown or chicken stock	300 ml	750 ml
Tomato paste	15 ml	38 ml
Fresh coriander, finely chopped	½ tsp	1¼ tsp
Salt and black pepper		

Energy	Cals	Fat	Sat fat	Carb	Sugar	Protein	Fibre	Sodium
190 kJ	45 kcal	1.8 g	0.1 g	6.1 g	5.2 g	1.2 g	2.6 g	0.5 g

Using vegetable stock.

1 Place the onions, carrot, pepper, tomato, ground coriander, garlic, ginger and curry paste into a suitable pan. Cover with the stock.
2 Bring to the boil and simmer for approximately 15 minutes.
3 Add the tomato paste.
4 Place in a blender and blend until smooth.
5 Add the finely chopped coriander and the seasoning. Correct the consistency.

57 Apple sauce

Ingredient	8 portions
Cooking apples	400 g
Sugar	50 g
Butter or margarine	25 g

Energy	Cals	Fat	Sat fat	Carb	Sugar	Protein	Fibre	Sodium
276 kJ	65 kcal	2.6 g	1.6 g	11.0 g	11.0 g	0.2 g	1.1 g	0.0 g

Using butter.

1 Peel, core and wash the apples.
2 Place with other ingredients in a covered pan and cook to a purée.
3 Pass through a sieve or liquidise.

58 Tomato sauce (*sauce tomate*)

Ingredient	Makes 500 ml
Carrots, chopped into mirepoix	90 g
Celery, chopped into mirepoix	30 g
Clove of garlic, chopped	½
Vegetable oil	25 g
Butter	25 g
Thyme	1 g
Bay leaf	½
Tomato purée	12 g
Plum tomatoes	200 g
Chicken stock	750 g
Juniper berries	2
Cream	75 g
Gastric (50/50 sherry vinegar and sugar, heated to dissolve the sugar)	5 g

1 Sweat the carrots, celery and garlic in the oil and butter.
2 Add the thyme, bay leaf and tomato purée, and cook for 5 minutes.
3 Add the plum tomatoes and cook for 5 minutes.
4 Add the chicken stock and juniper berries, reduce by a third.
5 Remove the mirepoix. Strain through a chinois.
6 Finish with the cream, bring to the boil and blitz.
7 Season with salt and gastric.

59 Cranberry sauce

Ingredient	8 portions
Cranberries	400 g
Water	100 ml
Sugar	50 g

1 Simmer all ingredients together in a covered pan (not iron or aluminium) until soft.
2 The sauce may be sieved or liquidised if required.

Variation

Half orange juice and half water, plus some grated orange zest, may be used. Alternatively, use half orange juice and half port wine.

Energy	Cals	Fat	Sat fat	Carb	Sugar	Protein	Fibre	Sodium
138 kJ	32 kcal	0.1 g	0.0 g	8.3 g	8.3 g	0.2 g	1.9 g	0.0 g

60 Hollandaise sauce

Ingredient	Makes 500 g
Peppercorns, crushed	12
White wine vinegar	3 tbsp
Egg yolks	6
Clarified butter	325 g
Salt and cayenne pepper	

1. Place the peppercorns and vinegar in a small pan and reduce to one-third.
2. Add 1 tablespoon of cold water and allow to cool. Add the egg yolks.
3. Put on a bain-marie and whisk continuously to a sabayon consistency.
4. Remove from the heat and gradually whisk in the clarified butter.
5. Add seasoning and pass through muslin or a fine chinois.
6. Store in an appropriate container at room temperature for no more than 2 hours.

Note
Egg-based sauces should not be kept warm for more than two hours. After this time, they should be thrown away. They are best made fresh to order.

Faults
If you add oil or butter too fast when making hollandaise or mayonnaise, the sauce may curdle because the lecithin has had insufficient time to coat the droplets. This can be rectified by adding the broken sauce to more egg yolks.

Variation
- Mousseline sauce – a hollandaise base with lightly whipped cream.
- Maltaise sauce – a hollandaise base with lightly grated zest and juice of one blood orange.

61 Béarnaise sauce

1. Place the shallots, tarragon, peppercorns and vinegar in a small pan and reduce to one-third.
2. Add 1 tablespoon of cold water and allow to cool. Add the egg yolks.
3. Put on a bain-marie and whisk continuously to a sabayon consistency.
4. Remove from the heat and gradually whisk in the clarified butter.
5. Add seasoning. Pass through muslin or a fine chinois.
6. To finish, add the chopped chervil and tarragon.
7. Store in an appropriate container.

Note
Egg-based sauces should not be kept warm for more than two hours. After this time, they should be thrown away. They are best made fresh to order.

Professional tip
This sauce should be twice as thick as hollandaise.

Variation
- Choron sauce – add 200 g tomato concassé, well dried. Do not add the chopped tarragon and chervil to finish.
- Foyot or valois sauce – add 25 g warm meat glaze.
- Paloise sauce – use chopped mint stalks in place or the tarragon in the reduction. To finish, add chopped mint instead of the chervil and tarragon.

Ingredient	Makes 500 ml
Shallots, chopped	50 g
Tarragon	10 g
Peppercorns, crushed	12
White wine vinegar	3 tbsp
Egg yolks	6
Clarified butter	325 g
Salt and cayenne pepper	
Chervil and tarragon to finish, chopped	

Stocks, soups and sauces 5

62 Salsa verde

Ingredient	8 portions
Mint, coarsely chopped	1 tbsp
Parsley, coarsely chopped	3 tbsp
Capers, coarsely chopped	3
Clove of garlic (optional)	1
Dijon mustard	1 tsp
Lemon, juice of	½
Extra virgin olive oil	120 ml
Salt	

Energy	Cals	Fat	Sat fat	Carb	Sugar	Protein	Fibre
281 kJ	69 kcal	7.5g	1.1g	0.2g	0.1g	0.1g	0.0g

Per tablespoon.

1 In a large bowl, mix all the ingredients together and check the seasoning.

Serve with grilled fish.

63 Melted butter sauce (*beurre fondu*)

Ingredient	4 portions	10 portions
Butter	200g	500g
Water or white wine	2 tbsp	5 tbsp

- **Method 1**: boil the butter and water together gently until combined, then pass through a fine strainer.
- **Method 2**: melt the butter in the water and carefully strain off the fat, leaving the water and sediment in the pan.

Note

Usually served with poached fish and certain vegetables (e.g. blue trout, salmon, asparagus, sea kale).

Energy	Cals	Fat	Sat fat	Carb	Sugar	Protein	Fibre
388 kJ	94 kcal	10.3g	6.5g	0.1g	0.1g	0.1g	0.0g

64 Horseradish sauce (*sauce raifort*)

Ingredient	8 portions
Horseradish	25 g
Vinegar or lemon juice	1 tbsp
Salt, pepper	
Cream or crème fraiche, lightly whipped	125 ml

1 Wash, peel and rewash the horseradish. Grate finely.
2 Mix all the ingredients together.

Serve with roast beef, smoked trout, eel or halibut.

> **Professional tip**
> It is essential to blend the ingredients without over-mixing them, in order to get a good flavour.

Energy	Cals	Fat	Sat fat	Carb	Sugar	Protein	Fibre	Sodium
135 kJ	33 kcal	3.0g	1.9g	0.7g	0.6g	0.7g	0.3g	0.0g

Using cream.

65 Sweet and sour sauce

Ingredient	4 portions	10 portions
White vinegar	375 ml	1 litre
Brown sugar	150 g	375 g
Tomato ketchup	125 ml	300 ml
Light soy sauce	1 tbsp	2½ tbsp
Seasoning		

1 Boil the vinegar and sugar in a suitable pan.
2 Add the tomato ketchup, soy sauce and seasoning.
3 Simmer for a few minutes then use as required. This sauce may also be lightly thickened with cornflour or another thickening agent.

Energy	Cals	Fat	Sat fat	Carb	Sugar	Protein	Fibre	Sodium
823 kJ	194 kcal	0.0g	0.0g	47.8g	47.4g	1.0g	0.4g	0.8g

66 Gribiche sauce

Ingredient	500 g
Hard-boiled eggs, sieved	2
Vegetable oil	325 ml
French mustard	1 tsp
White wine vinegar	100 ml
Capers, chopped	30 g
Gherkins, chopped	30 g
Parsley, chopped	½ tsp
Chives, chopped	½ tsp
Basil, chopped	½ tsp
Seasoning	

This is an emulsified sauce. The mustard is a natural emulsifying agent.

1. Place the sieved egg yolks in a basin and add the mustard and vinegar.
2. Whisk together with a balloon whisk.
3. Slowly add the oil, whisking continuously.
4. When the emulsion is formed, add the remainder of the ingredients and season.

Serve with steamed fish, fried fish, cold meats, chicken and gammon.

6 Eggs

Recipes included in this chapter

No.	Recipe	Page
1	Soft-boiled eggs in the shell (*oeufs à la coque*)	137
2	Soft-boiled eggs out of the shell (*oeufs mollets*)	137
3	Hard-boiled eggs (*oeufs durs*)	138
4	Scrambled eggs (*oeufs brouillés*)	138
5	Fried eggs (*oeufs frits*)	139
6	Eggs en cocotte	139
7	Eggs Benedict	140
8	Quail Scotch eggs	141
9	Eggs sur le plat	142
10	Scotch eggs	142
11	Omelette (*omelette nature*)	144
12	Spanish omelette	145
13	Feta, mint, lentil and pistachio omelette	146
14	Duck egg frittata with sweetcorn and beans	147
15	Poached duck egg, asparagus, cured ham, grain mustard dressing	148
16	Poached quail eggs with smoked haddock chowder	149

Eggs are a very versatile ingredient and are used extensively in hors d'oeuvres, meat and poultry dishes, soups, pasta, egg dishes, salads, fish dishes, sweets and pastries, sauces and savouries. They are useful as a main dish as they provide the energy, fat, minerals and vitamins needed for growth and repair of the body.

Fried, scrambled, poached and boiled eggs, and omelettes, are mainly served at breakfast, but a variety of egg dishes may also be served for lunch, high tea, supper and snacks.

Most egg products are available in liquid, frozen or spray-dried form. Whole eggs are used primarily for cake production, where their foaming and coagulation properties are required. Egg whites are used for meringues and light sponges, where their foaming property is crucial.

The structure of eggs

The outer shell of an egg is composed mainly of calcium carbonate; they are lined with membranes and have a number of pores for gas exchange. These pores are covered by a wax-like layer known as the cuticle. This cuticle protects against microbial invasion and controls water loss.

The egg white is divided into a thick layer around the yolk and a thinner layer next to the shell. The thick layer anchors the yolk, together with the chalaza, in the middle of the egg, where it is less vulnerable to microbial attack. The egg white has an important function as it possesses special antibacterial properties, which, under normal circumstances, prevent the growth and multiplication of micro-organisms that have entered the shell. The yolk is rich in nutrients and is the part of the egg that is most vulnerable to micro-organisms.

Egg yolks are high in saturated fat, while egg whites are made up of protein and water.

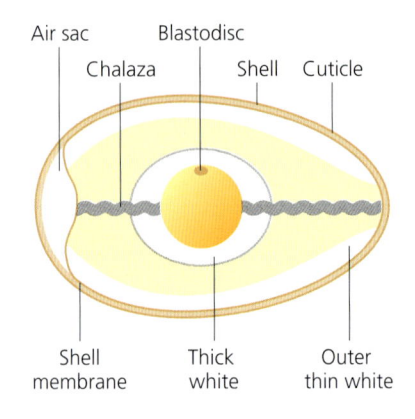

Table 6.1 The composition of eggs (approximate percentages)

	Whole egg	White	Yolk
Water	73	87	47
Protein	12	10	15
Fat	11	0	33
Minerals	1	0.5	2
Vitamins	3	2.5	3

Eggs 6

Types of eggs

Almost all of the eggs used for culinary purposes come from hens, but eggs from turkeys, geese, ducks, guinea fowl, quail and gulls are also edible.

Quails' eggs are used in a variety of ways, for example: as a garnish on many hot and cold dishes; and as a starter or main course, such as a salad of assorted leaves with hot wild mushrooms and poached quail eggs, or tartlet of quail eggs on chopped mushrooms coated with hollandaise sauce.

Purchasing and quality points

When buying eggs the following points should be noted:
- The eggshell should be clean, well shaped, strong and slightly rough.
- When eggs are broken there should be a high proportion of thick white to thin white. If an egg is kept, the thick white gradually changes into thin white, and water passes from the white into the yolk.
- The yolk should be firm, round (not flattened) and of a good, even colour. As eggs are kept the yolk loses strength and begins to flatten, water evaporates from the egg and is replaced by air.
- Hens can pass salmonella bacteria into their eggs and therefore cause food poisoning. To reduce this risk, pasteurised eggs may be used where appropriate (pasteurised eggs are washed, sanitised and then broken into sterilised containers; with the yolks and whites either separated or together they are strained and pasteurised – that is, heated to 63 °C for one minute – then rapidly cooled).
- Always purchase fresh eggs from sources where there is no salmonella contamination or from a low-risk supplier. Look for the 'Lion' quality mark on the egg shell and egg box – it shows that the eggs have been produced to the highest standards of food safety, including a programme of vaccination against *Salmonella enteritidis*. Always buy eggs from a reputable retailer where they will have been transported and stored at the correct temperature (below 20 °C).
- Cracked eggs should not be used.

Candling of eggs is a method that is used for checking the quality of eggs. The egg is illuminated with a light so the flaws can be seen, including the yolk position and size, the size of the air sac and the presence of blood or meat spots.

The Code of Practice for Lion Quality eggs covers breeding flocks and hatcheries, pullet rearing and laying birds, including both hygiene and animal welfare requirements, farm handling of eggs, distribution of eggs from farms, feeding, hen disposal, packing centres, procedures, advice to retailers, consumers and caterers, and environmental policy and enforcement. For more information on the British Lion Quality mark see www.lioneggfarms.co.uk.

Quality grading

Under European law eggs are graded for quality using the following system:
- Grade A – naturally clean, fresh eggs, internally perfect with intact shells and an air sac not exceeding 6 mm in depth.
- Grade B – eggs that have been downgraded because they have been cleaned or preserved, or because they are internally imperfect, cracked or have an air sac exceeding 6 mm but not more than 9 mm in depth. Grade B eggs are broken out and pasteurised.
- Grade C – eggs that are fit for breaking for manufacturing purposes but cannot be sold in their shells to the public.

Sizes

Hens' eggs are now graded in four sizes in the UK – small, medium, large and very large – as shown in Table 6.2 below.

Table 6.2 Hens' egg sizes

Egg size	Weight	Old size
Very large	73 g	Size 0 to size 1
Large	63–73 g	Size 1 to size 3
Medium	53–63 g	Size 3 to size 5
Small	53 g and under	Size 5 to size 7

The size of the eggs does not affect their quality, but it does affect their price. Once eggs have been tested for quality, then weighed and graded (see Purchasing and quality points below) they are packed into boxes. The wholesale price of eggs is quoted per 'long hundred' (120). All egg boxes leaving the packing station are dated.

135

Preparing and cooking eggs

Make sure the eggs are fresh and always cook them according to the recipe. Take special care when undercooking eggs so that the yolks are soft.

Cooking eggs using different methods will affect the taste and texture. Egg dishes can be very flavoursome and use a range of herbs and spices, especially when preparing scrambled eggs and omelettes.

Environmental officers advise that eggs should be cooked well done and should reach an internal temperature of 72°C. However, eggs cooked to this temperature are overcooked and often have a rubbery texture. Most people expect eggs to be served at a lower temperature, but they should be cooked thoroughly to reduce the risk of food poisoning from salmonella.

Always choose the correct tools and equipment when cooking egg dishes, especially when scrambling, poaching, frying, boiling and baking. Always have the correct equipment to hand.

> **Food safety** ⚠️
> - Hands should be washed before and after handling eggs.
> - Preparation surfaces, utensils and containers should be cleaned regularly and always cleaned between preparation of different dishes.

Healthy options when making egg dishes

When preparing egg dishes such as omelettes, scrambled eggs or eggs sur le plat, use olive oil instead of butter. When finishing egg dishes, fromage frais or natural yoghurt can be used instead of cream in some recipes.

Holding and serving temperatures

When possible, always serve eggs to order. Do not have egg dishes such as fried eggs and scrambled eggs on a buffet for long periods as they will tend to lose moisture and dry out, changing their texture and flavour and therefore becoming inedible.

As explained above, it is best that eggs are cooked to order and are cooked through. Do not leave eggs cooked and on a hot buffet for long periods – leave for no more than 20 minutes.

Egg dishes should be consumed as soon as possible after preparation or, if not for immediate use, refrigerated at 5°C or below.

Storing eggs

Eggs should be stored in a cool but not too dry place (0–5°C is ideal) where the humidity of the air and the amount of carbon dioxide present are controlled. Eggs will keep for up to nine months under these conditions.

Most eggs have date stamps and must not be used after that date. Stocks should be rotated: first in, first out.

Because eggshells are porous, eggs will absorb any strong odours; therefore, they should not be stored near strong-smelling foods such as onions, fish and cheese.

Test yourself

1. State four quality points to look for when buying fresh eggs.
2. Describe the process for cooking a poached egg.
3. State what you could do when preparing and cooking scrambled eggs to make the dish healthier.
4. At what temperature should egg dishes be held for service?
5. How should an egg dish not for immediate use be stored?

Egg recipes

1 Soft-boiled eggs in the shell (*oeufs à la coque*)

Allow 1 or 2 eggs per portion.

Method 1 (soft)

1. Place the eggs in cold water and bring to the boil.
2. Simmer for 2–2½ minutes, then remove from the water.
3. Serve at once in an egg cup.

Method 2 (medium soft)

1. Plunge the eggs in boiling water, then reboil.
2. Simmer for 4–5 minutes.
3. Serve at once in an egg cup.

Energy	Cals	Fat	Sat fat	Carb	Sugar	Protein	Fibre	Sodium
595 kJ	143 kcal	9.6g	2.7g	0.0g	0.0g	14.1g	0.0g	0.2g

Using 2 eggs per portion.

2 Soft-boiled eggs out of the shell (*oeufs mollets*)

Hard-boiled eggs (left) and soft-boiled eggs (right) – recipes 2 and 3

Energy	Cals	Fat	Sat fat	Carb	Sugar	Protein	Fibre	Sodium
595kJ	143kcal	9.6g	2.7g	0.0g	0.3g	14.1g	0.0g	0.2g

Using 2 eggs per portion.

Allow 1 or 2 eggs per portion.

1. Plunge the eggs into boiling water, then bring back to the boil.
2. Simmer for 4½–5 minutes. Refresh immediately.
3. Remove the shells carefully.
4. Reheat when required for 30 seconds in hot salted water.

3 Hard-boiled eggs (oeufs durs)

Energy	Cals	Fat	Sat fat	Carb	Sugar	Protein	Fibre	Sodium
595 kJ	143 kcal	9.6g	2.7g	0.0g	0.0g	14.1g	0.0g	0.2g

Using 2 eggs per portion.

Allow 1 or 2 eggs per portion.

1. Plunge the eggs into a pan of boiling water.
2. Reboil and simmer for 8–10 minutes.
3. Refresh until cold under running water.
4. Remove the shell carefully if required.

Note

If high temperatures or a long cooking time are used to cook eggs, iron in the yolk and sulphur compounds in the white are released to form an unsightly blackish ring around the yolk. Stale eggs will also show a black ring round the yolk.

4 Scrambled eggs (oeufs brouillés)

1. Break the eggs in a basin, add milk (if using), lightly season with salt and pepper and thoroughly mix with a whisk.
2. Melt half the butter in a thick-bottomed pan, add the eggs and cook over a gentle heat, stirring continuously until the eggs are lightly cooked.
3. Remove from the heat, correct the seasoning and mix in the remaining butter. (A tablespoon of cream may also be added at this point.)

Serve in individual egg dishes or on a slice of freshly butter toast with the crust removed.

Ingredient	4 portions	10 portions
Eggs	6–8	15–20
Milk (optional)	2 tbsp	5 tbsp
Salt, pepper		
Butter or oil	50g	125g

Energy	Cals	Fat	Sat fat	Carb	Sugar	Protein	Fibre
1,105 kJ	263 kcal	22.9g	8.7g	0.5g	0.5g	13.9g	0.0g

Using hard margarine instead of butter.

Variation

Scrambled eggs may be served with smoked salmon (as shown).

Note

If scrambled eggs are cooked too quickly or for too long the protein will toughen, the eggs will discolour because of the iron and sulphur compounds being released, and syneresis (separation of water from the eggs) will occur. This means that they will be unpleasant to eat. The heat from the pan will continue to cook the eggs after it has been removed from the stove; therefore, the pan should be removed from the heat just before the eggs are cooked.

Healthy eating tips

- Try to keep the butter used in cooking to a minimum and serve with unbuttered toast.
- Garnish with a grilled tomato.

5 Fried eggs (*oeufs frits*)

Allow 1 or 2 eggs per portion.

1 Melt a little fat in a frying pan. Add the eggs.
2 Cook gently until lightly set. Serve on a plate or flat dish.

Professional tip

To prepare an excellent fried egg, it is essential to use a fresh high-quality egg, to maintain a controlled low heat and to use a high-quality fat (butter or oil, such as sunflower oil).

Food safety

Lightly cooked eggs do not reach high enough temperatures to kill all bacteria that may be present. Do not serve lightly cooked eggs to people in high-risk groups: very young children, elderly people, pregnant women or people who are ill.

Energy	Cals	Fat	Sat fat	Carb	Sugar	Protein	Fibre	Sodium
1,014 kJ	245 kcal	20.5g	4.7g	0.0g	0.0g	15.0g	0.0g	0.2g

Using 2 eggs per portion. Fried in sunflower oil.

6 Eggs en cocotte

1 Butter the appropriate number of egg cocottes.
2 Break an egg carefully into each and season.
3 Place the cocottes in a sauté pan containing 1 cm water.
4 Cover with a tight-fitting lid, place on a fierce heat so that the water boils rapidly.
5 Cook for 2–3 minutes until the eggs are lightly set, then serve.

Variation

- Half a minute before the cooking is completed, add 1 tsp of cream to each egg and complete the cooking.
- When cooked, add 1 tsp of *jus-lié* to each egg.
- Place diced cooked chicken, mixed with cream, in the bottom of the cocottes; break the eggs on top of the chicken and cook.
- As above, using tomato concassé in place of chicken.

Ingredient	4 portions	10 portions
Butter	25g	60g
Eggs	4	10
Salt, pepper		

Energy	Cals	Fat	Sat fat	Carb	Sugar	Protein	Fibre
534 kJ	127 kcal	11.2g	5.2g	0.0g	0.0g	6.8g	0.0g

7 Eggs Benedict

Ingredient	4 portions	10 portions
Cooking medium (see note)		
Large eggs	8	20
Butter, unsalted	2 tbsp	5 tbsp
Plain English muffins, split and toasted	4	10
Smoked bacon or sweet cure bacon, cooked	12 slices	30 slices
Hollandaise sauce	200 g	500 g

Energy	Cals	Fat	Sat fat	Carb	Sugar	Protein	Fibre	Sodium
3910 kJ	943 kcal	77.0g	37.8g	24.8g	2.2g	39.2g	1.4g	2.1g

1. Bring the cooking medium to a slight simmer.
2. Crack an egg into a cup and carefully slide it into the hot poaching liquid. Quickly repeat with all the eggs.
3. Poach the eggs for 3 minutes, turning them occasionally with a spoon, until the whites are firm.
4. Using a slotted spoon, remove the eggs and transfer to a kitchen towel. Lightly dab the eggs with the towel to remove any excess water.
5. While the eggs are poaching, butter the muffins and place two halves on each plate.
6. Reheat the bacon and place on top of the muffins, then top with the drained eggs.
7. To finish, lightly spoon over a generous helping of warm hollandaise sauce and serve immediately, or serve the hollandaise separately.

Note

The cooking bath must be deep and must have a minimum of 15 per cent distilled or white wine vinegar added.

8 Quail Scotch eggs

Ingredient	4 portions	10 portions
Quail eggs	12	30
Sausage meat	750 g	1750 g
Dijon mustard	50 g	125 g
Chives, chopped	5 g	12 g
Chervil, chopped	5 g	12 g
Egg	1	3
Sea salt	10 g	25 g
Ground white pepper	1 pinch	2 pinches
Vegetable oil, for frying		
Coating		
Egg, beaten	1	3
Flour	200 g	500 g
Salt	10 g	25 g
Breadcrumbs	100 g	250 g

Energy	Cals	Fat	Sat fat	Carb	Sugar	Protein	Fibre	Sodium
3,998 kJ	957 kcal	58.0 g	14.7 g	71.0 g	2.6 g	39.0 g	4.0 g	2.3 g

1 Place the eggs in boiling water for 2½ minutes, and refresh immediately in ice water before peeling.
2 In a large bowl, combine the sausage meat with the Dijon mustard, chives, chervil, egg, salt and white pepper.
3 Place the mixture on to a sheet of baking parchment/greaseproof paper and lay another sheet on top. Using a rolling pin, gently roll over the top baking sheet in order to roll out the meat to approximately 1 cm thickness.
4 Remove the baking sheets and divide the meat into 12 portions. Place a peeled quail egg on each portion of meat and roughly mould the meat around the egg, being careful not to overlap too much. Repeat for each egg.
5 Pané in seasoned flour, egg and breadcrumbs, rolling the eggs in your hand to keep their shape. Chill the eggs in the fridge until required.
6 To cook the Scotch eggs, deep fry between 170 and 180 °C until golden brown.
7 Remove the eggs from the oil and drain using kitchen roll. The Scotch eggs should retain their liquid centre.
8 Serve with an appropriate dipping sauce, such as a flavoured mayonnaise or a sweet chilli dressing.

Variation
The sausage meat could be replaced with white crab meat for a seafood variation.

Healthy eating tips
Instead of deep frying, bake the scotch eggs at 180 °C for 30 minutes. This will lead to a more solidly cooked egg, but you will need this time to ensure the sausage meat is cooked.

9 Eggs sur le plat

Allow 1 or 2 eggs per portion.

1. Take a china *sur le plat* dish. Add a teaspoon of olive oil or butter. Heat it on the side of the stove, until it is moderately hot.
2. Break in 1 or 2 eggs. Allow them to set on the stove.
3. Transfer to the oven for 2–4 minutes to finish cooking.

Note

A *sur le plat* dish is a shallow porcelain dish used for cooking and serving eggs.

Energy	Cals	Fat	Sat fat	Carb	Sugar	Protein	Fibre	Sodium
875 kJ	211 kcal	16.9g	6.3g	0.0g	0.0g	14.8g	0.0g	0.2g

Using butter and two eggs.

10 Scotch eggs

1. Place the eggs, still in their shells, in a pan of water.
2. Place over a high heat and bring to the boil, then reduce the heat to simmer for approximately 9 minutes.
3. Drain and refresh the eggs under cold running water, then peel.
4. Mix the sausage meat with the thyme, parsley and spring onion in a bowl, season well with salt and freshly ground black pepper.
5. Divide the sausage meat mixture into four and flatten each out on a clean surface into ovals about 12 cm long and 8 cm at the widest point.
6. Roll the boiled egg in the seasoned flour.
7. Place each egg on to a sausage meat oval, then wrap the sausage meat around the egg, making sure the coating is smooth and completely covers the egg.
8. Dip each meat-coated egg in the beaten egg, covering the entire surface area.
9. Roll in the breadcrumbs to coat completely.
10. Heat the oil in a deep heavy-bottomed pan, to 180 °C.

Ingredient	4 portions	10 portions
Eggs	4	10
Pork sausage meat	275g	700g
Fresh thyme leaves	1 tsp	2½ tsp
Fresh parsley, chopped	1 tsp	2½ tsp
Spring onion, very finely chopped	1	2½
Plain flour, seasoned	125g	300g
Egg, beaten	1	2½
Breadcrumbs	250g	625g
Salt and freshly ground black pepper		
Vegetable oil for deep frying		

11 Carefully place each Scotch egg into the hot oil and deep fry for 6–8 minutes, until golden and crisp and the sausage meat is completely cooked.

12 Carefully remove from the oil with a slotted spoon and drain on kitchen paper.

To serve, cut the egg in half and season slightly with rock salt. Scotch eggs can be served hot, warm or cold.

Energy	Cals	Fat	Sat fat	Carb	Sugar	Protein	Fibre	Sodium
2906 kJ	692 kcal	30.9g	8.5g	80.2g	4.7g	28.2g	2.0g	1.2g

Variation

For a **vegetarian** version of the traditional pork Scotch egg, follow the same method as above, replacing the sausage meat with 350g of dry mashed potato.

A **fish** version can be made. Follow the same method as above, using 300g fish mousse (this works best using salmon) instead of sausage meat.

1 Flatten out an oval of the sausage meat mixture.

2 Flour the egg and wrap the meat around it until it is completely covered.

3 Dip in flour, then beaten egg.

4 Roll the egg in the breadcrumbs.

5 The egg should be completely coated in breadcrumbs, ready for frying.

Practical Cookery 14th edition

11 Omelette (*omelette nature*)

1. Break the eggs into a basin, season lightly with salt and pepper.
2. Beat well with a fork, or whisk until the yolks and whites are thoroughly combined and no streaks of white can be seen.
3. Heat the omelette pan; wipe thoroughly clean with a dry cloth.
4. Add the butter; heat until foaming but not brown.
5. Add the eggs and cook quickly, moving the mixture continuously with a fork until lightly set; remove from the heat.
6. Half fold the mixture over at right angles to the handle.
7. Tap the bottom of the pan to bring up the edge of the omelette.
8. With care, tilt the pan completely over so as to allow the omelette to fall into the centre of the dish or plate.
9. Neaten the shape if necessary and serve immediately.

Ingredient	1 portion
Eggs	2–3
Salt, pepper	
Butter or oil	10 g

Energy	Cals	Fat	Sat fat	Carb	Sugar	Protein	Fibre
990 kJ	236 kcal	20.2 g	9.1 g	0.0 g	0.0 g	13.6 g	0.0 g

1. Whisk the eggs until the yolks and whites are combined.
2. Move the mixture continuously while it cooks. 
3. Carefully tip the omelette out of the pan. 

Variation

Variations to omelettes can easily be made by adding the ingredient that the guest or dish may require. For example:
- fine herbs (chopped parsley, chervil and chives)
- mushroom (cooked, sliced, wild or cultivated)
- cheese (25 g grated cheese added before folding)
- tomato (incision made down centre of cooked omelette, filled with hot tomato concassé; served with tomato sauce)
- bacon (grill and then julienne into small strips and fold in at the end).

Healthy eating tips
- Use salt sparingly and serve with plenty of starchy carbohydrate and vegetables or salad.

12 Spanish omelette

Ingredient	1 portion
Eggs	2–3
Salt, pepper	
Butter, or oil	10g
Tomato concassé	50g
Onions, cooked	100g
Red pepper, diced	100g
Parsley, chopped	

Energy	Cals	Fat	Sat fat	Carb	Sugar	Protein	Fibre	Sodium
1,726 kJ	416 kcal	30.9g	11.2g	10.9g	8.2g	24.6g	2.5g	0.8g

1 Make up an omelette following recipe 11, steps 1 to 5, but including the tomato, onion, red pepper and parsley with the eggs.

2 Sharply tap the pan on the stove to loosen the omelette and toss it over as for a pancake.

This omelette is cooked and served flat. Many other flat omelettes can be served with a variety of ingredients.

When the butter is foaming, add the egg mixture

The omelette is tipped out flat

13 Feta, mint, lentil and pistachio omelette

Ingredient	4 portions	10 portions
Vegetable oil	4 tbsp	10 tbsp
Brown lentils, cooked	400 g	1 kg
Sorrel	20 leaves approximately	50 leaves
Seasoning		
Feta cheese, crumbled	50 g	125 g
Fresh mint, chopped	2 tbsp	5 tbsp
Pistachio nuts, toasted	2 tbsp	5 tbsp
Eggs	12	30

Energy	Cals	Fat	Sat fat	Carb	Sugar	Protein	Fibre	Sodium
2007 kJ	481 kcal	32.8g	8.1g	17.5g	0.8g	30.3g	5.4g	0.4g

For the filling:

1 Heat the oil in a pan. Add the lentils and the sorrel, season with salt and pepper. Stir until the sorrel is wilted.
2 Remove from the heat; add the feta cheese, mint and pistachio nuts.

For the omelette:

1 Beat the eggs well, add a teaspoon of water or cream to every three eggs.
2 Heat sufficient oil or butter in an omelette pan and proceed to make the omelettes.
3 When nearly cooked through, tilt the omelette pan and start to fold the omelette.
4 Add the filling and continue to finish folding the omelette.

Serve on plates garnished with mint leaves and wedges of lemon or lime.

14 Duck egg frittata with sweetcorn and beans

Ingredient	4 portions	10 portions
Olive oil	15 ml	40 ml
Spring onions, finely chopped	4	10
Green chilli, finely chopped	1	3
Small new potatoes, cooked and sliced	300 g	750 g
Duck eggs	4	10
Dill, finely chopped	1 tsp	2½ tsp
Seasoning		
Frozen sweetcorn	150 g	375 g
Broad beans, cooked and peeled	150 g	375 g
Goats' cheese, sliced	50 g	125 g
Watercress	1 small bunch	1 large bunch

Energy	Cals	Fat	Sat fat	Carb	Sugar	Protein	Fibre	Sodium
1,304 kJ	312 kcal	17.1 g	5.1 g	21.2 g	3.7 g	18.3 g	4.1 g	0.4 g

1 Heat the oil in a suitable pan, add the onions and chilli, and cook for 2 minutes.
2 Add the cooked sliced potatoes. Cook for a further 2 minutes.
3 Beat the eggs in a suitable bowl, and add the dill and seasoning.
4 Add the sweetcorn and beans to the pan. Stir well.
5 Add the eggs and cook until just starting to set.
6 Add the sliced goats' cheese, placing evenly across the frittata.
7 Remove from the heat, place under the salamander and cook until golden brown.
8 Turn out on to a suitable dish and serve garnished with watercress.

15 Poached duck egg, asparagus, cured ham, grain mustard dressing

Ingredient	4 portions	10 portions
Grain mustard	25 g	60 g
Olive oil	50 ml	125 ml
Honey	1½ tbsp	4 tbsp
White wine vinegar	10 ml and 2 tbsp	25 ml and 4 tbsp
Asparagus spears	16	40
Duck eggs	4	10
Salt and black pepper		
Cured ham	4 slices	10 slices
Chives, finely chopped	1 tbsp	2½ tbsp

Energy	Cals	Fat	Sat fat	Carb	Sugar	Protein	Fibre	Sodium
1,189kJ	287kcal	23.6g	4.4g	7.2g	7.1g	11.3g	0.8g	1.4g

1 Combine the mustard, olive oil, honey and 10 ml of vinegar, and mix well to create the vinaigrette. Set aside.

2 Prepare the asparagus by removing the woody bases and peeling the asparagus spears.

3 Bring two large pans of water to the boil and heavily season one of them with salt. Add 2 tbsp of vinegar to the other one.

4 Crack the eggs into four individual cups and, using a whisk, stir the vinegar water vigorously to create a whirlpool. Working quickly, gently place the eggs one by one into the centre of the whirlpool and allow the water to simmer.

5 Poach the eggs for approximately 3 minutes until still runny inside. Lift from the water with a slotted spoon and keep warm.

6 In the last minute of egg poaching time, place the asparagus in the salted water and boil for 1 minute until tender. Remove, season with salt and pepper and keep warm.

7 Using four warm plates, divide the asparagus spears and place a slice of ham over them. Top with a warm egg and drizzle with the vinaigrette. Season the top of the eggs with salt and pepper, and sprinkle with some chopped chives.

Note

The eggs and the asparagus can be part cooked (blanched) and refreshed (in iced water) before reheating (réchauffé) for service.

16 Poached quail eggs with smoked haddock chowder

Ingredient	4 portions	10 portions
Smoked haddock	550 g	1375 g
Milk	500 ml	1250 g
Water	500 ml	1250 g
Thyme sprig	1	3
Bay leaf	1	3
Butter	50 g	125 g
Onion, finely chopped	50 g	125 g
Flour	25 g	62 g
Seasoning		
Lemon juice	1	3
Quail eggs	8	20
Parsley, finely chopped	1 tbsp	3 tbsp

Energy	Cals	Fat	Sat fat	Carb	Sugar	Protein	Fibre
1,063 kJ	254 kcal	13.2 g	7.2 g	5.9 g	1.0 g	27.9 g	0.6 g

1 Place the smoked haddock in a suitable pan, covering with the milk and water. Season lightly. Add the thyme and bay leaf.
2 Bring to boil and simmer gently for approximately 5 minutes.
3 In a saucepan, melt the butter. Add the onion and sweat without colour.
4 Remove the haddock from the cooking liquor, take off the skin and reserve.
5 Add the flour to the onions and stir well. Gradually add the cooking liquor, discarding the bay leaf and the thyme. This will produce a smooth, slightly thickened soup.
6 Add half the haddock. Liquidise thoroughly and pass through a sieve.
7 Flake the rest of the haddock and add to the soup. Season and add the lemon juice.
8 Poach the quail eggs. Place 2 eggs in each serving bowl, ladle the soup on top and sprinkle with chopped parsley.

7 Rice, pulses and grains

Recipes included in this chapter

No.	Recipe	Page
	Rice	
1	Plain boiled rice	158
2	Steamed rice	158
3	Braised or pilaff rice	159
4	Braised rice with mushrooms (*riz pilaff aux champignons*)	160
5	Risotto with Parmesan (*risotto con Parmigiano*)	160
6	Indian-style rice (pilau)	161
7	Brown rice (tabbouleh)	162
8	Rice salad (*salade de riz*)	162
9	Brown rice salad	163
10	Asian rice salad	164
	Pulses	
11	Bean goulash	165
12	Mexican bean pot	166
	Grains	
13	Crisp polenta and roasted Mediterranean vegetables	167
14	Polenta and lentil cakes with roasted vegetables and cucumber and yoghurt sauce	168
15	Lentil and goats' cheese salad	169
16	Couscous with meat and vegetables	170
17	Couscous fritters with feta (*amuse bouche*)	171
18	Couscous salad with roasted vegetables and mixed herbs	172

Rice

Rice is one of the world's most important crops: it is the main food crop for about half the world's population. A hot, wet atmosphere is required for the cultivation of rice, and it is grown chiefly in India, Southeast Asia, South America, Italy and the southern states of the USA. In order to grow, it needs more water than any other cereal crop.

Rice is used in a variety of dishes, both starters and main courses.

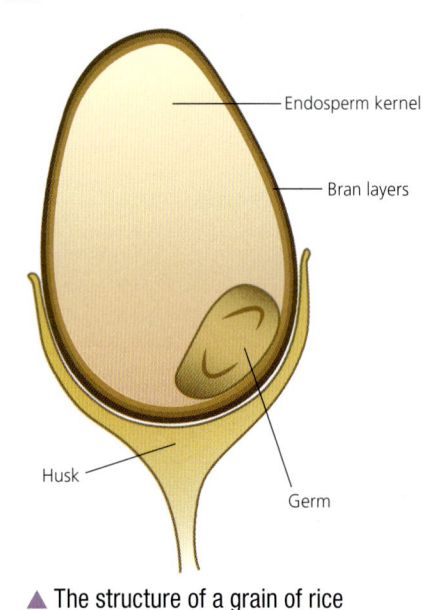

▲ The structure of a grain of rice

Rice varieties

There are around 250 different varieties of rice. The main ones are described below.

- **Long-grain**: a narrow, pointed grain that has had the full bran and most of the germ removed so that it is less fibrous than brown rice. Because of its firm structure, which helps to keep the grains separate when cooked, it is suitable for plain boiling and savoury dishes such as kedgeree and curry.
- **Short-grain**: a short, rounded grain with a soft texture, suitable for sweet dishes and risotto.
- **Round**: rice that has an even, round grain.
- **Brown grain**: any rice that has had the outer covering removed, but retains its bran and, as a result, is more nutritious and contains more fibre. It takes longer to cook than long-grain rice. The nutty flavour of brown rice lends itself to some recipes but does not substitute well in traditional dishes such as paella, risotto or puddings.

Many other types of rice are now widely available, which can add different colours and textures to dishes. Some of these are described below.

- **Arborio**: an Italian short-grain rice. It is used in risottos because it can absorb a good deal of cooking liquid without becoming too soft.

- **Basmati**: a narrow long-grain rice with a distinctive flavour, suitable for serving with Indian dishes. Basmati rice should be soaked before being cooked to remove excess starch.
- **Wholegrain rice**: the whole unprocessed grain of the rice.
- **Wild rice**: this is actually an aquatic grass, not a rice.
- **Easy-cook rice**: traditional rice is milled direct from the field; this rice is steamed under pressure before it is milled, which hardens the grain and reduces the possibility of overcooking. The raw rice is golden in colour and turns white during cooking.
- **Aromatic rice**: special rice with a distinct flavour and aroma. Its quality and flavour can differ from one year to the next based on the harvest and climate change.
- **Jasmine rice**: this aromatic rice originates from Thailand; it is soft and sticky when cooked and is sometimes known as sticky rice.

> **Professional tip**
> Many chefs prefer to use jasmine rice when making sushi as it sticks together and therefore is easier to shape.

- **American aromatic rice**: this type of aromatic rice is now becoming available in several varieties.
- **Japonica rice**: this rice is grown in California and available as red, brown and black rice. It is commonly used in Japanese culinary work and Caribbean cuisine. When cooked it is moist, sticky and firm.

Other rice products include:
- **Rice paper**: edible paper made from milled rice, used in pastry work for nougat and macaroons, etc.
- **Rice wine**: made from fermented wine; sake is the most famous rice wine and is drunk extensively in Japan. Mirin is a sweet rice wine used in rice dishes and culinary work. Shaoxing is a Chinese rice wine.
- **Rice cakes**: rice cakes are best known in Japan and the countries of the Pacific Rim, where rice production is the economic staple and the grain forms the basis for many meals and foods.
- **Rice noodles**: these are made from rice flour. They come in a range of shapes and sizes and styles similar to pasta shapes. They are made by blending rice flour and water, rolling out the mixture, cutting or extruding it. The noodles are then usually dried. Fresh noodles are often cut into wide ribbons that are used in soups and stir fries. Sometimes ingredients such as mung bean flour may be added to rice noodles to change their consistency and appearance. The noodles cook up slightly transparent, and tend to be chewy and slightly resilient. Examples include laksa noodles, rice fluke noodles, rice sticks, rice vermicelli and rice river noodles.

Quality points to look for in rice
- No split grains.
- Good colour.
- Free from infestation, moisture and foreign bodies.

Preparing and cooking rice

Most rice purchased today does not require washing. However, the washing and soaking of rice removes any excess starch, which tends to cloud the cooking medium. Washing impure rice removes debris, dirt and impurities.

Rice grains are porous and absorb water easily. Rice should be slightly undercooked (to the bite), known professionally as al denté, unless if the rice is being moulded.

When boiling rice, cook in a large quantity of water and drain well. Often the rice is refreshed in cold running water or ice water then drained and stored in the refrigerator. However, it is not advisable to reheat rice due to the risk of food poisoning with *Bacillus cereus*.

Rice introduces texture, flavour and carbohydrate content to dishes. The resulting texture and flavour depends on the cooking method and temperature used. The following cooking methods can be used when cooking rice dishes:
- boiling
- steaming
- frying
- stewing
- braising
- microwaving
- baking.

Rice absorbs liquid easily. Use the information in Table 7.1 as a guide to liquid absorption to achieve the exact texture and overall result required.

Table 7.1 Liquid to rice proportions

Cooking method	Liquid to rice proportion
Boiling	3:1 or 4:1
Pilaff (braised)	2:1
Risotto	3:1
Paella	4:1
Sushi	1:5
Wild rice	4:1

As the grains cook, starch is released and naturally thickens the liquid. This is particularly important when making risotto and sushi.

Cooking risotto

When cooking risotto (for example, see recipe 5), arborio is the easiest rice to find, but vialone and carnaroli are other Italian types that can be used. Do not attempt to use pudding, patna or Japanese rice, despite their similar appearance to Italian rice.

A perfect risotto is not a pile of stodgy rice on a plate, sitting like a glutinous mound, nor is it a soupy liquid mess lying flat on the plate. It should be just about moundable, fighting to hold its little peaks from collapsing back into the rest. All the liquid should be combined with the rice to give a creamy-type consistency. Finish with butter and cream.

Storage

Uncooked rice can be stored on the shelf in a tightly sealed container. The shelf life of brown rice is shorter than that of white rice (the bran layers contain oil that can become rancid). Refrigerator storage is recommended for longer shelf life. It is not recommended to store cooked rice but it can be frozen for up to 6 months.

Once cooked, keep rice hot (above 65°C for no longer than two hours) or cool it quickly (within 90 minutes) and keep it cool, below 5°C. If this is not done, the spores of *Bacillus cereus* (a bacterium found in the soil) may revert to bacteria and multiply in the cooked rice.

Pulses

Pulses are one of the most versatile commodities. They can be used extensively in a wide range of dishes. Imaginative and experimental use of different herbs, spices, flavourings and vegetables can give individual variation to pulse recipes.

Pulses are defined as annual leguminous crops, which yield from 1 to 12 grains or seeds of variable size, shape and colour within a pod. The term 'pulse' is reserved for crops harvested solely for the dry grain. This therefore excludes green beans and green peas, which are considered vegetable crops. Also excluded are crops that are grown mainly for oil extraction (oil seeds such as soybeans and peanuts), and crops that are used exclusively for sowing (for example clovers and alfalfa).

All pulses, except for soybeans, are very similar in nutritional content. They are rich in protein, carbohydrate and fibre, and low in fat, which is mostly of the unsaturated kind. They are also an important source of some B vitamins and contain iron. Fresh pulses contain vitamin C, but this declines after harvesting and virtually all is lost from dried pulses. They are 20 to 25 per cent protein, which is double that found in wheat and three times that found in rice.

Types of pulses

Beans

- **Aduki**: small, round, deep red, shiny, nutty and sweet (they are used in Japanese confectionery).
- **Black**: glistening black skins, creamy flesh.
- **Black-eyed**: small white beans with a savoury, creamy flavour, and with a black 'scar' where they were joined to the pod. Used a lot in American and African cooking, they are the essential ingredient in the traditional southern-style dish 'Hoppin John' – a mixture of black-eyed beans, bacon and white rice traditionally eaten on New Year's Day.
- **Broad**: also known as fava beans; strongly flavoured.
- **Borlotti**: Italian beans with a mild, bittersweet flavour; they're used in regional stews and often mixed with rice, and are particularly good in soups such as minestrone and *pasta e fagioli*.
- **Butter**: also known as lima beans, available large or small.
- **Cannellini**: Italian haricot, slightly larger than the English.
- **Dutch brown**: light brown in colour.
- **Flageolet**: pale green, kidney-shaped with a delicate flavour.
- **Ful mesdames**: also known as Egyptian brown beans; small, brown and knobbly, known as the field bean in the UK.
- **Haricot**: white, smooth and oval; used for baked beans.
- **Mung**: small and olive green in colour; good flavour; available split, whole and skinless. Widely used sprouted for their shoots.
- **Pinto**: the original ingredient of Mexican refried beans; an orange-pink bean with rust-coloured specks that grows freely across South America and throughout the American southwest; the bean is

creamy-white in colour with a fluffy texture when cooked, and is good in soups, salads and rich stews.
- **Red kidney**: normally dark red-brown, this kidney-shaped bean holds its shape and colour and is therefore great in mixed bean salads and stews, including the traditional chilli con carne.
- **Soissons**: finest haricot beans.
- **Soy**: soybeans are very high in nutrients, especially protein, and they contain all the essential amino acids. They are processed into many forms: soy flour, TVP (meat substitute), tofu (curd), oils, margarine, soy milk and soy sauce.

Peas

- **Blue**: also known as marrowfat peas; pleasant flavour, floury texture, retain shape when cooked.
- **Chickpeas**: shaped like hazelnuts, they have a tasty nutty flavour when cooked. Chickpeas are used all over the world in dishes such as the Indian *kabli chana* or Spanish *caldo gallego*. Chickpeas are a key ingredient of hummus – a traditional Greek dip of cooked chickpeas, tahini (sesame seed paste), oil and garlic. They can be bought and soaked from dried, but canned chickpeas do just as well for most recipes.
- **Split green**: a sweeter variety than the blue pea; cook to a purée easily.
- **Split yellow**: cook to a purée easily.

Both yellow and green split peas are used for vegetable purées and soups.

Lentils

Lentils, varying in size and colour, can form a nutritious basis for a meal. Larger brown or green lentils retain their shape during cooking and are particularly good in soups. Red and yellow lentils cook down well, can be puréed, and are used a great deal in Indian cooking (such as in a spicy dhal). Tiny green puy lentils have a distinctive flavour and also keep their shape and colour when cooked.

- **Orange**: several types, which vary in size and shade, and may be sold whole or split.
- **Green or continental**: retain shape after cooking, available in small or large varieties.
- **Yellow**: of Asian origin, often used as a dhal accompaniment to curry dishes.
- **Red**: purée easily, used for soups and stews, etc.
- **Indian brown**: red lentils from which the seed coat has not been removed; they purée easily.

- **Puy**: dark French lentils, which vary in size; they retain their shape when cooked and are considered the best of their type.
- **Dhal**: the Hindi word for dried peas and beans; also the name of a spicy lentil dish.

Preparing and cooking pulses

Allow about 55 g dry weight per person – once soaked and cooked they will at least double in weight.

Most dried pulses need soaking for several hours before they can be cooked; exceptions are all lentils, green and yellow split peas, black-eyed beans and mung beans. Soaking times vary from 4 to 12 hours. It is usually most convenient to soak pulses overnight.

Always discard the soaking water, rinse the pulses and cook them in fresh water without any salt (salt toughens the skins and makes for longer cooking). Changing the water will also help to reduce the flatulence some people suffer after eating pulses. Adding a pinch of aniseed, caraway, dill or fennel seeds is also supposed to help with this.

Dried kidney beans need to be cooked carefully – soak them for at least eight hours. After soaking, drain and rinse them, discarding the soaking water. Put them into a pan with cold water to cover and bring to the boil – the beans must be boiled for 10 minutes to destroy toxins; after this, simmer until cooked (approximately 45–60 minutes). The beans should have an even, creamy texture throughout – if the centre is still hard and white, they require longer cooking.

Soybeans should be soaked for at least 12 hours, drained and rinsed then covered with fresh water and brought to the boil. Soybeans should be boiled for the first hour of cooking; they can then be simmered for the remaining two to three hours that it takes to cook them.

> **Food safety**
> It is not safe to eat raw or undercooked kidney beans or soybeans.

When preparing pulses and lentils, cook them in sparkling bottled water. The sparkling motion helps ensure even cooking through momentum; the reason for using bottled water over tap water is the reduced calcium. In hard-water areas there is a lot of calcium, which blocks the pores of pulses, causing beans to 'boil in their jackets' and burst, making the pulses undesirable. Bottled water allows the fluid to pass through the tiny pores and cook evenly.

Storage

One advantage of dried pulses is that they store very well for long periods if kept in a dry, airtight container away from light. However, it is best to eat them as fresh as possible. Pulses toughen on storage and older ones will take longer to cook.

- Store fresh pulses in a refrigerator at a temperature below 5 °C.
- Store frozen pulses in a freezer at a temperature below −18 °C.
- Store dried pulses in clean airtight containers off the floor in the dry store.
- Unpack tinned pulses and check that the tins are sound and undamaged.
- When storing cooked pulses, keep them covered and in a refrigerator at a temperature below 5 °C.
- To prevent the risk of cross-contamination, store cooked pulses away from any raw foods.

Grains

Cereals are important crops and are the oldest farmed agricultural products. Grain is the name given to the edible fruit of cereals. In many countries grains are the main staple food, as they are inexpensive and readily available. Cereals are used in a range of dishes and food products, including breads, soups and stews.

Grains are a rich source of carbohydrate and supply most of their food energy as starch. They are also a significant source of protein. Wholegrain cereals are good sources of dietary fibre, essential fatty acids and other important nutrients.

The whole grain is made up of three parts: the bran, the endosperm and the germ:

- The bran is the outer layers of the cereal. Bran contains a high amount of dietary fibre and some B vitamins (B_1, thiamine, and B_3, niacin). It also contains the minerals zinc, copper and iron, as well as protein and other chemicals.
- The endosperm is the middle layer and is the largest section of the grain. It is the main energy supply and is rich in carbohydrates, protein and B vitamins.
- The germ is the smallest part of the grain. As the name suggests, it develops into the new plant. It is rich in B vitamins, minerals, vitamin E and other chemicals.

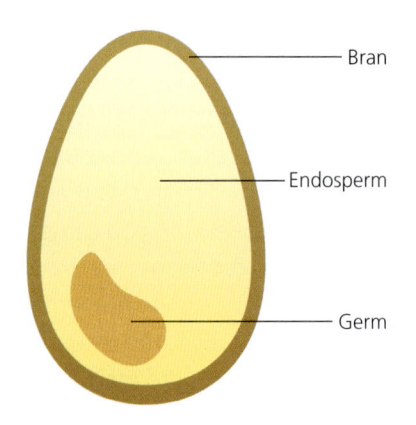

Types of grain

Barley

Barley grows in a wider variety of climatic conditions than any other cereal. Usually found in the shops as **whole** or **pot barley** (or **polished pearl barley**) you can also buy **barley flakes** or **kernels**. It can be cooked on its own (one part grain to three parts water for 45–60 minutes) as an alternative to rice, pasta or potatoes, or added to stews. Malt extract is made from sprouted barley grains.

Barley must have its fibrous hull removed before it is eaten (hulled barley). Hulled barley still has its bran and germ and is considered to be a whole grain, making it a popular health food. Pearl barley is hulled barley that has been processed further to remove the bran.

Buckwheat

When roasted, the seeds of buckwheat are dark reddish-brown. It can be cooked (one part grain to two parts water for 6 minutes, leave to stand for 6 minutes) and served like rice, or it can be added to stews and casseroles. **Buckwheat flour** can be added to cakes, muffins and pancakes, where it imparts a distinctive flavour. Soba noodles, made from buckwheat, are an essential ingredient in Japanese cooking. Buckwheat is gluten free.

Corn/maize

Fresh corn – available in the form of sweetcorn and corn on the cob – is eaten as a vegetable. The dried grain is most often eaten as cornflakes or popcorn. The flour made from corn (**cornmeal**) is used to make Italian polenta, and can be added to soups, pancakes and muffins. Cook polenta (one part grain to three parts

Rice, pulses and grains   7

▲ From left to right: barley, millet and buckwheat

water, for 15–20 minutes), stirring carefully to avoid lumps. Use it like mashed potato: it is quite bland, so try stirring in tasty ingredients such as Gorgonzola or Parmesan and fresh herbs, or press it when cold, cut into slices, brush with garlicky olive oil and grill. You can also get ready-made polenta. Tortillas are made from maize meal, as are quite a lot of snack foods. Don't confuse cornmeal with **refined corn starch/flour**, used for thickening. Corn is gluten free.

Oats

There are various grades of **oatmeal**, including **rolled oats** and **jumbo oat flakes**. All forms can be used to make porridge, combined with nuts to make a nut roast, or added to stews. Oatmeal is low in gluten so can't be used to make bread, but can be mixed with wheat flour to add flavour and texture to bread, muffins and pancakes. Oatmeal contains some oils and can become rancid, so watch the best-before date.

Oatmeal is created by grinding oats into a coarse powder; various grades are available depending on the thoroughness of the grinding (including coarse, pinhead and fine). The main uses of oats are:
- as an ingredient in baking
- in the manufacture of bannocks or oatcakes
- as a stuffing for poultry
- as a coating for some cheeses
- as an ingredient of black pudding
- for making traditional porridge.

Millet

Millet is a group of small-seeded cereal crops or grains widely grown around the world for food and fodder. The main millet varieties are:
- pearl millet
- foxtail millet
- proso millet (also known as common millet, broom corn millet, hog millet or white millet)
- finger millet.

Coeliac patients can replace certain cereal grains (such as wheat) in their diets by consuming millets in various forms, including breakfast cereals.

In western India, millet flour (called 'bajari' in Marathi) has been commonly used with 'jowar' (sorghum) flour for hundreds of years to make the local staple flatbread, 'bhakri'.

Millet can often be used in place of buckwheat, rice or quinoa.

The protein content in millet is very close to that of wheat; both provide about 11 per cent protein by weight. Millets are rich in B vitamins – especially B_3 (niacin), B_6 and B_9 (folic acid) – calcium, iron, potassium, magnesium and zinc. Millets contain no gluten, so they cannot rise to make bread. When combined with wheat or xanthan gum (for those who have coeliac disease), though, they can be used to make raised bread. Alone, they are suited to flatbread.

Millet is an alternative to rice but the tiny grains need to be cracked before they will absorb water easily. Before boiling, sauté them with a little vegetable oil for 2–3 minutes until some are seen to crack, then add water carefully (one part grain to three parts water). Bring to the boil and simmer for 15–20 minutes until fluffy. **Millet flakes** can be made into porridge or added to muesli. **Millet flour** is available, and it is sometimes also made into pasta.

Wheat

This is the most familiar cereal in the UK today, used for bread, cakes, biscuits, pastry, breakfast cereals and pasta. **Wheat grains** can be eaten whole (cook one part grain to three parts water for 40–60 minutes) and have a satisfying, chewy texture. **Cracked** or **kibbled wheat** is the dried whole grains cut by steel blades. **Bulgar wheat** is parboiled before cracking, has a light texture and only needs rehydrating by soaking in boiling water or stock. **Semolina** is a grainy yellow flour ground from durum or hard wheat, and is the main ingredient of dried Italian pasta. **Couscous** is made from semolina grains that have been rolled, dampened and coated with finer wheat flour. Soak in two parts of water/stock to rehydrate; traditionally, it is steamed after soaking. **Strong wheat flour** (with a high gluten content) is required for yeasted breadmaking. **Plain flour** is used for general cooking including cakes and pastry. **Wheat flakes** can be used for porridge, muesli and flapjacks.

Quinoa

Quinoa is an ancient crop that fed the South American Aztecs for thousands of years, and has recently been cultivated in the UK. It's a seed that is high in protein, making it useful for vegetarians.

The small, round grains look similar to millet but are pale brown in colour. The taste is mild and the texture firm and slightly chewy. It can be cooked like millet and absorbs twice its volume in liquid. Cook for 15 minutes (one part grain to three parts water); it's ready when all the grains have turned from white to transparent, and the spiral-like germ has separated. Use in place of more common cereals or pasta, or in risottos, pilaff and vegetable stuffings. It may be used in place of rice and is served in salads and some stuffings.

Rye

Rye is the only cereal (apart from wheat and barley) that has enough gluten to make a yeasted loaf. However, with less gluten than wheat, **rye flour** makes a denser, richer-flavoured bread. It's more usual to mix rye flour with wheat flour. **Rye grains** should be cooked using one part grain to three parts water for 45–60 minutes. **Kibbled rye** is often added to granary-type loaves. Rye grains can be added to stews, and **rye flakes** are good in muesli.

Spelt

Originating in the Middle East, Spelt is closely related to common wheat and has been popular for decades in eastern Europe. It has an intense nutty, wheaty flavour. The flour is excellent for breadmaking and spelt pasta is becoming more widely available.

Quality points to look for in grains

Grains should always look and smell faintly sweet or have no aroma at all. If you detect a musty or oily scent, the grains have passed their peak and should not be purchased.

Buy grains that are well packaged and sealed tightly. Check the use-by date.

Preparing and cooking grains

Grains should first be washed under cold water in a colander to remove any dust or foreign bodies. Look for any unusual infestation such as insects. The dry grain does not need to be soaked.

Grains can vary in cooking time depending on the age of the grain. Grains are usually boiled, or steamed, but may be braised or stewed. As the grain is heated, it absorbs the water, swells and bursts, cooking at between 60°C and 70°C. Grains such as couscous, bulgar wheat and millet only usually require boiling water to be poured on to them, stirred and cooled. Cooking softens the grains. Whole grains take longer to cook than grains that have been processed.

Grains may be cooked in water or soaked in wine or fruit juice; they may also be steamed. Consider too the trend of baking porridge oats and oat flakes, polenta and cornmeal, soaked or parboiled, poured into a lined baking sheet, usually on a silicone mat, and baked in the oven. As the grains are baked the water will cook the product, evaporate and the result is a dry baked grain.

Storage

Cereals are best stored in airtight containers in a cool, dark, dry place. Whole grains can be stored for up to two years; flaked or cracked grains and flours should be used within two to three months of purchase.

Whole grains must be stored more carefully than refined grains, since the healthy oils found largely in the germ of the whole grain can be negatively affected by heat, light and moisture. Because each grain has a different fat content, their shelf life varies.

Intact grains will keep for up to six months in a cool dry store, or up to one year in a freezer.

Wholegrain flours and meals spoil more quickly than intact grains because their protective bran layer has been broken up and air can reach all parts of the grain, causing oxidation. If stored properly they will keep for one to three months in a cool, dry store, or up to two to six months in a freezer.

Test yourself

1. State three quality points to look for when buying rice.
2. How much liquid to rice would you use when cooking risotto?
3. Describe how to store uncooked rice.
4. Describe how you would prepare dried chickpeas before cooking.
5. Describe how to store dried pulses.
6. Describe the preparation and cooking process for red kidney beans.
7. List three quality points to look for when buying grains.
8. State two foods for which barley can be used as an alternative.
9. Describe how to cook polenta by boiling.
10. What is an appropriate cooking method for rye?

Rice recipes

1 Plain boiled rice

Allow 100 g of rice (dry weight) for 4 portions.

1. Pick and wash the long-grain rice. Add to plenty of boiling salted water.
2. Stir to the boil and simmer gently until tender (approximately 12–15 minutes).
3. Pour into a sieve and rinse well under cold running water, then boiling water. Drain and leave in the sieve, placed over a bowl and covered with a cloth.
4. Place on a tray in the hotplate and keep hot.
5. Serve separately in a vegetable dish.

Energy	Cals	Fat	Sat fat	Carb	Sugar	Protein	Fibre	Sodium
363 kJ	86 kcal	0.3g	0.1g	19.0g	0.0g	1.8g	0.4g	0.3g

2 Steamed rice

Allow 100 g of rice (dry weight) for 4 portions.

1. Place the washed rice into a saucepan and add water until the water level is 2.5 cm above the rice.
2. Bring to the boil over a fierce heat until most of the water has evaporated.
3. Turn the heat down as low as possible, cover the pan with a lid and allow the rice to complete cooking in the steam.
4. Once cooked, the rice should be allowed to stand in the covered steamer for 10 minutes.

Energy	Cals	Fat	Sat fat	Carb	Sugar	Protein	Fibre
358 kJ	84 kcal	0.3g	0.1g	18.7g	0.0g	1.8g	0.4g

3 Braised or pilaff rice

Ingredient	4 portions	10 portions
Butter or oil	50 g	125 g
Onion, chopped	25 g	60 g
Rice, long grain, white or brown	100 g	250 g
White stock (preferably chicken)	200 ml	500 ml
Salt, mill pepper		

Energy	Cals	Fat	Sat fat	Carb	Sugar	Protein	Fibre
774 kJ	184 kcal	10.4 g	4.5 g	22.1 g	0.3 g	1.9 g	0.6 g

Using white rice and hard margarine. Using brown rice and hard margarine, 1 portion provides: 769 kJ/183 kcal energy, 10.9 g fat, 4.6 g saturated fat, 20.7 g carbohydrates, 0.7 g sugar, 1.9 g protein and 1.0 g fibre.

1. Place half the butter or oil into a small sauteuse. Add the onion.
2. Cook gently without colouring for 2–3 minutes. Add the rice.
3. Cook gently without colouring for 2–3 minutes.
4. Add twice the amount of stock to rice.
5. Season, cover with buttered paper, bring to the boil.
6. Place in a hot oven (230–250 °C) for approximately 15 minutes, until cooked.
7. Remove immediately into a cool sauteuse.
8. Carefully mix in the remaining butter or oil with a two-pronged fork.
9. Correct the seasoning and serve.

Cook the rice gently without colouring

Add the stock

Cover with buttered paper, with a small hole at the centre

Note
It is usual to use long-grain rice for pilaff because the grains are firm and there is less likelihood of them breaking up and becoming mushy. During cooking, the long-grain rice absorbs more liquid, loses less starch and retains its shape as it swells; short or medium grains may split at the ends and become less distinct in outline.

Variation
Pilaff may also be infused with herbs and spices such as cardamom.

Professional tip
Cook the rice for the exact time specified in the recipe. If it cooks for longer, it will be overcooked and the grains will not separate.

Healthy eating tips
- Use an unsaturated oil (sunflower or olive). Lightly oil the pan and drain off any excess after the frying is complete.
- Keep the added salt to a minimum.

4 Braised rice with mushrooms (riz pilaff aux champignons)

Ingredients are as for braised or pilaff rice (recipe 3) with the addition of 50–100 g well-washed, sliced button mushrooms (or wild mushrooms).

1. Place 25 g butter in a small sauteuse. Add the onion.
2. Cook gently without colour for 2–3 minutes.
3. Add the rice and button mushrooms.
4. Complete as for braised or pilaff rice (recipe 3) from step 4.

Energy	Cals	Fat	Sat fat	Carb	Sugar	Protein	Fibre	Sodium
849 kJ	203 kcal	11.7g	6.9g	22.0g	0.5g	3.5g	0.9g	0.2g

Using 75 g of button mushrooms.

5 Risotto with Parmesan (risotto con Parmigiano)

Ingredient	4 portions	10 portions
Chicken stock	1.2 litres	3 litres
Butter	80g	200g
Onion, peeled and finely chopped	½	1¼
Arborio rice	240g	600g
Parmesan, freshly grated	75g	180g
Salt, pepper		

Energy	Cals	Fat	Sat fat	Carb	Sugar	Protein	Fibre
2,598 kJ	621 kcal	36.2g	14.1g	49.9g	4.2g	23.0g	0.3g

1. Bring the stock to a simmer, next to where you will cook the risotto. Take a wide, heavy-bottomed pan or casserole, put half the butter in over a medium heat and melt.
2. Add the onion and sweat until it softens and becomes slightly translucent.
3. Add the rice and stir with a heat-resistant spatula until it is thoroughly coated in butter (about 2 minutes). Then take a soup ladle of hot stock and pour it into the rice.
4. Continue to cook and stir until this liquid addition is completely absorbed (about 3 minutes).
5. Repeat this procedure several times until the rice has swollen and is nearly tender. The rice should not be soft but neither should it be chalky. Taste and wait: if it is undercooked, it will leave a gritty, chalky residue in your mouth.
6. Normally the rice is ready about 20 minutes after the first addition of stock.
7. Add the other half of the butter and half the Parmesan off the heat. Stir these in, season and cover. Leave to rest and swell a little more for 3 minutes. Serve immediately after this in soup plates, with more Parmesan offered separately.

This is the classic risotto.

Rice, pulses and grains   7

Healthy eating tips
- Use an unsaturated oil (sunflower or olive), instead of butter, to sweat the onion. Lightly oil the pan and drain off any excess after the frying is complete.
- Additional salt is not necessary.
- Serve with a large salad and tomato bread.

Professional tip
Add the stock slowly, to give the rice time to absorb the liquid.

Stir regularly during cooking.

Variation
Risotto variations include:
- **saffron or Milanese-style**: soak ¼ teaspoon saffron in a little hot stock and mix into the risotto near the end of the cooking time; bone marrow is also sometimes added.
- **seafood**: add any one or a mixture of cooked mussels, shrimp, prawns, etc., just before the rice is cooked; also use half fish stock, half chicken stock.
- **mushroom**: garnish with cooked mushrooms
- **asparagus**: garnish with freshly cooked asparagus heads.

Risotto may be served as an *amuse-bouche* (bite-sized appetiser).

6 Indian-style rice (pilau)

Ingredient	4 portions	10 portions
Basmati rice	300 g	750 g
Ghee	1 tbsp	2½ tbsp
Bay leaves	2	5
Cloves	5	12
Green cardamom pods	5	12
Cassia bark (5 cm piece)	1	2
Fennel seeds	1 tsp	2½ tsp
Cumin seeds	½ tsp	1 tsp
Brown cardamom pods	1	2
Star anise	1	2
Water, boiling	570 ml	1,425 ml

Energy	Cals	Fat	Sat fat	Carb	Sugar	Protein	Fibre
1,315 kJ	315 kcal	5.8g	3.3g	60.0g	0.0g	.59g	0.0g

1 Wash and drain the rice.
2 Heat the ghee in a large thick-based saucepan and stir fry the spices for 30 seconds.
3 Add the rice and very gently stir fry, being careful not to breaking the grains of rice.
4 Add to the boiling water and stir around.
5 Place a lid on top and turn down to the lowest heat.
6 Leave for 8 minutes – the water should have been completely absorbed.
7 Check the rice. If it is done, remove from the heat and gently fluff up with a fork.
8 If the rice is still brittle in the middle, replace the lid and leave for a further 2 minutes, adding a little more water if necessary.

7 Brown rice (tabbouleh)

Ingredient	4 portions	10 portions
Brown basmati rice	150 g	375 g
Sprigs of fresh thyme	2	5
Celery, chopped	300 g	750 g
Large eggs	4	10
Olive oil	3 tbsp	8 tbsp
Large lemon, zest and juice	2	5
Red onion, finely chopped	1	3
Medium tomatoes, blanched, skinned, deseeded and cut into a small concassé	2	5
Seedless cucumber, peeled, cored and cut into brunoise	½	1½
Flat-leaf parsley, chopped	3 tbsp	7½ tbsp
Fresh mint, chopped	1 tbsp	2½ tbsp
Fresh coriander, chopped	1 tbsp	2½ tbsp
Pomegranate, seeds only	1	3
Salt and freshly ground black pepper		

Energy	Cals	Fat	Sat fat	Carb	Sugar	Protein	Fibre	Sodium
1,386 kJ	331 kcal	16.2 g	2.7 g	34.1 g	6.9 g	12.1 g	5.8 g	0.3 g

1 Simmer the rice with the thyme and celery for 20 minutes until tender. Drain and leave to cool.
2 Meanwhile, boil the eggs for 7 minutes before refreshing in ice-cold water. Peel off the shell and slice the eggs into quarters.
3 Transfer the rice into a bowl. Add the olive oil, lemon zest and juice, red onion, tomato and cucumber, and stir to mix the ingredients through the rice.
4 Carefully add the parsley, mint, coriander (leaving some to sprinkle on top) and pomegranate, and season to taste.
5 Serve with the quartered eggs on top.

8 Rice salad (*salade de riz*)

Ingredient	4 portions	10 portions
Tomatoes	100 g	250 g
Rice, cooked	100 g	250 g
Peas, cooked	50 g	125 g
Vinaigrette	1 tbsp	2½ tbsp
Salt, pepper		

Energy	Cals	Fat	Sat fat	Carb	Sugar	Protein	Fibre
906 kJ	216 kcal	6.9 g	1.1 g	34.6 g	3.3 g	5.9 g	8.3 g

For 4 portions.

1 Skin and deseed the tomatoes; cut into 0.5 cm dice.
2 Mix with the rice and peas.
3 Add the vinaigrette and correct the seasoning.

Healthy eating tips
- This dish is high in starchy carbohydrate and can be varied with different/additional vegetables.
- Lightly dress with vinaigrette and add salt sparingly.

Professional tip
Cook the rice so that it still has a bite, with the grains separate, not sticking together; it should not feel starchy in the mouth.

Rice, pulses and grains

9 Brown rice salad

Energy	Cals	Fat	Sat fat	Carb	Sugar	Protein	Fibre	Sodium
1,127 kJ	270 kcal	16.3g	2.3g	28.1g	6.9g	4.2g	3.5g	0.3g

Ingredient	4 portions	10 portions
Brown rice	100g	250g
Salt		
Boiling water	175g	440g
Vinaigrette	1 tbsp	2½ tbsp
Tomatoes	100g	250g
Peas, cooked	50g	125g
Haricots verts, cooked and finely sliced	25g	60g
Cucumber, finely chopped	5cm	12cm
Spring onions, very finely chopped	3	7
Red dessert apple, chopped but not peeled	1	2½
Walnuts, finely chopped	25g	60g
Mixed peppers, deseeded, cut into fine dice	25g	60g

1 Place the rice into a saucepan with a sprinkle of salt and cover with boiling water.
2 Bring the water back to the boil; stir once, put a lid on and simmer very gently for approximately 35–40 minutes, until all the liquid has been absorbed.
3 Empty the rice into a salad bowl, fluff it up with a fork and pour three-quarters of the vinaigrette over while it's still hot. Leave to cool.
4 While the rice is cooling, blanch the tomatoes, remove the skins and cut into quarters. Remove the seeds and cut in 0.5cm dice.
5 Once the rice is cool, mix in the tomatoes and all the other ingredients, adding the remaining vinaigrette. Check the seasoning and keep in a cool place until needed.

10 Asian rice salad

Ingredient	4 portions	10 portions
Flat-leaf parsley, finely chopped	2 tbsp	5 tbsp
Coriander, finely chopped	2 tbsp	5 tbsp
Mint, finely chopped	1 tbsp	2½ tbsp
Garlic clove, finely chopped	1	4
Ginger, finely chopped	1 tsp	3 tsp
Soy sauce	2 tbsp	5 tbsp
Lime juice	1	3
Honey	1 tbsp	2½ tbsp
Peanut oil	4 tbsp	10 tbsp
Brown rice, cooked	400 g	1 kg
Courgettes, diced	1	3
Peas, cooked	125 g	300 g
Spring onions, shredded	2	5
Coriander leaves to garnish		

Energy	Cals	Fat	Sat fat	Carb	Sugar	Protein	Fibre	Sodium
1,197 kJ	286 kcal	13.5g	2.7g	35.2g	12.4g	5.9g	3.7g	0.8g

1 Blitz the herbs, garlic, ginger, soy sauce, lime juice and honey in a food processor.
2 Slowly add the oil.
3 In a bowl add the rice, courgettes, peas and spring onions. Mix well.
4 Stir in the herb dressing.
5 Serve garnished with coriander leaves.

Note
In case of allergen concerns, oils other than peanut oil could be used.

Rice, pulses and grains   7

Pulse recipes

11 Bean goulash

Ingredient	4 portions	10 portions
Red kidney or haricot beans, dried	200 g	500 g
Sunflower oil	60 ml	150 ml
Onion, finely chopped	50 g	125 g
Clove of garlic, crushed	1	2–3
Paprika	25 g	60 g
Red peppers	2	5
Green pepper	1	2–3
Yellow pepper	1	2–3
Button mushrooms, sliced	200 g	500 g
Tomato purée	50 g	125 g
Vegetable stock	750 ml	2 litre
Bouquet garni	1	2
Seasoning		
Small turned potatoes, cooked	8	20
Parsley, chopped, to serve		

Energy	Cals	Fat	Sat fat	Carb	Sugar	Protein	Fibre
1,728 kJ	411 kcal	17.9 g	2.7 g	50.0 g	7.3 g	17.3 g	18.5 g

1 Soak the beans for 24 hours in cold water. Drain, place into a saucepan. Cover with cold water, boil for at least 10 minutes and then simmer until tender.
2 Heat the oil in a sauté pan, sweat the onion and garlic without colour for 2–3 minutes; add the paprika and sweat for a further 2–3 minutes.
3 Add the peppers (cut in halves, with seeds removed and cut into 1 cm dice). Add the button mushrooms; sweat for a further 2 minutes.
4 Add the tomato purée, vegetable stock and bouquet garni. Bring to the boil and simmer until the pepper and mushrooms are cooked.
5 Remove the bouquet garni. Add the drained cooked beans, correct the seasoning and stir.
6 Garnish with potatoes (or gnocchi) and chopped parsley.
7 Serve wholegrain pilaff or wholemeal noodles separately.

Healthy eating tips
- Use less sunflower oil to sweat the onions.
- Add only a pinch of salt.
- Serve with rice or noodles and a green salad or mixed vegetables.

12 Mexican bean pot

Ingredient	4 portions	10 portions
Red kidney or haricot beans, dried	300 g	750 g
Onions, finely chopped	100 g	250 g
Carrots, sliced	100 g	250 g
Tomato, skinned, deseeded and diced	200 g	500 g
Cloves of garlic, crushed and chopped	2	5
Paprika	10 g	25 g
Dried marjoram	3 g	9 g
Small fresh chilli, finely chopped	1	2–3
Small red pepper, finely diced	1	2–3
Yeast extract	5 g	12 g
Chives, chopped		
Seasoning		

Energy	Cals	Fat	Sat fat	Carb	Sugar	Protein	Fibre
672 kJ	161 kcal	1.2 g	0.2 g	27.0 g	4.6 g	12.3 g	14.0 g

1. Soak the beans in cold water for 24 hours. Drain. Place into a saucepan, cover with cold water, bring to the boil and simmer gently.
2. When three-quarters cooked, add all the other ingredients except the chopped chives.
3. Continue to simmer until all is completely cooked.
4. Serve sprinkled with chopped chives.

Healthy eating tips
- No added salt is needed; there is plenty in the yeast extract.
- Serve with a selection of colourful vegetables.

Grain recipes

13 Crisp polenta and roasted Mediterranean vegetables

Ingredient	4 portions	10 portions
Polenta		
Water	200 ml	500 ml
Butter	30 g	75 g
Polenta flour	65 g	160 g
Parmesan, grated	25 g	60 g
Egg yolks	1	2
Crème fraiche	110 g	275 g
Seasoning		
Roasted vegetables		
Red peppers	2	5
Yellow peppers	2	5
Courgettes	2	5
Red onions	2	5
Vegetable oil	200 ml	500 ml
Seasoning		
Clove of garlic	1	3
Thyme, sprigs	2	5

Energy	Cals	Fat	Sat fat	Carb	Sugar	Protein	Fibre	Sodium
3,267 kJ	790 kcal	71.4 g	18.9 g	28.6 g	14.0 g	10.1 g	6.6 g	0.1 g

To make the polenta:

1 Bring the water and the butter to the boil.
2 Season the water well and whisk in the polenta flour.
3 Continue to whisk until very thick.
4 Remove from the heat and add the Parmesan, egg yolk and crème fraiche.
5 Whisk until all incorporated; check the seasoning.
6 Set in a lined tray.
7 Once set, cut using a round cutter or cut into squares.
8 Reserve until required.

To make the roasted vegetables:

1 Roughly chop the vegetables into large chunks. Ensure the seeds are removed from the peppers.
2 Toss the cut vegetables in the oil and season well.
3 Place the vegetables in an oven with the aromats for 30 minutes at 180 °C.
4 Remove from the oven and drain. Reserve until required.

To serve:

1 To serve the dish, shallow-fry the polenta in a non-stick pan until golden on both sides.
2 Warm the roasted vegetables and place them in the middle of the plate. Place the polenta on top.
3 Finish with rocket salad and balsamic dressing.

Professional tip

Line the tray with cling film and silicone paper before pouring in the polenta – this will stop it from sticking to the tray when it sets.

14 Polenta and lentil cakes with roasted vegetables and cucumber and yoghurt sauce

Ingredient	4 portions	10 portions
Puy lentils	250 g	625 g
Vegetable stock	250 ml	625 ml
Fine polenta	75 g	187 g
Parmesan cheese, grated	25 g	62 g
Egg, beaten	1	3
Salt and pepper		
Leeks, finely chopped and blanched	75 g	187 g
Clove of garlic, crushed and finely chopped	1	3
Olive oil	3 tbsp	8 tbsp
Sauce		
Cucumber, peeled	250 g	625 g
Natural yoghurt	250 ml	625 ml
Mint, chopped	¼ tsp	1¼ tsp
Chives, chopped	1 tsp	2½ tsp

Energy	Cals	Fat	Sat fat	Carb	Sugar	Protein	Fibre
1,898 kJ	452 kcal	15.2 g	4.1 g	55.6 g	7.9 g	25.2 g	4.3 g

1 Wash the lentils and cook in salted water for about 25 minutes until tender but still firm. Drain well, refresh and drain again. Dry on a suitable cloth.
2 Bring the vegetable stock to the boil, add the polenta and cook gently, stirring until thickened.
3 Add the Parmesan and beaten egg; season.
4 Mix the lentils, polenta, leeks and garlic together.
5 Correct the seasoning, cool and shape into four (or ten) round cakes.
6 Place in the fridge and chill well for at least 1 hour.
7 Heat the olive oil in a suitable pan; gently fry the cakes for about 3–4 minutes on each side until heated through and well browned.
8 To make the sauce, liquidise the peeled cucumber with the yoghurt, and finish with chopped mint and chives.
9 To serve, place a small amount of the sauce on to a plate and place the cakes on top. Garnish the plate with freshly roasted vegetables.

Healthy eating tips
- No additional salt is needed.
- Use less olive oil to fry the cakes, and drain on kitchen paper.

15 Lentil and goats' cheese salad

Ingredient	4 portions	10 portions
Puy lentils	100 g	250 g
Bay leaf	1	2½
Spring onions, finely chopped	4	10
Red pepper, finely chopped	1	2½ tbsp
Parsley, chopped	1 tbsp	2½ tbsp
Cherry tomatoes, sliced in half	400 g	1 kg
Rocket leaves	200 g	500 g
Goats' cheese	100 g	250 g
Dressing		
Olive oil	1 tbsp	2½ tbsp
Balsamic vinegar	1 tbsp	2½ tbsp
Clear honey	2 tbsp	5 tbsp
Garlic clove, crushed and chopped	1	2½

Energy	Cals	Fat	Sat fat	Carb	Sugar	Protein	Fibre
907 kJ	216 kcal	9.2 g	4.1 g	22.8 g	10.5 g	11.9 g	4.5 g

1 Rinse the lentils and place in a saucepan. Add the bay leaf and cover with water. Bring to the boil and simmer for 20–30 minutes until tender.
2 Drain and then place in a bowl. Add the spring onions, red pepper, parsley and cherry tomatoes; mix well.
3 For the dressing, whisk together in a bowl the oil, vinegar, honey and garlic, and stir into the lentils.
4 Serve on a bed of rocket, with the goats' cheese sprinkled over.

Note

This dish provides a healthy, balanced starter.

16 Couscous with meat and vegetables

Ingredient	4 portions	10 portions
Couscous	200 g	500 g
Lean stewing lamb	400 g	1 kg
Stewing beef *or* chicken, cut for sauté	200 g	500 g
Olive oil	2 tbsp	5 tbsp
Onion, finely chopped	50 g	125 g
Clove of garlic, crushed and chopped	1	2–3
Celery, sliced	100 g	250 g
Leek, sliced	100 g	250 g
Carrot, diced (1 cm)	100 g	250 g
Chickpeas	25 g	60 g
Ground ginger (optional)	¼ tsp	½ tsp
Saffron (optional)	¼ tsp	½ tsp
Raisins	50 g	125 g
Courgettes, diced	100 g	250 g
Tomatoes, skinned, deseeded and diced	50 g	125 g
Parsley, chopped		
Tomato purée	50 g	125 g
Cayenne pepper		
Paprika	½ tsp	1 tsp
Butter	50 g	125 g

Energy	Cals	Fat	Sat fat	Carb	Sugar	Protein	Fibre
2,146 kJ	515 kcal	28.5g	12.6g	42.2g	14.7g	25.3g	2.8g

Using lamb and butter.

1. Soak the couscous in warm water for 10 minutes.
2. Fry the meat in the oil until browned and sealed. Remove quickly.
3. Fry the onions and garlic, then remove and drain.
4. Place the meat, onions and garlic into a saucepan, and add the celery, leeks, carrots and chickpeas. Cover with water and season.
5. Add the ginger and saffron, if using; bring to the boil and simmer for about 1 hour.
6. Drain the couscous, place in the top part of the couscousier and steam for 30 minutes. Alternatively, place the couscous in a metal colander lined with muslin. Fit into the top of the saucepan, making sure that the liquid from the stew does not touch the steamer as the couscous will become lumpy. Stir occasionally.
7. Add the raisins and courgettes to the stew, followed by the tomatoes, chopped parsley and tomato purée. Cook for a further 30 minutes.
8. Remove approx. 250 ml (625 ml) sauce from the stew and stir enough cayenne pepper in to it to make it strong and fiery. Finish with paprika.
9. To serve, pile the couscous into a suitable serving dish, preferably earthenware, add knobs of butter and work into the grains with a fork.
10. Carefully arrange the meat and vegetables over the couscous and pour the broth over. Serve the hot peppery sauce separately.
11. Alternatively, the couscous, meat and vegetables, broth and peppery sauce can be served in separate bowls.

Note

Pre-cooked couscous is also available.

Healthy eating tips

- No additional salt is needed.
- Add only a small amount of fat to the couscous before adding the meat and vegetables.
- The fat content will be reduced if skinned chicken is used or less lamb/beef and more vegetables.

17 Couscous fritters with feta (*amuse bouche*)

Ingredient	4 portions	10 portions
Couscous	80 g	200 g
Vegetable stock	100 ml	250 ml
Beaten egg	½	1¼
Natural yoghurt	1 tbsp	2½ tbsp
Feta cheese, cut into 1 cm dice	40 g	100 g
Tomatoes, skinned, deseeded and cut into small dice	25 g	60 g
Spring onions, finely chopped	2	5
Vegetable oil	1 tbsp	2½ tbsp

Energy	Cals	Fat	Sat fat	Carb	Sugar	Protein	Fibre	Sodium
533 kJ	128 kcal	6.9g	2.3g	11.8g	1.5g	5.2g	0.3g	0.2g

1. Place the couscous in a suitable bowl; pour in the boiling stock and stir. Allow to stand until the couscous absorbs the stock.
2. Add the egg and yoghurt, mix well and season. Fold in the feta cheese, tomatoes and spring onions.
3. Divide the mixture into the number of portions and shape into small cakes.
4. Shallow fry the fritters in vegetable oil on both sides until golden brown.
5. Serve as an *amuse bouche* on a fresh tomato sauce seasoned with chilli. Garnish each fritter with a suitable chutney, red onion, beetroot or fig.

18 Couscous salad with roasted vegetables and mixed herbs

Ingredient	4 portions	10 portions
Roasted vegetables (selection)	100 g	250 g
Couscous	250 g	625 g
Balsamic vinegar	1 tbsp	2½ tbsp
Olive oil	3 tbsp	8 tbsp
Lemon, juice of	¼	¾
Seasoning		
Fresh mint, chopped	½ tsp	1¼ tsp
Fresh coriander, chopped	½ tsp	1¼ tsp
Fresh thyme, chopped	½ tsp	1¼ tsp

Energy	Cals	Fat	Sat fat	Carb	Sugar	Protein	Fibre
1,248 kJ	300 kcal	12.5 g	1.7 g	42.2 g	8.6 g	6.6 g	3.8 g

1. Prepare the roasted vegetables.
2. Place the couscous in a suitable bowl and gently pour over 300 ml of boiling water (750 ml for 10 portions).
3. Stir well, cover and leave to stand for 5 minutes.
4. Separate the grains with a fork.
5. Add the balsamic vinegar, olive oil, lemon juice and seasoning.
6. Mix well, then stir in the chopped herbs.
7. Finish by adding the roasted vegetables.
8. Serve in a suitable bowl or use individual plates. For plated service, arrange the couscous neatly in the centre of the plate, arrange the roasted vegetables around, then garnish with fresh herbs.

Professional tip

When adding the vinegar and oil, add just enough to give the correct texture and flavour.

Healthy eating tips

- Use an unsaturated oil and lightly brush the vegetables when roasting.
- Use the minimum amount of salt.

8 Pasta and noodles

Recipes included in this chapter

No.	Recipe	Page
Pasta		
1	Fresh egg pasta dough	178
2	Spaghetti with tomato sauce (*spaghetti al pomodoro*)	179
3	Spaghetti bolognaise (*spaghetti alla bolognese*)	180
4	Penne arrabiata	181
5	Ravioli	182
6	Macaroni cheese	183
7	Spinach fettuccine with ham and cream cheese (*fettuccine verde con salsa cremona*)	184
8	Tagliatelle carbonara	184
9	Ravioli of squash and spinach with wild mushroom sauce	185
10	Lasagne	186
11	Vegetarian lasagne	188
12	Ricotta and spinach cannelloni with tomato and basil sauce	189
Gnocchi		
13	Potato gnocchi (*gnocchi piemontese*)	190
14	Parmesan gnocchi and tomato sauce	191

Pasta

Pasta is made from durum wheat, which has a 15 per cent protein content. This makes it a good alternative to rice and potatoes for vegetarians. Pasta also contains carbohydrates in the form of starch, which gives the body energy. Eating more pasta is in line with the recommendation to 'eat more starchy carbohydrates'.

Traditionally, pasta was eaten as a starter, but it is now used much more as a main course or stand-alone dish.

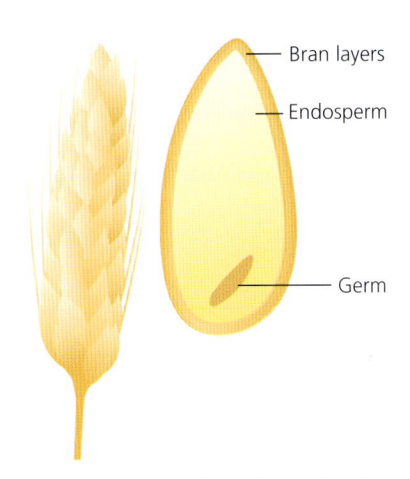

▲ The structure of a grain of wheat

Types of pasta

There are basically four types of pasta, each of which may be plain or flavoured with spinach or tomato:

1. dried durum wheat pasta
2. fresh egg pasta
3. semolina pasta
4. wholewheat pasta.

Dried pasta

There are an almost infinite number of types of dried pasta, especially if you include all the regional variations. Almost 90 per cent of the pasta eaten in Italy is dried.

Fresh pasta

Fresh pasta has a short shelf life as it contains eggs.

Stuffed pasta

Pasta that is to be stuffed must be rolled as thinly as possible. The stuffing should be pleasant in taste and plentiful in quantity. The edges of the pasta must be thoroughly sealed otherwise the stuffing will seep out during poaching.

The list of possible stuffings is almost endless as every district in Italy has its own variations and, with thought and experimentation, many more can be produced.

Examples of stuffed pasta include the following:
- **Agnolini**: small half-moon shapes, usually filled with ham and cheese or minced meat.
- **Cannelloni**: large tubes of pasta, poached that may be stuffed with a variety of fillings (e.g. ricotta cheese and spinach) and finished with an appropriate sauce.
- **Cappelletti**: shaped like little hats and usually filled as agnolini; they are available dried.
- **Ravioli**: usually square with serrated edges. A wide variety of fillings can be used (fish, meat, vegetarian, cheese, etc.).
- **Ravolini**: 'little ravioli', half the size of ravioli.
- **Tortellini**: a slightly larger version of cappelletti; also available in dried form.
- **Tortelloni**: a double-sized version of tortellini.

Quality points

When purchasing dried pasta the box or container should be sealed and the pasta unbroken. Check the 'best before' date. Dried pasta must be dry and not damp, have a good even colour with no signs of infestation. If you experience problems with the ingredients inform the supplier or your manger immediately. If in doubt, do not use them.

When purchasing fresh pasta it must be at or below 5 °C, evenly coloured, intact and not torn or damaged. The pasta must separate easily.

Ingredients for pasta dishes

A huge variety of ingredients may be used in pasta dishes. The list is almost endless, but may include:
- fish, e.g. smoked salmon, anchovies, tuna
- shellfish, e.g. shrimps, prawns, scallops, lobster, crab, cockles
- meat, e.g. smoked ham, sausage, salami, bacon, beef, chicken, duck
- offal, e.g. tongue, chicken livers
- herbs, e.g. parsley, rosemary, basil, tarragon, chives, marjoram
- spices, e.g. chillies, saffron, grated nutmeg
- vegetables, e.g. mushrooms, tomatoes, onions, fennel, courgettes, spring onions, peas, spinach, peppers, broad beans, broccoli
- nuts, e.g. pine nuts, walnuts, hazelnuts
- fruit, e.g. stoned olives, avocado, sultanas, lemon zest
- eggs
- capers
- cooked, dried beans
- Balsamic vinegar.

It is important to know what ingredients blend well together and complement the pasta without overpowering the main ingredient. Customers must also know what ingredients are in the dish in case they suffer from an allergy.

Preparing and cooking pasta dishes

Dried pasta

A rule of thumb for cooking dried pasta is to allow 100 g per portion as a main course; increase accordingly if larger portions are required.

Bring plenty of water (at least 4 litres for every 600 g of dry pasta) to a rolling boil. Add about 1 tbsp of salt per 4 litres of water, if desired. Add the pasta in small quantities to maintain the rolling boil. Stir frequently to prevent sticking. Do not cover the pan. Follow package directions for cooking time. Do not overcook. Pasta should be *al dente* (meaning literally 'to the tooth' – tender, yet firm). It should be slightly resistant to the bite, but cooked through. Drain pasta to stop the cooking action but do not rinse it unless the recipe specifically says to do so. For salads, drain and rinse pasta with cold water.

Fresh egg pasta

This requires less cooking time than dried pasta. When cooking fresh pasta, the addition of a few drops of olive oil in the water will help prevent the pasta pieces from sticking together.

Straining

Always strain pasta carefully as it is a delicate product. Use a colander or a spider.

Pasta and noodles 8

▲ Pasta-making equipment, left to right: pasta machine, ravioli cutter, ravioli tray and rolling pin

Making fresh pasta

1. Sift 400 g strong flour together with a pinch of salt.
2. Make a well in the flour; pour 4 beaten eggs into the well.
3. Gradually incorporate the flour.   
4. Mix until a dough is formed. Add olive oil to adjust to the required consistency. The amount of oil will vary according to the type of flour and the size of the eggs.
5. Pull and knead the dough until it is of a smooth elastic consistency.
6. Cover the dough and allow to rest in a cool place for 30 minutes.
7. After resting, knead the dough again.
8. Roll the dough out on a well-floured surface to a thickness of 0.5 mm.
9. Trim the sides and cut as required using a large knife.

Other cooking methods for pasta dishes

- **Baking**: this technique is used for dishes such as cannelloni and pasta bakes. These dishes have usually been cooked previously and require baking to finish the product. This technique requires the dish to cook evenly to give a well-distributed colour. After cooking, clean the dish before presenting it to the customer. Always check the internal temperature using a probe to ensure that it reaches a safe 75 °C.
- **Grilling**: this method is used to finish cooked pasta dishes that include a sauce topped with grated cheese.
- **Deep frying**: some pasta dishes may be deep fried; the pasta is first boiled and then coated before deep frying. An example is stuffed ravioli dipped in egg wash or butter milk, coated in breadcrumbs and then deep fried.

Sauces and accompaniments

Always mix sauces into pasta in a large bowl or saucepan to enable the ingredients to be well distributed throughout it. This is best done with a large spoon or, if cold, the pasta can be mixed by hand (make sure hands have been thoroughly washed; alternatively use food gloves).

Examples of sauces to go with pasta include:
- tomato sauce
- cream, butter or béchamel-based sauces
- rich meat sauce, e.g. bolognaise
- olive oil and garlic
- soft white or blue cheese
- pesto.

Cheeses used when pasta cooking include the following:
- **Parmesan**: the most popular hard cheese for use with pasta, ideal for grating. The flavour is best when it is freshly grated. If bought ready grated, or if it is grated and stored, the flavour deteriorates.
- **Pecorino**: a strong ewes' milk cheese, sometimes studded with peppercorns. Used for strongly flavoured dishes, it can be grated or thinly sliced.
- **Ricotta**: a creamy-white cheese made from the discarded whey of other cheeses. It is widely used in fillings for pasta such as cannelloni and ravioli, and for sauces.
- **Mozzarella**: traditionally made from the milk of the water buffalo. Mozzarella is pure white and creamy, with a mild but distinctive flavour, and usually round or pear-shaped. It will keep for only a few days in a container half-filled with milk and water.
- **Gorgonzola and dolcelatte**: distinctive blue cheeses that can be used in sauces.

All stuffed pasta should be served in or coated with a suitable sauce and, depending on the type of recipe, may be finished 'au gratin' by sprinkling with freshly grated Parmesan and browning lightly under the salamander.

Storing pasta

Dry pasta can be stored almost indefinitely, if kept in a tightly sealed package or a covered container in a cool, dry place, but you must observe the best-before date on the packaging.

Fresh egg pasta should be stored in the refrigerator at or below 5 °C; if it is not for immediate use it must be stored in a cool, dry place. Allow it to dry then keep it in a clean, dry container or bowl in a cool, dry store.

If cooked pasta is not to be used immediately, drain and rinse thoroughly with cold water. If the pasta is left to sit in water, it will continue to absorb water and become mushy. When the pasta is cool, drain and toss lightly with salad oil to prevent it from sticking and drying out. Cover tightly and refrigerate or freeze. Refrigerate the pasta and sauce separately or the pasta will become soggy. To reheat, put pasta in a colander and immerse in rapidly boiling water just long enough to heat through. Do not allow the pasta to continue to cook. Pasta may also be reheated in a microwave.

Always make sure you refresh the pasta in plenty of water so that the pasta is free flowing and does not stick together.

Shaped raw pasta is best stored in large containers sprinkled with semolina, layered with sheets of greaseproof or silicone paper or sheets of plastic in an airtight container.

Stuffed fresh pasta should be blanched, drained, frozen or chilled in small amounts which allows for easy separation. Frozen pasta will keep for up to three months but it is recommended that it is used within one month.

Food safety

Remember to store fresh pasta in the refrigerator at 5 °C. When cooked the core temperature must be 75 °C.

Noodles

Noodles are probably the world's oldest fast food; they are versatile and quick to cook. They may be steamed, boiled, pan-fried, stir fried or deep fried. Noodles are a staple food in southeast Asia but they are also very popular in the West.

Noodles are high in starch (carbohydrate). They provide some protein, especially those made from hard wheat and beans. The addition of egg also increases noodles' protein content.

Examples of the nutritional content of some noodles are given in Table 8.1.

Noodles can be made fresh or purchased dried.

Quality points

The basic quality points for dried noodles are:
- even and of a good colour
- no sign of moisture or discolouration.

Fresh noodles must:
- have a good colour
- be evenly cut and of the right thickness throughout.

Cooking noodles

As noodles take very little time to cook it is best to cook them to order.

Storing noodles

Store fresh noodles in a vacuum pouch or in a plastic sealed bag in the refrigerator. Dried noodles should be kept in a tightly sealed package or a covered container in a cool, dry place, but you must observe the best-before date on the packaging.

Table 8.1 Nutritional content of noodles

100 g dry weight	Calories	Carbohydrates	Protein	Fat	Sodium
Rice sticks	380	88%	6%	0	
Rice vermicelli	363	85.5%	7.3%	0	
Egg noodles	341	70%	11%	1.9%	0.8%
Wheat noodles	308	60% (plus fibre 10%)	12.5%	2%	0.8%
Bean thread	320	65%	20%	0	
Pasta	350	75%	11.5%	0.3%	

Source: Pat Chapman (1998) *Pat Chapman's Noodle Book*, Hodder & Stoughton Ltd.

Test yourself

1. State three quality points to look for when buying dried pasta.
2. State three pieces of equipment you would use when preparing fresh pasta.
3. Describe how to prepare fresh egg pasta dough.
4. What is the minimum legal temperature for holding cooked lasagne hot for service?
5. Describe how to store cooked pasta which is not for immediate use.
6. State two quality points to look for when buying fresh noodles.
7. Describe how to store uncooked fresh noodles.
8. Name three types of noodle.

Pasta recipes

1 Fresh egg pasta dough

Ingredient	4 portions	10 portions
Pasta flour	175 g	350 g
Whole eggs	1	2
Egg yolks	3	6

Energy	Cals	Fat	Sat fat	Carb	Sugar	Protein	Fibre
1,672 kJ	400 kcal	17.2 g	9.4 g	50.0 g	10.2 g	11.8 g	4.0 g

This is an alternative method to the one given earlier in the chapter.

1. Place all the ingredients into a food processor and mix quickly until a wet crumb mix appears; this should take no more than 30–45 seconds.
2. Tip the mix out on to a clean surface; this is where the working of the pasta begins. Knead it lightly.
3. The pasta dough may feel wet at this stage, however the working of the gluten will take the moisture back into the dry mass, leaving a velvety-smooth finish that is malleable and easy to work; most of this process should be carried out using a pasta machine.
4. Rest the dough for 30 minutes and then it is ready to use.
5. For a classic noodle shape, roll out to a thin rectangle 45 × 15 cm. Cut into 0.5 cm strips. Leave to dry.

> **Professional tip**
> - Do not knead the dough too much or it will become tough.
> - Let it rest before rolling it out.
> - The best way to roll out pasta dough to the correct thickness is to use a pasta machine.

Combine the ingredients into a wet crumb mix

Work and roll out the pasta using a pasta machine

A pasta machine with an attachment can be used to cut noodles

Pasta and noodles 8

2 Spaghetti with tomato sauce (*spaghetti pomodoro*)

1. Plunge the spaghetti into a saucepan containing boiling salted water. Allow to boil gently.
2. Stir occasionally with a wooden spoon. Cook for approximately 12–15 minutes, until *al dente*.
3. Drain well in a colander. Return to a clean, dry pan.
4. Mix in the butter and add the tomato sauce. Correct the seasoning.
5. Add the tomato concassé and 4–5 leaves of flat parsley or fresh basil torn into pieces with your fingers, and serve with grated cheese.

Professional tip

Cook pasta to an *al dente* texture.

Healthy eating tips

- Use very little or no salt as there is already plenty from the cheese.
- Reduce or omit the butter and serve with a large green salad.

Ingredient	4 portions	10 portions
Spaghetti	400 g	1 kg
Butter (optional) or olive oil	25 g	60 g
Tomato sauce (page 128)	250 ml	625 ml
Salt, mill pepper		
Tomato concassée, to serve		
Fresh basil or flat parsley, to serve		
Grated cheese, to serve		

Energy	Cals	Fat	Sat fat	Carb	Sugar	Protein	Fibre	Sodium
2,316 kJ	551 kcal	19.9 g	6.7 g	75.0 g	5.5 g	17.9 g	5.0 g	0.5 g

Using olive oil.

Place the spaghetti into boiling water

Drain the cooked pasta

Add the sauce to the pasta

3 Spaghetti bolognaise (*spaghetti alla bolognese*)

Ingredient	4 portions	10 portions
Butter or oil	20 g	50 g
Onion, chopped	50 g	125 g
Clove of garlic, chopped	1	2
Lean minced beef or tail end fillet, cut into 3 mm dice	400 g	1 kg
Jus-lié	125 ml	300 ml
Tomato purée	1 tbsp	2½ tbsp
Marjoram or oregano	Pinch	½ tsp
Mushrooms, diced	100 g	250 g
Salt, mill pepper		
Spaghetti	400 g	1 kg
Grated cheese, to serve		

Energy	Cals	Fat	Sat fat	Carb	Sugar	Protein	Fibre	Sodium
2,594 kJ	616 kcal	18.2 g	7.5 g	73.0 g	5.3 g	40.0 g	5.0 g	0.6 g

Using olive oil, and beef stock in place of the *jus-lié*.

1. Place half the butter or oil in a sauteuse.
2. Add the chopped onion and garlic, and cook for 4–5 minutes without colour.
3. Add the beef and cook, colouring lightly.
4. Add the *jus-lié*, the tomato purée and the herbs.
5. Simmer until tender.
6. Add the mushrooms and simmer for 5 minutes. Correct the seasoning.
7. Meanwhile, cook the spaghetti in plenty of boiling salted water.
8. Allow to boil gently, stirring occasionally with a wooden spoon.
9. Cook for approximately 12–15 minutes. Drain well in a colander.
10. Return to a clean pan containing the rest of the butter or oil (optional).
11. Correct the seasoning.
12. Serve with the sauce in centre of the spaghetti.
13. Serve grated cheese separately.

Variation

There are many variations on bolognaise sauce, e.g. substitute lean beef with pork mince or use a combination of both; add 50 g each of chopped carrot and celery; add 100 g chopped pancetta or bacon.

Healthy eating tips

- Use an unsaturated oil (sunflower or olive). Lightly oil the pan and drain off any excess after the frying is complete. Skim the fat from the finished dish.
- Season with the minimum amount of salt.
- Try using more pasta and extending the sauce with tomatoes.
- Serve with a large green salad.

Alternative recipe for bolognaise sauce

Ingredient	4 portions	10 portions
Olive oil	1 tbsp	2½ tbsp
Beef mince and pork mince	270 g	700 g
Onion, chopped	½	1
Mushrooms, sliced	100 g	250 g
Carrots, peeled and cut as for paysanne	1	2
Red wine	75 ml	180 ml
Beef stock or meat stock, reduced	100 ml	250 ml
Tomato purée	1 tbsp	2 tbsp
Tabasco sauce (optional)	½ tsp	1 tsp
Salt and freshly ground black pepper, to taste		
Fresh parsley, chopped	2 tbsp	5 tbsp
Fresh chives, chopped, to garnish		

1. Heat the olive oil in a frying pan, over a medium heat.
2. Add the beef and pork mince and the chopped onion and pan-fry for 4–6 minutes, stirring well, until the mince has browned and the onion has softened.
3. Add the mushrooms and carrots and cook for a further minute before adding the red wine, beef stock and tomato purée.
4. Add the Tabasco sauce and season to taste (optional).
5. Add the chopped parsley and cook for 2–4 minutes more to allow the wine and stock to reduce a little.
6. When mixing the pasta into the sauce, first drain the water thoroughly from the pasta then place into the bolognaise sauce.
7. Toss well, to evenly coat, then spoon into a serving bowl.
8. Garnish with the chopped chives, to serve (optional).

4 Penne arrabiata

Ingredient	4 portions	10 portions
Extra virgin olive oil	90 ml	225 ml
Onion, chopped	1	2½
Medium hot chillies, finely chopped	2	5
Cloves of garlic, chopped	1	2
Bacon lardons	100 g	250 g
Canned chopped plum tomatoes	600 g	1.5 kg
Tomato purée	1 tbsp	2½ tbsp
Salt, to taste		
Fresh/dried penne rigate pasta	400 g	1 kg
Basil leaves, shredded	5	12
Parmesan shavings, to serve		

Energy	Cals	Fat	Sat fat	Carb	Sugar	Protein	Fibre
2,263 kJ	539 kcal	24.1 g	4.4 g	65.7 g	10.2 g	19.3 g	2.8 g

1. Gently heat the olive oil in a frying pan. Add the onion, chilli and garlic and fry while stirring for one minute. Add the lardons and cook until golden.
2. Add the chopped tomatoes and tomato purée to the frying pan and simmer for 10–15 minutes, until the sauce has thickened a little. Season with salt to taste.
3. While the sauce is cooking, cook the pasta in large saucepan of boiling, salted water until *al dente* (fresh pasta will cook much more quickly than dried pasta). Drain the pasta and drizzle it with oil.
4. Add the basil to the sauce. Mix in the drained pasta.
5. Serve with shavings of Parmesan.

5 Ravioli

Ingredient	4 portions	10 portions
Flour	200 g	500 g
Salt		
Olive oil	35 ml	150 ml
Water	100 ml	250 ml

Energy	Cals	Fat	Sat fat	Carb	Sugar	Protein	Fibre
1,027 kJ	249 kcal	9.4 g	1.4 g	38.9 g	0.8 g	4.8 g	1.6 g

1. Sieve the flour and salt. Make a well. Add the liquid.
2. Knead to a smooth dough. Rest for at least 30 minutes in a cool place.
3. Roll out to a very thin oblong: 30 cm × 45 cm.
4. Cut in half and egg wash.
5. Place the stuffing in a piping bag with a large plain tube.
6. Pipe out the filling in small pieces, each about the size of a cherry, approximately 4 cm apart, on to one half of the paste.
7. Carefully cover with the other half of the paste and seal, taking care to avoid air pockets.
8. Mark each with the back of a plain cutter.
9. Cut in between each line of filling, down and across with a serrated pastry wheel.
10. Separate on a well-floured tray.
11. Poach in gently boiling salted water for approximately 10 minutes. Drain well.
12. Place in an earthenware serving dish.
13. Cover with 250 ml *jus-lié*, demi-glace or tomato sauce.
14. Sprinkle with 50 g grated cheese.
15. Brown under the salamander and serve.

Fresh egg pasta dough can also be used. If you have prepared the dough, start this recipe at step 3.
The photo shows ravioli stuffed with spinach and ricotta cheese, then poached. The ravioli has been drizzled with olive oil and garnished with micro herbs and slices of Parmesan.

Possible fillings

Here are some examples of stuffing for ravioli, tortellini and other pastas. Each recipe provides enough stuffing to use with 400 g of pasta.

Fish	
Fish, chopped, cooked	200 g
Mushrooms, chopped, cooked	100 g
Parsley, chopped	
Anchovy paste	

Spinach and ricotta	
Dry spinach, cooked, puréed	200 g
Ricotta cheese	200 g
Butter	25 g
Nutmeg	
Salt and pepper	

Pork and veal	
Lean pork mince, cooked	200 g
Lean veal mince, cooked	200 g
Butter	25 g
Cheese, grated	25 g
2 yolks or 1 egg	
Fresh white breadcrumbs	25 g
Salt and pepper	

Pasta and noodles

Ricotta and Parmesan	
Marjoram, chopped	Pinch
Ricotta cheese	150 g
Parmesan, grated	75 g
Egg	1
Nutmeg	
Salt and pepper	

Chicken	
Chicken, cooked, minced	200 g
Ham, minced	100 g
Butter	25 g
2 yolks or 1 egg	
Cheese, grated	25 g
Nutmeg, grated	pinch
Salt and pepper	
Fresh white breadcrumbs	25 g

Beef	
Beef or pork mince, cooked	200 g
Spinach, cooked	100 g
Onion, chopped, cooked	50 g
Oregano	
Salt and pepper	

6 Macaroni cheese

1. Plunge the macaroni into a saucepan containing plenty of boiling salted water.
2. Allow to boil gently and stir occasionally with a wooden spoon.
3. Cook for approximately 15 minutes and drain well in a colander.
4. Return to a clean pan containing the butter.
5. Mix with half the cheese and add the béchamel and mustard. Season.
6. Place in an earthenware dish and sprinkle with the remainder of the cheese.
7. Brown lightly under the salamander and serve.

Browning the macaroni well gives it a good flavour, texture and presentation.

Ingredient	4 portions	10 portions
Macaroni	400 g	1 kg
Butter or oil, optional	25 g	60 g
Grated cheese	100 g	250 g
Thin béchamel sauce	500 ml	1.25 litres
Diluted English or continental mustard	¼ tsp	1 tsp
Salt, mill pepper		

Energy	Cals	Fat	Sat fat	Carb	Sugar	Protein	Fibre	Sodium
2,748 kJ	654 kcal	26.7 g	12.6 g	81.0 g	6.9 g	22.2 g	4.2 g	0.5 g

Using olive oil.

Healthy eating tips
- Half the grated cheese could be replaced with a small amount of Parmesan (more flavour and less fat).
- Use semi-skimmed milk for the béchamel. No added salt is necessary.

Variation
Variations include the addition of cooked, sliced mushrooms, diced ham, sweetcorn, tomato, and so on. Macaroni may also be prepared and served as for any of the spaghetti dishes.

7 Spinach fettuccine with ham and cream cheese (fettuccine verde con salsa cremona)

Ingredient	4 portions	10 portions
Spinach fettuccine or other pasta	400 g	1 kg
Cream cheese, mashed	200 g	500 g
Single cream	2 tbsp	5 tbsp
Parmesan cheese, grated	50 g	125 g
Salt and pepper		
Butter, melted	50 g	125 g
Lean cooked ham, cut into thick julienne	100 g	250 g

Energy	Cals	Fat	Sat fat	Carb	Sugar	Protein	Fibre
3,183 kJ	760 kcal	42.2 g	25.4 g	76.3 g	2.7 g	23.7 g	3.1 g

1. Cook the fettuccine in plenty of boiling salted water.
2. Mix the cream cheese, cream and Parmesan, and season with salt and pepper.
3. Drain the fettuccine and return it to the pan.
4. Mix in the butter and cream cheese mixture. Add the ham. Toss and serve.

Healthy eating tips
- This sauce is high in fat and salt, so additional butter and salt is not necessary.
- For a lower-fat version, use a 'light' cream cheese.
- Serve with a large green salad.

8 Tagliatelle carbonara

Ingredient	4 portions	10 portions
Tagliatelle	300 g	750 g
Olive oil	1 tbsp	2½ tbsp
Cloves of garlic, peeled and crushed	2	5
Smoked bacon, diced	200 g	500 g
Eggs	4	10
Double or single cream	4 tbsp	150 ml
Parmesan cheese	4 tbsp	150 ml

Energy	Cals	Fat	Sat fat	Carb	Sugar	Protein	Fibre	Sodium
2,911 kJ	698 kcal	44.8 g	20.8 g	43.0 g	1.9 g	33.4 g	0.2 g	1.0 g

1. Cook the tagliatelle in boiling salted water until *al dente*. Refresh and drain.
2. Heat the oil in a suitable pan. Fry the crushed and chopped garlic. Add the diced, smoked bacon.
3. Mix together the beaten eggs, cream and Parmesan. Season with black pepper.
4. Add the tagliatelle to the garlic and bacon. Add the eggs and cream, stirring until the eggs cook in the heat. Serve immediately.

9 Ravioli of squash and spinach with wild mushroom sauce

For the ravioli

1 Peel the butternut squash, remove the seeds and chop the flesh roughly.
2 Cook the squash in the butter with the salt over a medium heat until soft.
3 Add the spinach and cook for a further minute.
4 Drain off the butter and chill the mixture until firm.
5 Once the mixture is firm, roll out and cut into 1 cm pieces.
6 Roll the pasta dough and make the ravioli to the required shape.
7 Place on a floured tray and reserve until required.

For the sauce

1 Sweat down the onions, fresh mushrooms, garlic and herbs in the butter for 10 minutes.
2 Add the dried cep and sweat for a further 5 minutes.
3 Add the Noilly Prat and reduce completely.
4 Add the vegetable stock and reduce by three-quarters.
5 Add the cream and bring to the boil. Remove the thyme and bay leaf.
6 Blitz the sauce until smooth, season and reserve until required.

To serve

1 Blanch the ravioli in simmering, salted water for 3 minutes.
2 Heat the sauce gently in a pan. Drain the ravioli and add to the sauce.
3 Garnish with the squash (reheated in the oven).
4 Finish with chopped chives and serve as required.

Ingredient	4 portions	10 portions
Squash and spinach ravioli		
Butternut squash	500 g	1.25 kg
Butter	100 g	250 g
Salt	10 g	25 g
Spinach	250 g	625 g
Pasta dough	400 g	1 kg
Wild mushroom sauce		
Onions, finely sliced	50 g	125 g
Button mushrooms, finely sliced	75 g	185 g
Wild mushrooms, sliced	60 g	150 g
Clove of garlic	½	1
Bay leaf	1	2
Sprig of thyme	1	2
Butter	10 g	25 g
Dried cep	5 g	12 g
Noilly Prat (dry vermouth)	75 g	185 g
Vegetable stock	200 ml	500 ml
Single cream	100 g	250 g
Salt and pepper		
Chives, chopped		

Energy	Cals	Fat	Sat fat	Carb	Sugar	Protein	Fibre	Sodium
2,469 kJ	590 kcal	30.8 g	17.6 g	62.0 g	6.6 g	15.8 g	4.2 g	1.3 g

Practical Cookery 14th edition

10 Lasagne

Ingredient	4 portions	10 portions
Lasagne sheets	200 g	500 g
Oil	1 tbsp	2½ tbsp
Streaky bacon, thin strips of	50 g	125 g
Onion, chopped	100 g	250 g
Carrot, chopped	50 g	125 g
Celery, chopped	50 g	125 g
Minced beef	200 g	500 g
Tomato purée	1 tbsp	2½ tbsp
Jus-lié or demi-glace	375 ml	1 litre
Clove of garlic	1	2½
Salt, pepper		
Marjoram	½ tsp	1½ tsp
Mushrooms, sliced	100 g	250 g
Béchamel sauce	250 ml	600 ml
Parmesan or Cheddar cheese, grated	25 g	125 g

Energy	Cals	Fat	Sat fat	Carb	Sugar	Protein	Fibre
2,416 kJ	575 kcal	28.7 g	11.4 g	56.1 g	10.0 g	26.7 g	5.8 g

1 Prepare the fresh egg pasta dough and roll out to 1 mm thick.
2 Cut into 6 cm squares.
3 Allow to rest in a cool place and dry slightly on a cloth dusted with flour.
4 Whether using fresh or ready-bought lasagne, cook in gently simmering salted water for approximately 3 minutes (fresh pasta) or 10 minutes (dried).
5 Refresh in cold water, then drain on a cloth.
6 Gently heat the oil in a thick-bottomed pan, add the bacon and cook for 2–3 minutes.
7 Add the onion, carrot and celery, cover the pan with a lid and cook for 5 minutes.
8 Add the minced beef, increase the heat and stir until lightly brown.
9 Remove from the heat and mix in the tomato purée.
10 Return to the heat, mix in the *jus-lié* or demi-glace, stir to boil.
11 Add the garlic, salt, pepper and marjoram, and simmer for 15 minutes. Remove the garlic.
12 Mix in the mushrooms, reboil for 2 minutes, then remove from the heat.
13 Butter an ovenproof dish and cover the bottom with a layer of the meat sauce.
14 Add a layer of lasagne and cover with meat sauce.
15 Add another layer of lasagne and cover with the remainder of the meat sauce.
16 Cover with the béchamel.
17 Sprinkle with cheese, cover with a lid and place in a moderately hot oven at 190 °C for approximately 20 minutes.
18 Remove the lid, cook for a further 15 minutes and serve in the cleaned ovenproof dish.

Note

This recipe can be made using 200 g of ready-bought lasagne or it can be prepared fresh using 200 g flour noodle paste. Wholemeal lasagne can be made using noodle paste made with 100 g wholemeal flour and 100 g strong flour.

Pasta and noodles   8

Brown the minced beef in a thick-bottomed pan

Place a layer of lasagne over a layer of meat sauce

Cover the final layer with béchamel

Variation

Traditionally, pasta dishes are substantial in quantity but because they are so popular they are also sometimes requested as lighter dishes. Obviously the portion size can be reduced but other variations can also be considered.

For example, freshly made pasta cut into 8–10 cm rounds or squares, rectangles or diamonds, lightly poached or steamed, well drained and placed on a light tasty mixture (e.g. a tablespoon of mousse of chicken or fish or shellfish, well-cooked dried spinach flavoured with toasted pine nuts and grated nutmeg or a duxelle mixture) using just the one piece of pasta on top or a piece top and bottom. A light sauce should be used (e.g. a measure of well-reduced chicken stock with a little skimmed milk, blitzed to a froth just before serving, pesto sauce, a drizzle of good-quality olive oil, or a light tomato sauce). The dish can be finished with a suitable garnish (e.g. lightly fried wild or cultivated sliced mushrooms).

Fillings for lasagne can be varied in many ways. Tomato sauce may be used instead of *jus-lié*.

Healthy eating tips

- Use an unsaturated oil (sunflower or olive). Lightly oil the pan and drain off any excess after the frying is complete. Skim the fat from the finished meat sauce.
- Season with the minimum amount of salt.
- The fat content can be proportionally reduced by increasing the ratio of pasta to sauce and thinning the béchamel.

Practical Cookery 14th edition

11 Vegetarian lasagne

1. Cook the lasagne sheets in boiling, salted water until *al dente*; refresh and drain.
2. Heat half the oil and sweat the onion and garlic.
3. Add the mushrooms and continue to cook without colour. Season.
4. Heat the remaining oil in a sauteuse, add the courgettes and lightly fry; sprinkle with the oregano. Cook until crisp, then add the tomatoes and tomato purée.
5. Add the broccoli and carrots, then mix in the pine kernels.
6. Make a cheese sauce using the béchamel and half the grated cheese; finish with the natural yoghurt.
7. Grease a suitable ovenproof dish well with the sunflower oil and place a layer of lasagne in the bottom.
8. Cover with a layer of mushrooms, then a layer of lasagne, then the broccoli and tomato mixture, then lasagne, then cheese sauce. Continue to do this, finishing with a layer of cheese sauce on the top.
9. Sprinkle with the remaining grated Parmesan.
10. Bake in a preheated oven at 180 °C for 20–25 minutes.

Ingredient	4 portions	10 portions
Sheets of lasagne	10	30
Sunflower oil	125 ml	300 ml
Onions, finely chopped	100 g	250 g
Cloves of garlic, chopped	2	5
Mushrooms, sliced	200 g	500 g
Salt and pepper		
Medium-sized courgettes, cut into 1 cm dice	2	5
Oregano	3 g	9 g
Tomatoes, skinned, deseeded and diced	200 g	500 g
Tomato purée	2 tbsp	5 tbsp
Broccoli, cut into small florets, blanched and refreshed	300 g	750 g
Carrots, cut into 0.5 cm dice, blanched and refreshed	100 g	250 g
Pine nuts	25 g	60 g
Béchamel sauce	250 ml	625 ml
Parmesan cheese, grated	50 g	125 g
Natural yoghurt	250 ml	625 ml

Healthy eating tips
- Try using a mixture of white and green lasagne.
- Use as little oil as possible to sweat the onion.
- Make the béchamel with semi-skimmed milk.
- No added salt is needed.

Energy	Cals	Fat	Sat fat	Carb	Sugar	Protein	Fibre
2,993 kJ	713 kcal	46.2 g	8.5 g	54.6 g	16.5 g	22.9 g	11.8 g

12 Ricotta and spinach cannelloni with tomato and basil sauce

1. Preheat the oven to 190 °C.
2. Cook the lasagne sheets in a large pan of boiling, salted water for the time stated on the packaging. Refresh immediately in ice-cold water.
3. Pick the spinach to de-branch it. Blanch by plunging it into rapidly boiling water for 20 seconds before refreshing it in ice-cold water.
4. Drain the spinach and squeeze out the excess water, then chop roughly.
5. Beat the ricotta with a spoon until soft, stir in the spinach and season well with salt and pepper.
6. Using a piping bag, pipe the ricotta mixture down one side of each lasagne sheet and roll it up to form a filled tube. Cover and chill in a refrigerator.
7. Place the cannelloni into a lightly oiled baking dish.
8. Pour the tomato sauce over the prepared cannelloni, and sprinkle with freshly shredded basil and the grated Parmesan.
9. Bake at 190 °C for 20 minutes and serve.

Ingredient	4 portions	10 portions
Dried plain or spinach lasagne sheets	12	30
Fresh spinach	350 g	850 g
Ricotta cheese	200 g	500 g
Salt and pepper		
Tomato sauce (page 128)	200 ml	500 ml
Basil, shredded	1 tbsp	2 tbsp
Parmesan cheese, grated	50 g	125 g

Energy	Cals	Fat	Sat fat	Carb	Sugar	Protein	Fibre	Sodium
1,913 kJ	454 kcal	14.6 g	6.3 g	61.0 g	6.5 g	23.8 g	3.1 g	0.3 g

De-branch the spinach

Stir the chopped spinach into the beaten ricotta

Pipe the ricotta mixture down one side of the lasagne sheet

Carefully lift the edge of the sheet with a knife, then roll the cannelloni by hand

Gnocchi recipes

13 Potato gnocchi (*gnocchi piemontese*)

1. Bake or boil the potatoes in their jackets.
2. Remove the skins and mash with a fork or pass through a sieve.
3. Mix with the flour, egg, butter and seasoning while hot.
4. Mould into balls the size of walnuts.
5. Dust well with flour and flatten slightly with a fork.
6. Poach in gently boiling water until they rise to the surface. Drain carefully.
7. Dress in a buttered earthenware dish, cover with tomato or any other pasta sauce.
8. Sprinkle with grated cheese, brown lightly under the salamander and serve.

Ingredient	4 portions	10 portions
Potatoes	300 g	1 kg
Flour, white or wholemeal	100 g	250 g
Egg and egg yolk, beaten	1	2
Butter	25 g	60 g
Salt and pepper		
Nutmeg, grated		
Tomato sauce (page 128)	250 ml	625 ml
Grated cheese, to serve		

Healthy eating tips

No added salt is necessary.

Energy	Cals	Fat	Sat fat	Carb	Sugar	Protein	Fibre
1,045 kJ	248 kcal	9.7 g	4.7 g	35.2 g	2.1 g	7.2 g	2.1 g

Using white flour.

Ingredients for gnocchi

Combine the mashed potato with the other ingredients while hot

Mould the mixture into balls, then flatten with a fork

Drop the gnocchi into gently boiling water and poach them

14 Parmesan gnocchi and tomato sauce

Ingredient	4 portions	10 portions
Parmesan gnocchi		
Desiree potatoes, cooked	350 g	875 g
Parmesan cheese	75 g	185 g
Egg yolks	2	5
Butter	10 g	25 g
Salt and pepper		
Pasta flour	125 g	300 g
Tomato sauce		
Carrot	75 g	185 g
Celery	20 g	50 g
Butter	25 g	60 g
Vegetable oil	25 g	60 g
Clove of garlic	½	1
Sprig of thyme	1	2
Juniper berries	1	2
Bay leaf	1	2
Plum tomatoes	200 g	500 g
Tomato purée	10 g	25 g
Vegetable stock	500 ml	1.25 litres
Cream	25 g	60 g
Sherry vinegar, to taste		
Fresh herbs, e.g. basil, and Parmesan to finish		

Energy	Cals	Fat	Sat fat	Carb	Sugar	Protein	Fibre	Sodium
1814 kJ	433 kcal	25.0 g	11.1 g	41.0 g	6.4 g	14.7 g	4.0 g	0.7 g

Excluding juniper berries; using ¼ tsp sherry vinegar and 10 g shaved Parmesan to garnish per 4 portions.

For the Parmesan gnocchi:
1. Place the potatoes in an oven at 180 °C for 1 hour.
2. Grate the Parmesan using a fine grater.
3. Discard the potato skins and pass the cooked potato through a drum sieve.
4. Add the Parmesan, egg yolks, butter and seasoning.
5. Mix until smooth but do not overwork.
6. Incorporate the flour until it is all absorbed.
7. Wrap the dough in cling film and allow to rest for 30 minutes.
8. Roll and shape into 1 cm pieces.
9. Blanch the gnocchi in simmering water until they float.
10. Refresh the gnocchi and reserve until required.

For the tomato sauce:
1. Cut the carrot and celery into small pieces.
2. Heat the butter and oil in a pan, sweat down the carrot and celery with the garlic, thyme, juniper berries and bay leaf for 10 minutes.
3. Roughly chop the tomatoes and add to the pan with the tomato purée. Cook for 15 minutes.
4. Add the vegetable stock and reduce by half.
5. Add the cream and reduce by half.
6. Remove the bay leaf and thyme, add the sherry vinegar, then blitz until smooth.
7. Reserve until required.

To finish:
1. Gently sauté the gnocchi in a little oil, and warm the sauce gently.
2. Combine the two together and finish with fresh herbs and shaved Parmesan.

9 Fish and shellfish

Recipes included in this chapter

No.	Recipe	Page
	Grilled fish dishes	
1	Grilled tuna, rocket and fennel salad	211
2	Grilled fillets of sole, plaice or haddock	212
3	Whole grilled mackerel with tomatoes, basil and shaved fennel	212
4	Whole sole grilled with traditional accompaniments	213
5	Sardines with tapenade	214
	Poached fish dishes	
6	Poached salmon	215
7	Poached smoked haddock	215
8	Poached turbot, brill, halibut or cod (on the bone)	216
9	Délice of flat white fish Dugléré	217
10	Fillets of fish in white wine sauce (filets de poisson vin blanc)	218
11	Fillets of fish mornay (filets de poisson mornay)	219
12	Fillets of fish Véronique	220
13	Fish kedgeree	221
	Baked fish dishes	
14	Baked cod with a herb crust	222
15	Baked hake with tomatoes and olives	223
16	Cod boulangère	224
17	Fish pie	225
	Steamed fish dishes	
18	Salmon en papillote with crushed new potatoes	226
19	Steamed fish with garlic, spring onions and ginger	227
20	Steamed halibut with lime and fennel	228
21	Steamed clams in saffron and spring green broth	229
	Deep-fried fish dishes	
22	Frying batters (pâtes à frire) for fish	230
23	Fried fish in batter	231
24	Deep-fried fish coated with breadcrumbs	231
25	Goujons of plaice	232
26	Salmon fishcakes	232
	Shallow-fried fish dishes	
27	Shallow-fried fish	234
28	Shallow-fried sole with shrimp and caper dressing	235
29	Fish meunière	236
30	Pan-fried fillets of sole with rocket and broad beans	237
31	Pan-fried skate with capers and beurre noir	238
32	Nage of red mullet with baby leeks	239
33	Barramundi with garlic, ginger and lemon butter and pak choi	240
34	Thai fishcakes	241
	Boiled shellfish dishes	
35	Mussels in white wine sauce (moules marinière)	242
36	Clam chowder	243
	Fried shellfish dishes	
37	Crab cakes with chilli lime dipping sauce	244
38	Prawns with chilli and garlic	245
	Grilled shellfish dishes	
39	Scallops and bacon	246
	Cold fish and shellfish dishes	
40	Dressed crab	247
41	Smoked salmon	248
42	Oysters	248
43	Cold salmon	249
44	Fish salad (salade de poisson)	250
45	Sea bass ceviche	251
46	Soused herring and mackerel	252
47	Crab, lobster or prawn cocktail (cocktail de crabe, homard, crevettes, crevettes roses)	252
48	Potted shrimps	253
49	Fruits de mer	254

Fish

Types and varieties

Fish are vertebrates (animals with a backbone) and are split into two primary groups: **flat** and **round** fish. From this they can be split again into subgroups or secondary groups:

192

- **Oily fish** have bodies that are round in shape and include herring, mackerel, salmon, tuna and sardines. They are **pelagic** fish, which means that they are found midwater.
- **White fish** can be round, such as cod, whiting, hake, pollock and sea bass, or flat, such as plaice, sole and turbot. They are **demersal** fish, which means that they are found at or near the bottom of the sea.
- **Shellfish**.

Many people choose to eat fish in preference to meat because of health considerations and, consequently, consumption of fish has been steadily increasing. This popularity has resulted in a far greater selection becoming available and, due to swift and efficient transport, well over 200 types of fish are on sale throughout the year.

Fish is plentiful in the UK because it is surrounded by water, although overfishing and pollution are having a detrimental effect on supplies of certain fish. Most catches are made off Iceland or Scotland, in the North Sea, Irish Sea and the English Channel. Salmon are caught in certain English and Scottish rivers, and are also extensively farmed. Frozen fish is imported from Scandinavia, Canada and Japan, and other countries worldwide; Canada and Japan both export frozen salmon to Britain.

Unfortunately, due to overfishing, the supply of fish is not unlimited and it is now necessary to have fish farms (such as those for trout and salmon, turbot, bass and cod) to supplement natural sources. This is not the only problem: due to contamination by humans and industry, seas and rivers are becoming increasingly polluted, affecting both the supply and the suitability of fish – particularly shellfish – for human consumption.

Quality points when choosing and buying fish

Fresh fish can be bought by the kilogram, number of fillets or number of whole fish of the weight that is required. For example, 30 kg of salmon could be ordered as 2 × 15 kg, 3 × 10 kg or 6 × 5 kg, the number of whole fish, or portions such as fillets, suprêmes or darnes. Frozen fish can be purchased whole (gutted), filleted, cut or prepared in a wide variety of different ways. The checklists below summarise the main points to look for when choosing and buying fish.

Whole fish
These should have:
- clear, bright eyes, not sunken
- bright red gills
- no missing scales; scales should be firmly attached to the skin
- moist skin (fresh fish feels slightly slippery)
- shiny skin with bright natural colouring
- a stiff tail
- firm flesh
- a fresh sea smell and no trace of ammonia smell.

Fish fillets
These should be:
- neatly trimmed with firm flesh
- firm and closely packed together, not ragged or gaping
- a translucent white colour if they are from a white fish, with no discoloration.

Smoked fish
These should have:
- a glossy appearance
- firm flesh and not sticky
- a pleasant, smoky smell.

Frozen fish
This should:
- be frozen hard with no signs of thawing
- be in packaging that is not damaged
- show no evidence of freezer burn (this shows as dull, white, dry patches).

Seasonality
The quality of fish can vary due to local climatic and environmental conditions. Generally, all fish spawn over a period of four to six weeks. During spawning, they use up a lot of their reserves of fat and protein in the production of eggs. This has the effect of making their flesh watery and soft. Fish in this condition are termed 'spent fish'. This takes anything between one and two months, depending on local environmental conditions. Imported and frozen fish is available all year.

Availability
Naturally, prevailing weather conditions have an enormous bearing on fishing activities. The full range of species may not always be available during stormy weather, for instance.

Dealing with problems with fish
If you find there are problems with fish or shellfish and they are not of the quality, quantity, cut or type required, inform a supervisor or head chef immediately.

Practical Cookery 14th edition

Table 9.1 Seasonality of fish

	JAN	FEB	MAR	APR	MAY	JUN	JUL	AUG	SEP	OCT	NOV	DEC
Bream	●	●	●	●	○	○	○	●	●	●	●	●
Brill	●	●	●	●	○	●	●	●	●	●	●	●
Cod	●	●	○	○	●	●	●	●	●	●	●	●
Eel						●	●	●	●	●	●	
Grey mullet	●	●	○	○	●	●	●	●	●	●	●	●
Gurnard	●	●	●	●	●	●	●	●	●	●	●	●
Haddock	●	●	●	●	●	●	●	●	●	●	●	●
Hake	●	●	○	○	○	●	●	●	●	●	●	●
Halibut	●	●	●	○	○	●	●	●	●	●	●	●
Herring	●	●	●	●	●	●	●	●	●	●	●	●
John Dory	●	●	●	●	●	●	●	●	●	●	●	●
Mackerel	●	●	○	○	●	●	●	●	●	●	●	●
Monkfish	●	●	●	●	●	●	●	●	●	●	●	●
Plaice	●	●	○	○	●	●	●	●	●	●	●	●
Red mullet			●	●	●	●	●	●	●	●	●	
Salmon (farmed)	●	●	●	●	●	●	●	●	●	●	●	●
Salmon (wild)					●	●	●	●	●			
Sardines	●	●	●	●	●			●	●	●	●	●
Sea bass	●	●	●	●	○	○	●	●	●	●	●	●
Sea trout					●	●	●	●	○	○	○	
Skate	●	●				●	●	●	●	●	●	●
Squid	●								●	●	●	●
Sole (Dover)	○	●	●						●	●	●	●
Sole (lemon)	●	●	●	●	●	●	●	●				
Trout						●	●	●	●	●	●	●
Tuna	●	●	●	●	●	●	●	●	●	●	●	●
Turbot	●	●	●	○	○	○	●	●	●	●	●	●
Whiting	●	●								●	●	●

Key:
- Available ● (darker)
- At best ● (lighter)
- ○ Spawning and roeing – this can deprive the flesh of nutrients and will decrease the yield.

This applies when checking deliveries or when you are about to use fish already in storage.

Storing fish

Once caught, fish has a shelf life of 10 to 12 days if properly refrigerated at a temperature between 0 °C and 4 °C. If the fish is delivered whole with the innards still in the fish, it should be gutted and the cavity washed well before it is stored.

Use the fish as soon as possible after delivery, but it can be stored overnight. Rinse, pat dry, cover with cling film and store in a refrigerator just for fish or at the bottom of a multi-use refrigerator. Make sure the fish is covered or wrapped, labelled and dated. Fish may also be vacuum packed before chilling. For fish products that do not need to be used immediately, use in rotation: this means using older items before the newly delivered items.

Ready-to-eat cooked fish, such as hot-smoked mackerel, cooked prawns and crab, should be stored on shelves above other raw foodstuffs to avoid cross-contamination.

> **Food safety** ⚠
>
> - Store fresh fish on trays covered with cling film and labelled in a refrigerator, preferably at a temperature of 1–2 °C. This also applies to prepared raw fish.
> - To avoid the risk of cross-contamination, fish should be stored in a separate refrigerator away from other foods; cooked and raw fish must be kept separate.
> - Frozen fish should be stored in a freezer at −18 °C. Frozen fish should be defrosted in a deep container, covered with cling film and at the bottom of the refrigerator. Do not defrost at kitchen temperatures.
> - Keep smoked fish well wrapped in a refrigerator to avoid the strong smell permeating other items.
> - Fish offal and bones present a high risk of contamination and must not be mixed or stored with raw prepared fish.

Preservation of fish

Fish deteriorates quickly after it has been caught and over many years ways have been sought to preserve fish for longer. The following are some of the ways that fish (and shellfish) can be preserved.

Freezing

Fish is either frozen at sea or as soon as possible after reaching port. The freezing process should be fast because the longer it takes to freeze, the larger and more angular the ice crystals become, which breaks the protein strands. This results in liquid leaking out when the fish is defrosted, leaving an inferior product. When fish is frozen quickly, the ice crystals are small, and there is less leakage and less damage. Most fish should be defrosted before being cooked but some prepared fish products, such as frozen, breadcrumbed scampi or plaice, can be cooked from frozen. Plaice, halibut, turbot, haddock, pollack, sole, cod, trout, salmon, herring, whiting, scampi, smoked haddock and kippers, as well as a wide range of prepared products, are available frozen.

Frozen fish should be checked for:
- no evidence of freezer burn
- undamaged packaging
- minimum fluid loss during defrosting
- flesh still firm after defrosting.

Frozen fish should be stored at −18 °C to −20 °C and defrosted overnight in a refrigerator. It should *not* be defrosted in water as this spoils the taste and texture of the fish, and valuable water-soluble nutrients are lost. Fish should not be refrozen as this will impair its taste and texture, as well as being a food safety risk.

Canning

It is usually the oily fish that are canned. Sardines, salmon, anchovies, pilchards, tuna, herring and herring roe (eggs) are canned in either their own juice (e.g. salmon), in oil, a sauce, brine or spring water. In some countries bottling is popular for fish such as herrings; this is a similar process to canning.

Salting

In the UK, the salting of fish is usually accompanied by a smoking process.
- Cured herrings are packed in salt.
- Caviar – the slightly salted roe of the sturgeon – is sieved, canned and refrigerated.

In some Caribbean countries salted dried fish, especially cod, has been popular for many years and this is now available in numerous other countries. It needs to be soaked in plenty of cold water for several hours before use.

Pickling

Herrings pickled in vinegar are filleted, rolled and skewered, and known as rollmops.

Smoking

Fish that is to be smoked may be gutted or left whole. It is then soaked in a strong salt solution (brine) and, in some cases, a dye is added to improve colour. After this, it is drained, hung on racks in a kiln and exposed to smoke for five or six hours.

Smoked fish should be wrapped well and kept separate from other fish to prevent the smell and dye penetrating other foods.

Cold smoking takes place at a temperature of no more than 33 °C (this is to avoid cooking the flesh). Therefore, all cold-smoked fish is raw and is usually cooked before being eaten, the exceptions being smoked salmon and cold-smoked trout.

Hot-smoked fish is cured at a temperature between 70°C and 80°C in order to cook the flesh, so does not require further cooking.

Choose fish with a pleasant smoky smell and a bright glossy surface. The flesh should be firm; sticky or soggy flesh means that the fish may have been of low quality or under smoked. Smoked fish still needs refrigeration or freezing.

Healthy eating tips
Salted, pickled and smoked fish has a high salt content so there is no need to add additional salt when cooking.

Preparation

When preparing fish and shellfish it is important to always select the correct tools and equipment to enable you to work professionally and achieve a good finish. Fish is a delicate product and some, such as fillets of flat white fish, can be very delicate. Choosing your equipment well and handling the fish carefully will help to prevent damage and wastage. Do not over handle the fish and, when prepared, place neatly on a tray, cover and refrigerate until needed. Correct equipment will also allow for safe working practices and reduce the risks of cross-contamination.

Preparation equipment may include: chef's knife, filleting knife, oyster knife, scissors/secateurs, fish tweezers, chopping boards, bowls, trays, spoons and other items as required. Assemble all of your equipment before you start the task.

Unless otherwise stated, as a guide allow 100 g fish off the bone and approximately 200 to 300 g on the bone for a portion (check the recipe).

All fish should be washed under running cold water before and after preparation.

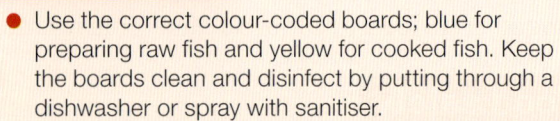

Food safety
- Use the correct colour-coded boards; blue for preparing raw fish and yellow for cooked fish. Keep the boards clean and disinfect by putting through a dishwasher or spray with sanitiser.
- If possible keep other equipment used just for raw fish use. If this is not possible, wash and sanitise equipment before and immediately after each use.
- Unhygienic equipment, utensils and preparation areas increase the risk of cross-contamination.
- Use a dishwasher to clean and disinfect equipment after use and wash hands thoroughly.
- For cleaning, use disposable single-use cloths where possible along with sanitiser.

There are various methods of preparing, cutting and filleting fish and these are described below.

Trimming and scaling
Whole fish are trimmed to remove the scales, fins and head using fish scissors and a knife. If the head is to be left on (as in the case of a salmon for a cold buffet), the gills and the eyes are removed.

Gutting
If the fish needs to be gutted, the following procedure should be used.
1. Cut from the vent to two-thirds along the fish.
2. Draw out the intestines with the fingers or, in the case of a large fish, use the hook handle of a utensil such as a ladle.
3. Ensure that the blood lying along the main bone is removed, then wash and drain thoroughly.
4. If the fish is to be stuffed then it may be gutted by removing the innards through the gill slits, so leaving the stomach skin intact, forming a pouch in which to put the stuffing. When this method is used, care must be taken to ensure that the inside of the fish is clear of all traces of blood.

Fish and shellfish | **9**

Skinning and filleting

The following sequences demonstrate how to prepare and fillet a round or flat fish, and how to skin and prepare a whole Dover sole. These fish have already been gutted and cleaned.

When you fillet a fish, remove the first fillet by cutting along the backbone from head to tail. Then reverse the fish and remove the second fillet by cutting from tail to head.

Coating and marinating

Fish and shellfish can be coated with items such as flour, egg and breadcrumbs (*pane*), milk and flour or batter before cooking. They may also be marinated – placed in a prepared mixture which may include herbs, spices, seasonings, fruit juice or zest, oil, wine and other ingredients – to achieve the required flavour.

Filleting a round fish (salmon)

1. Remove the head and clean thoroughly. 
2. Remove the first fillet by cutting along the backbone from head to tail. Keeping the knife close to the bone, remove the fillet.
3. After both fillets have been removed, remove the rib cavity bones and trim the fish neatly. 

Boning a round fish (trout)

Remove the pin bones from the fillet

197

Filleting a flat fish (turbot)

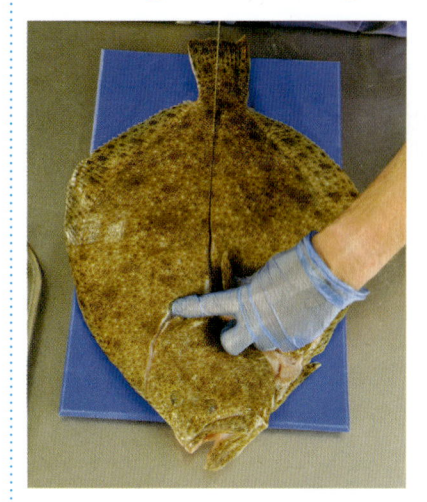

1. Using a filleting knife, make an incision from the head to tail. Cut around the gill and backbone.

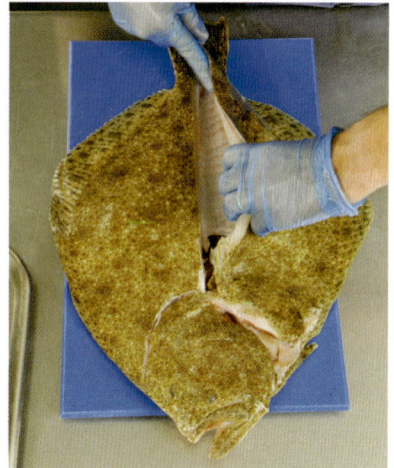

2. Remove the first fillet, holding the knife almost parallel to the work surface and keeping the knife close to the bone.

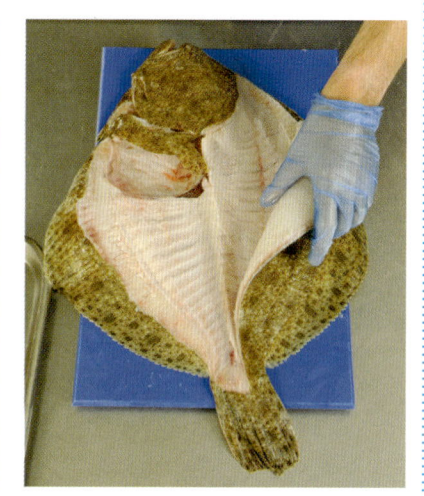

3. Repeat for the second fillet.

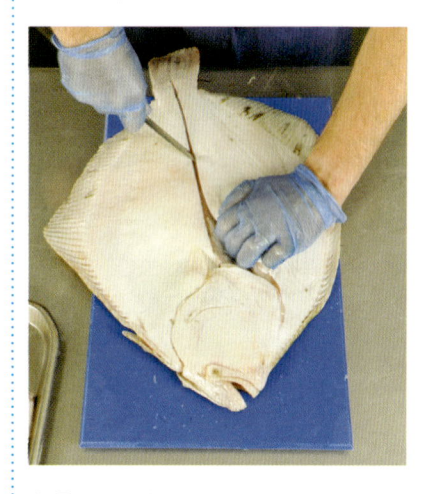

4. Turn the fish over and repeat, removing the last two fillets.

5. Hold the fillet firmly at the tail end. Cut the flesh as close to the tail as possible, as far as the skin. Keep the knife parallel to the work surface, grip the skin firmly and move the knife from side to side to remove the skin.

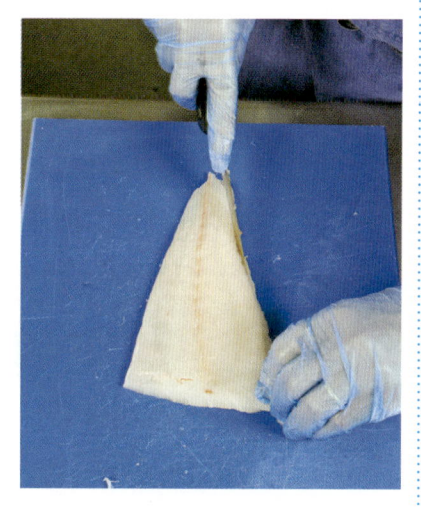

6. Trim the fillets neatly.

Preparing a whole Dover sole

1 Score the skin just above the tail.

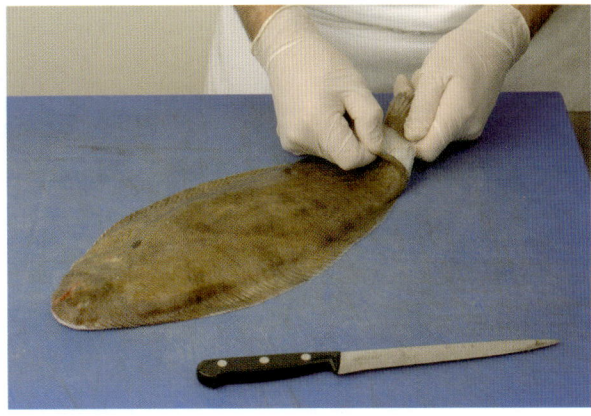

2 Hold the tail firmly, then cut and scrape the skin until sufficient is lifted to be gripped.

3 Pull the skin away from the tail to the head. Both the black and white skins may be removed in this way.

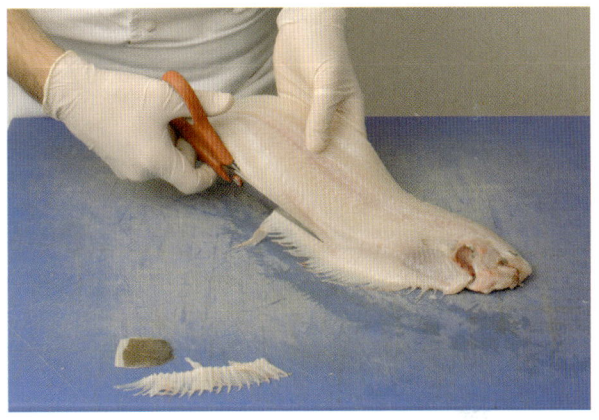

4 Trim the tail and side fins with fish scissors.

5 Remove the eyes. Clean and wash the fish thoroughly. The fish is shown here with all the parts that were removed.

Cuts of fish

Fish may be cut and portioned depending on their size, shape and the menu requirements. The usual fish cuts are:

- **Fillets**: cuts of fish free from bone. There will be two fillets from a round fish (one from each side of the spine) and four from a flat fish (two from each side).
- **Steaks**: thick slices of fish on or off the bone.
- **Darnes**: steaks of round fish (salmon, cod) cut through the bone.
- **Tronçons**: steaks of flat fish (turbot, halibut) cut through the bone. If cut from a large fish, these may then be cut into halves or quarters.
- **Suprêmes**: prime cuts of fish without bone and skin, for example cut from skinless fillets of salmon, turbot or brill.
- **Goujons**: filleted fish cut into strips approximately 8 × 0.5 cm.
- **Délice**: fillets of fish neatly folded with the skinned side facing inwards.
- **Paupiette**: fillets of fish, such as sole, plaice or whiting, spread with a stuffing and rolled.
- **Plaited** (*en tresse*): for example, sole fillets cut into three even pieces lengthwise to within 1 cm of the top, and neatly plaited.

Practical Cookery 14th edition

▲ Cuts of fish: (clockwise from top left) darne, tronçon, fillet, paupiettes, suprême, goujons

Portion control

There are a number of ways that can be used to achieve good portion control with fish, for example:
- specified size and weight of a whole fish, such as trout, sea bass or dover sole per portion
- specified cut sizes of darnes, tronçons and suprêmes used as a portion
- number of fillets from small fish, for example two fillets from a plaice as a portion
- number of shellfish items, for example six king prawns, four scallops or half a lobster making a portion
- number and size of paupiettes or délice offered as a portion
- dividing a fish pie into equal-sized portions
- filling an individual pie dish or serving dish or pastry case
- using a ladle to measure the portion size of a fish stew or soup.

> **Professional tip**
>
> The fish or shellfish dish you cook needs to meet the dish requirements as required by your supervisor or head chef. It must also meet the requirements and descriptions on the menu (this is a legal requirement). So if the menu says Dover sole you cannot use lemon sole instead unless you change the menu. You must also meet cooking method requirements, when a menu states grilled fish it must be grilled not oven baked. The customer too will have expectations of the dish you are preparing and cooking, and it is important to achieve the required quality to meet those expectations.

Cooking methods

The texture of various fish and shellfish varies greatly: some are very fragile and can break easily when cooking, so handle carefully and choose a suitable cooking method. For example, plaice fillets are very soft and delicate so are not suitable for stewing or roasting. Your recipes will provide good guidelines to suitable cooking methods.

Fish is very economical on fuel because it cooks quickly. When cooked, fish loses its translucent look and takes on an opaque appearance. It will also flake easily, so should be handled with care to stop it breaking up.

Fish can easily become dry and lose its flavour if overcooked, so it is important to consider methods of cookery carefully. Overcooked, dry fish will be far less enjoyable to eat and is less attractive than fish that is cooked properly. The correct cooking method must also be selected to ensure the fish meets dish requirements and menu descriptions.

To maintain the quality and food safety of fish dishes it is advisable to check the internal temperature using a temperature probe. It is recommended that all fish should be cooked to a minimum internal temperature of 63 °C. This is for whole fish and cuts of fish. Prepared fish dishes such as fish pie or fishcakes should be cooked to a minimum of 75 °C.

Because fish cooks so quickly, an experienced chef will be able to tell when certain types of fish are cooked by touch (touch temperature).

Fish and shellfish

> **Food safety**
> Environmental health officers may require higher temperatures.

The following are the main cooking methods used for fish.

Frying

Frying is probably the most popular method of cooking fish. Described below are the three main types of frying.

Shallow frying

The fish should be seasoned and lightly coated with flour before frying, in order to protect it and seal in the flavour. Use a mixture of oil and butter when frying, and turn the fish only once during cooking, to avoid it breaking up.

This method is suitable for small whole fish, cuts or fillets cooked in oil or fat in a frying pan. The fish can also be lightly coated with semolina, matzo meal, oatmeal or breadcrumbs before frying. If the frying medium is to be butter, it must be clarified otherwise there is a risk that the fish may burn. Oil is the best medium, to which a little butter may be added for flavour.

Deep frying

This method is suitable for small whole white fish, cuts and fillets, as well as made-up items such as fishcakes. All white fish are suitable for deep frying in batter, including cod, pollack, haddock and skate. Depending on size, the fish may be left whole or may be portioned or filleted.

The fish should be seasoned and coated before frying, usually with a batter or an egg and breadcrumb mixture to form a surface that prevents penetration of the cooking fat or oil into the fish. It also adds a crisp texture to the fish. Use a thermostatically controlled deep fryer no more than half-filled with oil; heat the oil to 175 °C. Test the temperature before serving the fish. Drain the fish on absorbent paper after cooking.

Coatings can be either:
- flour, egg and breadcrumbs (*pane*)
- milk and flour
- batter.

Stir-frying

This is a very fast and popular method of cooking where the fish is cooked along with suitable vegetables and perhaps noodles, bean shoots or rice. Spices, flavourings and suitable sauces may also be added. Use a wok or deep frying pan and a high cooking temperature. Food should be cut into thin strips and all prepared before cooking begins. This method is well suited to firm-fleshed fish cut into strips or shellfish.

Grilling

Grilling, or griddling, is cooking under radiant heat, and is a fast and convenient method suitable for fillets or small whole fish. When grilling whole fish, trim and prepare neatly and descale. Cut through the flesh at the thickest part of the fish to allow even cooking. Lightly oil and season fish or fillets and, to avoid breaking, do not turn more than once.

Poaching

Poaching is suitable for:
- whole fish such as salmon, trout or bass
- certain cuts on the bone such as salmon, turbot, brill, halibut, cod and skate
- fillets, suprêmes or fish prepared into délice or paupiette.

In each case, the prepared fish should be completely immersed in the cooking liquid, which can be either water, water and milk, or fish stock (for white fish), or a court bouillon (water, vinegar, onion, carrot, thyme, bay leaf, parsley stalks and peppercorns) for oily fish. Most kinds of fish can be cooked in this way and should be poached gently for 5–8 minutes, depending on the thickness of the fish.

Whole fish are covered with a cold liquid and brought to the boil, then cooked just below simmering point. Cut fish are usually placed in the liquid when it is at simmering point then cooked just below simmering point. The resulting liquid is ideal for use in sauces and soups.

When poaching smoked fish, place in cold, unsalted water and bring to simmering point, then lower the temperature slightly. This liquid will be salty and may not be suitable for use in stocks and sauces.

Sous-vide

This method, where the fish is sealed in a vacuum pack and cooked in a water bath, has become a popular way to cook fish. It helps to reduce moisture loss and also allows the fish to cook with a marinade or sauce if required.

Boiling

Boiling is used mainly for shellfish and, as many shellfish are sold already cooked, this is often done at sea or soon after landing because shellfish can deteriorate quickly.

Shellfish are often boiled from live and include: lobsters, crabs, oysters, langoustines, crayfish, clams, cockles, mussels, prawns and shrimps.

Roasting

Roast fish frequently appears on restaurant menus but, because fish is much more delicate than meat, only whole fish or larger, firmer cuts are suitable for roasting and care must be taken not to overcook. The fish may be brushed with oil or clarified butter before cooking and may be raised a little from the base of the pan using vegetables. More usually the fish is placed skin down in the hot cooking pan to add colour and texture, or the skin is seared in hot oil first then cooked skin side up. The fish is usually basted with the pan juices as it cooks.

When the fish is cooked and removed, the tray can be deglazed with a suitable wine (usually a dry white) and fish stock to form the base of an accompanying sauce.

Fish can also be coated in a light crust of breadcrumbs mixed with a good oil, butter, lemon juice, freshly chopped herbs (such as parsley, tarragon, chervil or rosemary), a duxelle-based mixture or a light coating of creamed horseradish.

The cooked fish may be served with a sauce or salsa, or placed on a bed of creamed or flavoured mashed potato with a compound butter sauce and quarters of lemon.

Baking

Many fish (whole, portioned or filleted) may be oven-baked. To retain their natural moisture it is necessary to protect the fish from direct heat and this may be done by coating. Prepared fish dishes, such as fish pies and en croute items, are also finished by baking.

There are various ways of preparing fish for baking:
- whole fish need to be scaled, gutted and washed, then may be stuffed with items such as a duxelle-based mixture, flavoured breadcrumbs, fish mousses, herbs or vegetables, such as onion or fennel
- wrapped in pastry (puff or filo)
- coated with a crumb mixture
- completely covered with a thick coating of dampened sea salt, which is removed before serving
- topping or finishing a prepared dish such as a fish pie or seafood with puff pastry, mashed potato or a sauce.

For a whole fish or cuts of fish proceed as follows:

1 Depending on the size and shape of the fish, 100 to 150 g thick portions can be cut, leaving the skin on (this helps to retain the natural moisture of the fish).
2 Place the prepared portions in a greased ovenproof dish, brush with oil and bake slowly, skin side up (this may be seared in hot oil first); alternatively, place skin side down in a hot pan to sear it.
3 Add herbs such as parsley, rosemary or thyme, and finely sliced vegetables such as mushrooms, onions, shallots.
4 The fish can then be served, for example on a bed of creamy or flavoured mashed potato with a suitable sauce, a compound butter or a salsa.

Steaming

Small whole fish, fish cuts or fillets are good cooked in this way. Preparation is usually simple, with the fish just being seasoned then placed in a steamer tray lined with greaseproof paper or in a small steamer over simmering water covered with a lid. Cook for 10 to 15 minutes, depending on the thickness of the fish or the fillets.

Steaming can also be done by putting the food between two plates and placing the plates over a pan of simmering water.

Fish is prepared as for poaching. Any fish that can be poached or boiled may also be cooked by steaming. This method has a number of advantages:
- it is an easy method of cooking
- because it is quick, it conserves flavour, colour and nutrients
- it is suitable for large-scale cookery.

Any cooking liquor from the steamed fish may be strained off, reduced and incorporated into a sauce. Preparation can also include adding finely cut ingredients (such as ginger, spring onions, garlic, mushrooms and soft herbs), lemon juice and dry white wine, either to the fish on the steamer dish before cooking or when the fish is served.

Braising and stewing

These tend to be less popular methods for cooking fish but generally whole fish or larger cuts of fish can be braised in a closed container covering or half covering the fish with a suitable liquid (such as those used for poaching). Vegetables such as onion, shallot and fennel may be added along with herbs, spices, lemon or lime.

Fish and shellfish 9

Stewing of fish may be similar to braising but in many countries there are traditional fish stews using a variety of fish and shellfish along with onions, shallots, tomatoes, garlic and a variety of other ingredients. Examples of these would be bouillabaisse from France, cataplana from Portugal, the Italian-American dish cioppino, and moqueca from Brazil.

Table 9.2 gives examples of some of the 200-plus fish types that are available, divided into oily and white varieties. It also shows which methods of cookery are suitable for each fish.

Table 9.2 Examples of fish types available and suitable cooking methods

	Baking	Boiling	Deep frying	Grilling	Poaching	Roasting	Shallow (pan) frying	Steaming	Stir-frying
Oily fish									
Barracuda				✓			✓		
Dorade (red sea bream)	✓			✓			✓		✓
Emperor bream	✓			✓			✓		
Herring				✓			✓		
Mackerel	✓			✓	✓				
Marlin	✓			✓					
Monkfish	✓						✓		✓
Red mullet	✓				✓		✓		
Red snapper	✓				✓		✓		
Salmon	✓	✓		✓	✓	✓	✓	✓	✓
Sardines							✓		
Trout	✓			✓			✓		
Tuna				✓	✓		✓		✓
Whitebait			✓						
White fish									
Cod	✓	✓	✓	✓	✓	✓	✓	✓	
Coley		✓	✓	✓	✓		✓		
Dover sole			✓	✓	✓		✓		
Grouper				✓		✓	✓		
Haddock	✓		✓	✓	✓		✓		
Hake	✓			✓	✓		✓		
Halibut	✓			✓	✓		✓	✓	✓
Huss			✓	✓	✓				
John Dory	✓				✓		✓		
Lemon sole	✓		✓	✓	✓		✓		
Plaice	✓		✓	✓	✓		✓		
Pollock	✓	✓		✓	✓		✓	✓	
Sea bass	✓			✓	✓		✓	✓	
Shark	✓			✓		✓	✓		✓
Skate		✓	✓	✓			✓		
Swordfish	✓			✓			✓		✓
Turbot	✓	✓	✓	✓	✓	✓	✓		✓

203

Healthy eating options when preparing and cooking fish (and shellfish)

Fish is a naturally healthy food because it is a high protein food that is low in fat; in fact it is as good a source of protein as meat. Oily fish (sardines, mackerel, herring, salmon, sardines) contain the fat-soluble vitamins A and D in their flesh as well as omega-3 fatty acids (the unsaturated fatty acids that are essential for good health). It is recommended that we eat more oily fish. Owing to its fat content, oily fish is not as easily digestible as white fish, however.

The flesh of white fish does not contain any fat (and vitamins A and D are only present in the liver, which is why it is used in cod liver or halibut liver oil).

If the small bones in sardines, whitebait and canned salmon are eaten they provide calcium and phosphorus.

The preparation and cooking methods selected can change the nutritional content of a fish dish however. For example, by taking white fish and seasoning it, coating it in batter and deep frying it, you have increased the salt, carbohydrate and fat content significantly.

Healthy options when preparing and cooking fish include:
- Do not add salt in preparation, cooking and finishing.
- Use low-fat cooking options such as steaming, poaching and grilling.
- Reduce fat and salt content in coatings and marinades.
- Use oils and butter sparingly when grilling or baking fish.
- Avoid high-fat, salty sauces and adding extra butter before serving.

Shellfish

Shellfish, such as lobsters and crabs, are all invertebrates, which means that they do not have an internal skeleton. They are split into two main groups:
- **Molluscs** have either an external hinged double shell (for example, scallops and mussels) or a single spiral shell (for example, winkles and whelks), or have soft bodies with an internal shell, such as squid and octopus (these are called cephalopods).
- **Crustaceans** have tough outer shells that act like armour, and also have flexible joints to allow quick movement (for example, crab and lobster).

Choosing and buying shellfish

Shellfish are prized for their tender, fine-textured flesh, which can be prepared in a variety of ways. They are prone to rapid spoilage however, because they contain quantities of certain proteins (amino acids) that encourage bacterial growth.

To ensure freshness and best flavour it may be preferable to choose live shellfish and cook them yourself. This is increasingly possible with modern transportation, especially air freight, which allows shellfish to be transported around the world quickly.

Consider the following points when choosing shellfish:
- The shells should not be cracked or broken.
- The shells of mussels and oysters should be tightly shut; open shells that do not close when tapped sharply should be discarded.
- Lobsters, crabs and prawns should have a good colour and be heavy for their size.
- Lobsters and crabs should have all their limbs in place.

Storing shellfish

All shellfish start to spoil as soon as they have been removed from their natural environment, therefore the longer shellfish are stored the more they will deteriorate due to the bacteria present (see the guidelines on choosing and buying, above). Best practice would be to cook immediately and store as for cooked fish. Shellfish can be blanched quickly to remove the shell and membrane (especially in lobsters), but they will still need to be stored as a raw product as they will require further cooking.

Bear in mind the following quality, purchasing and storage points:
- Where possible, shellfish should be purchased live to ensure freshness.
- Shellfish should be kept in suitable containers, covered with cling film or damp cloths, and stored in a refrigerator.
- Shellfish should be cooked as soon as possible after purchasing.

Cooking shellfish

The flesh of fish and shellfish is different to meat and, as a consequence, their muscle make-up is very different too, making the connective tissue very fragile, the

Table 9.3 Seasonality of shellfish

	JAN	FEB	MAR	APR	MAY	JUN	JUL	AUG	SEP	OCT	NOV	DEC
Crab (brown cock)	At best	At best	At best	At best	Available	Available	Available	Available	Available	Available	Available	
Crab (spider)	Available	Available	Available	Available		At best	At best	At best	At best	Available	Available	Available
Crab (brown hen)		Available	Available	Available	Available		Available	Available	Available	Available	Available	Available
Clams		Available	Available	Available	Available	Available	Available	Available	Available	Available	Available	
Cockles		Available	Available	Available	Available	Available	Available	Available	Available	Available	Available	Available
Crayfish (signal)					Available	Available	Available	Available	Available	Available		
Lobster	Available	Available							Available	Available	Available	Available
Langoustines				Available	Available	Available	Available	Available	Available	Available		
Mussels	Available	Available	Available	Available					Available	Available	Available	Available
Oysters (rock)	Available	Available	Available	Available					Available	Available	Available	Available
Oysters (native)	Available	Available	Available	Available					Available	Available	Available	Available
Prawns						Available	Available	Available	Available	Available	Available	
Scallops	Available	Available	Available	Available	Available		Available	Available	Available	Available	Available	Available

Key:
Available (dark shell)
At best (light shell)

muscle fibres shorter and the fat content relatively low. Generally, care should be taken when cooking and shellfish should be cooked as little as possible, to the point that the protein in the muscle groups just coagulates. Beyond this point the flesh tends to dry out, leading to toughening and a dry texture. Shellfish are known for their dramatic colour change when being cooked, from blue/grey to a vibrant orange colour. This is because they contain red and yellow pigments called carotenoids, bound to molecules of protein. Once heat is applied, the bonds are broken and the bright colour appears.

Shrimps and prawns

These are often bought cooked, either in the shells or peeled. Smell is a good guide to freshness. Shrimps and prawns can be used for garnishes, decorating fish dishes, cocktails, sauces, salads, hors d'oeuvres, omelettes, and snack and savoury dishes. They can also be used for a variety of hot dishes, including stir-fries, risotto and curries. Potted shrimps are also a popular dish. Freshly cooked prawns in their shells may also be served cold accompanied by a mayonnaise-based sauce, such as garlic mayonnaise. **King prawns** are a larger variety that can also be used in any of the above ways.

Raw and cooked shrimps and prawns are prepared by having the head, carapace (upper shell), legs, tail section and the dark intestinal vein running down the back removed.

Scampi, crayfish and Dublin Bay prawns

Scampi, crayfish and Dublin Bay prawns are also known as Norway lobster or langoustine, and are sold fresh, frozen, raw or cooked. Their tails are prepared like shrimps and they are used in a variety of ways: salads, rice dishes, stir-fries, deep fried, poached and served with a number of different sauces. They are also used as garnishes for hot and cold fish dishes.

Freshwater crayfish are also known as *écrevisse*. These are small freshwater crustaceans with claws, found in lakes and lowland streams. They are prepared and cooked like shrimps and prawns, and used in many dishes, including soup. They are often used whole to garnish hot and cold fish dishes.

▲ Remove the cord from each langoustine before cooking

Lobster

Although there many different lobster varieties around the world, the two main ones are the American lobster, which tends to be the largest, and the European lobster, which is usually smaller. Their preferred habitat is hard surfaces or crevices on the sea bed at depths of around 20 to 60 metres. Lobsters grow very slowly and can live up to 100 years. As they grow they shed their hard shell and form another one. Maturity is reached at about five years old and at a length of 18 to 20 cm. They can weigh up to 9 kg but are usually around 2 to 3 kg. They have ten limbs (decapods), two of which are the two large front claws (one is used for cutting and one for crushing).

Purchasing points

Purchase alive, with both claws attached, to ensure freshness.

- Lobsters should be heavy in proportion to their size.
- The coral of the hen lobster is necessary to give the required colour for certain soups, sauces and lobster dishes.
- Hen lobsters are distinguished from cock lobsters by their broader tails.

Cooking lobsters

1. Wash then plunge the lobsters into a pan of boiling salted water containing 60 ml vinegar to 1 litre of water.
2. Cover with a lid, reboil, then allow to simmer for 15 to 20 minutes according to size.
3. Overcooking can cause the tail flesh to toughen and the claw meat to become hard and fibrous.
4. Allow to cool in the cooking liquid when possible.

Some advice for the humane killing of lobsters is to place them in the freezer for one hour before cooking to numb them. Some chefs prefer to kill the lobster instantly by plunging the tip of a sharp knife straight down and through the lobster, right behind the eyes. There is also a device called the Crustastun, which uses an electric current to stun and painlessly kill shellfish such as lobsters, crabs and langoustines before cooking. The machine can make a large crustacean unconscious in less than 0.3 seconds and kill it in five to ten.

Cleaning a cooked lobster

1. Remove the claws and the pincers from the claws.
2. Crack the claws and joints, and remove the meat.
3. Cut the lobster in half by inserting the point of a large knife 2 cm above the tail on the natural central line.
4. Cut through the tail firmly.
5. Turn the lobster around and cut through the upper shell (carapace).
6. Remove the halves of the sac (which contains grit) from each half. This is situated at the top, near the head.
7. Using a small knife, remove the intestinal trace from the tail and wash if necessary.

Preparing a cooked lobster

Remove the claws and legs

Cut the lobster in half

Remove the meat from the cleaned lobster

Uses

Lobsters are served cold in cocktails, lobster mayonnaise, hors d'oeuvres, salads, sandwiches and in halves on cold buffets. They are used hot in soups, sauces, rice dishes, stir-fry dishes and in numerous ways served in the half-shell with various sauces. They are also used to garnish fish dishes.

Crawfish

These are sometimes referred to as 'spiny lobsters' but, unlike lobsters, they have no claws and their meat is solely in the tail. Crawfish vary considerably in size from 1 to 3 kg; they are cooked as for lobsters and the tail meat can be used in any of the lobster recipes. Because of their impressive appearance whole dressed crawfish are sometimes used on special cold buffets. They are very expensive and are also available frozen.

Squid

Squid is a cephalopod; they are traditionally popular in Mediterranean cuisine but have increased in popularity through the rest of Europe. It is available all year round fresh or frozen. Squid vary in size, from 5 to 7 cm in length, to up to 25 cm. The ink sac and transparent cartilage need to be removed and the main body is often cut into rings for cooking. Squid needs to be cooked very quickly or by a slow moist method otherwise it can be tough.

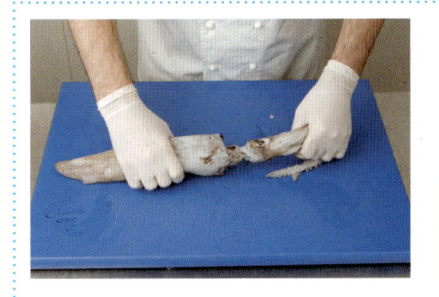

1 Pull the head away from the body, together with the innards.

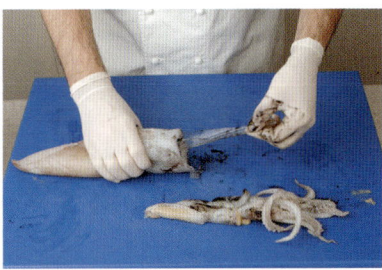

2 Taking care not to break the ink bag, remove the long transparent blade of cartilage (the backbone or quill).

3 Cut the tentacles just below the eye and remove the small round cartilage at the base of the tentacles.

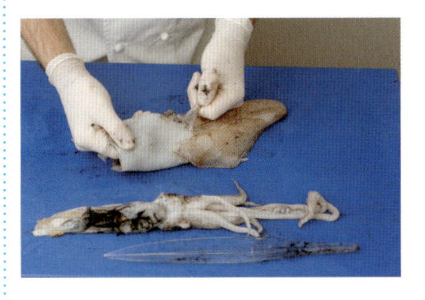

4 Scrape or peel off the reddish membrane that covers the pouch, rub with salt and wash under cold water.

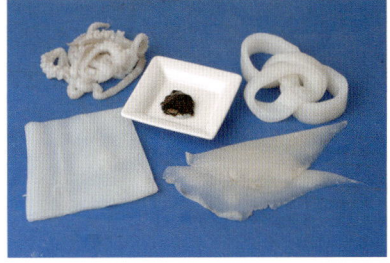

5 Discard the head, innards and pieces of cartilage. Cut up the squid as required.

Crab

There are an estimated 4,000 species of edible of crab. The meat from crab is very different in the claws and the main body. Crab claws have a sweet, dense white meat similar to lobster while the flesh from under the main body shell is soft, rich and brown. Male crabs tend to have larger claws and more white meat.

European brown crabs, the most widely available across Europe and available year-round, reach 20 to 25 cm across and have large front claws with dark pincers, a red or brown shell and red legs.

Atlantic blue crabs have a blue/brown shell and tend to be smaller than European brown crabs at 10 to 15 cm.

Dungeness crabs can reach up to 20 cm and have plenty of good white, dense meat in the claws. The meat in the shell tends to be different from other crabs and is pale grey/green in colour. It is popular in the west of the United States.

Spider crabs are popular in France and Spain, and do look like a big spider. The meat has a good flavour but it has no large claws (so no white claw meat).

Purchasing points

- Buy alive where possible to ensure freshness.
- Ensure that both claws are attached.
- Crabs should be heavy in relation to size.

Cooking

Cook as for lobsters.

Uses

Crab meat can be served simply with bread and salad, used cold for hors d'oeuvres, cocktails, salads, sandwiches and dressed crab. Used hot, it can be covered with a suitable sauce and served with rice, in *bouchées* or pancakes, or made into crab fishcakes.

Cockles

Cockles are enclosed in small, attractive, cream-coloured shells. As they live in sand it is essential to purge them by washing well under cold running water and leaving them in cold salted water (changed frequently) until no traces of sand remain.

Cockles can be cooked either by steaming, boiling in unsalted water, on a preheated griddle, or as for any mussel recipe. They should be cooked only until the shells open.

They can be used in soups, sauces, salads, stir-fries and rice dishes, and as garnish for fish dishes.

Mussels

Mussels are bivalves, which means they have a double outer shell hinged at the top. Mussels can be from either sea or freshwater (rivers and lakes) but the sea varieties are by far the most widely used. Mussels are now extensively farmed, cultivated on wooden frames in the sea, producing tender, delicately flavoured plump flesh. They are produced off British coasts and also imported from France, Holland and Belgium. French mussels are small; Dutch and Belgian mussels are plumper. The production of mussels is considered to be ecologically sound, which means that the species is not threatened or damaging to the environment.

Purchasing points

- The shells must be tightly closed, indicating the mussels are alive.
- They should be of a good size.
- There should not be an excessive number of barnacles attached.
- They should smell fresh.

Storage

Mussels should be kept in containers, covered with damp cloths or cling film, and stored in a refrigerator. Do not store mussels in water.

Cooking

1. Scrape the shells to remove any barnacles, etc. Remove the byssus threads ('beards').
2. Wash well in several changes of water and drain in a colander.
3. Prepare a cooking liquid of shallots, butter, garlic and herbs along with fish stock.
4. Cook the mussels in the liquid in a large pan with a tightly fitting lid until they open, which usually takes 4 to 5 minutes. Remove the mussels and check they have all opened; throw away any that are still closed.
5. Strain the liquid, whisk in some cream and serve with the mussels still in their shells.

Alternatively, place 25 g chopped shallot or onion for each litre of mussels into a thick-bottomed pan with a tight-fitting lid. Add the mussels, cover with the lid and cook on a fierce heat for 4 to 5 minutes until the shells open completely. Remove the mussels from their shells. Retain the carefully strained liquid to make a sauce to serve with the mussels.

Uses

Mussels can be used for soups, sauces and salads, and cooked in a wide variety of hot dishes.

Scallops

Scallops are bivalves with a fan-shaped shell. They vary in size from 15 cm for great scallops, around 8 cm for bay scallops, and to queen scallops that are the size of cockles. Inside is the round white flesh and the orange coral (the roe), which is often discarded. Scallops are popular and the prices tend to remain high, especially for hand-dived scallops rather than those caught by a dredging trawler. They are prepared by prising the two halves of the shell apart and removing the white flesh and the orange roe if required.

Scallops in their shells should be covered with damp cloths and kept in a refrigerated cold room or fish refrigerator.

Cooking

Scallops should only be cooked lightly, otherwise they shrink and toughen.

- Poach gently for two to three minutes in fish stock or dry white wine with a little onion, carrot, thyme, bay leaf and parsley. Serve with a suitable sauce (for example white wine or mornay).
- Lightly fry on both sides for a few seconds in butter or oil in a very hot pan (if the scallops are very thick they can be cut in half sideways) and serve with a suitable garnish (sliced wild or cultivated mushrooms, or a fine brunoise of vegetables and tomato) and a liquid that need not be thickened (white wine and fish stock, or a cream- or butter-mounted sauce). Fried scallops can also be served hot on a plate of salad leaves.
- Deep fry, either egg and crumbed or passed through a light batter and served with segments of lemon and a suitable sauce.
- Wrap in thin streaky bacon and place on skewers for grilling or barbecuing.

Whelks

The common whelk is familiar around the coast of Britain. It is actually a gastropod, which means it has a large, strong flat foot to move around on. Whelks are also equipped with a siphon, which is used for breathing and feeling around for food.

British winkles

The main types of British winkle, which can be readily identified on rocky shores, are:

- small periwinkle: approximately 4 mm
- rough periwinkle: at least four different subspecies, with the largest reaching 30 mm
- flat periwinkle.

Oysters

Oysters are highly regarded saltwater bivalves found near the bottom of the sea; the upper shell (valve) is flattish and attached by a ligament hinge to the lower, bowl-shaped shell. A number of different species available, including native, flat or rock oysters, with Colchester and Whitstable being significant oyster areas in the UK. Traditionally oysters are eaten raw so it is essential that they are very fresh and cleaned/purged well. Preparation usually involves prising the two halves of the shell apart with a small, pointed oyster knife. The oysters may then be served with lemon and other condiments.

Oysters are high in protein and low in fat; they are rich in zinc and contain many other nutrients such as calcium, iron, copper, iodine, magnesium and selenium.

Purchasing points

They should smell fresh and the shells should be clean, bright and unbroken. The shells should be tightly closed or should close when tapped.

Storage

Oysters should be stored at a low temperature (1 °C to 2 °C). Unopened live oysters can be kept in the fish refrigerator covered with wet cloths or cling film for two to three days; discard any that open. Do not store in an airtight container or under fresh water as this will cause them to die. Shucked oysters (ones that have been removed from their shells) can be kept refrigerated in a sealed container for four to five days.

Ready prepared shellfish

Shellfish are increasingly available ready prepared in a number of ways, such as breadcrumbed and frozen prawns and scampi, or shellfish wrapped in puff or filo pastry, mussels, cooked and vacuum packed in a sauce, crab cakes, sushi and many more. Shellfish are great favourite for canapés and many of these are now available ready prepared.

Test yourself

1. What are the differences between oily and white fish? Give three examples of each.
2. At what temperatures should a) fresh fish and b) frozen fish be stored?
3. How would you defrost fish that has been frozen?
4. Describe how you would skin a Dover sole.
5. What are the quality points you would look for in a delivery of fresh fish? If you thought there were problems with the quality, what would you do?
6. If you had been asked to fillet and skin five whole plaice, what equipment would you get ready?
7. List four cooking methods that could be used for white fish and four for oily fish.
8. List five types of fish suitable for deep frying.
9. Describe the following cuts of fish and suggest a method for cooking each of them:
    a. délice
    b. tronçon
    c. darne
    d. goujon.
10. Describe how you would prepare mussels for cooking.
11. How would you prepare and cook scallops?
12. What are the quality points you would look for with lobsters? How would you prepare them?

Fish and shellfish

Grilled fish recipes

1 Grilled tuna, rocket and fennel salad

Energy	Cals	Fat	Sat fat	Carb	Sugar	Protein	Fibre	Sodium
1,619 kJ	388 kcal	24.3 g	4.3 g	4.2 g	3.7 g	38.4 g	4.5 g	0.6 g

Ingredient	4 portions	10 portions
For the salad		
Rocket salad, washed and picked	400 g	1 kg
Fennel bulb	1	2
Green beans, cooked and refreshed	200 g	500 g
Baby spinach	100 g	250 g
Coriander, picked	50 g	125 g
For the dressing		
Dijon mustard	1 tsp	3 tsp
Cider vinegar	1 tsp	3 tsp
Olive oil	3 tbsp	7 tbsp
Sunflower oil	3 tbsp	7 tbsp
Lemon juice	1 tsp	2 tsp
Lime juice	1 tsp	2 tsp
Seasoning		
For the fish		
Tuna steaks (150 g, no skin or blood line)	4	10
Olive oil	50 ml	125 ml
Sea salt, fresh milled black pepper		
Lemon	1	2

For the salad:

1. Ensure all the leaves are well washed and picked.
2. Cut the root and top off the fennel, leaving the main bulb.
3. Thinly slice the fennel on a mandolin. Place in cold water with plenty of ice (this will make the fennel very crisp and curly, giving the salad some height).
4. Place all the salad ingredients into a large bowl ready to dress with the dressing.

For the dressing:

1. Place the mustard and vinegar in a bowl then slowly whisk in the oil.
2. To finish, adjust the taste with the lemon juice, lime juice and seasoning.
3. To dress, mix the salad and dressing well, check the seasoning and divide the salad equally between four/ten plates.

For the tuna:

1. Before you start to cook the tuna, ensure that the salad is dressed and on the serving plate.
2. Lightly brush the tuna steaks with the oil and season.
3. Ensure the grill is hot. Place two steaks on at a time (this is manageable as the tuna cooks very quickly).
4. Turn after 30 seconds and cook until the centre half of the tuna is still pink.
5. Remove and place on the salad. Repeat for the other steaks. Serve with a wedge of lemon.

Note

This recipe lends itself well to other fish such as salmon, sea bass, turbot, trout, hake and monkfish.

2 Grilled fillets of sole, plaice or haddock

1. Remove the black skin from sole and plaice. Wash the fillets and dry them well.
2. Pass through flour, shake off surplus and brush with oil.
3. Place on hot grill bars, a griddle or a greased baking sheet if grilling under a salamander. Brush occasionally with oil. Turn the fish carefully and grill on both sides. Do not overcook.

Serve with lemon slices with the rind removed.

Energy	Cals	Fat	Sat fat	Carb	Sugar	Protein	Fibre	Sodium
802 kJ	191 kcal	7.8g	1.0g	3.9g	0.1g	26.6g	0.2g	0.1g

Professional tip

Oil the grill bars well, so that the fish does not stick.

3 Whole grilled mackerel with tomatoes, basil and shaved fennel

Energy	Cals	Fat	Sat fat	Carb	Sugar	Protein	Fibre	Sodium
2,067 kJ	497 kcal	39.4g	7.8g	3.9g	3.8g	32.4g	2.2g	0.2g

Based on sardines rather than mackerel.

Ingredient	4 portions	10 portions
For the mackerel		
Medium mackerel, head and guts removed	4	10
Olive oil	50 ml	125 ml
Freshly milled pepper		
For the salad		
Olive oil	50 ml	125 ml
Baby plum tomatoes, cut in half	400 g	1 kg
Fennel bulb, shaved on a mandolin	1	2
Baby spinach	100 g	250 g
Lemon, juice of	1	2
Basil leaves, torn	6	15

For the mackerel:

1. Ensure that the fish is clean. Score the flesh of each fish in the deepest part (near the head), about 3 mm into the fish but not through to the bone. (This scoring is called *ciseler* – it helps the fish to cook more evenly and can be used with most methods of cooking whole fish.)
2. Brush with the oil and place on a moderate grill. (Wrap the tail in foil to ensure that it doesn't burn.)
3. Turn the fish over to cook the other side, removing the foil. At this point, start making the salad.
4. Once the fish is cooked, dress the plates with the salad and lay the fish on top. Drizzle the pan juices over and around the fish and serve.

For the salad:

1. Heat the oil in a pan and add the tomatoes and fennel. Cook on a hot heat.
2. Remove from the heat, stir in the spinach and allow it to wilt.
3. Season with salt, pepper and a dash of lemon juice. Finish with basil leaves.

4 Whole sole grilled with traditional accompaniments

Ingredient	4 portions	10 portions
Whole sole, skin removed	4	10
Butter for grilling	200 g	500 g
Seasoning		
Parsley butter	100 g	250 g
Lemons, peeled and cut into wedges	1	3

Energy	Cals	Fat	Sat fat	Carb	Sugar	Protein	Fibre	Sodium
3,058 kJ	740 kcal	65.4 g	39.1 g	1.0 g	0.9 g	36.9 g	0.3 g	0.7 g

1. Ensure the fish is clean of roe, scales and skin.
2. Place on a buttered grilling tray and rub soft butter into the flesh.
3. Season and place under the grill.
4. When the butter starts to brown slightly, remove from the grill and turn the fish over carefully, using a roasting fork or a long pallet knife.
5. With a spoon, baste the flesh of the uncooked side and continue cooking. The tail end will cook faster than the head end – the tail should therefore be cooked in the less-hot area towards the front of the grill.
6. To check whether the fish is done, place your thumb just behind the gill area and you should feel the flesh ease away from the bone.
7. Finish with parsley butter and a wedge of lemon.

> **Professional tip**
>
> Remember that sole is a delicate fish, so be careful not to overcook it. This is a classic recipe for slip, Dover and lemon sole – there is no need to modernise it.

5 Sardines with tapenade

Ingredient	4 portions	10 portions
Sardines	8–12	20–30
For the tapenade		
Kalamata olives	20	50
Capers	1 tbsp	2½ tbsp
Lemon juice	1 tsp	2½ tsp
Olive oil	2 tsp	5 tsp
Anchovy paste (optional)	½ tsp	1¼ tsp
Freshly ground black pepper		

Energy	Cals	Fat	Sat fat	Carb	Sugar	Protein	Fibre	Sodium
3,167 kJ	757 kcal	44.0g	12.4g	0.0g	0.0g	90.5g	0.8g	1.0g

Using additional olives in place of capers.

1 Finely chop the olives and capers. Add the lemon juice, olive oil, anchovy paste and black pepper. Mix well.
2 Allow 2–3 sardines per portion. Clean the sardines and grill them on both sides, either on an open flame grill or under the salamander.
3 When cooked, smear the tapenade on top. The tapenade can be heated slightly before spreading.

Variation
A little chopped basil and a crushed chopped clove of garlic may also be added to the tapenade.

Cleaned sardines

Grilled sardines, before the tapenade is added

Poached fish dishes

6 Poached salmon

Depending on the size of the salmon, either a whole or half a darne would be served as a portion.
See page 249 for a court bouillon recipe.

1. Place the prepared and washed darnes of salmon in a court bouillon, just below simmering, for approximately 5 minutes.
2. Drain well and carefully remove the centre bone and outer skin. Ensure that the fish is cleaned of any cooked blood.

Serve with a suitable sauce (e.g. hollandaise or pesto) or melted herb butter, and thinly sliced cucumber.

Energy	Cals	Fat	Sat fat	Carb	Sugar	Protein	Fibre	Sodium
1,284 kJ	309 kcal	20.6g	5.5g	0.3g	0.3g	30.4g	0.1g	0.1g

7 Poached smoked haddock

Ingredient	4 portions	10 portions
Smoked haddock fillets	400–600 g	1–1.5 kg
Milk and water, mixed		

This is a popular breakfast dish and is also served as a lunch and a snack dish.

1. Cut fillets into even portions, place into a shallow pan and just cover with half milk and water.
2. Poach gently for a few minutes until cooked.
3. Drain well and serve.

Variation

- When cooked, garnish with slices of peeled tomato or tomato concassé, lightly coat with cream, flash under the salamander and serve.
- Top with a poached egg.
- When cooked, lightly coat with Welsh rarebit mixture, brown under the salamander and garnish with peeled slices of tomato or tomato concassé.

Energy	Cals	Fat	Sat fat	Carb	Sugar	Protein	Fibre	Sodium
702 kJ	168 kcal	7.6g	4.6g	1.4g	1.4g	23.4g	0.0g	1.0g

For a 125 g portion.

8 Poached turbot, brill, halibut or cod (on the bone)

1. Place the prepared fish into a shallow pan of simmering, lightly salted water containing lemon juice (the citric acid helps to make the flesh firm and white and gives a gentle flavour).
2. Allow to poach gently. The cooking time depends on the thickness of the fish. Do not overcook.
3. Remove with a fish slice, remove the skin, drain and serve.
4. Garnish with picked parsley and plain boiled potatoes, and serve with a suitable sauce (e.g. hollandaise, herb butter, shrimp or mushroom).

Energy	Cals	Fat	Sat fat	Carb	Sugar	Protein	Fibre	Sodium
1,412 kJ	353 kcal	9.5g	2.5g	0.3g	0.3g	62.0g	0.0g	0.2g

Place the fish into the gently simmering liquid

Allow the fish to poach

Lift out the fish and remove any black skin

Fish and shellfish 9

9 Délice of flat white fish Dugléré

Ingredient	4 portions	10 portions
Fillets of flat white fish (e.g. sole, plaice)	400–600 g	1–1.5 kg
Fish stock for poaching	approx. 200 ml	approx. 500 ml
For the sauce		
Butter	25 g	60 g
Shallots, finely chopped	20 g	50 g
Fish stock	60 ml	150 ml
Dry white wine	60 ml	150 ml
Whipping cream	200 ml	500 ml
Butter, sliced and kept cold on ice	50 g	125 g
Tomatoes, skinned and neatly diced (concassé)	2	5
Parsley, chopped finely	10 g	20 g

Energy	Cals	Fat	Sat fat	Carb	Sugar	Protein	Fibre	Sodium
1974 kJ	475 kcal	38.0g	23.0g	3.5g	3.2g	28.0g	0.7g	0.6g

Using 150 g plaice.

1. Skin the fish, trim and wash.
2. Fold the fillets neatly, ensuring the skinned side is facing inwards (délice).
3. Using a wide, shallow pan, poach the délice gently in fish stock for 4–6 minutes (depending on the thickness of the fillet).
4. To make the sauce, sweat the finely chopped shallots with the butter in a saucepan, until translucent.
5. Add the fish stock and reduce by one-third.
6. Add the dry white wine and reduce again by half.
7. Add the whipping cream and reduce by one-third, until the cream starts to thicken the sauce to a coating consistency.
8. Add the cold, sliced butter and ripple the sauce over the butter until the butter has emulsified into the sauce (monté). Check the seasoning and adjust accordingly. Do not allow the sauce to reboil as the butter will split and the sauce will become greasy.
9. Add the neatly cut tomato concassé and finely chopped parsley to the sauce.
10. To serve, drain the fish well and place neatly on a plate; carefully coat each délice with the sauce and serve.

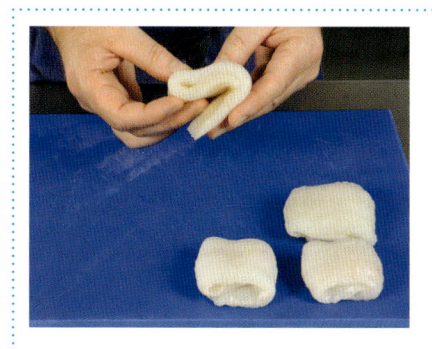

Fold each fillet into a délice

Sweat the finely chopped shallots

Coat each délice with sauce

Practical Cookery 14th edition

10 Fillets of fish in white wine sauce (*filets de poisson vin blanc*)

1. Skin and fillet the fish, trim and wash.
2. Butter and season an earthenware dish.
3. Sprinkle with the sweated chopped shallots and add the fillets of fish.
4. Season, add the fish stock, wine and lemon juice.
5. Cover with buttered greaseproof paper.
6. Poach in a moderate oven at 150–200 °C for 7–10 minutes.
7. Drain the fish well; dress neatly on a flat dish or clean earthenware dish.
8. Bring the cooking liquor to the boil with the velouté.
9. Correct the seasoning and consistency and pass through double muslin or a fine strainer.
10. Mix in the butter then, finally, add the cream.
11. Coat the fillets with the sauce. Garnish with flat parsley or *fleurons* (puff paste crescents).

Ingredient	4 portions	10 portions
Fillets of white fish (100–150 g)	4	10
Butter, for dish and greaseproof paper		
Shallots, finely chopped and sweated	10 g	25 g
Fish stock	60 ml	150 ml
Dry white wine	60 ml	150 ml
Lemon, juice of	¼	½
Fish velouté	250 ml	625 ml
Butter	50 g	125 g
Cream, lightly whipped	2 tbsp	5 tbsp

Energy	Cals	Fat	Sat fat	Carb	Sugar	Protein	Fibre
1,421 kJ	342 kcal	24.0 g	12.8 g	5.8 g	0.9 g	25.9 g	0.2 g

Professional tip

In this recipe, the shallots should be sweated before use; however, if they are very finely chopped, they could be added raw.

Healthy eating tips

- Keep the added salt to a minimum.
- Reduce the amount of butter and cream added to finish the sauce.
- Less sauce could be added, plus a large portion of potatoes and vegetables.

Variation

Add to the fish before cooking:
- fish *bonne-femme*: 100 g thinly sliced white button mushrooms and chopped parsley
- fish *bréval*: as for *bonne-femme* plus 100 g diced, peeled and deseeded tomatoes.

11 Fillets of fish mornay (*filets de poisson mornay*)

Ingredient	4 portions	10 portions
White fish fillets	500–600 g	1.5 kg
Butter, for dish and greaseproof paper		
Fish stock	125 ml	300 ml
Béchamel sauce	250 ml	625 ml
Egg yolk or sabayon	1	3
Grated cheese, preferably Gruyère or Parmesan	50 g	125 g
Salt and cayenne pepper		
Butter	25 g	60 g
Cream, lightly whipped	2 tbsp	5 tbsp

Energy	Cals	Fat	Sat fat	Carb	Sugar	Protein	Fibre
1,309 kJ	315 kcal	19.3 g	9.3 g	5.5 g	0.7 g	29.9 g	0.2 g

1 Prepare the fillets; place in a buttered, seasoned earthenware dish or shallow pan, such as a sauté pan.
2 Add the fish stock, cover with buttered paper.
3 Cook in a moderate oven at 150–200 °C for approximately 5–10 minutes.
4 Drain the fish well, place in a clean earthenware or flat dish.
5 Bring the béchamel to the boil, add the reduced cooking liquor, whisk in the egg yolk and remove from the heat. Add half of the cheese and correct the consistency. Do not reboil, otherwise the egg will curdle.
6 Correct the seasoning and pass through a fine strainer.
7 Mix in the butter and cream; check the consistency.
8 Mask the fish with the sauce, sprinkle with the remaining grated cheese and gratinate under the salamander.

Healthy eating tips
- Reduce the amount of butter and cream added to finish the sauce.
- Less sauce could be served, plus a large portion of potatoes and vegetables.

Variation
Classical variations include:
- Fillets of fish Walewska – place a slice of cooked lobster on each fish fillet before coating with the sauce; after the dish is browned decorate each fillet with a slice of truffle.
- Fillets of fish Florentine – proceed as for fillets mornay, placing the cooked fish on a bed of well-drained and heated dry leaf spinach.

Practical Cookery 14th edition

12 Fillets of fish Véronique

1. Skin and fillet the fish, trim and wash.
2. Butter and season an earthenware dish.
3. Sprinkle with the sweated chopped shallots and add the fillets of fish.
4. Season, add the fish stock, wine and lemon juice.
5. Cover with buttered greaseproof paper.
6. Poach in a moderate oven at 150–200 °C for 7–10 minutes.
7. Drain the fish well and retain the cooking liquor. Dress the fish neatly on a flat dish or clean earthenware dish.
8. Bring the cooking liquor to the boil with the velouté and egg yolk or sabayon.
9. Correct the seasoning and consistency, and pass through double muslin or a fine strainer.
10. Mix in the butter then, finally, add the cream.
11. Coat the fillets with the sauce. Glaze under the salamander.
12. Arrange the grapes neatly on the dish.

Ingredient	4 portions	10 portions
Fillets of white fish (100–150 g)	4	10
Butter, for dish and greaseproof paper		
Shallots, finely chopped, sweated in a little butter/oil	10 g	25 g
Fish stock	60 ml	150 ml
Dry white wine	60 ml	150 ml
Lemon, juice of	½	1
Fish velouté	250 ml	625 ml
Egg yolk or spoonful of sabayon	1	2½
Butter	50 g	125 g
Cream, lightly whipped	2 tbsp	5 tbsp
White grapes, blanched, skinned and pipped	50 g	125 g

Energy	Cals	Fat	Sat fat	Carb	Sugar	Protein	Fibre
1,077 kJ	256 kcal	19.3 g	10.7 g	6.9 g	2.1 g	11.8 g	0.4 g

Professional tip
Plaice and sole are very good in this dish.

Chill the grapes well before use, so that they provide a real contrast of flavour.

Healthy eating tips
- Keep the added salt to a minimum.
- Reduce the amount of butter and cream added to finish the sauce.
- Less sauce could be added plus a large portion of potatoes and vegetables.

Fish and shellfish   9

13 Fish kedgeree

Ingredient	4 portions	10 portions
Fish (usually smoked haddock or fresh salmon)	400 g	1 kg
Milk for poaching		
Rice pilaff (see page 159)	200 g	500 g
Eggs, hard-boiled	2	5
Butter	50 g	125 g
Salt, pepper		
Chives, chopped	1 tsp	2 tsp
Curry sauce, to serve	250 ml	625 ml

Energy	Cals	Fat	Sat fat	Carb	Sugar	Protein	Fibre
1,974 kJ	472 kcal	28.2 g	15.3 g	29.3 g	4.7 g	25.7 g	1.2 g

Using smoked haddock.

This dish is traditionally served for breakfast, lunch or supper. The fish used should be named on the menu (e.g. salmon kedgeree).

1. Poach the fish in milk. Remove all skin and bone. Flake the fish.
2. Cook the rice pilaff. Cut the eggs into dice.
3. Combine the eggs, fish and rice and heat in the butter. Correct the seasoning and add the chives.

Serve hot with a sauceboat of curry sauce.

Healthy eating tips
- Reduce the amount of butter used to heat the rice, fish and eggs.
- Garnish with grilled tomatoes and serve with bread or toast.

Remove the skin from the poached fish

Flake the fish

Dice the hard-boiled eggs

221

Practical Cookery 14th edition

Baked fish dishes

14 Baked cod with a herb crust

1. Place the prepared, washed and dried fish on a greased baking tray or ovenproof dish.
2. Combine the ingredients for the herb crust (the mustard, breadcrumbs, butter, margarine or oil, cheese, parsley and seasoning) and press evenly over the fish.
3. Bake in the oven at 180 °C for approximately 15–20 minutes until cooked and the crust is a light golden-brown.

Serve either with lemon quarters or a suitable salsa (see page 131) or sauce, e.g. tomato or egg.

Ingredient	4 portions	10 portions
Cod fillets, 100–150 g each	4	10
Herb mustard	1 tsp	2½ tsp
Fresh breadcrumbs	100 g	250 g
Butter, margarine or oil	100 g	250 g
Cheddar cheese, grated	100 g	250 g
Parsley, chopped	1 tsp	1 tbsp
Salt, pepper		

Professional tip

Add a little bit of beaten egg to the breadcrumb mixture; this will help bind the mixture together.

Healthy eating tips

- Use a little sunflower oil when making the herb crust.
- Cheese is salty – no added salt is needed.
- Serve with a large portion of tomato or cucumber salsa and new potatoes.

Energy	Cals	Fat	Sat fat	Carb	Sugar	Protein	Fibre
1,882 kJ	452 kcal	30.8 g	18.7 g	12.7 g	0.8 g	31.7 g	0.4 g

Using mustard powder (1 tsp) for herb mustard.

Fish and shellfish 9

15 Baked hake with tomatoes and olives

Ingredient	4 portions	10 portions
Baby plum vine tomatoes	300 g	750 g
Olive oil	100 ml	250 ml
Cloves of garlic, unpeeled	6	15
Black olives, stoned	16	40
Hake fillets (200 g, skin on, bones removed)	4	10

Energy	Cals	Fat	Sat fat	Carb	Sugar	Protein	Fibre	Sodium
1,659 kJ	400 kcal	29.9 g	4.3 g	4.3 g	2.5 g	28.6 g	2.1 g	0.4 g

1 Preheat the oven to 175 °C.
2 Put the tomatoes in a small roasting pan, drizzle with the olive oil and add the garlic.
3 Roast for 15 minutes, then add the olives.
4 Move the mixture aside and add the hake fillets to the pan, skin side down.
5 Baste them with a little of the olive oil in the pan and bake for 8–10 minutes, depending on the thickness of the fillets, until just firm and flaking easily.
6 Remove the pan from the oven and squeeze the roasted garlic cloves out of their skins.
7 Gently mix them with the tomatoes and olives, trying not to break up the tomatoes too much.
8 Season the tomato mixture and spoon on to four plates. Place a piece of baked hake on top of each.
9 Serve with braised cabbage and mashed potato.

Note

Kalamata olives are best – they have a subtle flavour.

Cod, pollock or haddock may be used instead of hake.

223

16 Cod boulangère

Ingredient	4 portions	10 portions
Onion	1	2
Oil	50 ml	125 ml
Sea salt, freshly milled black pepper		
Potatoes	750 g	2 kg
Thyme		
Lemon, zest and juice of	1	2
Fish stock, hot	400 ml	1 litre
Butter	100 g	250 g
Cod fillets (100 g, skinless, boneless)	4	10
Fresh peas	300 g	750 g
Chives, chopped		

Energy	Cals	Fat	Sat fat	Carb	Sugar	Protein	Fibre	Sodium
2,650 kJ	636 kcal	35.7 g	15.1 g	44.1 g	5.4 g	37.3 g	8.7 g	0.6 g

1. Peel the onions and slice them approximately 3 mm thick.
2. Heat the oil in a thick-bottomed pan, place in the onions and cook slowly until a light golden-brown. (Do not fast-fry the onions – this is a caramelisation process to reveal their natural sugars.)
3. Meanwhile, preheat the oven to 190 °C.
4. Grease a shallow baking tin with a little butter and season well with freshly milled black pepper and sea salt.
5. Peel the potatoes and slice them finely (3 mm thick).
6. Once the onions are softened, arrange the potato and onion in alternate layers on the bottom of the baking dish, also adding the thyme throughout.
7. Mix the lemon juice and zest with the hot fish stock and pour over the potatoes and onion.
8. Randomly place knobs of butter over the top of the potatoes.
9. Cover the baking dish with foil and bake in the oven for 55 minutes.
10. While the potatoes are cooking, prepare the cod by cutting it into large, bite-sized chunks and place in the fridge.
11. When the potatoes are cooked (check with the point of a knife), arrange the fish over the top of the potatoes, recover with the foil and cook for another 10 minutes.
12. Remove the foil and sprinkle over the peas, recover and place back in the oven for a further 3 minutes.
13. Remove from the oven, take off the foil, clean the outer rim of the dish if required, sprinkle with the chopped chives and serve.

17 Fish pie

Ingredient	4 portions	10 portions
Béchamel (thin) (see page 112)	250 ml	625 ml
Cooked fish (free from skin and bone)	200 g	500 g
Mushrooms, cooked and diced	50 g	125 g
Egg, hard-boiled and chopped	1	2½
Parsley, chopped		
Salt, pepper		
Potatoes, mashed or duchess	200 g	500 g
Egg wash or milk, to finish		

Energy	Cals	Fat	Sat fat	Carb	Sugar	Protein	Fibre
879 kJ	209 kcal	12.0 g	5.3 g	11.9 g	3.2 g	14.1 g	0.9 g

1. Bring the béchamel to the boil.
2. Add the fish, mushrooms, egg and parsley. Correct the seasoning.
3. Place in a buttered pie dish.
4. Carefully spread or pipe the potato on top. Brush with egg wash or milk.
5. Brown in a hot oven and use a food probe to check that the temperature is 75 °C.

Cook the fish, mushrooms and egg in the béchamel

Pipe mashed potato over the top before baking

Healthy eating tips
- Keep the added salt to a minimum.
- This is a healthy main course dish, particularly when served with plenty of vegetables.

Variations
Suitable fish include cod, haddock, pollock, plaice, sole, gurnard and monkfish.

Many variations can be made to this recipe with the addition of:
- prawns or shrimps
- herbs such as dill, tarragon or fennel
- raw fish poached in white wine, the cooking liquor strained off, double cream added in place of béchamel and reduced to a light consistency.

Steamed fish dishes

18 Salmon en papillote with crushed new potatoes

Ingredient	4 portions	10 portions
For the potatoes		
New potatoes	20	50
Olive oil	50 ml	125 ml
Dill, finely chopped	1 tsp	2 tsp
Sea salt, freshly milled black pepper		
For the salmon		
Olive oil	2 tbsp	5 tbsp
Cloves of garlic, thinly sliced	2	5
Red chilli, deseeded, finely chopped	1	2
Large shallots, thinly sliced	1	2
Carrot, peeled and cut into thin matchsticks	1	2
Sugarsnap peas, halved lengthways	16	40
Purple sprouting broccoli stems	8	20
Flat-leaf parsley stems	2	5
Suprêmes of salmon (200 g, skin on, pin boned)	4	10
Rock salt		
White wine	200 ml	500 ml

1. Preheat one oven to 190 °C and another to 220 °C.
2. For timing purposes, start with the potatoes. Boil them until they are just cooked but not soft.
3. Crush roughly with the back of a fork and place on a lightly oiled baking tray. Sprinkle with the olive oil and black pepper. Put aside until the salmon is in the oven.
4. Cut two pieces of tin foil per portion, each measuring about 23 cm².
5. Place half of the foil squares on a work surface and drizzle with the olive oil.
6. Sprinkle over the garlic, chilli and shallots and arrange the vegetables and salmon suprêmes on top.
7. Season with the rock salt.
8. Place the remaining foil squares on top of the fish, lining up with the base foil.
9. Bring together the edges of the bottom foil with the top and fold together, then repeat to form a watertight seal (this is the essence of the cooking method). Before making the last fold to seal each parcel, pour in 50 ml of white wine.
10. Place on a baking sheet and bake at 190 °C for 10–12 minutes. Meanwhile, in the hotter oven, further cook the potatoes for 12 minutes until crisp and golden.
11. To serve, sprinkle the potatoes with the chopped dill and serve with the parcels of salmon.

Energy	Cals	Fat	Sat fat	Carb	Sugar	Protein	Fibre
3,032 kJ	727 kcal	41.4 g	6.7 g	36.1 g	7.2 g	46.8 g	6.9 g

Fish and shellfish 9

Note

The term 'en papillotte' means 'butterfly' and traditionally this method of cookery was all about the theatre at the restaurant table.

The ingredients were placed on a piece of parchment paper (today's greaseproof paper, or aluminium foil), shaped like a heart or a butterfly (both sides symmetrical). The edges of the paper were brushed with oil and crimped together, forming a waterproof seal. Once placed in the oven, the moisture from the ingredients inflates the parchment pouch like a pillow and cooks the dish in its own juices. This is then taken straight to the table and opened in front of the diner, allowing the aromas to escape, creating great theatre and sensory stimulation.

This method of cookery still has its place in the modern world of gastronomy, however there is less theatre in the room. The parcel is likely to be opened in the kitchen and served on the plate, thus harnessing the natural cooking juices from the ingredients to create a naturally light and clean-tasting dish.

19 Steamed fish with garlic, spring onions and ginger

1. Wash and dry the fish well; rub *lightly* with salt on both sides.
2. Put the fish on to plates, scatter the ginger evenly on top.
3. Cover the plates tightly, place into the steamer and steam gently until just cooked (5–15 minutes, according to the thickness of the fish).
4. Remove the plates, sprinkle on the spring onions and soy sauce.
5. Brown the garlic slices in the hot oil and pour over the dish.

Garlic and ginger have intense flavours, so they must be chopped very finely.

Healthy eating tips
- Steaming is a healthy way of cooking.
- Serve with a large portion of rice or noodles and stir-fried vegetables.

Variation

This is a Chinese recipe that can be adapted in many ways – for example, replace the spring onions and garlic and use thinly sliced mushrooms, diced tomato (skinned and deseeded), finely chopped shallots, lemon juice, white wine, chopped parsley, dill or chervil.

Ingredient	4 portions	10 portions
White fish fillets, e.g. cod, sole	400 g	1 kg
Salt		
Fresh ginger, freshly chopped	1 tbsp	2½ tbsp
Spring onions, finely chopped	2 tbsp	5 tbsp
Light soy sauce	1 tbsp	2½ tbsp
Cloves of garlic, peeled and thinly sliced	4	10
Oil	1 tbsp	2½ tbsp

Energy	Cals	Fat	Sat fat	Carb	Sugar	Protein	Fibre
468 kJ	112 kcal	3.5 g	0.7 g	1.2 g	0.4 g	18.7 g	0.1 g

Using two cloves of garlic.

20 Steamed halibut with lime and fennel

Ingredient	4 portions	10 portions
Halibut fillet, skinned (or use any other white fish such as pollack, cod, haddock)	4 × 100 g	10 × 100 g
Spring onions, thinly sliced	4	10
Salt and black pepper		
Red chilli, deseeded and cut into very thin slices	½	1½
Lime juice	3 tbsp	8 tbsp
Olive oil or sunflower oil	3 tbsp	8 tbsp
Limes cut into rounds	1	3
Bay leaves	2	6
Cloves of garlic, finely chopped	1	2½
Coriander, chopped	1 tbsp	2½ tbsp
Fennel bulb, very thinly sliced	1	2½
Thai fish sauce (Nam Pla)	1 tbsp	2½ tbsp

Energy	Cals	Fat	Sat fat	Carb	Sugar	Protein	Fibre	Sodium
914 kJ	219 kcal	13.3g	1.9g	2.2g	1.6g	22.8g	2.1g	0.1g

1. Mix together the lime juice, oil, garlic and fish sauce and marinate the fish in this for 30 minutes, spooning the mixture over the fish frequently.
2. Remove the fish from the marinade and scatter each piece with spring onion, coriander, chilli and a slice of lime.
3. Season the fennel and place in a steamer tray, small steamer or between two plates over simmering water.
4. Top with the fish, make sure it is well covered and steam gently for 5–10 minutes until the fish is cooked and the fennel tender.
5. Remove the fish and continue to cook the fennel if necessary.
6. Divide the fennel between the plates and top each with fish.

21 Steamed clams in saffron and spring green broth

Ingredient	4 portions	10 portions
Fish stock	700 ml	1750 ml
Chorizo, ½ cm diced	75 g	190 g
Garlic clove, crushed and chopped	1	2
Saffron strands	½ tsp	2 tsp
Spring greens, 2 heads	150 g	375 g
Live clams	1000 g	2500 g
Fresh parsley, finely chopped	2 tbsp	5 tbsp
Olive oil	40 ml	100 ml
Lemon	1	3

Energy	Cals	Fat	Sat fat	Carb	Sugar	Protein	Fibre	Sodium
1,059kJ	255kcal	18.5g	14.2g	5.6g	2.7g	16.3g	2.5g	0.9g

Using mussels instead of clams.

1 Place the stock, chorizo, garlic and saffron in a suitable pan and bring to the boil.
2 Add the greens. Cover and cook for approximately 2 minutes.
3 Add the clams. Cover and cook over a high heat for approximately 4 to 5 minutes until the clams have opened. Stir in the chopped parsley.
4 Serve in suitable bowls, dividing the greens and the clams equally.
5 Ladle over the stock, drizzle with olive oil and serve with wedges of lemon.

Deep-fried fish dishes

22 Frying batters (*pâtes à frire*) for fish

Recipe A

Ingredient	4 portions	10 portions
Flour	200 g	500 g
Salt		
Yeast	10 g	25 g
Water or milk	250 ml	625 ml

1. Sift the flour and salt into a basin.
2. Dissolve the yeast in a little of the water.
3. Make a well in the flour. Add the yeast and the liquid.
4. Gradually incorporate the flour and beat to a smooth mixture.
5. Allow to rest for at least 1 hour before using.

Batter mixed to the right consistency

Recipe B

Ingredient	4 portions	10 portions
Flour	200 g	500 g
Salt		
Egg	1	2–3
Water or milk	250 ml	625 ml
Oil	2 tbsp	5 tbsp

1. Sift the flour and salt into a basin. Make a well. Add the egg and the liquid.
2. Gradually incorporate the flour and beat to a smooth mixture.
3. Mix in the oil. Allow to rest before using.

Recipe C

Ingredient	4 portions	10 portions
Flour	200 g	500 g
Salt		
Water or milk	250 ml	625 ml
Oil	2 tbsp	5 tbsp
Egg whites, stiffly beaten	2	5 tbsp

1. As for recipe B, but fold in the egg whites just before using.

Note

Other ingredients can be added to batter, for example chopped fresh herbs, grated ginger, garam masala or beer.

Fish and shellfish   9

23 Fried fish in batter

1. Pass the prepared, washed and well-dried fish through flour, shake off the surplus and pass through the batter (see recipe 22).
2. Place carefully away from you into the hot deep-fryer at 175 °C until the fish turns a golden-brown. Remove and drain well.

Serve with lemon quarters and tartare sauce.

> **Professional tip**
> Remove any excess batter before frying; too much batter will make the dish too heavy.

Energy	Cals	Fat	Sat fat	Carb	Sugar	Protein	Fibre
1,736 kJ	415 kcal	14.0g	1.8g	41.6g	3.5g	33.2g	2.1g

Pass the prepared fish through the batter

Shake off any excess and then lower carefully into the fryer

24 Deep-fried fish coated with breadcrumbs

1. Pass the fillets through flour, beaten egg and fresh white breadcrumbs. (Pat the surfaces well to avoid loose crumbs falling into the oil, burning and spoiling both the oil and the fish.)
2. Deep fry at 175 °C, until the fish turns a golden-brown. Remove and drain well.
3. Serve with lemon wedges and tartare sauce.

Energy	Cals	Fat	Sat fat	Carb	Sugar	Protein	Fibre	Sodium
1,356 kJ	324 kcal	19.5g	2.0g	14.0g	0.5g	24.2g	0.8g	0.2g

231

25 Goujons of plaice

1. Cut fillets of plaice into strips approximately 8 × 0.5 cm. Wash and dry well.
2. Pass through flour, beaten egg and fresh white breadcrumbs. Pat the surfaces well so that there are no loose crumbs which could fall into the oil and burn.
3. Deep fry at 175–180 °C, then drain well.

Serve with lemon quarters and a suitable sauce (e.g. tartare).

Professional tip
Keep the coating ingredients (flour, egg and breadcrumbs) separate. Shake off any excess flour and egg before dipping the fish into the breadcrumbs.

Other fish, e.g. sole or salmon, may be used instead of plaice.

Energy	Cals	Fat	Sat fat	Carb	Sugar	Protein	Fibre	Sodium
1,094 kJ	261 kcal	13.8g	0.0g	13.8g	0.0g	21.3g	0.6g	0.3g

26 Salmon fishcakes

Ingredient	4 portions	10 portions
Salmon fillet, skinned and boneless	400 g	1 kg
Butter	50 g	125 g
Lemon, juice of	1	2
Spring onions	3	8
Flat-leaf parsley	10 g	25 g
Dill	sprig	sprig
Cooked mashed potato (make sure this is fairly dry)	225 g	560 g
Eggs, beaten	1	2
Crème fraiche	1 tbsp	2½ tbsp
Thai fish sauce (*nam pla*) – optional	Few drops	1 tsp
Plain flour, seasoned		
Eggs, beaten		
Breadcrumbs		

Energy	Cals	Fat	Sat fat	Carb	Sugar	Protein	Fibre
1,821 kJ	438 kcal	30.2g	13.6g	18.0g	1.5g	24.5g	1.6g

1 Place the salmon in an oiled roasting tin, season with salt and pepper, dot with butter and squeeze the lemon juice over.
2 Bake at 200 °C for approximately 7 minutes.
3 Allow the salmon to cool a little, then flake into bite-sized pieces.
4 Chop the spring onions and herbs.
5 Add the salmon to the mashed potato, and mix in the herbs, spring onion, beaten egg and crème fraiche. Add a little *nam pla* if using and season.
6 Form into neat, even-sized cake shapes (a ring mould could be used), place on a tray lined with cling film and chill thoroughly for several hours.
7 Coat with seasoned flour, egg and breadcrumbs (*pané*), chill well again or the formed cakes can be frozen.
8 Cook in a deep fryer as required and drain on kitchen paper.
9 Serve with a suitable sauce or salsa and/or mixed salad leaves.

One way to divide the mixture is to form it into a long roll

Divide the roll into even pieces

Mould each piece into a ball

Pass the balls through seasoned flour, beaten egg and breadcrumbs

Flatten each cake firmly and shake off surplus crumbs

Deep fry until golden brown

Practical Cookery 14th edition

Shallow-fried fish dishes

27 Shallow-fried fish

1. Prepare, clean, wash and dry the fish well.
2. Pass through flour and shake off all surplus. (If using non-stick pans it is not necessary to flour the fish.)
3. Heat the frying medium, such as oil, in a frying pan.
4. Shallow-fry on both sides (presentation side first), then serve.

> **Professional tip**
>
> Do not overcrowd the pan because this may cause the temperature of the oil to fall, which will affect the efficient cooking of the fish.

Energy	Cals	Fat	Sat fat	Carb	Sugar	Protein	Fibre	Sodium
1,056 kJ	251 kcal	13.2g	1.7g	7.8g	0.2g	26.0g	0.4g	0.2g

Pass the fish through seasoned flour

Place carefully into the pan, presentation side first

Turn the fish gently, once, during cooking

> **Variation**
>
> When cooked, sprinkle with a mixture of grated lemon zest, finely chopped garlic and chopped parsley (known as gremolata).

28 Shallow-fried sole with shrimp and caper dressing

Ingredient	4 portions	10 portions
Lemon sole (350 g)	4	10
Ground cumin, toasted	5 g	12 g
Sea salt, freshly milled black pepper		
Plain flour	200 g	500 g
Sunflower oil	100 ml	250 ml
For the dressing		
Shrimps, cooked and peeled	100 g	250 g
Small capers	75 g	200 g
Butter, cut into small cubes	150 g	375 g
Olive oil	50 ml	125 ml
Parsley, chopped	2 tbsp	5 tbsp
Lemon, juice of	1	2

Energy	Cals	Fat	Sat fat	Carb	Sugar	Protein	Fibre	Sodium
4,655 kJ	1117 kcal	74.9 g	25.2 g	39.7 g	1.6 g	74.5 g	2.3 g	1.0 g

1 Fillet the fish and trim the fillets to neaten them.
2 Mix the cumin, salt, pepper and flour together.
3 Before you start cooking the fish, make sure the other components of the dish are ready, as the sole will cook quickly.
4 Heat the oil in a non-stick pan large enough to cook one portion (four fillets). Pass the fillets through the flour, ensuring that the whole fillet is coated.
5 Place the fillets into the hot oil, presentation side first, and cook until golden. Turn and cook for a further 10 seconds, remove and place on an oven tray (they will be flashed in the oven just before serving).
6 Repeat the process for the other portions.
7 Add the dressing ingredients, except the parsley and lemon juice, to the pan, and heat until the butter foams and brings out the flavour of the capers.
8 Squeeze in the lemon juice and add the parsley.
9 Flash the sole in a moderate oven. Spoon the dressing over the sole to serve. Accompany with purple sprouting broccoli or green salad.

29 Fish meunière

Ingredient	4 portions	10 portions
White fish fillets, skinned	400–600 g	1–1.5 kg
Large lemons	2	5
Clarified butter	100 g	250 g
Parsley, chopped	1 tsp	2 tsp

Energy	Cals	Fat	Sat fat	Carb	Sugar	Protein	Fibre
1,314 kJ	313 kcal	24.1 g	10.3 g	3.1 g	0.0 g	21.2 g	0.1 g

Many fish, whole or filleted, may be cooked by this method: for example, sole, sea bass, bream, fillets of plaice, trout, brill, cod, turbot, herring and scampi.

1. Prepare and clean the fish, wash and drain.
2. Pass through seasoned flour, shaking off all surplus.
3. Shallow-fry on both sides, presentation side first, in hot clarified butter or oil.
4. Dress neatly on an oval flat dish or plate/plates.
5. Peel a lemon, removing the peel, white pith and pips.
6. Cut the lemon into slices and place one on each portion.
7. Squeeze some lemon juice on the fish.
8. Allow 10–25 g butter per portion and colour in a clean frying pan to the nut-brown stage (*beurre noisette*).
9. Pour over the fish.
10. Sprinkle with chopped parsley and serve.

Professional tip
When the butter has browned, try adding a squeeze of lemon juice or a splash of white wine for extra flavour.

Healthy eating tips
- Use a small amount of unsaturated oil to fry the fish.
- Use less *beurre noisette* per portion. Some customers will prefer the finished dish without the additional fat.

Variation
Variations include the following:
- **Fish meunière with almonds**: as for fish meunière, adding 10 g of almonds cut in short julienne or coarsely chopped into the meunière butter just before it begins to turn brown. This method is usually applied to trout.
- **Fish belle meunière**: as for fish meunière, with the addition of a grilled mushroom, a slice of peeled tomato and a soft herring roe (passed through flour and shallow-fried), all neatly dressed on each portion of fish.
- **Fish Doria**: as for fish meunière, with a sprinkling of small turned pieces of cucumber carefully cooked in 25 g of butter in a small covered pan, or blanched in boiling salted water.
- **Fish Grenobloise**: as for fish meunière, the peeled lemon being cut into segments, neatly dressed on the fish, with a few capers sprinkled over.
- **Fish Bretonne**: as for fish meunière, with a few picked shrimps and cooked sliced mushrooms sprinkled over the fish.

For each of these classical dishes, chefs may wish to add some chopped herbs for flavour; for example, add chopped dill to fish Doria.

30 Pan-fried fillets of sole with rocket and broad beans

Ingredient	4 portions	10 portions
Oil for frying		
Sole fillets, trimmed	16	40
Seasoning		
Butter	200 g	500 g
Broad beans, cooked and shelled	250 g	625 g
Rocket, picked and washed	300 g	750 g
Vinaigrette	50 ml	125 ml

Energy	Cals	Fat	Sat fat	Carb	Sugar	Protein	Fibre	Sodium
2,710 kJ	654 kcal	54.2 g	28.0 g	5.1 g	1.4 g	36.6 g	6.6 g	0.6 g

Note

This is a very simple and quick dish. Any salad or greens, if they are quickly cooked or lightly dressed, can go with this dish.

1. Heat a little oil in a non-stick pan.
2. Place the fillets of sole on a tray and season on both sides.
3. Place the fish in the pan carefully (presentation side down).
4. Cook for 1 minute on a medium/high heat, and then carefully turn the fish, remove the pan from the heat and allow the residual heat to finish the cooking.
5. Place the sole fillets (four per portion) on serving plates and keep warm.
6. Place the butter in the cooking pan, heat to the *noisette* stage, add the broad beans and cook for 30 seconds to 1 minute just to reheat them.
7. Mask the fish with the *noisette* butter and the beans. Finish with a dressed rocket salad.

31 Pan-fried skate with capers and *beurre noir*

1. Place a skillet on the hottest part of the stove and an empty sauté pan to the side of the stove, achieving a moderate heat (this is for the *beurre noir*).
2. Ensure the skate wings are fresh, and free from ammonia aromas and skin. Season them with salt and pepper.
3. Add the vegetable oil to the skillet and place in the skate wings; cook with colour for 1–2 minutes and then carefully turn. At this point, ease the skillet to a cooler point of the stove while the *beurre noir* cooks.
4. Place the butter in the sauté pan and allow to foam (at this point remove the skate and place on the serving dish).
5. Add the lemon, parsley and capers to the *beurre noir* and stir well.
6. To finish, nap over the skate wing and serve.

Note

Because skate pass urine through their wings, if they are not extremely fresh they will start to smell of ammonia after three to four days. This is a key indicator of their freshness.

Ingredient	4 portions	10 portions
Skate, skinless fillets (approx. 160 g each)	4	10
Seasoning		
Vegetable oil	50 ml	125 ml
Butter	175 g	450 g
Lemons, juice of	2	5
Flat-leaf parsley, chopped	2 tbsp	5 tbsp
Small capers	100 g	250 g

Energy	Cals	Fat	Sat fat	Carb	Sugar	Protein	Fibre	Sodium
2,395 kJ	579 kcal	51.9 g	24.7 g	0.8 g	0.8 g	27.1 g	1.2 g	1.0 g

Based on olives in place of capers.

Fish and shellfish | **9**

32 Nage of red mullet with baby leeks

Ingredient	4 portions	10 portions
Mussels, cooked and removed from shell	16	40
Lemons, juice of	2	5
Baby spinach	200 g	500 g
Baby leeks	12	30
Baby asparagus, spears of	12	30
Green beans, pieces of	2 tbsp	5 tbsp
Red mullet fillets (approximately 120 g each), pin bones and scales removed	4	10
Nage		
Large onion	1	3
Carrots, peeled	2	5
Celery sticks	2	5
Leeks	2	5
Cloves of garlic	1	3
Half white and half pink peppercorns	12	30
Star anise	1	3
White wine	375 ml	950 ml
Noilly Prat	375 ml	950 ml
Chervil	10 g	25 g
Parsley	10 g	25 g
Tarragon	10 g	25 g
Chives, chopped	1 tbsp	3 tbsp

Energy	Cals	Fat	Sat fat	Carb	Sugar	Protein	Fibre	Sodium
2,172 kJ	519 kcal	9.2 g	0.9 g	26.8 g	19.7 g	46.2 g	13.1 g	0.6 g

1. In a large pan place the onions, carrots, celery and leeks, which have been cut into 2 cm pieces.
2. Just cover the vegetables with water. Bring to the boil. Simmer for 4–5 minutes. Remove from the heat and add the rest of the ingredients.
3. Cover with cling film and allow to cool to room temperature. Place into a plastic container and store in the fridge overnight to develop flavour.
4. Pass through a fine sieve. Any surplus nage can be frozen for later use.
5. To finish, place 500 ml of the vegetable nage in a pan, add the mussels, a squeeze of lemon, spinach, baby leeks, asparagus and green beans.
6. Bring to the boil, check the seasoning and retain.
7. Heat a non-stick pan with a little vegetable oil. Season the mullet fillets and cook for 1 minute on each side (thickness dependent), starting with the skin side down.
8. Divide the vegetable garnish between the bowls. Place the red mullet on top of the vegetable garnish and, returning the pan the mullet was cooked in to the stove, pour in the nage.
9. When the nage has returned to the boil, spoon over the fish and garnish. Serve immediately.

> **Professional tip**
>
> This dish is open to many substitutions of fish and shellfish but one key point to remember is that the nage should not be allowed to overpower the main ingredients.

239

Practical Cookery 14th edition

33 Barramundi with garlic, ginger and lemon butter and pak choi

Ingredient	4 portions	10 portions
Olive oil	75 ml	200 ml
Barramundi fillets (200 g, skin off)	4	10
Seasoning		
Small heads of pak choi	8	20
Salted butter	100 g	250 g
Garlic, small cloves, chopped	1	2
Root ginger, cut into 2–3/6–8 pieces	50 g	125 g
Fresh lemon juice	3 tbsp	7 tbsp
Fresh basil leaves, chopped	5	12

Energy	Cals	Fat	Sat fat	Carb	Sugar	Protein	Fibre	Sodium
3,174 kJ	766 kcal	62.2 g	19.7 g	7.9 g	6.9 g	44.3 g	6.8 g	0.3 g

Using spring greens instead of pak choi.

Note
Barramundi can be used in any recipe calling for a white fish such as cod, bass or haddock, or red snapper.

1. Bring a pan of salted water to the boil.
2. Heat the oil in a non-stick frying pan.
3. Season the fish fillets and place in the hot oil. Cook for 2 minutes and then turn, removing the pan from the heat. Allow the residual heat to finish the cooking process.
4. Meanwhile, blanch the pak choi for 2 minutes in the boiling water, until vibrant green. Drain.
5. Remove the fish from the pan and keep it warm. Return the pan to the heat and add the butter, garlic and ginger. Cook for 2 minutes until the garlic is soft and the ginger has imparted its flavour. Remove the ginger and add the lemon juice and basil.
6. Mix well and add the pak choi. Ensure that all the flavours are incorporated well.
7. Serve the fish and pak choi with the dressing from the pan over the top.

34 Thai fishcakes

Ingredient	4 portions	10 portions
Salmon, filleted and skinned	100 g	250 g
Cod, filleted and skinned	100 g	250 g
Sesame oil	½ tsp	1¼ tsp
Cloves of garlic	2	5
Root ginger, grated	1 tbsp	2¼ tbsp
Red chillies (small)	½	1
Soy sauce	1 tsp	1½ tsp
Lemon grass	12 g	30 g
Salt	2 g	5 g
Pepper	2 g	5 g
Lime juice	2 tsp	5 tsp
Sunflower oil for cooking	2 tsp	5 tsp

Energy	Cals	Fat	Sat fat	Carb	Sugar	Protein	Fibre
395 kJ	95 kcal	5.8 g	0.9 g	0.7 g	0.2 g	10.0 g	0.1 g

1. Place all ingredients, except the oil for cooking, in a food processor, blend until bound together and smooth.
2. Turn out and divide into 12 small cakes for four portions (30 for ten portions). The cakes should be at least 2 cm thick.
3. Heat the oil in a suitable pan. Place the fish cakes in, allowing approximately 3 minutes each side. Drain on kitchen paper after frying.
4. Serve immediately garnished with flat-leaf parsley and Thai cucumber salad.

Healthy eating tips
- No added salt is needed.
- Serve with plenty of fragrant Thai rice and extra vegetables.

Boiled shellfish dishes

35 Mussels in white wine sauce (*moules marinière*)

Ingredient	4 portions	10 portions
Shallots, chopped	50 g	125 g
Parsley, chopped	1 tbsp	2 tbsp
White wine	60 ml	150 ml
Strong fish stock	200 ml	500 ml
Mussels	2 kg	5 kg
Butter	25 g	60 g
Flour	25 g	60 g
Seasoning		

Energy	Cals	Fat	Sat fat	Carb	Sugar	Protein	Fibre	Sodium
1,900 kJ	452 kcal	14.3 g	5.3 g	18.1 g	0.9 g	61.4 g	0.6 g	1.5 g

1 Take a thick-bottomed pan and add the shallots, parsley, wine, fish stock and the cleaned mussels.
2 Cover with a tight-fitting lid and cook over a high heat until the shells open.
3 Drain off all the cooking liquor in a colander set over a clean bowl to retain the cooking juices.
4 Carefully check the mussels and discard any that have not opened.
5 Place in a dish and cover to keep warm.
6 Make a roux from the flour and butter; pour over the cooking liquor, ensuring it is free from sand and stirring continuously to avoid lumps.
7 Correct the seasoning and garnish with more chopped parsley.
8 Pour over the mussels and serve.

Variation

For an eastern influence add a little red chilli and replace the parsley with coriander.

Fish and shellfish 9

36 Clam chowder

Ingredient	4 portions	10 portions
Clams		
Shallots, finely diced	2 medium	5 medium
Butter	50 g	125 g
Clams, shells tightly closed	500 g	1250 g
White wine or dry vermouth	20 ml	50 ml
Chowder		
Vegetable oil	50 ml	125 ml
Smoked bacon, cut into 1 cm dice	50 g	125 g
Medium onion, cut into 1 cm dice	1	3
Medium carrot, cut into 1 cm dice	1	3
Garlic cloves, finely chopped	2	5
Celery sticks, cut into 1 cm dice	1	3
Medium potato, peeled and cut into 1 cm dice	1	3
Medium yellow pepper, cut into 1 cm dice	1	3
Chicken stock	1 litre	2½ litres
Whipping cream	100 ml	250 ml
Butter	50 g	125 g

Energy	Cals	Fat	Sat fat	Carb	Sugar	Protein	Fibre	Sodium
2,367 kJ	571 kcal	47.0 g	21.5 g	21.5 g	8.4 g	14.5 g	5.4 g	1.0 g

Using salted butter and white wine, and mussels instead of clams.

For the clams

1 Take a large saucepan with a tight-fitting lid and place over a medium heat with the shallots and butter. Cook for 1 minute without letting the shallots colour.

2 Add the washed clams, shake the pan, then add the wine and place the lid on the pan immediately. Leave the clams to steam for 1–2 minutes so that they open and exude an intense liquor.

3 Remove the lid and make sure all the clams are open. Remove the pan from the heat and discard any with closed shells.

4 Place a colander over a large bowl and pour the contents of the pan into the colander, reserving the liquor for the chowder.

5 Allow the clams to cool. Pick out the meat and discard the shells. Store the clam meat in an airtight container in the fridge until you are ready to serve the chowder.

For the chowder

1 In a large saucepan, heat the oil. When hot, add the bacon and cook for about 5 minutes until crisp and brown.

2 Using a perforated spoon, transfer the bacon onto kitchen paper to drain. Add the onion, carrot, garlic, celery and potato to the saucepan, reduce the heat to medium-low and cook the vegetables for 3–4 minutes without colouring.

3 Add the peppers and cook for 5 minutes. Pour in the chicken stock and the reserved liquor from the clams.

4 Bring to the boil and simmer for 10 minutes or until the volume of liquid has reduced by about half.

5 Add the cooked bacon and the cream, then bring to the boil and reduce for a further 2 minutes until the soup thickens slightly.

6 Just before serving whisk in the butter.

Healthy eating tips

For the clams, the butter can be replaced with olive oil.

For the chowder, the whipping cream and butter could be replaced with fromage frais, low-fat crème fraîche or natural yoghurt.

243

Fried shellfish dishes

37 Crab cakes with chilli lime dipping sauce

Ingredient	30–40 cakes
Crab cakes	
Crab meat	350 g
Uncooked prawns, shelled and deveined	650 g
Red curry paste	1 tbsp
Egg	1
Spring onions	2
Fresh coriander, finely chopped	2 tbsp
Lemon grass, finely chopped	2 tsp
Red Thai chilli, deseeded and chopped	1
Vegetable oil	2 tbsp
Dipping sauce	
Lime juice	2 tbsp
Water	2 tbsp
Fish sauce (*nam pla*)	2 tsp
Kaffir lime leaf, chopped	1
Red Thai chilli, deseeded and finely chopped	1

For the crab cakes:

1 In a food processor, place the crab, prawns, curry paste, egg, spring onion, coriander, lemon grass and chilli. Combine all ingredients until mixed together.
2 Shape into small cakes.
3 Heat the oil in a shallow pan and fry the crab cakes on both sides until golden brown. Drain, then place on a suitable dish with the dipping sauce (see below).

For the dipping sauce:

1 Combine all ingredients in a suitable bowl.
2 Stir well.

Energy	Cals	Fat	Sat fat	Carb	Sugar	Protein	Fibre
557 kJ	133 kcal	5.6 g	0.7 g	1.2 g	0.4 g	19.6 g	0.1 g

38 Prawns with chilli and garlic

Ingredient	4 portions	10 portions
Clove of garlic, crushed	1	3
Lime, juice of	1	2½
Lemon, juice of	½	1¼
Mild red chillies, deseeded and finely chopped	2	5
Olive oil	1 tbsp	3 tbsp
Honey	1 tbsp	3 tbsp
Extra large prawns, raw, shells on, heads removed	32	80
Black pepper		
To serve		
Salsa verde (see page 131)	100 ml	250 ml
Garlic bread	4 slices	10 slices
Green salad		

Energy	Cals	Fat	Sat fat	Carb	Sugar	Protein	Fibre	Sodium
728 kJ	173 kcal	3.8g	0.6g	6.6g	6.3g	28.6g	0.1g	0.3g

1. In a shallow dish, mix together the garlic, lime juice, lemon juice, chillies, olive oil and honey.
2. Make an incision (don't cut all the way through – leave the prawn intact) in the back of each prawn and remove the entrails. Wash and dry well.
3. Add the prawns to the oil/chilli mix, season with black pepper and marinate in the fridge for 30 minutes.
4. Meanwhile, prepare the green salad, salsa verde and garlic bread.
5. Remove the prawns from the marinade and heat a small amount of oil in a non-stick frying pan.
6. Place the prawns in the pan and cook until pink and cooked through, basting with any leftover marinade while cooking.
7. To serve, place warm garlic bread on plates and pile the prawns up on top, allowing the cooking juices to run into the bread. Drizzle with salsa verde and serve with the salad.

Grilled shellfish dishes

39 Scallops and bacon

Ingredient	4 portions	10 portions
Large scallops, shelled, roe and skirt removed, washed	12	30
Pancetta bacon rashers (rind off)	12	30
Olive oil	50 ml	125 ml
Lemon	1	2½
Asparagus sticks, peeled, blanched for 1 minute and refreshed	16	40
Seasoning		

Energy	Cals	Fat	Sat fat	Carb	Sugar	Protein	Fibre	Sodium
1,705 kJ	410 kcal	26.8g	6.9g	5.9g	2.8g	36.4g	2.3g	1.3g

1 Wrap the scallops in the pancetta, pin with a cocktail stick and season (be mindful that the pancetta is salty).
2 Heat the oil in a non-stick pan, place the scallops in and cook until golden-brown. Squeeze the lemon over the scallops and allow the juice to evaporate slightly.
3 Remove from the pan and retain with all the pan juices.
4 Return the pan to the heat and add the asparagus, cooking for a further 2 minutes.
5 To serve, divide the asparagus on to plates. Top with the scallops, pour over the pan juices and serve.

Cold fish and shellfish dishes

40 Dressed crab

Ingredient	1 portion
Whole crab, cooked	1 (200–300 g)
Salt, pepper	
Worcester sauce	
Mayonnaise	
Fresh white breadcrumbs	
Decoration as required, e.g. parsley and hard-boiled egg	

Energy	Cals	Fat	Sat fat	Carb	Sugar	Protein	Fibre	Sodium
1,974 kJ	474 kcal	28.6g	4.4g	0.8g	0.7g	53.1g	0.7g	1.2g

1. Remove large claws and sever at the joints.
2. Remove the flexible pincer from the claw.
3. Crack or saw carefully and remove all flesh.
4. Remove flesh from two remaining joints with the handle of spoon.
5. Carefully remove the soft undershell.
6. Discard the gills (dead man's fingers) and the sac behind the eyes.
7. Scrape out all the inside of the shell and pass through a sieve.
8. Season with salt, pepper, Worcester sauce and a little mayonnaise; thicken lightly with fresh white breadcrumbs.
9. Trim the shell by tapping carefully along the natural line.
10. Scrub the shell thoroughly and leave to dry.
11. Dress the brown meat down the centre of the shell.
12. Shred the white meat, taking care to remove any small pieces of shell.
13. Dress neatly on either side of the brown meat.
14. Decorate as desired, using any of the following: chopped parsley, hard-boiled white and yolk of egg, anchovies, capers, olives.
15. Serve the crab on a flat dish garnished with lettuce leaves, quarters of tomato and the crab's legs.
16. Serve a vinaigrette or mayonnaise sauce separately.

41 Smoked salmon

Allow 35–50 g per portion.

1. A side of smoked salmon must be carefully trimmed to remove the dry outside surface before service. Remove all bones (a pair of pliers is useful for this).
2. Carve the salmon on the slant, as thinly as possible.
3. Dress neatly, overlapping, on a plate or dish, decorated with sprigs of parsley Accompaniments include brown bread and butter, and lemon.

Energy	Cals	Fat	Sat fat	Carb	Sugar	Protein	Fibre
149 kJ	36 kcal	1.1 g	0.3 g	0.0 g	0.0 g	6.4 g	0.0 g

Note

Other smoked fish served as hors d'oeuvres include halibut, eel, conger eel, trout, mackerel, herring (buckling), cod's roe and sprats.

Healthy eating tips

Oily fish (such as salmon, trout, mackerel, rollmops and sprats) are high in omega-3 fatty acids, which are beneficial for health.

42 Oysters

Ingredient	4 portions
Rock or native oysters	24
Lemon	1
To accompany	
Brown bread and butter	
Tabasco or chilli sauce	

Note

Make sure the oysters have been grown in or fished from clean waters, and take note of the famous rule only to use them when there is an 'r' in the month, although rock oysters are available throughout the year.

Energy	Cals	Fat	Sat fat	Carb	Sugar	Protein	Fibre	Sodium
192 kJ	45 kcal	0.9 g	0.2 g	2.7 g	1.0 g	6.8 g	0.4 g	0.3 g

Excluding accompaniments.

Fish and shellfish 9

1. Select only those oysters that are tightly shut and have a fresh smell (category A is best, which means the waters they have grown in are clean).
2. To open an oyster, only the point of the oyster knife is used. Hold the oyster with a thick oven cloth to protect your hand.
3. With the oyster in the palm of your hand, push the point of the knife about 1 cm deep into the 'hinge' between the 'lid' and the body of the oyster.
4. Once the lid has been penetrated, push down. The lid should pop open. Lift up the top shell, cutting the muscle attached to it.
5. Remove any splintered shell from the flesh and solid shell.
6. Return each oyster to its shell and serve on a bed of crushed ice with chilli sauce, brown bread and lemon.

43 Cold salmon

Salmon may be obtained in varying weights from 3.5–15 kg: 0.5 kg of uncleaned salmon yields 2–3 portions. Size is an important consideration, depending on whether the salmon is to be cooked whole or cut into darnes. A salmon of any size may be cooked whole. When required for darnes, a medium-sized salmon is more suitable.

For the court bouillon

1. Simmer all the ingredients for 30–40 minutes.
2. Pass through a strainer, use as required.

Cooking for service in darnes or portions

1. Cook the salmon in the court bouillon, either whole or cut into darnes.
2. Allow to cool thoroughly in the cooking liquid to keep it moist. Divide a whole salmon into eight even portions; for darnes, remove the centre bone and cut each darne in half, if required.
3. Except when whole, remove the centre bone, the skin and brown surface, and dress neatly on a flat dish.
4. Peel and slice the cucumber and neatly arrange a few slices on each portion.
5. Garnish with quarters of lettuce and quarters of tomatoes.
6. Serve the sauce or mayonnaise in a sauceboat separately.

Energy	Cals	Fat	Sat fat	Carb	Sugar	Protein	Fibre	Sodium
2,141 kJ	517 kcal	40.3g	6.5g	5.1g	4.5g	33.0g	1.8g	1.2g

Ingredient	2–3 portions	8–10 portions
Cooking liquid (court bouillon)		
Water	1 litre	2.5 litres
Salt	10 g	25 g
Carrots, sliced	50 g	125 g
Bay leaf	2–3	5–8
Parsley stalks		
Vinegar	60 ml	150 ml
Peppercorns	6	15
Onions, sliced	50 g	125 g
Sprig of thyme		
Salmon for service in darnes or portions		
Salmon, cleaned	500 g	1.25 kg
Court bouillon (see above)	400 ml	1 litre
Cucumber	¼	½
Large lettuce	½	1
Tomatoes	80 g	200 g
Mayonnaise or green sauce	100 ml	250 ml

> **Professional tip**
> Always allow the salmon to remain in the court bouillon until cold.

Cooking and presenting salmon whole

1. Scrape off all scales, from tail to head, using the back of a knife.
2. Remove all gills and clean out the head.
3. Remove the intestines and clear the blood from the backbone.
4. Trim off all fins. Wash well.
5. Place in a salmon kettle and cover with cold court bouillon.
6. Bring slowly to the boil, skim, then simmer very gently.
7. Allow the following approximate simmering times:
   - 3.5 kg – 15 minutes
   - 7 kg – 20 minutes
   - 10.5 kg – 25 minutes
   - 14 kg – 30 minutes.
8. Allow the cooked salmon to cool, then remove it from the liquid. Carefully remove the skin and the dark layer under the skin (which is cooked blood). The now bared salmon flesh should be perfectly smooth.
9. Make sure the salmon is well drained and place it on to the serving dish or board.
10. The salmon is now ready for decorating and garnishing. Keep this to the minimum and avoid over-covering the fish and the dish. Neatly overlapping thin slices of cucumber (the skin may be left on or removed), quartered tomatoes (which can be peeled and neatly cut), small pieces of hearts of lettuce can, if artistically set out, give a quick, neat-looking, appetising appearance. Remember though, time is money – there is no justification for spending a lot of time cutting fiddly little pieces of many different items to form patterns that often look untidy.

44 Fish salad (salade de poisson)

Ingredient	4 portions	10 portions
Cooked fish, free from skin and bone	200 g	500 g
Egg, hard-boiled	1	2–3
Cucumber (optional)	50 g	125 g
Lettuce	½	1
Parsley or fennel, chopped		
Salt, pepper		
Vinaigrette	1 tbsp	2–3 tbsp

Energy	Cals	Fat	Sat fat	Carb	Sugar	Protein	Fibre
978 kJ	233 kcal	13.5 g	3.0 g	1.5 g	1.4 g	26.4 g	1.3 g

For 4 portions.

1. Flake the fish.
2. Cut the egg and cucumber into 0.5 cm dice and finely shred the lettuce
3. Mix ingredients together and add the parsley.
4. Correct the seasoning and mix in the vinaigrette.
5. It may be decorated with lettuce, anchovies and capers.

Healthy eating tips
Use salt sparingly.

Note
Be careful not to overcook the fish.

45 Sea bass ceviche

Ingredient	4 portions	10 portions
Sea bass fillet, skinless, free of bone	400 g	1 kg
Large lime, juice only	1	2½
Yuzu juice	2 tbsp	5 tbsp
Coriander leaves, finely chopped	1 tbsp	2½ tbsp
Shallots, finely chopped	2	5
Ginger, shredded	1 tsp	2½ tsp
Red chilli, deseeded, finely chopped	1	2½
Sugar	1 tsp	2½ tsp
Light pomace oil or vegetable oil	1 tsp	2½ tsp
To serve		
Sea salt		
Crunchy raw salad of carrot, fennel and celeriac		

Energy	Cals	Fat	Sat fat	Carb	Sugar	Protein	Fibre	Sodium
540 kJ	128 kcal	3.8g	0.6g	3.8g	3.5g	19.8g	0.5g	0.3g

1 In a shallow, non-metallic tray, combine all the ingredients except the fish.
2 Slice the fish at a 45 degree angle, 5 mm thick.
3 Place the fish into the curing liquid. Refrigerate for 20 minutes until the edges of the fish turn white (do not leave too long as the fish will cure through and resemble rollmops).
4 To finish, lay the fish neatly on a plate with a little of the curing garnish and juice.
5 Season with a little sea salt and serve with a crunchy salad.

Note

Yuzu is a citrus fruit grown in east Asia – the juice is available in bottles.

Practical Cookery 14th edition

46 Soused herring or mackerel

Ingredient	4 portions	10 portions
Herrings or mackerel	2	5
Salt, pepper		
Button onions	25 g	60 g
Carrots, peeled and fluted	25 g	60 g
Bay leaf	½	1½
Peppercorns	6	15
Thyme	1 sprig	2 sprigs
Vinegar	60 ml	150 ml

Energy	Cals	Fat	Sat fat	Carb	Sugar	Protein	Fibre
605 kJ	144 kcal	11.1 g	2.4 g	0.8 g	0.8 g	10.3 g	0.3 g

1 Clean, scale and fillet the fish.
2 Wash the fillets well and season with salt and pepper.
3 Roll up with the skin outside. Place in an earthenware dish.
4 Peel and wash the onion. Cut the onion and carrots into neat, thin rings.
5 Blanch for 2–3 minutes.
6 Add to the fish with the remainder of the ingredients.
7 Cover with greaseproof paper and cook in a moderate oven for 15–20 minutes.
8 Allow to cool, place in a dish with the onion and carrot.
9 Garnish with picked parsley, dill or chives.

Healthy eating tips
- Serve with plenty of salad vegetables and bread or toast (optional butter or spread).
- Keep added salt to a minimum.

47 Crab, lobster, shrimp or prawn cocktail (*cocktail de crabe, homard, crevettes, crevettes roses*)

Ingredient	4 portions	10 portions
Lettuce	½	1¼
Prepared shellfish	100–150 g	250–350 g
Shellfish cocktail sauce	125 ml	300 ml

Energy	Cals	Fat	Sat fat	Carb	Sugar	Protein	Fibre
966 kJ	230 kcal	21.0 g	3.2 g	0.6 g	0.6 g	9.6 g	0.3 g

Professional tip
Portion control is important so that this dish does not cost too much to produce. The cocktail needs to be presented well.

Fish and shellfish

1. Wash, drain well and finely shred the lettuce, avoiding long strands. Place about 2 cm deep in cocktail glasses or dishes.
2. Add the prepared shellfish: crab (shredded white meat only); lobster (cut into 2 cm dice); shrimps (peeled and washed); prawns (peeled, washed and, if large, cut into two or three pieces).
3. Coat with sauce.
4. Decorate with an appropriate piece of the content, such as a prawn, with the shell on the tail removed, placed on the edge of the glass of a prawn cocktail. A more modern presentation is to serve the cocktail plated.

48 Potted shrimps

Ingredient	4 portions	10 portions
Butter	100 g	250 g
Chives, chopped	2 tbsp	5 tbsp
Cayenne pepper, to taste		
Brown shrimps, peeled	600 g	1.5 kg
Clarified butter	6 tbsp	15 tbsp

Energy	Cals	Fat	Sat fat	Carb	Sugar	Protein	Fibre	Sodium
3,887 kJ	942 kcal	92.9g	58.1g	1.1g	0.7g	25.7g	0.1g	0.9g

This is a real seaside dish, full of flavour and eaten with plenty of brown bread and butter. Lobster or langoustine can be used – although timings will need to be adapted accordingly. The traditional seasoning for potted shrimps is ground mace.

1. Put the butter, chives and cayenne pepper in a medium-sized pan and leave to melt over a gentle heat.
2. Add the peeled shrimps and stir over the heat for a couple of minutes until they have heated through, but don't let the mixture boil.
3. Divide the shrimps and butter between four small ramekins. Level the tops and then leave them to set in the refrigerator.
4. Spoon over a thin layer of clarified butter and leave to set once more. Serve with plenty of brown toast or crusty brown bread.

Professional tip
- Do not let the mixture boil (step 2) – if it does, the shrimps will become tough.
- Remove from the fridge and allow to warm slightly before serving, to bring out the flavour.

49 Fruits de mer

Ingredient	4 portions	10 portions
Lobster, cooked	1	2½
Crab, cooked	1	2½
Large prawns, cooked	12	30
Winkles, raw	100 g	250 g
Fresh clams	200 g	500 g
Fresh cockles	200 g	500 g
Mussels, live	200 g	500 g
Langoustines, live	6	10
White wine	75 ml	200 ml
Parsley stalks	4	10
Shallots, roughly chopped	2	5
Salt		
Oysters	12	30
For the sauces		
Mayonnaise	250 ml	625 ml
Garlic cloves, finely chopped	2	5
Tomato ketchup	2 tsp	5 tsp
Brandy	1 tbsp	2½ tbsp
Tabasco sauce		
Red wine vinegar	100 ml	250 ml
Shallots, finely chopped	2	5
To serve		
Sprigs of parsley and lemon wedges, to garnish		
Chorizo sausage, warm, to garnish (optional)		

Energy	Cals	Fat	Sat fat	Carb	Sugar	Protein	Fibre	Sodium
3,440 kJ	828 kcal	56.5 g	8.7 g	6.8 g	3.7 g	65.6 g	0.9 g	2.3 g

To prepare the seafood

1. Cut the lobster in half lengthways. Remove the stomach and give the claws a crack to break the shell.
2. Open the crab, remove the 'dead man's fingers' and cut the body into four. Give the claws a few cracks to break the shell – this will make getting the meat out at the table easier.
3. Put the prawns, winkles, clams, cockles, mussels and langoustines into a pan with the white wine, parsley stalks, shallots and salt. Bring to the boil, cover and steam for 4 minutes until the mussels, clams and cockles open. Remove from the water and put on a tray to cool.
4. Open the oysters with an oyster knife.
5. Place a generous portion of crushed ice on a tray. Arrange the lobster, crab, langoustines, clams, mussels, cockles, winkles, prawns and oysters on the ice, garnishing with lemon and parsley.

Note

Dead man's fingers are the crab's gills. You can see them inside the crab: they are grey and shaped like fingers.

To make the sauces

1. Divide the mayonnaise into thirds. Set one third to one side.
2. Mix the chopped garlic into another third of the mayonnaise.
3. To make seafood sauce, mix the tomato ketchup, the brandy and a dash of Tabasco into the remaining mayonnaise.
4. To make shallot vinegar, mix together the red wine vinegar and the shallots.

Serve the fruits de mer with the mayonnaise, aioli (garlic mayonnaise), seafood sauce, shallot vinegar, lemon wedges and Tabasco, and chorizo sausage if desired.

10 Meat and offal

Recipes included in this chapter

No.	Recipe	Page
	Grilled lamb dishes	
1	Lamb satay	279
2	Grilled lamb cutlets (*côtelettes d'agneau grillées*)	280
3	Mixed grill	280
4	Lamb kebabs (*shish kebab*)	281
5	Grilled loin or chump chops, or noisettes of lamb	282
	Fried lamb dishes	
6	Lamb rosettes with thyme and blueberries	282
7	Noisettes of lamb with baby ratatouille	283
8	Lamb valentine steaks with fresh hummus	283
9	Samosas	284
	Braised lamb dishes	
10	Braised lamb chump chops (*chops d'agneau braisés*)	286
11	Braised lamb shanks	287
12	Hot pot of lamb or mutton	288
	Lamb stews	
13	Brown lamb or mutton stew	289
14	Irish stew	290
	Roast lamb dishes	
15	Roast leg of lamb with mint, lemon and cumin	291
16	Roast saddle of lamb with rosemary mash	292
17	Best end of lamb with breadcrumbs and parsley	292
18	Slow-cooked shoulder of lamb with potatoes boulangère	293
19	Pot-roast shoulder of lamb with gratin forcemeat	294
	Lamb combined cooking	
20	Shepherd's pie	295
	Grilled beef dishes	
21	Grilled beef	296
22	Hamburger, American style	296
	Fried beef dishes	
23	Tournedos	298
24	Sirloin steak with red wine (*entrecôte bordelaise*)	298
25	Beef stroganoff	299
26	Hamburg or Vienna steak	300
	Braised beef dishes	
27	Carbonnade of beef	301
28	Beef bourguignon	302
29	Braised beef (*boeuf braisé*)	304
	Steamed/boiled beef dishes	
30	Boiled silverside, carrots and dumplings	305
31	Steak pudding	306
	Beef stew dishes	
32	Goulash	308
	Baked beef dishes	
33	Cornish pasties	309
34	Steak pie	310
	Roast beef dishes	
35	Roast wing of beef	312
36	Yorkshire pudding	313
37	Slow-cooked sirloin with lyonnaise onions and carrot purée	314
	Fried veal dishes	
38	Escalope of veal	315
39	Breadcrumbed veal escalope with ham and cheese (*escalope de veau cordon bleu*)	316
40	Veal escalope with Parma ham and mozzarella cheese (*involtini di vitello*)	317
	Braised veal dishes	
41	Fricassée of veal	318
42	Braised shin of veal (*osso buco*)	320
	Fried pork dishes	
43	Pork escalope with calvados sauce	321
44	Sweet and sour pork	322
45	Stir-fried pork fillet	323
	Braised pork dishes	
46	Sauerkraut, ham hock and lentils	323

255

	Boiled pork dishes	
47	Boiled bacon	326
	Roast pork dishes	
48	Roast leg of pork	326
49	Roast pork belly with shallots and champ potatoes	327
50	Slow-roast belly of pork	328
51	Sage and onion dressing for pork	328
52	Spare ribs in barbecue sauce	329
53	Roast joint of bacon	329
	Offal dishes	
54	Calf's liver and bacon (*foie de veau au lard*)	330
55	Grilled lambs' kidneys (*rognons grillés*)	331
56	Devilled lambs' kidneys	331
57	Braised calf's cheeks with vegetables	332
58	Braised beef cheek in red wine	333
59	Shallow-fried lambs' sweetbreads	334
	Pâté	
60	Liver pâté (pâté de foie)	335
	Cold meats	
61	Chicken salad	336
62	Raised pork pie	337
63	Veal and ham pie	338
64	Terrine of bacon, spinach and mushrooms	339

Meat

Butcher's meat used today is largely a product of selective breeding and feeding techniques – animals are reared carefully to reach high standards and meet specific needs. Present-day demand is for lean and tender meat – modern cattle, sheep and pigs are well-fleshed yet compact creatures, and there is an increase in use of specific-named breeds on restaurant tables.

Full information on meat, including cattle, sheep and pigs, can be found at:
- www.qmscotland.co.uk
- www.eblex.org.uk
- www.bpex.org.uk

The structure of meat

Meat and its fat content varies considerably. The fat is found round the outside of meat, in **marbling** (the white flecks of fat throughout the lean muscle) and inside the meat fibres. The visible fat (saturated) should be trimmed off as much as possible before cooking.

To cook meat properly it is important to understand its structure:
- Meat comprises fibres bound by connective tissue.
- Connective tissue (elastin) is yellow and collagen white.
- Yellow tissue needs to be removed.
- Small fibres are present in tender cuts and younger animals.
- Coarser fibres are present in tougher cuts and older animals.
- Fat assists in providing flavour and moistens meat during roasting and grilling.
- Tenderness, flavour and moistness are increased if meat is hung after slaughter and before being used.

Quality points when choosing and buying meat

Meat is a natural product and therefore not uniform, varying in quality from carcass to carcass. Flavour, texture and appearance are determined by the type of animal and the way it has been fed.

There is no reason to think that flavour is obtained only in meat that possesses a higher proportion of fat, although fat does give a characteristic flavour to meat and helps to keep it moist during roasting. Neither is the colour of meat any guide to quality. Consumers are inclined to choose light-coloured meat – bright-red beef, for example – because they think that it will be fresher than an alternative dark-red piece. Freshly butchered beef is bright red because the pigment in the tissues, myoglobin, has been chemically affected by the oxygen in the air. After several hours the colour changes to dark red or brown as the pigment is further oxidised to become metamyoglobin. The colour of fat can vary from almost pure white in lamb to bright yellow in beef. Colour depends on the feed, on the breed and, to a certain extent, on the time of year.

The most useful guide to tenderness and quality is knowledge of the cuts of meat and their location on the carcass. The various cuts are described below, but in principle the leanest and most tender cuts – the **prime cuts** – come from the hindquarters. The **coarse cuts** – meat from the neck, legs and forequarters; those parts of the animal that have had plenty of muscular exercise and where fibres have become hardened – provide meat for braising and stewing. Many consider these cuts to have more flavour, although they require slow cooking to make them tender. The meat from young animals is generally more tender.

Animals may be injected before slaughter with an enzyme, such as papin, which softens the fibres and muscles. This speeds up a natural process: meat contains its own enzymes that gradually break down the protein cell walls as the carcass ages; that is why meat is hung for 10 to 20 days in controlled conditions of temperature and humidity before being offered for sale. Meat that has been aged longer is more expensive as the cost of refrigeration is high and the meat itself shrinks because of evaporation and the trimming of the outside hardened edges.

Kosher and halal meat

Meat that is sold as kosher or halal must have been slaughtered according to the food laws of Judaism (kosher) or Islam (halal).

Kosher slaughter is done by a quick, deep stroke across the throat with a sharp blade. This is considered painless, causes unconsciousness within two seconds and is widely recognised as the most humane method of slaughter possible. The animal is bled completely, and the meat soaked in suet and water to remove any residual blood, because blood must not be consumed in a kosher diet.

Halal slaughter is done by cutting the throat or piercing the hollow of the throat, causing a quick death with the least pain possible. The blood is completely drained from the carcass. Halal slaughter is preceded by a prayer.

Storing meat

Meat that is chilled is kept at a temperature just above freezing point in a controlled atmosphere. Meat should be hung and stored between 0 °C and 1 °C.

Chilled meat cannot be kept in the usual type of cold room for more than a few days, although sufficient time must be allowed for the meat to hang, enabling it to become tender. Beef can be stored for up to three weeks, veal for one to three weeks, lamb for 10 to 15 days, and pork 7 to 14 days.

> **Food safety**
>
> Store uncooked meat, offal and poultry on trays to prevent dripping, ideally in separate refrigerators, at a temperature of 1 °C to 4 °C. If separate refrigerators are not available, then store in separate areas of the refrigerator, with uncooked meat at the bottom and cooked meat above it.

Other preservation methods

Freezing

Small carcasses, such as lamb and mutton, can be frozen without affecting their quality. They can be kept frozen until required and then thawed out before being used. Some beef is frozen, but it is inferior in quality to chilled beef.

Canning

Large quantities of meat are canned; corned beef is an example with a very high protein content. Pork is used for tinned luncheon meat. Ham cuts are also available in cans.

Salting

The salt draws out moisture and creates an environment in which bacteria find it difficult to multiply. If salted in cold weather (so that the meat does not spoil while the salt has time to take effect), salted meat can last for years. Salting is still used with bacon, before the meat is smoked, and hams. It is also used for some beef products, for example dried beef, corned beef and pastrami, which are made by soaking beef in a 10 per cent salt water brine for several weeks. Meat can be pickled in brine; this method of preservation may be applied to silverside, brisket and ox tongues.

Preparing meat

Refer to the sections on different types of meat below for further detail on preparation methods. The following food safety points should be taken into account to reduce the risk of cross-contamination when preparing meat:

- When preparing uncooked meat, offal or poultry, and then cooked food, or changing from one type of meat, offal or poultry to another, equipment, working areas and utensils must be thoroughly cleaned or changed.
- Where colour-coded boards are used, it is essential to always use the correct colour-coded boards for the preparation of foods, and different ones for cooked foods.
- Clean all work surfaces with detergent and sanitiser to kill bacteria. This is particularly important when handling poultry and pork.

For information on maintaining a safe and secure working environment; a professional and hygienic appearance; and clean food production areas, equipment and utensils, as well as food hygiene, please refer to Chapters 1 and 2.

Tenderising meat

The tenderness of meat depends on the following factors.

- **The size of the muscle fibres:** the smaller and narrower the fibres, the more tender is the meat.
- **Amount of connective tissue:** tough meat contains more connective tissue than tender meat. The older the animal, and the greater its levels of activity during life, the higher the amount of connective tissue.
- **Length of time for hanging:** after slaughter, meat is hung for several days to make it more tender. During hanging:
  - the glycogen in the muscle tissue is converted into lactic acid
  - the pH of the meat falls from 7.4 to 5.5, which causes partial denaturation of the fibre proteins
  - enzyme action causes a partial breakdown of the proteins, which increases tenderness and contributes to the flavour of the meat.
- **Activity of the animal before death:** animals must be rested before slaughter. If they are not, the supply of glycogen to the muscle tissues is reduced and less lactic acid is produced during hanging, which will have the effect of making the meat tougher to eat.

Meat may be tenderised by the chef in the following ways:

- **physically**, by pounding the meat with a meat hammer; cutting and mincing helps to break down the fibres and the connective tissue
- **chemically**, using marinades such as lemon juice, vinegar or wine; this helps to coagulate proteins
- **using enzymes**, which break down proteins; meat-tenderising products contain papain, a protein-splitting enzyme extracted from the papaya plant.

Cooking meat

Meat is an extremely versatile product that can be cooked in a multitude of ways and matched with practically any vegetable, fruit and herb. The cut (shin, steak, brisket and so on), the method of cooking (roasting, braising, grilling) and the time and temperature all affect the way the meat will taste.

Raw meat is difficult to chew because the muscle fibre contains an elastic protein (collagen), which is softened only by mincing – as in steak tartare – or by cooking. When you cook meat, the protein gradually **coagulates** as the internal temperature increases. At 77°C coagulation is complete, the protein begins to harden and further cooking makes the meat tougher.

> **Professional tip**
>
> Meat bones are useful for giving flavour to soups and stocks, especially beef ones with plenty of marrow. Veal bones are gelatinous and help to enrich and thicken soups and sauces. Fat can be rendered down for frying or used as an ingredient, such as suet or lard used in pastry.

Time and temperature in meat cookery

Since tenderness combined with flavour is the aim in meat cookery, much depends on the ratio of time and temperature. In principle, slow cooking retains the juices and produces a more tender result than fast cooking at high temperatures. There are, of course, occasions when high temperatures are essential: for instance, you need to grill a steak under a hot flame for a very limited time to obtain a crisp, brown surface and a pink, juicy interior – using a low temperature would not give you the desired result. But, in potentially tough cuts, such as breast of lamb, or where there is a quantity of connective tissue (e.g. neck of lamb), a slow rate of cooking converts the tissues to gelatine and helps to make the meat more tender. Meat containing bone will take longer to cook because bone is a poor conductor of heat.

Tough or coarse cuts of meat should be cooked by braising, pot roasting or stewing. Marinating in a suitable marinade, such as wine and wine vinegar, helps to tenderise the meat and imparts an additional flavour. Searing meat in hot fat or in a hot oven before roasting or stewing helps to produce a crisp exterior by coagulating the protein but does not, as is widely supposed, seal in the juices. However, if the external temperature is too high and cooking prolonged, rapid evaporation and contraction of the meat will cause considerable loss of juices and fat. Salt sprinkled on meat before cooking will also hasten loss of moisture since salt absorbs water.

When fibrous proteins are heated they contract and squeeze out the associated water. For example, when a steak is cooked the proteins contract, therefore squeezing out all the water/juices. If the heat is increased or continues, the steak will become dry and the eating quality will be impaired. Cuts of meat also contain elastin and collagen: elastin (the muscle group associated with tendons and arteries) is extremely stretchy and further cooking adds to its strength; collagen (the main muscle proteins, which amount to the highest proportion of mass in the muscle) is tough and chewy. Meat that has a higher proportion of both, usually from the major and highly worked muscle groups, would not be suitable for prime cooking (e.g. grilling or frying). However, these cuts of meat may be cooked for longer at the correct temperature (braising), dissolving the collagen as it is water soluble, forming gelatine and offering a tasty joint of meat.

Prime cuts, such as beef fillets, have little collagen in their make-up (approximately 3 per cent) and do not require long cooking to tenderise them. Although most chefs would adopt a high temperature for a short period on the prime cuts, this does not always lead to a perfect result. Due to the lack of fat and collagen in such cuts of meat, high heat will dry out the muscle fibres and, consequently, the eating quality is impaired. A lower temperature and longer in the oven will produce a gradual heat, therefore there is less extreme coagulation in the tissues and less fluid will be squeezed out in the process.

Sirloin of beef has more collagen than fillet (it is essentially a worked muscle group) and is generally cooked on a high heat, either roasted or pan-fried. Using a slow cooking method, however, you can prepare sirloin that is extremely tender, full of moisture, with a roasted outer and a flavoursome roasted meat taste. An average sirloin joint for roasting can weigh from 2 kg to 5 kg whole off the bone. The method is to seal the meat on the outside, as you would normally, place into a preheated oven at 180 °C, cook for 10 minutes, then reduce the temperature to 64 °C (the oven door may need to be open at this stage). Once the oven has come down to 64 °C, close the door and cook for a further 1 hour and 50 minutes. This will give you an extremely tender piece of sirloin.

To maintain the quality and safety of meat and poultry dishes, it is advisable to check internal temperatures using a probe. The recommended temperatures are shown in Table 10.1.

Table 10.1 Recommended internal temperatures

Meat	Recommended internal temperature
Beef	rare 52 °C, medium 57 °C, well done 62 °C
Duck	pink 57 °C; well done 62 °C
Lamb	pink 57 °C, well done 62 °C
Pork	73 °C
Turkey/chicken	77 °C
Veal	62 °C

Environmental health officers may require higher temperatures.

The Maillard reaction

A series of chemical reactions, known as the Maillard reaction, happen when proteins are heated with sugars to temperatures above 140 °C. This is why a good flavour develops when meat cooks.

Always ensure that the outside of the meat is cooked at a high temperature (until it is a dark brown colour), in order to develop the flavour. Cook meats with little connective tissue for only a short time. Seal the outside so that it is browned and so that the inside does not become tough (e.g. by grilling, frying or roasting).

Meats with lots of connective tissue should be cooked for longer so that all the connective tissue breaks down and the bundles of coagulated muscle proteins fall apart, tenderising the meat (e.g. by stewing or braising).

Griddling meat, poultry and game

Griddling is sometimes referred to as indoor barbequing because it gives the food a slightly smoky, charred taste. A griddle can be a solid piece of built-in equipment, or you can use a griddle pan.

Griddling requires only a small amount of oil. Usually only prime cuts of meat, poultry and game are griddled, and these are often marinated beforehand. Examples are sirloin and fillet steaks, chicken breasts, pork chops, lamb cutlets and venison steaks.

Follow the guidelines listed below when griddling.
- Make sure the griddle is clean before placing the food on it.
- Brush oil directly onto the food, rather than the griddle.
- Do not move the food around too much. If you want the quadrillage effect, turn the food at right angles halfway through the cooking on each side.
- Wipe the griddle clean after use.

Lamb and mutton

Lamb is the meat from a sheep under a year old; above that age the animal is called a 'hogget' and its meat becomes mutton. The lamb carcass provides smaller cuts of more tender meat than mutton. Mutton needs to be well ripened by long hanging before cooking and, as it is usually fatty, needs a good deal of trimming as well.

Lamb has a very thin, parchment-like covering on the carcass, known as the 'fell', which is usually left on roasts to help them maintain their shape during cooking. It should, however, be removed from chops. The flesh of a younger lamb is usually more tender. A good way to judge age is through weight – especially with legs of lamb: the highest quality weighs about 2.3 kg and never more than 4 kg. Smaller chops are also more tender and, therefore, more expensive.

> **Professional tip**
>
> Mutton fell out of favour in the UK for some years but has recently become more popular, backed by the Mutton Renaissance campaign, which was supported by several well-known chefs and the Prince of Wales. Using mutton is good for food sustainability – because the animals are not killed young they are larger than lambs and have a higher yield.

Quality points

- Good-quality lamb should have fine, white fat, with pink flesh where freshly cut; in mutton the flesh is a deeper colour.
- A good-quality animal should be compact and evenly fleshed.
- The lean flesh should be firm, of a pleasing dull-red colour and of a fine texture or grain.
- There should be an even distribution of surface fat, which should be hard, brittle and flaky in structure and a clear white colour.
- In a young animal the bones should be pink and porous, so that when cut a degree of blood is shown in their structure. As the sheep grows older, the bones become hard, dense and white, and inclined to splinter when chopped.

Portions and cuts

As a guide, when ordering allow approximately 100 g meat off the bone per portion, and 150 g on the bone per portion. It must be clearly understood, however, that the weights given can only be approximate. They must vary according to the quality of the meat and also according to the purpose for which the meat is being butchered. For example, a chef will often cut differently from a shop butcher (a chef frequently needs to consider the presentation of the particular joint, while the butcher is more often concerned with economical cutting). In the text that follows, simple orders of dissection are given for each carcass. In general, bones need to be removed only when preparing joints, so as to facilitate carving. The bones are used for stock and the excess fat can be rendered down for second-class dripping.

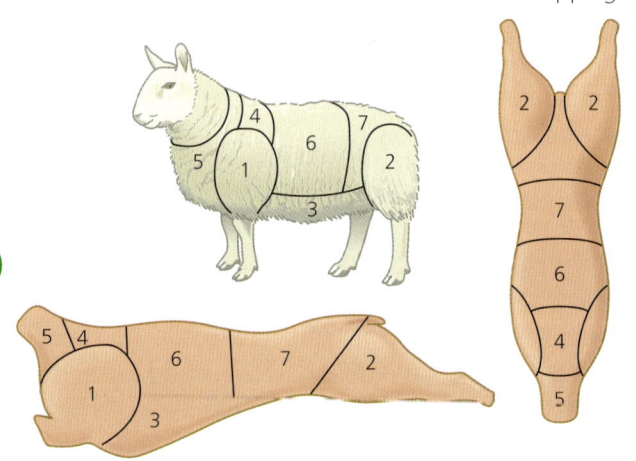

▲ Joints of lamb, viewed from different angles – see Table 10.2 for an explanation of the numbers

Table 10.2 Lamb and mutton joints, their uses and weights

Joint	Uses	Approx. weight (kg) Lamb	Mutton
Whole carcass		16	25
Shoulder (1)	Roasting, stewing	3	4.5
Leg (2)	Roasting (mutton boiled)	3.5	5.5
Breast (3)	Roasting, stewing	1.5	2.5
Middle neck (4)	Stewing	2	3
Scrag-end (5)	Stewing, broth	0.5	1
Best end/rack (6)	Roasting, grilling, frying	2	3
Saddle (7)	Roasting, grilling, frying	3.5	5.5

The order of dissection of a lamb carcass:

1. Remove the shoulders.
2. Remove the breasts.
3. Remove the middle neck and scrag.
4. Remove the legs.
5. Divide the saddle from the best end.

Meat and offal 10

Table 10.3 Common cooking methods for lamb

Joint	Methods of cookery
Saddle	Roast, pot roast
Loin	Roast
Fillet	Grill, fry
Loin chop	Grill, fry, stew, braise
Chump chop	Grill, fry, stew, braise
Kidney	Grill, sauté

Preparing a shoulder of lamb

- **Boning**: remove the blade bone and upper arm bone (see diagram) and tie with string; the shoulder may be stuffed before tying.
- **Cutting for stews**: bone out, cut into even 25–50 g pieces.
- **For roasting**: remove the pelvic or aitchbone; clean and trim the knucklebone so as to leave approximately 3 cm of clean bone; trim off excess fat and tie with string if necessary.

Health and safety

Wear a safety apron for protection when using a boning knife. If you are doing a great deal of boning then consider protective gloves as well.

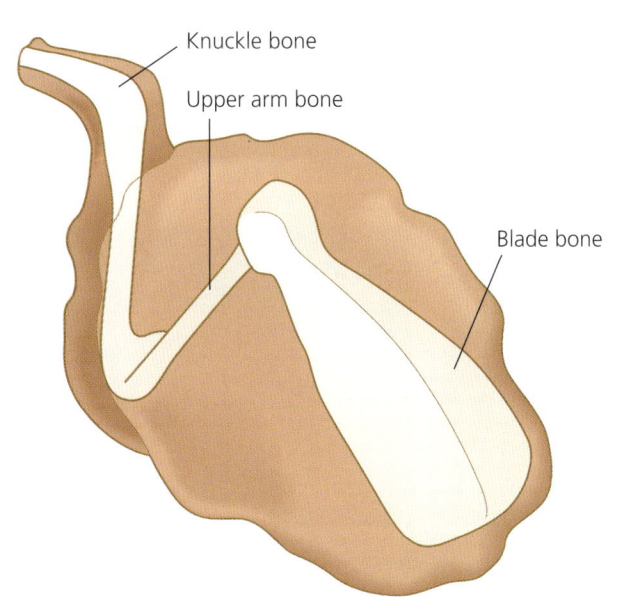

▲ Shoulder of lamb, showing three bones

Preparing breasts of lamb

- Remove excess fat and skin.
- **For roasting**: bone, stuff and roll; tie with string.
- **For stewing**: cut into even 25–50 g pieces.

Preparing middle neck

- **For stewing**: remove excess fat, excess bone and gristle; cut into even 50 g pieces; this joint, when correctly butchered, can give good uncovered second-class cutlets.

Preparing scrag-end

- **For stewing**: this can be chopped down the centre, the excess bone, fat and gristle removed, and cut into even 50 g pieces, or boned out and cut into pieces.

Preparing a saddle of lamb

The saddle may be divided as follows:

- remove the skin, starting from head to tail and from breast to back
- split down the centre of the backbone to produce two loins
- each loin can be roasted whole, boned and stuffed, or cut into loin and chump chops.

A full saddle is illustrated below. For large banquets it is sometimes better to remove the chumps and use short saddles. Saddles may also be boned and stuffed.

If the saddle is to be roasted:

- skin and remove the kidney
- trim the excess fat and sinew
- cut off the flaps, leaving about 15 cm each side so as to meet in the middle under the saddle
- remove the aitch, or pelvic, bone
- score neatly and tie with string.

For presentation the tail may be left on, protected with foil and tied back. The saddle can also be completely boned, stuffed and tied.

▲ Saddle of lamb

261

Preparing a loin of lamb

If the loin is to be roasted:
- skin and remove excess fat and sinew
- remove the pelvic bone and tie with string.

If the loin is to be boned and stuffed:
- remove the skin, excess fat and sinew
- bone out
- replace the fillet, season and stuff if required, and tie with string.

Preparing lamb chops

- **Loin chops**: skin the loin, remove the excess fat and sinew, then cut into chops approximately 100–150 g in weight. A first-class loin chop should have a piece of kidney skewered in the centre.
- **Double loin chop (Barnsley chop)**: these are cut approximately 2 cm across a saddle on the bone. When trimmed they are secured with a skewer and may include a piece of kidney in the centre of each chop.
- **Chump chops**: these are cut from the chump end of the loin. Cut into approximately 150 g chops and trim where necessary.
- **Noisettes**: this is a cut from a boned-out loin. Cut slantwise into approximately 2 cm thick slices, bat out slightly, and trim into a cutlet shape.
- **Rosettes**: this is a cut from a boned-out loin approximately 2 cm thick. It is shaped round and tied with string.
- **Valentine**: this is a cut from a boned-out loin. Cut slantwise into approximately 4 cm thick slices, then cut in half through top, about two-thirds through but keeping the meat connected at bottom, and fold out into heart shape (often called a butterfly cut).

▲ Lamb loin chops

▲ Left to right: rosette, valentine, noisette, Barnsley (double loin) chop

Preparing a best end (rack) of lamb

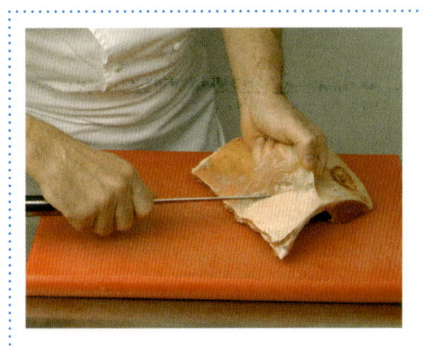

1. Remove the bark/skin, working from head to tail and from breast to back. Leave as much fat as possible on the joint.

2. Mark or score the fat, 2 cm from the end of the bones.

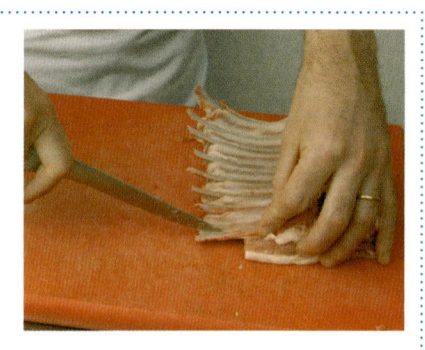

3. Score down the middle of the back of each bone, scoring the cartilage.

Meat and offal

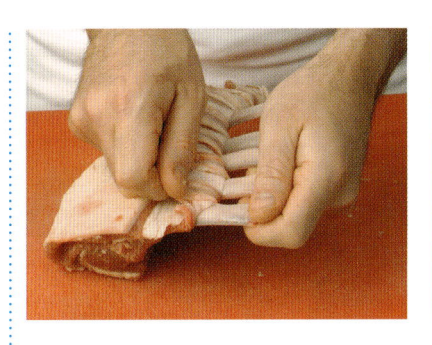

4 Pull the skin fat and meat from the bone (to bring out the bone ends – this is an alternative to scraping them).

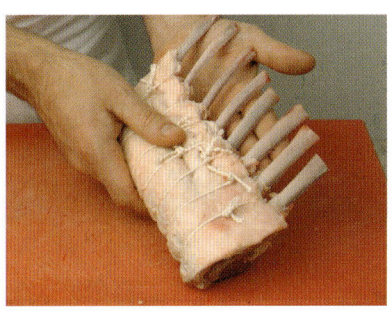

5 Remove the elastin as shown, then clean the sinew from between the rib bones.

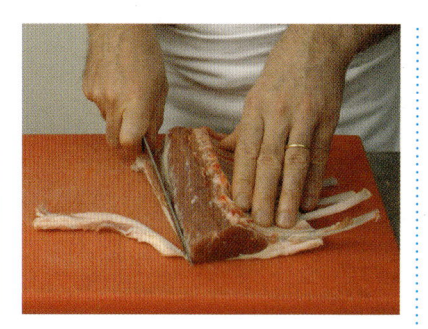

6 Trim the overall length of the bones to two and a half times the length of the nut of meat. Score the fat neatly to approximately 2 mm deep and tie the joint.

To make the best end into cutlets, prepare as for roasting, excluding the scoring, and divide evenly between the bones. Alternatively, the cutlets can be cut from the best end and prepared separately.

A single cutlet consists of one bone, and a double cutlet two bones, so a six-bone best end yields six single or three double cutlets.

▲ Lamb cutlets

Carving and serving roast lamb

Roast leg
Holding the bone, carve with a sharp knife at an angle of 45 degrees and take off each slice as it is cut. Continue in this manner along the joint, turning it from side to side as the slices get wider.

Shoulder
To obtain reasonable-sized slices of meat, carve the flesh side, not the skin side, of the joint. Having obtained the slices, carve round the bones. Due to the awkward shape of the bone structure, the shoulder is normally boned out, rolled and tied before cooking to facilitate carving.

Roast saddle
- **Carving on the bone**: there are two usual ways of carving the saddle, one is by carving lengthways either side of the backbone, the other by making a deep cut lengthwise either side of the backbone and then slicing across each loin. It is usual to carve the saddle in thick slices.
- **Carving off the bone**: for economical kitchen carving it is often best to bone the loins out whole, carve into slices, then reform on the saddle bone.
- The fillets may be left on the saddle or removed; in either case they are carved and served with the rest of the meat.

Roast loin
- **On the bone**: proceed as for the saddle.
- **Boned-out**: cut in slices across the joint; the slices are cut slightly thicker when stuffed.

Roast best end (rack)
Divide into cutlets by cutting between bones.

Service
All roast joints are served garnished with watercress and a sauceboat of roast gravy separately. When carved, serve a little gravy over the slices as well as offering a sauceboat of gravy. Mint sauce should be served with roast lamb and redcurrant jelly should be available. For roast mutton, redcurrant jelly and/or onion sauce should be served, with mint sauce available.

Beef

Quality points

- The lean meat should be bright red with small flecks of white fat (marbled).
- The fat should be firm, brittle in texture, creamy-white in colour and odourless. Older animals and dairy breeds have fat that is usually a deeper-yellow colour.

Butchery

A side of beef weighs approximately 180 kg. A whole side is divided between the wing ribs and the fore ribs.

Dissection of a hindquarter of beef

1. Remove the rump suet and kidney.
2. Remove the thin flank.
3. Divide the loin and rump from the leg (topside, silverside, thick flank and shin).
4. Remove the fillet.
5. Divide the rump from the sirloin.
6. Remove the wing ribs.
7. Remove the shin.
8. Bone out the aitchbone.
9. Divide the leg into the three remaining joints (silverside, topside and thick flank).

Table 10.4 Joints, uses and weights of a hindquarter of beef

Joint	Uses	Approx. weight (kg)
Shin	Consommé, beef tea, stewing	7
Topside	Braising, stewing, second-class roasting	10
Silverside	Pickled in brine then boiled	14
Thick flank	Braising and stewing	12
Rump	Grilling and frying as steaks, braised in the piece	10
Sirloin	Roasting, grilling and frying in steaks	9
Wing ribs	Roasting, grilling and frying in steaks	5
Thin flank	Stewing, boiling, sausages	10
Fillet	Roasting, grilling and frying in steaks	3
Fat and kidney	Fat: rendered for frying and basting, using in pastry	10
	Kidney: pies, puddings, braising	

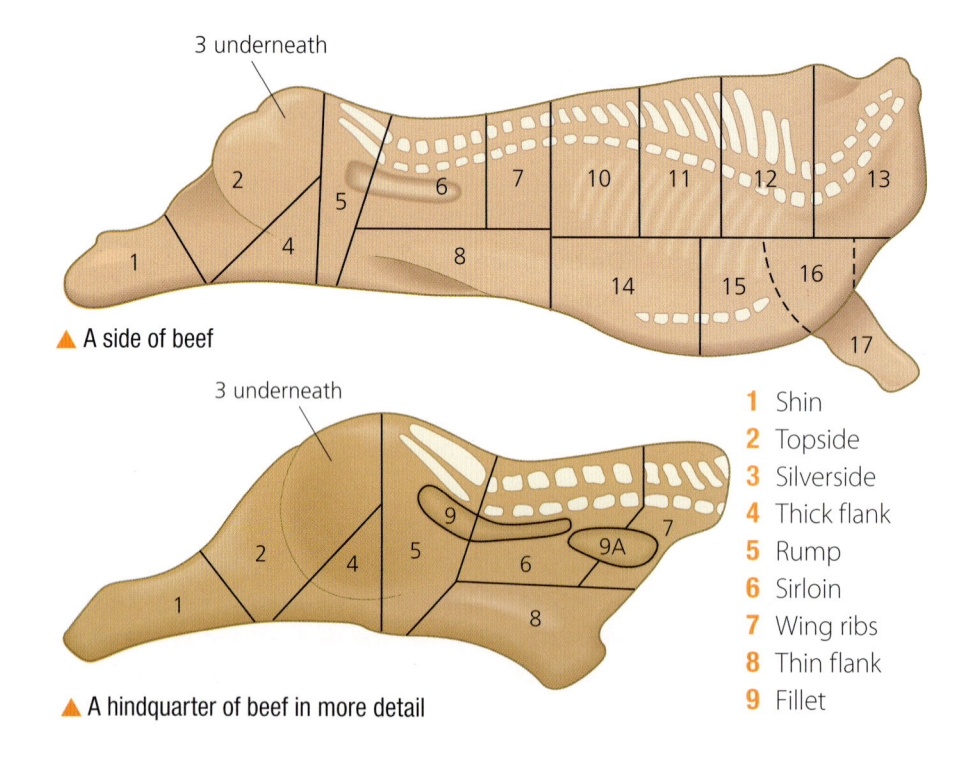

▲ A side of beef

▲ A hindquarter of beef in more detail

1 Shin
2 Topside
3 Silverside
4 Thick flank
5 Rump
6 Sirloin
7 Wing ribs
8 Thin flank
9 Fillet
9A Fat and kidney
10 Fore rib
11 Middle rib
12 Chuck rib
13 Sticking piece
14 Plate
15 Brisket
16 Leg of mutton cut
17 Shank

Meat and offal

Preparing joints from a hindquarter of beef

- **Shin**: bone out, remove excess sinew; cut or chop as required.
- **Topside**: for roasting and braising remove excess fat, cut into joints and tie with string; for stewing cut into dice or steaks as required.
- **Silverside**: remove the thigh bone; this joint is usually kept whole and pickled in brine prior to boning.
- **Thick flank**: as for topside.
- **Rump**: bone out; cut off the first outside slice for pies and puddings. Cut into approximately 1.5 cm slices for steaks. The point steak – considered the most tender – is cut from the pointed end of the slice.

Dissection of a forequarter of beef

1. Remove the shank.
2. Divide in half down the centre.
3. Take off the fore ribs.
4. Divide into joints.

Table 10.5 Joints, uses and weights of a forequarter of beef

Joint	Uses	Approx. weight (kg)
Fore rib	Roasting and braising	8
Middle rib	Roasting and braising	10
Chuck rib	Stewing and braising	15
Sticking piece	Stewing and sausages	9
Plate	Stewing and sausages	10
Brisket	Pickled in brine and boiled, pressed beef	19
Leg of mutton cut	Braising and stewing	11
Shank	Consommé, beef tea	6

Preparing cuts of beef

The cuts of beef vary considerably, from very tender fillet steak through to tough brisket or shin, and there is a greater variety of cuts in beef than for any other type of meat. While their names may vary, there are 14 primary cuts from a side of beef, each one composed of muscle, fat, bone and connective tissue. The least developed muscles, usually from the inner areas, can be roasted or grilled, while leaner and more sinewy meat is cut from the more highly developed external muscles. Exceptions are rib and loin cuts, which come from external but basically immobile muscles.

Knowing where the cuts come from helps to designate the cooking method.

- **Fillet** is taken from the back of the animal; this is the most tender part, cut from the centre of the sirloin. It is usually cut into steaks and can be fried or grilled.
- **Sirloin** is either roasted as a joint or cut into boneless steaks; it is more tender than rump but not as tender as fillet. Sirloin steaks are suitable for grilling or frying.
- **Rump** is a good-quality cut though it is less tender than fillet or sirloin. It is suitable for roasting, grilling or frying.
- **Rib** is sold on the bone or unboned and rolled. It is suitable for roasting.
- **Topside** is a lean, tender cut from the hindquarters. It is suitable for braising or pot roasting.
- **Silverside** is taken from the hindquarters; this is a cut from the round. It can be pot roasted or used for traditional boiled beef.
- **Flank** is a boneless cut from the mid-to-hindquarters; it is suitable for braising or stewing.
- **Skirt** is a boneless, rather gristly cut. It is usually stewed or made into mince.
- **Brisket** is a cut from the fore end of the animal, below the shoulder. Quite a fatty joint, it is sold on or off the bone or salted. It is suitable for slow roasting.

▲ Fillet and loin of beef

265

Sirloin

If the sirloin is to be roasted whole on the bone (*l'aloyau de boeuf*):

- Saw through the chine bone.
- Lift back the covering fat in one piece for approximately 10 cm.
- Trim off the sinew and replace the covering fat.
- Tie with string if necessary.
- Ensure that the fillet has been removed.

To roast the whole sirloin boned out:

- Remove the fillet and bone out the sirloin. Remove the sinew.
- Remove the excess fat and sinew from the boned side.
- This joint may be roasted open or rolled and tied with string.

Sirloin may be cut into various steaks for grilling or frying:

- **Minute steaks**: cut into 1 cm slices, flatten with a cutlet bat dipped in water, making as thin as possible, then trim.
- **Sirloin steaks (entrecôte)**: cut into 1 cm-thick slices and trim (approximate weight 150 g).
- **Double sirloin steaks**: cut into 2 cm-thick slices and trim (approximate weight 250–300 g).
- **Porterhouse steaks**: cut including the bone from the rib end of the sirloin.
- **T-bone steaks**: cut from the rump end of the sirloin, including the bone and fillet.

▲ T-bone steaks

Fillet

As a fillet of beef can vary from 2.5–4.5 kg it follows that there must be considerable variation in the number of steaks obtained from it. In this list of the different fillet steaks, it is assumed that a 3 kg fillet is used.

- **Chateaubriand**: double fillet steak 3 to 10 cm thick, two to four portions (average weight 300 g to 1 kg). Cut from the head of the fillet, trim off all the nerves and leave a little fat on the steak.
- **Fillet steaks**: approximately four steaks of 100 to 150 g each, 1.5 to 2 cm thick. These are trimmed as for chateaubriand.
- **Tournedos**: approximately six to eight at 100 g each, 2 to 4 cm thick. Continue cutting down the fillet. Remove all the nerve and fat tissue, and tie each tournedos with string.
- **Tail of fillet** is another possible cut. The tail of a 3 kg fillet will weigh approximately 0.5 kg. Remove all fat and sinew, and slice or mince as required. This cut is useful for dishes that need small pieces of tender beef, such as stir-fries.

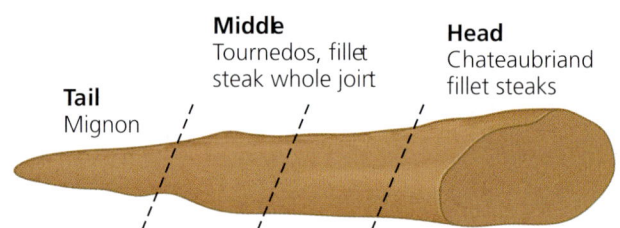

▲ Cuts of fillet of beef

The whole fillet may be roasted or pot roasted (*poêlé*). Remove the head and tail of the fillet, leaving an even centre piece from which all the nerve and fat is removed. This may be larded by inserting pieces of fat bacon, cut into long strips, with a larding needle.

Wing rib (*côte de boeuf*)

This joint usually consists of the last three rib bones, which, because of their curved shape, act as a natural trivet. Because of its prime quality it is a first-class roasting joint, hot or cold, particularly when it is to be carved in front of the customer.

Meat and offal 10

To prepare, the chine needs to be removed from the joint	Cut seven-eighths of the way through the spine or chine bone and remove the nerve	Saw through the rib bones on the underside, 5–10 cm from the end, to finish removing the chine
Trim and clean the top bone	Remove the elastin	Tie the bone firmly back with string; it will act as a trivet

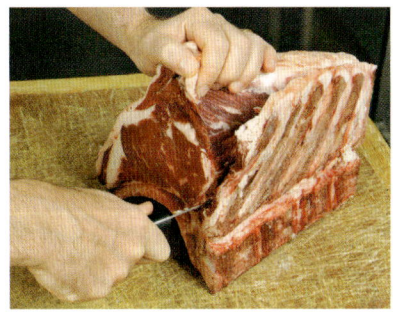

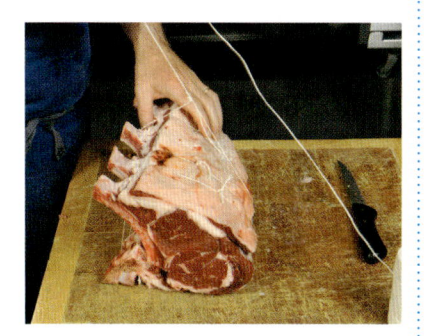

Fore ribs and middle ribs from the forequarter are prepared in the same way as wing rib.

Other cuts

- **Thin flank** from the hindquarter: trim off excessive fat and cut or roll as required.

- **Chuck ribs, sticking piece, brisket, plate, leg of mutton cut** and **shank** are all cuts from the forequarter. Bone out, remove excess fat and sinew, and use as required.

Table 10.6 Best beef cuts for pan-frying, grilling and griddling

Type of steak	Description
Rib-eye steaks	Large, slightly rounded 2.5 cm thick steaks, cut from the eye of the fore rib. They carry a little more fat than other types of steak but are the most flavoursome.
Sirloin steaks	Lean and tender boneless steaks, cut about 2.5 cm thick, with a thin layer of fat running along one edge. These are suitable for all methods of quick cooking and have a great flavour. Similar to T-bone steaks, although they are larger than sirloin steaks.
Porterhouse steaks	Cut on the bone from the rib end of the sirloin. They are large steaks, cut about 5 cm thick, and are usually cooked to serve two people.
Entrecôte	The French term for a steak cut from the middle of the sirloin.
Rump steaks	Large, longer cuts of steak, usually about 2.5 cm thick. A firmer texture than cuts from the sirloin but much more flavour.
Fillet steaks	Very lean, round steaks that are usually cut to about 4 cm thick. They are the most expensive because the tenderness is guaranteed.
Chateaubriand steak	A large piece of fillet (500 g or so) cut from the thicker end of the fillet, most often roasted to serve two or more people.

Type of steak	Description
Tournedos	The French term for small, compact round steaks cut from the centre of the fillet.
Filet mignon	A smaller steak, cut from the narrower end of the fillet.
Frying steaks	Thin slices of inexpensive steak taken from the top rump, and best suited to very quick cooking. Must not be overcooked, as this cut tends to be a little tough.
Feather steaks	These lesser-known, thinly sliced steaks cut from the blade are best suited to very quick cooking. Also referred to as the 'inquisitive foodies' steak', as it is not a well-known cut. It is taken from the shoulder blade, so there are only two in every cow. The cut is small, but packs lots of sweet flavour. Should only be cooked rare, otherwise it will toughen.
Hanger steak	Prized for its full flavour, this cut is taken from the plate (the lower belly region). Sometimes referred to as the 'butcher's steak', because butchers would often keep it for themselves rather than offer it for sale.

Barbecue cooking

1. **Choice of meat**: some fat is required for flavour, but not too much. Ensure size and thickness are uniform to allow even cooking. Suitable cuts include: T-bone steaks, rib steaks, double lamb chops and noisettes, well-trimmed pork cutlets and steaks.
2. **Seasoning**: add salt and pepper, and brush lightly with oil before placing on the barbecue. Take care when using marinades as some may contain glucose, which burns easily. Try marinating with wine and herbs; avoid marinating oils, which may ignite and spoil the barbecue.
3. **Choice and preparation of barbecue**: gas is the preferred choice for temperature control. Allow time to preheat the barbecue (30 minutes for gas, 1½ hours for charcoal). If cooking on charcoal, always wait for the flames to go out and the embers to start glowing before starting to cook.
   - Secure a layer of tinfoil over the barbecue.
   - Wait until the grill bars are hot or the charcoal embers glow.
   - Remove tin foil and brush the grill bars with a firm, long-handled wire brush to remove any unwanted debris.
4. **Cooking**: place the seasoned and lightly oiled meat at a 45° angle on the barbecue and seal one side. Rotate through another 45°, allow to cook, then turn the meat and repeat the process: this creates attractive markings on the meat. Control the temperature and do not let the meat burn or blacken unnecessarily. Only cook as much meat as required at one time; if left for too long it will dry out and become tough. Use a meat probe to ensure the desired internal temperature is reached. 'Made-up' items such as burgers and sausages must be cooked thoroughly to the centre.
5. Serve with fresh, crisp vegetables or salads and traditional barbecue dips and sauces.

Food safety

Burgers and sausages should be cut open, checked and cooked for longer if necessary. Barbecued food may look well cooked when it isn't.

Testing whether beef is cooked

Roast joints

When using a temperature probe, insert it into the part of the joint that was thickest before the food was placed in the oven. The internal temperature reached should be as follows:
- rare meat: 55–60 °C
- medium done: 66–71 °C
- well done: 78–80 °C.

To test without a temperature probe:
- remove the joint from the oven and place on a plate or dish
- firmly press the surface of the meat so that some juice issues
- check the colour of the juice: *red* indicates the meat is underdone; *pink* indicates the meat is medium done; *clear* indicates that the meat is cooked through.

Grilled beef

The degrees of cooking for grilled meat are:
- very rare (or blue): cooked over a fierce heat for a few seconds on each side
- rare: the cooked meat has a reddish tinge
- medium: the cooked meat is slightly pinkish
- well done: thoroughly cooked with no sign of pinkness.

Meat and offal 10

When using a temperature probe, insert it into the part of the meat that was thickest before the food was placed under the grill. The internal temperature reached should be as follows:

- rare: 45–50 °C
- medium: 55–60 °C
- well done: 75–77 °C

You can also check how well done grilled meat is by using finger pressure. The springiness, or resilience, of the meat and the amount of blood issuing from it indicates the degree to which it is cooked. This calls for experience, but if the meat is placed on a plate and tested, then the more underdone the steak, the greater the springiness and the more blood will be shown on the plate.

Veal

Veal is obtained from good-quality carcasses weighing around 100 kg. This quality of veal is required for first-class cookery and is produced from calves slaughtered at between 12 and 24 weeks.

Veal is available all year round.

Quality points

- The flesh should be pale pink in colour and firm in structure – not soft or flabby.
- Cut surfaces should be slightly moist, not dry.
- Bones, in young animals, should be pinkish white, porous and with a degree of blood in their structure.
- The fat should be firm and pinkish white.
- The kidney should be firm and well covered with fat.

Where applicable, when offering veal on a menu, give the origin and breed of the veal.

The veal carcass

The average weight of English or Dutch milk-fed veal calves is 18 kg. The joints of veal are shown in the diagram and Table 10.7.

The order of dissection for a veal carcass is as follows:
1 Remove the shoulders.
2 Remove the breast.
3 Take off the leg.
4 Divide the loin and best end from the scrag and neck end.
5 Divide the loin from the best end.

Table 10.7 Uses and weights of veal joints and offal

Joint	Uses	Approx. weight (kg)
Knuckle (1)	Osso buco, sauté, stock	2
Leg (2)	Roasting, braising, escalopes, sauté	5
Loin (3)	Roasting, frying, grilling	3.5
Best end (4)	Roasting, frying, grilling	3
Shoulder (5)	Braising, stewing	5
Neck end (6)	Stewing, sauté	2.5
Scrag (7)	Stewing, stock	1.5
Breast (8)	Stewing, roasting	2.5
Kidneys	Stewing (pies and puddings), sauté	–
Liver	Frying	–
Sweetbreads	Braising, frying	–
Head	Boiling, soup	4
Brains	Boiling, frying	–
Bones	Stock	–

Dissecting a leg of veal

1 Remove the knuckle by dividing the knee joint (at A on the diagram) and cut through the meat away from the cushion line (from A to B).
2 Remove the aitchbone at thick end of the leg, separating it at the ball and socket joint.

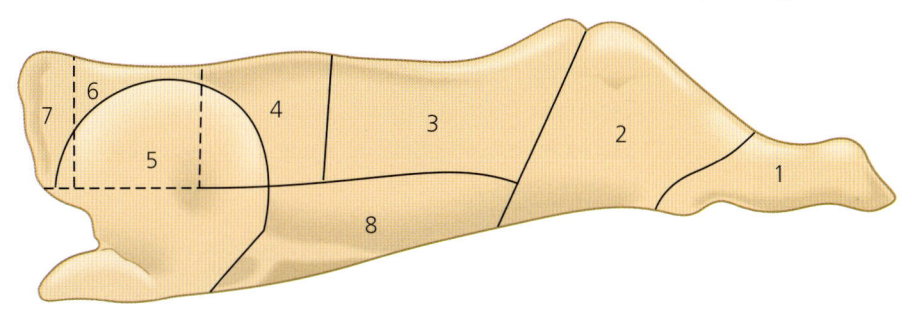

▲ A side of veal – see Table 10.7 for an explanation of the numbers

3. Remove all the outside skin and fat, thus exposing the natural seams. It will now be seen that the thigh bone divides the meat into two-thirds and one-third (thick flank).
4. Stand the leg on the thick flank with point D (on the diagram) uppermost. Divide the cushion from the under cushion, following the natural seam, using the hand and the point of a knife. Having reached the thigh bone, remove it completely.
5. When the boned leg falls open, the three joints can easily be seen joined only by membrane. Separate and trim the cushion, removing the loose flap of meat.
6. Trim the under cushion, removing the layer of thick gristle. Separate into three small joints through the natural seams. It will be seen that one of these will correspond with the round in silverside of beef.
7. Trim the thick flank by laying it on its round side and making a cut along the length about 2.5 cm deep. A seam is reached and the two trimmings can be removed.

The anticipated yield of escalopes from this size of leg would be 6.25 kg, that is, 55 × 100 g or 75 × 80 g, serving 1 or 2 escalopes per portion.

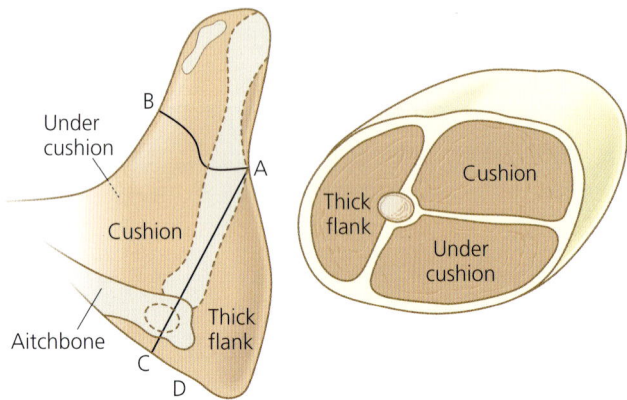

▲ Dissection of a leg of veal

Preparing joints and cuts of veal

Shin
- For stewing (on the bone; *osso buco*): cut and saw into 2–4 cm thick slices through the knuckle.
- For sauté: bone out and trim, then cut into even 25 g pieces.

Leg
- For braising or roasting whole: remove the aitch bone, clean and trim 4 cm off the knuckle bone. Trim off the excess sinew.
- To braise or roast the nut: remove all the sinew; if there is insufficient fat on the joint then bard (tie fat around it, for example, bacon) thinly and secure with string.
- Escalopes: remove all the sinew, cut into large 50–75 g slices against the grain and bat out thinly.
- For sauté: remove all the sinew and cut into 25 g pieces.

Loin and best end
- For roasting: bone out and trim the flap, roll out and secure with string. This joint may be stuffed before rolling.
- For frying: trim and cut into cutlets.

▲ Veal escalopes

Table 10.8 Joints of a leg of veal

Cuts	Weight	Proportion	Uses	Corresponding joint in beef
Cushion or nut	2.75 kg	15%	Escalopes, roasting, braising, sauté	Topside
Under cushion or under nut	3 kg	17%	Escalopes, roasting, braising, sauté	Silverside
Thick flank	2.5 kg	14%	Escalopes, roasting, braising, sauté	Thick flank
Knuckle (whole)	2.5 kg	14%	Osso buco, sauté	
Bones (thigh and aitch)	2.5 kg	14%	Stock, *jus-lié*, sauces	
Usable trimmings	2 kg	11%	Pies, stewing	

Boning a loin of veal

The loin

Using a boning knife, carefully remove the fillet

The joint and the fillet

Bring the loin down from the rib to the backbone, and trim the rib bones

Trim the excess fat and sinew from the meat

The fillet, boned loin and bones (which can be used for stock)

Shoulder
- For braising: bone out as for lamb; usually stuffed.
- For stewing: bone out, remove all the sinew and cut into 25 g pieces.

Neck end and scrag
For stewing or sauté: bone out and remove all the sinew; cut into approximately 25 g pieces.

Breast
- For stewing: as for neck end.
- For roasting: bone out, season, stuff and roll up, then tie with string.

Pork

The keeping quality of pork is less than that of other meat; therefore it must be handled, prepared and cooked with great care. Pork should always be well cooked, reaching at least 75 °C in the centre.

Where applicable, name the origin and breed of the pork (e.g. Gloucester Old Spot, Tamworth) on the menu.

Quality points
- Lean flesh should be pale pink, firm and of a fine texture.
- The fat should be white, firm, smooth and not excessive.
- Bones should be small, fine and pinkish.
- The skin or rind should be smooth.

The pork carcass

The cuts of pork are shown in the diagram below and their uses in Table 10.9.

Practical Cookery 14th edition

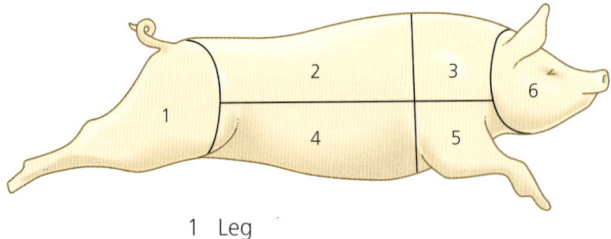

1. Leg
2. Loin
3. Spare rib of neck
4. Belly
5. Shoulder
6. Head

▲ Pig carcass dissection

Table 10.9 Joints, uses and weights of pork

Joint	Uses	Approx. weight (kg)
Leg	Roasting, boiling	5
Loin	Roasting, frying, grilling	6
Spare rib	Roasting, pies	1.5
Belly	Pickling, boiling, stuffed, rolled and roasted	2
Shoulder	Roasting, sausages, pies	3
Head	Brawn	4
Trotters	Grilling, boiling	
Kidneys	Sauté, grilling	
Liver	Frying, pâté	

At five to six weeks old a piglet is known as a sucking or suckling pig. Its weight is then between 5 and 10 kg.

The order of dissection for a pig carcass is:
1. Remove the head.
2. Remove the trotters.
3. Remove the leg.
4. Remove the shoulder.
5. Remove the spare ribs.
6. Divide the loin from the belly.

Preparing joints and cuts of pork

Leg

- **For roasting**: remove the pelvic or aitch bone, trim and score the rind neatly – that is, with a sharp-pointed knife make a series of 3 mm-deep incisions approximately 2 cm apart all over the skin of the joint; trim and clean the knuckle bone.

- **For boiling**: it is usual to pickle the joint either by rubbing dry salt and saltpetre (potassium nitrate) into the meat or by soaking it in a brine solution; then remove the pelvic bone, trim and secure with string if necessary.

Loin

- **For roasting (on the bone)**: saw down the chine bone in order to facilitate carving; trim the excess fat and sinew and score the rind in the direction that the joint will be carved; season and secure with string.

- **For roasting (boned out)**: remove the fillets and bone out carefully; trim off the excess fat and sinew, score the rind and neaten the flap. Season, replace the filet mignon, roll up and secure the string. This joint is sometimes stuffed.

- **Chops for grilling or frying**: remove the skin, excess fat and sinew, then cut and saw or chop through the loin in approximately 1 cm-thick slices; remove the excess bone and trim neatly.

▲ Boned leg of pork

▲ Loin of pork

Meat and offal

▲ Pork chops

Spare rib

- **For roasting**: remove the excess fat, bone and sinew, and trim neatly.
- **For grilling**: remove the excess fat, bone and sinew, cut into individual ribs or leave as a rack, and marinade for at least 2 hours.
- **For pies**: remove the excess fat and sinew, bone out and cut as required.

Shoulder

- **For roasting**: the shoulder is usually boned out, the excess fat and sinew removed, seasoned, scored and rolled with string; it may be stuffed and can also be divided into two smaller joints.
- **For sausages or pies**: skin, bone out and remove the excess fat and sinew; cut into even pieces or mince.

Belly

Boning a pork belly

Pork belly before it is prepared for roasting

Remove all the small rib bones

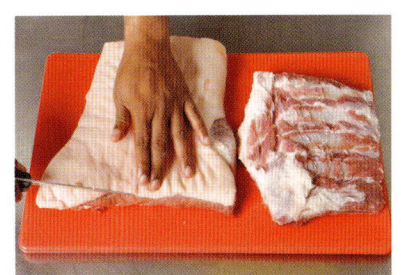

Cut the fat

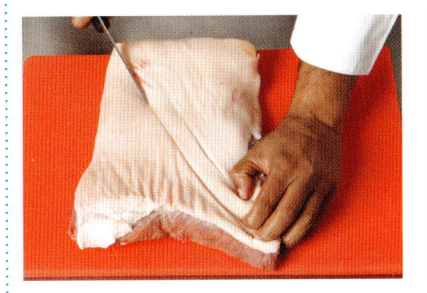

Score the fat

Season with salt, pepper and chopped sage

Roll and secure with string; this joint may be stuffed

Bacon

Bacon is the cured flesh of a bacon-weight pig that is specifically reared for bacon (because its shape and size yield economic bacon joints). Bacon is cured either by dry salting and then smoking or by soaking in brine followed by smoking. Green bacon is brine-cured but not smoked; it has a milder flavour but does not keep for as long as smoked bacon.

Depending on the degree of salting during the curing process, bacon joints may or may not require soaking in cold water before being cooked.

Do not confuse ham with gammon. Ham is meat taken from the carcass *before* salting or smoking and cooking, where gammon is taken from the carcass *after* brining and smoking.

Quality

- There should be no sign of stickiness.
- There should be a pleasant smell.
- The rind should be thin, smooth and free from wrinkles.
- The fat should be white, smooth and not excessive in proportion to the lean meat.
- The lean meat should be a deep-pink colour and firm.

Preparing bacon joints and cuts

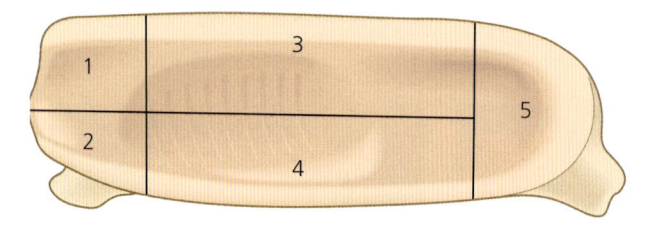

1 Collar
2 Hock
3 Back
4 Streaky
5 Gammon

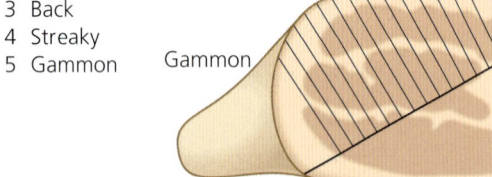

▲ A side of bacon

Table 10.10 Cuts, uses and weights of bacon

Joint	Uses	Approx. weight (kg)
Collar	Boiling, grilling	4.5
Hock	Boiling, grilling	4.5
Back	Grilling, frying	9
Streaky	Grilling, frying	4.5
Gammon	Boiling, grilling, frying	7.5

Collar

- **For boiling**: remove bone (if any) and tie with string.
- **Rashers for grilling**: remove the rind, trim off the outside surface and cut into thin slices (rashers) across the joint.

Hock

Leave whole or bone out and secure with string. The hock is usually boiled.

Back and streaky bacon

- **Rashers for grilling**: remove all bones and rind, and cut into thin rashers.
- **Rashers or chops for frying**: remove the rind, trim off the outside surface and cut into rashers or chops of the required thickness.

Gammon

Cut fairly thick slices from the middle of the gammon. Trim them and remove the rind. Slices of gammon are usually grilled or fried.

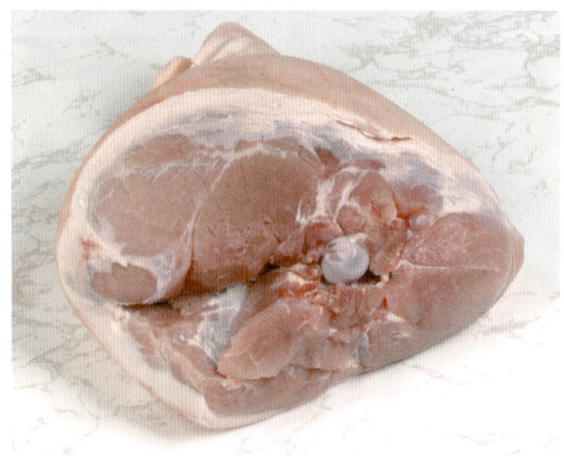

▲ Gammon

Meat and offal

▲ Gammon steaks

Offal and other edible parts of the carcass

Offal is the name given to the edible parts taken from the inside of a carcass of meat, including the liver, kidneys, heart and sweetbreads. Tripe, brains, tongue, head and oxtail are also sometimes included under this term.

Fresh offal (unfrozen) should be purchased as required and can be refrigerated under hygienic conditions at a temperature of 1–4°C. Frozen offal must be kept in a deep freeze at −18°C or below, and defrosted in a refrigerator as required.

Liver

Liver is low in fat, a good source of protein and iron, and also contains vitamins A and D.

- **Calf's liver** is considered the best in terms of tenderness and flavour. It is also the most expensive.
- **Lamb's liver** is mild in flavour, light in colour and tender. Sheep's liver, being from an older animal, is firmer in substance, deeper in colour and has a stronger flavour.
- **Ox** or **beef liver** is the cheapest and, if taken from an older animal, can be coarse in texture and strong in flavour. It is usually braised.
- **Pig's liver** has a strong, full flavour and is used mainly for pâté recipes.

Quality points

- Liver should look fresh, moist and smooth, with a pleasant colour and no unpleasant smell.
- Liver should not be dry or contain an excessive number of tubes.

Preparing liver

- Remove the skin if possible.
- Remove the gristle and tubes.
- Cut into thin slices on the slant.

Kidneys

The nutritional value of kidney is similar to that of liver.

- **Lamb's kidneys** are light in colour, delicate in flavour and ideal for grilling and frying.
- **Sheep's kidneys** are darker in colour and stronger in flavour.
- **Calf's kidneys** are light in colour, delicate in flavour and used in a variety of dishes.
- **Ox kidney** is dark in colour, strong in flavour, and is either braised or used in pies and puddings (mixed with beef).
- **Pig's kidneys** are smooth, long and flat, and have a strong flavour.

Quality points

- Suet – the saturated fat in which kidneys are encased – should be left on, otherwise the kidneys will dry out. The suet should be removed when kidneys are being prepared for cooking.
- Both suet and kidneys should be moist and have no unpleasant smell.

Preparing kidneys

Skin them and remove the fat and gristle, then cut as required:

- **For grilling**: split the kidney three-quarters of the way through lengthwise. Cut out and discard the gristle. Skewer.
- **For sauté**: cut slantways.
- **For calves' or pigs' kidneys**: cut down the middle lengthwise. Remove the sinew. Cut into thin slices or neat dice.

275

Preparing kidneys for grilling

Skin the kidneys, and remove any fat and gristle

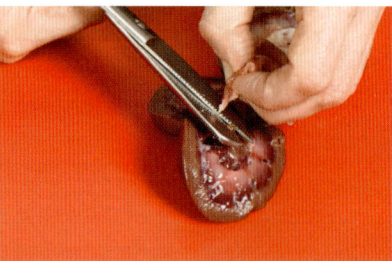

Lift up and cut out the white sinew in the centre

Split the kidney three-quarters of the way through, and open it up

Kidneys before, during and after preparation

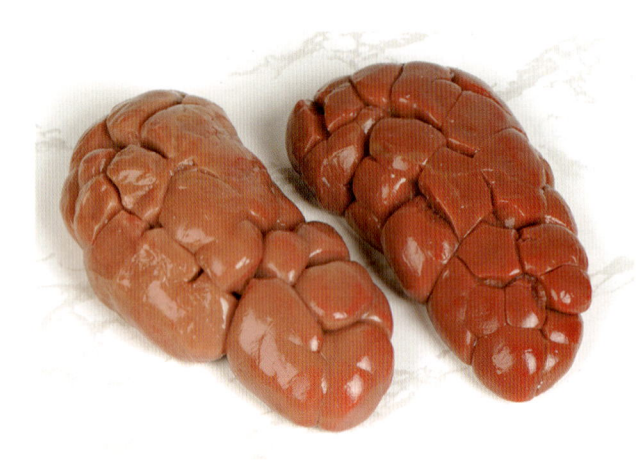

▲ Veal kidneys

Hearts

Hearts are a good source of protein, which is needed for growth and repair of the body.
- **Lamb's hearts** are small and light; they are normally served whole.
- **Sheep's hearts** are dark and solid; they can be dry and tough unless cooked carefully.
- **Ox** or **beef hearts** are dark coloured and solid, and tend to be dry and tough.
- **Calf's hearts**, coming from a younger animal, are lighter in colour and more tender.

Before cooking, remove the arterial tubes and excess fat. Most hearts need slow braising to tenderise them.

Quality points
- Hearts should not be too fatty and should not contain too many tubes.
- When cut they should be moist, not sticky, and with no unpleasant smell.

Sweetbreads

Sweetbreads are the pancreas gland (heart bread) and thymus gland (neck bread). The heart bread is round, plump and of better quality than the neck bread, which is long and uneven in shape. Calf's heart bread, considered the best, weighs up to 600 g, while lamb's heart bread weighs up to 100 g.

Sweetbreads are an easily digested source of protein, which makes them valuable for use in invalid diets.

Quality points
- Heart and neck breads should be fleshy and of a good size.
- They should be creamy-white in colour and have no unpleasant smell.

Meat and offal

Preparing sweetbreads
- Soak in cold salted water for two to three hours to remove blood, which would darken the sweetbreads during cooking. Use several changes of water for calves' sweetbreads.
- Wash well, blanch, trim and refresh.
- For calves' sweetbreads, peel off the membrane and connective tissue.
- The sweetbreads can then be pressed between two trays with a weight on top, and refrigerated.

▲ Veal sweetbreads

Tripe
Tripe is the stomach lining or white muscle of the ox, consisting of the rumen or paunch and the honeycomb tripe (considered the best). Sheep tripe, which is darker in colour, is obtainable in some areas. Tripe contains protein, is low in fat and high in calcium.

Tripe should be fresh, with no signs of stickiness or unpleasant smell. To prepare it, wash it well and soak in cold water, then cut into even pieces. Boil or simmer until tender.

Tongues
Ox, lamb and sheep tongues are those most used in cooking. Ox tongues are usually salted then soaked before being cooked. Lamb tongues are cooked fresh.

Tongues must be fresh and have no unpleasant smell and there should not be an excess of waste at the root end. To prepare them for cooking remove the bone and gristle from the throat end and soak in cold water for two to four hours. If salted, soak for three to four hours.

Oxtail
Oxtails usually weigh 1.5–2 kg and should be lean with not too much fat. There should be no sign of stickiness and no unpleasant smell. To prepare the tail, cut between the natural joints then trim off excess fat. The large pieces may be split in two.

Suet
Suet is the fat that surrounds the kidneys. Beef suet should be creamy-white, brittle and dry. Other meat fat should be fresh, not sticky, and with no unpleasant smell.

Bone marrow
Marrow is obtained from the bones of the leg of beef. It should be of good size, firm, creamy-white and odourless. Sliced, poached marrow may be used as a garnish for some meat dishes and savouries.

Bones
Bones must be fresh, not sticky, with no unpleasant smell, and preferably meaty (as they are used for stock, the foundation for so many preparations).

Pigs' trotters
To prepare trotters, boil in water for a few minutes then scrape with the back of a knife to remove the hairs. Wash off in cold water and split in half.

Table 10.11 Uses of beef offal

Offal	Uses
Bones	Beef stocks
Heart	Braising
Kidney	Stewing, soup
Liver	Braising, frying
Suet	Suet paste and stuffing, or rendered down for first-class dripping
Sweetbread	Braising, frying
Tail	Braising, soup
Tongue	Pickled in brine, boiling, braising
Tripe	Boiling, braising

Other meat preparations

Forcemeat

This is a term given to numerous mixtures of meats (usually veal and pork) and poultry, game, fish, vegetables and bread. Forcemeats range from a simple sausagemeat to the finer mixtures used in the making of hot mousses (ham, chicken, fish) and soufflés. Also included are mixtures of bread, vegetables and herbs, which are alternatively referred to as stuffings.

Forcemeats are used for galantines, raised pies, terrines, meatballs and a wide variety of other dishes.

Crépinettes

These are small sausages, usually made from a forcemeat of veal, lamb, pork or chicken, encased either in caul (a thin membrane of fat from the intestines) or paper-thin slices of salt pork. Other ingredients are sometimes added (e.g. chopped mushrooms or truffles). Crépinettes are usually covered with melted butter or good quality oil, coated with fresh white breadcrumbs and grilled, sautéed or cooked in the oven. Traditionally they are served with potato purée and a well-flavoured demi-glace sauce.

Test yourself

1. List two quality points to look for when buying beef.
2. Describe how to store uncooked meat in a refrigerator.
3. Describe the stages in the preparation of a best end of lamb.
4. What are the benefits of sealing meat before cooking?
5. Give two reasons why braising is a suitable cooking method for neck of veal.
6. Describe the stages in the preparation and cooking of a leg of pork.
7. List four quality points to look for when buying pork.
8. List two quality points to look for when buying calves' liver.
9. Why is braising the most appropriate cooking method for hearts?
10. Describe how to prepare sweetbreads for cooking.

Lamb dishes

1 Lamb satay

Ingredient	To make 10	To make 20
Lamb fillets or loin of lamb	250 g	500 g
Clove of garlic, crushed and chopped	1	2
Thai fish sauce	1 tsp	2 tsp
Sweet chilli sauce	1 tbsp	2 tbsp
Fresh ginger, grated	1 tsp	2 tsp
Lime juice	30 ml	60 ml
Peanut butter (coarse)	1 tbsp	2 tbsp
Ground cumin	½ tsp	1 tsp
Ground turmeric	½ tsp	1 tsp
Sauce		
White vinegar	30 ml	60 ml
Caster sugar	1 tbsp	2 tbsp
Sweet chilli sauce	3 tsp	1 tbsp
Unsalted, roasted peanuts	3 tsp	1 tbsp
Fresh coriander leaves, finely chopped	3 tsp	1 tbsp

Energy	Cals	Fat	Sat fat	Carb	Sugar	Protein	Fibre	Sodium
1,624 kJ	391 kcal	29.3 g	10.2 g	13.3 g	11.7 g	19.6 g	2.4 g	0.7 g

1 Prepare the lamb, cutting it into thin strips.
2 In a bowl place the garlic, sauces, ginger, lime juice, peanut butter and spices. Mix well.
3 Put the lamb into the marinade, stir and put in refrigerator for 3 hours or overnight.
4 Meanwhile, soak some bamboo skewers in water for about an hour to prevent scorching.
5 Thread the lamb on to the skewers. Grill the lamb skewers, turning once until cooked and nicely coloured.
6 Prepare the sauce by placing the vinegar and sugar in a small pan, stirring until the sugar has dissolved. Bring to the boil and simmer for 2 minutes. Stir in the remaining ingredients.
7 Serve the lamb on a suitable platter on banana leaves (optional) with the dipping sauce in a bowl in the centre.

2 Grilled lamb cutlets (côtelettes d'agneau grillées)

1. Season the cutlets lightly with salt and mill pepper.
2. Brush with oil or fat.
3. If the grill is heated from below, place the prepared cutlet on the greased, preheated bars. Cook for approximately 5 minutes, turn and complete the cooking.
4. If using a salamander, place the cutlets on a greased tray, cook for approximately 5 minutes, turn and complete the cooking.
5. Serve dressed, garnished with a deep-fried potato and watercress. A compound butter (e.g. parsley, herb or garlic) may also be served.
6. Each cutlet bone may be capped with a cutlet frill.

Healthy eating tips
When served with boiled new potatoes and boiled or steamed vegetables, the dish becomes more 'balanced'.

Energy	Cals	Fat	Sat fat	Carb	Sugar	Protein	Fibre	Sodium
1,493 kJ	357 kcal	20.7 g	9.8 g	0.0 g	0.0 g	42.8 g	0.0 g	0.1 g

3 Mixed grill

Ingredient	4 portions	10 portions
Sausages	4	10
Cutlets	4	10
Kidneys	4	10
Tomatoes	4	10
Mushrooms	4	10
Streaky bacon, rashers	4	10
Deep-fried potato, to serve		
Watercress, to serve		
Parsley butter, to serve		

Energy	Cals	Fat	Sat fat	Carb	Sugar	Protein	Fibre
2,050 kJ	488 kcal	40.8 g	19.3 g	0.0 g	0.0 g	30.4 g	0.0 g

1 portion (2 cutlets). With deep-fried potatoes, parsley and watercress, 1 portion provides: 3,050 kJ/726 kcal energy, 59.2 g fat, 26.6 g saturated fat, 20.2 g carbohydrates, 2.5 g sugar, 29.5 g protein and 4.9 g fibre.

These are the usually accepted items for a mixed grill, but it will be found that there are many variations to this list (e.g. steaks, liver, a Welsh rarebit and fried egg).

1 Grill in the order listed above.
2 Dress neatly on an oval flat dish or plates.

Garnish with deep-fried potato, watercress and a slice of compound butter on each kidney or offered separately.

> **Professional tip**
>
> The items must be cooked in the order listed above, so that they are all fully and evenly cooked at the end.

> **Healthy eating tips**
>
> Add only a small amount of compound butter and serve with plenty of potatoes and vegetables.

4 Lamb kebabs (*shish kebab*)

Energy	Cals	Fat	Sat fat	Carb	Sugar	Protein	Fibre	Sodium
1,544 kJ	372 kcal	25.1g	9.9g	7.2g	5.9g	29.6g	2.0g	0.1g

1 Cut the meat into cubes and place on skewers with squares of green pepper, tomato, onion and bay leaves in between. The pieces of lamb and vegetables must be cut evenly so that they will cook evenly
2 Sprinkle with chopped thyme and cook over a hot grill.

Serve with pilaff rice, or with chickpeas and finely sliced raw onion.

> **Note**
>
> Kebabs, a dish of Turkish origin, are pieces of food impaled and cooked on skewers over a grill or barbecue. There are many variations and different flavours can be added by marinating the kebabs in oil, wine, vinegar or lemon juice with spices and herbs for 1–2 hours before cooking.
>
> Kebabs can be made using tender cuts, or mince of lamb and beef, pork, liver, kidney, bacon, ham, sausage and chicken, using either the meats individually or combining two or three. Vegetables and fruit can also be added (e.g. onion, apple, pineapple, peppers, tomatoes, aubergine). Kebabs can be made using vegetables exclusively (e.g. peppers, onion, aubergine, tomatoes). Kebabs are usually served with a pilaff rice (see page 159).
>
> The ideal cuts of lamb are the nut of the lean meat of the loin, best end or boned-out meat from a young shoulder of lamb.

> **Variation**
>
> Miniature kebabs (one mouthful) can be made, impaled on cocktail sticks, grilled and served as an amuse-bouche, or as a hot snack at receptions.
>
> Fish kebabs can be made using a firm fish, such as monkfish or tuna, and marinating in olive oil, lemon or lime juice, chopped fennel or dill, garlic and a dash of Tabasco or Worcester sauce.

5 Grilled loin or chump chops, or noisettes of lamb

1. Season the chops or noisettes lightly with salt and mill pepper.
2. Brush with oil and place on hot greased grill bars or place on a greased baking tray.
3. Cook quickly for the first 2–3 minutes on each side, in order to seal the pores of the meat.
4. Continue cooking steadily, allowing approximately 12–15 minutes in all.

A compound butter may also be served, together with deep-fried potatoes.

Variation

Sprigs of rosemary or other herbs may be laid on the chops during the last few minutes of grilling to impart flavour.

Energy	Cals	Fat	Sat fat	Carb	Sugar	Protein	Fibre	Sodium
1,338 kJ	320 kcal	16.1 g	7.4 g	0.0 g	0.0 g	43.8 g	0.0 g	0.1 g

6 Lamb rosettes with thyme and blueberries

Ingredient	4 portions	10 portions
Lamb rosettes	8	20
Olive oil	2 tbsp	5 tbsp
Red wine	250 ml	625 ml
Fresh thyme	4 sprigs	10 sprigs
Lamb stock	250 ml	625 ml
Blueberries	200 g	500 g
Salt and pepper		

Energy	Cals	Fat	Sat fat	Carb	Sugar	Protein	Fibre	Sodium
3197 kJ	771 kcal	63.0 g	28.0 g	6.1 g	4.6 g	35.0 g	1.3 g	0.4 g

Using lamb cutlets and beef stock.

1. Shallow-fry the rosettes in the olive oil.
2. Deglaze the pan with the wine, then add the thyme.
3. Add the lamb stock and reduce to a sauce consistency.
4. Add the blueberries, then season.
5. Serve the lamb with the blueberries and the sauce.

Note

Risotto makes a suitable accompaniment.

7 Noisettes of lamb with baby ratatouille

Ingredient	4 portions	10 portions
Noisettes of lamb	8	20
Vegetable oil for frying		
Baby ratatouille (see recipe on page 450, but cut the vegetables into 0.75 cm dice)	400 g	1 kg

Energy	Cals	Fat	Sat fat	Carb	Sugar	Protein	Fibre
1,666 kJ	400 kcal	29.3 g	9.3 g	3.8 g	3.2 g	30.7 g	2.4 g

1 Prepare the noisettes of lamb.
2 Shallow-fry the seasoned noisettes in vegetable oil on both sides until just pink.
3 Drain on kitchen paper. Serve on a bed of baby ratatouille.
4 Garnish with fresh basil or some fresh chopped mixed herbs (parsley, chervil, tarragon, etc).

8 Lamb valentine steaks with fresh hummus

Ingredient	4 portions	10 portions
Lamb steaks	8	20
Olive oil	2 tbsp	5 tbsp
For the hummus		
Canned chickpeas	600 g	1.5 kg
Cloves of garlic, crushed and chopped	4	10
Ground cumin	1 tsp	2½ tsp
Lemon juice	½ tsp	1¼ tsp
Mint leaves, chopped	1 tsp	2½ tsp
Extra virgin olive oil	10 tbsp	25 tbsp
Tahini paste	2 tbsp	5 tbsp

Energy	Cals	Fat	Sat fat	Carb	Sugar	Protein	Fibre	Sodium
4,099 kJ	985 kcal	72.0 g	18.4 g	24.6 g	1.7 g	60.0 g	9.1 g	0.4 g

Using 100 g lamb valentine steak.

1 Prepare the valentine steaks.
2 To make the hummus, drain and rinse the chickpeas. Purée in a food processor with the garlic, cumin, lemon juice, mint, olive oil and tahini paste.
3 Lightly season the valentines. Shallow-fry in olive oil until golden brown and slightly pink.
4 Serve on individual plates on a bed of hummus, garnished with fresh mint. Alternatively, serve the steaks on plates with the hummus piped as a rosette, and a circle of lamb jus around.

9 Samosas

Energy	Cals	Fat	Sat fat	Carb	Sugar	Protein	Fibre	Sodium
2,740 kJ	682 kcal	43.9g	15.2g	49.5g	2.0g	25.5g	3.0g	0.5g

Using short paste and lamb filling.

Filling 1: potato

Ingredient	4 portions	10 portions
Potatoes, peeled	200 g	500 g
Vegetable oil	1½ tsp	3¾ tsp
Black mustard seeds	½ tsp	1¼ tsp
Onions, finely chopped	50 g	125 g
Fresh ginger, finely chopped	12 g	30 g
Fennel seeds	1 tsp	2½ tsp
Cumin seeds	¼ tsp	1 tsp
Turmeric	¼ tsp	1 tsp
Frozen peas	75 g	187 g
Salt, to taste		
Water	1 tbsp	2½ tbsp
Fresh coriander, finely chopped	1 tsp	2½ tsp
Garam masala	½ tsp	2½ tsp
Pinch of cayenne pepper		

1 Cut the potatoes into 0.5 cm dice; cook in water until only just cooked.
2 Heat the oil in a suitable pan, add the mustard seeds and cook until they pop.
3 Add the onions and ginger. Fry for 7–8 minutes, stirring continuously until golden brown.
4 Stir in the fennel, cumin and turmeric; add the potatoes, peas, salt and water.
5 Reduce to a low heat, cover the pan and cook for 5 minutes.
6 Stir in the coriander; cook for a further 5 minutes.
7 Remove from the heat, stir in the garam masala and the cayenne seasoning.
8 Remove from the pan, place into a suitable bowl to cool before using.

Filling 2: lamb

Ingredient	4 portions	10 portions
Saffron	½ tsp	1¼ tsp
Boiling water	2½ tsp	6¼ tsp
Vegetable oil	3 tsp	7½ tsp
Fresh ginger, finely chopped	12 g	30 g
Cloves of garlic, crushed and chopped	2	5
Onions, finely chopped	50 g	125 g
Salt, to taste		
Lean lamb, minced	400 g	1 kg
Pinch of cayenne pepper		
Garam masala	1 tsp	2½ tsp

1 Infuse the saffron in the boiling water; allow to stand for 10 minutes.
2 Heat the vegetable oil in a suitable pan. Add the ginger, garlic, onions and salt, stirring continuously. Fry for 7–8 minutes, until the onions are soft and golden brown.
3 Stir in the lamb, add the saffron with the water. Cook, stirring the lamb until it is cooked.
4 Add the cayenne and garam masala, reduce the heat and allow to cook gently for a further 10 minutes.
5 The mixture should be fairly tight with very little moisture.
6 Transfer to a bowl and allow to cool before using.

Meat and offal

To make the samosas

Ingredient	16–20 pasties	40–50 pasties
Short pastry made from ghee fat and fairly strong flour (the dough must be fairly elastic)	400 g	1 kg
Or filo or spring roll pastry		

Healthy eating tips
- Use the minimum of salt in the potato filling. No added salt is necessary with the lamb.
- Use a small amount of unsaturated oil to fry the mustard seeds, onions and lamb.
- Drain off the excess fat before adding the water.

Note
Allow 4 or 5 samosas for a portion. They can also be served individually as finger food.
The samosas may be made in advance, covered with cling film or plastic, and refrigerated before being deep fried.
Samosas can be garnished with coriander leaves and served with chutney.

1 Cut the paste into strips approx. 18 × 7 cm. Fold over the end of the pastry.

2 Eggwash the upper side of the pastry, then fold over the top part to form a pocket.

3 Flip over the pocket, ease it open and fill it.

4 Once completely full, eggwash the top edge and the flap of pastry.

5 Fold over the pastry and wrap it round the seal the samosa.

6 Deep fry until golden brown and crisp.

10 Braised lamb chump chops (*chops d'agneau braisés*)

1. Fry the seasoned chops in a sauté pan quickly on both sides in hot fat.
2. When turning the chops, add the mirepoix (onion and carrot).
3. Draw aside and drain off the surplus fat.
4. Add the flour and mix in, singe in the oven or on top of the stove. (Alternatively, use flour that has been browned in the oven.)
5. Add the tomato purée and the hot stock, and stir with a kitchen spoon until thoroughly mixed.
6. Add the bouquet garni and garlic, if using. Season, skim and allow to simmer; cover with a lid.
7. Cook (preferably in the oven), skimming off all oil and scum.
8. When cooked, transfer the chops to a clean pan.
9. Correct the seasoning and consistency of the sauce.
10. Skim off any oil and pass the sauce through a fine strainer over the chops.
11. Serve sprinkled with chopped parsley.

Ingredient	4 portions	10 portions
Lamb chops	4	10
Salt and pepper		
Sunflower or olive oil		
Onion, diced	100 g	250 g
Carrot, diced	100 g	250 g
Flour (white or wholemeal)	25 g	60 g
Tomato purée	1 level tsp	2½ level tsp
Brown stock	500 ml	1.25 litre
Bouquet garni	1	2
Clove of garlic, optional	1	2½
Parsley, chopped		

Energy	Cals	Fat	Sat fat	Carb	Sugar	Protein	Fibre
1,452 kJ	349 kcal	23.4 g	10.8 g	9.4 g	3.8 g	25.8 g	1.2 g

Healthy eating tips
- Trim fat from the chops before frying.
- Use the minimum amount of salt.
- Lightly oil the pan with an unsaturated oil to fry the chops. Drain off any excess fat after the frying is complete.
- Serve with a large portion of vegetables.

Variation
Lamb steaks cut from the chump end of the leg can also be cooked in this way. Variations include the following additions after the sauce has been strained:
- cooked pulses (e.g. haricot, butter or flageolet beans)
- neatly cut cooked vegetables (e.g. carrots, turnips, swede, green beans or peas).

11 Braised lamb shanks

Ingredient	4 portions	10 portions
Lamb shanks	4	10
Olive oil for braising (to fill casserole about 1 cm deep)		
Leeks, roughly chopped	1	2½
Celery sticks, roughly chopped	2	5
Carrots, roughly chopped	2	5
Onions, roughly chopped	2	5
Garlic head, broken into cloves (unpeeled)	1	2½
Bay leaf	1	2½
Thyme sprig	1	2½
Rosemary sprig	1	2½
Red wine	375 ml	1 litre
Chicken stock	600 ml	1.5 litres

Energy	Cals	Fat	Sat fat	Carb	Sugar	Protein	Fibre	Sodium
3098 kJ	742 kcal	24.2g	7.4g	10.5g	8.1g	98.3g	4.0g	0.3g

1 Take a casserole (or oven-proof dish) and place on the hob over a high heat. Pour in the olive oil and, when hot, add the lamb shanks, turning occasionally until brown.
2 Once browned, remove the lamb from the pot and tip in the leek, celery, carrot, onion and garlic cloves. Stir them all together and add the bay leaf, thyme and rosemary. These ingredients will all add flavour to the dish but won't be served at the end.
3 Once the vegetables are lightly browned, place the lamb back into the pot, allowing it to rest on top of the vegetables.
4 Pour in the red wine and chicken stock and bring to the boil.
5 Cover the pot with a lid or kitchen foil and place in the oven at 150 °C to braise for 2 hours 30 minutes, or up to 5 hours depending on the amount of lamb being used. When the meat is cooked, the bone can easily be turned out of the meat (if you would like to present the bone, only give it a small turn to check if the lamb is ready, as it will be difficult to re-insert the bone once removed).
6 Pass the cooking stock through a fine sieve and reduce to the correct consistency (coats the back of a spoon).
7 Serve the lamb shanks with the cooking juices poured over the top.

The lamb can be served with mashed potato and roast vegetables.

12 Hot pot of lamb or mutton

Ingredient	4 portions	10 portions
Stewing lamb	500 g	1.25 kg
Salt, pepper		
Onions, thinly sliced	100 g	250 g
Potatoes, thinly sliced	400 g	1 kg
Brown stock	1 litre	2.5 litres
Oil (optional)	25 g	60 g
Parsley, chopped		

Energy	Cals	Fat	Sat fat	Carb	Sugar	Protein	Fibre
1,505 kJ	360 kcal	17.0 g	6.4 g	22.0 g	1.8 g	29.0 g	2.5 g

Using sunflower oil.

1. Trim the meat and cut into even pieces.
2. Place in a deep earthenware dish. Season with salt and pepper.
3. Lightly sauté the onions in the oil, if desired. Mix the onion and approximately three-quarters of the potatoes together.
4. Season and place on top of the meat; cover three parts with stock.
5. Neatly arrange an overlapping layer of the remaining potatoes on top, sliced about 2 mm thick.
6. Thoroughly clean the edges of the dish and place to cook in a hot oven at 230–250 °C until lightly coloured.
7. Reduce the heat and continue cooking for approximately 1½–2 hours.
8. Press the potatoes down occasionally during cooking.
9. Serve with the potatoes brushed with butter or margarine and sprinkle with the chopped parsley.

Note

Neck chops or neck fillet make a succulent dish.

When the dish is ready, the top layer of potatoes should be golden brown.

Variation

Try:
- using leek in place of onion
- adding 200 g lambs' kidneys
- quickly frying off the meat and sweating the onions before putting in the pot
- adding 100–200 g sliced mushrooms
- adding a small tin of baked beans or a layer of thickly sliced tomatoes before adding the potatoes
- using sausages in place of lamb.

Chop the lamb into even-sized pieces

Layer the potatoes over the lamb

Pour over the stock

13 Brown lamb or mutton stew

Ingredient	4 portions	10 portions
Stewing lamb or mutton	500 g	1.25 kg
Oil	2 tbsp	5 tbsp
Salt, pepper		
Carrot, chopped	100 g	250 g
Onion, chopped	100 g	250 g
Clove of garlic (if desired)	1	2½
Flour (white or wholemeal)	25 g	60 g
Tomato purée	1 level tbsp	2½ level tbsp
Brown stock (mutton stock or water)	500 g	1.25 litre
Bouquet garni		
Parsley, chopped, to serve		

Energy	Cals	Fat	Sat fat	Carb	Sugar	Protein	Fibre
1,320 kJ	314 kcal	18.7 g	6.2 g	9.4 g	3.2 g	27.9 g	1.3 g

Using sunflower oil.

1. Trim the meat and cut into even pieces.
2. Partly fry off the seasoned meat in the oil, then add the carrot, onion and garlic, and continue frying.
3. Drain off the surplus fat, add the flour and mix.
4. Singe in the oven or brown on top of the stove for a few minutes, or add previously browned flour.
5. Add the tomato purée and stir with a wooden spoon.
6. Add the stock and season.
7. Add the bouquet garni, bring to the boil, skim and cover with a lid.
8. Simmer gently until cooked (preferably in the oven) for approximately 1–2 hours, until the lamb is tender.
9. When cooked, place the meat in a clean pan.
10. Correct the sauce and pass it on to the meat.
11. Serve sprinkled with chopped parsley.

Fry the lamb, onions and carrots

Mix in the flour

Add the stock and bring to the boil

Healthy eating tips
- Trim off as much fat as possible before frying.
- Use the minimum amount of salt to season the meat.
- Serve with plenty of potatoes and vegetables.

Professional tip
- Make sure the oil is hot before placing the meat in the pan to brown quickly all over.
- Do not allow the meat to boil in the oil, because this will spoil the flavour and texture.

14 Irish stew

Ingredient	4 portions	10 portions
Stewing lamb (scrag, middle neck or shoulder)	500 g	1.25 kg
Salt, pepper		
Bouquet garni		
Potatoes	400 g	1 kg
Onions	100 g	250 g
Celery	100 g	250 g
Savoy cabbage	100 g	250 g
Leeks	100 g	250 g
Button onions	100 g	250 g
Parsley, chopped		

Energy	Cals	Fat	Sat fat	Carb	Sugar	Protein	Fibre
1,339 kJ	319 kcal	11.2 g	5.2 g	26.1 g	5.7 g	30.2 g	5.0 g

1. Trim the meat and cut into even pieces. Blanch and refresh.
2. Place in a shallow saucepan, cover with water, bring to the boil, season with salt and skim. If tough meat is being used, allow ½–1 hour stewing time before adding any vegetables.
3. Add the bouquet garni. Turn the potatoes into barrel shapes.
4. Cut the potato trimmings, onions, celery, cabbage and leeks into small neat pieces and add to the meat; simmer for 30 minutes.
5. Add the button onions and simmer for a further 30 minutes.
6. Add the potatoes and simmer gently with a lid on the pan until cooked.
7. Correct the seasoning and skim off all fat.
8. Serve sprinkled with chopped parsley.

Professional tip
Keep the meat and vegetables covered with liquid during cooking, to keep the dish consistent and tasty.

Variation
Alternatively, a more modern approach is to cook the meat for 1½–2 hours until almost tender, then add the vegetables and cook until all are tender. Optional accompaniments include Worcester sauce and/or pickled red cabbage.

Healthy eating tips
- Trim as much fat as possible from the stewing lamb.
- Use the minimum amount of salt.
- Serve with colourful seasonal vegetables to create a 'healthy' dish.

Ingredients for Irish stew  | Boil the meat  | Add the vegetables

15 Roast leg of lamb with mint, lemon and cumin

Ingredient	4 portions	10 portions
Mint	25 g	62.5 g
Lemons, juice of	2	5
Cumin	2 tsp	5 tsp
Olive oil	4 tbsp	10 tbsp
Leg of lamb	3.5 kg	2 × 3.5 kg

Energy	Cals	Fat	Sat fat	Carb	Sugar	Protein	Fibre
2,192 kJ	524 kcal	39.1 g	13.7 g	0.3 g	0.3 g	29.7 g	0.0 g

Using a 225 g portion of lamb.

1 Place the mint, lemon juice, cumin and olive oil in a food processor. Carefully blend the mint, lemon juice, cumin and olive oil to give maximum flavour.
2 Rub the mixture into the lamb and place in a suitable roasting tray.
3 Roast the lamb at 200 °C for 15 minutes then reduce the temperature to 180 °C until the required degree of cooking is achieved (see page 259).

Serve on a bed of boulangère potatoes or dauphinoise potatoes and a suitable green vegetable, e.g. leaf spinach with toasted pine nuts, or with a couscous salad.

Ingredients for roast leg of lamb with mint, lemon and cumin

Place the leg of lamb in a roasting tray and rub with the mint and lemon mixture

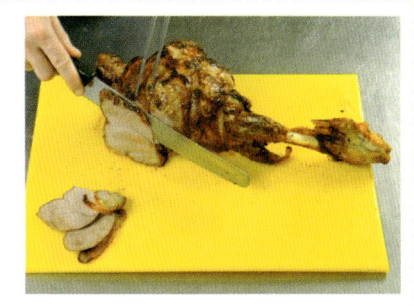

Carving a leg of lamb

16 Roast saddle of lamb with rosemary mash

Ingredient	4 portions	10 portions
Saddle of lamb, boned		
Milk	250 ml	625 ml
Rosemary	2 sprigs	5 sprigs
Potatoes, mashed	1.3 kg	3.25 kg

Energy	Cals	Fat	Sat fat	Carb	Sugar	Protein	Fibre	Sodium
3,215 kJ	770 kcal	45.7 g	22.1 g	58.9 g	4.7 g	34.4 g	5.6 g	0.2 g

1. Bone the saddle of lamb and roast in the normal way.
2. Bring the milk to the boil with the rosemary. Remove from the heat, cover and leave to infuse for 10–15 minutes.
3. To make the rosemary mash, prepare a potato purée using the milk infused with rosemary.

17 Best end of lamb with breadcrumbs and parsley

Energy	Cals	Fat	Sat fat	Carb	Sugar	Protein	Fibre	Sodium
2530 kJ	612 kcal	51.3 g	24.2 g	6.6 g	0.5 g	31.2 g	0.2 g	0.2 g

Using butter.

1. Lightly brush the joint with oil and season it.
2. Roast the best end at 220 °C for 15–20 minutes.
3. Cover the fat surface of the meat with a mixture of the fresh white breadcrumbs mixed with plenty of chopped parsley, an egg and the melted butter or margarine.
4. Return to the oven for approximately 10 minutes to complete the cooking, browning carefully.

> **Professional tip**
> Cook the lamb until it is pink. Carefully bind the breadcrumbs with herbs and beaten egg, so that they will hold together during cooking.

> **Variation**
> Try:
> - mixed fresh herbs used in addition to parsley
> - adding finely chopped garlic
> - chopped fresh herbs, shallots and mustard.

Ingredient	6 portions
Best end of lamb, French trimmed	2
Oil	
Seasoning	
Fresh white breadcrumbs	50 g
Parsley, chopped	2 tbsp
Egg	1
Butter or margarine, melted	50 g

Meat and offal 10

18 Slow-cooked shoulder of lamb with potatoes boulangère

Ingredient	4 portions	10 portions
Boned shoulder of lamb, rolled and tied	1	3
Olive oil	1 tbsp	3 tbsp
Salt, pepper		
Rosemary, sprigs	6	18
Thyme, sprigs	6	18
Cloves of garlic	4	10
Mirepoix	400 g	1 kg
Bay leaves	1	3
Red wine or dry cider	250 ml	625 ml
Brown stock	300 ml	750 ml
Redcurrant jelly	1 tbsp	2 tbsp

Energy	Cals	Fat	Sat fat	Carb	Sugar	Protein	Fibre	Sodium
1,815 kJ	437 kcal	30.8g	14.5g	2.2g	0.3g	27.6g	0.4g	0.6g

1 For instructions on how to prepare potatoes boulangère for baking, see page 425.
2 Rub the lamb with oil, and season with salt and pepper. Place in a suitable roasting tray and cook in an oven at 200 °C for 15 minutes.
3 Remove from the oven and reduce the temperature to 140 °C.
4 Add the remaining ingredients to the roasting tray.
5 Cook for 2 hours, basting every 20 minutes.
6 Remove the lamb from the roasting tray and return it to the oven on a rack. Place the potatoes boulangère directly below the lamb. Cook for ½–1 hour, until the lamb is tender and sticky.
7 To finish the sauce, once the lamb is removed from the roasting tray, reduce the cooking liquor to the required consistency. Add the strained redcurrant jelly, mix well, correct seasoning, then strain.

19 Pot-roast shoulder of lamb with gratin forcemeat

Energy	Cals	Fat	Sat fat	Carb	Sugar	Protein	Fibre	Sodium
3537 kJ	850 kcal	54.0g	24.0g	42.0g	12.5g	51.0g	6.2g	0.6g

Using beef stock and chicken liver.

Ingredient	10 portions
Lamb shoulder, boned	3 kg
Gratin forcemeat (see below)	300 g
Salt	1 tsp
Pepper	½ tsp
Wholewheat flour	3 tbsp
Oil	3 tbsp
Brown stock	500 mls
Potatoes, turned	10
Carrots, turned	10
Button onions	10
Worcestershire sauce	1 tsp

1. Preheat the oven to 160°C.
2. Stuff shoulder with forcemeat and tie.
3. Dredge the lamb with seasoned flour.
4. Heat oil in a large roast pot over medium high heat.
5. Add the floured lamb to hot pan and brown evenly on all sides.
6. Pour stock to cover lamb.
7. Cover the pot and place in the preheated oven. Slow cook the lamb for 2½ to 3 hours.
8. During the last 45 minutes, add the vegetables to the pot. Cover and continue to cook until meat and vegetables are tender.
9. Remove the cooked lamb and vegetables from the pot to a serving platter.
10. Strain the cooking liquor and adjust the consistency; this can be thickened if desired.
11. Finish with Worcestershire sauce and season to taste.

Sautéed forcemeat (gratin forcemeat)

Ingredient	Makes 300 g
Chicken liver or calves' liver (free from skin and sinews)	150 g
Pork fat, diced	5 g
Mushroom trimmings	50 g
Sautéed shallots	25 g
Butter	50 g
Spice salt	5 g
Pinch thyme and marjoram	
Brandy	10 mls

1. Brown the pork fat in the butter, to set firm. Remove from pan and set to one side.
2. Sauté the liver in the same pan to set.
3. Return pork back to the pan.
4. Add mushrooms, sautéed shallots and seasonings.
5. Sauté all together, then flame with brandy.
6. Remove from heat and allow to cool.
7. Place all ingredients in food processor and blend. The forcemeat is then ready to use.

> **Professional tip**
>
> This forcemeat could also be used to stuff a loin of lamb or skirt of beef rolled and then pot roasted, or served on croutons to accompany poultry or game dishes.

20 Shepherd's pie

Ingredient	4 portions	10 portions
Onions, chopped	100 g	250 g
Oil	35 ml	100 ml
Lamb or mutton (minced), cooked	400 g	1 kg
Salt, pepper		
Worcester sauce	2–3 drops	5 drops
Potatoes, cooked	400 g	1 kg
Butter or margarine	25 g	60 g
Milk or egg wash		
Jus-lié or demi-glace	125–250 ml	300–600 ml

Energy	Cals	Fat	Sat fat	Carb	Sugar	Protein	Fibre
1,744 kJ	415 kcal	25.3 g	9.1 g	22.1 g	2.5 g	26.3 g	1.6 g

Using sunflower oil, with hard margarine in topping.

1. Cook the onion in the oil without colouring.
2. Add the cooked meat from which all fat and gristle has been removed.
3. Season and add Worcester sauce (sufficient to bind).
4. Bring to the boil; simmer for 10–15 minutes.
5. Place in an earthenware or pie dish.
6. Prepare the potatoes – mix with the butter or margarine, then mash and pipe, or arrange neatly on top.
7. Brush with the milk or egg wash.
8. Colour lightly under a salamander or in a hot oven.
9. Serve accompanied with a sauceboat of *jus-lié*.

Note

This dish prepared with cooked beef is known as **cottage pie**.

Pipe the potato carefully so that the meat is completely covered.

When using reheated meats, care must be taken to heat thoroughly and quickly.

Healthy eating tips

- Use an oil rich in unsaturates (olive or sunflower) to lightly oil the pan.
- Drain off any excess fat after the lamb has been fried.
- Try replacing some of the meat with baked beans or lentils, and add tomatoes and/or mushrooms to the dish.
- When served with a large portion of green vegetables, a healthy balance is created.

Variation

Try:
- adding 100–200 g sliced mushrooms
- adding a layer of thickly sliced tomatoes, then sprinkling with rosemary
- mixing a tin of baked beans in with the meat
- sprinkling with grated cheese and browning under a salamander
- varying the flavour of the mince by adding herbs or spices
- varying the potato topping by mixing in grated cheese, chopped spring onions or herbs, or by using duchess potato mixture
- serving lightly sprinkled with garam masala and with grilled pitta bread.

Beef dishes

21 Grilled beef

Energy	Cals	Fat	Sat fat	Carb	Sugar	Protein	Fibre
706 kJ	168 kcal	6.0g	2.7g	0.0g	0.0g	28.6g	0.0g

1 Lightly season the steaks with salt and pepper, and brush on both sides with oil.
2 Place on hot, preheated and greased grill bars.

The following cuts may be cooked in this way:
- rump steak
- point steak
- double fillet steak (chateaubriand)
- fillet steak
- tournedos
- porterhouse or T-bone steak
- sirloin steak (entrecôte)
- double sirloin steak
- minute steak
- rib eye steak.

Allow approximately 100–150 g per portion, although in many establishments these weights will be exceeded.

3 Turn halfway through the cooking and brush occasionally with oil. Cook to the degree ordered by the customer (see page 269).
4 Serve garnished with watercress and deep-fried potatoes, and offer a suitable sauce such as compound butter or sauce béarnaise.

22 Hamburger, American style

Energy	Cals	Fat	Sat fat	Carb	Sugar	Protein	Fibre	Sodium
1,868 kJ	450 kcal	32.4g	13.9g	0.0g	0.0g	39.4g	0.0g	0.2g

Hamburgers – now more commonly known as burgers – were originally made using 200 g of minced beef per portion.

The meat used should be pure beef with 20–25 per cent beef fat by weight. Less fat than this will result in a tough, dry hamburger. If more fat is used the hamburgers will be unpalatable, nutritionally undesirable and will shrink considerably during cooking.

296

1 Pass the meat through a mincer twice. This makes a more tender product.
2 Lightly mix the mince with any desired seasoning or ingredients (over-mixing will make the hamburger tough).
3 Mould the mixture into patties. Mark the top with crossed lines using a knife.
4 Grill until cooked thoroughly to the centre, reaching 75 °C. Do not prick the hamburgers while cooking, as the juices will seep out leaving a dry product.

Note

Mini burgers (one mouthful) can be served as hot canapés at receptions.

Variation

Variations in seasonings and ingredients can be added to the minced beef, but traditionally the sauces and garnishes offered are sufficient. These can include: ketchup, mustard, mayonnaise, chilli sauce, horseradish, cheese, raw onion rings, lettuce, avocado slices, bacon, and various pickles and relishes. Freshly fried chips and/or cut pieces of raw vegetables (e.g. carrot, celery, spring onions) can be added.

The bun may be plain or seeded (sesame seeds).

Alternative fillings can include:
- cheese – either on its own or added to the beef
- egg – a freshly fried egg, or added to the beef
- chicken – a freshly grilled portion of chicken, either minced or in the piece
- fish – a freshly grilled portion of a whole fish (cod or haddock)
- vegetables – a selection of freshly grilled or fried vegetables (e.g. onions, peppers, aubergines, mushrooms).

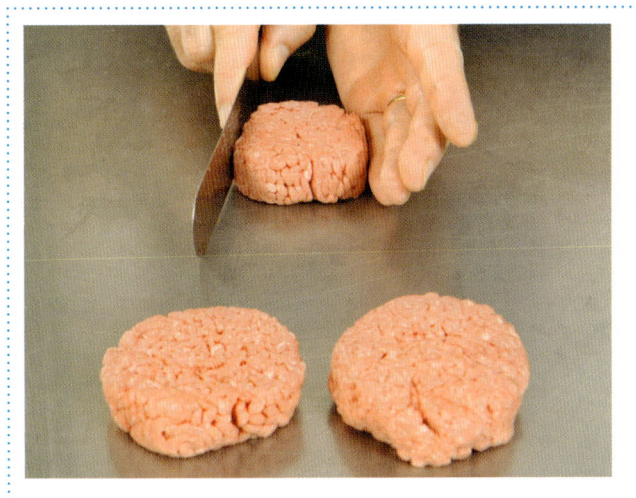

Mould the mixture into shape

Mark the top of each burger before grilling it

23 Tournedos

Note
Traditionally, tournedos are cooked underdone and served on a round croûte of bread fried in butter.

Healthy eating tips
- Use little or no salt to season the steaks.
- Fry in a small amount of an unsaturated oil and drain off all excess fat after frying.
- Serve with plenty of boiled new potatoes or a jacket potato and a selection of vegetables.

Variation
Tournedos can be served with a variety of sauces, such as chasseur, red wine or mushroom, and numerous garnishes (e.g. diced cubed potatoes, wild or cultivated mushrooms). The photo shows **tournedos Rossini** – the tournedos are served with foie gras, Parma ham, girolles, truffle and a Madeira jelly.

Energy	Cals	Fat	Sat fat	Carb	Sugar	Protein	Fibre	Sodium
1,540 kJ	366 kcal	13.2g	4.8g	0.0g	0.0g	61.8g	0.0g	0.2g

Tournedos are cut from the middle of a fillet of beef and are usually 100–150g in weight.

1. Lightly season and shallow-fry on both sides in a sauté pan.
2. Serve with an appropriate garnish or sauce (see Variation).

24 Sirloin steak with red wine (*entrecôte bordelaise*)

Ingredient	4 portions	10 portions
Butter or oil	50 g	125 g
Sirloin steaks (approximately 150–200 g each)	4	10
Red wine	60 ml	150 ml
Red wine sauce (see page 124)	250 ml	625 ml
Parsley, chopped		

Energy	Cals	Fat	Sat fat	Carb	Sugar	Protein	Fibre
3,013 kJ	717 kcal	62.2g	21.6g	6.0g	3.0g	26.1g	1.4g

Using sunflower oil and 150g raw steak per portion. Using sunflower oil and 200g raw steak per portion provides: 3584 kJ/853 kcal energy, 73.6g fat, 26.2g saturated fat, 6.0g carbohydrates, 3.0g sugar, 34.4g protein and 1.4g fibre.

Meat and offal 10

1. Heat the butter or oil in a sauté pan.
2. Lightly season the steaks on both sides with salt and pepper.
3. Fry the steaks quickly on both sides, keeping them underdone.
4. Dress the steaks on a serving dish.
5. Pour off the fat from the pan.
6. Deglaze with the red wine. Reduce by half and strain.
7. Add the red wine sauce, reboil and correct the seasoning.
8. Coat the steaks with the sauce.
9. Sprinkle with chopped parsley and serve.

Traditionally, two slices of beef bone marrow, poached in stock for 2–3 minutes, would be placed on each steak.

Professional tip
Cook the steaks to order (and make the sauce by deglazing the pan and reducing), not in advance.

Healthy eating tips
- Use little or no salt to season the steaks.
- Fry in a small amount of an unsaturated oil and drain off all excess fat after frying.
- Serve with plenty of boiled new potatoes or a jacket potato and a selection of vegetables.

25 Beef stroganoff

Ingredient	4 portions	10 portions
Fillet of beef (tail end)	400 g	1 kg
Butter or oil	50 g	125 g
Salt, pepper		
Shallots, finely chopped	25 g	60 g
Dry white wine	125 ml	300 ml
Cream	125 ml	300 ml
Lemon, juice of	¼	½
Parsley, chopped		

Energy	Cals	Fat	Sat fat	Carb	Sugar	Protein	Fibre
1,364 kJ	325 kcal	23.7 g	7.9 g	1.7 g	1.7 g	21.2 g	0.3 g

Using sunflower oil.

1. Cut the meat into strips approximately 1 × 5 cm.
2. Place the butter or oil in a sauteuse over a fierce heat.
3. Add the beef strips, lightly season with salt and pepper, and allow to cook rapidly for a few seconds. The beef should be brown but underdone.
4. Drain the beef into a colander. Pour the butter back into the pan.
5. Add the shallots, cover with a lid and allow to cook gently until tender.
6. Drain off the fat, add the wine and reduce to one-third.
7. Add the cream and reduce by a quarter.
8. Add the lemon juice and the beef strips; do not reboil. Correct the seasoning.
9. Serve lightly sprinkled with chopped parsley. Accompany with rice pilaff (see page 159).

Healthy eating tips
- Use little or no salt to season the meat.
- Fry in a small amount of an unsaturated oil.
- Serve with a large portion of rice and a salad.

299

26 Hamburg or Vienna steak

Ingredient	4 portions	10 portions
Onion, finely chopped	25 g	60 g
Butter or oil	10 g	25 g
Lean minced beef	200 g	500 g
Small egg	1	2–3
Breadcrumbs	100 g	250 g
Cold water or milk	2 tbsp (approximately)	60 ml (approximately)

Energy	Cals	Fat	Sat fat	Carb	Sugar	Protein	Fibre
681 kJ	162 kcal	6.7 g	1.9 g	12.7 g	1.0 g	13.8 g	1.0 g

1 Cook the onion in the fat without colour, then allow to cool.
2 Add to the rest of the ingredients and mix in well.
3 Divide into even pieces and, using a little flour, make into balls, flatten and shape round.
4 Shallow-fry in hot fat on both sides, reducing the heat after the first few minutes, making certain they are cooked right through.
5 Serve with a light sauce, such as piquant sauce (see page 120).

The 'steaks' may be garnished with French-fried onions and sometimes with a fried egg.

Healthy eating tips
- Use a small amount of an unsaturated oil to cook the onion and to shallow-fry the meat.
- The minced beef will produce more fat, which should be drained off.
- Serve with plenty of starchy carbohydrate and vegetables.

Meat and offal | **10**

27 Carbonnade of beef

Ingredient	4 portions	10 portions
Lean beef (topside)	400 g	1 kg
Salt, pepper		
Flour (white or wholemeal)	25 g	60 g
Dripping or oil	25 g	60 g
Onions, sliced	200 g	500 g
Beer	250 ml	625 ml
Caster sugar	10 g	25 g
Tomato purée	25 g	60 g
Brown stock		

Energy	Cals	Fat	Sat fat	Carb	Sugar	Protein	Fibre
1,037 kJ	247 kcal	9.1 g	1.8 g	14.0 g	8.1 g	24.7 g	1.1 g

1 Cut the meat into thin slices.
2 Season with salt and pepper and pass through the flour.
3 Quickly colour on both sides in hot fat and place in a casserole.
4 Fry the onions to a light brown colour. Add to the meat.
5 Add the beer, sugar and tomato purée and sufficient brown stock to cover the meat.
6 Cover with a tight-fitting lid and simmer gently in a moderate oven at 150–200 °C until the meat is tender (approximately 2 hours).
7 Skim, correct the seasoning and serve.

Slice the meat thinly

Pass each slice through the flour

Pour the liquid over the browned meat and onions

Healthy eating tips
- Trim off as much fat as possible before frying and drain off all surplus fat after frying.
- Use the minimum amount of salt to season the meat.
- Skim all fat from the finished sauce.
- Serve with plenty of potatoes and vegetables.

Note
Carbonnade of beef is usually served with braised red cabbage. Serve separately.

28 Beef bourguignon

Ingredient	4 portions	10 portions
Beef		
Beef shin pre-soaked in red wine (see below) for 12 hours	600 g	1.5 kg
Inexpensive red Bordeaux wine	1 bottle	2 bottles
Olive oil	50 ml	125 ml
Onion	100 g	250 g
Carrot	100 g	250 g
Celery sticks	75 g	180 g
Leek	100 g	250 g
Cloves of garlic	2	5
Sprig fresh thyme	1	2
Bay leaf	1	2
Seasoning		
Veal/brown stock to cover		
Garnish		
Button onions, cooked	150 g	300 g
Cooked bacon lardons	150 g	300 g
Button mushrooms, cooked	150 g	300 g
Parsley, chopped	2 tsp	5 tsp
To finish		
Mashed potato	300 g	750 g
Washed, picked spinach	300 g	750 g
Cooked green beans	250 g	625 g

Energy	Cals	Fat	Sat fat	Carb	Sugar	Protein	Fibre	Sodium
2,838 kJ	681 kcal	33.3 g	9.1 g	20.1 g	7.2 g	44.9 g	8.0 g	0.9 g

1 Preheat the oven to 180 °C.
2 Remove the meat from the wine. Trim the beef shin of all fat and sinew, and cut into 2.5 cm-thick rondelles.
3 Heat a little oil in a thick-bottomed pan and seal/brown the skin. Place in a large ovenproof dish.
4 Meanwhile, reduce the red wine by half.
5 Peel and trim the vegetables as appropriate, then add them to the pan that the beef has just come out of and gently brown the edges. Then place this, along with the garlic and herbs, in the ovenproof dish with the meat.
6 Add the reduced red wine to the casserole, then pour in enough stock to cover the meat and vegetables. Bring to the boil, then cook in the oven preheated to 180 °C for 40 minutes; after that, turn the oven down to 90–95 °C and cook for a further 4 hours until tender.
7 Remove from the oven and allow the meat to cool in the liquor. When cold, remove any fat. Reheat gently at the same temperature to serve.
8 Heat the garnish elements separately and sprinkle over each portion. Serve with a mound of mashed potato, wilted spinach and buttered green beans. Finish the whole dish with chopped parsley.

Variation

Other joints of beef can be used here; beef or veal cheek can be used, reducing the time for the veal, or modernise the dish by using the slow-cooked fillet preparation and serving the same garnish.

Professional tip

Shallow fry the beef in hot oil to brown it all over, but do not let it boil in the oil. Then allow it to stew gently in the red wine.

Meat and offal

Marinate the beef

Gently brown the vegetables

Brown the meat

Pour in stock to cover the meat and vegetables

29 Braised beef (*boeuf braisé*)

Ingredient	4 portions	10 portions
Lean beef (topside or thick flank)	400 g	1 kg
Dripping or oil	25 g	60 g
Onions, sliced and lightly fried	100 g	250 g
Carrots, sliced and lightly fried	100 g	250 g
Brown stock	500 ml	1.25 litres
Salt and pepper		
Bouquet garni	1	2
Tomato purée	25 g	60 g
Demi-glace or *jus-lié*	250 ml	625 ml

Energy	Cals	Fat	Sat fat	Carb	Sugar	Protein	Fibre
1,380 kJ	329 kcal	14.3 g	3.3 g	26.8 g	4.7 g	24.7 g	2.4 g

Using sunflower oil.

Method 1

1. Trim and tie the joint securely.
2. Season and colour quickly on all sides in hot fat to seal the joint.
3. Place the lightly fried, sliced vegetables into a small braising pan (any pan with a tight-fitting lid that may be placed in the oven) or in a casserole.
4. Place the joint on to the vegetables.
5. Add the stock, which should come two-thirds of the way up the meat, and season lightly.
6. Add the bouquet garni and tomato purée and, if available, add a few mushroom trimmings.
7. Bring to the boil, skim and cover with a lid. Cook in a moderate oven at 150–200 °C.
8. After approximately 1½ hours' cooking, remove the meat.
9. Add the demi-glace or *jus-lié*, reboil, skim and strain.
10. Replace the meat; do not cover, but baste frequently and continue cooking for approximately 2–2½ hours in all. Braised beef should be well cooked (allow 35 minutes per 0.5 kg plus 35 minutes). To test if cooked, pierce with a trussing needle – it should penetrate the meat easily and there should be no sign of blood.
11. Remove the joint and correct the colour, seasoning and consistency of the sauce.
12. To serve: remove the string and carve slices across the grain. Pour some of the sauce over the slices and serve the remainder of the sauce in a sauceboat.

Method 2

As for Method 1, but when the joint and vegetables are browned, sprinkle with 25 g (60 g for 10 portions) flour and singe in the oven; add the tomato purée, stock and bouquet garni; season and complete the recipe.

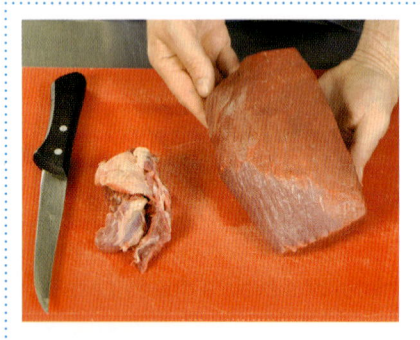

Trim the joint neatly

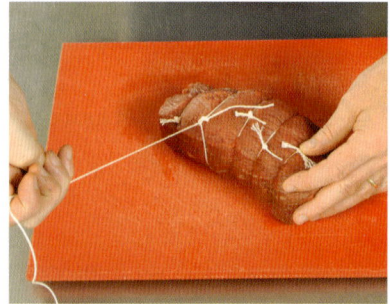

Tie the joint securely before braising it

Place the joint in the pan on a layer of vegetables

Meat and offal | **10**

Note

Suitable garnishes include spring vegetables or pasta. Red wine may be used in place of stock.

Healthy eating tips

- Trim off as much fat as possible before frying and drain off all surplus fat after frying.
- Use the minimum amount of salt.
- Skim all fat from the finished sauce.
- Serve with plenty of potatoes and vegetables.

30 Boiled silverside, carrots and dumplings

Ingedient	4 portions	10 portions
Silverside, pre-soaked in brine	400 g	1 kg
Onions	200 g	500 g
Carrots	200 g	500 g
Suet paste	100 g	250 g

Energy	Cals	Fat	Sat fat	Carb	Sugar	Protein	Fibre
1,068 kJ	254 kcal	10.17 g	4.6 g	15.5 g	5.5 g	26.3 g	2.6 g

Note

A large joint of silverside is approximately 6 kg; for this size of joint, soak it overnight and allow 25 minutes cooking time per 0.5 kg plus 25 minutes.

The beef is salted because this gives the desired flavour. The meat is usually salted before it is delivered to the kitchen.

Healthy eating tips

Adding carrots, onions, boiled potatoes and a green vegetable will give a healthy balance.

Variation

Herbs can be added to the dumplings.

Boiled brisket and tongue can be served with the silverside.

French-style boiled beef is prepared using unsalted thin flank or brisket with onions, carrots, leeks, celery, cabbage and a bouquet garni, all cooked and served together, accompanied with pickled gherkins and coarse salt.

1. Soak the meat in cold water for 1–2 hours to remove excess brine.
2. Place in a saucepan and cover with cold water, bring to the boil, skim and simmer for 45 minutes.
3. Add the whole prepared onions and carrots and simmer until cooked.
4. Divide the suet paste into even pieces and lightly mould into balls (dumplings).
5. Add the dumplings and simmer for a further 15–20 minutes.
6. Serve by carving the meat across the grain, garnish with carrots, onions and dumplings, and moisten with a little of the cooking liquor.

31 Steak pudding

Ingredient	4 portions	10 portions
Suet paste (see page 525)	200 g	500 g
Prepared stewing beef (chuck steak)	400 g	1 kg
Worcester sauce	1 tsp	2½ tsp
Parsley, chopped	1 tsp	2½ tsp
Salt, pepper		
Onion, chopped (optional)	50–100 g	125–250 g
Water	125 ml approximately	300 ml approximately.

Energy	Cals	Fat	Sat fat	Carb	Sugar	Protein	Fibre
1,369 kJ	326 kcal	17.3 g	7.8 g	20.6 g	1.0 g	23.0 g	1.1 g

1. Line a greased ½ litre basin with three-quarters of the suet paste and retain one-quarter for the top.
2. Mix all the other ingredients, except the water, together.
3. Place in the basin with the water to within 1 cm of the top.
4. Moisten the edge of the suet paste, cover with the top and seal firmly.
5. Cover with greased greaseproof paper and also, if possible, foil or a pudding cloth tied securely with string.
6. Cook in a steamer for at least 3½ hours for a four-portion pudding, or approximately 1½ hours for individual puddings.
7. Serve with the paper and cloth removed, clean the basin, place on a round flat dish and fasten a napkin round the basin.

Extra gravy should be served separately. If the gravy in the pudding is to be thickened, the meat can be lightly floured.

Healthy eating tips
- Use little or no salt as the Worcester sauce contains salt.
- Trim off as much fat as possible from the raw stewing beef.
- Serve with plenty of potatoes and vegetables.

Variation
Try:
- adding 50–100 g ox or sheep's kidneys cut in pieces with skin and gristle removed
- adding 50–100 g sliced or quartered mushrooms
- making the steak pudding with a cooked filling; in which case, simmer the meat until cooked in brown stock with onions, parsley, Worcester sauce and seasoning; cool quickly and proceed as above, steaming for 1–1½ hours.

Meat and offal 10

Line the basin with suet paste

Fill the basin, then cover the top with paste

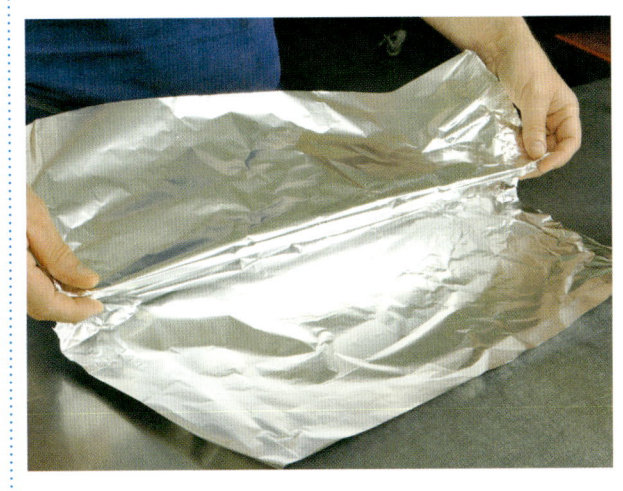

Make a foil cover for the basin, with a fold to allow it to expand

Tie the cover over the basin securely

Practical Cookery 14th edition

32 Goulash

Ingredient	4 portions	10 portions
Prepared stewing beef	400 g	1 kg
Lard or oil	35 g	100 g
Onions, chopped	100 g	250 g
Flour	25 g	60 g
Paprika	10–25 g	25–60 g
Tomato purée	25 g	60 g
Stock or water	750 ml (approximately)	2 litres (approximately)
Turned potatoes or small new potatoes	8	20
Choux paste (see page 520)	125 ml	300 ml

Energy	Cals	Fat	Sat fat	Carb	Sugar	Protein	Fibre
1,625 kJ	389 kcal	20.4 g	6.0 g	26.1 g	3.9 g	26.9 g	1.7 g

1 Remove excess fat from the beef. Cut into 2 cm square pieces.
2 Season and fry in the hot fat until slightly coloured. Add the chopped onion.
3 Cover with a lid and sweat gently for 3–4 minutes.
4 Add the flour and paprika and mix in with a wooden spoon.
5 Cook out in the oven or on top of the stove. Add the tomato purée, mix in.
6 Gradually add the stock, stir to the boil, skim, season and cover.
7 Allow to simmer, preferably in the oven, for approximately 1½–2 hours until the meat is tender.
8 Add the potatoes and check that they are covered with the sauce. (Add more stock if required.)
9 Re-cover with the lid and cook gently until the potatoes are cooked.
10 Skim and correct the seasoning and consistency. A little cream or yoghurt may be added at the last moment.
11 Serve sprinkled with a few gnocchis made from choux paste (see page 520), reheated in hot salted water or lightly tossed in butter or margarine. Alternatively, garnish with turned potatoes.

Healthy eating tips
- Trim off as much fat as possible before frying and drain all surplus fat after frying.
- Use the minimum amount of salt to season the meat.
- Serve with a large side salad.

Meat and offal 10

33 Cornish pasties

Ingredient	4 portions	10 portions
Short paste (see page 507)	200 g	500 g
Potato (raw), finely diced	100 g	250 g
Raw beef, chuck or skirt, cut into thin pieces	100 g	250 g
Onion or leeks, chopped	50 g	125 g
Swede (raw), finely diced (optional)	50 g	125 g
Egg wash		

Energy	Cals	Fat	Sat fat	Carb	Sugar	Protein	Fibre
1,217 kJ	290 kcal	16.2 g	6.0 g	29.3 g	1.2 g	8.7 g	1.8 g

1. Roll out the short paste to 3 mm thick and cut into rounds 12 cm in diameter.
2. Mix the remaining ingredients together, moisten with a little water and place in the rounds in piles. Brush the edges with egg wash.
3. Fold in half and seal; flute the edge and brush evenly with egg wash.
4. Cook in a moderate oven at 150–200 °C for ½–1 hour.
5. Serve with a suitable sauce/gravy, or hot or cold as a snack.

Note

The filling can be made from cooked meat that has been quickly chilled and held at 3 °C.

Healthy eating tips

- Adding baked beans, tomatoes and/or mushrooms will 'dilute' the fat from the meat.
- Serve with a large portion of vegetables.

Variation

Variations include:
- potato, onion or leek, and turnip or swede, with fresh herbs
- bacon, hard-boiled eggs and leeks
- lamb, carrot and potato
- apples, cinnamon, cloves, brown sugar, cider
- puff pastry.

Ingredients for Cornish pasties

Place the filling on to the pastry

Fold the pastry over and seal the edge

309

34 Steak pie

Ingredient	4 portions	10 portions
Prepared stewing beef (chuck steak)	400 g	1 kg
Oil or dripping	50 ml	125 ml
Onion, chopped (optional)	100 g	250 g
Worcester sauce, few drops		
Parsley, chopped	1 tsp	2½ tsp
Water, stock, red wine or dark beer	125 ml	300 ml
Salt, pepper		
Cornflour	10 g	25 g
Short, puff or rough puff paste (see pages 507, 526 and 529)	100 g	250 g

Energy	Cals	Fat	Sat fat	Carb	Sugar	Protein	Fibre
1,442 kJ	346 kcal	22.2g	2.9g	13.6g	1.8g	24.3g	0.4g

Using puff pastry (McCance data).

1 Cut the meat into 2 cm strips then cut into squares.
2 Heat the oil in a frying pan until smoking, add the meat and quickly brown on all sides.
3 Drain the meat off in a colander.
4 Lightly fry the onion.
5 Place the meat, onion, Worcester sauce, parsley and the liquid in a pan, season lightly with salt and pepper.
6 Bring to the boil, skim, then allow to simmer gently until the meat is tender.
7 Dilute the cornflour with a little water, stir into the simmering mixture, reboil and correct seasoning.
8 Place the mixture into a pie dish and allow to cool.
9 Cover with the paste, egg wash and bake at 200 °C for approximately 30–45 minutes.

Meat and offal 10

Dice the steak evenly

Coat the meat in cornflour before frying it

Cover the top with paste and trim off the excess

Press gently to ensure a seal between the paste and the dish

Healthy eating tips
- Use little or no salt as the Worcester sauce contains salt.
- Fry in a small amount of an unsaturated oil and drain off all excess fat after frying.
- There will be less fat in the dish if short paste is used.
- Serve with boiled potatoes and plenty of vegetables.

Variation
Try:
- adding 50–100 g ox or sheep's kidneys with skin and gristle removed and cut into neat pieces
- adding 50–100 g sliced or quartered mushrooms
- adding 1 heaped teaspoon of tomato purée and some mixed herbs
- in place of cornflour, the meat can be tossed in flour before frying off
- in place of plain flour, 25–50 per cent wholemeal flour may be used in the pastry.

Practical Cookery 14th edition

35 Roast wing of beef

Ingredient	10 portions
Wing rib of beef	1 × 2 kg
Beef dripping	25 g
Yorkshire puddings (see recipe 36), prepared English mustard or horseradish sauce, to serve	
Gravy	
Carrots (for the mirepoix)	50 g
Onion (for the mirepoix)	50 g
Red wine	200 ml
Plain flour	30 g
Beef stock	300 ml

Energy	Cals	Fat	Sat fat	Carb	Sugar	Protein	Fibre
3,185 kJ	758 kcal	31.0 g	13.0 g	31.6 g	4.5 g	90.0 g	1.6 g

1 Preheat the oven to 195 °C.
2 Place the dripping in a heavy roasting tray and heat on the stove top.
3 Place the beef in the tray and brown well on all sides.
4 Place in the oven on 195 °C for 15 minutes then turn down to 75 °C for 2 hours.
5 Remove and allow to rest before carving.

For the gravy

1 Remove the beef. Place the tray with the fat, sediment and the juice back on the stove.
2 Add the mirepoix and brown well.
3 Add the red wine and reduce by two-thirds.
4 Mix the flour and a little stock together to form a viscous batter-like mix.
5 Add the stock to the roasting tray and bring to the boil.
6 Pour in the flour mix and whisk into the liquid in the tray.
7 Bring to the boil, simmer and correct the seasoning.
8 Pass through a sieve and retain for service.

To complete

Slice the beef and warm the Yorkshire puddings (see recipe 36), serve with the gravy, horseradish and mustard.

> **Professional tip**
>
> This dish would work well with most vegetables or potatoes. As an alternative, why not add slightly blanched root vegetables to the roasting tray at the start of the beef cooking, remove and reheat for service? They will obtain maximum flavour from the beef and juices.

36 Yorkshire pudding

Ingredient	4 portions	10 portions
Flour	85 g	215 g
Eggs	2	5
Milk	85 ml	215 ml
Water	40 ml	100 ml
Dripping or oil	20 g	50 g

Energy	Cals	Fat	Sat fat	Carb	Sugar	Protein	Fibre	Sodium
730 kJ	174 kcal	9.3 g	2.1 g	17.5 g	1.3 g	6.3 g	0.9 g	0.1 g

1 Place the flour and eggs into a mixing bowl and mix to a smooth paste.
2 Gradually whisk in the milk and water and place in the refrigerator for 1 hour. Preheat the oven to 190 °C.
3 Heat the pudding trays in the oven with a little dripping or oil in each well.
4 Carefully ladle the mixture in, up to about two-thirds full.
5 Place in the oven and slowly close the door (if you have a glass-fronted door it will be easy to monitor progress; if not, after about 30 minutes check the puddings). The myth about opening the door during cooking has an element of truth in it – however, it is slamming and the speed at which the door is opened that have most effect, so have just a small, careful peek to check and see if they are ready.
6 For the last 10 minutes of cooking, invert the puddings (take out and turn upside down in the tray) to dry out the base.
7 Serve immediately.

> **Professional tip**
> The oven, and the oil, must be very hot before the mixture is placed into the pudding tray; if they are not hot enough, the puddings will not rise.

37 Slow-cooked sirloin with lyonnaise onions and carrot purée

Ingredient	4 portions	10 portions
Beef		
Sirloin, outer skin removed, with fat tied back on	1 kg	3 kg
Oil	50 ml	125 ml
Clove of garlic, sliced	1	2
Sprigs of thyme	1	2
Bay leaves	1	2
Lyonnaise onions		
Onions	200 g	500 g
Seasoning		
Carrot purée		
Medium-sized carrots	600 g	1.5 kg
Star anise	1	2
To serve		
Jus de viande (meat juice)	150 ml	375 ml
Sprigs of chervil		

Energy	Cals	Fat	Sat fat	Carb	Sugar	Protein	Fibre	Sodium
2,436 kJ	584 kcal	26.9 g	7.4 g	13.5 g	11.2 g	72.5 g	5.9 g	0.8 g

For the beef:

1 Preheat the oven to 180 °C. Season the beef and heat the oil in the pan. Add the garlic, thyme, bay leaves and the beef.
2 Place the beef in the oven for 15 minutes. Remove and turn the oven down to 70 °C. When the oven has reached this new temperature, return the beef to it for a further 1 hour 10 minutes.
3 While the beef is cooking, make the lyonnaise onions and carrot purée (see below) and keep warm.

For the onions:

1 Finely slice the onions and put them into a large induction pan while cold.
2 Put on medium heat and season.
3 When the onions are starting to colour, turn down and cook slowly for approximately 2 hours.
4 Cool and refrigerate.

For the carrot purée:

1 Peel the carrots. Liquidise half of them into carrot juice and place the juice into a small pan.
2 Cut the remaining carrots into equal slices of about 1 cm and place into the carrot juice.
3 Boil the carrots, ensuring that you scrape down the sides of the pan.
4 For the last 8 minutes of cooking, before all the liquid has completely evaporated, drop in the star anise. Pass, retaining the juice.
5 Remove the star anise and blitz the purée for 7 minutes, adding the retained juice.

To finish:

1 When the beef is cooked, remove from the oven and carve evenly. Place a portion of carrot purée and lyonnaise onions on each plate. Top with the beef and pour over the jus de viande (meat juice), garnish with sprigs of chervil and serve.

Meat and offal | **10**

Veal dishes

38 Escalope of veal

Ingredient	4 portions	10 portions
Nut or cushion of veal	400 g	1 kg
Seasoned flour	25 g	60 g
Egg	1	2½
Breadcrumbs	50 g	125 g
Oil, for frying	50 g	125 g
Butter, for frying	50 g	125 g
Beurre noisette (optional)	50 g	125 g
Jus-lié (page 126)	60 ml	150 ml

Energy	Cals	Fat	Sat fat	Carb	Sugar	Protein	Fibre
2,079 kJ	495 kcal	39.8 g	11.4 g	10.3 g	0.5 g	24.7 g	1.0 g

Fried in sunflower oil, using butter to finish.

Veal escalope Holstein

1 Trim and remove all sinew from the veal.
2 Cut into four even slices and bat out thinly using a little water.
3 Flour, egg and crumb. Shake off surplus crumbs. Mark with a palette knife.
4 Place the escalopes into shallow hot fat and cook quickly for a few minutes on each side.
5 Dress on a serving dish or plate.
6 An optional finish is to pour over 50 g *beurre noisette* (nut-brown butter) and finish with a cordon of *jus-lié*.

The escalopes need to be batted out thinly. Excess breadcrumbs must be shaken off before the escalopes are placed into the hot fat.

Healthy eating tips
- Use an unsaturated oil to fry the veal.
- Make sure the fat is hot so that less will be absorbed into the crumb.
- Drain the cooked escalope on kitchen paper.
- Use the minimum amount of salt.
- Serve with plenty of starchy carbohydrate and vegetables.

Variation

Escalope of veal Viennoise: as for this recipe, but garnish the dish with chopped yolk and white of egg and chopped parsley; on top of each escalope place a slice of peeled lemon decorated with chopped egg yolk, egg white and parsley, an anchovy fillet and a stoned olive; finish with a little lemon juice and nut-brown butter.

Veal escalope Holstein: prepare and cook the escalopes as for this recipe; add an egg fried in butter or oil, and place two neat fillets of anchovy criss-crossed on each egg; serve.

Escalope of veal with spaghetti and tomato sauce: prepare escalopes as for this recipe, then garnish with spaghetti with tomato sauce (page 179), allowing 10 g spaghetti per portion.

39 Breadcrumbed veal escalope with ham and cheese (*escalope de veau cordon bleu*)

1. Trim and remove all sinew from the veal.
2. Cut into eight even slices (20 slices for ten portions) and bat out thinly using a little water.
3. Place a slice of ham and a slice of cheese on to four of the veal slices (ten slices for ten portions), cover with the remaining veal slices and press together firmly.
4. Flour, egg and crumb. Shake off all surplus crumbs and shape like a diamond. Mark on one side with crossed lines using a palette knife.
5. Place the escalopes marked side down into the hot oil (with butter if desired) and cook quickly for a few minutes on each side, until golden brown.
6. An optional finish is to serve coated with *beurre noisette* (nut-brown butter) and a cordon of *jus-lié*.

Ingredient	4 portions	10 portions
Nut or cushion of veal	400 g	1 kg
Cooked ham, sliced	4	10
Gruyère cheese, sliced	4	10
Seasoned flour	25 g	60 g
Egg, beaten	1	2½
Breadcrumbs	50 g	125 g
Oil	50 g	125 g
Butter (optional)	100 g	250 g
Beurre noisette (optional)	50 g	125 g
Jus-lié	60 ml	150 ml

Note
Veal escalopes may be cooked plain (not crumbed), in which case they are only slightly batted out.

Healthy eating tips
- No added salt is needed as there is plenty in the ham and cheese.
- This is a high-fat dish so serve with plenty of starchy carbohydrates and vegetables to 'dilute' the fat.

Energy	Cals	Fat	Sat fat	Carb	Sugar	Protein	Fibre
2,632 kJ	627 kcal	48.1 g	16.3 g	12.0 g	1.3 g	37.1 g	0.7 g

Fried in sunflower oil, using butter to finish.

Bat out the escalopes

Layer the veal, ham and cheese

Coat the escalope with breadcrumbs and mark on one side

40 Veal escalope with Parma ham and mozzarella cheese (*involtini di vitello*)

Ingredient	4 portions	10 portions
Small, thin veal escalopes	400 g (8 in total)	1 kg (20 in total)
Flour (for dusting)		
Parma ham, thinly sliced	100 g	250 g
Mozzarella cheese, thinly sliced	200 g	500 g
Fresh sage leaves	8	20
or		
dried sage	1 tsp	2½ tsp
Salt, pepper		
Butter or oil	50 g	125 g
Parmesan cheese, grated		

Energy	Cals	Fat	Sat fat	Carb	Sugar	Protein	Fibre
1,642 kJ	394 kcal	26.1 g	15.5 g	0.1 g	0.1 g	39.8 g	0.0 g

1 Sprinkle each slice of veal lightly with flour and flatten.
2 Place a slice of Parma ham on each escalope.
3 Add several slices of mozzarella cheese to each.
4 Add a sage leaf or a light sprinkling of dried sage.
5 Season, roll up each escalope and secure with a toothpick or cocktail stick. Make sure the ham and cheese are well sealed within the escalope before cooking.
6 Melt the butter in a sauté pan, add the escalopes and brown on all sides.
7 Transfer the escalopes and butter to a suitably sized ovenproof dish.
8 Sprinkle generously with grated Parmesan cheese and bake in a moderately hot oven at 190 °C for 10 minutes.
9 Clean the edges of the dish and serve.

Healthy eating tips
- Use a small amount of oil to fry the escalopes and drain the cooked escalopes on kitchen paper.
- No added salt is necessary as there is plenty of salt in the cheese.
- Serve with plenty of vegetables.

Layer the veal, ham and cheese, then roll them up

Transfer the fried escalopes to an ovenproof dish and sprinkle with cheese

41 Fricassée of veal

Ingredient	4 portions	10 portions
Boned stewing veal (shoulder or breast)	400 g	1 kg
Butter or oil	35 g	90 g
Flour	25 g	60 g
White veal stock	500 ml	1.25 litres
Salt, pepper		
Egg yolk	1	2–3
Cream (dairy or vegetable)	2–3 tbsp	5–7 tbsp
Squeeze of lemon juice		
Parsley, chopped, to finish		

Energy	Cals	Fat	Sat fat	Carb	Sugar	Protein	Fibre
992 kJ	236 kcal	13.6g	7.5g	5.3g	0.4g	23.3g	0.2g

Using butter.

1. Trim the meat. Cut into even 25 g pieces.
2. Sweat the meat gently in the butter without colour in a sauté pan.
3. Mix in the flour and cook out without colour.
4. Allow to cool.
5. Gradually add boiling stock just to cover the meat, stir until smooth.
6. Season, bring to the boil, skim.
7. Cover and simmer gently on the stove until tender (approximately 1½–2 hours).
8. Pick out the meat into a clean pan. Correct the sauce.
9. Pass on to the meat and reboil. Mix the yolk and cream in a basin.
10. Add a little of the boiling sauce, mix in and pour back on to the meat, shaking the pan until thoroughly mixed; do not reboil. Add the lemon juice.
11. Serve, finished with chopped parsley and heart-shaped croutons fried in butter or oil.

Professional tip

After adding the flour, cook carefully so that it does not colour.

Add the liaison of yolks and cream carefully. Do not allow the sauce to boil after this, because it will curdle.

Meat and offal

Ingredients for fricassée of veal

Cook the meat and flour

Add the stock and continue to cook

Add the liaison of egg yolk and cream

Healthy eating tips
- Add the minimum amount of salt.
- Brush the croutons with olive oil and bake them, or serve with sippets (small, thin pieces of toasted bread).
- A large serving of starchy carbohydrates and vegetables will help to proportionally reduce the fat content.

Variation

Add mushrooms and button onions. Proceed as for this recipe but, after 1 hour's cooking, pick out the meat, strain the sauce back on to the meat and add 2 small button onions per portion. Simmer for 15 minutes, add 2 small white button mushrooms per portion, washed and peeled if necessary, then complete the cooking. Finish and serve as in this recipe. This is known as *fricassée de veau à l'ancienne*.

42 Braised shin of veal (*osso buco*)

Ingredient	4 portions	10 portions
Salt and ground pepper		
Plain flour	45 g	112 g
Thick slices of veal shin on the bone	4 × 200 g	10 × 200 g
Butter	50 g	125 g
Oil	2 tbsp	5 tbsp
White wine	150 ml	375 ml
Plum tomatoes	450 g	1.1 kg
Light veal or chicken stock	300 ml	750 ml
Sprigs of parsley and thyme		
Bay leaf	1	1

Energy	Cals	Fat	Sat fat	Carb	Sugar	Protein	Fibre
1,732 kJ	413 kcal	19.7 g	8.5 g	12.5 g	3.9 g	47.3 g	1.5 g

1. Preheat the oven to 180 °C.
2. Season the flour and use to coat the meat well on both sides.
3. Heat the butter and oil in a casserole, add the veal and fry, turning once, until browned on both sides. Add the wine and cook, uncovered, for 10 minutes. Blanch, peel and chop the tomatoes, and add along with the stock and herbs.
4. Cover and cook in the centre of the oven until the meat is very tender and falls away from the marrow bone in the middle.

Delicious served with sauté potatoes or with a *risotto alla Milanese*.

Note

Part of the attraction of this dish is the marrow found in the bones. Although very rich, it is a special treat. Traditionally, *osso buco* is served with a gremolata, which is a combination of chopped parsley, garlic and lemon zest that is added to the dish at the very end. It has been omitted from this recipe, offering you a simple base.

Pork dishes

43 Pork escalope with calvados sauce

Ingredient	4 portions	10 portions
Crisp eating apples (e.g. russet)	2	5
Cinnamon	¼ tsp	¾ tsp
Lemon juice	1 tbsp	2½ tbsp
Brown sugar	2 tsp	5 tsp
Butter, melted	25 g	60 g
Pork escalopes	4 × 100 g	10 × 100 g
Butter or oil	50 g	125 g
Shallots or onions, finely chopped	50 g	125 g
Calvados	30 ml	75 ml
Double cream or natural yoghurt	125 ml	300 ml
Salt, cayenne pepper		
Basil, sage or rosemary, chopped		

Energy	Cals	Fat	Sat fat	Carb	Sugar	Protein	Fibre
1,856 kJ	447 kcal	34.2 g	20.3 g	12.7 g	12.5 g	22.8 g	1.1 g

Using lean meat only, and double cream.

Variation

Calvados can be replaced with twice the amount of cider and reduced by three-quarters as an alternative.

Add a crushed clove of garlic and 1 tablespoon of continental mustard (2–3 cloves and 2½ tablespoons for 10 portions).

1. Core and peel the apples.
2. Cut into 0.5 cm-thick rings and sprinkle with a little cinnamon and a few drops of lemon juice.
3. Place on a baking sheet, sprinkle with brown sugar and a little melted butter, and caramelise under the salamander or in the top of a hot oven.
4. Lightly sauté the escalopes on both sides in the butter.
5. Remove from the pan and keep warm.
6. Add the chopped shallots to the same pan, cover with a lid and cook gently without colouring (use a little more butter if necessary).
7. Strain off the fat, leaving the shallots in the pan, and deglaze with the calvados.
8. Reduce by a half and then add the cream or yoghurt, seasoning and herbs.
9. Reboil, correct the seasoning and consistency, and pass through a fine strainer on to the meat.
10. Garnish with slices of caramelised apple.

Special care must be taken not to overheat if using yoghurt, otherwise the sauce will curdle.

Healthy eating tips

- Use a little unsaturated oil to sauté the escalopes.
- Add the minimum amount of salt.
- Try using yoghurt stabilised with a little cornflour, or half cream and half yoghurt.

44 Sweet and sour pork

Ingredient	4 portions	10 portions
Loin of pork, boned	250 g	600 g
Sugar	12 g	30 g
Dry sherry	70 ml	180 ml
Soy sauce	70 ml	180 ml
Cornflour	50 g	125 g
Vegetable oil, for frying	70 ml	180 ml
Oil	2 tbsp	5 tbsp
Clove of garlic	1	2½
Fresh root ginger	50 g	125 g
Onion, chopped	75 g	180 g
Green pepper, in 1 cm dice	1	2½
Chillies, chopped	2	5
Sweet and sour sauce (see page 132)	210 ml	500 ml
Pineapple rings (fresh or canned)	1	3
Spring onions	2	5

Energy	Cals	Fat	Sat fat	Carb	Sugar	Protein	Fibre
3,067 kJ	730 kcal	43.9 g	9.2 g	69.7 g	54.7 g	13.4 g	1.6 g

1. Cut the boned loin of pork into 2 cm pieces.
2. Marinate the pork for 30 minutes in the sugar, sherry and soy sauce.
3. Pass the pork through cornflour, pressing the cornflour in well.
4. Deep fry the pork pieces in oil at 190 °C until golden brown, then drain. Add the tablespoons of oil to a sauté pan.
5. Add the garlic and ginger, and fry until fragrant.
6. Add the onion, pepper and chillies, sauté for a few minutes.
7. Stir in the sweet and sour sauce, bring to the boil.
8. Add the pineapple cut into small chunks, thicken slightly with diluted cornflour. Simmer for 2 minutes.
9. Deep fry the pork again until crisp. Drain, mix into the vegetables and sauce or serve separately.
10. Serve garnished with rings of spring onions or button onions.

Professional tip

It is important to allow the pork enough time to marinate.

Meat and offal | **10**

45 Stir-fried pork fillet

Ingredient	4 portions	10 portions
Shallots, finely chopped	2	5
Clove of garlic (optional), chopped	1	2½
Button mushrooms, sliced	200 g	500 g
Olive oil		
Pork fillet	400 g	1 kg
Chinese five-spice powder	1 pinch	2½ pinches
Soy sauce	1 tbsp	2½ tbsp
Clear honey	2 tsp	5 tsp
Dry white wine	2 tbsp	5 tbsp
Salt, pepper		

Energy	Cals	Fat	Sat fat	Carb	Sugar	Protein	Fibre
831 kJ	199 kcal	9.8g	2.2g	5.1g	4.2g	22.9g	0.8g

1 Gently fry the shallots, garlic and sliced mushrooms in a little oil in a frying pan or wok.
2 Add the pork cut into strips, stir well, increase the heat, season and add the Chinese five-spice powder; cook for 3–4 minutes then reduce the heat.
3 Add the soy sauce, honey and wine, and reduce for 2–3 minutes.
4 Correct the seasoning and serve.

Healthy eating tips
- No extra salt is needed, as soy sauce is added.
- Adding more vegetables and a large portion of rice or noodles can reduce the overall fat content.

46 Sauerkraut, ham hocks and lentils

Sauerkraut is made by a process of pickling called lacto-fermentation. The bacteria and yeasts needed for the fermentation process are found on the cabbage leaves. No additional bacteria are added for this reaction to take place.

The process of making sauerkraut begins by washing and finely slicing white cabbage. It is put into a large pot, a specific amount of salt is mixed in and it is mashed with a cabbage masher. This allows the cabbage juices to be extracted: it produces enough to cover the cabbage in liquid. It is important for the cabbage to be completely covered in liquid to keep air out – any cabbage exposed to air would spoil during the fermentation process.

323

Using salt in this way is a process that can extract the natural juices of many ingredients by breaking down the cell structure. In meat, this 'tightening action' affects the myosin protein, while in vegetables it breaks down the cell wall structure – commonly done when preparing cauliflower for piccalilli or aubergine for ratatouille.

The cabbage, covered with its juices, is put into a large, covered, airtight container and allowed to ferment for four to six weeks. The bacteria and yeast begin the fermentation process. Over time, the lactic acid bacteria become active, converting the sugars in the cabbage into lactic acid. The sauerkraut is ready when the desired 'sourness' is obtained.

Sauerkraut can keep for several months if it is stored in an airtight container and stored at or below 13°C. Refrigeration is not essential, but it greatly increases the shelf life of the sauerkraut. Many commercial producers also use pasteurisation to further increase its shelf life.

If you can plan ahead, then this is a worthwhile recipe to make. It highlights some of the near-forgotten culinary techniques that are making a comeback at every level of gastronomy.

Below there are two methods for making sauerkraut: traditional and modern. Alternatively, use 600g of ready-made sauerkraut for this ham hock recipe.

Sauerkraut – traditional method

Ingedient	8–10 portions
Head of white cabbage	1
Salt	40g

1 Finely slice the cabbage. Mix with the salt and mash down, encouraging the cell structure to break down and extracting the natural liquid from the cabbage.

2 Ensure that the cabbage is completely covered with the liquid.

3 Place the cabbage in a covered container (not air sealed as the bacteria need air movement) for four to six weeks, until the cabbage takes on the natural sourness.

4 Store in an airtight jar for up to six months at 13°C, or place in the fridge if a longer shelf life is required.

Sauerkraut – modern interpretation

Ingredient	8–10 portions
Head of white cabbage	1
Salt	10g
Oil	50ml
Butter	50g
Streaky bacon, cut into lardons	300g
Shallots, sliced	2
Juniper berries	5
Alsace-style wine	250ml
Chicken stock	1 litre

1 Shred the cabbage and place in a colander over a dish. Sprinkle with the salt and leave to extract the liquid for an hour.

2 Squeeze out the remaining liquid by hand, wash the cabbage and pat dry with kitchen towel.

3 Heat the oil and butter in a pan and add the bacon. Cook until the bacon is crisp and has released its fat into the pan.

4 Add the cabbage and cook until soft, without colour.

5 Add the juniper, and then deglaze with the wine and reduce until half the liquid has evaporated.

6 Add the chicken stock and reduce the heat until the cabbage mix is soft and has absorbed the liquid (you may have to regularly top up with a little water to aid the cooking).

For the ham hocks

Ingredient	8–10 portions
Ham hocks, about 1.3 kg	2
Onion, quartered	1
Carrots, quartered lengthways	2
Celery sticks, cut into thirds crossways	2
Fresh thyme, few sprigs	
Bay leaf	

1. Before starting the cooking process, blanch the hocks to rinse away any impurities and excess salt.
2. Put the joints in a large saucepan, cover with cold water and bring to the boil.
3. Reduce the heat and simmer for 1 minute, then carefully move the pan to the sink and drain off the hot water.
4. Refresh the hams under cold running water for a minute or so, then tip out the water.
5. Put the blanched hams in the pan, and add the onion, carrots, celery sticks, thyme and bay leaf.
6. Pour in enough fresh cold water to cover and bring to a simmer.
7. The pan can now be covered with its lid and the hams cooked, keeping the liquor at a gentle simmer for 3 hours.
8. To check if the hams are cooked, pull out the small bone close to the large one – it should be loose and come out easily.
9. Rest the hams in the stock for 15–20 minutes.
10. Lift out the hams and set aside until cool enough to handle. Wrap in cling film to retain the moisture.
11. Retain 900 ml of the stock to cook the lentils.
12. About 10 minutes before the lentils are ready, strip off the skin and fat from the hams with a knife, then remove the meat from the bones and cut it into rough pieces or shred it with your fingers.

For the lentils

Ingredient	8–10 portions
Puy lentils	250 g
Butter	75 g
Large onion, peeled and finely diced	1
Large carrot, peeled and finely diced	1
Celery stick, finely diced	1
Fresh parsley, coarsely chopped	1 heaped tbsp
Stock from cooking the hams, strained	900 ml

1. First blanch the lentils by plunging them into a pan of boiling water, then drain into a sieve and refresh under the cold tap. (This process not only rinses the lentils well, it also speeds up the entire braising process and stops the lentils breaking before the cooking process has finished.)
2. Melt the butter in a medium saucepan. Add the diced onion, carrot and celery, cover the pan and cook without colouring for 5–6 minutes.
3. Tip in the blanched lentils, then pour in the reserved stock from the hams.
4. Bring the lentils to a simmer and cook for about 30 minutes, until tender. Check occasionally and top up with more stock if needed.

To finish

Warm the sauerkraut gently in a pan and place on a large serving plate. Scatter the shredded ham over the top of the cabbage. Add the coarsely chopped parsley to the lentils, and season with a twist of pepper, then scatter the lentils over the dish and serve with crusty sourdough bread.

Energy	Cals	Fat	Sat fat	Carb	Sugar	Protein	Fibre	Sodium
2295 kJ	550 kcal	31.0 g	12.4 g	29.0 g	12.4 g	40.0 g	10.7 g	2.4 g

Using the traditional method and a pork leg joint.

47 Boiled bacon

1. Soak the bacon in cold water for 24 hours before cooking. Change the water.
2. Bring to the boil, skim and simmer gently (approximately 25 minutes per 0.5 kg, plus another 25 minutes). Allow to cool in the liquid.
3. Remove the rind and brown skin; carve.
4. Serve with a little of the cooking liquor.

Boiled bacon may be served with pease pudding (a purée of yellow split peas) and a suitable sauce such as parsley (see page 113). It may also be served cold, or used as an ingredient in other dishes.

Energy	Cals	Fat	Sat fat	Carb	Sugar	Protein	Fibre
1,543 kJ	367 kcal	30.5g	12.2g	0.0g	0.0g	23.1g	0.0g

Using 113 g per portion.

48 Roast leg of pork

Energy	Cals	Fat	Sat fat	Carb	Sugar	Protein	Fibre
1,357 kJ	323 kcal	22.4g	8.9g	0.0g	0.0g	30.4g	0.0g

113 g portion.

1. Prepare leg for roasting (see page 272).
2. Moisten with water, oil, cider, wine or butter and lard, then sprinkle with salt, rubbing it well into the cracks of the skin. This will make the crackling crisp.
3. Place on a trivet in a roasting tin with a little oil or dripping on top.
4. Start to cook in a hot oven at 230–250 °C, basting frequently.
5. Gradually reduce the heat to 180–185 °C, allowing approximately 25 minutes per 0.5 kg plus another 25 minutes. Pork must always be well cooked. If using a probe, the minimum temperature should be 75 °C for 2 minutes.
6. When cooked, remove from the pan and prepare a roast gravy from the sediment (see page 124).
7. Remove the crackling and cut into even pieces for serving.

Serve the joint garnished with picked watercress and accompanied by roast gravy, sage and onion dressing and apple sauce. If to be carved, proceed as for roast lamb (see page 263).

Variation

Other joints can also be used for roasting (e.g. loin, shoulder and spare rib).

49 Roast pork belly with shallots and champ potatoes

Ingredient	4 portions	10 portions
Pork belly	1.2 kg	3 kg
Salt, pepper		
Olive oil	1 tbsp	2½ tbsp
Shallots	20	50
Butter	70 g	175 g
Potatoes, peeled and chopped	1 kg	2.5 kg
Spring onions, chopped	8	20
Double cream	4 tbsp	10 tbsp

Energy	Cals	Fat	Sat fat	Carb	Sugar	Protein	Fibre	Sodium
2,680 kJ	645 kcal	50.5 g	18.3 g	0.0 g	0.0 g	47.8 g	0.0 g	0.2 g

1. Place the pork on a rack in a roasting tray; season and oil. Roast in the oven for 10 minutes at 200 °C and then for 3–3½ hours at 140 °C.
2. Peel the shallots, fry gently in half the butter until caramelised. Keep warm.
3. Purée the potatoes.
4. Melt the remaining butter in a pan and sauté the spring onions until soft. Add the spring onion and the butter to the potato purée.
5. Add the cream and mix well.
6. Serve the pork with the caramelised shallots and potato.
7. Serve with a reduced brown stock flavoured with cider; alternatively, a red wine sauce may be served.

50 Slow-roast belly of pork

Ingredient	4 portions	10 portions
Pork belly	1.2 kg	3 kg
Salt and pepper		

1. Preheat the oven to 145 °C.
2. Season the pork with salt and pepper.
3. Place on a rack in a large roasting tray, skin-side up.
4. Roast for 4½–5 hours, then remove from the tray.
5. Pour off excess fat and make a gravy.
6. Carve into thick slices and serve with apple sauce, sage and onion dressing and a suitable potato and vegetable.

Energy	Cals	Fat	Sat fat	Carb	Sugar	Protein	Fibre
3,216 kJ	774 kcal	60.6g	21.9g	0.0g	0.0g	57.3g	0.0g

51 Sage and onion dressing for pork

Ingredient	4 portions	10 portions
Onion, chopped	50 g	125 g
Pork dripping	50 g	125 g
White breadcrumbs	100 g	250 g
Chopped parsley, pinch		
Powdered sage, good pinch		
Salt, pepper		

Healthy eating tips
- Use a small amount of unsaturated oil instead of dripping.
- Add the minimum amount of salt.

Energy	Cals	Fat	Sat fat	Carb	Sugar	Protein	Fibre	Sodium
865 kJ	204 kcal	12.9g	6.3g	20.6g	1.9g	2.7g	0.2g	0.2g

1. Cook the onion in the dripping without colour.
2. Combine all the ingredients. Dressing is usually served separately.

Professional tip
Modern practice is to refer to this as a dressing if served separately to the meat, but as stuffing if used to stuff the meat.

Meat and offal

52 Spare ribs in barbecue sauce

1. Sweat the onion and garlic in the oil without colour.
2. Mix in the vinegar, tomato purée, honey, stock, Worcester sauce, mustard and thyme, and season with salt.
3. Allow the barbecue sauce to simmer for 10–15 minutes.
4. Place the prepared spare ribs fat side up on a trivet in a roasting tin.
5. Brush the spare ribs liberally with the barbecue sauce.
6. Place in a moderately hot oven: 180–200 °C.
7. Cook for ¾–1 hour.
8. Baste generously with the barbecue sauce every 10–15 minutes.
9. The cooked spare ribs should be brown and crisp.
10. Cut the spare ribs into individual portions and serve.

Ingredient	4 portions	10 portions
Onion, finely chopped	100 g	250 g
Clove of garlic, chopped	1	2
Oil	60 ml	150 ml
Vinegar	60 ml	150 ml
Tomato purée	150 g	375 g
Honey	60 ml	150 ml
Brown stock	250 ml	625 ml
Worcester sauce	4 tbsp	10 tbsp
Dry mustard	1 tsp	2½ tsp
Pinch thyme		
Salt		
Spare ribs of pork	2 kg	5 kg

Energy	Cals	Fat	Sat fat	Carb	Sugar	Protein	Fibre
6,151 kJ	1,465 kcal	12.6 g	37.3 g	20.3 g	17.1 g	63.5 g	0.3 g

Using sunflower oil.

Professional tip
Apply plenty of barbecue sauce before and during cooking, to give the ribs a good flavour.

Healthy eating tips
- Sweat the onion and garlic in a little unsaturated oil.
- No added salt is necessary as the Worcester sauce is salty.

53 Roasted joint of bacon

1. Soak the joint in cold water for 24 hours.
2. Remove from the water. Dry well.
3. Place on a roasting tray and roast for approximately 25 minutes per 0.5 kg, plus another 25 minutes.
4. Remove from the oven and allow to stand for 5 minutes before carving.
5. Use the sediment to make roast gravy (see page 124), having checked for saltiness.
6. The joint may be cooked in foil and, for the last 25–30 minutes, cooked out of the foil.

Energy	Cals	Fat	Sat fat	Carb	Sugar	Protein	Fibre
1,021 kJ	245 kcal	14.8 g	4.9 g	0.0 g	0.0 g	28.0 g	0.0 g

Offal dishes

54 Calf's liver and bacon (*foie de veau au lard*)

Ingredient	4 portions	10 portions
Calf's liver	300 g	750 g
Flour		
Oil, for frying	50 g	125 g
Streaky bacon	50 g	125 g
Jus-lié	125 ml	300 ml

Energy	Cals	Fat	Sat fat	Carb	Sugar	Protein	Fibre
998 kJ	238 kcal	13.4 g	5.0 g	2.8 g	2.7 g	26.9 g	1.1 g

1 Skin the liver and remove the gristle.
2 Cut in slices on the slant.
3 Pass the slices of liver through flour and shake off the excess.
4 Quickly fry on both sides in hot oil.
5 Remove the rind and bone from the bacon and grill on both sides.
6 Serve the liver and bacon with a cordon of *jus-lié* and a separate sauceboat of *jus-lié*.

Note
Liver dishes are often cooked so that the liver is still pink in the centre. It is safer to cook to a higher core temperature, especially if the dish is for anyone in a high-risk group (see Chapter 1).

Variation
Lamb's liver may be cooked in the same way. Variations include the following:
- Fry in butter and sprinkle with powdered sage or chopped fresh sage.
- Fry in butter, remove the liver then deglaze the pan with raspberry vinegar and powdered thyme.
- When cooked, sprinkle with chopped parsley and a few drops of lemon juice.
- Flour, egg and breadcrumb the liver before cooking.
- The liver may be lightly brushed with oil and grilled.

Healthy eating tips
- Bacon is salty, so no added salt is needed.
- Use a little unsaturated oil to fry the liver, and drain off any excess fat.
- Serve with boiled new potatoes and a variety of vegetables.

Meat and offal **10**

55 Grilled lambs' kidneys (*rognons grillés*)

1. Season the prepared skewered kidneys (as for lamb kebabs, see recipe 4).
2. Brush with melted butter or oil.
3. Place on preheated, greased grill bars or on a greased baking tray.
4. Grill fairly quickly on both sides (approximately 5–10 minutes depending on size).
5. Serve with parsley butter, picked watercress and straw potatoes.

Energy	Cals	Fat	Sat fat	Carb	Sugar	Protein	Fibre
614 kJ	147 kcal	10.3g	5.9g	0.1g	0.1g	13.7g	0.0g

Healthy eating tips
- Use the minimum amount of salt.
- Serve with plenty of starchy carbohydrates and vegetables.

56 Devilled lambs' kidneys

Ingredient	4 portions	10 portions
Lambs' kidneys	8	20
Olive oil	1 tbsp	2½ tbsp
Salt, pepper		
Amontillado sherry	60 ml	150 ml
White wine vinegar	1 tbsp	2½ tbsp
Redcurrant jelly	1 tsp	2½ tsp
Worcester sauce	3 drops	7 drops
Double cream	1 tbsp	2½ tbsp
English mustard	1 tsp	2½ tsp
Mixed herbs, chopped		

Energy	Cals	Fat	Sat fat	Carb	Sugar	Protein	Fibre	Sodium
692 kJ	165 kcal	8.1g	2.7g	2.5g	2.4g	17.3g	0.0g	0.4g

1. Prepare the kidneys: cut in half, remove the white ducts then cut into quarters.
2. Heat the oil in the pan. Season the kidneys and place in the pan. When cooked, remove.
3. Add the sherry to the pan and bring to the boil, then add the vinegar and redcurrant jelly.
4. Add the Worcester sauce and season.
5. Add the cream and mustard. Simmer and reduce to a sauce consistency.
6. Add the kidneys and warm through.
7. Serve on a bed of pilaff rice (see page 159), garnished with chopped herbs.

331

57 Braised calf's cheeks with vegetables

Ingredient	4 portions	10 portions
Calf's cheeks	800 g	2 kg
Salt, pepper		
Olive oil or vegetable oil	2 tbsp	5 tbsp
Ground cumin	½ tsp	1¼ tsp
White peppercorns	½ tsp	1¼ tsp
Cloves	4	10
Celery, 5 mm dice	1 stick	2½ sticks
Bay leaves	2	5
Cloves of garlic	8	20
Leeks, finely shredded	1	2½
Onions, chopped	1	2½
Shallots, quartered	2	5
Savoy cabbage	400 g	1 kg
Dry white wine	500 ml	1.25 litres
Cider	350 ml	875 ml
Chopped chives	½ tsp	1¼ tsp

Energy	Cals	Fat	Sat fat	Carb	Sugar	Protein	Fibre	Sodium
2208 kJ	527 kcal	20.0g	6.3g	13.5g	10.8g	49.0g	6.0g	0.4g

Using stewing steak in place of cheeks.

1. Season the cheeks.
2. Heat the oil in a suitable pan. Sear the cheeks on all sides. Remove and keep warm. Add to the pan the cumin, peppercorns, cloves, celery, bay leaves, garlic, leeks, onions and shallots. Cook until the vegetables start to brown.
3. Add the cabbage and cook until wilted and slightly brown.
4. Add half the white wine and three-quarters of the cider.
5. Return the cheeks to the pan. Cover and braise in the oven for about 2½ hours, until the meat is tender.
6. Remove the cheeks and vegetables from the juices. Set aside and keep warm.
7. Strain the juices and return to the pan. Then add the remaining wine and cider. Bring to the boil and reduce to a sauce consistency.
8. Return the cheeks to the pan and simmer, basting with the sauce until it is syrupy and the meat is glazed.
9. To serve, place the vegetables on plates with the cheeks on top. Mask with the sauce and sprinkle with chopped chives.
10. Serve with polenta or couscous.

58 Braised beef cheek in red wine

Ingredient	4 portions	10 portions
Beef cheek, cut into 12 large pieces	450 g	1200 g
Seasoned flour	65 g	175 g
Vegetable oil	35 ml	85 ml
Carrots, roughly diced	100 g	250 g
Onion, roughly diced	100 g	250 g
Red wine	750 ml	1.75 l
Garlic cloves, chopped	3	7
Bouquet garni	1	2
Salt and pepper		

Energy	Cals	Fat	Sat fat	Carb	Sugar	Protein	Fibre	Sodium
2,098 kJ	503 kcal	21.9 g	0.4 g	17.5 g	3.8 g	26.4 g	2.3 g	0.6 g

1 Preheat the oven to 160 °C.
2 Gently roll the pieces of meat in the seasoned flour. Heat the vegetable oil in a large, heavy, heatproof casserole dish until very hot then brown the meat quickly and evenly. Add the diced carrots and onions, cover and sweat gently for 10 minutes.
3 Remove the excess cooking fat either by tipping the pan and using a spoon or by holding the lid over the casserole and carefully pouring the fat away. Deglaze the dish with the red wine and bring to the boil. Add the garlic, bouquet garni and season.
4 Replace the lid and cook in the oven for approximately 2½ hours, until the meat is very tender. Stir regularly during cooking, adding a little water if there is too much evaporation.
5 Remove the casserole dish from the oven. Lift out the pieces of meat with a slotted spoon and place in another pan, then pass the sauce through a fine sieve over the meat. Discard the vegetables and the bouquet garni.
6 Adjust the seasoning and consistency of the sauce as required.
7 Serve with creamy mashed potatoes and seasonal green vegetables.

59 Shallow-fried lambs' sweetbreads

Ingredient	4 portions	10 portions
Sweetbreads	8	20
Seasoned flour		
Oil	50 ml	125 ml
Butter	50 g	125 g
Lemon, juice of	1	2½
Parsley, chopped	½ tsp	1¼ tsp

Energy	Cals	Fat	Sat fat	Carb	Sugar	Protein	Fibre	Sodium
1,635 kJ	396 kcal	36.0g	11.0g	0.4g	0.4g	17.6g	0.1g	0.4g

1 Trim the sweetbreads, then blanch them for 30 seconds. Pass through seasoned flour.
2 Shallow-fry in oil for 2 minutes, turning.
3 Add butter to pan (*beurre noisette*), then add the lemon juice and chopped parsley.
4 Drain and serve.

Pâté

60 Liver pâté (*pâté de foie*)

Ingredient	4 portions	10 portions
Liver (chicken, pig, calf, lamb, etc.)	100 g	250 g
Butter or oil	25 g	60 g
Onion, chopped	10 g	25 g
Cloves of garlic	1	2½
Sprigs of parsley, thyme, chervil		
Fat pork	50 g	125 g
Salt, pepper		
Fat bacon	25 g	60 g

Energy	Cals	Fat	Sat fat	Carb	Sugar	Protein	Fibre
896 kJ	213 kcal	19.1 g	8.5 g	0.7 g	0.1 g	9.8 g	0.0 g

1. Cut the liver into 2 cm pieces.
2. Toss quickly in the butter or oil in a frying pan over a fierce heat for a few seconds with the onion, garlic and herbs.
3. Allow to cool.
4. Pass the liver and fat pork together through a mincer, twice. Season.
5. Line an earthenware terrine with wafer-thin slices of fat bacon.
6. Place the mixture into the terrine. Cover with fat bacon.
7. Stand in a tray half-full of water and bring to simmering point.
8. Cook in a moderate oven for 1 hour. Use a temperature probe to check that the centre reaches 75 °C.
9. Blast chill. When quite cold, cut into 0.5 cm slices and serve on lettuce leaves. Usually served accompanied with freshly made toast.

Note

This is a typical recipe for a homemade terrine, often seen on the menu as *pâté maison*.

Healthy eating tips

- Use an unsaturated oil (sunflower or olive). Lightly oil the pan and drain off any excess after the frying is complete.
- The bacon is high in salt so very little (or no) added salt is necessary.

Cold meats

61 Chicken salad

Ingredient	4 portion	10 portion
Fresh chicken	1.5 kg	3.75 kg
Black peppercorns	10	25
Bay leaves	3	7
Cumin seeds, ground	2 tsp	5 tsp
Almonds, sliced	25 g	60 g
For the dressing		
Greek yoghurt	2 tbsp	5 tbsp
Mayonnaise	3 tbsp	7 tbsp
Lemons, juice and zest of	2	5
Cucumber, peeled and diced	1	2½
Fresh basil, picked and torn	25 g	60 g
To serve		
Mixed salad leaves	100 g	250 g
Vinaigrette	20 ml	50 ml

Energy	Cals	Fat	Sat fat	Carb	Sugar	Protein	Fibre	Sodium
4,752 kJ	1,148 kcal	95.2g	27.3g	3.6g	2.7g	70.0g	0.7g	0.4g

1 Place the chicken in a large saucepan and cover with water.
2 Add the peppercorns and bay leaves and bring to a gentle simmer. Poach gently for about 40 minutes and leave it to cool in the liquid.
3 Once cool, take the chicken out of the pan, remove the skin and shred the meat. Cover and place in a refrigerator.
4 Dry fry the cumin and almonds in a hot pan and leave to cool.
5 To make the dressing, mix the yoghurt, mayonnaise and lemon zest and juice in a large bowl.
6 Add the chicken, cucumber, cumin and almonds with the torn basil. Mix well and serve on a bed of the mixed salad leaves tossed lightly in vinaigrette.

62 Raised pork pie

Ingredient	4 portions	10 portions
Hot water paste		
Strong plain flour	250 g	500 g
Salt		
Lard or margarine (alternatively use 100 g lard and 25 g butter or margarine)	125 g	300 g
Water	125 ml	300 ml
Filling		
Shoulder of pork, without bone	300 g	1 kg
Bacon	100 g	250 g
Allspice (or mixed spice) and chopped sage	½ tsp	1½ tsp
Salt, pepper		
Bread, soaked in milk	50 g	125 g
Stock or water	2 tbsp	5 tbsp
Egg wash		
Stock, hot	125 ml	375 ml
Gelatine	5 g	12.5 g
Picked watercress and salad to serve		

Energy	Cals	Fat	Sat fat	Carb	Sugar	Protein	Fibre	Sodium
3,005 kJ	721 kcal	47.7 g	19.3 g	49.2 g	1.7 g	26.7 g	2.7 g	1.2 g

For the pastry:

1 Sift the flour and salt into a basin. Make a well in the centre.
2 Boil the fat with the water and pour immediately into the flour.
3 Mix with a wooden spoon until cool enough to handle.
4 Mix to a smooth paste and use while still warm.

For the filling:

1 Cut the pork and bacon into small even pieces and combine with the rest of the main ingredients.
2 Keep one-quarter of the paste warm and covered.
3 Roll out the remaining three-quarters and carefully line a well-greased raised pie mould. Ensure that there is a thick rim of pastry.
4 Add the filling and press down firmly.
5 Roll out the remaining pastry for the lid and egg wash the edges of the pie.
6 Add the lid, seal firmly, neaten the edges, cut off any surplus paste; decorate if desired.
7 Make a hole 1 cm in diameter in the centre of the pie; brush all over with egg wash.
8 Bake in a hot oven (230–250 °C) for approximately 20 minutes.
9 Reduce the heat to moderate (150–200 °C) and cook for 1½–2 hours in all.
10 If the pie colours too quickly, cover with greaseproof paper or foil. Remove from the oven and carefully remove tin. Egg wash the pie all over and return to the oven for a few minutes.
11 Remove from the oven and fill with approximately 125 ml of good hot stock in which 5 g of gelatine has been dissolved.

Serve when cold, garnished with picked watercress and offer a suitable salad.

63 Veal and ham pie

Ingredient	4 portions	10 portions
Hot water paste (see recipe 62)	125 ml	310 ml
Ham or bacon	150 g	375 g
Salt, pepper		
Egg, hard-boiled	1	2½
Lean veal	250 g	625 g
Parsley and thyme	½ tsp	1¼ tsp
Lemon, grated zest of	1	2½
Stock or water	2 tbsp	5 tbsp
Bread, soaked in milk	50 g	125 g
Gelatine	5 g	12.5 g

Energy	Cals	Fat	Sat fat	Carb	Sugar	Protein	Fibre
607 kJ	144 kcal	4.5 g	1.5 g	3.8 g	0.8 g	22.4 g	0.1 g

Proceed as for raised pork pie (recipe 62) but place the shelled egg in the centre of the mixture. Serve when cold, garnished with picked watercress and offer a suitable salad.

Partly fill the pie, then place egg(s) into the centre

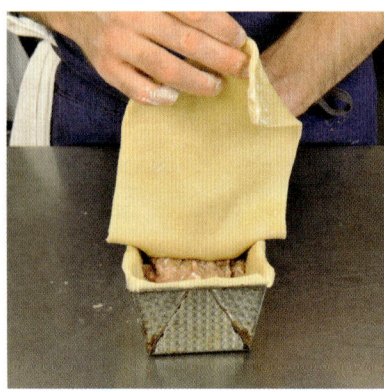

Add the pastry lid and seal it firmly

Pour gelatine dissolved in stock into the pie after baking

64 Terrine of bacon, spinach and mushrooms

Ingredient	12 portions
Collar of bacon	1 kg
Carrot	1
Onion clouté	1
Bouquet garni	1
Celery	2 sticks
Peppercorns	8
Fresh spinach	500 g
Butter	50 g
Mushrooms (preferably morels)	200 g

Energy	Cals	Fat	Sat fat	Carb	Sugar	Protein	Fibre
1,436 kJ	347 kcal	30.4 g	7.2 g	1.2 g	1.0 g	17.0 g	1.4 g

Using common mushrooms.

1. If necessary soak the bacon overnight. Drain.
2. Place the bacon in cold water, bring to the boil, add the carrot, onion, bouquet garni, celery and peppercorns.
3. Simmer until tender.
4. Pick some large leaves of spinach to line the terrine dish. Blanch the leaves, refresh and drain.
5. Lightly cook the rest of the spinach gently; refresh, drain and shred.
6. Alternatively, shred the spinach raw, quickly cook in butter, drain and then blast chill.
7. Cook the mushrooms in a little butter, season and chill well.
8. When cool, remove the bacon from the cooking liquor and chop into small pieces.
9. Line the terrine with cling film, then the spinach leaves. Layer with bacon, mushrooms and spinach. Cover with spinach leaves and cling film. Wait for 12 hours or overnight.
10. When ready, turn out, slice and serve on plates, with leek and mushroom vinaigrette served separately.

Healthy eating tips
- Soaking the bacon overnight will remove some of the salt.
- Use only a little butter to cook the mushrooms.
- Use a minimum amount of salt to season the vinaigrette.
- Serve with warm bread rolls, butter optional.

11 Poultry and game

Recipes included in this chapter

No.	Recipe	Page
	Shallow-fried chicken dishes	
1	Chicken sauté chasseur	354
2	Crumbed breast of chicken with asparagus (*suprême de volaille aux pointes d'asperges*)	355
3	Paella	356
4	Chicken palak	357
	Deep-fried chicken dishes	
5	Deep-fried chicken	358
6	Chicken Kiev	358
	Grilled chicken dishes	
7	Chicken spatchcock (*poulet grillé à la crapaudine*)	359
8	Grilled chicken (*poulet grillé*)	360
	Braised or steamed chicken dishes	
9	Braised chicken leg forestière	361
10	Steamed ballotine of chicken with herb stuffing and red wine jus	362
11	Fricassée of chicken	363
	Poached chicken dishes	
12	Chicken à la king	364
13	Poached suprême of chicken with Madeira and mushroom café cream sauce	365
14	Confit chicken leg with leeks and artichokes	366
	Roast chicken dishes	
15	Roast chicken with dressing (*poulet rôti à l'anglaise*)	367
	Casserole chicken dishes	
16	Chicken in red wine (*coq au vin*)	368
	Baked or tandoori chicken dishes	
17	Chicken pie	369
18	Tandoori chicken	370
	Turkey dishes	
19	Roast turkey	371
20	Turkey escalopes	372
	Duck dishes	
21	Duck breast steaks with cherries	372
22	Confit duck leg with red cabbage and green beans	373
23	Roast duck or duckling (*canard ou caneton rôti*)	374
24	Sage and onion stuffing for duck	375
25	Cranberry and orange dressing for duck	375
	Cold dish	
26	Terrine of chicken with vegetables	376
	Goose dish	
27	Roast goose	377
	Guinea fowl dish	
28	Suprêmes of guinea fowl with a pepper and basil coulis	377
	Game dishes	
29	Pot au feu of pigeon	378
30	Roast partridge	379
31	Traditional-contemporary roast grouse	380
32	Pot-roasted quail with roast carrots and mashed potato	381
33	Stuffed roast quail	382
34	Braised baron of rabbit with olives and tomatoes	383
35	German-style saddle of hare	384
36	Medallions of venison with buttered cabbage and haricots blancs	385
37	Medallions of venison with celeriac purée and braised red cabbage	386

Poultry

The term 'poultry' is applied to all domestic fowl bred for food, and includes turkeys, geese, ducks, fowls and pigeons.

The flesh of poultry is more easily digested than that of butchers' meat. It contains protein and is therefore useful for building and repairing body tissues and providing heat and energy. The fat content is low and it contains a high percentage of unsaturated fatty acids.

Originally, fowl were classified according to size and feeding by specific names as shown in Table 11.1.

Poultry and game

Table 11.1 Traditional classification of fowl

Fowl	Weight (kg)	Number of portions
Single baby chicken (poussin)	0.3–0.5	1
Double baby chicken (poussin)	0.5–0.75	2
Small roasting chicken	0.75–1	3–4
Medium roasting chicken	1–2	4–6
Large roasting or boiling chicken	2–3	6–8
Capon	3–4.5	8–12
Old boiling fowl	2.5–4	

There is approximately 15 to 20 per cent bone in poultry.

Storing poultry

Chilled birds should be stored between 1°C and 4°C. Oven-ready birds are eviscerated (gutted and cleaned) and should be stored in a refrigerator. Frozen birds must be kept in a deep freeze until required, but must be completely thawed, preferably in a refrigerator, before being cooked. This procedure is essential to reduce the risk of food poisoning: chickens are potential carriers of salmonella and campylobacter, and if birds are cooked from the frozen state there is a risk that the centre of the bird will not reach the required degree of heat to kill off these pathogens.

When using frozen poultry, check that:
- the packaging is undamaged
- there are no signs of freezer burn, which is indicated by white patches on the skin
- frozen birds are defrosted by moving them from the freezer to a refrigerator.

Preparing poultry

Refer to the sections below for different types of poultry for specific preparation methods. For information on maintaining a safe and secure working environment; a professional and hygienic appearance; clean food production areas, equipment and utensils; and food hygiene when preparing and cooking poultry, please refer to Chapters 1 and 2.

Additional health and safety points to reduce the risk of cross-contamination when preparing poultry are as follows:
- When preparing uncooked poultry or game and then cooked food – or changing from one type of meat, poultry or game to another – equipment, working areas and utensils must be thoroughly cleaned or changed.
- If colour-coded boards are used, it is essential that you always use the correct colour-coded boards for the preparation of raw or cooked poultry.
- Unhygienic equipment, utensils and preparation areas increase the risk of cross-contamination and danger to health.
- Store uncooked poultry and game on trays to prevent dripping, in a separate refrigerator, at a temperature of 1–4°C, preferably at the lower temperature. When separate refrigerators are not available then store in the bottom of the refrigerator.
- Wash all work surfaces with a bactericidal detergent to kill bacteria. This is particularly important when handling poultry and game.

Cooking, holding and serving poultry

Refer to Chapter 10 for the principles related to cooking meat. All poultry must be cooked until it reaches a core temperature of 75°C, even if this is not stated in the recipe. When holding cooked poultry and game dishes this should be above 65°C.

Chicken

The different types of chicken are:
- **Spring chickens**: poussin 4–6 weeks old, used for roasting and grilling.
- **Broiler chickens**: 3–4 months old, used for roasting, grilling and casseroles.
- **Medium roasting chickens**: fully grown, tender, prime birds, used for roasting, grilling, sauté, casseroles, suprêmes and pies.
- **Large roasting or boiling chickens**: used for roasting, boiling, casseroles and galantine.
- **Capons**: specially bred, fattened cock birds used for roasting.
- **Old hens**: used for stocks and soups.

341

Quality points

- Plump breast, pliable breast bone and firm flesh.
- Skin white and unbroken. Broiler chickens have a faint bluish tint.
- Corn-fed are yellow. Free-range have more colour, a firmer texture and more flavour.
- Bresse chickens are specially bred in France and are highly regarded for their quality and flavour.
- Old birds have coarse scales, large spurs on the legs and long hairs on the skin.

Trussing

To truss a bird for roasting:

1 Place the bird on its back.

2 To facilitate carving, remove the wishbone.

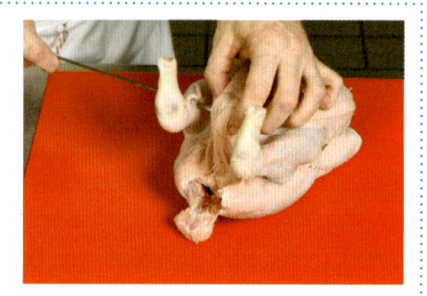

3 Insert a trussing needle through the bird, midway between the leg joints.

4 Thread the needle through the tendon and breast.

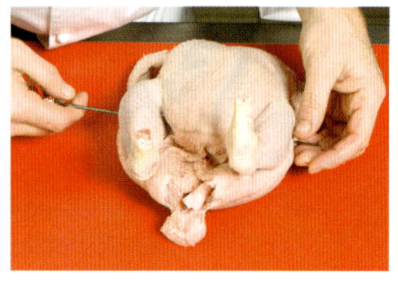

5 The needle comes out by the wing.

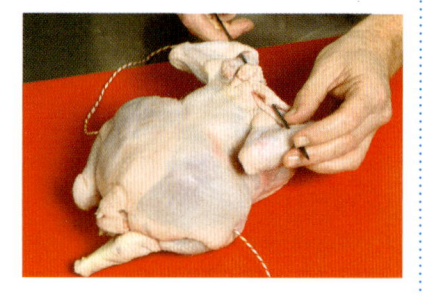

6 Turn over the chicken.
7 Run the needle under the skin through the wing, crown and other wing.

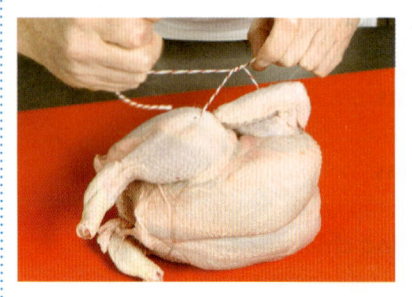

8 The string ends at the same place it started. Tie the ends of the string securely.

9 The trussed bird will hold its shape during roasting.

Poultry and game

To truss for boiling or pot roasting:
- Proceed as for roasting.
- Cut the leg sinew just below the joint.
- Bend back the legs so that they lie parallel to the breast and secure when trussing, *or* insert the legs through incisions made in the skin at the rear end of the bird, and secure when trussing.

Cutting chicken

Chicken is cut into pieces as shown in the diagram. The leg is cut into two parts: drumstick and thigh.

1 Wing	**2** Breast	**3** Thigh
4 Drumstick	**5** Winglet	**6** Carcass

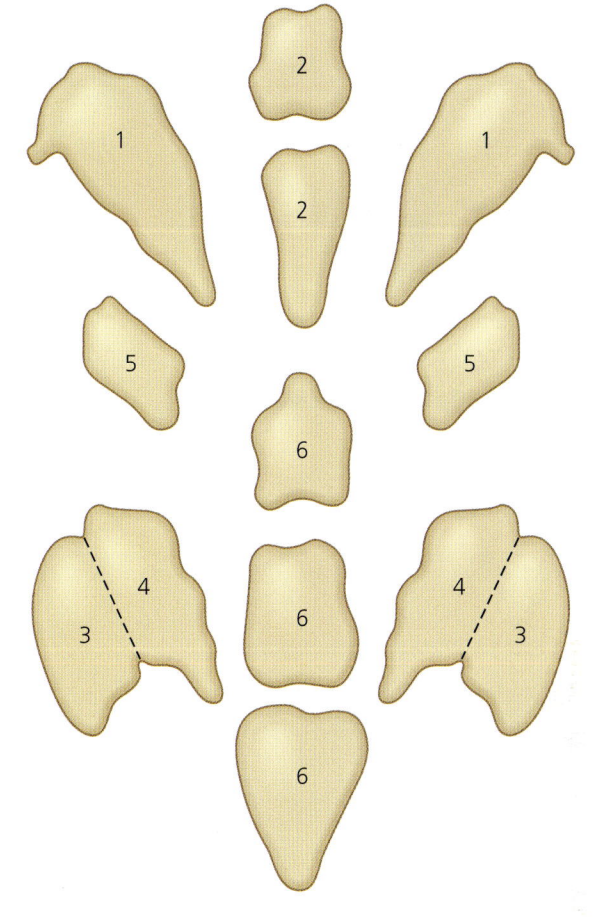

▲ Cuts of chicken

Cutting chicken for sauté, fricassée, pies, etc.

1 Remove the winglets.

2 Remove the legs from the carcass, cutting around the oyster.

3 Cut off the feet.

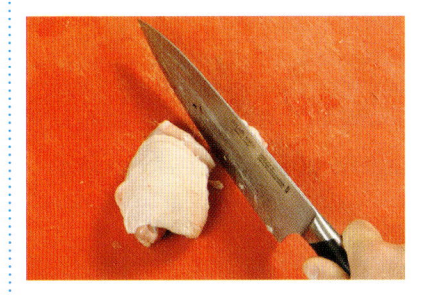

4 Separate the thigh from the drumstick.

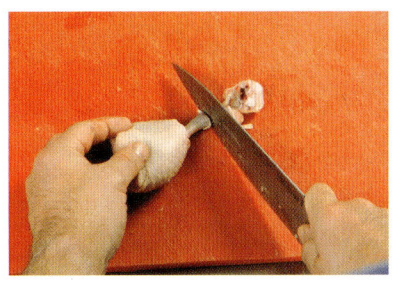

5 Trim the drumstick neatly.

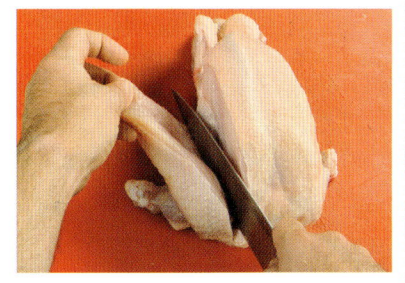

6 Remove each breast from the carcass.

343

7 Separate the wing from the breast and trim it.

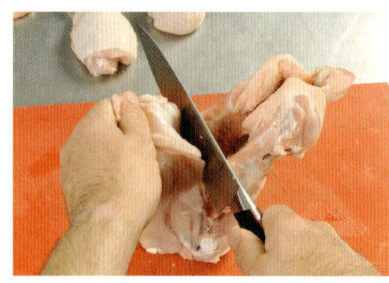

8 Cut into the cavity, splitting the carcass (this may be used for stock).

9 Cut each breast in half.

10 Chicken cut for sauté, on the bone: thighs, drumsticks, breasts, winglets and wings.

Preparing a spatchcock chicken

To prepare chicken for grilling:
- Remove the wishbone.
- Cut off the claws at the first joint.
- Place the bird on its back.
- Insert a large knife through the neck end and out of the vent.
- Cut through the backbone and open out.
- Remove back and rib bones.

The chicken may then be grilled whole (spatchcock, see recipe 7) or cut into pieces.

Insert the knife through the neck end

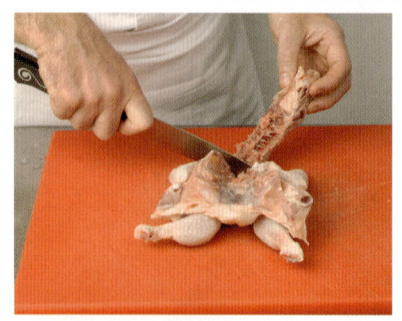

Remove the backbone

Spatchcock chicken ready for cooking

Preparing chicken suprêmes

A suprême is the wing and half the breast of a chicken with the trimmed wing bone attached to the white meat. One chicken yields two suprêmes. To cut suprêmes, use a chicken weighing 1.25 to 1.5 kg. Removing the skin is optional.

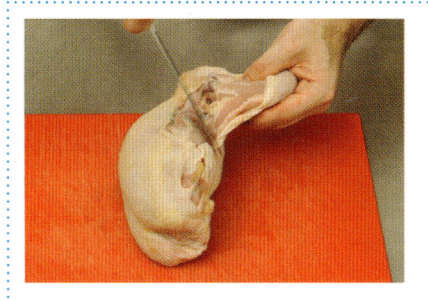

1 Cut off both the legs.

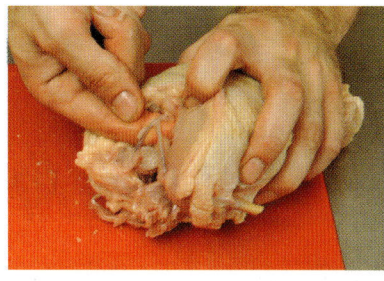

2 Scrape the wing bone bare, adjoining the breasts. Cut off the winglets near the joints, leaving 1.5 to 2 cm of bare bone attached. Then remove the wishbone.

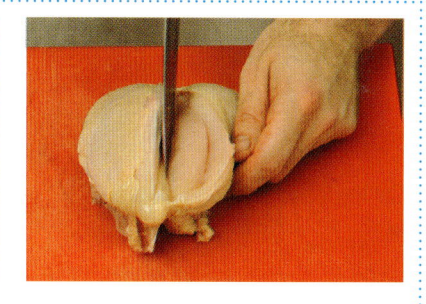

3 Cut the breasts close to the breastbone and follow the bone down to the wing joint.

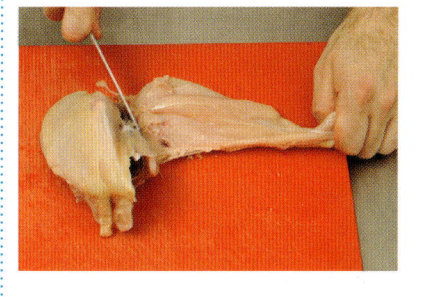

4 Cut through the joint. Pull the suprêmes off, using the knife to assist.

5 To finish, lift the fillets from the suprêmes and remove the sinew from each. Make an incision lengthways, along the thick side of the suprêmes; open and place the fillets inside. Close, lightly flatten with a bat moistened with water, and trim if necessary.

Stuffing and tying a ballotine

A ballotine is a boned, stuffed leg of bird.

Cut the leg open around the bone.	Start to separate the knuckle from the meat. (Scrape the bone.)	Lift the knuckle away (tunnel boning).
Cut the bone below the knuckle.	Fill the cavity of the thigh and drumstick with stuffing.	Close up in a neat shape and secure with string.

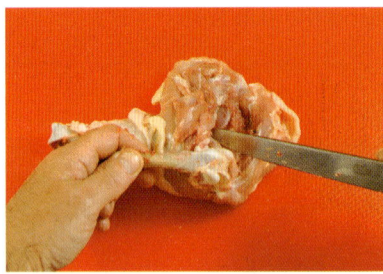

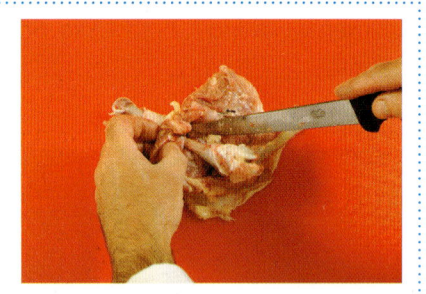

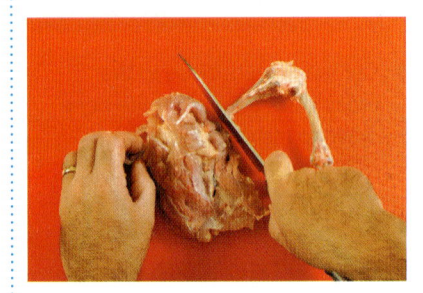

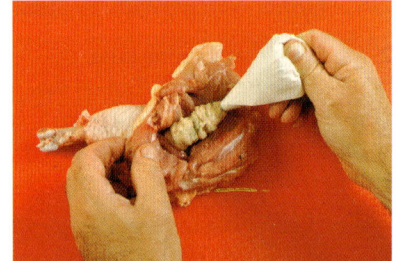

Ballotines of chicken may be cooked and served using any of the recipes for chicken sauté presented in this chapter.

Cutting cooked chicken

To cut up a cooked chicken (roasted or boiled):

- Remove the legs and cut in two (drumstick and thigh).
- Remove the wings.
- Separate the breast from the carcass and divide in two.
- Serve a drumstick with a wing and the thigh with the breast.

Turkey

Turkeys can vary in weight from 3.5 to 20 kg. They are trussed in the same way as chicken for roasting. The wishbone should always be removed before trussing in order to facilitate carving. The sinews should be drawn out of the legs. Allow 200 g per portion raw weight.

When cooking a large turkey, the legs are often removed, boned, rolled and tied before roasting. The whole breast still on the bone is known as a crown. Suprêmes can be removed as for other poultry and then used in similar ways, slicing across the breast to form an escalope which would normally be batted out with a cutlet bat to gain an even slice that can then be filled, coated and cooked.

Stuffings may be rolled in foil, steamed or baked and thickly sliced. If a firmer stuffing is required, mix in one or two raw eggs before cooking.

Quality points

- Large full breast with undamaged skin and no signs of stickiness.
- Legs smooth with supple feet and a short spur.
- As birds age the legs turn scaly and the feet harden.

Poultry and game 11

Preparing a large turkey for roasting

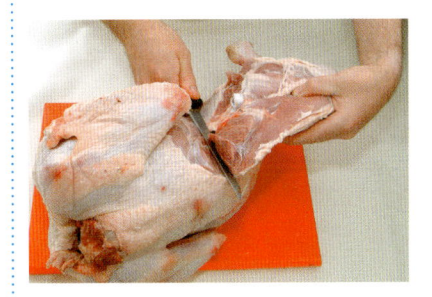

1 Remove the legs; cooking them separately will reduce the cooking time and enable the legs and breast to cook more evenly.

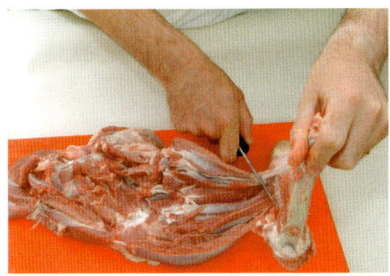

2 Remove the leg bones.

3 Stuff and roll each leg if required.

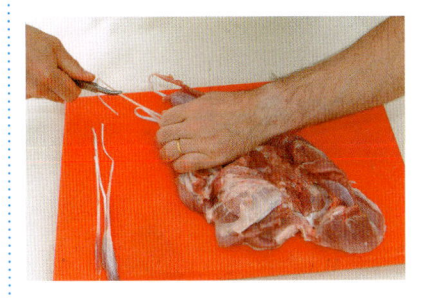

4 Tie the stuffed legs securely.

5 Cut the remainder of the bird in half, again to reduce the cooking time.

6 The two halves, ready for roasting, with one leg left whole and the other boned, stuffed and rolled.

Preparing a chicken or turkey crown

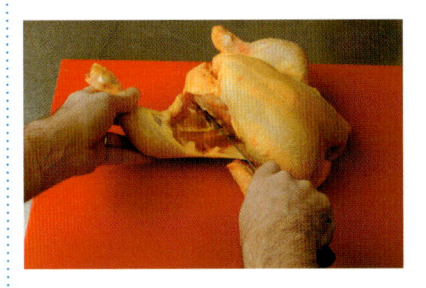

1 Cut off the legs.

2 Sever the leg at the joint with a sharp tap of the knife.

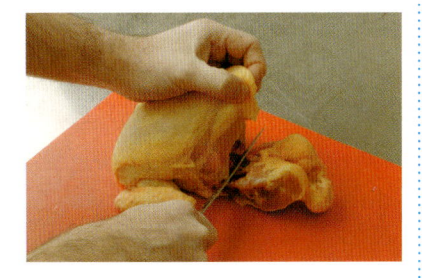

3 Cut off the front of the bird, leaving the crown.

4 A prepared crown: this is useful for roasting when only a few portions are required or the legs are not wanted.

347

Tunnel boning a turkey or chicken

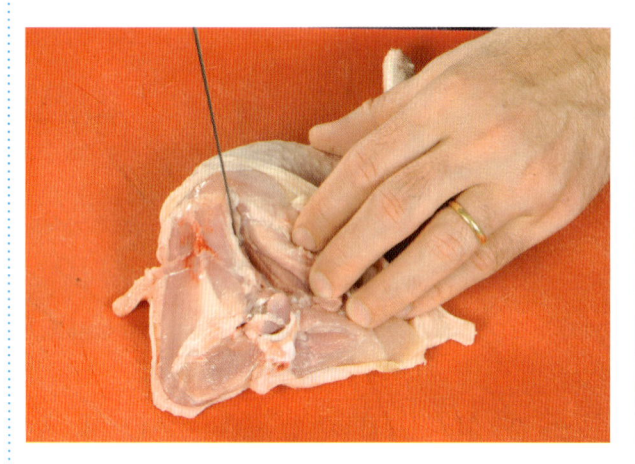

1 Cut around the exposed end of the bone.

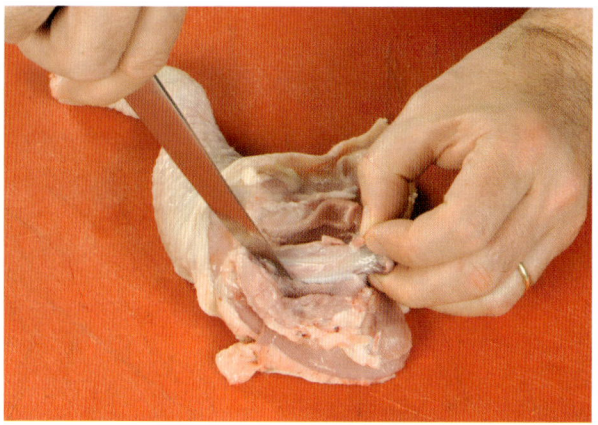

2 Scrape and cut, gently parting the flesh from the bone.

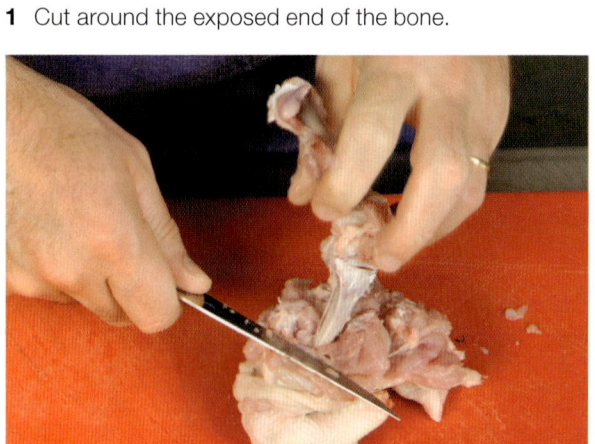

3 Push the meat down as it is freed, and lift the bone out.

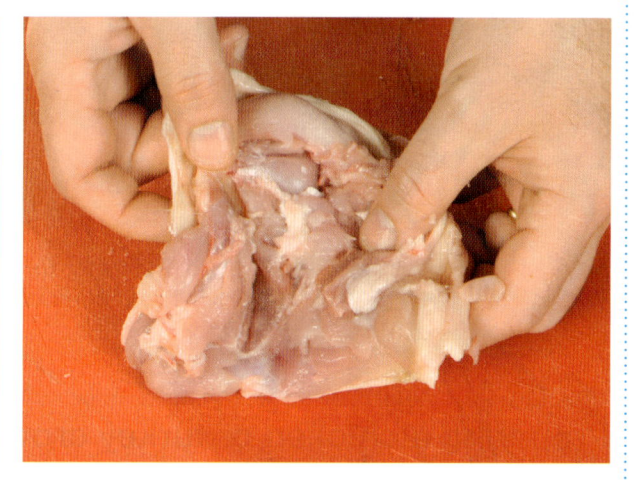

4 The de-boned leg.

Duck and geese

Approximate sizes are as follows:
- **duckling**: 1.5–2 kg
- **duck**: 3–4 kg
- **gosling**: 3 kg
- **goose**: 6 kg.

Quality points

- Plump breasts.
- Webbed feet tear easily.
- Lower back bends easily.
- Feet and bill should be yellow.

Ducks and geese are prepared for roasting in the same way as chickens. The gizzard is not split but trimmed off with a knife.

Game

The word game is used, for culinary purposes, to describe animals or birds that are hunted for food, although many birds and animals categorised as game are now being bred domestically, such as squab (pigeon), duck and venison. There are two types of game:

1 **Feathered**: often purchased plucked and dressed ready for cooking.
2 **Furred**: purchased skinned and pre-jointed in most kitchens.

Wild animals, because of their diet and general lifestyle, have more of certain enzymes in their tissues than poultry, which break down or metabolise meat proteins; they become active about 24 hours after the animal has been killed, softening the meat and making it gelatinous and more palatable (as well as giving the characteristic 'gamey' flavour). They also contain micro-organisms (anaerobes), which also help to break down the proteins.

Poultry and game 11

Choosing and buying

The most important factor when buying game is to know its 'life age' and its 'hanging age', since this will determine the method of cookery to be used. Indications of age are by no means infallible, but there are some general guidelines when buying young birds – soft-textured feet, pliable breastbones – and young partridges have pointed flight feathers (the first large feather of the wing), while in older birds these feathers are more rounded. There are many other distinctive guidelines you can use when selecting game, however the grading of game is a specialised subject and best left to the experts.

The seasons for game are shown in Table 11.2.

Table 11.2 Seasonality of game

	JAN	FEB	MAR	APR	MAY	JUN	JUL	AUG	SEP	OCT	NOV	DEC
Furred												
Hare	At best	At best	Available	Available	Available	Available	Available	Available	Available	Available	Available	Available
Rabbit	Available	Available	Available	Available	Available	Available	Available	Available	Available	Available	Available	Available
Venison	Available	Available	Available	Available	Available	Available	Available	Available	Available	Available	Available	Available
Feathered												
Goose (wild)	Available									At best	At best	At best
Goose (farmed)	Available								Available	At best	At best	At best
Grouse									12th	At best	At best	At best
Mallard	Available									Available	Available	Available
Moorhen	Available									Available	Available	Available
Partridge (English grey leg)	At best									At best	At best	At best
Partridge (French red leg)	Available									Available	Available	Available
Pheasant	At best									At best	At best	At best
Pigeon (farmed)	Available	Available	Available	Available	Available	Available	Available	Available	Available	Available	Available	Available
Pigeon (English wood)	Available	Available	Available	At best	At best	At best	At best	At best	At best	At best	Available	Available
Quail	Available	Available	Available	Available	At best	At best	At best	At best	At best	Available	Available	Available
Snipe	Available							12th	At best	At best	At best	At best
Teal	Available											
Woodcock	Available									At best	At best	At best

Key:
- Available (bird icon)
- At best (bird icon)

Storing and hanging game

Game bought from a game dealer will probably have been hung correctly. If, however, you require your game (or any other meat that benefits from hanging) to be hung specifically for you, speak to your butcher or game dealer. The general rules are to hang in a cool, dry, airy place, protected from flies to prevent maggot infestation. You should hang the carcass until you detect the first whiff of tainting. In Britain, birds are usually hung from their heads, feet down, and rabbits and other game are hung with their heads down.

However, there is no real need to hang game, due to the metabolic enzymes present so, if you object to the strong flavour that hanging promotes, a short hanging period (or no hanging at all) may be preferable.

Current legislation does not allow the hanging or plucking of game in a normal kitchen environment.

Game should be well wrapped and careful consideration given to its age; strict labelling is essential because, when in prime condition, the meat may have a slightly tainted smell, which may be difficult to discern from the smell that denotes the meat is past its best.

Drawing and washing

This is the process that is carried out when the bird is sold with all its entrails still inside. To remove, make a small lateral incision into the backside of the bird, then insert your forefinger and index finger, and roll them around the inner cavity of the bird. This loosens the membrane that holds in the innards. When loose, remove from the wider backside and discard. Ensure that all the innards are removed, that the cavity is empty, then wash and dry well.

Check for any shot that could be present and remove before completing preparations ready for cooking.

Cooking game

Game meat responds best to roasting. Young game birds in particular should be trussed and roasted; it is traditional to leave them unstuffed. Due to the low fat content of game, especially wild non-domestic varieties, added fat in the form of sliced streaky bacon, lardons and the like can be wrapped around the bird to help baste it while cooking and therefore retain moisture. Older, tougher game or high-worked muscle groups, such as a haunch of venison, should be casseroled/stewed or made into pies or terrines. Marinating in oil, vinegar or wine with herbs and spices helps to make tough meat more tender; it may also enhance the taste and it speeds up the action of the metabolic enzyme that breaks game down.

As game birds are deficient in fat, a thin slice of fat bacon (bard) should be tied over the breast during cooking to prevent it from drying out; this is also placed on the breast when serving.

The preparation techniques for poultry, such as stuffing ballotines, also apply to game birds.

Roast game birds are served with gravy; bread sauce and browned breadcrumbs (toasted or fried) are served separately.

Roast pheasant, partridge or grouse may also be served in the traditional manner: on a croûte of fried bread, garnished with thick round pieces of toasted French bread spread with game farce, game chips and picked watercress.

Game birds

Pheasant

One of the most common game birds, pheasants are found in the hedgerows and open farmland across the country. Young birds are reared and then released. An average weight of 1.5 to 2 kg will serve two; they are often served roasted although chefs sometimes remove the legs and cook separately.

Partridge

Two varieties are used in the UK, with the red-legged being slightly larger than the grey-legged. They have an average weight of around 500 g per bird and are cooked as for pheasant.

Grouse

Red grouse are found in the hills and mountains feeding on heather. The grouse season starts on the 12th of August each year, which is considered to be the start of the hunting season for game. With an average weight of around 750 g per bird, they are served roasted or pot roasted with appropriate garnishes and sauce.

Pigeon

As pigeons do not have gall bladders it is not necessary to remove their livers when they are drawn and cleaned. Tender young pigeons (less than 12 months old) can be roasted, pot roasted or split open and grilled and served (for example, with a Robert, charcutière or devilled sauce).

Young pigeons can be cut in half, flattened slightly, seasoned, shallow-fried in butter, and cooked and finished as for sautés of chicken (for example, chasseur, bordelaise).

Quail

Only plump birds with firm white fat should be selected. When prepared the entrails are drawn, but the heart and liver are retained inside the birds. They may be roasted, spit roasted, cooked 'en casserole' or poached in a rich, well-flavoured chicken or veal stock (or a combination of both). Quails may also be boned out from the back and stuffed with a forcemeat.

Hare and rabbits

The rabbit is distinguished from the hare by its shorter ears, feet and body. The ears of good-quality hare and rabbits should tear easily. With old hare, the lip is more pronounced than in young animals.

Preparation of wild rabbit

1 Carefully remove the fur.
2 Cut an incision along the belly.
3 Remove the intestines.
4 Clean out the forequarter, removing all traces of blood.

Venison

Venison is the name given to the meat of deer, with the main types available being red deer, fallow deer and roe deer. Of these three, the meat of the roebuck is considered to have the best and most delicate eating quality. The prime cuts are the legs, loins and best ends. The shoulder of young animals can be boned, rolled and roasted but, if in any doubt as to its tenderness, it should be cut up and used for stewed or braised dishes.

Venison is available from most catering butchers. The cuts and joints of venison are shown in the diagram and Table 11.3.

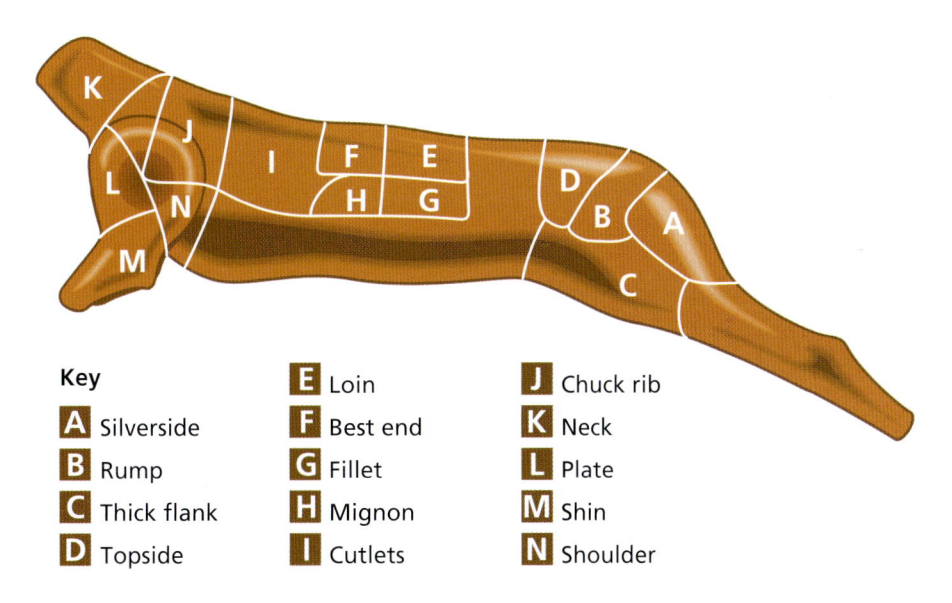

Key
- **A** Silverside
- **B** Rump
- **C** Thick flank
- **D** Topside
- **E** Loin
- **F** Best end
- **G** Fillet
- **H** Mignon
- **I** Cutlets
- **J** Chuck rib
- **K** Neck
- **L** Plate
- **M** Shin
- **N** Shoulder

▲ Cuts and joints of venison

Table 11.3 Cuts and joints of venison

Cut	Joints	Approx. weight	Uses
Haunch	Silverside	2 kg	Stewing, braising
	Topside	2 kg	Roasting, braising
	Thick flank	1.5 kg	Stewing
	Rump dice, escalopes	1.5 kg	Roasting, braising, frying
Saddle	Saddle	8 kg	Roasting, braising, frying
	Loin	1.4 kg	
	Noisettes	1 kg	
	Chops	1 kg	
	Filet mignon	0.5 kg	
Best end	Best end cutlets	1.5 kg	Frying, roasting, braising
Fillet	Fillet	1 kg	Escalopes, medallions, steaks
Shin	Shin	0.5 kg	Dice, mince, stewing
Neck	Neck	2 kg	Grilling, dice, mince, stewing
Shoulder	Shoulder	4 kg	Roasting/stewing, braising, dice, mince, burgers, sausages
	Chuck rib	2 kg	

The nutritional value of venison is compared with other meats in Table 11.4. It is a good meat to use when planning healthier menus as it contains very little fat. The fat in venison is mainly polyunsaturated and therefore lower in cholesterol.

Venison is also a good source of protein, as 100 g of venison supplies 68.5 per cent of the daily value for protein for only 179 calories and 1.4 g of saturated fat. It is also a source of iron, vitamin B_{12} and other B vitamins.

Quality points

- The flesh should be dark red in colour.
- The flesh should be dry and firm.
- The carcass should have a good amount of flesh and a close grain texture.
- The flesh should be lean, with little fat.
- There should be no unpleasant smell.

After slaughter, carcasses should be hung well in a cool place for several days and, when cut into joints, are usually marinated before being cooked. Joints of venison should be well fleshed and a dark brownish-red colour.

Cooking and serving cutlets

Venison cutlets (cut from the best end) and chops (cut from the loin) are usually well trimmed and cooked by shallow-frying, provided that the meat is tender. If in doubt, they should be braised.

After they are cooked they should be removed from the pan, the fat poured off and the pan deglazed with stock, red wine, brandy, Madeira or sherry, which is then added to the accompanying sauce.

A spicy, peppery sauce is usually offered, which can be varied by the addition of extra ingredients (for example,

Table 11.4 Nutritional information: venison and other meats

Meat	Fat g/100 g	Protein g/100 g	Iron mg/100 g	Cholesterol mg/100 g
Venison	1.6	22.2	3.3	29
Chicken	2.1	22.3	0.7	90
Pork	2.2	21.7	0.8	64
Lamb	12.3	19.0	0.25	78
Beef	12.9	20.4	1.3	48

cream, yoghurt, redcurrant jelly, cooked beetroot, sliced button or wild mushrooms, cooked pieces of chestnut, and so on).

Accompaniments can include, for example, a purée of a root vegetable (e.g. celeriac, turnip, swede, carrot, parsnip, or any combination of these).

Cooking and serving steaks

Venison steaks, or escalopes, are cut from the boned-out nuts of meat from the loins, trimmed well and thinned slightly with a meat bat.

The escalopes can be quickly shallow-fried and finished as for cutlets and chops, and served with a variety of accompanying sauces and garnishes.

Cooking and serving haunch of venison

The haunch may be roasted or braised. It is popular served hot or cold.

Wild boar

For good quality, buy animals obtained from suppliers using as near as possible 100 per cent pure breeding stock wild boars that are free to roam and forage for food, rather than those that have been penned and fed.

Animals aged between 12 and 18 months old, weighing 60 to 75 kg on the hoof, are best slaughtered in the late summer when their fat content is lower. The meat should be hung for seven to ten days before being used.

Young boar up to the age of six months are sufficiently tender for cooking in noisettes and cutlets, and joints for roasting. The prime cuts of older animals (e.g. leg, loin, best end) can be marinated and braised.

Boar's head is prepared by boning the head and stuffing it with a forcemeat to which strips of ox tongue, foie gras, truffles and pistachio nuts can be added. The head is tied securely in a cloth and simmered gently. When cooled it is completely coated and the tusks are re-inserted. Boar's head is a traditional Christmas cold buffet dish served with a spicy sauce (e.g. Cumberland).

Test yourself

1. List five quality points for a good quality chicken.
2. At what temperature should prepared poultry be chilled for storage?
3. State three considerations when roasting a chicken.
4. What is the safe internal temperature required for cooked poultry?
5. Explain why shallow frying is an appropriate cooking method for turkey escalopes.
6. Briefly describe how to truss a turkey.
7. State why you would baste a whole duck when roasting.
8. Describe how to store game birds.
9. List three quality points you should look for when buying venison.
10. Describe how you can keep game birds moist during cooking.

Chicken dishes

1 Chicken sauté chasseur

Ingredient	4 portions	10 portions
Butter or oil	50 g	125 g
Salt, pepper		
Chicken, 1.25–1.5 kg, cut for sauté	1	2½
Shallots, chopped	10 g	25 g
Button mushrooms, washed and sliced	100 g	250 g
Dry white wine	3 tbsp	8 tbsp
Jus-lié, demi-glace or reduced brown stock	250 ml	625 ml
Tomato concassé	200 g	500 g
Parsley and tarragon, chopped		

Energy	Cals	Fat	Sat fat	Carb	Sugar	Protein	Fibre
2,430 kJ	579 kcal	45.8 g	20.7 g	2.1 g	1.6 g	37.6 g	1.5 g

Using butter.

1 Place the butter or oil in a sauté pan on a fairly hot stove.
2 Season the pieces of chicken and place in the pan in the following order: drumsticks, thighs, wings and breast.
3 Cook to a golden brown on both sides.
4 Cover with a lid and cook on the stove or in the oven until tender. Dress neatly in a suitable dish.
5 Add the shallots to the sauté pan, rubbing them into the pan sediment to extract the flavour. Cover with a lid and cook on a gentle heat for 1–2 minutes.
6 Add the washed, sliced mushrooms and cover with a lid. Cook gently for 3–4 minutes, without colour. Drain off the fat.
7 Add the white wine and reduce by half. Add the *jus-lié*, demi-glace or reduced stock.
8 Add the tomatoes. Simmer for 5 minutes.
9 Correct the seasoning and pour over the chicken.
10 Sprinkle with chopped parsley and tarragon and serve.

Ballotines of chicken chasseur can be prepared as above or lightly braised (as shown).

Professional tip

The leg meat takes longer to cook than the breast meat, which is why the drumsticks and thighs should be added first.

Add the soft herbs and tomatoes just before serving.

Healthy eating tips

- Use a minimum amount of salt to season the chicken.
- The fat content can be reduced if the skin is removed from the chicken.
- Use a little unsaturated oil to cook the chicken, and drain off all excess fat from the cooked chicken.
- Serve with a large portion of new potatoes and seasonal vegetables.

Poultry and game — 11

Place the chicken into the hot pan

Cook the shallots in the pan that was used for the chicken – they will pick up the sediment and flavour

2 Crumbed breast of chicken with asparagus (*suprême de volaille aux pointes d'asperges*)

Ingredient	4 portions	10 portions
Suprêmes of chicken	4 × 125 g	10 × 125 g
Egg	1	2
Breadcrumbs (white or wholemeal)	50 g	125 g
Oil	50 g	125 g
Butter or margarine	100 g	250 g
Jus-lié	60 ml	150 ml
Asparagus	200 g	500 g

Energy	Cals	Fat	Sat fat	Carb	Sugar	Protein	Fibre
1,831 kJ	439 kcal	26.4 g	8.9 g	15.7 g	1.5 g	35.5 g	1.3 g

1 Pané the chicken suprêmes. Shake off all surplus crumbs.
2 Neaten and mark on one side with a palette knife.
3 Heat the oil and 50 g (125 g for 10 portions) of the butter or margarine in a sauté pan.
4 Gently fry the suprêmes to a golden brown on both sides (6–8 minutes). Use a probe to check that the centre has reached 75 °C.
5 Dress the suprêmes on a flat dish and keep warm.
6 Mask the suprêmes with the remaining butter cooked to the nut-brown stage.
7 Surround the suprêmes with a cordon of *jus-lié*.
8 Garnish each suprême with a neat bundle of asparagus points (previously cooked, refreshed and reheated with a little butter).

Healthy eating tips
- Use a minimum amount of salt.
- Remove the skin from the suprêmes and fry in a little unsaturated vegetable oil. Drain on kitchen paper.
- Try omitting the additional cooked butter.
- Serve with plenty of boiled new potatoes and vegetables.

3 Paella

Ingredient	4 portions	10 portions
Lobster, cooked	400 g	1 kg
Squid	200 g	500 g
Gambas (Mediterranean prawns), cooked	400 g	1 kg
Mussels	400 g	1 kg
White stock	1 litre	2.5 litres
Pinch of saffron		
Onion, finely chopped	50 g	125 g
Clove of garlic, finely chopped	1	2–3
Red pepper, diced	50 g	125 g
Green pepper, diced	50 g	125 g
Roasting chicken, cut for sauté	1.5 kg	3.75 kg
Olive oil	60 ml	150 ml
Short-grain rice	200 g	500 g
Thyme		
Bay leaf		
Seasoning		
Tomatoes, skinned, deseeded and diced	200 g	500 g
Lemon wedges, to finish		

Energy	Cals	Fat	Sat fat	Carb	Sugar	Protein	Fibre
3,383 kJ	804 kcal	31.0 g	6.2 g	48.8 g	3.8 g	85.7 g	1.3 g

Using chicken.

1 Prepare the lobster: cut it in half, remove the claws and legs, discard the sac and trail. Remove the meat from the claws and cut the tail into 3–4 pieces, leaving the meat in the shell.
2 Clean the squid: pull the body and head apart, and extract the transparent 'pen' from the body. Rinse well, pulling off the thin purple membrane on the outside. Remove the ink sac. Cut the body into rings and the tentacles into 1 cm lengths.
3 Prepare the gambas by shelling the body.
4 Boil the mussels in water or white stock until the shells open. Shell the mussels and retain the cooking liquid.
5 Boil the white stock and mussel liquor together, infused with saffron. Simmer for 5–10 minutes.
6 Sweat the finely chopped onion in a little oil in a suitable pan, without colour. Add the garlic and the peppers.
7 Sauté the chicken in olive oil until cooked and golden brown, then drain.
8 Add the rice to the onions and garlic and sweat for 2 minutes.
9 Add about 200 ml white stock and mussel liquor.
10 Add the thyme, bay leaf and seasoning. Bring to the boil then cover with lightly oiled greaseproof paper and a lid. Cook for 5–8 minutes in a moderate oven (180 °C).
11 Add the squid and cook for another 5 minutes.
12 Add the tomatoes, chicken and lobster pieces, mussels and gambas. Stir gently, cover with a lid and reheat the rice in the oven.
11 Correct the consistency of the rice if necessary by adding more stock, so that it looks sufficiently moist without being too wet. Correct the seasoning.
12 When all is reheated and cooked, place in a suitable serving dish, decorate with four (ten) gambas and four (ten) mussels halved and shelled. Finish with wedges of lemon.

Poultry and game — 11

Note

A raw lobster may be used for a traditional paella, which should be prepared as follows. Remove the legs and claws, and crack the claws. Cut the lobster in half crosswise, between the tail and the carapace. Cut the carapace in two lengthwise. Discard the sac. Cut across the tail in thick slices through the shell. Remove the trail, wash the lobster pieces and cook with the rice.

Healthy eating tips

- To reduce the fat, skin the chicken and use a little unsaturated oil to sweat the onions and fry the chicken.
- No added salt is necessary.
- Serve with a large green salad.

4 Chicken palak (chicken fried with spinach and spices)

Ingredient	4 portions	10 portions
Chicken, 1.5 kg, cut for sauté	1	2
Ghee, butter or oil	50 g	125 g
Onion, finely chopped	50 g	125 g
Clove of garlic, crushed and chopped	1	2–3
Fresh ginger	25 g	60 g
Green chilli	1	2½
Ground cumin	1 tsp	2½ tsp
Ground coriander	1 tsp	2½ tsp
Spinach, washed and finely chopped	250 g	625 g
Tomatoes, skinned, deseeded and diced	200 g	500 g
Chicken stock	250 ml	625 ml

Energy	Cals	Fat	Sat fat	Carb	Sugar	Protein	Fibre
1,575 kJ	378 kcal	21.9 g	9.5 g	4.4 g	3.5 g	41.3 g	1.9 g

Estimated edible meat used; butter used.

Healthy eating tips

- Skin the chicken and fry in a small amount of unsaturated oil.
- Skim excess fat from the finished dish.
- Serve with plenty of rice, dhal, chapatis and a vegetable dish.

1 Gently fry the chicken in the fat until golden brown.
2 Remove the chicken; fry the onion and garlic until lightly browned. Add the ginger, chilli and spices, and sweat for 3 minutes.
3 Stir in the spinach, add the tomatoes and season. Add the chicken pieces.
4 Add the chicken stock and bring to the boil.
5 Cover with a lid and cook in a moderate oven (180 °C) for 30 minutes or until the chicken is tender. Stir occasionally, adding more stock if necessary.
6 Serve in a suitable dish with rice, chapatis and dhal.

5 Deep-fried chicken

1 Cut the chicken as for sauté. Alternatively, the chicken may be boned.
2 Coat with flour, egg and crumbs (pané), or pass them through a light batter (see page 452) to which herbs can be added.
3 Deep fry in hot oil (approx. 170–180 °C) until golden brown and cooked through – about 5 minutes. When the chicken is cooked, a probe in the thickest part will read 75 °C+, and the juices will run clear when the chicken is pierced.

For suprêmes, make an incision, stuff with a compound butter, flour, egg and crumb, and deep fry as in chicken Kiev (recipe 6).

Healthy eating tips
The fat content can be reduced if the skin is removed from the chicken.

Energy	Cals	Fat	Sat fat	Carb	Sugar	Protein	Fibre
1,754 kJ	421 kcal	28.6g	6.1g	14.5g	0.4g	27.2g	0.5g

6 Chicken Kiev

Ingredient	4 portions	10 portions
Suprêmes of chicken	4 × 150 g	10 × 150 g
Butter	100 g	250 g
Seasoned flour	25 g	65 g
Eggs	2	5
Breadcrumbs	100 g	250 g

1 Make an incision along the thick sides of the suprêmes. Insert 25 g cold butter into each. Season.
2 Pass through seasoned flour, egg wash and crumbs, ensuring complete coverage. Egg wash and crumb twice if necessary.
3 Deep fry until completely cooked. When the chicken is cooked, a probe in the thickest part will read 75 °C+, and the juices will run clear when the chicken is pierced. Drain and serve.

Energy	Cals	Fat	Sat fat	Carb	Sugar	Protein	Fibre	Sodium
2,094 kJ	500 kcal	26.1g	14.4g	24.4g	0.9g	43.4g	1.0g	0.5g

Poultry and game 11

Carefully make an incision in the top of the suprême

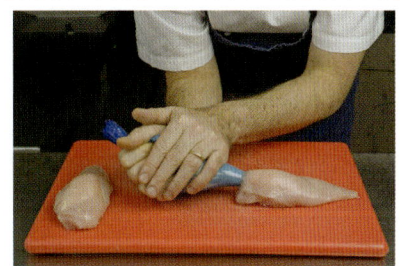

Stuff with softened butter

Dip the chicken in egg and flour and then coat with breadcrumbs

Variation
Additional ingredients may be added to the butter before insertion:
- chopped garlic and parsley
- fine herbs such as tarragon or chives
- liver paté.

Professional tip
The butter must be pushed well into the suprême, and the incision must be sealed, or the butter will leak out during cooking.

7 Chicken spatchcock (*poulet grillé à la crapaudine*)

Ingredient	4 portions	10 portions
Chicken, 1.25–1.5 kg	1	2½

Energy	Cals	Fat	Sat fat	Carb	Sugar	Protein	Fibre
1,560 kJ	372 kcal	24.1g	8.0g	0.0g	0.0g	38.9g	0.0g

Healthy eating tips
- Use a minimum amount of salt to season the chicken.
- The fat content can be reduced if the skin is removed from the chicken.
- Use a small amount of an unsaturated oil to brush the chicken.
- Serve with a large portion of potatoes and vegetables.

1. Cut horizontally from below the point of the breast over the top of the legs down to the wing joints, without removing the breasts. Fold back the breasts.
2. Snap and reverse the backbone into the opposite direction so that the point of the breast now extends forward.
3. Flatten slightly. Remove any small bones.
4. Skewer the wings and legs in position.
5. Season with salt and mill pepper.
6. Brush with oil or melted butter.
7. Place on preheated grill bars or on a flat tray under a salamander.
8. Brush frequently with melted fat or oil during cooking and allow approximately 15–20 minutes on each side.
9. Test if cooked by piercing the drumstick with a needle or skewer – there should be no sign of blood.

Serve garnished with picked watercress and offer a suitable sauce separately (e.g. devilled sauce or a compound butter).

8 Grilled chicken (*poulet grillé*)

Energy	Cals	Fat	Sat fat	Carb	Sugar	Protein	Fibre
975 kJ	234 kcal	15.7g	4.3g	0.0g	0.0g	23.3g	0.0g

Based on chicken with bone, wing and leg quarters.

1. Season the chicken with salt and mill pepper, and prepare for grilling (see page 344).
2. Brush with oil or melted butter or margarine, and place on preheated greased grill bars or on a barbecue or a flat baking tray under a salamander.
3. Brush frequently with melted fat during cooking; allow approximately 15–20 minutes each side.
4. Test if cooked by piercing the drumstick with a skewer or trussing needle; there should be no sign of blood issuing from the leg.
5. Serve garnished with picked watercress and offer a suitable sauce separately.

Healthy eating tips
- Use a minimum of salt and an unsaturated oil.
- Garnish with grilled tomatoes and mushrooms.
- Serve with Delmonico potatoes and green vegetables.

Variation

Grilled chicken is frequently garnished with streaky bacon, tomatoes and mushrooms.

The chicken may be marinated for 2–3 hours before grilling, in a mixture of oil, lemon juice, spices, herbs, freshly grated ginger, finely chopped garlic, salt and pepper. Chicken or turkey portions can also be grilled and marinated beforehand if wished (breasts or boned-out lightly battened thighs of chicken).

Poultry and game

9 Braised chicken leg forestière

Energy	Cals	Fat	Sat fat	Carb	Sugar	Protein	Fibre	Sodium
1,878 kJ	448 kcal	15.9g	3.9g	16.9g	8.7g	49.9g	3.6g	1.0g

Note

These quantities will produce a moderate portion to be served as part of a three-course meal. Allow two chicken legs per person for a hearty portion.

Ingredient	4 portions	10 portions
Chicken legs	4	10
Salt and pepper		
Olive oil	2 tbsp	5 tbsp
Onions, sliced fairly thickly	2	5
Smoked bacon, thickly sliced rashers cut into lardons	3	8
Clove of garlic, crushed	1	2
Whole button or small chestnut mushrooms (if larger, cut in half)	100 g	250 g
Oyster mushrooms, sliced in half	100 g	250 g
Plain flour	1½ tbsp	4 tbsp
Tomato purée	1 tbsp	2½ tbsp
Red wine	250 ml	625 ml
Brown chicken stock	400 ml	1 litre
Tomatoes, blanched, peeled, concassé	3	7½
Fresh tarragon and parsley, chopped	15 g	35 g

1. Season the chicken with salt and pepper. Heat the olive oil in a lidded sauté pan or shallow casserole and pan-fry the chicken over a medium-high heat, turning, until golden on both sides.
2. Remove from the pan and keep to one side. You will need about 2 tablespoons of fat left in the pan to cook the onions so, if the legs have released a lot of fat, drain off the excess.
3. Add the onions and fry for 2–3 minutes before adding the bacon, garlic and mushrooms to the pan. Continue to stir until they have a little colour and the mushrooms are beginning to soften.
4. Sprinkle over the flour and stir until the flour has lightly browned.
5. Stir in the tomato purée and then gradually add the red wine and chicken stock, stirring until the liquid has fully mixed into the flour and purée paste.
6. Return the chicken to the pan and bring to a simmer. Place a lid on the pan and continue to cook, allowing the sauce to just simmer for about 1 hour, or until the meat is completely tender.
7. To finish, remove the chicken legs, place on to a plate or tray and keep in a warm place, e.g. the side of the stove. Skim the sauce of any further excess fat and adjust the consistency as necessary.
8. Adjust the seasoning before adding the tomatoes.
9. Place the chicken legs back into the sauce and scatter over the chopped herbs before serving.

10 Steamed ballotine of chicken with herb stuffing and red wine jus

Ingredient	4 portions	10 portions
Chicken legs	4	10
Forcemeat		
Minced chicken	120 g	300 g
Parsley	1 tsp	2½ tsp
Tarragon	1 tsp	2½ tsp
Chives	1 tsp	2½ tsp
Chervil	1 tsp	2½ tsp
Salt and pepper		
Red wine jus		
Shallots, sliced	75 g	190 g
Butter	25 g	60 g
Garlic, finely chopped	5 g	10 g
Red wine	175 ml	440 ml
Chicken stock	175 ml	440 ml
Veal or beef jus	125 ml	310 ml
Bay leaves	1	2½
Thyme, sprigs	½	1

Energy	Cals	Fat	Sat fat	Carb	Sugar	Protein	Fibre	Sodium
1,626 kJ	390 kcal	24.9 g	8.5 g	1.8 g	0.9 g	33.4 g	0.5 g	1.1 g

Variation

Instead of the traditional chicken legs, ballotines can be made using:
- chicken suprêmes, batted out, stuffed and rolled
- chicken breasts: make an incision in the thicker part and fill this with forcemeat.

These ballotines are cooked in the same way.

1. Remove the thighbone and the knuckle joint from the chicken legs.
2. Prepare the forcemeat by mixing all of the herbs with the minced chicken. Season the mix and divide it evenly between the chicken legs.
3. Season the legs then stuff them with the forcemeat. Roll the leg into a neat cylinder and either tie the leg in place or roll tightly in cling film and tie off the ends.
4. Steam the legs for 30–45 minutes or until the core temperature reaches 84 °C.
5. Allow the chicken legs to rest so they will stay in shape.
6. When the chicken legs have rested and cooled slightly, remove the string or cling film and dry them.
7. Heat a sauté pan with oil and butter, add the chicken legs and brown the skin. Slice and serve with the sauce.

For the red wine jus:
1. Caramelise the shallots in the butter until golden, adding the garlic at the end.
2. Strain off any excess butter, deglaze the pan with the red wine and reduce by half.
3. Add the chicken stock and veal jus and reduce to a sauce consistency, adding the aromats for the last 5 minutes.
4. Pass through a muslin cloth and serve over the sliced ballotines.

11 Fricassée of chicken

Ingredient	4 portions	10 portions
Chicken, 1.25–1.5 kg	1	2–3
Salt, pepper		
Butter, margarine or oil	50 g	125 g
Flour	35 g	90 g
Chicken stock	0.5 litre	1.25 litres
Egg yolks	2	5
Cream or non-dairy cream	4 tbsp	10 tbsp
Parsley, chopped		

Energy	Cals	Fat	Sat fat	Carb	Sugar	Protein	Fibre
2,699 kJ	643 kcal	51.3 g	23.3 g	7.4 g	0.6 g	38.2 g	0.4 g

Using butter.

1. Cut the chicken as for sauté (page 343); season with salt and pepper.
2. Place the butter in a sauté pan. Heat gently.
3. Add the pieces of chicken. Cover with a lid.
4. Cook gently on both sides without colouring. Mix in the flour.
5. Cook out carefully without colouring. Gradually mix in the stock.
6. Bring to the boil and skim. Allow to simmer gently until cooked.
7. Mix the yolks and cream in a basin (liaison).
8. Pick out the chicken into a clean pan.
9. Pour a little boiling sauce on to the yolks and cream and mix well.
10. Pour all back into the sauce, combine thoroughly but do not reboil.
11. Correct the seasoning and pass through a fine strainer.
12. Pour over the chicken, reheat without boiling.
13. Serve sprinkled with chopped parsley and garnish with heart-shaped croutons, fried in butter, if desired.

Professional tip

Sauté the chicken lightly. Add the liaison of yolks and cream carefully. Do not allow the sauce to come back to the boil once the liaison has been added, or it will curdle.

Variation

Fricassée de volaille à l'ancienne: a fricassée of chicken with button onions and mushrooms can be made in a similar way, with the addition of 50–100 g button onions and 50–100 g button mushrooms. They are peeled and the mushrooms left whole, turned or quartered depending on size and quality. The onions are added to the chicken as soon as it comes to the boil and the mushrooms 15 minutes later. Heart-shaped croutons may be used to garnish. This is a classic dish.

Healthy eating tips

- Keep added salt to a minimum throughout the cooking.
- Use a little unsaturated oil to cook the chicken, and drain off all excess fat after cooking.
- Try oven-baking the croutons brushed with olive oil.
- The sauce is high in fat, so serve with plenty of starchy carbohydrate and vegetables.

12 Chicken à la king

1. Wash, peel and slice the mushrooms.
2. Cook them without colour in the butter or oil.
3. If using raw pepper, discard the seeds, cut the pepper into dice and cook with the mushrooms.
4. Cut the chicken into small, neat slices.
5. Add the chicken to the mushrooms and pepper.
6. Drain off the fat. Add the sherry.
7. Add the velouté and bring to the boil.
8. Finish with the cream and correct the seasoning.
9. Place in a serving dish and decorate with small strips of cooked pepper.

Use a velouté with a good chicken flavour, to create the best sauce.

Ingredient	4 portions	10 portions
Button mushrooms	100 g	250 g
Butter or oil	25 g	60 g
Red pepper, skinned	50 g	125 g
Chicken, boiled or steamed	400 g	1.25 kg
Sherry	30 ml	75 ml
Chicken velouté	125 ml	150 ml
Cream or non-dairy cream	30 ml	75 ml

Energy	Cals	Fat	Sat fat	Carb	Sugar	Protein	Fibre
1,226 kJ	292 kcal	16.7 g	7.8 g	3.2 g	0.8 g	30.4 g	0.9 g

Using butter or hard margarine.

Variation

Try adding 1 or 2 egg yolks to form a liaison with the cream, mixed into the boiling mixture at the last possible moment and immediately removed from the heat.

Chicken à la king may be served in a border of golden-brown duchess potato, or a pilaff of rice (see page 159) may be offered as an accompaniment. It is suitable for a hot buffet dish.

Healthy eating tips

- Use the minimum amount of salt.
- Remove the skin from the cooked chicken.
- Try reducing or omitting the cream used to finish the sauce.
- Serve with plenty of rice and vegetables or salad.

Slice the mushrooms and dice the red pepper

Neatly slice the cooked chicken

Add the velouté during cooking

13 Poached suprême of chicken with Madeira and mushroom café cream sauce

1. Sauté the shallots and mushrooms in butter until golden brown.
2. Divide the mushroom and shallots into equal piles in a shallow pan – place each of the trimmed chicken suprêmes on to one pile.
3. Add the Madeira and bring to the boil.
4. Add the reduced chicken stock, bring back to the boil and cover with buttered greaseproof paper.
5. Place the chicken in a preheated oven at 170 °C and cook for 12 minutes, or until the core temperature reaches 75 °C. (In the suprême with the wing bone, ensure that the meat near the bone reaches 82 °C.)
6. When cooked, remove the chicken from the pan and set aside.
7. Leave the mushrooms in the pan for the sauce. Reduce the cooking liquor until it begins to thicken naturally.
8. Add the cream and reduce to a sauce consistency.
9. Season and serve with the chicken suprêmes.

Note
The café cream sauce of Madeira wine, chicken stock and double cream is also known as café au lait.

Ingredient	4 portions	10 portions
Shallots, finely chopped	40 g	100 g
Button mushrooms, sliced	160 g	400 g
Butter	40 g	100 g
Chicken suprêmes	4	10
Madeira wine	2 tbsp	5 tbsp
Brown chicken stock	250 ml	625 ml
Double cream	200 ml	500 ml

Energy	Cals	Fat	Sat fat	Carb	Sugar	Protein	Fibre
2,126 kJ	512 kcal	37.3 g	22.4 g	2.5 g	2.2 g	38.2 g	0.8 g

14 Confit chicken leg with leeks and artichokes

Ingredient	4 portions	10 portions
Confit oil	1 litre	2.5 litres
Cloves of garlic	4	10
Bay leaf	1	3
Sprig of thyme		
Chicken legs, 200 g	4	10
Vegetable oil	50 ml	125 ml
Globe artichokes, prepared, cooked and cut into quarters	4	10
Whole leeks, blanched	2	5
Brown chicken stock	250 ml	625 ml
Butter	50 g	125 g
Chives, chopped	1 tbsp	2½ tbsp
Seasoning		

Energy	Cals	Fat	Sat fat	Carb	Sugar	Protein	Fibre	Sodium
3,622 kJ	875 kcal	75.9g	3.6g	43.3g	3.6g	43.3g	2.6g	0.8g

1 Gently heat the confit oil, add the garlic, bay and thyme.
2 Put the chicken legs in the oil and place on a medium to low heat, ensuring the legs are covered.
3 Cook gently for 3–3½ hours.
4 To test if the legs are cooked, squeeze the flesh on the thigh bone and it should just fall away.
5 When cooked, remove the legs carefully and place on a draining tray.
6 Heat the vegetable oil in a medium sauté pan, add the artichokes and leeks, colour slightly and then add the brown chicken stock.
7 Reduce the heat to a simmer and cook for 4–5 minutes; meanwhile place the confit leg on a baking tray and place in a preheated oven at 210 °C; remove when the skin is golden brown (approximately 5 minutes), taking care as the meat is delicate.
8 Place the chicken in a serving dish or on a plate, check the leeks and artichokes are cooked through, and bring the stock to a rapid boil, working in the butter to form an emulsion.
9 Add the chopped chives to the sauce and nap over the chicken legs.

Note
Confit oil is half olive oil and half vegetable oil, infused with herbs, garlic, whole spices or any specific flavour you wish to impart into the oil. The foodstuff picks up the flavour through slow cooking in the oil.

Professional tip
This dish utilises the less popular chicken legs; it is not only very cost-effective but has great depth of flavour due to the work the muscle group has done.

Poultry and game

After cooking in oil, squeeze the thigh to determine whether it is done

Remove from the oven when the chicken is golden brown

Add butter to the stock to form an emulsion

15 Roast chicken with dressing (*poulet rôti à l'anglaise*)

Ingredient	4 portions (per chicken)
Chicken, 1.25–1.5 kg	1
Salt and pepper	
Oil or butter	100 g
Onion, chopped	25 g
Chopped parsley, pinch	
Powdered thyme, pinch	
Breadcrumbs (white or wholemeal)	50 g
Liver from the chicken, raw, chopped (optional)	

Energy	Cals	Fat	Sat fat	Carb	Sugar	Protein	Fibre
1,363 kJ	327 kcal	20.4 g	3.7 g	6.7 g	0.7 g	29.5 g	0.3 g

Based on average edible portion of roasted meat (100 g).

1 Lightly season the chicken inside and out with salt.
2 Place on its side in a roasting tin.
3 Cover with 50 g of the oil or butter.
4 Place in a hot oven for approximately 20–25 minutes, then turn on to the other side.
5 Cook for a further 20–25 minutes. Baste frequently.
6 To test whether the chicken is fully cooked, pierce it with a fork between the drumstick and thigh, and hold it over a plate. The juice issuing from the chicken should not show any sign of blood. If using a temperature probe, insert in the thickest part of the leg; it should read 75 °C. Place the cooked chicken breast-side down to retain all the cooking juices.
7 To make the dressing, gently cook the onion in the remaining oil or butter without colour.
8 Season and add the herbs and breadcrumbs.
9 Mix in the liver if using.
10 Correct the seasoning and bake or steam the dressing separately, for approximately 20 minutes, until thoroughly cooked and reaching 75 °C.

Professional tip
Arranging the chicken so that it cooks sitting on one leg, then the other, and then the breast, ensures that the whole bird cooks evenly.

Healthy eating tips
- Use unsaturated oil to cook the onion.
- Keep the added salt to a minimum.
- Serve with plenty of potatoes and vegetables.

16 Chicken in red wine (*coq au vin*)

Ingredient	4 portions	10 portions
Roasting chicken, 1.5 kg	1	2–3
Lardons	50 g	125 g
Small chipolatas	4	10
Button mushrooms	50 g	125 g
Butter	50 g	125 g
Sunflower oil	3 tbsp	7 tbsp
Small button onions	12	30
Red wine	500 ml	900 ml
Beurre manié		
Butter	25 g	60 g
Flour	10 g	25 g

Energy	Cals	Fat	Sat fat	Carb	Sugar	Protein	Fibre
4,794 kJ	1,141 kcal	95.7 g	32.9 g	16.6 g	2.3 g	49.0 g	1.7 g

Using sunflower oil and hard margarine.

1. Cut the chicken as for sauté (see page 343). Blanch the lardons.
2. If the chipolatas are large, divide into two.
3. Wash and cut the mushrooms into quarters.
4. Sauté the lardons, mushrooms and chipolatas in a mixture of butter and oil. Remove when cooked.
5. Lightly season the pieces of chicken and place in the pan in the correct order (see recipe 1) with button onions. Sauté until almost cooked.
6. Place in a casserole with the mushrooms and lardons.
7. Drain off the fat from the sauté pan. Deglaze with the red wine and stock; bring to the boil.
8. Transfer the liquid to the casserole (just covering the chicken); cover with a lid and finish cooking.
9. Remove the chicken and onions, place into a clean pan.
10. Lightly thicken the liquor with a *beurre manié* of butter and flour by whisking small pieces of it into the simmering liquid.
11. Pass the sauce over the chicken and onions, add the mushrooms, chipolatas and lardons. Correct the seasoning and reheat.
12. Add the *beurre manié* slowly, mixing well, to create a thick, smooth sauce.

Healthy eating tips
- Use a well-seasoned pan to dry-fry the lardons and chipolatas, then add the mushrooms.
- Drain all the fat from the cooked chicken.
- Garnish with oven-baked croutons and serve with plenty of starchy carbohydrate and vegetables.

Sauté the other ingredients before the chicken

Sauté the chicken pieces and onion in the same pan

Add a *beurre manié*

17 Chicken pie

Ingredient	4 portions	10 portions
Chicken, 1.25–1.5 kg	1	2–3
Salt, pepper		
Streaky bacon	100 g	250 g
Button mushrooms, washed and sliced	100 g	250 g
Onion, chopped	1	2½
Chicken stock	250 ml	625 ml
Chopped parsley, pinch		
Hard-boiled egg, chopped	1	2½
Cold chicken stock		
Puff pastry (page 526)	200 g	500 g

Energy	Cals	Fat	Sat fat	Carb	Sugar	Protein	Fibre
3,357 kJ	799 kcal	62.6 g	25.1 g	16.4 g	1.9 g	43.3 g	1.8 g

Using hard margarine in the pastry.

1 Cut the chicken as for sauté (see page 343) or bone out completely and cut into 4 × 1 cm pieces.
2 Season lightly with salt and pepper.
3 Wrap each piece in very thin streaky bacon. Place in a pie dish.
4 Add the mushrooms and remainder of the ingredients, except the pastry.
5 Add sufficient cold stock to barely cover the chicken.
6 Cover with puff pastry and allow to rest in a refrigerator.
7 Egg wash and bake at 200 °C for approximately 30 minutes, until the pastry has set and the juice is simmering.
8 Reduce the heat to 160–180 °C and continue cooking for 1 hour.

Note

If the pie is to be served cold, a soaked leaf of gelatine can be laid on the chicken before covering with pastry.

Healthy eating tips

- Add little or no salt – the bacon is salty.
- Remove the skin from the chicken.
- Serve with plenty of starchy carbohydrates and a large mixed salad.

Practical Cookery 14th edition

Wrap the chicken pieces in bacon

Pour stock over the pie filling

Egg wash the edge of the pie dish and lay the pastry over

Press down gently at the edges to form a seal

Trim off the excess and then crimp the edges with your fingers

18 Tandoori chicken

Ingredient	4 portions	10 portions
Chicken, cut as for sauté (page 343)	1.25–1.5 kg	3–4 kg
Salt	1 tsp	2½ tsp
Lemon, juice of	1	2½
Natural yoghurt	300 ml	850 ml
Small onion, chopped	1	2½
Clove of garlic, peeled	1	2½
Ginger, piece of, peeled and quartered	5 cm	12 cm
Fresh hot green chilli, sliced	½	1
Garam masala	2 tsp	5 tsp
Ground cumin	1 tsp	2½ tsp
Red and yellow colouring, few drops each		

Energy	Cals	Fat	Sat fat	Carb	Sugar	Protein	Fibre
1,436 kJ	342 kcal	14.1 g	4.6 g	10.1 g	8.6 g	44.6 g	0.3 g

Estimated edible meat used; vegetable oil used.

Professional tip
If cooking in a tandoor oven, make sure the chicken is secure on the skewer, so that it cannot slip off during cooking.

Healthy eating tips
- Skin the chicken and reduce the salt by half.
- Serve with rice and vegetables.

370

Poultry and game 11

1. Cut slits bone-deep in the chicken pieces.
2. Sprinkle the salt and lemon juice on both sides of the pieces, lightly rubbing into the slits; leave for 20 minutes.
3. Combine the remaining ingredients in a blender or food processor.
4. Brush the chicken pieces on both sides, ensuring the marinade goes into the slits. Cover and refrigerate for 6–24 hours.
5. Preheat the oven to the maximum temperature.
6. Shake off as much of the marinade as possible from the chicken pieces; place on skewers and bake for 15–20 minutes or until cooked.

Serve with red onion rings and lime or lemon wedges.

Turkey dishes

19 Roast turkey

Ingredient	4 portions	10 portions
Turkey, with legs on	1 small bird	4–5 kg
Sea salt and freshly ground black pepper		
Unsalted butter, melted	250 g	625 g

Energy	Cals	Fat	Sat fat	Carb	Sugar	Protein	Fibre
1,076 kJ	257 kcal	9.6 g	3.2 g	0.0 g	0.0 g	42.0 g	0.0 g

Professional tip

The secret to keeping turkey moist is to baste as much as you can and, when the turkey is cooked, place it on its breast, breast-side down, allowing all the cavity juices to penetrate the meat.

1. Adjust an oven rack to its lowest position and remove the other racks in the oven. Preheat to 165 °C.
2. Remove turkey parts from neck and breast cavities and reserve for other uses, if desired. Dry bird well with paper towels, inside and out. Salt and pepper inside the breast cavity.
3. Set the bird on a roasting rack in a roasting pan, breast-side up, brush generously with half the butter and season with salt and pepper. Tent the bird with foil.
4. Roast the turkey for 2 hours. Remove the foil and baste with the remaining butter. Increase the oven temperature to 220 °C and continue to roast until an instant-read thermometer registers 75 °C in the thigh of the bird, about 45 minutes more.
5. Remove turkey from the oven and set aside to rest for 15 minutes before carving. Carve and serve with roast gravy, cranberry sauce, bread sauce, and either or both sausage meat and chestnut dressing and parsley and thyme dressing. Chipolata sausages and rolled rashers of grilled bacon may also be served.

20 Turkey escalopes

1. Cut 100 g slices from boned-out turkey breast and lightly flour. Gently cook on both sides in butter or oil with a minimum of colour; alternatively flour, egg and crumb the slices and shallow fry.
2. Serve with a suitable sauce and/or garnish (e.g. pan-fried turkey escalope cooked with oyster mushrooms and finished with white wine and cream).

Energy	Cals	Fat	Sat fat	Carb	Sugar	Protein	Fibre	Sodium
1,712 kJ	414 kcal	37.0g	14.0g	5.9g	0.2g	14.8g	0.3g	0.1g

Professional tip

The oil or fat must be hot enough before the escalopes are placed in the pan. If it is too cool, the breadcrumbs will absorb the fat and the dish will be greasy.

Duck dishes

21 Duck breast steaks with cherries

Ingredient	4 portions	10 portions
Duck breasts, skinned and scored	4	10
Olive oil for frying		
Cherries	300 g	750 g
Raspberry vinegar	4 tbsp	10 tbsp
Bramble jelly or redcurrant jelly	4 tbsp	10 tbsp
Extra virgin olive oil	2 tbsp	5 tbsp

Energy	Cals	Fat	Sat fat	Carb	Sugar	Protein	Fibre	Sodium
1,432 kJ	341 kcal	15.3g	3.8g	21.5g	21.5g	30.3g	0.9g	0.2g

1. Season and shallow-fry the duck breasts in olive oil, skin side down, and finish in the oven at 200 °C if required.
2. Meanwhile, place the cherries, vinegar and jelly in a pan and heat gently until the jelly has melted. Simmer and remove from the heat.
3. Stir in the extra virgin olive oil.
4. Carve the breasts into slices and serve on top of the sauce with the cherries and an accompaniment of vegetables.

22 Confit duck leg with red cabbage and green beans

1. Gently heat the confit oil, add the garlic, bay leaf and thyme.
2. Put the duck legs in the oil and place on a medium to low heat, ensuring the legs are covered.
3. Cook gently for 4–4½ hours (if using goose, 5–6½ hours may be needed).
4. To test if the legs are cooked, squeeze the flesh on the thigh bone and it should just fall away.
5. When cooked, remove the legs carefully and place on a draining tray.
6. When drained, put the confit leg on a baking tray and place in a preheated oven at 210 °C; remove when the skin is golden brown (approximately 9–10 minutes), taking care as the meat is delicate.
7. Heat the butter in a medium sauté pan and reheat the green beans.
8. Place the braised cabbage in a small pan and reheat slowly.
9. Place the duck leg in a serving dish or plate along with the red cabbage and green beans.

Ingredient	4 portions	10 portions
Confit oil	1 litre	2.5 litres
Cloves of garlic	4	10
Bay leaf	1	3
Sprig of thyme	1	2
Duck legs	4 × 200 g	10 × 200 g
Butter	50 g	125 g
Green beans, cooked and trimmed	300 g	750 g
Braised red cabbage	250 g	625 g
Seasoning		

Energy	Cals	Fat	Sat fat	Carb	Sugar	Protein	Fibre	Sodium
3,859 kJ	932 kcal	83.0 g	28.0 g	7.7 g	6.4 g	39.2 g	4.2 g	0.3 g

Professional tip

Confit oil is 50/50 olive oil and vegetable oil infused with herbs, garlic, whole spice or any specific flavour you wish to impart into the oil; then, through slow cooking in the oil, the foodstuff picks up the flavour.

Confit duck legs can be prepared up to three or four days in advance. Remove them carefully from the fat they are stored in, clean off any excess fat and place directly into the oven. This is a great timesaver in a busy service.

23 Roast duck or duckling (canard ou caneton rôti)

1. Lightly season the duck inside and out with salt.
2. Truss and brush lightly with oil.
3. Place on its side in a roasting tin, with a few drops of water.
4. Place in a hot oven for 20–25 minutes.
5. Turn on to the other side.
6. Cook for a further 20–25 minutes. Baste frequently.
7. To test if cooked, pierce with a fork between the drumstick and thigh and hold over a plate. The juice issuing from the duck should not show any signs of blood. If using a probe, the temperature should be 62 °C. If the duck is required pink, the temperature should be 57 °C.
8. Prepare the roast gravy with the stock and the sediment in the roasting tray. Correct the seasoning, remove the surface fat.
9. Serve garnished with picked watercress. Accompany with a sauceboat of hot apple sauce, a sauceboat of gravy, and game chips. Also serve a sauceboat of sage and onion dressing (recipe 24).

Ingredient	4 portions	10 portions
Duck	1	2–3
Salt		
Oil		
Brown stock	0.25 litres	600 ml
Salt, pepper		
Watercress, bunch	1	2
Apple sauce (page 127)	125 ml	300 ml

Energy	Cals	Fat	Sat fat	Carb	Sugar	Protein	Fibre
3,083 kJ	734 kcal	60.5g	16.9g	8.2g	7.8g	40.0g	1.4g

With apple sauce and watercress.

Note

Arrange the duck to cook sitting on one leg, then the other leg and then the breast, so the whole bird cooks evenly.

The temperatures in this recipe reflect industry standards for cooking duck. For food safety reasons, it is advisable to cook duck to higher temperatures.

Healthy eating tips

- Use the minimum amount of salt to season the duck and the roast gravy.
- Take care to remove all the fat from the roasting tray before making the gravy.
- This dish is high in fat and should be served with plenty of boiled new potatoes and a variety of vegetables.

24 Sage and onion dressing for duck

Ingredient	4 portions	10 portions
Onion, chopped	100 g	250 g
Duck fat or butter	100 g	250 g
Powdered sage	¼ tsp	½ tsp
Parsley, chopped	¼ tsp	½ tsp
Salt, pepper		
White or wholemeal breadcrumbs	100 g	250 g
Duck liver (optional), chopped	50 g	125 g

Energy	Cals	Fat	Sat fat	Carb	Sugar	Protein	Fibre	Sodium
1,346 kJ	320 kcal	26.0 g	8.4 g	22.0 g	2.7 g	2.9 g	1.0 g	0.2 g

Using duck fat and omitting liver.

1 Gently cook the onion in the fat without colour. Add the chopped liver (if required) and fry until cooked.
2 Add the herbs and seasoning. Mix in the crumbs. Form into thick sausage shapes, in foil.
3 Place in a tray and finish in a hot oven at 180 °C for approximately 5–10 minutes. Check with a probe that the centre has reached 75 °C.

Serve separately with roast duck.

25 Cranberry and orange dressing for duck

Ingredient	4 portions	10 portions
Cranberries	400 g	1 kg
Granulated sugar	50 g	125 g
Red wine	125 ml	310 ml
Red wine vinegar	2 tbsp	5 tbsp
Orange zest and juice	2	5

Energy	Cals	Fat	Sat fat	Carb	Sugar	Protein	Fibre
398 kJ	93 kcal	0.2 g	0.0 g	22.7 g	22.7 g	1.3 g	4.2 g

1 Place the cranberries in a suitable saucepan with the rest of the ingredients.
2 Bring to the boil and simmer gently for approximately 1 hour, stirring from time to time.
3 Remove from the heat and leave to cool. Use as required.

Note

The dressing may be liquidised if a smooth texture is required.

Cold dish

26 Terrine of chicken with vegetables

Ingredient	8–10 portions
Carrots, turnips and swedes, peeled and cut into 7 mm dice	50 g of each
Broccoli, small florets	50 g
Baby corn, cut into 7 mm rounds	50 g
French beans, cut into 7 mm lengths	50 g
Chicken (white meat only), minced	400 g
Egg whites	2
Double cream	200 ml
Salt, mill pepper	

Energy	Cals	Fat	Sat fat	Carb	Sugar	Protein	Fibre
930 kJ	226 kcal	17.3 g	9.4 g	2.0 g	1.8 g	15.5 g	0.9 g

1. Blanch all the vegetables individually in boiling salted water, ensuring that they remain firm. Refresh in cold water, and drain well.
2. Blend the chicken and egg whites in a food processor until smooth. Turn out into a large mixing bowl and gradually beat in the double cream.
3. Season with salt and mill pepper, and fold in the vegetables.
4. Line a lightly greased 1-litre terrine with cling film.
5. Spoon the farce into the mould and overlap the cling film.
6. Cover with foil, put the lid on and cook in a bain-marie in a moderate oven for about 45 minutes. Use a temperature probe to check that the centre has reached 75 °C.
7. When cooked, remove the lid and leave to cool overnight.

Healthy eating tips
- Keep the added salt to a minimum.
- Serve with plenty of salad vegetables and bread or toast (optional butter or spread).

Cut the vegetables into neat dice, rounds and florets

Line the terrine with cling film and spoon in the mixture

Cover the mixture with cling film and press down gently

Goose dish

27 Roast goose

The average weight of a goose is 5–6 kg.

1. Clean and truss the goose as for a chicken (see page 342).
2. Roast the goose using the same procedure for roasting a duck (recipe 23), with the oven at 200–230 °C. Turn it down to 180 °C after 20 minutes. Allow 15–20 minutes per 0.5 kg.

Energy	Cals	Fat	Sat fat	Carb	Sugar	Protein	Fibre
9,541 kJ	2,305 kcal	210.5g	60.0g	0.0g	0.0g	103.1g	0.0g

Guinea fowl dish

28 Suprêmes of guinea fowl with a pepper and basil coulis

Ingredient	4 portions	10 portions
Red peppers	3	7½
Olive oil	150 ml	375 ml
Fresh basil, chopped	2 tbsp	5 tbsp
Salt, pepper		
Guinea fowl suprêmes (approximately 150 g each)	4	10

Energy	Cals	Fat	Sat fat	Carb	Sugar	Protein	Fibre
904 kJ	216 kcal	4.7g	1.3g	7.8g	7.3g	35.8g	0.5g

Using chicken instead of guinea fowl.

1. Skin the peppers by brushing with oil and gently scorching in the oven or under the grill. Alternatively, use a blowtorch with great care. Once scorched, peel the skin from the peppers, cut in half and deseed.
2. Place the peppers in a food processor, blend with the olive oil and pass through a strainer.
3. Add the chopped basil and season.
4. Season the guinea fowl and either shallow-fry or grill.
5. Pour the coulis on to individual plates. Place the guinea fowl on top and serve immediately.

Game dishes

29 Pot au feu of pigeon

Ingredient	4 portions	10 portions
Squabs, legs removed	6 (approx. 2 kg)	10 (approx. 3.5 kg)
Carrot, peeled and cut into 4 laterally	1	3
Celery stick, cut into 4	1	3
Baby turnips	8	20
Medium turnips, peeled and blanched	2	4
Leek, washed, cut in rounds	1	3
Small shallots, peeled and left whole	8	20
Smoked streaky bacon, rind removed	100g	250g
Chicken/game stock	400 ml	1 litre
Bouquet garni with 4 black peppercorns and 1 clove of garlic	1	3
Salt		

Energy	Cals	Fat	Sat fat	Carb	Sugar	Protein	Fibre
1,545 kJ	367 kcal	11.2g	3.4g	11.1g	10.0g	56.2g	4.8g

1. Place the squab legs in a large casserole and arrange the vegetables tightly in one layer with the legs, add the bacon then cover with the stock to about 4 cm above the ingredients (you may need to top this up with water).
2. Add the muslin-wrapped bouquet garni. Season with salt and bring to a gentle boil.
3. Skim off any impurities, cover with a lid (leaving a small gap) and simmer gently for 50 minutes.
4. Skim off any fat or impurities, then add the squab breasts and cook for a further 12 minutes.

Note

This is a social dish, designed to be placed in the middle of the table and served with warm, crusty bread, mashed potato or buttered new potatoes.

Arrange the squab legs and vegetables in the pan

Cover with stock

Add the breasts later, as they need less time to cook

Poultry and game | 11

30 Roast partridge

Ingredient	4 portions	10 portions
Grey-legged partridges (approx. 400g each), oven-ready, with livers	4	10
Unsalted butter	20 g	50 g
Groundnut oil or vegetable oil	20 g	50 g
Salt and freshly ground pepper		
Roasting juices from veal, pork or beef	70 ml	175 ml
Water	50 ml	125 ml

Energy	Cals	Fat	Sat fat	Carb	Sugar	Protein	Fibre
2,495 kJ	596 kcal	26.7 g	7.6 g	0.3 g	0.1 g	88.5 g	0.0 g

Note

Simply roasted partridge is a great autumnal or winter base for most accompaniments: braised cabbage, roast carrots, parsnips and so on.

1. Shorten the wings and sear the partridges under a flame to remove the feather stubs. Remove any trace of gall from the liver. Wash briefly, pat dry and reserve.
2. In a roasting tray sear the wing bones and the partridges in the butter and oil for 2 minutes on each side and 2 minutes on the breast (6 minutes in total) until they are brown.
3. Season with salt and pepper, and roast in the preheated oven for 5–10 minutes, according to the size of the partridges.
4. Remove from the oven and place the partridges on a cooling wire, breast-side down. Cover loosely with aluminium foil and allow to rest.
5. In the same roasting tray, fry the livers in the remaining butter and oil until well done, and reserve. Spoon out the excess fat and add the roasting juices and water to the winglets, bring to the boil then simmer for 5 minutes.
6. Taste and season with salt and pepper, then strain through a fine sieve.
7. Serve with roasted seasonal vegetables (e.g. roast parsnips, carrots and braised cabbage). Suggested accompaniments include bread sauce, roast gravy, watercress and game chips. The fried livers may be puréed and served on croûtes of toasted bread as an accompaniment.

31 Traditional-contemporary roast grouse

Ingredient	4 portions	10 portions
Grouse		
Young grouse (approx. 750 g each)	4	10
Sage leaves	4	10
Butter	20 g	50 g
Salt and pepper		
Stock		
Oil	30 ml	75 ml
Reserved grouse wings and giblets		
Large onion, diced	1	2½
Celery stick, diced	1	2½
Carrot, diced	1	2½
Red wine	250 ml	625 ml
Water		
Thyme, sprig of		
Bay leaf	1	2½
Brandy		
Toast		
Small slices of bread	16	40
Duck fat		
To serve		
Bread sauce		
Watercress, bunches	1	2
Game chips		

Energy	Cals	Fat	Sat fat	Carb	Sugar	Protein	Fibre
3,932 kJ	943 kcal	24.7 g	7.1 g	63.8 g	9.5 g	107.4 g	5.6 g

Nutritional analysis includes accompaniments.

Note
Good-quality grouse that has not been over-hung is essential. The meat will already have a strong, pungent flavour from the birds' diet of heather.

1 Trim the wings from the young grouse, draw and reserve the livers, hearts and giblets. Season birds liberally inside and out, and put the livers and hearts back in with a sage leaf and a knob of butter. Preheat the oven to 210 °C.

2 Brown the wings and the remaining giblets in the oil with the onion, celery and carrot. Deglaze pan with red wine, cover with water and simmer for 30 minutes with the thyme and bay leaf. Strain and reserve.

3 Meanwhile, fry the bread in duck fat. Make the bread sauce and pick through the watercress.

4 Seal the birds in a little hot oil until golden, then place them at the top of the oven and roast. Cook until a probe inserted between the leg and the cavity reads 75 °C, or until the juices run clear.

5 Remove from the pan and leave the birds to rest for 10 minutes.

6 Put the roasting tray over a flame, add a splash of brandy and the stock, and allow to bubble down to a thin gravy.

7 A traditional way to serve grouse is to scoop out the livers and hearts, mash these up and serve on the toast. Place a bunch of the watercress into the grouse's cavity and put the bird and toast on to a plate with some bread sauce and game chips. Pour a little of the gravy over each bird and serve the remaining gravy separately. Alternatively, serve with apple sauce.

Bread sauce

Milk	600 ml
Onion, studded with cloves and bay leaf	1
Peppercorns	6
Fresh white breadcrumbs	100 g
Butter	50 g

1 Heat the milk to boiling point. Infuse the onion and peppercorns in the milk for 30 minutes, then remove.

2 Strain the milk and stir in the breadcrumbs.

3 Heat gently for 10 minutes until thick.

4 Stir in the butter and season.

32 Pot-roasted quail with roast carrots and mashed potato

Ingredient	4 portions	10 portions
Quails (approx. 75 g each)	8	20
Pancetta, thinly sliced	8 slices (approx. 160 g)	20 slices (approx. 420 g)
Fresh sage leaves	8	20
Vegetable oil	15 ml	40 ml
Butter	20 g	50 g
Salt and freshly ground pepper		
Carrots, peeled and cut into quarters	100 g	250 g
Oil	30 ml	75 ml
Dry white wine	125 ml	310 ml
Red wine	125 ml	310 ml
Brown stock	250 ml	625 ml
Unsalted butter	50 g	125 g
Portions of mashed potato	4 (200 g)	10 (500 g)
Chives, chopped	1 tsp	2 ½ tsp

Energy	Cals	Fat	Sat fat	Carb	Sugar	Protein	Fibre	Sodium
3,076 kJ	742 kcal	56.0 g	19.7 g	11.5 g	3.9 g	38.0 g	1.2 g	1.2 g

Chicken was used in place of quail.

1. Wash the quails thoroughly inside and out, then place them in a large colander to drain for at least 20 minutes; pat the quail dry.
2. Stuff the cavity of each bird with 1 slice of pancetta and 1 sage leaf.
3. Put the oil in a large, thick-bottomed roasting pan on a high heat. When the fat is hot, add all of the quails in a single layer and cook until browned on one side, gradually turning them, and continue cooking until they are evenly browned all over.
4. Lightly sprinkle the quails with salt and pepper, then add the carrots and cook for a couple of minutes until a slight colour appears.
5. Add the wine and brown stock then turn the birds once; let the wine bubble for about 1 minute then lower the heat to moderate and partially cover the pan. Cook the quail until the meat feels very tender when poked with a fork and comes away from the bone (approximately 35 minutes).
6. Check from time to time that there are sufficient juices in the pan to keep the birds from sticking; if this does occur, add 1 to 2 tablespoons of water at a time. When the quails are done, transfer them to a warmed tray and reserve.
7. Turn up the heat and reduce the cooking juices to a glaze – enough to coat all the birds, scraping the bottom of the pan with a spoon to loosen any cooking residues.
8. Add the unsalted butter and whisk in to form an emulsion; at this point, if the sauce splits or is too thick, add a little water and reboil.
9. Remove the carrots from the pan and place neatly on the plate with the mashed potato.
10. Pass the juices then pour them over the quail, sprinkle with chopped chives and serve immediately.

Stuff the cavity of the quail

Practical Cookery 14th edition

33 Stuffed roast quail

Ingredient	4 portions	10 portions
Quail	4	10
Forcemeat (see below)	200 g	500 g
Forcemeat		
Finely minced pork (half lean, half fat)	400 g	900 g
Quail and chicken livers	50 g	125 g
Shallot or onion, chopped	25 g	60 g
Mushroom, chopped	400 g	1 kg
Pinch of thyme		
Bay leaf	½–1	4
Salt, pepper, mixed spice		

Only plump birds with firm white fat should be selected. When prepared, the entrails are drawn but the heart and liver are retained inside the birds.

Bone out from the back, stuff with a forcemeat, made as described here, then cook by roasting, spit roasting, in a casserole or by poaching in a rich stock.

Energy	Cals	Fat	Sat fat	Carb	Sugar	Protein	Fibre	Sodium
753kJ	181kcal	11.2g	3.3g	0.2g	0.0g	19.6g	0.2g	0.1g

Assuming 75 g edible meat per quail.

1. Gently fry the pork to extract the fat.
2. Increase the heat, add the livers and the remainder of the ingredients.
3. Fry quickly to brown the livers.
4. Allow to cool, then pass through a sieve or mince finely.

Note

For food safety reasons, it is safer not to leave the livers pink. However, this will affect the overall eating quality.

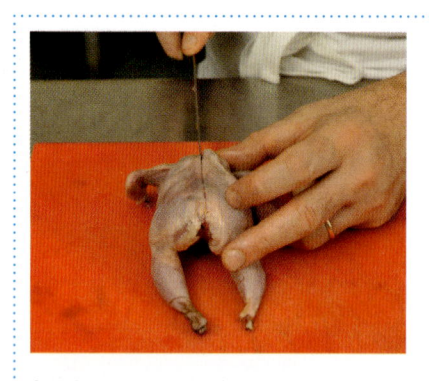

Cut down the back of the bird

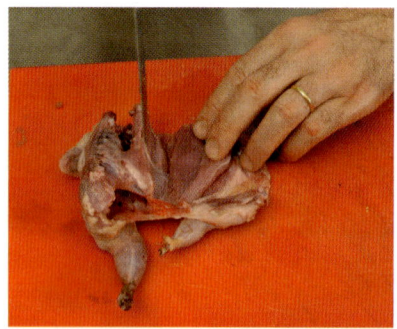

Bone it out from the back

Stuff the quail with farce

Poultry and game 11

34 Braised baron of rabbit with olives and tomatoes

Ingredient	4 portions	10 portions
Farm-raised rabbit barons (approx. 750–800 g each), including bones and trim for gravy	2	5
Carrot	1	2½
Onion	1	2½
Celery stick	1	2½
Olive oil	90 ml	225 ml
Balsamic vinegar	15 ml	40 ml
Caster sugar	10 g	25 g
Dry white wine	750 ml	1.9 litres
Butter, to brown the meat	125 ml	310 ml
Basil leaves	12	30
Black olives	32	80
Sun-dried tomato pieces	8	20
Salt and pepper		

Energy	Cals	Fat	Sat fat	Carb	Sugar	Protein	Fibre
2,365 kJ	568 kcal	41.0g	8.4g	5.5g	4.8g	44.6g	0.9g

Variation

The ingredients that give this recipe a Mediterranean influence (basil, olives and sun-dried tomatoes) can be omitted or substituted with a British theme – for example woodland mushrooms and parsnips – and served with braised cabbage.

1 Prepare the rabbits well ahead of time: cut the rabbits across at the point where the ribs end and chop the forequarters into small pieces.
2 Cut the vegetables into a mirepoix.
3 In a large saucepan, brown the bones and mirepoix in 2 tablespoons (or 5 tablespoons) of the olive oil.
4 Add the vinegar and sugar, and toss to coat. Cook until light brown.
5 Pour over almost all the white wine, reserving about 150 ml (or 375 ml) for deglazing the roasting pan later. Boil hard to reduce until the liquid has a syrupy consistency.
6 Just cover with cold water, return to the boil and skim.
7 Simmer for 1½ hours.
8 Pass the resulting stock into a bowl, wash out the saucepan and return the stock to it.
9 Bring back to the boil, skim again and, once more, return to a slow simmer until reduced by half. Reserve.
10 Cut the rabbit legs into two (thigh and drumstick), and the rack into two.
11 In a large saucepan, brown the meat cuts in foaming butter; when golden brown, add the finished stock and cook for a further 1½ hours (approximately).
12 When cooked, pass the sauce through a fine strainer, bring to the boil and reduce by half.
13 While reducing, put the rabbit into a casserole/serving dish, julienne the basil and remove the stones from the olives.
14 When the sauce is reduced by half, add the tomatoes, olives and basil. Correct the seasoning, pour over the rabbit and serve.

Note

A baron is the rear end of the rabbit – the rack and the two hind legs.

383

35 German-style saddle of hare

Ingredient	4 portions	10 portions
For the marinade		
Carrot, finely sliced	200 g	400 g
Onion, finely sliced	200 g	400 g
Celery, finely sliced	100 g	200 g
Cloves of garlic	2	5
Parsley stalks	25 g	60 g
Sprig of thyme		
Bay leaf	½	1
Cloves	2	5
Peppercorns	12	30
Red wine	500 ml	1.25 litres
Wine vinegar	125 ml	310 ml
Oil	125 ml	310 ml
For the hare		
Saddles of hare	2–4	5–10
Salt, pepper		
Cream	125 ml	310 ml
Lemon juice		

Energy	Cals	Fat	Sat fat	Carb	Sugar	Protein	Fibre
3,561 kJ	859 kcal	60.6 g	14.3 g	9.4 g	7.1 g	47.3 g	3.6 g

1. Season the hare with salt and pepper, and place into a suitable container (e.g. stainless steel or china).
2. Cover with the marinade ingredients.
3. Refrigerate, turning the joints over frequently, for approximately 24 hours.
4. Remove the saddles from the marinade and dry thoroughly.
5. Remove the vegetables from the marinade and place into a roasting tray. Place the saddles on top of the vegetables and roast in the oven at 180 °C.
6. When the saddle is three-quarters cooked, remove the vegetables.
7. Add the cream to the roasting tray and continue cooking. Baste the meat frequently with the cream. Keep the meat pink.
8. Remove the saddles from the tray. Separate the meat from the bone and slice each side into four pieces.
9. Add a few drops of lemon juice to the cooking liquor, correct the seasoning and consistency, and pass through a fine strainer. Serve the sauce with the saddles.

Suitable accompaniments include: cabbage; braised chestnuts or chestnut purée; Brussels sprouts with chestnuts; purée of celeriac, celeriac and parsnips or celeriac and onion; buttered noodles.

Note

The saddle is a joint cut from the back of the hare, usually in a similar way to a short saddle of lamb – that is, a pair of uncut loins. All skin and sinew must be removed and the joint trimmed before use. If desired, the joint may be larded with pork fat.

A saddle of hare yields one or two portions, depending on its size.

It is not essential to marinade the saddle if obtained from a young hare but, if there is any doubt as to its tenderness, or if it is to be kept for a few days, then the joint should be marinated, as in this recipe.

Variation

- After the saddle is removed, the roasting tray can be deglazed with brandy, whisky or gin.
- Sliced mushrooms (cultivated or wild) can be added to the sauce.

36 Medallions of venison with buttered cabbage and haricots blancs

Energy	Cals	Fat	Sat fat	Carb	Sugar	Protein	Fibre	Sodium
4,068 kJ	976 kcal	62.0 g	34.0 g	31.8 g	10.0 g	72.0 g	8.2 g	1.6 g

Using salted butter and 250 g venison medallion.

Medallions of venison

1 Preheat the oven to 190 °C.
2 Heat approximately half of the oil in a heavy frying pan and sear the venison loin, add salt and pepper, place in the oven in an ovenproof pan or on a baking tray, and cook for 6–8 minutes medium rare or according to taste.

Haricots blancs

1 Cook all the ingredients together in a vacuum pack bag in the steamer for 25–30 minutes (approximately).
2 Allow to chill for 1 hour, then place in the fridge until required for the buttered cabbage.

Buttered cabbage

1 Sweat the shallots, garlic and aromats in the remaining oil.
2 Add the cabbage and sweat for a further 5 minutes.
3 Add the butter and stock, and reduce until emulsified and cooked.
4 To finish, season with salt add the cooked haricots blancs.

To complete the dish

Serve the venison on a bed of the buttered cabbage on suitable plates. This dish may be finished with a cordon of red jus.

Ingredient	4 portions	10 portions
Vegetable oil	25 ml	75 ml
Medallions of venison	4	10
Haricots blancs		
Beans, soaked	200 g	500 g
Chicken stock	100 ml	250 ml
Clove of garlic	½	1
Bay leaf	½	1
Thyme	1 g	2 g
Buttered cabbage		
Shallots, finely sliced	200 g	500 g
Garlic cloves, crushed and chopped	1	2
Bay leaves	1	2
Thyme	1 g	2 g
Cabbage, stalk removed	600 g	1500 g
Butter	240 g	600 g
Chicken stock	240 ml	600 ml
Salt	8 g	20 g

Ingredients for medallions of venison with buttered cabbage and haricots blancs

Sweat the cabbage with shallots, garlic and aromats

Sear the venison in a hot pan using tongs to turn it as it sears

Once the venison has relaxed, carve into medallions

37 Medallions of venison with celeriac purée and braised red cabbage

Celeriac purée

1. Cook the celeriac with the milk and butter in a vacuum pack bag for 40 minutes in the steamer.
2. Place the contents of the bag into the thermomix (or food processor) and add the cream.
3. Blitz for 8 minutes and then pass through a fine sieve (drum if available).
4. Season with salt and add the vinegar.
5. Chill and keep for service.

Alternatively, if you do not have a thermomix produce a traditional celeriac purée.

Braised red cabbage

1. Salt the cabbage for 10 minutes and then wash in water.
2. Dry in a cloth and then add the rest of the ingredients, retaining half the oil for step 3.
3. Place in a suitable pan, lightly oiled with olive oil. Braise in the oven at 150–200 °C for 1 hour.

To complete the dish

1. Prepare the medallions as for recipe 36.
2. Serve on suitable plates with the celeriac and cabbage. The plates may be finished with a cordon of game jus or red wine jus.

Ingredient	4 portions	10 portions
Medallions of venison	4	10
Celeriac purée		
Celeriac, in 2 cm dice	550 g	1400 g
Milk	300 ml	750 ml
Butter	50 g	125 g
Cream	200 ml	500 ml
Salt (approx.)	2 g	5 g
Vinegar		
Braised red cabbage		
Red cabbage	150 g	375 g
Salt, pepper		
Butter	50 g	125 g
Cooking apples, finely chopped	100 g	250 g
Caster sugar	10 g	25 g
Vinegar or red wine	50 ml	125 ml
Olive oil	25 ml	62 ml

Energy	Cals	Fat	Sat fat	Carb	Sugar	Protein	Fibre	Sodium
2,896 kJ	694 kcal	42.0 g	22.3 g	13.9 g	13.1 g	62.0 g	7.1	0.7 g

Using salted butter, semi-skimmed milk, single cream and red wine.

Healthy eating tip

For the celeriac purée, semi-skimmed milk could be used and natural yoghurt could be used instead of cream.

12 Vegetables and vegetable protein

Recipes included in this chapter

No.	Recipe	Page
	Root vegetables	
1	Buttered carrots (*carottes au beurre*)	398
2	Carrots in cream sauce (*carottes à la crème*)	398
3	Purée of carrots (*purée de carottes*)	399
4	Beetroot (*betterave*)	399
5	Goats' cheese and beetroot tarts with salad of watercress	400
6	Parsnips (*panais*)	401
7	Buttered celeriac, turnip or swede	401
8	Purée of celeriac, turnips, swede or parsnips	402
9	Salsify	402
	Bulbs	
10	Fried onions (*oignons sautées ou oignons lyonnaise*)	403
11	Caramelised button onions	403
12	Braised fennel with black olives and cardamom	404
13	Braised leeks with garlic and olives	404
14	French-fried onions (*oignons frites à la française*)	405
	Flower heads	
15	Broccoli	406
16	Cauliflower (*chou-fleur nature*)	407
17	Cauliflower au gratin	407
	Fungi	
18	Grilled mushrooms (*champignons grillés*)	408
19	Stuffed mushrooms (*champignons farcis*)	408
	Seeds and pods	
20	Broad beans	409
21	Mangetout	409
22	French beans (*haricots verts*)	410
23	French-style peas (*petit pois à la française*)	410
24	Corn on the cob	411
25	Okra in cream sauce	412
26	Okra curry	412
	Tubers	
27	Plain boiled potatoes (*pommes nature*)	413
28	Parsley potatoes (*pommes persillées*)	413
29	New potatoes (*pommes nouvelles*)	414
30	Mashed potatoes (*pommes purées*)	415
31	Duchess potatoes	416
32	Steamed potatoes in their jackets (*pommes vapeur*)	417
33	Baked jacket potatoes (*pommes au four*)	417
34	Roast potatoes (*pommes rôties*)	418
35	Chateau potatoes	418
36	Fried or chipped potatoes	419
37	Sauté potatoes	420
38	Sauté potatoes with onions (*pommes lyonnaise*)	421
39	New potato rissoles (*pommes nouvelles rissolées*)	422
40	Parmentier potatoes	422
41	Noisette potatoes (*pommes noisettes*)	423
42	Cocotte potatoes (*pommes cocotte*)	423
43	Fondant potatoes	424
44	Savoury potatoes (*pommes boulangères*)	425
45	Macaire potatoes (potato cakes)	426
46	Byron potatoes (*pommes Byron*)	427
47	Croquette potatoes	427
48	Swiss potato cakes (*rösti*)	428
49	Potatoes cooked in milk with cheese	429
50	Potatoes with bacon and onions	429
51	Delmonico potatoes	430
52	Jerusalem artichokes in cream sauce (*topinambours à la crème*)	430
	Leafy vegetables	
53	Spring greens (*choux de printemps*)	431
54	Leaf spinach (*épinards en branches*)	431
55	Spinach purée	432
56	Cabbage (*chou vert*)	432
57	Braised red cabbage (*choux à la flamande*)	433
58	Brussels sprouts (*choux de bruxelles*)	434
	Stems	
59	Artichoke bottoms	434
60	Globe artichokes	436

61	Asparagus points or tips	437
62	Asparagus wrapped in puff pastry with Gruyère	437
63	Braised chicory	439
64	Shallow-fried chicory	439
65	Kohlrabi	440

Vegetable fruits

66	Tomato concassé	440
67	Stuffed tomatoes	442
68	Fried aubergine (*aubergine frite*)	443
69	Stuffed aubergine	443
70	Marrow	444
71	Marrow provençale	444
72	Shallow-fried courgettes	445
73	Deep-fried courgettes	445
74	Fettuccine of courgette with chopped basil and balsamic vinegar	446
75	Courgette flowers	446
76	Roast butternut squash	447
77	Roast squash or pumpkin with cinnamon and ginger	448
78	Stuffed peppers (*piment farci*)	449

Mixed vegetable dishes

79	Mixed vegetables (*macédoine* or *jardinière de legumes*)	450
80	Ratatouille	450
81	Ratatouille pancakes with a cheese sauce	451
82	Roasted vegetables	452
83	Tempura	452
84	Vegetable biryani	454
85	Vegetable curry with rice pilaff	455

Vegetable protein

86	Crispy deep-fried tofu	456
87	Chinese vegetable and seitan stir-fry	456
88	Papaya and soya bean salad	457
89	Thai-style Quorn and vegetable curry	458

Other vegetarian dishes

90	Cheese fritters (*beignets au fromage*)	459
91	Cheese soufflé (*soufflé au fromage*)	460

Salads

92	Salad leaves	461
93	Mixed salad (*salade panachée*)	461
94	Green salad (*salade verte*)	462
95	French salad (*salade française*)	462
96	Radishes (*radis*)	463
97	Cucumber	463
98	Tomatoes (*tomates*)	464
99	Tomato salad (*salade de tomates*)	464
100	Tomato and cucumber salad (*salade de tomates et concombres*)	465
101	Beetroot salad (*salade de betterave*)	465
102	Coleslaw	466
103	Potato salad	466
104	Waldorf salad	467
105	French bean salad (*salade de haricots verts*)	468
106	Vegetable salad/Russian salad	468
107	Greek-style mushrooms	469
108	Haricot bean salad	469
109	Three bean salad	470
110	Caesar salad	470
111	Niçoise salad	471
112	Avocado and bacon salad	471

Vegetables

Vegetable is a culinary term that generally refers to the edible part of a plant. All parts of herbaceous plants eaten as food by humans, in whole or in part, are normally considered to be vegetables. Mushrooms, though categorised as fungi, are also commonly considered vegetables. In general, vegetables are thought of as being savoury, not sweet, although there are many exceptions. In most countries they are associated with poultry, meat or fish as part of a meal or as an ingredient. Nuts, grains, herbs, spices and culinary fruits (see below) are not normally considered to be vegetables. Some vegetables are botanically classed as fruits – tomatoes are berries and avocados are drupes – but both are commonly used as vegetables because they are not sweet.

Vegetables can include leaves (lettuce), stems (asparagus), roots (carrots), flowers (broccoli), bulbs (garlic), seeds (peas and beans) and vegetable fruits (such as cucumbers, squash, pumpkins and capsicums).

- A **root** is the part of the plant growing down into the soil to support the plant and take up water and nutrients.
- A **stem** is the part of the plant usually above the ground that bears the buds, leaves, flowers and fruit (although it can be underground). A young stem is called a shoot.
- A **bulb** is an organ in some plants which consist of an underground axis with many thick overlapping leaves.
- A **flower** is the reproductive part of the plant, often brightly coloured to attract insects.

Vegetables and vegetable protein

- A **tuber** is an underground stem used for storing food; it is also able to produce new plants.
- A **leaf** is the part of the plant that makes food by photosynthesis.
- A **pod** is the part in some plants where the seeds are developed, for example pea pods.
- A **seed** is the reproductive mechanism of the plant.
- **Fruits** are the part of the flowering plant that contains the seeds.

Vegetables are an important part of our diet, so it is essential to pay attention to quality, purchasing, storage and efficient preparation and cooking if the nutritional content of vegetables is to be conserved.

The nutrient content of different types of vegetables varies considerably. With the exception of pulses, vegetables provide little protein or fat, but they do contain water-soluble vitamins such as vitamin B and vitamin C, fat-soluble vitamins including vitamin A and vitamin D, as well as carbohydrates and minerals. Root vegetables contain starch or sugar for energy, a small but valuable amount of protein, some mineral salts and vitamins. They are also useful sources of cellulose and water. Green vegetables are rich in mineral salts and vitamins, particularly vitamin C and carotene. The greener the leaf, the larger the quantity of vitamins present. The chief mineral salts are calcium and iron.

Vegetables are also an excellent source of antioxidants, which can lower the risk of heart disease, cancer and diabetes-related damage, and even slow down the body's natural ageing process.

Purchasing and selection

The purchasing of vegetables is affected by:
- the perishable nature of the products
- varying availability owing to seasonal fluctuations, and supply and demand
- the effects of preservation (for example, freezing, drying and canning).

Fresh vegetables are living organisms and will lose quality quickly if not stored and handled properly. Automation in harvesting and packaging speeds the handling process and helps retain quality.

Quality points

Root vegetables must be:
- clean, free from soil
- firm, not soft or spongy
- sound
- free from blemishes
- of an even size
- of an even shape.

Green vegetables must be absolutely fresh and have leaves that are bright in colour, crisp and not wilted. In addition:
- cabbages and Brussels sprouts should be compact and firm
- cauliflowers should have closely grown flowers, a firm white head and not too much stalk or too many outer leaves
- peas and beans should be crisp and of medium size; pea pods should be full and beans not stringy
- blanched stems must be firm, white, crisp and free from soil.

Potatoes must be inspected and selected before buying or on delivery.
- Choose firm, smooth ones.
- Avoid excessively wrinkled, withered, cracked potatoes.
- Do not buy those that have a lot of sprouts or green areas.

Grading

The EU vegetable quality grading system is as follows:
- **Extra class**: produce of the highest quality
- **Class 1**: produce of good quality
- **Class 2**: produce of reasonably good quality
- **Class 3**: produce of low market quality.

Seasonal availability

With the advances and development of transportation and refrigeration, fruit and vegetables can be purchased from all over the world and therefore, in many cases, seasons do not exist: for example, we can enjoy strawberries all year round. However, the UK strawberry season starts in late May/early June – local strawberries are full of flavour, while often imported strawberries lack flavour. For this reason, purchasing locally from local farms and specialist growers is popular, so knowing when vegetables are in season is important.

Provenance (knowing where our food comes from) has also become increasingly important as the consumer is now more concerned about the environment and carbon omissions; restricting the amount of food

Table 12.1 UK vegetable availability according to season

Spring (March, April, May)	Summer (June, July, August)	Autumn (September, October, November)	Winter (December, January, February)
Asparagus	Aubergine	Beetroot	Beetroot
Cauliflower	Beetroot	Carrots	Brussels sprouts
Cucumber	Broad beans	Celeriac	Cabbage
Jersey royal new potatoes	Broccoli	Fennel	Cauliflower
Purple sprouting broccoli	Carrots	Field mushrooms	Celeriac
Radishes	Courgettes	Kale	Chicory
Savoy cabbage	Cucumber	Leeks	Fennel
Sorrel	Fennel	Lettuce	Jerusalem artichokes
Spinach	Fresh peas	Marrows	Kale
Spring greens	Garlic	Potatoes	Leeks
Spring onions	Green beans	Pumpkins	Parsnips
Watercress	Lettuce and salad leaves	Rocket	Potatoes
	New potatoes	Sorrel	Red cabbage
	Radishes	Squashes	Swede
	Rocket	Sweet corn	Turnips
	Runner beans	Tomatoes	
	Salad onions	Watercress	
	Sorrel		
	Tomatoes		
	Watercress		

Source: Love British Food (www.lovebritishfood.co.uk)

travelling around the world as aircraft cargo has become an important issue. Consumers are also interested in the traceability of food – where it comes from, how it is grown and the welfare of farm workers. EU regulations require the food industry to trace the food, how food is farmed and how the animals are looked after and fed.

Storing vegetables

The fresher the vegetables, the better the flavour, so ideally they should not be stored at all. However, as storage is necessary in many cases, it should be for the shortest time possible.

Many root and non-root vegetables that grow underground can be stored over winter in a root cellar or other similarly cool, dark and dry place, to prevent the growth of mould, greening and sprouting. Care should be taken to understand the properties and vulnerabilities of the particular roots to be stored. These vegetables can last through to early spring and be almost as nutritious as when fresh.

Leafy vegetables lose moisture, and vitamin C degrades rapidly, during storage. They should be stored for as short a time as possible in a cool place in either a plastic bag or sealed plastic container. Green vegetables lose vitamin C quickly if they are bruised, damaged, stored for too long, prepared too early or overcooked.

- Store all vegetables in a cool, dry, well-ventilated room at an even temperature of 4–8 °C, which will help to minimise spoilage. Check vegetables daily and discard any that are unsound.
- Remove root vegetables from their sacks and store in bins or racks.
- Store green vegetables on well-ventilated racks.
- Store salad vegetables in a cool place and leave in their containers.
- Store frozen vegetables between −18 °C and −20 °C. Keep a check on use-by dates, damaged packages and any signs of freezer burn.
- You can store potatoes for several months without affecting their quality; they should be stored at a constant temperature (3 °C). If it is not possible to store them in this way, buying fresh potatoes regularly is best practice. There are three essential rules to bear in mind when storing potatoes: dry, dark and cool. You should avoid light as this will cause sprouting and, eventually, the greening effect, which contains mild toxins; if you have inadvertently purchased potatoes with this green tinge, remove the green bits and

Vegetables and vegetable protein 12

the rest of the potato is then fine to use. The storage of a potato is perhaps the most important aspect of its life – the closer the temperature is to freezing point, the quicker the potato starch coverts to sugar, producing a sweet flesh, but a loss of structure and, often, discoloration.

Food safety ⚠

- If vegetables are stored at the incorrect temperature micro-organisms may develop.
- If vegetables are stored in damp conditions moulds may develop.
- To prevent bacteria from raw vegetables passing on to cooked vegetables, store them in separate areas.
- Thaw out frozen vegetables correctly and *never* refreeze them once they have thawed out.

Preparing vegetables

Vegetables should be washed to remove any residue, chemicals and impurities before peeling. Peeling removes the outer skin of the vegetable or fruit; not all vegetables and fruit require peeling – this will depend on the type of fruit and vegetables and the recipe.

Cuts of vegetables

The size and shape to which the vegetables are cut may vary according to their type and use.

1 Large mirepoix
2 Small mirepoix
3 Paysanne
4 Sliced courgette
5 Turned vegetables
6 Finely diced onion
7 Tomato petals
8 Tomato concassé (gros brunoise)
9 Carrot block
10 Carrot strips
11 Julienne
12 Brunoise
13 Large block of mooli
14 Flat block
15 Jardinière
16 Macédoine

▲ Cuts of vegetables

391

Cutting vegetables into julienne (strips)

1 Cut the vegetables into 2 cm lengths (short julienne).

2 Cut the lengths into thin slices.

3 Cut the slices into thin strips.

4 Double the length gives a long julienne, used for garnishing (e.g. salads, meats, fish and poultry dishes).

Cutting vegetables into brunoise (small dice)

1 Cut the vegetables into convenient-sized lengths.

2 Cut the lengths into 2 mm slices.

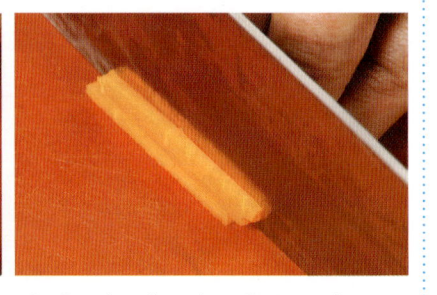

3 Cut the slices into 2 mm strips.

4 Cut the strips into 2 mm squares.

Vegetables and vegetable protein

There are at least four accepted methods of cutting **paysanne**. In order to cut economically, the shape of the vegetables should dictate which method to choose. All are cut thinly.
- 1 cm sided triangles.
- 1 cm sided squares.
- 1 cm diameter rounds.
- 1 cm diameter rough-sided rounds.

Concassé means roughly chopped. Skinned and deseeded tomatoes are roughly chopped for many food preparations (see recipe 66). The term is also used to refer to skinned and deseeded tomatoes that are cut into neat strips or cubes and used as a garnish.

Ready-prepared potatoes

Potatoes are obtainable in many convenience forms: peeled, turned, cut into various shapes for frying, or scooped into balls (*Parisienne*) or olive shaped.
- Chips are available fresh, frozen, chilled or vacuum packed.
- Frozen potatoes are available as croquettes, hash browns, sauté and roast.
- Mashed potato powder and flakes are also available.

Cooking vegetables

Approximate times only are given in the recipes in this chapter for the cooking of vegetables, as quality, age, freshness and size all affect the length of cooking time required. Young, freshly picked vegetables will need to be cooked for a shorter time than vegetables that have been allowed to grow older and that may have been stored after picking.

As a general rule, all root vegetables (with the exception of new potatoes) are started off by cooking in cold salted water. Vegetables that grow above the ground are started in boiling salted water; this is so that they may be cooked as quickly as possible for the minimum period of time, so that maximum flavour, food value and colour are retained.

Blanching

Delicate vegetables – particularly green vegetables – can be blanched in salted boiling water and then refreshed in ice-cold water to arrest the cooking process. The main reason for this is because, between the temperatures of 66 °C and 77 °C, chlorophyll is unstable. Chlorophyll is the green pigment in any plant that photosynthesises. For this reason it is important to get through this temperature zone as quickly as possible.

Steaming

All vegetables cooked by boiling may also be cooked by steaming. The vegetables are prepared in exactly the same way as for boiling, placed into steamer trays, lightly seasoned with salt and steamed under pressure for the minimum period of time in order to conserve maximum food value and retain colour. High-speed steam cookers are ideal for this purpose and, because of the speed of cooking they offer, batch cooking (cooking in small quantities throughout the service) can be practised instead of cooking large quantities prior to service, refreshing and reheating.

Frying

Many vegetables are cooked from raw by the stir-fry method, a quick and nutritious method of cooking. Vegetables may also be deep fried with a protective coating, such as tempura vegetables in a tempura batter. Vegetables may also be shallow fried in butter or vegetable oil, for example shallow-fried courgettes.

Health and safety

Make sure that vegetables are dry before being placed into hot oil. Make sure that every chef knows the fire drill and that they are confident in the procedures and systems for frying. Always have a spider and basket at hand when you are deep frying in order to remove the food quickly and safely if there is a problem. Always wear protective clothing when frying: it is safer to wear a chef's jacket with long sleeves rather than short sleeves.

Stewing

Stewing is an old, traditional method of cooking vegetables. The vegetables are cut into even pieces, gently sweated on the stove in a little oil, then a stock or tomato juice is added and allowed to simmer on the stove or in an oven.

The stewed vegetables may be flavoured with chopped herbs and/or spices. A classical stewed vegetable dish is ratatouille, which consists of aubergines, peppers, courgettes, onions and tomatoes in their juices.

Braising

Vegetables that are most suitable for braising include potatoes, onions, cabbage, fennel, and celery. In most cases vegetables are blanched (potatoes are the exception) and placed in a shallow pan with stock to come two-thirds of the way up, so not covering the vegetable.

> **Healthy eating tips**
> - Cook vegetables *al dente*.
> - Cook, reheat and serve immediately.
> - Use olive oil in place of butter.
> - Avoid the use of cream – use fromage frais or yoghurt instead.
> - Do not over-season – reduce the amount of salt used in cooking vegetables.

Cooking potatoes

Potatoes are tubers. They can have white, brown, purple or red skin, and white or golden flesh. Several named varieties of potato are grown in the UK and these will be available according to the season. The different varieties have differing characteristics and some are more suitable for certain methods of cooking than others (see chart and Table 12.2). The careful selection of potatoes to suit the job in hand is essential.

Cooked potatoes may have different textures, depending on whether they are 'waxy' or 'floury' varieties. This is due to changes that happen to the potato cells during cooking. These differences influence the performance of the potato when cooked in different ways (for example, boiling versus roasting).

- 'Waxy' potatoes are more solid than floury potatoes and hold their shape when boiled, but do not mash well. They are particularly suitable for baked and layered potato dishes such as boulangère potatoes. Popular varieties include Cara and Charlotte. Waxy potatoes are translucent and may have a moist and pasty feel.
- 'Floury' potatoes are especially popular in the UK. They are brighter and granular in appearance, leaving a drier feel. They are suitable for baking, mashing and chipping as they have a soft, dry texture when cooked. They are not suitable for boiling, however, because they tend to disintegrate. Popular varieties of floury potato include King Edward and Maris Piper.

During cooking, the starch in the potato starts to absorb water and swell in size. Potatoes need to be cooked for sufficient time to gelatinise the starch or they will look and taste undercooked.

Table 12.2 Potato varieties and recommended cooking methods

Variety	Methods of cookery
Cara	Boil, bake, chip, wedge
Charlotte	Boil, salad use
Desiree	Boil, roast, bake, chip, mash, wedge
Golden Wonder	Boil, roast, crisps
King Edward	Boil, bake, roast, mash, chip
Maris Piper	Boil, roast, bake, chip
Pink Fir Apple	Boil, salad use
Premiere	Boil
Record	Crisps
Romano	Boil, bake, roast, mash
Saxon	Boil, bake, chip
Wilja	Boil, bake, chip, mash

- **Baking**: long slow cooking is best for baked potatoes. The skin becomes very crisp and turns darker because the starch just below the skin converts to sugar, which browns in heat. Make sure you cut a slit in the potato as soon as it comes out of the oven so the interior doesn't steam, which makes for a heavier consistency.
- **Mashing**: mashed potatoes can be made from many varieties of potato. The starch in the potatoes, once again, absorbs water and swells during the cooking process. Then, when the potato is mashed or riced, the cells break open, releasing more starch, which makes the potatoes creamy and smooth. If you boil potatoes for mashing, return them to the hot pan after draining and shake over a medium heat for 2–3 minutes to dry the potatoes. Whatever the cooking method, add butter when you begin mashing. The butter coats the cells and the starch so they absorb less liquid, making the potatoes less gluey and fluffier. The slower the mash is cooked the better for the starch as it has more structure in the final mixing process, allowing the potato to hold in more fat/liquid than if cooked by the more traditional quicker method. Bring the potatoes up to the boil from cold as normal and boil for 2–3 minutes, remove and rinse in cold water, then repeat the process of boiling from cold and turn the heat down, not even to a simmer. This will obviously take longer but will reduce the water absorption rate dramatically due to the starch wall created by the first process.

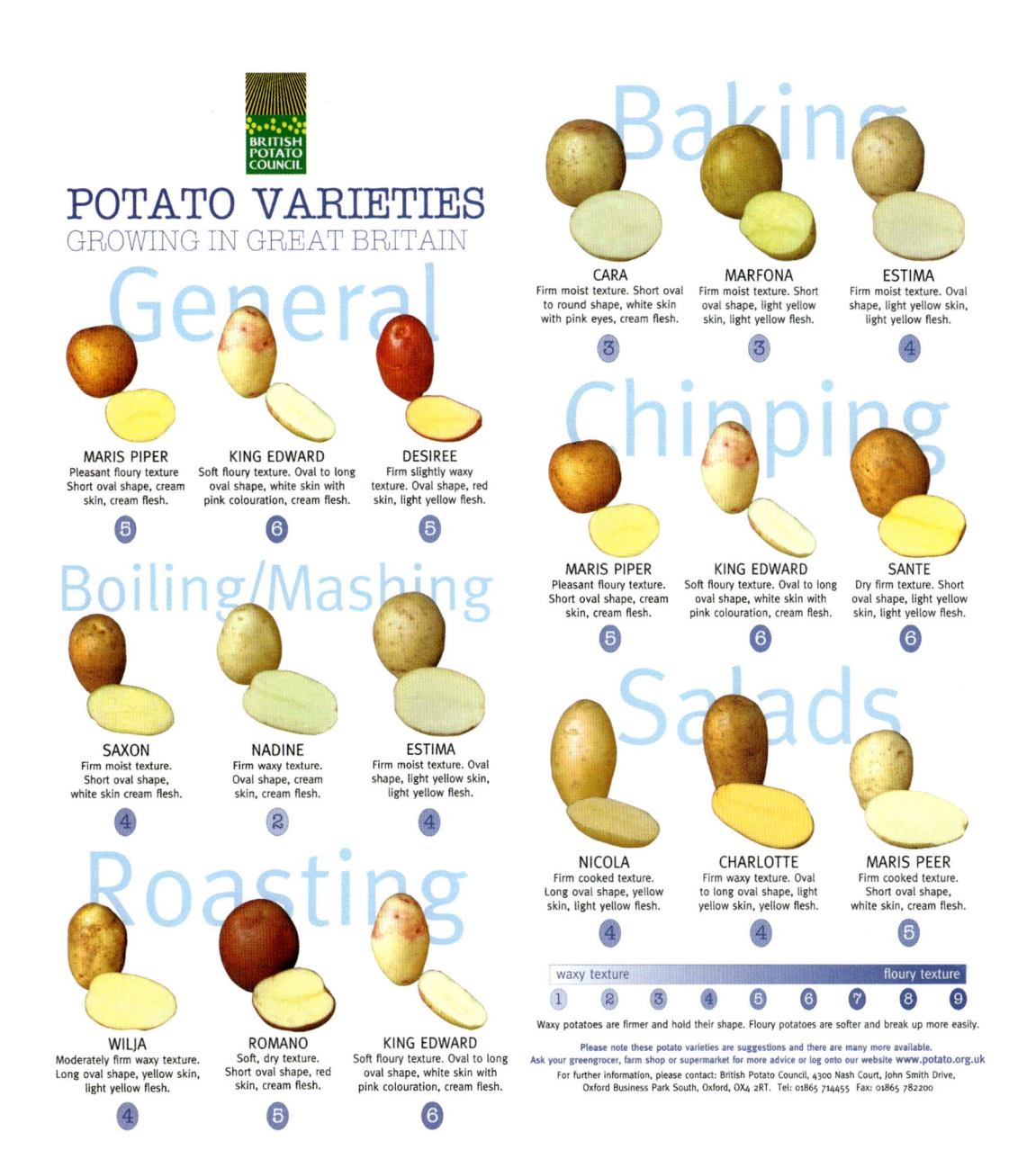

Vegetables and vegetable protein

POTATO VARIETIES GROWING IN GREAT BRITAIN

General

MARIS PIPER — Pleasant floury texture. Short oval shape, cream skin, cream flesh. ⑤

KING EDWARD — Soft floury texture. Oval to long oval shape, white skin with pink colouration, cream flesh. ⑥

DESIREE — Firm slightly waxy texture. Oval shape, red skin, light yellow flesh. ⑤

Boiling/Mashing

SAXON — Firm moist texture. Short oval shape, white skin cream flesh. ④

NADINE — Firm waxy texture. Oval shape, cream skin, cream flesh. ②

ESTIMA — Firm moist texture. Oval shape, light yellow skin, light yellow flesh. ④

Roasting

WILJA — Moderately firm waxy texture. Long oval shape, yellow skin, light yellow flesh. ④

ROMANO — Soft, dry texture. Short oval shape, red skin, cream flesh. ⑤

KING EDWARD — Soft floury texture. Oval to long oval shape, white skin with pink colouration, cream flesh. ⑥

Baking

CARA — Firm moist texture. Short oval to round shape, white skin with pink eyes, cream flesh. ③

MARFONA — Firm moist texture. Short oval shape, light yellow skin, light yellow flesh. ③

ESTIMA — Firm moist texture. Oval shape, light yellow skin, light yellow flesh. ④

Chipping

MARIS PIPER — Pleasant floury texture. Short oval shape, cream skin, cream flesh. ⑤

KING EDWARD — Soft floury texture. Oval to long oval shape, white skin with pink colouration, cream flesh. ⑥

SANTE — Dry firm texture. Short oval shape, light yellow skin, light yellow flesh. ⑥

Salads

NICOLA — Firm cooked texture. Long oval shape, yellow skin, light yellow flesh. ④

CHARLOTTE — Firm waxy texture. Oval to long oval shape, light yellow skin, yellow flesh. ④

MARIS PEER — Firm cooked texture. Short oval shape, white skin, cream flesh. ⑤

waxy texture ① ② ③ ④ ⑤ ⑥ ⑦ ⑧ ⑨ floury texture

Waxy potatoes are firmer and hold their shape. Floury potatoes are softer and break up more easily.

Please note these potato varieties are suggestions and there are many more available. Ask your greengrocer, farm shop or supermarket for more advice or log onto our website www.potato.org.uk
For further information, please contact: British Potato Council, 4300 Nash Court, John Smith Drive, Oxford Business Park South, Oxford, OX4 2RT. Tel: 01865 714455 Fax: 01865 782200

- **Roasting**: roast potatoes are simply cut into chunks and parboiled slowly until just cooked on the inside. Drain and toss in a liberal amount of olive oil and seasoning, then roast at a high temperature (220 °C) for 15 minutes. Remove, turn the temperature down to 180 °C and baste every 5 minutes to ensure a crisp coat all over. Once cooked serve immediately, as prolonged holding will inevitably cause the inside to steam, making the outside soft and leathery.

Yield

- 0.5 kg of old potatoes will yield approximately three portions.
- 0.5 kg of new potatoes will yield approximately four portions.
- 1.5 kg of old potatoes will yield approximately ten portions.
- 1.25 kg of new potatoes will yield approximately ten portions.

Finishing vegetable dishes

It is important to finish vegetable dishes at the point of service to retain their temperature and, for green vegetables, so that they retain their colour. There are a variety of finishes for vegetable dishes based on the individual recipes. Some vegetables are simply brushed with butter or olive oil, while some are finished with pine nuts, chopped mixed herbs, cream, cheese sauce, toasted almonds or toasted breadcrumbs with mixed herbs.

Holding and serving

As soon as vegetables have been cooked or reheated for service, serve immediately at the correct temperature (at least 65 °C). Vegetables such as French beans, broccoli and carrots loose heat very quickly. Vegetables on a buffet service must be served in batches and replenished regularly. Do not leave vegetables out on a hotplate for long periods as green vegetables will lose their colour as well as their vitamin C content.

Vegetable protein

According to the Vegetarian Society, vegetarian diets are consistent with dietary guidelines and can meet recommended dietary allowances for nutrients. You can get enough protein from a vegetarian diet as long as the variety of foods and the amounts consumed are adequate. Alternative sources of essential nutrients when following a vegetarian diet include fruits and vegetables; cereals, grains and pulses; nuts and seeds; dairy products such as milk, cheese and eggs; and vegetable protein.

Soya products

The soybean is an important global food source from which many products are made. Its leguminous seeds are high in protein and contain important amino acids, which are essential and cannot be made in the body. Soya flour is used to boost the protein content of a variety of dishes.

Tofu (also known as bean curd) is a product of the soybean. To produce tofu, soybeans are boiled, puréed and pressed through a sieve to produce soya milk. The milk is then processed in a similar way to soft cheese.

There are different types of tofu, depending on how much water has been pressed out of it. The more water is pressed out, the firmer it becomes, and the more fat and protein it contains. The most common types of tofu are silken, soft, medium, firm, extra firm and super firm.

- **Silken tofu:** undrained, unpressed Japanese-style tofu has the highest water content. It has different consistencies depending on how much soy protein it contains. Silken tofu is used in creamy and blended foods such as smoothies, desserts, puddings and salad dressings. It can also be used as an egg substitute in baking.
- **Regular tofu:** pressed, with a spongy texture. It comes in a number of varieties depending on how much water is pressed out.
- **Soft tofu:** the Chinese-style equivalent to silken tofu. It is used in the same way as silken tofu.
- **Medium tofu:** soft and delicate, and denser than silken tofu. It works well in soups such as miso.
- **Firm tofu:** absorbs flavours well and can be stir- and pan-fried. It can be used as a substitute for ricotta cheese.
- **Extra firm tofu:** holds its shape well, is good for slicing and dicing, and is used for shallow and deep frying. It can also be baked and grilled, crumbled and used as a substitute for ground meat.
- **Super firm tofu:** a very dense tofu with a high protein content.

Always keep tofu in a refrigerator and follow the instructions on the packet from the supplier.

Tempeh

Tempeh is a fermented soybean product that is cooked and pressed. It is similar to tofu but has a firmer texture and is purchased chilled.

Textured vegetable protein (TVP)

This meat substitute is manufactured from protein derived from wheat, oats, cottonseed, soybean and other sources. The main source of TVP is the soybean, due to its high protein content.

TVP is used mainly as a meat extender, replacing from 10 to 60 per cent of fresh meat. Some caterers on very tight budgets make use of it, but its main use is in food manufacturing.

By partially replacing the meat in certain dishes – such as casseroles, stews, pies, pasties, sausage rolls, hamburgers, meat loaf and pâté – it is possible to reduce costs, meet nutritional targets and serve food that is acceptable in appearance.

Soya protein can also be useful when making vegetarian dishes.

Mycoprotein

This meat substitute is produced from a plant that is a distant relative of the mushroom. Mycoprotein contains protein and fibre, and is the result of a fermentation process similar to the way yoghurt is made. It may be used as an alternative to chicken or beef or in vegetarian dishes. The most common brand is Quorn.

It is a low-fat, high-protein food that can be used in a variety of dishes (for example, oriental stir-fries) and does not shrink during preparation and cooking. Quorn mince or pieces can be substituted for chicken or minced meats. Its mild savoury flavour means that it complements the herbs and spices in a recipe and it is able to absorb flavour. Frozen Quorn may be cooked straight from the freezer or may be defrosted overnight in the refrigerator. Once thawed, it must be stored in the refrigerator and used within 24 hours.

Seitan

Seitan (also called wheat meat or wheat gluten) is produced from wheat and has a high gluten content. It can be used as a vegetarian alternative and as a meat substitute, and is high in protein. Asian restaurants use seitan as 'mock meat'.

Seitan can be prepared by hand using either wholewheat flour or vital wheat gluten; it is made by rinsing away the starch in the wheat, leaving high-protein gluten.

Quality points for vegetable protein

- Check the expiry date.
- There should be no unpleasant smell.
- There should be no discoloration (good colour).
- Tofu should be kept in the refrigerator.
- Soya must be free from foreign bodies.
- Packaging should be undamaged.

Test yourself

1. State two quality points to look for when buying leeks.
2. List five vegetables that are in season in autumn.
3. Describe the following cuts of vegetables:
   a macédoine
   b jardinière
   c julienne
   d paysanne.
4. Describe the preparation and cooking of braised red cabbage.
5. How should fresh green vegetables be stored?
6. What is meant by 'blanching' of vegetables and why is it done?
7. Describe two ways to make vegetable dishes healthier.
8. What is the difference between the method of boiling for green vegetables, such as broccoli, and root vegetables, such as potatoes?
9. Describe how tofu should be stored.
10. List three quality points you should look for when buying soya.

Root vegetables

1 Buttered carrots (carottes au beurre)

Ingredient	4 portions	10 portions
Carrots	400 g	1 kg
Salt		
Sugar		
Butter	25 g	60 g
Parsley, chopped		

Energy	Cals	Fat	Sat fat	Carb	Sugar	Protein	Fibre
297 kJ	71 kcal	5.1 g	3.3 g	5.8 g	5.8 g	0.7 g	2.8 g

Healthy eating tips

Use the minimum amount of salt.

1 Peel and wash the carrots.
2 Cut into neat, even pieces, turned barrel shapes or batons.
3 Place in a pan with a little salt, a pinch of sugar and the butter. Barely cover with water.
4 Cover with buttered paper and allow to boil steadily in order to evaporate all the water.
5 When the water has completely evaporated check that the carrots are cooked; if not, add a little more water and continue cooking. Do not overcook.
6 Toss the carrots over a fierce heat for 1–2 minutes in order to give them a glaze.
7 Serve sprinkled with chopped parsley.

2 Carrots in cream sauce (carottes à la crème)

Ingredient	4 portions	10 portions
Carrots	400 g	1 kg
Salt		
Butter	25 g	60 g
Parsley, chopped		
Cream sauce (page 112)	100 ml	250 ml

1 Prepare and cook carrots as for buttered carrots (see recipe 1).
2 Mix with the cream sauce, correct the seasoning and serve.

Energy	Cals	Fat	Sat fat	Carb	Sugar	Protein	Fibre
511 kJ	123 kcal	8.2 g	4.6 g	11.5 g	7.8 g	1.4 g	2.5 g

Using a cream sauce based on béchamel with single cream added 40:10.

Vegetables and vegetable protein — 12

Note
The cream sauce can be based on a béchamel sauce with single cream added in a ratio of 40:10. It could be made with wholemeal flour, skimmed milk and natural yoghurt.

Healthy eating tips
- Use the minimum amount of salt.
- Try replacing half the cream sauce with natural yoghurt.

---

3 Purée of carrots (*purée de carottes*)

Ingredient	4 portions	10 portions
Carrots	600 g	1.5 kg
Salt, pepper		
Butter	25 g	60 g

1 Wash, peel and rewash the carrots. Cut into pieces.
2 Barely cover with water, add a little salt. Simmer gently or steam until tender.
3 Drain well. Pass through a sieve or mouli.
4 Return to the pan, reheat and mix in the butter, correct the seasoning and serve.

Healthy eating tips
Use the minimum amount of salt.

Energy	Cals	Fat	Sat fat	Carb	Sugar	Protein	Fibre
410 kJ	99 kcal	5.6 g	3.4 g	11.9 g	11.1 g	0.9 g	3.6 g

---

4 Beetroot (*betterave*)

1 Select medium-sized or small beetroots; carefully twist off the green leaves (do not cut).
2 Wash well in cold water, cover with water and simmer gently until the skin is easily removed by rubbing between the fingers.

Note
Do not cut or prick with a knife as the beetroots will 'bleed' and turn pale.

Variation
Beetroot may also be cooked in a steamer, or baked.

It may be served hot:
- in cream sauce
- coated in herb-flavoured oil
- coated in butter and marmalade.

Energy	Cals	Fat	Sat fat	Carb	Sugar	Protein	Fibre
92 kJ	22 kcal	0.0 g	0.0 g	5.0 g	5.0 g	0.9 g	1.3 g

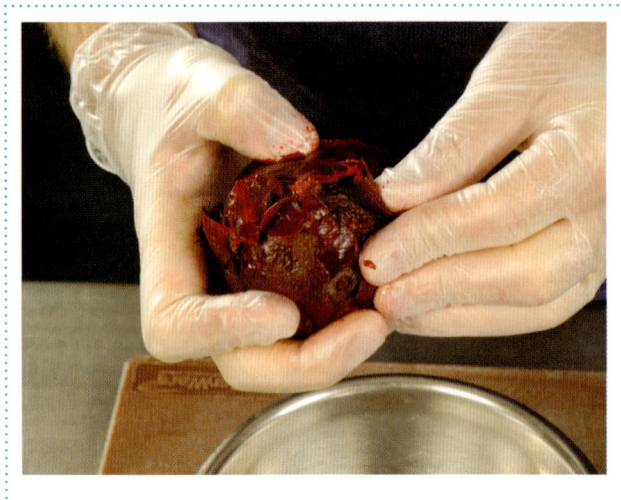

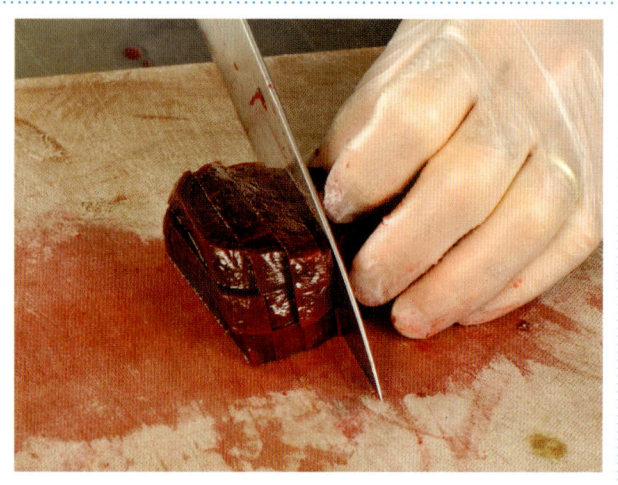

Peel the cooked beetroot, wearing gloves to avoid staining your skin

Cut into neat dice

5 Goats' cheese and beetroot tarts with salad of watercress

Ingredient	4 portions	10 portions
Puff pastry	400 g	1 kg
Shallots	150 g	375 g
Beetroot, cooked	200 g	500 g
Goats' cheese	200 g	500 g
Watercress, bunch	1	2

Energy	Cals	Fat	Sat fat	Carb	Sugar	Protein	Fibre
2,377 kJ	568 kcal	37.7 g	9.0 g	43.6 g	7.5 g	18.6 g	1.8 g

1. Roll the puff pastry to a thickness of 3 mm.
2. Chill the rolled puff pastry for 10 minutes.
3. Finely slice the shallots and sweat down without colour.
4. Cut the puff pastry into 4 discs approximately 150 mm in diameter.
5. Chill the pastry discs for 10 minutes.
6. Dice the cooked beetroot into pieces 10 × 10 mm.
7. To make the tarts, place the shallots on the pastry discs.
8. Cook at 180 °C for 12 minutes.
9. Once cooked, remove from the oven and top with the diced beetroot and crumbled goats' cheese.
10. To finish the dish, place the tarts on plates and finish with picked watercress and vinaigrette.

Vegetables and vegetable protein 12

6 Parsnips (*panais*)

1 Wash well. Peel the parsnips and rewash well.
2 Cut into quarters lengthwise, remove the centre root if tough.
3 Cut into neat pieces and cook in lightly salted water until tender, or steam.
4 Drain and serve with melted butter or in a cream sauce.

Variation

Parsnips may be roasted in the oven in a little fat (as shown here) or in with a joint, and can be cooked and prepared as a purée.

Energy	Cals	Fat	Sat fat	Carb	Sugar	Protein	Fibre
235 kJ	56 kcal	0.0g	0.0g	13.5g	2.7g	1.3g	2.5g

Professional tip

For great roast parsnips, blanch them for 2 minutes, drain, then roast in hot olive oil.

7 Buttered celeriac, turnip or swede

1 Peel and wash the vegetables.
2 Cut into neat pieces or turn barrel shaped.
3 Place in a pan with a little salt, a pinch of sugar and the butter. Barely cover with water.
4 Cover with a buttered paper and allow to boil steadily in order to evaporate all the water.
5 When the water has completely evaporated, check that the vegetables are cooked; if not, add a little more water and continue cooking. Do not overcook.
6 Toss the vegetables over a fierce heat for 1–2 minutes to glaze.
7 Drain well, and serve sprinkled with chopped parsley.

Ingredient	4 portions	10 portions
Celeriac, turnips or swedes	400 g	1 kg
Salt, sugar		
Butter	25 g	60 g
Parsley, chopped		

Energy	Cals	Fat	Sat fat	Carb	Sugar	Protein	Fibre
253 kJ	60 kcal	5.4g	3.3g	2.5g	2.5g	0.7g	1.9g

8 Purée of celeriac, turnips, swede or parsnips

Ingredient	4 portions	10 portions
Celeriac, turnips, swede or parsnips	600 g	1.5 kg
Salt, pepper		
Butter	25 g	60 g

1. Wash, peel and rewash the vegetables. Cut into pieces if necessary.
2. Barely cover with water; add a little salt.
3. Simmer gently until tender, or steam. Drain well.
4. Pass through a sieve or mouli, or use a food processor.
5. Return to the pan, reheat and mix in the butter; correct the seasoning and serve.

Energy	Cals	Fat	Sat fat	Carb	Sugar	Protein	Fibre
395 kJ	95 kcal	5.9 g	3.3 g	9.2 g	6.4 g	1.8 g	4.7 g

Using mixed vegetables and 25 g butter.

Variation
Combination vegetable purées can include, for example, swede and carrot, and parsnip and potato.

---

9 Salsify

Ingredient	4 portions	10 portions
Flour	10 g	20 g
Cold water	0.5 litres	1 litre
Salt, to taste		
Lemon, juice of	½	1

Energy	Cals	Fat	Sat fat	Carb	Sugar	Protein	Fibre
76 kJ	18 kcal	0.0 g	0.0 g	2.8 g	2.8 g	1.9 g	0.0 g

0.5 kg will yield 2–3 portions.

1. Wash, peel and rewash the salsify.
2. Cut into 5 cm lengths.
3. Cook in a blanc (see below). Do not overcook. Salsify may then be served brushed with melted butter, or coated in mornay sauce (see page 113), sprinkled with grated cheese and browned under a salamander. It may also be passed through batter and deep fried.

To make the blanc:

1. Mix the flour and water together.
2. Add the salt and lemon juice. Pass through a strainer.
3. Place in a pan, bring to the boil, stirring continuously.

Vegetables and vegetable protein — 12

Bulbs

10 Fried onions (oignons sautées ou oignons lyonnaise)

Ingredient	2 portions	4 portions
Onions	500 g	1 kg
Oil	25–50 g	50–100 g
Salt		

1 Peel and wash the onions; cut into halves and slice finely.
2 Cook slowly in the oil in a frying pan, turning frequently until tender and browned; season lightly with salt.

Healthy eating tips
- Use a little unsaturated oil to cook the onion.
- Use the minimum amount of salt.

Energy	Cals	Fat	Sat fat	Carb	Sugar	Protein	Fibre
681 kJ	162 kcal	12.9 g	2.4 g	10.4 g	10.4 g	1.8 g	2.6 g

Using peanut oil.

11 Caramelised button onions

Ingredient	4 portions	10 portions
Butter or vegetable oil	50 g	125 g
Button onions	250 g	700 g
Water or brown stock	100 ml	250 ml
Sugar	50 g	125 g

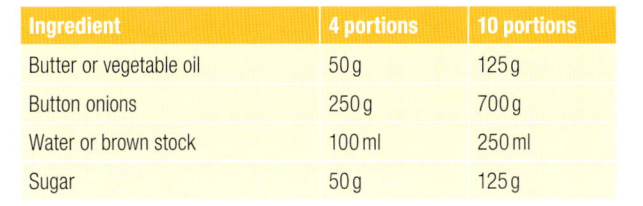

Energy	Cals	Fat	Sat fat	Carb	Sugar	Protein	Fibre	Sodium
713 kJ	171 kcal	10.8 g	6.5 g	18.4 g	16.7 g	1.2 g	1.2 g	0.5 g

1 Place the butter or oil in a shallow pan.
2 Fry the button onions quickly to a light golden brown colour.
3 Barely cover with water or brown stock. Add the sugar. Cook the button onions until they are tender and the liquid has reduced with the sugar to a light caramel glaze. Carefully coat the onions with the glaze.

Professional tip
The important thing is to reduce the stock and sugar until they form a light caramel syrup.

12 Braised fennel with black olives and cardamom

Ingredient	4 portions	10 portions
Fennel bulbs, medium	2	5
Olive or vegetable oil	2 tbsp	5 tbsp
Cloves of garlic, crushed or chopped	1	2½
Black olives, stoned and halved	8	20
Cardamom pods	2	5
Thyme, sprigs	1	2½
Chicken stock	300 ml	750 ml
White wine	300 ml	750 ml
Seasoning		

Energy	Cals	Fat	Sat fat	Carb	Sugar	Protein	Fibre	Sodium
531 kJ	128 kcal	6.9g	0.9g	3.3g	2.6g	1.7g	4.2g	0.6g

1 Prepare the fennel: remove any tough outer leaves and cut into quarters vertically.
2 Heat the oil in a suitable pan, add the fennel, and sweat without colour for 5–10 minutes.
3 Add the garlic, olives, cardamom and thyme. Add the stock and white wine, and season. Bring to the boil.
4 Cover with a lid and braise in an oven at 180–200 °C for approximately 1 hour, until tender.
5 When cooked, remove.

Note

Braised fennel may be served with a variety of meat and fish dishes. It may be coated with a cream, cheese, red wine or Madeira sauce.

Variation

- The fennel can be blanched for 2 minutes in boiling water and refreshed before sweating.
- Cinnamon or mixed spice may be used in place of cardamom.

13 Braised leeks with garlic and olives

Ingredient	4 portions	10 portions
Leeks, large	4	10
Butter	50g	125g
Cloves of garlic, crushed or chopped	4	10
Chicken stock	250 ml	625 ml
Thyme, sprigs	1	2½
Bay leaves	1	2½
White wine	125 ml	310 ml
Salt and pepper		
Green olives, quartered	50g	125g

Energy	Cals	Fat	Sat fat	Carb	Sugar	Protein	Fibre	Sodium
778 kJ	188 kcal	13.2g	7.1g	7.5g	5.5g	5.1g	5.0g	0.7g

1. Trim the leeks and discard any withered leaves.
2. Cut the leeks in half lengthways, but keeping them attached at the root. Wash well.
3. Blanch the leeks in boiling water for 2 minutes, then refresh.
4. Melt the butter in a suitable pan. Sweat the garlic.
5. Place the leeks in the pan; add all other ingredients except the olives. The chicken stock should almost cover the leeks. Season.
6. Bring to the boil and cover.
7. Place in a moderate oven at 180 °C for approximately 20 minutes.
8. When cooked, remove the thyme and bay leaf, and add the olives.
9. Serve as a vegetable or as a garnish to accompany roast meats, fish or pasta.

Note

After blanching the leeks it may be necessary to fold them in half before braising.

Variation

- Leeks may also be boiled in salted water for approximately 10–15 minutes.
- Leeks may be served with a cream sauce, parsley sauce or a cheese sauce.
- Coat the leeks with a red wine sauce, sometimes garnished with mushrooms.

14 French-fried onions (*oignons frites à la française*)

1. Peel and wash the onions.
2. Cut into 2 mm slices, against the grain. Separate into rings.
3. Pass through milk and seasoned flour.
4. Shake off the surplus. Deep fry in hot fat at 185 °C.
5. Drain well on kitchen paper, season lightly with salt and serve.

Healthy eating tips

- Make sure the oil is hot so that less is absorbed into the onions.
- Drain on kitchen paper.
- Use the minimum amount of salt.

Energy	Cals	Fat	Sat fat	Carb	Sugar	Protein	Fibre
661 kJ	159 kcal	11.7g	1.6g	12.3g	3.5g	2.0g	1.0g

Using 50 g onions, to give 83.5 g finished weight.

Slice the onions thinly

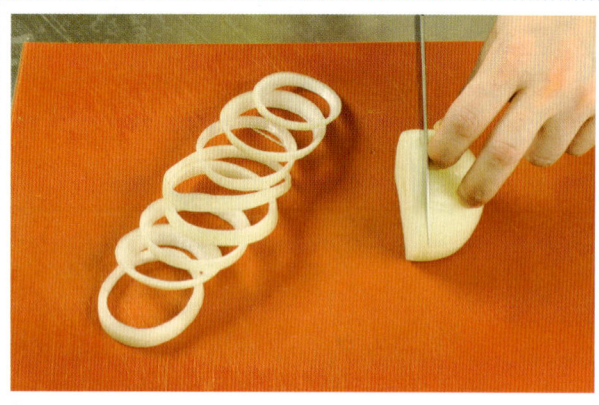

Pass each piece through milk and then seasoned flour

Flower heads

15 Broccoli

1 Cook in lightly salted water, or steam.

1 kg of raw broccoli yields approximately 8 portions.

Because of their size, green and purple broccoli need less cooking time than cauliflower. Broccoli is usually broken down into florets and, as such, requires very little cooking: once brought to the boil, 1–2 minutes should be sufficient. This leaves the broccoli slightly crisp.

Tenderstem broccoli is increasingly popular. It has long, slim, evenly sized stems and small flower heads, so it cooks quickly. The distinctive flavour is similar to asparagus. Green and purple varieties are available, and, because of the uniform shape, they can be presented very attractively.

Energy	Cals	Fat	Sat fat	Carb	Sugar	Protein	Fibre	Sodium
125 kJ	30 kcal	1.0g	0.3g	1.4g	1.1g	3.9g	4.6g	0.2g

406

Vegetables and vegetable protein   12

16 Cauliflower (*chou-fleur nature*)

Variation

- **Boiled or steamed cauliflower** may be served with 250 ml of cream sauce, 100 g of melted butter or 125 ml of hollandaise sauce. Serve the sauce in a sauceboat.
- **Buttered cauliflower** is brushed with 25–50 g melted butter before serving and can be sprinkled with chopped parsley.
- **Fried cauliflower**: cut the cooked cauliflower into four portions then lightly colour on all sides in 25–50 g butter.

Energy	Cals	Fat	Sat fat	Carb	Sugar	Protein	Fibre
142 kJ	34 kcal	0.9g	0.2g	3.0g	2.5g	3.6g	1.8g

Using no additions.

Allow one medium-sized cauliflower for four portions.
1. Trim the stem and remove the outer leaves.
2. Hollow out the stem with a peeler or cut into florets. Wash.
3. Cook in lightly salted boiling water, or steam, for approximately 10–15 minutes. Do not overcook (if cut into florets, cook for only 3–5 minutes).
4. Drain well and serve cut into four even portions.

17 Cauliflower au gratin

1. Cut the cooked cauliflower into four.
2. Reheat in a pan of hot salted water (*chauffant*), or reheat in butter in a suitable pan.
3. Place in vegetable dish or on a greased tray.
4. Coat with 250 ml of mornay sauce (see page 113).
5. Sprinkle with grated cheese.
6. Brown under the salamander and serve.

Healthy eating tips

No additional salt is needed as cheese is added.

Energy	Cals	Fat	Sat fat	Carb	Sugar	Protein	Fibre
632 kJ	150 kcal	10.4g	3.9g	8.6g	3.8g	6.3g	2.0g

407

Fungi

18 Grilled mushrooms (*champignons grillés*)

Ingredient	4 portions	10 portions
Grilling mushrooms (flat mushrooms)	200 g	500 g
Salt, pepper		
Butter, margarine or oil	50 g	125 g

1 Peel the mushrooms, remove the stalks; wash and drain well.
2 Place on a tray and season lightly with salt and pepper.
3 Brush with melted fat or oil and grill on both sides for 3–4 minutes. Serve with picked parsley.

Energy	Cals	Fat	Sat fat	Carb	Sugar	Protein	Fibre
499 kJ	119 kcal	12.8 g	1.7 g	0.0 g	0.0 g	0.9 g	1.3 g

Using sunflower oil.

Healthy eating tips
Use the minimum amount of salt.

19 Stuffed mushrooms (*champignons farcis*)

1 Peel the mushrooms, remove stalks and wash well.
2 Retain 8 or 12 of the best mushrooms (20 to 30 for ten portions). Finely chop the remainder with the well-washed peelings and stalks.
3 Cook the shallots, without colour, in a little fat.
4 Add the chopped mushrooms and cook for 3–4 minutes (duxelle).
5 Grill the mushrooms as in recipe 18.
6 Place the duxelle in the centre of each mushroom.
7 Sprinkle with a few breadcrumbs and some melted butter.
8 Reheat in the oven or under the salamander and serve.

Ingredient	4 portions	10 portions
Grilling mushrooms	300 g	750 g
Shallots, chopped	10 g	25 g
Butter, margarine or oil	50 g	125 g
Breadcrumbs	25 g	60 g

Energy	Cals	Fat	Sat fat	Carb	Sugar	Protein	Fibre
577 kJ	137 kcal	13.1 g	1.8 g	3.2 g	0.3 g	1.9 g	2.1 g

Using sunflower oil.

Healthy eating tips
Use a little unsaturated oil to cook the shallots.

Variation
Mushrooms may be stuffed with ratatouille or a forcemeat.

Vegetables and vegetable protein | **12**

Seeds and pods

20 Broad beans

Remove the inner shells of broad beans

Energy	Cals	Fat	Sat fat	Carb	Sugar	Protein	Fibre
344 kJ	81 kcal	0.6g	0.1g	5.0g	0.4g	7.9g	6.5g

100 g portion.

0.5 kg will yield about 2 portions.

1. Shell the beans and cook in boiling salted water for 10–15 minutes until tender. Do not overcook.
2. If the inner shells are tough, remove before serving.

Variation

Try:
- brushing with butter
- brushing with butter then sprinkling with chopped parsley
- binding with 500 ml cream sauce or fresh cream.

Professional tip

The modern technique is to take the beans out of their pod and outer skin before serving – this reveals the bright green, tender beans.

21 Mangetout

0.5 kg of mangetout will yield 4–6 portions.

1. Top and tail, wash and drain.
2. Cook in boiling salted water for 2–3 minutes, until slightly crisp.
3. Serve whole, brushed with butter.

Energy	Cals	Fat	Sat fat	Carb	Sugar	Protein	Fibre	Sodium
94 kJ	22 kcal	0.1g	0.0g	2.8g	2.4g	3.1g	0.0g	0.0g

409

22 French beans (haricots verts)

0.5 kg will yield 3–4 portions.

1. Top and tail the beans, carefully and economically.
2. Using a large sharp knife cut the beans into strips 5 cm × 3 mm.
3. Wash.
4. Cook in lightly salted boiling water, or steam, for 5–10 minutes, until tender.
5. Do not overcook. Drain well and serve.

Energy	Cals	Fat	Sat fat	Carb	Sugar	Protein	Fibre
646 kJ	154 kcal	2.9 g	0.5 g	28.5 g	2.1 g	5.1 g	5.9 g

Variation

Variations include:
- brushing the beans with butter
- gently tossing the cooked beans in butter over heat without colour
- combining 400 g cooked French beans with 50 g shallow-fried onions
- combining 400 g cooked French beans with 100 g cooked flageolet beans.

23 French-style peas (petit pois à la française)

Ingredient	4 portions	10 portions
Peas (in the pod)	1 kg	2.5 kg
Spring or button onions	12	40
Lettuce, small	1	2–3
Butter	25 g	60 g
Salt		
Caster sugar	½ tsp	1 tsp
Flour	5 g	12 g

Energy	Cals	Fat	Sat fat	Carb	Sugar	Protein	Fibre
515 kJ	123 kcal	5.6 g	3.4 g	12.9 g	5.8 g	5.9 g	5.7 g

1. Shell and wash the peas and place in a sauteuse.
2. Peel and wash the onions, shred the lettuce and add to the peas with half the butter, a little salt and the sugar.
3. Barely cover with water. Cover with a lid and cook steadily, preferably in the oven, until tender.
4. Correct the seasoning.
5. Mix the remaining butter with the flour, making a *beurre manié*, and place it into the boiling peas in small pieces until thoroughly mixed; serve.

When using frozen peas, allow the onions to almost cook before adding the peas.

Vegetables and vegetable protein | 12

Shell the peas and discard the pods

Place the prepared ingredients into the sauteuse

Add a *beurre manié* at the end of the cooking time

24 Corn on the cob

Allow 1 cob per portion.

1. Trim the stem.
2. Cook in lightly salted boiling water for 10–20 minutes or until the corn is tender. Do not overcook.
3. Remove the outer leaves and fibres.
4. Serve with a sauceboat of melted butter.

Creamed sweetcorn can be made by removing the corn from the cooked cobs, draining well and binding lightly with cream (fresh or non-dairy), béchamel sauce or yoghurt.

Energy	Cals	Fat	Sat fat	Carb	Sugar	Protein	Fibre
646 kJ	154 kcal	2.9g	0.5g	28.5g	2.1g	5.1g	5.9g

25 Okra in cream sauce

1. Top and tail the okra.
2. Blanch in lightly salted boiling water, or steam; drain.
3. Sweat in the margarine or butter for 5–10 minutes, or until tender.
4. Carefully add the cream sauce.
5. Bring to the boil, correct the seasoning and serve in a suitable dish.

Okra may also be served brushed with butter or sprinkled with chopped parsley.

Professional tip
Okra can become glutinous (slimy) when it is cooked in a sauce. To avoid this, wash the okra and let them dry before cooking.

Ingredient	4 portions	10 portions
Okra ('ladies' fingers')	400 g	1.25 kg
Butter or margarine	50 g	125 g
Cream sauce	250 ml	625 ml

Energy	Cals	Fat	Sat fat	Carb	Sugar	Protein	Fibre
928 kJ	221 kcal	20.2 g	9.8 g	5.7 g	5.7 g	4.4 g	3.2 g

Using hard margarine.

Healthy eating tips
- Use a little unsaturated oil to sweat the okra.
- Try using half cream sauce and half yoghurt, adding very little salt.

---

26 Okra curry

Ingredient	4 portions	10 portions
Okra, small	450 g	1.15 kg
Vegetable oil	2 tbsp	5 tbsp
Cumin seeds	2 tsp	5 tsp
Onions, finely chopped	110 g	275 g
Mild curry paste	1 tbsp	2½ tbsp
Tomatoes, medium, skinned, deseeded, finely chopped	3	8
Fresh coriander, chopped	1 tbsp	2½ tbsp
Red pepper, diced	½	1¼
Green pepper, diced	½	1¼
Fresh red chillies, finely sliced	2	5
Brown sugar	1 tbsp	2½ tbsp
Salt, to taste		

Energy	Cals	Fat	Sat fat	Carb	Sugar	Protein	Fibre	Sodium
722 kJ	173 kcal	10.4 g	1.1 g	16.3 g	14.3 g	5.3 g	8.2 g	0.3 g

Vegetables and vegetable protein 12

1. Very carefully and lightly wash the okra. Pat dry and leave intact.
2. Heat the oil in a wok or frying pan to a medium heat, add the cumin seeds and fry for 30 seconds.
3. Add the onion and curry paste and stir-fry for 5 minutes.
4. Add the tomato, coriander, peppers, chillies and sugar, and continue to stir-fry for 5 minutes.
5. While stir-frying, trim the okra to remove the tops and tails.
6. Add the trimmed okra to the other ingredients and gently stir-fry until cooked through (approximately 3–4 minutes).
7. Season and serve.

Tubers

27 Plain boiled potatoes (pommes nature)

1. Wash, peel and rewash the potatoes.
2. Cut or turn into even-sized pieces, allowing 2–3 pieces per portion.
3. Cook carefully in lightly salted water for approximately 20 minutes.
4. Drain well and serve.

Energy	Cals	Fat	Sat fat	Carb	Sugar	Protein	Fibre
487 kJ	116 kcal	0.1g	0.0g	28.6g	0.6g	2.0g	1.5g

Using old potatoes.

28 Parsley potatoes (pommes persillées)

1. Wash, peel and rewash the potatoes.
2. Cut or turn into even-sized pieces, allowing 2–3 pieces per portion.
3. Cook carefully in lightly salted water for approximately 20 minutes.
4. Drain well. Brush with melted butter and sprinkle with chopped parsley.

Energy	Cals	Fat	Sat fat	Carb	Sugar	Protein	Fibre
798 kJ	190 kcal	8.3g	5.2g	28.6g	0.6g	2.1g	1.5g

Using old potatoes and 10g butter per portion.

29 New potatoes (*pommes nouvelles*)

Method 1

1. Wash the potatoes, and boil or steam in their jackets until cooked.
2. Cool slightly, peel while warm and place in a pan of cold water.
3. When required for service add a little salt and a bunch of mint to the potatoes; heat through slowly.
4. Drain well; serve brushed with melted butter and sprinkled with chopped mint, or decorate with blanched, refreshed mint leaves.

Method 2

1. Scrape the potatoes and wash well.
2. Place in a pan of lightly salted boiling water with a bunch of mint and boil gently until cooked (about 20 minutes). Serve as above.

Energy	Cals	Fat	Sat fat	Carb	Sugar	Protein	Fibre
383 kJ	91 kcal	0.1g	0.0g	22.0g	0.8g	1.9g	2.4g

Note

The starch cells of new potatoes are immature; to help break down these cells new potatoes are cooked in water that is already boiling. This also helps to preserve vitamin C (ascorbic acid) in the potatoes.

30 Mashed potatoes (*pommes purées*)

Ingredient	4 portions	10 portions
Floury potatoes	0.5 kg	1.25 kg
Butter	25 g	60 g
Milk, warm	30 ml	85 ml

Energy	Cals	Fat	Sat fat	Carb	Sugar	Protein	Fibre
763 kJ	182 kcal	7.1 g	4.4 g	29.0 g	1.1 g	2.4 g	1.5 g

Using old potatoes, butter and whole milk.

1. Wash, peel and rewash the potatoes. Cut to an even size.
2. Cook in lightly salted water, or steam.
3. Drain off the water, cover and return to a low heat to dry out the potatoes.
4. Pass through a medium sieve or a ricer.
5. Return the potatoes to a clean pan.
6. Add the butter and mix in with a wooden spoon.
7. Gradually add warm milk, stirring continuously until a smooth creamy consistency is reached.
8. Correct the seasoning and serve.

Professional tip
Drain the potatoes as soon as they are cooked. If they are left standing in water, they will become too wet and spoil the texture of the dish.

Healthy eating tips
- Add a minimum amount of salt.
- Add a little olive oil in place of the butter, and use semi-skimmed milk.

Variation
Try:
- dressing in a serving dish and surrounding with a cordon of fresh cream
- placing in a serving dish, sprinkling with grated cheese and melted butter, and browning under a salamander
- adding 50 g diced cooked lean ham, 25 g diced red pepper and chopped parsley
- adding lightly sweated chopped spring onions
- using a good-quality olive oil in place of butter
- adding a little garlic juice (use a garlic press)
- adding a little fresh chopped rosemary or chives
- mixing with equal quantities of parsnip
- adding a little freshly grated horseradish or horseradish cream.

Pass the cooked potato through a sieve

Add milk to the potatoes and combine

31 Duchess potatoes

Ingredient	4 portions	10 portions
Floury potatoes	600 g	1.5 kg
Egg yolks	1	3
Butter	25 g	60 g
Salt, pepper		

Energy	Cals	Fat	Sat fat	Carb	Sugar	Protein	Fibre
819 kJ	195 kcal	8.2 g	3.3 g	28.6 g	0.6 g	3.5 g	1.5 g

Using old potatoes, whole milk, hard margarine.

1. Wash, peel and rewash the potatoes. Cut to an even size.
2. Cook in lightly salted water.
3. Drain off the water, cover and return to a low heat to dry out the potatoes.
4. Pass through a medium sieve or a special potato ricer or mouli.
5. Place the potatoes in a clean pan.
6. Add the egg yolks and stir in vigorously with a kitchen spoon.
7. Mix in the butter. Correct the seasoning.
8. Place in a piping bag with a large star tube and pipe out into neat spirals, about 2 cm in diameter and 5 cm tall, on to a lightly greased baking sheet.
9. Place in a hot oven at 230 °C for 2–3 minutes in order to firm the edges slightly.
10. Remove from the oven and brush with egg wash.
11. Brown lightly in a hot oven or under the salamander.

Note

At step 3, it is important to return the drained potatoes to the heat, so that they are as dry as possible.

Add egg yolks to the mashed potato

Pipe the potato into neat spirals, ready for baking

32 Steamed potatoes in their jackets (*pommes vapeur*)

1 Wash the potatoes well.
2 Place the potatoes into a steamer tray, sprinkle with salt and steam until tender.
3 When steaming new potatoes, add some sprigs of mint.
4 Drain before serving or peeling for sauté.

Professional tip
- Choose the most suitable varieties for steaming: Saxon, Nadine, Estima, Maris Piper or Desiree. Steaming retains more flavour than boiling.
- Always choose evenly sized potatoes so that they will cook in the same amount of time.
- If the potato is going to be cooked further, e.g. sauté, it is best to leave the skin on during steaming. The skin will protect the flesh of the potato from the steam.

Energy	Cals	Fat	Sat fat	Carb	Sugar	Protein	Fibre	Sodium
424 kJ	150 kcal	0.3g	0.0g	23.1g	0.8g	2.7g	2.3g	0.1g

33 Baked jacket potatoes (*pommes au four*)

1 Select good-sized potatoes; allow 1 potato per portion.
2 Scrub well and make a 2 mm-deep incision round the potato.
3 Place the potato, on a small mound of ground (sea) salt to help keep the base dry, on a tray in a hot oven at 230–250 °C for about 1 hour. Turn the potatoes over after 30 minutes.
4 Test by holding the potato in a cloth and squeezing gently; if cooked it should feel soft.

Healthy eating tips
- Potatoes can be baked without sea salt.
- Fillings based on vegetables with little or no cheese or meat make a healthy snack meal.

Energy	Cals	Fat	Sat fat	Carb	Sugar	Protein	Fibre
401 kJ	94 kcal	0.2g	0.0g	21.8g	0.9g	2.7g	1.6g

Using medium potato, 180g analysis given per potato.

Professional tip
Lightly scoring the potatoes will help to make sure that they cook evenly.

The potatoes can also be microwaved. Prick the skins first. Cook on full power for 5 minutes per potato. Wrap in foil and leave to rest for 3 minutes.

Variation
Split and filled with any of the following: grated cheese, minced beef or chicken, baked beans, chilli con carne, cream cheese and chives, mushrooms, bacon, ratatouille, prawns in mayonnaise, coleslaw, and so on.

The cooked potatoes can also be cut in halves lengthwise, the potato spooned out from the skins, seasoned, mashed with butter, returned to the skins, sprinkled with grated cheese and reheated in an oven or under the grill.

Practical Cookery 14th edition

34 Roast potatoes (*pommes rôties*)

1. Wash, peel and rewash the potatoes.
2. Cut into even-sized pieces (allow 3–4 pieces per portion).
3. Heat a good measure of oil or dripping in a roasting tray.
4. Add the well-dried potatoes and lightly brown on all sides.
5. Season lightly with salt and cook for about 1 hour in a hot oven at 230–250 °C.
6. Turn the potatoes over after 30 minutes.
7. Cook to a golden brown. Drain and serve.

> **Professional tip**
> Roast potatoes can be parboiled for 10 minutes, refreshed and well dried before roasting. This will cut down on the cooking time and can also give a crisper potato.

Energy	Cals	Fat	Sat fat	Carb	Sugar	Protein	Fibre
956 kJ	228 kcal	7.0g	1.1g	39.6g	0.9g	4.1g	1.5g

Using old potatoes and peanut oil for 1 portion (125 g raw potato).

> **Healthy eating tips**
> - Brush the potatoes with peanut or sunflower oil, with only a little in the roasting tray.
> - Drain off all the fat when cooked.

35 Chateau potatoes

1. Select small, even-sized potatoes and wash them.
2. Turn the potatoes into barrel-shaped pieces about the same size as fondant potatoes (recipe 43).
3. Place in a saucepan of boiling water for 2–3 minutes, then refresh immediately. Drain in a colander.
4. Finish as for roast potatoes. Use a non-stick tray, lightly oiled greaseproof paper or non-stick mat for the roasting.

Energy	Cals	Fat	Sat fat	Carb	Sugar	Protein	Fibre	Sodium
839 kJ	200 kcal	5.9g	0.7g	34.4g	1.2g	4.2g	3.5g	0.0g

36 Fried or chipped potatoes

Energy	Cals	Fat	Sat fat	Carb	Sugar	Protein	Fibre
1,541 kJ	367 kcal	15.8g	2.8g	54.1g	0.0g	5.5g	1.5g

Using old potatoes and peanut oil.

1. Prepare and wash the potatoes.
2. Cut into slices 1 cm thick and 5 cm long.
3. Cut the slices into strips 5 × 1 × 1 cm.
4. Wash well and dry in a cloth.
5. Cook in a frying basket without colour in moderately hot oil (165 °C).
6. Drain and place on kitchen paper on trays until required.
7. When required, place in a frying basket and cook in hot oil (185 °C) until crisp and golden.
8. Drain well, season lightly with salt and serve.

Note

Because chips are so popular, the following advice from the Potato Marketing Board is useful.
- Cook chips in small quantities; this will allow the oil to regain its temperature more quickly; chips will then cook faster and absorb less fat.
- Do not let the temperature of the oil exceed 199 °C as this will accelerate the fat breakdown.
- Use oils high in polyunsaturates for a healthier chip.
- Ideally use a separate fryer for chips and ensure that it has the capacity to raise the fat temperature rapidly to the correct degree when frying chilled or frozen chips.
- Although the majority of chipped potatoes are purchased frozen, the Potato Marketing Board recommends the following potatoes for those who prefer to make their own chips: Maris Piper, Cara and Desiree. King Edward and Santé are also good choices.

Healthy eating tips

- Chipped potatoes may be blanched twice, first at 140 °C, followed by a re-blanch at 160 °C until lightly coloured.
- Blanch in a steamer until just cooked, drain and dry well – final temperature 165 °C.

Practical Cookery 14th edition

37 Sauté potatoes

1. Select medium even-sized potatoes. Scrub well.
2. Plain boil or cook in the steamer. Cool slightly and peel.
3. Cut into 3 mm slices.
4. Toss in hot shallow oil in a frying pan until lightly coloured; season lightly with salt.
5. Serve sprinkled with chopped parsley.

Maris piper or Cara potatoes are good varieties for this dish.

Energy	Cals	Fat	Sat fat	Carb	Sugar	Protein	Fibre
1,249 kJ	297 kcal	11.4g	1.3g	46.8g	0.4g	4.9g	1.7g

Using old potatoes and sunflower oil.

Healthy eating tips
- Use a little hot sunflower oil to fry the potatoes.
- Add little or no salt; the customer can add more if required.

Cut the potatoes into 3 mm slices

Toss the slices in hot oil to cook (sauté)

420

38 Sauté potatoes with onions (*pommes lyonnaise*)

Allow 0.25 kg onion to 0.5 kg potatoes.

1. Shallow-fry the onions slowly in 25–50 g oil, turning frequently, until tender and nicely browned; season lightly with salt.
2. Prepare sauté potatoes as for recipe 37.
3. Combine the two and toss together.
4. Serve as for sauté potatoes.

Energy	Cals	Fat	Sat fat	Carb	Sugar	Protein	Fibre	Sodium
1,098 kJ	261 kcal	9.4g	1.1g	41.5g	6.4g	5.4g	5.3g	0.3g

Finely slice the onions

Sauté the potatoes and onions together

39 New potato rissoles (*pommes nouvelles rissolées*)

1. Boil or steam new potatoes, then drain them.
2. Fry to a golden brown in oil or butter, or a combination of both.

Energy	Cals	Fat	Sat fat	Carb	Sugar	Protein	Fibre
610 kJ	145 kcal	6.1g	1.1g	22.0g	0.8g	1.9g	2.4g

40 Parmentier potatoes

0.5 kg will yield 2–3 portions.

1. Select medium to large potatoes.
2. Wash, peel and rewash.
3. Trim on three sides and cut into 1 cm slices.
4. Cut the slices into 1 cm strips.
5. Cut the strips into 1 cm dice.
6. Wash well and dry in a cloth.
7. Cook in hot shallow oil in a frying pan until golden brown.
8. Drain, season lightly and serve sprinkled with chopped parsley (optional).

Energy	Cals	Fat	Sat fat	Carb	Sugar	Protein	Fibre
1,819 kJ	433 kcal	33.5g	6.3g	32.8g	0.7g	2.3g	1.7g

Using peanut oil.

Vegetables and vegetable protein | **12**

41 Noisette potatoes (*pommes noisettes*)

0.5 kg will yield two portions.

1. Wash, peel and rewash the potatoes.
2. Scoop out balls with a noisette spoon. Blanch the balls in boiling water.
3. Cook in a little oil in a sauté pan or frying pan. Colour on top of the stove and finish cooking in the oven at 230–250 °C.

Energy	Cals	Fat	Sat fat	Carb	Sugar	Protein	Fibre	Sodium
993 kJ	236 kcal	6.3 g	0.7 g	42.0 g	1.5 g	5.1 g	3.4 g	0.0 g

Using 1 tbsp of vegetable oil.

42 Cocotte potatoes (*pommes cocotte*)

1. Proceed as for chateau potatoes (recipe 35), but with the potatoes a quarter the size.
2. Cook in a sauté pan or frying pan.

Energy	Cals	Fat	Sat fat	Carb	Sugar	Protein	Fibre	Sodium
839 kJ	200 kcal	5.9 g	0.7 g	34.4 g	1.2 g	4.2 g	3.5 g	0.0 g

Practical Cookery 14th edition

43 Fondant potatoes

Energy	Cals	Fat	Sat fat	Carb	Sugar	Protein	Fibre
956 kJ	228 kcal	7.0g	2.1g	39.6g	0.9g	4.1g	1.5g

Using old potatoes and hard margarine for 1 portion (125g raw potato).

> **Professional tip**
> To give the potatoes a good glaze, use a high-quality stock and baste during cooking.

1. Select small or even-sized medium potatoes.
2. Wash, peel and rewash.
3. Turn into 8-sided barrel shapes or cut thick rounds with a cutter, allowing 2–3 per portion, about 5cm long, end diameter 1.5cm, centre diameter 2.5cm.
4. Brush with melted butter or oil.
5. Place in a pan suitable for the oven.
6. Half cover with white stock, season lightly with salt and pepper.
7. Cook in a hot oven at 230–250°C, brushing the potatoes frequently with melted butter or oil.
8. When cooked, the stock should be completely absorbed by the potatoes.
9. Brush with melted butter or oil and serve.

Variation
Fondant potatoes can be lightly sprinkled with:
- thyme, rosemary or oregano (or this can be added to the stock)
- grated cheese (Gruyère and Parmesan or Cheddar)
- chicken stock in place of white stock.

> **Healthy eating tips**
> - Use a little unsaturated oil to brush over the potatoes before and after cooking.
> - No added salt is needed; rely on the stock for flavour.

Turn the potatoes into barrel shapes

Place in a pan, half covered with stock, to cook

44 Savoury potatoes (*pommes boulangères*)

Energy	Cals	Fat	Sat fat	Carb	Sugar	Protein	Fibre
595 kJ	142 kcal	5.3 g	2.2 g	22.3 g	1.8 g	2.8 g	2.4 g

Using 25 g hard margarine (using 50 g hard margarine: 787 kJ/187 kcal energy, 10.3 g fat, 4.4 g saturated fat, 22.3 g carbohydrates, 1.8 g sugar, 2.8 g protein and 2.4 g fibre).

Ingredient	4 portions	10 portions
Potatoes	400 g	1 kg
Onions	100 g	250 g
Salt, pepper		
White stock	125 ml	310 ml
Butter or oil	25–50 g	60–125 g
Parsley, chopped		

Healthy eating tips
- Use an unsaturated oil.
- Add the minimum amount of salt; the stock provides flavour.
- This dish can be used to accompany fattier meat dishes and will help to dilute the fat.

1 Cut the potatoes into 2 mm slices on a mandolin. Set aside the best slices to use for the top.
2 Peel, halve and finely slice the onions.
3 Mix the onions and potatoes together and season lightly with salt and pepper.
4 Place in a well-buttered shallow earthenware dish or roasting tin.
5 Barely cover with stock.
6 Neatly arrange overlapping slices of potato on top.
7 Brush lightly with oil.
8 Place in a hot oven at 230–250 °C for 20 minutes until lightly coloured.
9 Reduce the heat and allow to cook steadily, pressing down firmly from time to time with a flat-bottomed pan.
10 All of the stock should be cooked into the potato when it is ready. Allow approximately 1½ hours cooking time in all.
11 Serve sprinkled with chopped parsley. If cooked in an earthenware dish, clean the edges of the dish with a cloth dipped in salt, and serve in the dish.

Variation

This potato dish can be cooked under a joint of lamb (shoulder or leg). Place an oven rack with the meat on above the potatoes for the final 1½ hours of cooking. The juices from the meat will baste the potatoes as it cooks, then serve the lamb on top of the potato if the style of the restaurant dictates.

Leeks can be used in place of onions for variety.

45 Macaire potatoes (potato cakes, *pommes Macaire*)

0.5 kg will yield 2–3 portions.

1. Prepare and cook as for baked jacket potatoes (recipe 33).
2. Cut in halves, remove the centre with a spoon, and place in a basin.
3. Add 25 g butter per 0.5 kg, a little salt and milled pepper.
4. Mash and mix as lightly as possible with a fork.
5. Using a little flour, mould into a roll, then divide into pieces, allowing one or two per portion.
6. Mould into 2 cm round cakes. Quadrille with the back of a palette knife. Flour lightly.
7. Shallow-fry on both sides in very hot oil and serve.

Energy	Cals	Fat	Sat fat	Carb	Sugar	Protein	Fibre
4,392 kJ	1,047 kcal	65.7 g	14.7 g	109.8 g	2.7 g	11.4 g	10.8 g

Using hard margarine and sunflower oil.

Professional tip
Make sure the potato mixture is firm enough to be shaped, and fry the cakes in very hot oil, or they will lose their shape.

Variation
Additions to potato cakes can include:
- chopped parsley, fresh herbs or chives, or duxelle
- cooked chopped onion
- grated cheese

Place the potatoes on a baking tray with salt

Once baked, cut in half and scoop out the centre

Mould the potato into cakes

Vegetables and vegetable protein 12

46 Byron potatoes (*pommes Byron*)

1. Prepare and cook as for Macaire potatoes (recipe 45).
2. Using the back of a dessertspoon make a shallow impression on each potato.
3. Carefully sprinkle the centres with grated cheese. Make sure no cheese is on the edge of the potato.
4. Cover the cheese with cream.
5. Brown lightly under the salamander and serve.

Note

This is a classical variation on Macaire potatoes.

Energy	Cals	Fat	Sat fat	Carb	Sugar	Protein	Fibre
2,099 kJ	505 kcal	39.0g	18.7g	33.4g	1.8g	7.1g	2.4g

Analysis given per potato, using 1 tbsp each of cheese and double cream per person.

47 Croquette potatoes

1. Use a duchess mixture (see recipe 31) moulded into cylinder shapes 5 × 2 cm.
2. Pass through flour, egg wash and breadcrumbs. Chill.
3. Reshape with a palette knife and chill. Deep fry in hot deep oil (185°C) in a frying basket.
4. When the potatoes are a golden colour, drain well and serve.

Energy	Cals	Fat	Sat fat	Carb	Sugar	Protein	Fibre
1,699 kJ	405 kcal	25.4g	6.6g	40.8g	1.1g	6.0g	2.2g

Healthy eating tips
- Add the minimum amount of salt.
- Use peanut or sunflower oil to fry the croquettes, and drain on kitchen paper.

48 Swiss potato cakes (rösti)

1. Parboil in salted water (or steam) for approximately 5 minutes.
2. Cool, then shred into large flakes on a grater.
3. Heat the oil or butter in a frying pan.
4. Add the potatoes, and season lightly with salt and pepper.
5. Press the potato together and cook on both sides until brown and crisp.

Note

The potato can be made in a 4-portion cake or into individual rounds.

Ingredient	4 portions	10 portions
Potatoes, unpeeled	400 g	1 kg
Oil or butter	50 g	125 g
Salt, pepper		

Energy	Cals	Fat	Sat fat	Carb	Sugar	Protein	Fibre
700 kJ	168 kcal	10.5 g	6.5 g	17.3 g	0.7 g	2.2 g	1.3 g

Using butter.

Healthy eating tips

- Lightly oil a well-seasoned pan with sunflower oil to fry the rösti.
- Use the minimum amount of salt.

Variation

- The potato cakes may also be made from raw potatoes.
- Add sweated chopped onion.
- Add sweated lardons of bacon.
- Use two parts of grated potato to one part grated apple.

Shred the parboiled potatoes on a grater

Press into shape in the frying pan

Turn out carefully after cooking

Vegetables and vegetable protein 12

49 Potatoes cooked in milk with cheese

Ingredient	4 portions	10 portions
Potatoes	500 g	1.25 kg
Milk	250 ml	625 ml
Salt and pepper		
Grated cheese	50 g	125 g

1 Slice the peeled potatoes to 0.5 cm thick.
2 Place in an ovenproof dish and just cover with milk.
3 Season, sprinkle with grated cheese and cook in a moderate oven (190 °C) until the potatoes are cooked and golden brown.

Energy	Cals	Fat	Sat fat	Carb	Sugar	Protein	Fibre	Sodium
734 kJ	174 kcal	5.6 g	3.4 g	24.0 g	3.7 g	8.0 g	1.8 g	0.4 g

50 Potatoes with bacon and onions

Ingredient	4 portions	10 portions
Potatoes, peeled	400 g	1.25 kg
Streaky bacon (lardons)	100 g	250 g
Button onions	100 g	250 g
White stock	250 ml	625 ml
Salt, pepper		
Parsley, chopped		

Energy	Cals	Fat	Sat fat	Carb	Sugar	Protein	Fibre
836 kJ	199 kcal	10.1 g	3.8 g	22.2 g	1.8 g	6.4 g	2.5 g

Using old potatoes.

1 Cut the potatoes into 1 cm dice.
2 Cut the bacon into 0.5 cm lardons; lightly fry in a little fat together with the onions and brown lightly.
3 Add the potatoes, half cover with stock, season lightly with salt and pepper. Cover with a lid and cook steadily in the oven at 230–250 °C for approximately 30 minutes.
4 Correct the seasoning, serve in a vegetable dish, sprinkled with chopped parsley.

Healthy eating tips
- Dry-fry the bacon in a well-seasoned pan and drain off any excess fat.
- Add little or no salt.

429

Practical Cookery 14th edition

51 Delmonico potatoes

1. Wash, peel and rewash the potatoes.
2. Cut into 6 mm dice.
3. Barely cover with milk, season lightly with salt and pepper and allow to cook for 30–40 minutes.
4. Place in an earthenware dish, sprinkle with breadcrumbs and melted butter, brown in the oven or under the salamander and serve.

Energy	Cals	Fat	Sat fat	Carb	Sugar	Protein	Fibre
900 kJ	214 kcal	6.3g	3.7g	37.5g	2.7g	4.4g	2.0g

Using old potatoes and whole milk.

Dice the potatoes

Place in a dish, barely covered with milk, to cook

After baking, sprinkle with breadcrumbs and gratinate

52 Jerusalem artichokes in cream sauce (*topinambours à la crème*)

1. Wash and peel the artichokes, then rewash. Cut to an even size.
2. Barely cover with water, add a little salt and simmer until tender; do not overcook.
3. Drain well and add 250 ml (600 ml for 10 portions) cream sauce (see page 112).

Note
Cream sauce may be made using skimmed milk and natural yoghurt.

Energy	Cals	Fat	Sat fat	Carb	Sugar	Protein	Fibre	Sodium
641 kJ	141 kcal	5.6g	2.1g	21.4g	5.1g	4.9g	7.1g	0.5g

Healthy eating tips
- Use the minimum amount of salt.
- Try replacing half the cream sauce with natural yoghurt.

Vegetables and vegetable protein — 12

Leafy vegetables

53 Spring greens (*choux de printemps*)

0.5 kg will serve 3–4 portions; 1.25 kg will serve 8–10 portions.

Prepare and cook as for cabbage (recipe 56), for 10–15 minutes according to age and type. Do not overcook.

Energy	Cals	Fat	Sat fat	Carb	Sugar	Protein	Fibre	Sodium
103 kJ	25 kcal	0.9g	0.1g	2.0g	1.8g	2.4g	4.3g	0.1g

54 Leaf spinach (*épinards en branches*)

0.5 kg will yield two portions.

1 Remove the stems and discard them.
2 Wash the leaves carefully in plenty of water, several times if necessary.
3 Cook in lightly salted boiling water for 3–5 minutes; do not overcook.
4 Refresh under cold water, squeeze dry into a ball.
5 When required for service, either reheat and serve plain or place into a pan containing 25–50 g butter, loosen with a fork and reheat quickly without colouring.

Energy	Cals	Fat	Sat fat	Carb	Sugar	Protein	Fibre
512 kJ	123 kcal	10.8g	6.6g	1.4g	1.2g	5.2g	6.3g

Using 25 g butter per 0.5 kg.

431

55 Spinach purée

Variation

Creamed spinach purée can be made by mixing in 30 ml cream and 60 ml béchamel or natural yoghurt before serving. Serve with a border of cream.

An addition would be 1 cm triangle-shaped croutons fried in butter.

Spinach may also be served with toasted pine kernels or finely chopped garlic.

Energy	Cals	Fat	Sat fat	Carb	Sugar	Protein	Fibre
588 kJ	143 kcal	11.9g	6.7g	3.3g	3.1g	5.7g	4.2g

Using 25 g butter per 0.5 kg.

0.5 kg will yield 2 portions.
1. Remove the stems and discard them.
2. Wash the leaves very carefully in plenty of water, several times if necessary.
3. Wilt for 2–3 minutes, taking care not to overcook.
4. Place on a tray and allow to cool.
5. Pass through a sieve or mouli, or use a food processor.
6. Reheat in 25–50 g butter, mix with a kitchen spoon, correct the seasoning and serve.

56 Cabbage (*chou vert*)

0.5 kg will serve 3–4 portions; 1.25 kg will serve 8–10 portions.
1. Cut the cabbage in quarters.
2. Remove the centre stalk and outside leaves.
3. Shred and wash well.
4. Place into lightly salted boiling water.
5. Boil steadily or steam until cooked (approximately 5–10 minutes, according to age and type). Do not overcook.
6. Drain immediately in a colander and serve.

Energy	Cals	Fat	Sat fat	Carb	Sugar	Protein	Fibre
38 kJ	9 kcal	0.0g	0.0g	1.1g	1.1g	1.3g	2.5g

Note

Overcooking will lessen the vitamin content and also spoil the colour. This applies to cooking any green vegetable.

Vegetables and vegetable protein

57 Braised red cabbage (*choux à la flamande*)

1. Quarter, trim and shred the cabbage. Wash well and drain.
2. Season lightly with salt and pepper.
3. Place in a well-buttered casserole or pan suitable for placing in the oven (not aluminium or iron, because these metals will cause a chemical reaction that will discolour the cabbage).
4. Add the peeled and cored apples. Cut into 1 cm dice and sugar.
5. Add the vinegar and bacon (if using), cover with a buttered paper and lid.
6. Cook in a moderate oven at 150–200 °C for 1½ hours.
7. Remove the bacon (if used) and serve.

Energy	Cals	Fat	Sat fat	Carb	Sugar	Protein	Fibre
754 kJ	180 kcal	15.2 g	8.4 g	7.8 g	7.7 g	3.4 g	3.2 g

Ingredient	4 portions	10 portions
Red cabbage	300 g	750 g
Salt, pepper		
Butter	50 g	125 g
Cooking apples, peeled and cored	100 g	250 g
Caster sugar	10 g	25 g
Vinegar or red wine	125 ml	310 ml
Bacon trimmings (optional)	50 g	125 g

Strain off most of the liquid after braising

Variation
Other flavourings include 50 g sultanas, grated zest of one orange, pinch of ground cinnamon.

Healthy eating tips
The fat and salt content will be reduced by omitting the bacon.

433

58 Brussels sprouts (*choux de bruxelles*)

0.5 kg will serve 3–4 portions; 1.25 kg will serve 8–10 portions.

1. Using a small knife, trim the stems; remove any discoloured outer leaves. Wash well.
2. Cook in lightly salted boiling water, or steam, for 5–10 minutes according to size. Do not overcook.
3. Drain well in a colander and serve.

Note

Brussels sprouts with butter are cooked and served as outlined here, but brushed with 25–50 g melted butter (60–125 g for 10 portions). For Brussels sprouts with chestnuts, to every 400 g of sprouts add 100 g cooked peeled chestnuts.

Energy	Cals	Fat	Sat fat	Carb	Sugar	Protein	Fibre
82 kJ	20 kcal	0.0 g	0.0 g	1.9 g	1.8 g	3.1 g	3.2 g

Stems

59 Artichoke bottoms

1. Cut off the stalk and pull out all the underneath leaves.
2. With a large knife, cut through the artichoke leaving only 1.5 cm at the bottom of the vegetable.
3. With a small, sharp knife, while holding the artichoke upside down, peel carefully, removing all the leaf and any green part, keeping the bottom as smooth as possible. If necessary, smooth with a peeler.
4. Rub immediately with lemon and keep in lemon water or ascorbic acid solution.
5. Using a spoon or the thumb, remove the centre furry part, which is called the choke. The choke is sometimes removed after cooking.
6. Artichoke bottoms should always be cooked in a blanc (see below).

Energy	Cals	Fat	Sat fat	Carb	Sugar	Protein	Fibre	Sodium
100 kJ	23 kcal	0.2 g	0.1 g	4.2 g	1.2 g	2.5 g	0.9 g	0.1 g

Using blanc version 1.

Vegetables and vegetable protein   12

Pull out the stalk of the artichoke

Alternatively, cut the stalk off

Pull off the leaves at the bottom

Peel the artichoke

Remove the choke

Note

Artichoke bases may be served as a vegetable; they are sometimes filled with another vegetable (e.g. peas, spinach). When they are served ungarnished they are usually cut into quarters.

Blanc (version 1)

Ingredient	4 portions	10 portions
Flour	10 g	25 g
Cold water	0.5 litres	1.25 litre
Salt, to taste		
Lemon, juice of	½	1¼

1 Mix the flour and water together.
2 Add the salt and lemon juice. Pass through a strainer.
3 Place in a pan, bring to the boil, stirring continuously.

Blanc (version 2)

Ingredient	4 portions	10 portions
Water	0.5 litres	1.25 litres
Vitamin C (ascorbic acid) tablets	2	5
Oil	30 ml	75 ml
Salt		

1 Combine the ingredients.

Healthy eating tips

- Use the minimum amount of salt.

60 Globe artichokes

Energy	Cals	Fat	Sat fat	Carb	Sugar	Protein	Fibre
32 kJ	8 kcal	0.0g	0.0g	1.4g	1.4g	0.6g	0.0g

Not including sauce.

Allow 1 artichoke per portion.

1. Cut off the stems close to the leaves.
2. Cut off about 2 cm across the tops of the leaves.
3. Trim the remainder of the leaves with scissors or a small knife.
4. Place a slice of lemon at the bottom of each artichoke.
5. Secure with string.
6. Simmer in gently boiling, lightly salted water (to which a little ascorbic acid – one vitamin C tablet – may be added) until the bottom is tender (20–30 minutes).
7. Refresh under running water until cold.
8. Remove the centre of the artichoke carefully.
9. Scrape away all the furry inside (the choke) and leave clean.
10. Replace the centre, upside down.
11. Reheat by placing in a pan of boiling salted water for 3–4 minutes.
12. Drain and serve accompanied by a suitable sauce.

Artichokes may also be served cold with vinaigrette sauce.

> **Professional tip**
> Do not cook artichokes in an iron or aluminium pan because these metals cause a chemical reaction that will discolour them.

Vegetables and vegetable protein 12

61 Asparagus points or tips

Energy	Cals	Fat	Sat fat	Carb	Sugar	Protein	Fibre	Sodium
124 kJ	29 kcal	0.9g	0.1g	1.6g	1.6g	3.5g	1.6g	0.1g

1 kg of asparagus will yield approximately 8 portions.

1. Using the back of a small knife, carefully remove the tips of the leaves.
2. Scrape the stem, either with the blade of a small knife or a peeler.
3. Wash well. Tie into bundles of about 12 heads.
4. Cut off the excess stem.
5. Cook in lightly salted boiling water for approximately 5–8 minutes.
6. Test if cooked by gently pressing the green part of the stem, which should be tender; do not overcook.
7. Lift carefully out of the water. Remove the string, drain well and serve.

Note

Young thin asparagus, 50 pieces to the bundle, is known as sprew or sprue. It is prepared in the same way as asparagus except that, when it is very thin, the removal of the leaf tips is dispensed with. It may be served as a vegetable, perhaps brushed with butter.

Asparagus tips are also used in numerous garnishes for soups, egg dishes, fish, meat and poultry dishes, cold dishes, salad, and so on.

Professional tip

As the flavour of asparagus is mild and can be leached out very easily through the cooking medium, a method of cookery that ensures that no flavour is lost in the cooking process is microwaving.

1. To microwave, place a piece of cling film over a plate that will fit in the microwave and, more importantly, is microwave safe.
2. Spread the cling film with a little oil and salt, evenly place the asparagus on the plate in a single layer.
3. Cover the plate and asparagus with another piece of cling film, and microwave for 30-second stints until the asparagus is tender; serve immediately.

The benefit of this method is that it retains flavour and colour, and it can be cooked in minutes, as opposed to batch cooking, which will, invariably, cause the asparagus to lose flavour and colour the longer it is stored.

If larger-scale cooking is required, the more traditional method, boiling in lightly salted water, should be used: cooking, say, 100 portions of asparagus in the microwave should be avoided for obvious reasons!

62 Asparagus wrapped in puff pastry with Gruyère

Ingredient	4 portions	10 portions
Gruyère cheese	175 g	440 g
Parmesan, freshly grated	3 tbsp	7½ tbsp
Crème fraiche	250 ml	625 ml
Puff pastry (page 526)	350 g	875 g
Egg wash or milk, for brushing		
Asparagus, freshly cooked	350 g	875 g
Salt, pepper		
Watercress, to garnish		

Energy	Cals	Fat	Sat fat	Carb	Sugar	Protein	Fibre
2,017 kJ	485 kcal	37.7 g	15.0 g	23.4 g	2.5 g	15.9 g	0.8 g

1 Cut the Gruyère cheese into 1 cm dice. In a suitable bowl, mix the Parmesan cheese and crème fraiche; season.

2 Roll out the puff pastry to approximately 0.25 cm thick and cut into squares approximately 18 × 18 cm.

3 Brush the edges with egg wash or milk.

4 Divide the crème fraiche, putting equal amounts on to the centre of each square. Lay the asparagus on top. Place the diced Gruyère cheese firmly between the asparagus.

5 Fold the opposite corners of each square to meet in the centre, like an envelope. Firmly pinch the seams together to seal them. Make a small hole in the centre of each one to allow the steam to escape. Place on a lightly greased baking sheet.

6 Allow to relax for 20 minutes in the refrigerator. Brush with egg wash or milk, sprinkle with Parmesan.

7 Bake in a hot oven at 200 °C for approximately 20–25 minutes until golden brown.

8 Serve garnished with watercress.

Professional tip

Make sure the pastry parcels are well sealed so that the mixture does not escape during cooking.

Healthy eating tips

The puff pastry and cheese make this dish high in fat. Serve with plenty of starchy carbohydrate to dilute it.

Vegetables and vegetable protein | 12

63 Braised chicory

Ingredient	4 portions	10 portions
Fish or chicken stock	200 ml	500 ml
Chicory, medium heads	8	20
Fresh lemon juice	3 tbsp	7½ tbsp
Caster sugar	3 tbsp	7½ tbsp
Sea salt and freshly ground black pepper		
Butter	25 g	60 g

Energy	Cals	Fat	Sat fat	Carb	Sugar	Protein	Fibre
476 kJ	114 kcal	6.3g	3.7g	17.8g	13.5g	1.1g	1.8g

1 Have the stock ready and set aside.
2 Trim the chicory of any bruised outside leaves, then trim the ends and use a small, sharp knife to remove the bitter core at the base of each head.
3 Bring a pan of water to the boil and add the lemon juice, 1 tablespoon of the sugar and salt to taste. Blanch the chicory for 8–10 minutes and drain well.
4 Drain all the liquid from the chicory and, in a large frying pan, heat the butter and brown the chicory on all sides; deglaze with a little stock and simmer for a few minutes, basting the chicory at all times.
5 Arrange the heads in a single layer on a platter, sprinkle with the remaining sugar, and season with salt and pepper. Leave to cool for about 10 minutes.

64 Shallow-fried chicory

Energy	Cals	Fat	Sat fat	Carb	Sugar	Protein	Fibre
484 kJ	118 kcal	12.0g	7.3g	4.8g	1.3g	0.9g	1.5g

Using 37.5 g butter.

1 Trim the stem, remove any discoloured leaves, wash.
2 Cook as for braised chicory (recipe 63).
3 Drain, shallow-fry in a little clarified butter or vegetable oil and colour lightly on both sides.
4 Serve with 10 g per portion nut-brown butter, lemon juice and chopped parsley.

65 Kohlrabi

1. Trim off the stems and leaves – these may be used for soups.
2. Peel thickly at the root end and thinly at the top end. Wash.
3. Cut into even-sized pieces. Young kohlrabi can be cooked whole.
4. Simmer in well-flavoured stock until tender.

Variations
- Serve kohlrabi with cream sauce.
- Kohlrabi may be baked and stuffed.

Note

Kohlrabi is a stem that swells to a turnip shape above the ground. When grown under glass it is pale green in colour; when grown outdoors it is purplish.

Select kohlrabi with tops that are green, young and fresh. If the globes are too large they may be woody and tough.

It can be added to casseroles and stews.

Energy	Cals	Fat	Sat fat	Carb	Sugar	Protein	Fibre
77 kJ	18 kcal	0.2g	0.0g	3.1g	3.0g	1.2g	1.9g

Vegetable fruits

66 Tomato concassé

Ingredient	4 portions	10 portions
Tomatoes	400g	1.25kg
Shallots or onions, chopped	25g	60g
Butter or oil	25g	60g
Salt, pepper		

Energy	Cals	Fat	Sat fat	Carb	Sugar	Protein	Fibre	Sodium
237 kJ	57 kcal	5.3g	3.3g	2.1g	1.9g	0.5g	0.7g	0.3g

Using butter and onions.

Vegetables and vegetable protein

1. Plunge the tomatoes into boiling water for 5–10 seconds – the riper the tomatoes, the less time is required. Refresh immediately.
2. Remove the skins, cut in quarters and remove all the seeds.
3. Roughly chop the flesh of the tomatoes.
4. Meanwhile, cook the chopped onion or shallots without colour in the butter or oil.
5. Add the tomatoes and season lightly.
6. Simmer gently on the side of the stove until the moisture is evaporated.

> **Note**
>
> This is a cooked preparation that is usually included in the normal *mise-en-place* of a kitchen as it is used in a great number of dishes.
>
> Uncooked tomato concassée is often used for *mise-en-place*.

Blanch the tomatoes and then peel them

Cut each tomato into quarters

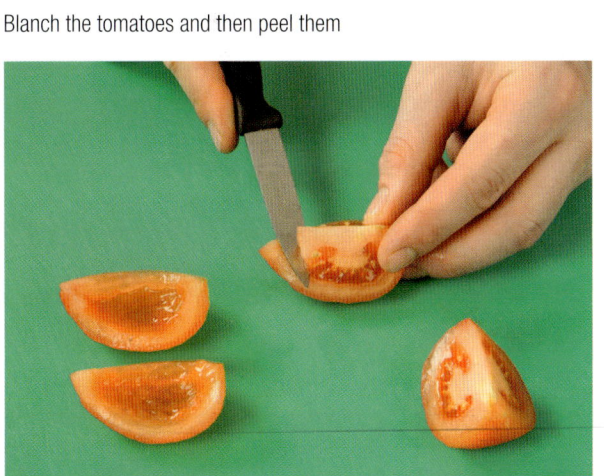

Remove the seeds from each petal

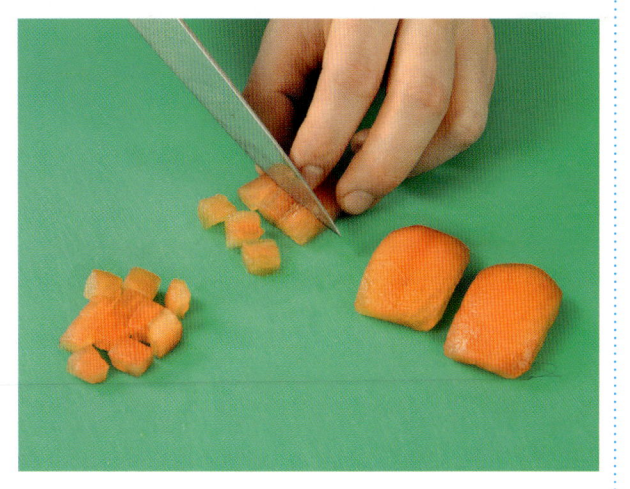

Roughly chop the tomatoes

Practical Cookery 14th edition

67 Stuffed tomatoes

1. Wash the tomatoes, remove the eyes.
2. Remove the top quarter of each tomato with a sharp knife.
3. Carefully empty out the seeds without damaging the flesh.
4. Place on a greased baking tray.
5. Cook the shallots in a little butter or oil without colour.
6. Add the washed chopped mushrooms; season with salt and pepper; add the garlic if using. Cook for 2–3 minutes.
7. Add a little of the strained tomato juice, the breadcrumbs and the parsley; mix to a piping consistency. Correct the seasoning. At this stage, several additions may be made (e.g. chopped ham, cooked rice).
8. Place the mixture in a piping bag with a large plain tube and pipe into the tomato shells. Replace the tops.
9. Brush with oil, season lightly with salt and pepper.
10. Cook in a moderate oven at 180–200 °C for 4–5 minutes.
11. Serve garnished with picked parsley or fresh basil or rosemary.

Ingredient	4 portions	10 portions
Tomatoes, medium-sized	8	20
Duxelle		
Shallots, chopped	10 g	25 g
Butter or oil	25 g	60 g
Mushrooms	150 g	375 g
Salt, pepper		
Clove of garlic, crushed (optional)	1	2–3
Breadcrumbs (white or wholemeal)	25 g	60 g
Parsley, chopped		

Energy	Cals	Fat	Sat fat	Carb	Sugar	Protein	Fibre
430 kJ	102 kcal	5.9 g	3.5 g	10.6 g	5.7 g	2.5 g	2.2 g

Healthy eating tips
- Use a small amount of an unsaturated oil to cook the shallots and brush over the stuffed tomatoes.
- Add the minimum amount of salt.
- Adding cooked rice to the stuffing will increase the amount of starchy carbohydrate.

Cut out the eye of the tomato

Slice off the top and remove the seeds from inside

Pipe in the filling and then replace the top

68 Fried aubergine (*aubergine frite*)

Allow half an aubergine per portion.

1 Remove alternate strips with a peeler.
2 Cut into 0.5 cm slices on the slant.
3 Pass through seasoned flour or milk and flour.
4 Shake off all surplus flour.
5 Deep fry in hot fat at 185 °C. Drain well and serve.

Energy	Cals	Fat	Sat fat	Carb	Sugar	Protein	Fibre
994 kJ	225 kcal	20.0g	3.8g	10.1g	5.9g	1.9g	5.2g

Note
Aubergines may also be shallow-fried, grilled or griddled.

69 Stuffed aubergine

Ingredient	4 portions	10 portions
Aubergines	2	5
Shallots, chopped	10g	25g
Oil or fat, to fry		
Mushrooms	100g	250g
Parsley, chopped		
Tomato concassé	100g	250g
Salt, pepper		
Demi-glace or *jus-lié*	125ml	300ml

Energy	Cals	Fat	Sat fat	Carb	Sugar	Protein	Fibre	Sodium
557 kJ	134 kcal	12.2g	1.5g	4.3g	3.8g	2.4g	4.5g	0.7g

1 Cut the aubergines in two lengthwise.
2 With the point of a small knife, make a cut round the halves approximately 0.5 cm from the edge, then make several cuts 0.5 cm deep in the centre.
3 Deep fry in hot fat at 185 °C for 2–3 minutes; drain well.
4 Scoop out the centre pulp and chop it finely.
5 Cook the shallots in a little oil or fat without colouring.
6 Add the well-washed mushrooms. Cook gently for a few minutes.
7 Mix in the pulp, parsley and tomato; season. Replace in the aubergine skins.
8 Sprinkle with breadcrumbs and melted butter. Brown under the salamander.
9 Serve with a cordon of demi-glace or *jus-lié*.

70 Marrow

1. Peel the marrow with a peeler or small knife.
2. Cut in half lengthwise.
3. Remove the seeds with a spoon.
4. Cut into even pieces, approximately 5 cm square.
5. Cook in lightly salted boiling water, or steam, for 10–15 minutes. Do not overcook.
6. Drain well and serve.

Variation

All the variations for cauliflower (recipes 16 and 17) may be used with marrow.

Energy	Cals	Fat	Sat fat	Carb	Sugar	Protein	Fibre
44 kJ	11 kcal	0.0g	0.0g	2.1g	2.0g	0.6g	0.9g

71 Marrow provençale

Ingredient	4 portions	10 portions
Marrow	400 g	1 kg
Onion, chopped	50 g	125 g
Clove of garlic, chopped	1	2–3
Oil or butter	50 g	125 g
Salt, pepper		
Tomato concassé	400 g	1 kg
Parsley, chopped		

Energy	Cals	Fat	Sat fat	Carb	Sugar	Protein	Fibre
524 kJ	126 kcal	10.6g	6.5g	6.4g	5.7g	1.8g	1.4g

1. Lightly peel the marrow, remove the seeds and cut into 2 cm dice.
2. Cook the onion and garlic in the oil in a pan for 2–3 minutes without colour.
3. Add the marrow and season lightly with salt and pepper.
4. Add the tomato concassé.
5. Cover with a lid and cook gently in the oven or on the side of the stove for 1 hour or until tender.
6. Sprinkle with chopped parsley and serve.

Note

Baby marrows may be served similarly, but reduce the cooking time to 5–10 minutes.

Healthy eating tips

- Use a little unsaturated oil to cook the onion.
- Use the minimum amount of salt.

Vegetables and vegetable protein · 12

72 Shallow-fried courgettes

1. Wash. Top and tail, and cut into round slices 3–6 cm thick.
2. Gently fry in hot oil or butter for 2 or 3 minutes, drain and serve.

Energy	Cals	Fat	Sat fat	Carb	Sugar	Protein	Fibre
456 kJ	111 kcal	10.7g	6.6g	1.9g	1.8g	1.9g	0.9g

Using butter.

73 Deep-fried courgettes

1. Wash. Top and tail, and cut into round slices 3–6 cm thick.
2. Pass through flour, or milk and flour, or batter, and deep fry in hot oil at 185 °C. Drain well and serve.

Energy	Cals	Fat	Sat fat	Carb	Sugar	Protein	Fibre
481 kJ	111 kcal	11.4g	1.4g	1.8g	1.7g	1.8g	0.9g

Using vegetable oil.

Professional tip

Make sure the oil is very hot before adding the courgette. Fry it quickly and drain it before serving.

445

Practical Cookery 14th edition

74 Fettuccine of courgette with chopped basil and balsamic vinegar

Ingredient	4 portions	10 portions
Courgettes, large	2	5
Olive oil	50 ml	125 ml
Olive oil, to finish	20 ml	50 ml
Balsamic vinegar, to finish	20 ml	50 ml
Basil leaves, shredded	2	5

1 Slice the courgettes finely lengthwise, using a mandolin (Japanese slicer).
2 Heat the olive oil in a suitable pan. Sauté the courgette slices quickly without colour for 35 seconds.
3 Place on suitable plates. Drizzle with olive oil and balsamic vinegar, and top with shredded basil leaves.

This may be served as a vegetarian starter or as a garnish for fish and meat dishes.

Energy	Cals	Fat	Sat fat	Carb	Sugar	Protein	Fibre	Sodium
745 kJ	181 kcal	17.9g	2.6g	1.9g	1.8g	1.8g	1.2g	0.0g

75 Courgette flowers

Ingredient	4 portions	10 portions
Flowering courgettes	4	10
Fish mousse (or other mousse, e.g. chicken, veal)	100 g	250 g
Corn oil		
Plain flour for dusting		
Batter		

Energy	Cals	Fat	Sat fat	Carb	Sugar	Protein	Fibre	Sodium
810 kJ	193 kcal	6.6g	1.2g	27.4g	2.2g	7.5g	1.5g	0.0g

Vegetables and vegetable protein | **12**

1. Gently break off the flowers from the courgettes, ensuring they stay intact.
2. Carefully snap out and discard the stigma from the flowers.
3. Place the fish mousse in a bowl, season lightly and mix.
4. Once the mousse is ready, place into a disposable piping bag.
5. Gently open the courgette flowers a little and pipe in the mousse until the flower is half full.
6. Twist the ends of the petals to seal in the mousse.
7. Place the filled flowers into a steamer or steaming basket over a pan of boiling water.
8. Steam for 2–3 minutes, then carefully immerse into a bowl of iced water to stop the cooking process.
9. Remove from the water, pat dry and store in an airtight container in the fridge for up to 2 hours.
10. Heat the oil for deep frying to 180 °C.
11. Roll the filled courgette flowers in plain flour; shake off the excess.
12. Dip them into batter then place them into the fryer for 1 minute until golden brown.
13. Drain briefly on some kitchen paper and serve.

Courgettes with flowers

76 Roast butternut squash

1. Peel the squash and cut it into thick, even pieces.
2. Place on a lightly oiled roasting tray and roast for approximately 20–25 minutes in a hot oven, until the flesh is soft and golden brown.

Energy	Cals	Fat	Sat fat	Carb	Sugar	Protein	Fibre	Sodium
342 kJ	81 kcal	4.1 g	0.5 g	10.4 g	5.6 g	1.4 g	2.5 g	0.0 g

Using 125 g of squash and 1 tsp vegetable oil per portion.

447

77 Roast squash or pumpkin with cinnamon and ginger

Ingredient	4 portions	10 portions
Butternut squash or pumpkin	500 g	1.25 kg
Butter or margarine	25 g	60 g
Olive oil	2 tbsp	5 tbsp
Ginger, peeled and freshly chopped	½ tsp	1¼ tsp
Ground cinnamon	½ tsp	1¼ tsp
Salt		
Caster sugar	10 g	25 g
Lemon, juice of	½	1¼

Energy	Cals	Fat	Sat fat	Carb	Sugar	Protein	Fibre	Sodium
519 kJ	125 kcal	11.0 g	4.2 g	6.0 g	5.3 g	1.1 g	1.7 g	0.0 g

1 Peel the squash, cut it in half and remove the seeds.
2 Cut the squash into 1.5 cm dice or into small wedges.
3 Place the butter into a suitable roasting pan and heat gently. Add the olive oil, ginger and cinnamon.
4 Add the squash gently and stir until the squash is coated in the spice mixture. Season and add the sugar.
5 Place in an oven at 200 °C until tender and golden brown.
6 When cooked, sprinkle with lemon juice.

Note

Garlic may be added to the spice mixture, and mixed spice may be used in place of cinnamon.

Peel and halve the squash, then remove the seeds

Cut the squash into even pieces

Stir the squash pieces into the warm butter and spices before roasting

78 Stuffed peppers (*piment farci*)

Ingredient	4 portions	10 portions
Red peppers, medium-sized	4	10
Carrots, sliced	50 g	125 g
Onions, sliced	50 g	125 g
Bouquet garni		
White stock	0.5 litres	1.25 litres
Salt, pepper		
Pilaff		
Rice (long grain)	200 g	500 g
Salt, pepper		
Onion, chopped	50 g	125 g
Butter	50 g	125 g

Energy	Cals	Fat	Sat fat	Carb	Sugar	Protein	Fibre
1,291 kJ	308 kcal	11.4 g	6.7 g	48.8 g	5.3 g	5.4 g	3.1 g

1. Place the peppers on a tray in the oven or under the salamander for a few minutes, or deep fry in hot oil at 180 °C, until the skin blisters.
2. Remove the skin; carefully cut off the top and empty out all the seeds.
3. Stuff with a well-seasoned pilaff of rice (ingredients as listed above), which may be varied by the addition of mushrooms, tomatoes, ham, and so on.
4. Replace the top of the peppers.
5. Place the peppers on the sliced carrot and onion in a pan suitable for the oven; add the bouquet garni, stock and seasoning. Cover with a buttered paper and a lid.
6. Cook in a moderate oven at 180–200 °C for 1 hour or until tender.
7. Serve garnished with picked parsley.

Healthy eating tips
- This dish is low in fat if the peppers are placed in the oven or under the salamander, not deep fried, and the butter/oil is kept to a minimum.
- Add little or no salt.
- If extra vegetables are added to the rice, and a vegetable stock used, this dish can be a useful vegetarian starter.

Briefly heat the peppers and then peel them

Cut off the top and empty out the seeds

Fill the pepper and then replace the stem

Mixed vegetable dishes

79 Mixed vegetables (*macédoine* or *jardinière de légumes*)

Ingredient	4 portions	10 portions
Carrots	100 g	250 g
Turnips	50 g	125 g
Salt		
French beans	50 g	125 g
Peas	50 g	125 g

Energy	Cals	Fat	Sat fat	Carb	Sugar	Protein	Fibre
58 kJ	14 kcal	0.1 g	0.0 g	2.5 g	1.7 g	1.0 g	2.1 g

1 Peel and wash the carrots and turnips; cut into 0.5 cm dice (macédoine) or batons (jardinière); cook separately in lightly salted water, do not overcook. Refresh.
2 Top and tail the beans; cut into 0.5 cm dice, cook and refresh, do not overcook.
3 Cook the peas and refresh.
4 Mix the vegetables and, when required, reheat in hot salted water.
5 Drain well, serve brushed with melted butter.

80 Ratatouille

Ingredient	4 portions	10 portions
Baby marrow (courgette)	200 g	500 g
Aubergines	200 g	500 g
Tomatoes	200 g	500 g
Oil	50 ml	125 ml
Onions, finely sliced	50 g	125 g
Clove of garlic, peeled and chopped	1	2
Red peppers, diced	50 g	125 g
Green peppers, diced	50 g	125 g
Salt, pepper		
Parsley, chopped	1 tsp	2–3 tsp

Energy	Cals	Fat	Sat fat	Carb	Sugar	Protein	Fibre
579 kJ	138 kcal	12.6 g	1.7 g	5.2 g	4.6 g	1.3 g	2.4 g

1 Trim off both ends of the marrow and aubergines.
2 Remove the skin using a peeler.
3 Cut into 3 mm slices.
4 Concassé the tomatoes (peel, remove seeds, roughly chop).
5 Place the oil in a thick-bottomed pan and add the onions.
6 Cover with a lid and allow to cook gently for 5–7 minutes without colour.

Vegetables and vegetable protein

7 Add the garlic, marrow and aubergine slices, and the peppers.
8 Season lightly with salt and mill pepper.
9 Allow to cook gently for 4–5 minutes, toss occasionally and keep covered.
10 Add the tomato and continue cooking for 20–30 minutes or until tender.
11 Mix in the parsley, correct the seasoning and serve. The vegetables need to be cut evenly so that they will cook evenly; it also improves the texture of the dish.

Healthy eating tips
- Use a little unsaturated oil to cook the onions.
- Use the minimum amount of salt.

Ingredients for ratatouille

Add the tomato to the vegetables during cooking (step 10)

81 Ratatouille pancakes with a cheese sauce

Ingredient	4 portions	10 portions
Ratatouille (recipe 80)		
Pancake batter		
Flour	100 g	250 g
Skimmed milk	250 ml	625 ml
Egg	1	2–3
Pinch of salt		
Sunflower margarine or butter, melted	10 g	25 g
Cheese sauce		
Skimmed milk	500 ml	1.25 litres
Sunflower oil	50 g	125 g
Flour	50 g	125 g
Onion, studded with cloves	1	2–3
Parmesan, grated	25 g	60 g
Egg yolk	1	2–3
Seasoning, cayenne		

1 Prepare and make the pancakes (one per portion).
2 Prepare the ratatouille (see recipe 80) and cheese sauce (see page 113).
3 Season with salt and cayenne pepper.
4 Fill the pancakes with the ratatouille, roll up and place on individual plates or on a service dish.
5 Coat with the cheese sauce and sprinkle with grated Parmesan. Finish by gratinating under the salamander.

Energy	Cals	Fat	Sat fat	Carb	Sugar	Protein	Fibre
2,398 kJ	571 kcal	35.8g	6.5g	46.1g	19.0g	19.6g	6.5g

Using margarine.

451

82 Roasted vegetables

Ingredient	4 portions	10 portions
Red onions, small	1	3
Red peppers	1	3
Yellow peppers	1	3
Courgettes	2	5
Aubergines	1	3
Cloves of garlic, coarsely chopped	1–2	2–4
Olive oil	1 tbsp	2½ tbsp
Balsamic vinegar	1 tbsp	2½ tbsp
Sea salt and freshly milled black pepper		
Fresh rosemary, roughly chopped		
Fresh basil, roughly chopped		

Energy	Cals	Fat	Sat fat	Carb	Sugar	Protein	Fibre
343 kJ	82 kcal	3.6g	0.6g	10.0g	8.6g	3.0g	3.8g

1 Peel the onions and cut into eight pieces. Cut the peppers into halves, deseed and cut each into approximately 4–6 even pieces. Cut the courgettes into 2 × 1 cm batons. Cut the aubergine into 2 × 1 cm batons.
2 Place all the vegetables (and the garlic) into a suitable roasting dish, sprinkle with the olive oil and balsamic vinegar.
3 Season lightly with sea salt and pepper.
4 Sprinkle with rosemary and basil.
5 Place in a preheated oven at 180 °C for approximately 15 minutes.
6 Serve immediately.

Note
These vegetables may also be chilled and served with a salad as a starter.

Healthy eating tips
Lightly brush the vegetables with the olive oil and add the minimum amount of salt.

83 Tempura

Ingredient	4 portions
Vegetable oil	500 ml
Courgettes, sliced	2
Sweet potato, scrubbed and sliced	1
Green pepper, seeds removed and cut into strips	1
Shiitake mushroom, stalks removed and halved if large	4
Onion, sliced as half moons	1
Parsley sprigs, to garnish	4
Batter (all ingredients must be stored in the fridge until just before mixing)	
Egg yolk	1
Ice-cold sparkling water	200 ml
Plain flour, sifted	100 g
Tentsuyu dipping sauce (optional)	
Dashi stock	200 ml
Mirin	3 tbsp
Soy sauce	3 tbsp
Ginger, grated	½ tsp

Energy	Cals	Fat	Sat fat	Carb	Sugar	Protein	Fibre
3,397 kJ	815 kcal	55.9g	7.4g	67.4g	5.3g	14.8g	5.0g

1. To prevent splattering during the frying, make sure to dry all deep fry ingredients thoroughly first with a kitchen towel.
2. For the batter, beat the egg yolk lightly and mix with the ice-cold water.
3. Add half the flour to the egg and water mixture. Give the mixture a few strokes. Add the rest of the flour all at once. Stroke the mixture a few times with chopsticks or a fork until the ingredients are loosely combined. The batter should be very lumpy. If over-mixed, tempura will be oily and heavy.
4. Heat the oil to 160 °C.
5. Dip the vegetables into plain flour and then into the batter, a few pieces at a time. Fry until just crisp and golden (about 1½ minutes).
6. Drain the cooked vegetables on a kitchen towel.
7. Serve immediately with a pinch of salt, garnished with parsley sprigs and lemon wedges, dry-roasted salt or with Tentsuyu dipping sauce in a small bowl with grated ginger. This dish can also be served with an accompaniment of grated white radish.
8. To make the Tentsuyu sauce (if required), combine the ingredients in a small saucepan; heat it through and leave to one side.

Any vegetables with a firm texture may be used for tempura.

Professional tip

The water and other batter ingredients must be ice cold.

The batter should be lumpy to give it texture. Do not over-mix it; this will make it oily and heavy.

Only fry a few pieces at once.

Healthy eating tips

Use sunflower or groundnut oil for frying.

Use sparkling water to make tempura batter

Cut a variety of vegetables into even pieces

Dip each piece into the batter and then deep fry it

84 Vegetable biryani

Ingredient	4 portions	10 portions
Basmati rice	400 g	1.25 kg
Oil	2 tbsp	5 tbsp
Cinnamon stick	½	1¼
Cardamom pods	4	10
Cloves	4	10
Onions, sliced	100 g	250 g
Cloves of garlic, crushed	1	2–3
Green chilli, finely chopped	1	2–3
Root ginger, grated	1 tbsp	2–3 tbsp
Mixed vegetables (e.g. carrots, celery, cauliflower, broccoli, French beans)	600 g	1.5 kg
Tomatoes, blanched, deseeded and chopped, or canned plum tomatoes	400 g	1.25 kg
Tomato purée	25 g	60 g
Salt, pepper		
Coriander leaves, chopped		

Energy	Cals	Fat	Sat fat	Carb	Sugar	Protein	Fibre
2,014 kJ	482 kcal	7.3 g	0.9 g	91.3 g	9.9 g	12.2 g	4.6 g

1. Wash, soak and drain the rice.
2. Partly cook the rice in boiling salted water for 3 minutes. Refresh and drain well.
3. Heat the oil in a suitably sized pan. Add the crushed cinnamon, cardamom and cloves, and sweat for 2 minutes.
4. Add the sliced onions, garlic, chilli and ginger. Continue to sweat until soft.
5. Prepare the vegetables: cut the carrots and celery into batons, the cauliflower and broccoli into florets and the French beans into 2.5 cm lengths.
6. Add the vegetables to the pan and fry for 2–3 minutes.
7. Add the tomatoes and tomato purée. Season.
8. Make sure there is sufficient moisture in the pan to cook the vegetables; usually a little water needs to be added. Ideally, though, the vegetables should cook in their own juices, combined with the tomatoes.
9. When the vegetables are partly cooked, layer them in a casserole or suitable pan with the rice. (Make sure that there is sufficient liquid to cook the rice.)
10. Cover the casserole and finish cooking in a moderate oven at 180 °C for about 20 minutes, or until the rice is tender.
11. Sprinkle with chopped coriander leaves and serve.

Note
A biryani is usually served with a side dish of vegetable curry.

Healthy eating tips
- Keep added salt to a minimum.
- Use a little unsaturated oil to sweat the spices, onions and vegetables.

85 Vegetable curry with rice pilaff

Ingredient	4 portions	10 portions
Mixed vegetables (e.g. cauliflower, broccoli, peppers, carrots, courgettes, mushrooms, aubergines)	600 g	1.5 kg
Butter or oil	100 g	250 g
Onions, chopped finely	150 g	375 g
Garam masala	25 g	60 g
Creamed coconut (or 50 g/125 g desiccated coconut)	25 g	60 g
Curry sauce made using vegetable stock	500 ml	1.5 litre
Rice pilaff (page 159)	100 g	250 g
Flaked almonds, roasted	50 g	125 g

Energy	Cals	Fat	Sat fat	Carb	Sugar	Protein	Fibre
1,814 kJ	432 kcal	35.5 g	7.4 g	23.5 g	16.3 g	6.4 g	6.7 g

1. Prepare the vegetables: cut the cauliflower and broccoli into small florets, blanch and refresh; cut the peppers in half, remove the seeds, cut into 1 cm dice; cut the carrots into large dice, blanch and refresh; and cut the courgettes into 1 cm dice. Leave the mushrooms whole; cut the aubergines into 1 cm dice.
2. Heat the butter or oil and sweat the onion.
3. Add the garam masala; sweat for approximately 2 minutes and add the coconut.
4. Add all the vegetables; sweat together for approximately 5 minutes.
5. Add the curry sauce, bring to the boil and simmer gently until all the vegetables are cooked but still crunchy in texture.
6. Make the rice pilaff according to the recipe on page 159. Add the roasted flaked almonds after cooking.
7. Serve the curry in a suitable dish with the rice pilaff, poppadoms and a curry tray with mango chutney.

Curry sauce

Ingredient	4 portions	10 portions
Onion, chopped	50 g	125 g
Clove of garlic, crushed	¼	½
Butter or oil	10 g	25 g
Flour	10 g	25 g
Curry powder	5 g	12 g
Tomato purée	5 g	12 g
Stock	375 ml	1 litre
Apple, chopped	25 g	60 g
Chutney, chopped	1 tbsp	2 tbsp
Desiccated coconut	5 g	12 g
Sultanas	10 g	25 g
Ginger root, grated *or*	10 g	25 g
Ground ginger	5 g	12 g
Salt		

1. Gently cook the onion and garlic in the fat in a small sauteuse without colouring.
2. Mix in the flour and curry powder. Cook gently to a sandy mixture.
3. Mix in the tomato purée, cool.
4. Gradually add the boiling stock and mix to a smooth sauce.
5. Add the remainder of the ingredients, season with salt, and simmer for 30 minutes. Skim and correct the seasoning.

Healthy eating tips

- Use a small amount of an unsaturated oil to sweat the onions.
- No added salt is necessary if the stock used contains yeast extract.

Vegetable protein

86 Crispy deep-fried tofu

Allow 50 g of firm tofu per portion.

1. Cut the firm tofu into cubes.
2. Coat the tofu cubes with any of the following: flour, egg and breadcrumbs; milk and flour; cornstarch; arrowroot.
3. Deep fry the tofu at 180 °C until golden brown. Drain.
4. Serve garnished with freshly grated ginger and julienne of herbs.

Serve with a tomato sauce flavoured with coriander.

Healthy eating tips
- Use an unsaturated oil to fry the tofu.
- Make sure the oil is hot so that less is absorbed.
- Alternatively, try dry-frying the tofu.

Energy	Cals	Fat	Sat fat	Carb	Sugar	Protein	Fibre
543 kJ	131 kcal	8.9 g	0.0 g	1.0 g	0.5 g	11.8 g	0.0 g

For a 50 g portion.

87 Chinese vegetable and seitan stir-fry

Ingredient	4 portions	10 portions
Hoisin sauce	70 ml	175 ml
Vegetable oil	30 ml	75 ml
Soy sauce	60 ml	150 ml
Rice vinegar	30 ml	75 ml
Sugar	30 g	75 g
Vegetable stock	400 ml	1 litre
Cornflour	30 g	75 g
Garlic cloves, chopped	3	7½
Fresh ginger, chopped	2 tsp	5 tsp
Seitan (see page 397), cut into 2 cm pieces	500 g	1.25 kg
Spring onions, chopped	8	20
Red pepper, shredded	2	5
Yellow pepper, shredded	2	5
Broccoli, cut into small florets	250 g	625 g
French beans	250 g	625 g

1. In a suitable saucepan whisk together the hoisin sauce, half the vegetable oil, half the soy sauce, the rice vinegar, sugar and vegetable stock. Bring to boil and add the cornflour (diluted in a little water to make a slurry). Add the garlic and ginger. Stir.
2. In a suitable wok, stir fry the seitan in the remaining vegetable oil, then add the remaining soy sauce. Stir fry for approximately 3 minutes. Add the spring onions, peppers, broccoli and French beans. Stir fry for a further 3 minutes.
3. Add the sauce mixture to the stir-fry; cooking until the vegetables are *al dente*.
4. Serve with freshly cooked noodles or pilaff rice.

88 Papaya and soya bean salad

1. In a suitable pan, add the oil and heat to a high temperature.
2. Add the spices. Stir well for 1 minute, then add the soya beans and cook for approximately 3 minutes. Allow to cool.
3. Put the diced papaya and cooked rice in a bowl, then add the cooled soya beans and spices.
4. Add seasoning and lime juice, and mix well.
5. Serve in a salad bowl.

Ingredient	4 portions	10 portions
Olive oil	30 ml	75 g
Ground coriander	5 g	12.5 g
Ground cardamom	5 g	12.5 g
Fennel seeds	5 g	12.5 g
Mustard seeds	5 g	12.5 g
Curry leaves	10 g	25 g
Soya beans, fresh or thawed from frozen	150 g	375 g
Papaya, peeled, seeded and diced	300 g	750 g
Cooked basmati rice	150 g	375 g
Seasoning		
Lime juice	1	2

Energy	Cals	Fat	Sat fat	Carb	Sugar	Protein	Fibre	Sodium
881 kJ	211 kcal	11.3 g	1.5 g	19.6 g	7.5 g	7.6 g	6.0 g	0.2 g

89 Thai-style Quorn and vegetable curry

Ingredient	4 portions	10 portions
Frozen Quorn pieces, defrosted	300 g	750 g
Light soy sauce	30 ml	75 ml
Vegetable oil	30 ml	75 ml
Thai green curry paste	30 g	75 g
Shallots, finely chopped	2	5
Green chilli, deseeded and finely chopped	1	3
Garlic cloves, crushed and chopped	3	7
Coconut milk	400 ml	1 litre
Baby corn	125 g	312 g
French beans, cut in half	125 g	312 g
Fresh asparagus, trimmed	100 g	250 g
Courgettes, sliced or cut into small wedges	1	2
Red pepper, deseeded and diced	1	2
Pak choi leaves	125 g	312 g
Lime juice	1	2
Fresh coriander, chopped	1 tbsp	2 tbsp
Spring onions, trimmed and chopped	2	5

1. Marinate the Quorn pieces in a suitable dish with the light soy sauce for at least 30 minutes.
2. Heat the oil in a wok. Add the green Thai curry paste and cook for 2 minutes, stirring frequently.
3. Add the shallots, chilli and garlic, and stir for 2 minutes. Stir in the marinated Quorn and cook for a further minute.
4. Add the coconut milk and bring to the boil. Add the baby corn, French beans, asparagus, courgettes and red pepper. Simmer for approximately 4 minutes.
5. Add the pak choi, cover with a lid and cook for 1 minute. Add the lime juice and half the coriander.
6. Sprinkle with the remaining coriander and chopped spring onions, and serve with steamed Thai jasmine rice.

Energy	Cals	Fat	Sat fat	Carb	Sugar	Protein	Fibre	Sodium
1,564 kJ	376 kcal	27.5 g	17.5 g	14.4 g	8.0 g	17.7 g	9.9 g	0.8 g

Vegetables and vegetable protein   12

Other vegetarian dishes

90 Cheese fritters (*beignets au fromage*)

1. Bring the water and butter to the boil in a thick-based pan. Remove from the heat.
2. Add the flour; mix with a kitchen spoon.
3. Return to a gentle heat and mix well until the mixture leaves the sides of the pan. Remove from the heat. Allow to cool slightly.
4. Gradually add the eggs, beating well. Add the cheese and season.
5. Using a spoon, scoop the mixture in pieces the size of a walnut and place into deep hot fat at 185 °C.
6. Allow to cook, with the minimum of handling, for about 10 minutes.
7. Drain and serve sprinkled with grated Parmesan.

Healthy eating tips
- Use sunflower margarine for the fritters.
- No extra salt is needed as the cheese has salt in it.
- Fry in hot sunflower oil and drain on kitchen paper.

Ingredient	4 portions	10 portions
Water	125 ml	310 ml
Butter	50 g	125 g
Flour, white or wholemeal	60 g	200 g
Eggs, medium	2	5
Parmesan cheese, grated	50 g	125 g
Salt, cayenne		

Energy	Cals	Fat	Sat fat	Carb	Sugar	Protein	Fibre
1,409 kJ	340 kcal	28.4 g	11.2 g	11.8 g	0.4 g	9.9 g	0.5 g

91 Cheese soufflé (soufflé au fromage)

Ingredient	4 portions	10 portions
Butter or margarine	25 g	60 g
Flour	15 g	50 g
Milk	125 ml	310 ml
Egg yolks	3	8
Salt, cayenne pepper		
Cheese, grated	50 g	125 g
Egg whites	4	10

Energy	Cals	Fat	Sat fat	Carb	Sugar	Protein	Fibre
3,223 kJ	767 kcal	60.2 g	28.2 g	17.6 g	6.1 g	39.7 g	0.5 g

Using hard margarine.

1. Melt the butter in a thick-based pan.
2. Add the flour and mix with a kitchen spoon.
3. Cook out for a few seconds without colouring.
4. Gradually add the cold milk and mix to a smooth sauce.
5. Simmer for a few minutes.
6. Add 1 egg yolk, mix in quickly; immediately remove from the heat.
7. When cool, add the remaining yolks. Season with salt and cayenne.
8. Add the cheese.
9. Place the egg whites and a pinch of salt (a pinch of egg white powder will help strengthen the whites) in a scrupulously clean bowl and whisk until stiff.
10. Add one-eighth of the whites to the mixture and mix well.
11. Gently fold in the remaining seven-eighths of the mixture; mix as lightly as possible. Place into a buttered soufflé case.
12. Cook in a hot oven at 220 °C for 25–30 minutes for a large soufflé or approximately 10 minutes for individual soufflés.
13. Remove from the oven, place on a round flat dish and serve immediately.

Healthy eating tips
- Use sunflower margarine and semi-skimmed milk to make the sauce.
- No added salt is needed as the cheese has salt in it.

Salads

92 Salad leaves

As these are eaten raw they may contain live food-poisoning bacteria; they must be thoroughly washed to remove any soil.

Lettuce (*laitue*) and iceberg lettuce

1. Trim off the root and remove the outside leaves.
2. Wash thoroughly and drain well.
3. The outer leaves can be pulled off and the hearts cut into quarters.

Cos lettuce (*laitue romaine*)

1. Trim off the root end and remove the outside leaves.
2. Wash thoroughly and drain well.
3. Cut into quarters.

Rocket

This is a small-leafed, sharp, peppery-tasting salad. Trim, wash well and drain.

Chicory (*endive belge*)

1. Trim off the root end.
2. Cut into 1 cm lengths; wash well and drain.

Curled chicory (*endive frisée*)

Thoroughly wash and trim off the stalk. Drain well.

Watercress (*cresson*)

Watercress, as the name suggests, is grown in water and, as there is always the danger that the water may have been polluted, it must be washed thoroughly in clean water.

Trim off the stalk ends, discard any discoloured leaves, wash thoroughly and drain.

Mustard and cress

1. Trim off the stalk ends of the cress.
2. Wash well and lift out of the water so as to leave the seed cases behind.
3. Drain well.

93 Mixed salad (*salade panachée*)

A typical mixed salad would consist of lettuce, tomato, cucumber, watercress, radishes, and so on – almost any kind of salad vegetable can be used.

Neatly arrange in a salad bowl; offer a vinaigrette separately.

94 Green salad (salade verte)

Any of the green salads – lettuce, cos lettuce, lamb's lettuce (also known as corn salad or mâche), curled chicory – or any combination of green salads may be used, and a few leaves of radicchio.
Neatly arrange in a salad bowl; serve with a vinaigrette separately.

95 French salad (salade française)

The usual ingredients are lettuce, tomato and cucumber, but these may be varied with other salad vegetables, and in some cases with quarters of egg.
A vinaigrette made with French mustard (French dressing) should be offered.

Vegetables and vegetable protein — 12

96 Radishes (*radis*)

Allow 3–5 radishes per portion.

1. Trim the green stems to about 2 cm long. Cut off the root end.
2. Wash well, drain. Cut into thin slices or serve whole. Dress neatly.

97 Cucumber

1. Peel the cucumber if desired.
2. Cut into thin slices and arrange neatly.
3. Lightly dress with vinaigrette or serve separately. Alternatively, cucumber may be sliced into 0.5 cm dice and bound with mayonnaise or yoghurt.

Note

This should not be served as a single hors d'oeuvre or main course.

Professional tip

To remove indigestible juices from the cucumber, slice and lightly sprinkle with salt. Allow the salt to draw out the water for approximately 1 hour, wash well under cold water and drain. This will make the cucumber limp.

Ingredient	4 portions	10 portions
Cucumber	½	1¼
Vinaigrette	1 tbsp	2½ tbsp

Energy	Cals	Fat	Sat fat	Carb	Sugar	Protein	Fibre	Sodium
80 kJ	20 kcal	1.7g	0.2g	0.7g	0.7g	0.3g	0.3g	0.0g

Healthy eating tips

- Vegetable-based salads are a healthy way to start a meal.
- Add the minimum amount of salt.

Practical Cookery 14th edition

98 Tomatoes (*tomates*)

Allow 1 tomato per portion.

1 Wash the tomatoes. Remove the eyes and slice thinly or cut into segments.
2 Dress neatly.

99 Tomato salad (*salade de tomates*)

Ingredient	4 portions	10 portions
Tomatoes	200 g	500 g
Lettuce	¼	½
Vinaigrette	1 tbsp	2½ tbsp
Onion or chives (optional), chopped	10 g	25 g
Parsley or mixed fresh herbs, chopped		

1 Peel the tomatoes if required. Slice thinly and arrange neatly on the lettuce leaves.
2 Sprinkle with the vinaigrette, onion (blanched if required) and parsley.

Variation

Alternate slices of tomato and mozzarella with basic dressing.

Energy	Cals	Fat	Sat fat	Carb	Sugar	Protein	Fibre
99 kJ	24 kcal	1.7 g	0.3 g	1.7 g	1.7 g	0.9 g	1.0 g

Vegetables and vegetable protein   12

100 Tomato and cucumber salad (*salade de tomates et concombres*)

Ingredient	4 portions	10 portions
Tomatoes	2	5
Cucumber	½	1¼
Vinaigrette	1 tbsp	2½ tbsp
Parsley or mixed fresh herbs, chopped		

1 Alternate slices of tomato and cucumber.
2 Sprinkle with the vinaigrette and parsley.

Professional tip
Blanch the tomatoes so that you can remove the skins, which are hard to digest.

Energy	Cals	Fat	Sat fat	Carb	Sugar	Protein	Fibre
112 kJ	27 kcal	2.0g	0.3g	1.9g	1.8g	0.5g	0.6g

101 Beetroot salad (*salade de betterave*)

Ingredient	4 portions	10 portions
Cooked beetroot, neatly cut or sliced	200g	500g
Onion or chives (optional), chopped	10g	25g
Vinaigrette	1 tbsp	2½ tbsp
Parsley, chopped		

Energy	Cals	Fat	Sat fat	Carb	Sugar	Protein	Fibre
134 kJ	32 kcal	2.0g	0.3g	3.2g	3.1g	0.7g	0.9g

1 Combine all the ingredients, except the parsley, blanching the onion if required.
2 Dress neatly and sprinkle with the chopped parsley.

Professional tip
- To cook the beetroot, blanch and then simmer it.
- Wear gloves when handling beetroot to avoid staining the skin.

Variation
Add 60–120 ml mayonnaise or natural yoghurt in place of vinaigrette (150–200 ml for 10 portions).

102 Coleslaw

Ingredient	4 portions	10 portions
White or Chinese cabbage	200 g	500 g
Carrot	50 g	125 g
Onion (optional)	25 g	60 g
Mayonnaise, natural yoghurt or fromage frais	125 ml	300 ml

Energy	Cals	Fat	Sat fat	Carb	Sugar	Protein	Fibre
629 kJ	150 kcal	14.8 g	2.2 g	2.9 g	2.9 g	1.5 g	1.8 g

Using mayonnaise.

1. Trim off the outside leaves of the cabbage.
2. Cut into quarters. Remove the centre stalk.
3. Wash the cabbage, shred finely and drain well.
4. Mix with a fine julienne of raw carrot and shredded raw onion. To lessen the harshness of raw onion, blanch and refresh.
5. Bind with mayonnaise, natural yoghurt or vinaigrette.

Healthy eating tips

Replace some or all of the mayonnaise with natural yoghurt and/or fromage frais.

Professional tip

Cut the cabbage into fine julienne to give the coleslaw a good, even texture.

103 Potato salad

Ingredient	4 portions	10 portions
Potatoes, cooked	200 g	500 g
Vinaigrette	1 tbsp	2½ tbsp
Onion or chive (optional), chopped	10 g	25 g
Mayonnaise or natural yoghurt	125 ml	300 ml
Salt, pepper		
Parsley or mixed fresh herbs, chopped		

Energy	Cals	Fat	Sat fat	Carb	Sugar	Protein	Fibre
503 kJ	120 kcal	8.7 g	1.3 g	10.0 g	0.3 g	1.0 g	0.7 g

Using mayonnaise.

1. Cut the potatoes into ½–1 cm dice; sprinkle with vinaigrette.
2. Mix with the onion or chive, add the mayonnaise and correct the seasoning. (The onion may be blanched to reduce its harshness.)
3. Dress neatly and sprinkle with chopped parsley or herbs.

This is not usually served as a single hors d'oeuvre or main course.

> **Professional tip**
> Mixing the potato, onion and mayonnaise gives a good flavour and texture, but be careful not to mix them too much or the potatoes will break up.

Variation

- Potato salad can also be made by dicing raw peeled or unpeeled potato, cooking them – preferably by steaming (to retain shape) – and mixing with vinaigrette while warm.
- Try adding two chopped hard-boiled eggs or 100 g of peeled dessert apple mixed with lemon juice, or a small bunch of picked watercress leaves.
- Potatoes may be cooked with mint and allowed to cool with the mint.
- Cooked small new potatoes can be tossed in vinaigrette with chopped fresh herbs (e.g. mint, parsley, chives).

104 Waldorf salad

Ingredient	4 portions	10 portions
Celery or celeriac	2 sticks/100 g	5 sticks/250 g
Russet apples	2	5
Walnuts, shelled and peeled	25 g	62 g
Mayonnaise		
Lettuce leaves, to serve		

Energy	Cals	Fat	Sat fat	Carb	Sugar	Protein	Fibre	Sodium
657 kJ	159 kcal	14.0 g	1.8 g	7.0 g	6.9 g	1.6 g	2.2 g	0.1 g

1. Dice celery or celeriac and crisp russet apples.
2. Mix with shelled and peeled walnuts and bind with mayonnaise.
3. Dress on quarters or leaves of lettuce (may also be served in hollowed-out apples).

When mixing in the mayonnaise, add just enough to give the right texture and flavour.

> **Healthy eating tips**
> Try using some yoghurt in place of the mayonnaise, which will proportionally reduce the fat.

Practical Cookery 14th edition

105 French bean salad (*salade de haricots verts*)

Ingredient	4 portions	10 portions
French beans, cooked	200 g	500 g
Vinaigrette	1 tbsp	2½ tbsp
Salt, pepper		

Combine all the ingredients.

> **Professional tip**
> Cook the beans *al dente*, so that the salad will have a crunchy texture.

Energy	Cals	Fat	Sat fat	Carb	Sugar	Protein	Fibre
125 kJ	30 kcal	1.9 g	0.3 g	2.5 g	1.2 g	0.9 g	2.0 g

> **Healthy eating tips**
> Add salt sparingly.

106 Vegetable salad/Russian salad

Ingredient	4 portions	10 portions
Carrots	100 g	250 g
Turnips	50 g	125 g
French beans	50 g	125 g
Peas	50 g	125 g
Vinaigrette	1 tbsp	2–3 tbsp
Mayonnaise or natural yoghurt	125 ml	300 ml
Salt, pepper		

Energy	Cals	Fat	Sat fat	Carb	Sugar	Protein	Fibre
392 kJ	93 kcal	8.8 g	1.3 g	2.5 g	2.1 g	1.3 g	3.0 g

Using mayonnaise.

1 Peel and wash the carrots and turnips, cut into 0.5 cm dice or batons.
2 Cook separately in salted water, refresh and drain well.
3 Top and tail the beans, and cut into 0.5 cm dice; cook, refresh and drain well.
4 Cook the peas, refresh and drain well.
5 Mix all the well-drained vegetables with vinaigrette and then mayonnaise.
6 Correct the seasoning. Dress neatly.

Do not overcook the vegetables, and drain them well before adding the dressing – otherwise the salad will be too wet.

> **Healthy eating tips**
> - Try half mayonnaise and half natural yoghurt.
> - Season with the minimum amount of salt.

Vegetables and vegetable protein | 12

107 Greek-style mushrooms

1. Combine all the ingredients except the mushrooms, to create a Greek-style cooking liquor.
2. Cook the mushrooms gently in the cooking liquor for 3 to 4 minutes.
3. Serve cold with the unstrained liquor.

Professional tip

Simmer the vegetables carefully so that they are correctly cooked and absorb the flavours.

Ingredient	4 portions	10 portions
Water	250 ml	625 ml
Olive oil	60 ml	150 ml
Lemon, juice of	1	1½
Bay leaf	½	1
Sprig of thyme		
Peppercorns	6	15
Coriander seeds	6	15
Salt		
Small white button mushrooms, cleaned	200 g	500 g

Variation

Other vegetables such as artichokes and cauliflower can also be cooked in this style, using the same liquor.
- For artichokes, peel and trim 6 artichokes for 4 portions (or 15 for 10); cut the leaves short and remove the chokes. Blanch the artichokes in water with a little lemon juice for 10 minutes, refresh, then simmer in the Greek-style liquor for 15–20 minutes.
- For cauliflower, trim and wash one medium cauliflower for 4 portions (2 for 10); break it into small sprigs about the size of cherries. Blanch the sprigs for about 5 minutes, refresh, then simmer in the Greek-style liquor for 5–10 minutes. Keep the cauliflower slightly undercooked and crisp.

Energy	Cals	Fat	Sat fat	Carb	Sugar	Protein	Fibre
587 kJ	142 kcal	15.2 g	2.2 g	0.4 g	0.3 g	1.0 g	0.6 g

108 Haricot bean salad

Ingredient	4 portions	10 portions
Haricot beans, cooked	200 g	500 g
Vinaigrette	1 tbsp	2½ tbsp
Parsley, chopped		
Onion, chopped and blanched if necessary	¼	½
Chives (optional)	15 g	40 g
Salt, pepper		

Energy	Cals	Fat	Sat fat	Carb	Sugar	Protein	Fibre
278 kJ	66 kcal	2.1 g	0.4 g	9.0 g	0.7 g	3.3 g	3.1 g

1. Combine all the ingredients.

This recipe can be used for any type of dried bean.

Healthy eating tips
- Lightly dress with vinaigrette.
- Add salt sparingly.

Practical Cookery 14th edition

109 Three-bean salad

Use 200 g (500 g for 10 portions) of three different dried beans (for example, red kidney, black-eyed, flageolet). Proceed as for a haricot bean salad (recipe 108).

Energy	Cals	Fat	Sat fat	Carb	Sugar	Protein	Fibre
1,849 kJ	440 kcal	8.7 g	1.1 g	63.4 g	6.3 g	30.9 g	36.0 g

For 4 portions.

110 Caesar salad

Ingredient	4 portions	10 portions
Cos lettuce (medium size)	2	5
Croutons, 2 cm square	16	40
Eggs, fresh	2	5
Dressing		
Garlic, finely chopped	1 tsp	2½ tsp
Anchovy fillets, mashed	4	10
Lemon juice	1 tsp	2½ tsp
Virgin olive oil	6 tbsp	15 tbsp
White wine vinegar	1 tbsp	2½ tbsp
Salt, black mill pepper		
To serve		
Parmesan, freshly grated	75 g	190 g

Energy	Cals	Fat	Sat fat	Carb	Sugar	Protein	Fibre
1,494 kJ	361 kcal	32.2 g	7.9 g	5.1 g	2.0 g	12.9 g	1.2 g

Using toast for croutons.

1. Separate the lettuce leaves, wash, dry thoroughly and refrigerate.
2. Lightly grill or fry (in good fresh oil) the croutons on all sides.
3. Plunge the eggs into boiling water for 1 minute, remove and set aside.
4. Break the lettuce into serving-sized pieces and place into a salad bowl.
5. Mix the dressing, break the eggs, spoon out the contents, mix with a fork, add to the dressing and mix into the salad.
6. Mix in the cheese, scatter the croutons on top and serve.

Professional tip
Because the eggs are only lightly cooked, they must be perfectly fresh, and the salad must be prepared and served immediately. In the interests of food safety, the eggs are sometimes hard boiled.

Alternatively, the salad may be garnished with hard-boiled gull's eggs.

Healthy eating tips
- No added salt is needed; anchovies and cheese are high in salt.
- Oven bake the croutons.
- Serve with fresh bread or rolls.

111 Niçoise salad

Ingredient	4 portions	10 portions
Tomatoes	100 g	250 g
French beans, cooked	200 g	500 g
Diced potatoes, cooked	100 g	250 g
Salt, pepper		
Vinaigrette	1 tbsp	2½ tbsp
Anchovy fillets	10 g	25 g
Capers	5 g	12 g
Stoned olives	10 g	25 g

Energy	Cals	Fat	Sat fat	Carb	Sugar	Protein	Fibre
217 kJ	52 kcal	2.4 g	0.4 g	6.3 g	1.2 g	1.7 g	2.5 g

1 Peel the tomatoes, deseed and cut into neat segments.
2 Dress the beans, tomatoes and potatoes neatly.
3 Season with salt and pepper. Add the vinaigrette.
4 Decorate with anchovies, capers and olives.

Healthy eating tips
- Lightly dress with vinaigrette.
- The anchovies are high in salt, so no added salt is necessary.

112 Avocado and bacon salad

Ingredient	4 portions	10 portions
Thin streaky bacon rashers, rind and excess fat trimmed	8	20
Fresh lemon juice	1 tbsp	2½ tbsp
Garlic clove, crushed finely	1	2½
Extra virgin olive oil	2 tbsp	5 tbsp
Salt and freshly ground black pepper		
Ripe avocados, medium	2	5
Snow pea sprouts, stems trimmed	50 g	125 g

Energy	Cals	Fat	Sat fat	Carb	Sugar	Protein	Fibre	Sodium
1,462 kJ	354 kcal	34.4 g	7.6 g	2.4 g	0.7 g	9.0 g	4.9 g	1.0 g

1 Grill the bacon rashers under a salamander until crisp. Transfer to a tray lined with kitchen paper and allow to cool.
2 Place the lemon juice and garlic in a mixing bowl and whisk in the olive oil. Season with salt and pepper.
3 Halve the avocados lengthways, remove the stones and peel the skin. Place the avocados on to a chopping board, cut side down, and cut in half lengthways, then crossways into slices 1 cm thick.
4 Layer the avocados, bacon and snow pea sprouts on serving plates, drizzling the dressing between the layers. Serve immediately.

13 Bread and dough products

Recipes included in this chapter

No.	Recipe	Page
	Bread doughs	
1	Wholemeal bread	476
2	Seeded bread rolls	477
3	Parmesan rolls	478
4	Red onion and sage rolls	478
5	Sundried tomato bread	479
6	Olive bread	480
7	Soda bread	481
8	Rye bread	482
9	Bagels	483
10	Cholla bread	484
11	Focaccia	484
12	Naan bread	485
13	Pizza	486
14	Pitta bread	487
15	Pitta bread without yeast	488
	Bread products	
16	Sandwiches	489
17	Wraps	490
18	Bagels	490
	Buns	
19	Bun dough	491
20	Bath buns	493
21	Hot cross buns	493
22	Swiss buns	494
23	Doughnuts	493
	Savarin doughs	
24	Savarin dough	495
25	Savarin with fruit	497
26	Marignans chantilly	497
27	Blueberry baba	497

Ingredients

The principal ingredients in bread and dough products are wheat flour and yeast. Bread and bread products form the basis of our diet and are staple products in our society. We eat bread at breakfast, lunch and dinner, as sandwiches, bread rolls, croissants, French sticks, and so on. Bread is also used as an ingredient for many other dishes, either as slices for sandwiches or toast, as fried bread or as breadcrumbs.

Dough consists of strong flour (flour with a high gluten and protein content), water, salt and yeast, which are kneaded together to the required consistency at a suitable temperature. It is then allowed to prove (to rise and increase in size), when the yeast produces carbon dioxide and water, which aerates the dough. When baked it produces a light, digestible product with flavour and colour.

Salted dough is more manageable than unsalted dough. Salt is usually added a few moments before the end of the kneading, since its function is to help expand the dough's volume.

Flour-based products provide energy and a variety of vitamins and minerals. Wholemeal bread products also provide roughage, an essential part of a healthy diet.

Dough

Fermentation

For dough to become leavened bread (bread that has risen, rather than flat bread) it must go through a fermentation process. This is brought about by the action of yeast, a living micro-organism rich in protein and vitamin B. The yeast reacts with enzymes in the dough, which converts sugar into alcohol, producing the characteristic flavour of bread. The action also produces carbon dioxide, which makes the bread rise.

Yeast requires ideal conditions for growth. These are:
- **warmth**: a good temperature for dough production is 22–30 °C
- **moisture**: the liquid should be added at approximately 37 °C – if it is cooler, the yeast may not activate; if it is any hotter it may kill the yeast
- **food**: this is obtained from the starch in the flour
- **time**: this is needed to allow the yeast to grow.

Dried yeast has been dehydrated and must be creamed with a little water before use. It will keep for several months in its dry state. Some types of dried yeast can be used straight from the packet.

Bread and dough products

Yeast will not survive in a high concentration of sugar or salt, and its growth will slow down in a very rich dough with a high fat and egg content.

When mixing yeast in water or milk, make sure that the liquid is at the correct temperature (37 °C), and disperse the yeast in the liquid (the word 'disperse' is used as living organisms cannot be dissolved).

Why does dough ferment?

It is interesting to understand why doughs ferment and what the effects are on the end product. In order to understand why yeast dough rises, it is important to note that the main ingredients of natural leavening are water, air and, most importantly, sugar, which is transformed into carbon dioxide and alcohol, and causes the leavening. The carbon dioxide forms bubbles inside the dough and makes it rise. Fermentation is a transformation undergone by organic matter (sugars).

Types of dough

Dough products come in a variety of forms and styles. The variety of flour alongside the additional ingredients incorporated, whether the dough is leavened or unleavened, provides dough products with their own unique qualities. The majority of doughs have some sort of leavening agent, usually yeast, or a starter, from which the natural yeast in flour is developed slowly over a long period of time and replaced with fresh flour and water as the required amount of the starter is used to produce the bread in question.

Some dough products do not require yeast as a raising agent. Soda bread, for example, uses bicarbonate of soda, an alkali which reacts with the acidic components within doughs and batters to release carbon dioxide. The carbon dioxide raises the product and helps with the development of texture. Other dough products, such as pitta bread and flatbreads, do not use a raising agent and are referred to as unleavened breads.

Enriched doughs

The basic bread dough of wheat flour, yeast and water may be enriched with fat, sugar, eggs, milk and numerous other ingredients. Some examples of enriched doughs are:

- **buns**: a rich dough enriched with eggs, butter and sugar, used for a wide variety of buns including Chelsea buns, Swiss buns and teacakes
- **savarin**: a rich yeast dough used for savarins, babas and marignans
- **brioche**: a rich yeast dough with a high butter (fat) content.

Laminated doughs

Croissants and Danish pastries are enriched doughs to which the fat is added by layering or lamination. This makes them softer to eat because the fat in the dough insulates the water molecules, keeping the moisture level higher during baking.

Danish pastries may be filled with frangipane, apple, custard, pastry cream, cherries and many other ingredients.

Speciality doughs

- **Blinis**: a type of savoury pancake traditionally made from buckwheat flour.
- **Naan bread**: a leavened Indian bread traditionally cooked in a tandoor (oven).
- **Pitta bread**: Middle Eastern and Greek unleavened bread.
- **Chapatti**: an Indian unleavened bread made from a fine ground wholemeal flour known as 'atta'.
- **Pizza dough**: this is traditionally made using '00 flour' – a fine flour produced from the central part of the wheat grain that produces light, crisp doughs. Pizza dough is often enriched with olive oil to provide moisture and flavour.

Convenience dough products

There are many different types of convenience dough product on the market.

- Fresh and frozen pre-proved dough products: for example, rolls, croissants, Danish pastries and French breads
- Bake-off products that are finished and ready for baking: these can be bought either frozen or fresh, or in modified atmosphere-packaged forms (in vacuum packs, for example). This process removes most of the oxygen around the product to slow down spoilage. Such products have to be kept refrigerated. They include garlic bread, bread rolls and Danish pastries.

Working with dough: quality points

- Fresh yeast should be removed from the refrigerator and used at room temperature.

- Check that all ingredients are weighed carefully.
- Work in a clean and tidy manner to avoid cross-contamination.
- Check all temperatures carefully.
- Note that wholemeal doughs absorb more water than white doughs; the volume of water absorbed by flour also varies according to its strength (the protein and bran content).
- When using machines, check that they are in good working order.
- Always remember the health and safety rules when using machinery.
- Divide the dough with a dough divider, hard scraper or hydraulic cutting machine. This is referred to as scaling the dough. This can be done by hand for smaller quantities.
- Check the divided dough pieces for weight. When weighing, remember that doughs lose up to 12.5 per cent of their water during baking.
- Keep the flour, bowl and liquid warm.
- Remember to knock the dough back (re-knead it) carefully once proved, as this will expel the gas and allow the yeast to be dispersed properly, coming back into direct contact with the dough.
- Proving allows the dough to ferment; the second prove is essential for giving dough products the necessary volume and a good flavour.
- Time and temperature are crucial when cooking dough products. Ensure the oven is at the correct temperature before placing the product in to bake.
- Always follow the manufacturer's instructions when using frozen dough products.
- Contamination can occur if doughs are defrosted incorrectly.

Faults in yeast doughs

If your dough has a close texture, this may be because:
- it was insufficiently proved
- it was insufficiently kneaded
- it contains insufficient yeast
- the oven was too hot
- too much water was added
- too little water was added.

If your dough has an uneven texture, this may be because:
- it was insufficiently kneaded
- it was over-proved
- the oven was too cool.

If your dough has a coarse texture, this may be because:
- it was over-proved, uncovered
- it was insufficiently kneaded
- too much water was added
- too much salt was added.

If your dough is wrinkled, this may be because it was over-proved.

If your dough is sour, this may be because:
- the yeast was stale
- too much yeast was used.

If the crust, is broken this may be because the dough was under-proved at the second stage.

If there are white spots on the crust, this may be because the dough was not covered before the second proving.

Storage of cooked dough products

Store dough products in clean, air-tight containers at room temperature or in a freezer for longer periods. Do not store in a refrigerator unless you want the bread to stale quickly for use as breadcrumbs. Staling will also occur quickly in products that contain a lot of fat and milk. Many commercial dough products contain anti-staling agents.

Crusty rolls and bread are affected by changes in storage conditions; they are softened by a damp environment and humid conditions, so should be stored in a dry environment to keep them crusty.

Bread

Today restaurants often offer a range of different flavoured breads. A wide variety is available internationally, with different nations and regions having their own speciality breads. Bread also plays an important part in many religious festivals, especially Christian and Jewish festivals.

Bulk fermentation

The traditional bread-making process is known as the bulk fermentation process. This was used by many bakers before the introduction of high-speed mixing and dough conditioners, which both eliminate the need for bulk fermentation time. However, this traditional method produces a fine flavour, which is evident in the final product.

Bulk fermentation time (BFT) is the term is used to describe the length of time that the dough is allowed to ferment in bulk. BFT is measured from the end of the mixing method to the beginning of the scaling (weighing) process. The length of BFT can be from one to six hours and is related to the level of salt and yeast in the recipe, as well as the dough temperature.

During the bulk fermentation process it is important that ideal conditions are adhered to:
- The dough must be kept covered to prevent the surface of the dough developing a skin.
- The appropriate temperature must be maintained and monitored to control the rate of fermentation.

Finishing and presentation

Depending of the type of product being made, there are a number of different finishes that can be applied to dough products. Certain breads, such as baguettes, are scored before they are baked, which helps to produce an appealing visual finish to the baked product.

Many breads are sprinkled with seeds, for example poppy, sesame and fennel, before they are baked. Others may have herbs added, such as the red onion and sage rolls that feature in this chapter, or are sprinkled with cheese, as seen with Parmesan rolls. A common but perhaps the most simple of finishes applied to breads is a light dusting of the same flour used to produce the bread. This is sieved over the bread once it has cooled and applies to many of the examples shown in this chapter.

Many dough products – including breads and laminated doughs, such as croissant and pain au chocolat – are brushed with egg wash before they are baked. This produces a light, golden-brown glaze during the baking process. Other products are glazed after baking, for example Swiss buns and Danish pastries, which are often finished with a fruit glaze and water icing. Other enriched doughs, such as Chelsea buns, are soaked with bun syrup while still hot after baking and sprinkled with nibbed sugar.

Allergies

Gluten is the protein found in wheat, barley and rye, and to a lesser extent in yeast. An increasing number of people are intolerant to gluten, which results in damage to the lining of the small intestine. This is known as coeliac disease and people who are intolerant must avoid the consumption of wheat and flour-based products.

Although it is essential to clearly list all potential allergens when making fermented dough products, the allergens that are most likely to be used in their production include:
- gluten – flours and any products made from wheat, rye, barley and oats
- nuts – such as hazelnuts and nibbed almonds added to garnish Danish pastries, for example
- sesame seeds – often sprinkled on the surface of breads and rolls
- eggs – used in the production of enriched doughs
- lactose – for example, milk used in place of water in the production of dough; cheese used to glaze breads; yoghurt used in speciality doughs, such as naan.

Beyond the basic preparation of fermented doughs, attention is also required with regard to the additional ingredients that are used to complete the product. It is vitally important to assess any of the other potential allergens that are incorporated into fermented doughs, as well as the dough itself.

Test yourself

1. What is meant by fermentation?
2. Name two types of speciality bread.
3. Why is temperature so important when making bread dough using yeast?
4. What is the raising agent used in soda bread?
5. What is the difference between strong and soft flour?
6. State the nutritional benefits of wholemeal flour.
7. Give two examples, with descriptions, of dough products in the following categories:
    a. enriched doughs
    b. laminated doughs
    c. speciality doughs.
8. Name three seeds that are often sprinkled on bread rolls before baking.
9. What is the difference between leavened and unleavened bread?
10. What is the meaning of the term 'scaling'?

Bread doughs

1 Wholemeal bread

Ingredient	Makes 2 loaves
Unsalted butter or oil	60 g
Honey	3 tbsp
Water, lukewarm	500 ml
Fresh yeast	25 g
or	
Dried yeast	18 g
Salt	1 tbsp
Flour, unbleached strong white	125 g
Flour, stoneground wholemeal	625 g

Energy	Cals	Fat	Sat fat	Carb	Sugar	Protein	Fibre
6,893 kJ	1,628 kcal	32.5 g	16.7 g	302.3 g	62.6 g	50.5 g	40.0 g

1. Melt the butter in a saucepan.
2. Mix together 1 tbsp of honey and 4 tbsp of the water in a bowl.
3. Disperse the yeast into the honey mixture.
4. In a basin, place the melted butter, remaining honey and water, the yeast mixture and salt.
5. Add the white flour and half the wholemeal flour. Mix well.
6. Add the remaining wholemeal flour gradually, mixing well between each addition.
7. The dough should pull away from the side of the bowl and form a ball. The resulting dough should be soft and slightly sticky.
8. Turn out on to a floured work surface. Sprinkle with white flour, knead well.
9. Brush a clean bowl with melted butter or oil. Place the dough in the bowl, cover with a damp cloth and allow to prove in a warm place. This will take approximately 1–1½ hours.
10. Knock back and further knead the dough. Cover again and rest for 10–15 minutes.
11. Divide the dough into two equal pieces.
12. Form each piece of dough into a cottage loaf or place in a suitable loaf tin.
13. Allow to prove in a warm place for approximately 45 minutes.
14. Place in a preheated oven, 220 °C and bake until well browned (approximately 40–45 minutes).
15. When baked, the bread should sound hollow and the sides should feel crisp when pressed.
16. Cool on a wire rack.

Variation

Alternatively, the bread may be divided into 50 g rolls, brushed with egg wash and baked at 200 °C for approximately 10 minutes.

Healthy eating tip

- Only a little salt is necessary to 'control' the yeast. Many customers will prefer less salty bread.

2 Seeded bread rolls

Ingredient	Makes 30 rolls
Strong flour	1 kg
Yeast	30 g
Water at 37 °C	600 ml
Salt	20 g
Caster sugar	10 g
Milk powder	20 g
Sunflower oil	50 g
Egg wash	
Poppy seeds	
Sesame seeds	

Energy	Cals	Fat	Sat fat	Carb	Sugar	Protein	Fibre	Sodium
633 kJ	150 kcal	3.4 g	0.5 g	26.0 g	1.2 g	5.3 g	1.4 g	0.3 g

Per roll.

1. Sieve the flour on to paper.
2. Dissolve the yeast in half the water.
3. Dissolve the salt, sugar and milk powder in the other half.
4. Add both liquids and the oil to the flour at once and mix on speed 1 for 5 minutes or knead by hand for 10 minutes.
5. Cover with cling film and leave to prove for 1 hour at 26 °C.
6. 'Knock back' the dough and scale into 50 g pieces.
7. Shape and place in staggered rows on a silicone paper-covered baking sheet.
8. Prove until the rolls almost double in size.
9. Egg wash carefully and sprinkle with seeds.
10. Bake immediately at 230 °C with steam for 10–12 minutes.
11. Break one open to test if cooked.
12. Allow to cool on a wire rack.

Professional tip

Instead of weighing out each 50 g piece of dough, weigh out 100 g pieces and then halve them.

Placing bread rolls in staggered rows means they are less likely to 'prove' into each other. The spacing allows them to cook more evenly and more will fit on the baking sheet.

Variation

Try using other types of seed such as sunflower, linseed or pumpkin.

For a beer glaze mix, together 150 ml beer with 100 g rye flour and brush on before baking.

3 Parmesan rolls

1. Follow method for seeded rolls (recipe 2) up to step 5.
2. Lightly flour work surface and roll the dough into a rectangle until 3 cm thick.
3. Make sure the dough is not stuck to the surface.
4. Brush with water and cover with Parmesan.
5. Using a large knife, cut into squares 6 × 6 cm.
6. Place on a silicone paper-covered baking sheet and leave to prove until almost double in size.
7. Bake at 230 °C for 10–12 minutes with steam.
8. Cool on a wire rack.

Ingredient	Makes 30 rolls
Bread roll dough (see recipe 2 but omit the seeds)	
Parmesan cheese, grated	200 g

Energy	Cals	Fat	Sat fat	Carb	Sugar	Protein	Fibre	Sodium
2,169 kJ	512 kcal	9.9 g	2.2 g	94.3 g	1.8 g	17.5 g	5.2 g	1.0 g

Professional tip

When making bread that requires rolling out as opposed to being individually shaped, it is helpful to decrease the liquid content by 10 per cent so it will be easier to process.

To ensure the squares are all the same size, mark a grid using the back of the knife before cutting.

4 Red onion and sage rolls

Ingredient	8 rolls	16 rolls
Red onion	½	1
Dried sage	¼ tsp	½ tsp
Bread roll dough (see recipe 2 but omit the seeds)		
Oil	1 tbsp	2 tbsp

Energy	Cals	Fat	Sat fat	Carb	Sugar	Protein	Fibre	Sodium
759 kJ	181 kcal	9.2 g	1.7 g	21.7 g	2.8 g	4.2 g	1.2 g	1.0 g

1. Finely dice the red onion. Sweat it, then leave to cool.
2. Chop the sage and add it to the onion.
3. Pin out bread dough in a rectangle. Spread the onion and sage mixture over seven-eighths of the dough. Egg wash the exposed edge.
4. Roll the dough as you would for a Swiss roll, and seal the edge.
5. Cut into 50 g slices.
6. Place the slices on a prepared baking sheet and egg wash. Bake in a preheated oven at 220 °C for approximately 10 minutes. Cool on a wire rack.

13 Bread and dough products

5 Sundried tomato bread

Ingredient	2 × 450 g loaves
Sun-dried tomatoes, chopped	100 g
Water, warm	300 ml
Bread flour	500 g
Salt	10 g
Skimmed milk powder	12.5 g
Butter	12.5 g
Yeast (fresh)	20 g
Sugar	12.5 g

Energy	Cals	Fat	Sat fat	Carb	Sugar	Protein	Fibre	Sodium
10,192 kJ	2,414 kcal	70.8 g	12.8 g	401.8 g	29.6 g	67.4 g	20.7 g	5.0 g

1 Soak the sun-dried tomatoes in boiling water for 30 minutes.
2 Sieve the flour, salt and skimmed milk powder.
3 Add the butter and rub through the dry ingredients.
4 Disperse the yeast into warm water, approximately 37 °C. Add and dissolve the sugar. Add to the above ingredients.
5 Mix until a smooth dough is formed. Check for any extremes in consistency and adjust as necessary until a smooth elastic dough is formed.
6 Cover the dough, keep warm and allow to prove.
7 After approximately 30–40 minutes, knock back the dough and mix in the chopped sun-dried tomatoes (well drained).
8 Mould and prove again for another 30 minutes (covered).
9 Divide the dough into two and mould round.
10 Rest for 10 minutes. Keep covered.
11 Remould into ball shape.
12 Place the dough pieces into 15 cm diameter hoops laid out on a baking tray. The hoops must be warm and lightly greased.
13 With the back of the hand flatten the dough pieces.
14 Prove at 38–40 °C in humid conditions, preferably in a prover.
15 Bake at 225 °C for 25–30 minutes.
16 After baking, remove the bread from the tins immediately and place on a cooling wire.

6 Olive bread

Ingredient	4 loaves
Starter	
Yeast	40 g
Water at 37 °C	180 ml
Strong flour	225 g
Sugar	5 g
Dough	
Strong flour	855 g
Sugar	40 g
Salt	20 g
Water at 37 °C	450 ml
Olive oil	160 ml
Green olives, cut into quarters	100 g

Energy	Cals	Fat	Sat fat	Carb	Sugar	Protein	Fibre	Sodium
5,174 kJ	1,229 kcal	44.2 g	6.5 g	188.3 g	3.5 g	30.9 g	15.9 g	5.2 g

1. For the starter, dissolve the yeast in the water, add the flour and sugar, mix well, cover and leave to ferment for 30 minutes.
2. For the dough, sieve the flour, sugar and salt into a mixing bowl, add the water followed by the starter and start mixing slowly.
3. Gradually add the oil and continue mixing to achieve a smooth dough.
4. Cover with cling film and prove for 1 hour or until double in size.
5. Knock back, add the olives and divide the dough into four.
6. Roll into long shapes and place on a baking sheet sprinkled with rice cones, return to the prover and leave until double in size.
7. Brush with olive oil and bake at 220 °C for 20–25 minutes.
8. When cooked, the bread should sound hollow when tapped on the base.
9. Leave to cool on a wire rack.

Bread and dough products 13

1 Make up the starter.
2 Starter ready for use after proving. 
3 Start mixing in the ingredients for the main dough, tearing up the starter. 
4 Continue mixing in the ingredients and working the dough. 
5 Shape the dough. 
6 Divide and roll into loaves. 

7 Soda bread

Ingredient	2 loaves
Flour, wholemeal	250 g
Flour (strong)	250 g
Bicarbonate of soda	1 tsp
Salt	1 tsp
Buttermilk	200 g
Water, warm	60 ml
Butter, melted	25 g

Energy	Cals	Fat	Sat fat	Carb	Sugar	Protein	Fibre	Sodium
8,341 kJ	1,970 kcal	39.8g	20.9g	357.8g	18.5g	67.9g	20.9g	3.6g

1 Sift the flours, salt and bicarbonate of soda into a bowl.
2 Make a well and add the buttermilk, warm water and melted butter.
3 Work the dough for about 5 minutes.
4 Mould into 2 round loaves and mark the top.
5 Bake at 200 °C for about 25 minutes. When the bread is ready, it should make a hollow sound when tapped.

8 Rye bread

Ingredient	1 loaf
Fresh yeast (or dried yeast may be used)	15 g
Water, warm	60 ml
Black treacle	1 tbsp
Vegetable oil	1 tbsp
Caraway seeds (optional)	15 g
Salt	15 g
Lager	250 ml
Rye flour	250 g
Unbleached bread flour	175 g
Polenta	
Egg wash	

Energy	Cals	Fat	Sat fat	Carb	Sugar	Protein	Fibre	Sodium
7,174 kJ	1,690 kcal	24.7 g	2.9 g	331.8 g	12.5 g	46.7 g	46.2 g	6.0 g

1. Disperse the yeast in the warm water (at approximately 37 °C).
2. In a basin mix the black treacle, oil, two-thirds of the caraway seeds (if required) and the salt. Add the lager. Add the yeast and mix in the sieved rye flour. Mix well.
3. Gradually add the bread flour. Continue to add the flour until the dough is formed and it is soft and slightly sticky.
4. Turn the dough on to a lightly floured surface and knead well.
5. Knead the dough until it is smooth and elastic.
6. Place the kneaded dough into a suitable bowl that has been brushed with oil.
7. Cover with a damp cloth and allow the dough to prove in a warm place until it is double in size. This will take about 1½–2 hours.
8. Turn the dough on to a lightly floured work surface, knock back the dough to original size. Cover and allow to rest for approximately 5–10 minutes.
9. Shape the dough into an oval approximately 25 cm long.
10. Place on to a baking sheet lightly sprinkled with polenta.
11. Allow the dough to prove in a warm place, preferably in a prover, until double in size (approximately 45 minutes to 1 hour).
12. Lightly brush the loaf with egg wash, sprinkle with the remaining caraway seeds (if required).
13. Using a small, sharp knife, make three diagonal slashes, approximately 5 mm deep into the top of the loaf.
14. Place in a preheated oven at 190 °C and bake for approximately 50–55 minutes.
15. When cooked, turn out. The bread should sound hollow when tapped and the sides should feel crisp.
16. Allow to cool.

Healthy eating tip
- Only a little salt is necessary to 'control' the yeast. Many customers will prefer less salty bread.

9 Bagels

Ingredient	10–12 bagels
Strong flour	450 g
Yeast	15 g
Water, warm	150 ml
Salt	10 g
Caster sugar	25 g
Oil	45 ml
Egg yolk	20 g
Milk	150 ml
Poppy seeds	

Energy	Cals	Fat	Sat fat	Carb	Sugar	Protein	Fibre	Sodium
670 kJ	158 kcal	2.1 g	0.5 g	32.7 g	5.0 g	6.2 g	1.6 g	0.8 g

1. Sieve the flour, place in a mixing bowl.
2. Make a well and add the yeast which has been dissolved in the water.
3. Mix a little of the flour into the yeast to form a batter, sprinkle over some of the flour from the sides and leave to ferment.
4. Mix together the salt, sugar, oil, egg yolk and milk.
5. When the batter has fermented add the rest of the ingredients and mix to achieve a smooth dough.
6. Cover and prove for 1 hour (BFT).
7. Knock back and scale at 50 g pieces, shape into rolls and make a hole in the centre using a small rolling pin.
8. Place on a floured board and prove for 10 minutes.
9. Carefully drop into boiling water and simmer until they rise to the surface.
10. Lift out and place on a silicone-covered baking sheet, egg wash, sprinkle or dip in poppy seeds and bake at 210 °C for 30 minutes.

Use a rolling pin to make a hole in the centre of each bagel

Poach the bagels in water

Egg wash the bagels and sprinkle with seeds before baking

Practical Cookery 14th edition

10 Cholla bread

1. Rub the butter or margarine into the sieved flour in a suitable basin.
2. Mix the sugar, salt and egg together.
3. Disperse the yeast in the water.
4. Add all these ingredients to the sieved flour and mix well to develop the dough. Cover with a damp cloth or plastic and allow to ferment for about 45 minutes.
5. Divide into 125–150 g strands and begin to plait as follows:

4–strand plait	5–strand plait
2 over 3	2 over 3
4 over 2	5 over 2
1 over 3	1 over 3

6. After moulding, place on a lightly greased baking sheet and egg wash lightly.
7. Prove in a little steam until double in size. Egg wash again lightly and decorate with maw seeds (poppy seeds).
8. Bake in a hot oven, at 220 °C for 25–30 minutes.

Ingredient	2 loaves
Butter or margarine	56 g
Flour (strong)	500 g
Caster sugar	18 g
Salt	1 tsp
Egg	1
Yeast	25 g

Energy	Cals	Fat	Sat fat	Carb	Sugar	Protein	Fibre	Sodium
4,876 kJ	1,154 kcal	30.1 g	16.1 g	198.1 g	13.1 g	35.0 g	10.3 g	1.2 g

11 Focaccia

Ingredient	1 loaf
Active dry yeast	2 packets (approx. 15 g)
Sugar	1 tsp
Lukewarm water (about blood temperature)	230 ml
Extra virgin olive oil, plus extra to drizzle on the bread	70 g
Salt	1½ tsp
Flour, unbleached all-purpose	725 g
Coarse salt	
Picked rosemary	

Energy	Cals	Fat	Sat fat	Carb	Sugar	Protein	Fibre	Sodium
12,915 kJ	3,052 kcal	78.7 g	11.5 g	553.6 g	14.7 g	66.7 g	30.0 g	5.6 g

484

1. Dissolve the yeast and sugar in half of the lukewarm water in a bowl; let sit until foamy. In another bowl, add the remaining water, the olive oil, and the salt.
2. Pour in the yeast mixture.
3. Blend in the flour, a quarter at a time, until the dough comes together. Knead on a floured board for 10 minutes, adding flour as needed to make it smooth and elastic. Put the dough in an oiled bowl, turn to coat well, and cover with a towel.
4. Let rise in a warm draught-free place for 1 hour, until doubled in size.
5. Knock back the dough, knead it for a further 5 minutes, and gently roll it out in to a large disc or sheet to approximately 2 cm thick.
6. Let rise for 15 minutes, covered. Oil your fingers and make impressions with them in the dough, 3 cm apart. Let prove for 1 hour.
7. Preheat the oven to 200 °C. Drizzle the dough with olive oil and sprinkle with coarse salt and picked rosemary.
8. Bake for 15–20 minutes in a very hot oven at 200 °C, until golden brown. Sprinkle with additional oil if desired. Cut into squares and serve warm.

12 Naan bread

Ingredient	6 portions
Flour (strong)	350 g
Caster sugar	1½ tsp
Salt	1 tsp
Baking powder	½ tsp
Fresh yeast	15 g
Warm milk (37 °C)	150 ml
Unsweetened plain yoghurt	150 ml
Butter, clarified	100 g
Poppy seeds	2 tbsp

Energy	Cals	Fat	Sat fat	Carb	Sugar	Protein	Fibre
1,619 kJ	386 kcal	20.5 g	12.0 g	48.3 g	5.0 g	10.1 g	1.8 g

With clarified butter – using ghee.

1. Sift the flour into a suitable bowl and add the sugar, salt and baking powder.
2. Mix the yeast into the warm milk and stir in the yoghurt. Mix thoroughly with the flour to form a dough.
3. Knead the dough until it is smooth. Cover with a clean cloth and leave to rise in a warm place for about 4 hours.
4. Divide the risen dough into 12 equal portions and, on a lightly floured surface, roll into balls.
5. Flatten the balls into oblong shapes, using both hands, and slapping the naan from one hand to the other.
6. Cook the naan bread on the sides of a tandoor oven or on a lightly greased griddle or heavy-bottomed frying pan.
7. Cook the naan on one side only. Brush the raw side with clarified butter and sprinkle with poppy seeds; turn over, cook the other side or brown under a salamander.

Note

This recipe comes from Punjab and goes well with tandoori meat dishes as well as vindaloos. Traditionally, naans are baked in clay ovens called a tandoor. They must be eaten fresh and hot, and served immediately.

Healthy eating tips

- Cook the bread without added fat.
- It is a useful accompaniment for fattier meat dishes.

13 Pizza

Ingredient	2 × 18 cm
Flour, strong white	200 g
Pinch of salt	
Margarine	12 g
Yeast	5 g
Water or milk at 24 °C	125 ml
Caster sugar	5 g
Onions, finely chopped	100 g
Cloves of garlic, crushed	2
Sunflower oil	60 ml
Plum tomatoes, canned	200 g
Tomato purée	100 g
Oregano	3 g
Basil	3 g
Sugar	10 g
Cornflour	10 g
Mozzarella cheese	100 g

1. Sieve the flour and the salt. Rub in the margarine.
2. Disperse the yeast in the warm milk or water; add the caster sugar. Add this mixture to the flour.
3. Mix well, knead to a smooth dough, place in a basin covered with a damp cloth and allow to prove until doubled in size.
4. Knock back, divide into two and roll out into two 18 cm discs. Place on a lightly greased baking sheet.
5. Sweat the finely chopped onions and garlic in the oil until cooked.
6. Add the roughly chopped tomatoes, tomato purée, oregano, basil and sugar. Bring to the boil and simmer for 5 minutes.
7. Dilute the cornflour in a little water, stir into the tomato mixture and bring back to the boil.
8. Take the discs of pizza dough and spread 125 g of filling on each one.
9. Sprinkle with grated mozzarella cheese or lay the slices of cheese on top.
10. Bake in a moderately hot oven at 180 °C, for about 10 minutes.

The pizza dough may also be made into rectangles so that it can be sliced into fingers for buffet work.

Energy	Cals	Fat	Sat fat	Carb	Sugar	Protein	Fibre
3,956 kJ	941 kcal	46.3 g	13 g	114.4 g	20.1 g	23.6 g	8.4 g

Using 100 per cent strong white flour.

Note

Pizza is a traditional dish originating from southern Italy. In simple terms it is a flat bread dough that can be topped with a wide variety of ingredients and baked quickly. The only rule is not to add wet ingredients, such as tomatoes, which are too juicy, otherwise the pizza will become soggy. Traditionally, pizzas are baked in a wood-fired brick oven, but they can be baked in any type of hot oven for 8–15 minutes depending on the ingredients. The recipe given here is a typical one.

Variation

Oregano is sprinkled on most pizzas before baking. This is a basic recipe and many variations exist. Some have the addition of olives, artichoke hearts, prawns, mortadella sausage, garlic sausage or anchovy fillets; other combinations include:
- mozzarella cheese, anchovies, capers and garlic
- mozzarella cheese, tomato and oregano
- ham, mushrooms, egg and parmesan cheese
- prawns, tuna, capers and garlic
- ham, mushrooms and olives.

14 Pitta bread

Ingredients	Makes 6 pittas
Strong white flour	250 g
Fresh yeast	15 g
Black onion seeds	20 g
Salt	1 tsp
Water	160 ml
Olive oil	2 tsp

Energy	Cals	Fat	Sat fat	Carb	Sugar	Protein	Fibre	Sodium
672 kJ	159 kcal	1.9 g	0.3 g	29.8 g	0.2 g	5.6 g	1.4 g	0.3 g

Onion seeds omitted.

1. Mix the flour, onion seeds and salt in a bowl.
2. Mix the yeast with a little of the water and pour into a well in the centre and allow to ferment (starts to bubble and rise).
3. Add 120 ml water and 1½ teaspoons of oil. Mix the ingredients together, and gradually add the remaining water and oil to form a soft dough. You may not need all of the water.
4. Lightly oil the table. Place the dough on top, and knead well to a smooth elastic dough.
5. Place in an oiled bowl. Cover with cling film and allow to prove until doubled in size.
6. Place on a lightly floured table and knock back. Divide into approximately six balls. Roll each ball into an oval shape, 3 to 5 mm thick.
7. Place on a lightly oiled and floured tray.
8. Bake in a hot oven 250 °C for approximately 5 to 10 minutes.

Mix the yeast with a little water and pour into a well in the centre; allow to ferment

Knead until a soft, smooth, elastic ball of dough is formed

Cover and allow the dough to prove until it has doubled in size

Divide the dough into six evenly-sized pieces

Roll each ball of dough into a long oval shape, approximately 3 to 5 mm thick

Bake in a hot oven for 5 to 10 minutes (depending on shape and size)

15 Pitta bread without yeast

Ingredient	Makes 4 pittas
Butter	50 g
Milk	185 ml
Strong white flour	300 g
Baking powder	5 g
Salt	½ tsp
Olive oil	25 ml

Energy	Cals	Fat	Sat fat	Carb	Sugar	Protein	Fibre	Sodium
1,811 kJ	432 kcal	18.2 g	8.1 g	57.0 g	2.5 g	10.2 g	2.5 g	0.4 g

Using unsalted butter and semi-skimmed milk.

1. Heat the butter and milk to blood heat. In a suitable bowl add this to the flour, baking powder and salt.
2. Work into a smooth dough.
3. Place on to a floured table and knead until smooth. If necessary, add extra flour.
4. Wrap in cling film and allow to relax for 30 minutes.
5. Unwrap and divide into four pieces. Roll into balls. Using a rolling pin, roll into rounds 0.3 cm thick.
6. Lightly oil a suitable pan. Cook for approximately 1 minute over a medium heat. Turn over and cook the other side. There should be smallish brown spots on both sides.
7. Brush with olive oil and serve.

Bread products

16 Sandwiches

For speed of production, sandwiches are made in bands by cutting the bread lengthways. Once filled, the crusts are removed and the sandwiches cut into fingers. Today, bakers will bake bread to your specification and slice it ready for use. The specification may also include speciality breads such as tomato, basil, walnut and olive bread.

Sandwiches may be made from every kind of bread, fresh or toasted, in a variety of shapes, and with an almost endless assortment of fillings. They may be garnished with potato or vegetable crisps and a little salad.

Sandwiches may also be cut into small cubes and a variety placed on a cocktail stick like a mini kebab.

Toasted sandwiches

These are made by inserting a variety of savoury fillings between two slices of hot, freshly buttered toast (for example, scrambled egg, bacon, fried egg, scrambled egg with chopped ham) or by inserting two slices of buttered bread with the required filling into a sandwich toaster.

Club sandwich

Energy	Cals	Fat	Sat fat	Carb	Sugar	Protein	Fibre	Sodium
3473 kJ	832 kcal	54.0g	18.3g	51.0g	4.5g	39.0g	3.1g	1.5g

Using 2 slices of bacon, 50 g chicken and 1 egg.

This is a filling of lettuce, grilled bacon, slices of hard-boiled egg, mayonnaise and slices of chicken layered between three slices of hot buttered toast.

Bookmaker sandwich

This is an underdone minute steak between two slices of hot buttered toast.

Double- and triple-decker sandwiches

Toasted and untoasted bread can be made into double-decker sandwiches, using three slices of bread with two separate fillings. Triple- and quadro-decker sandwiches may also be prepared. They may be served hot or cold.

Open sandwich or Scandinavian smorgasbord

These are prepared from a buttered slice of any bread, garnished with any type of meat, fish, eggs, vegetables or salad. Varieties of open sandwich include the following:
- smoked salmon, lettuce, potted shrimps, slice of lemon
- cold sliced beef, sliced tomato, fans of gherkins
- shredded lettuce, sliced hard-boiled egg, mayonnaise, cucumber
- pickled herring, chopped gherkin, capers (sieved), hard-boiled egg.

Bookmaker sandwich

A selection of open sandwiches

17 Wraps

Wraps are fillings wrapped in tortillas (plain or flavoured, for example, tomato or herb). A wide variety of fillings can be used, for example: chicken and roasted vegetables; beans and red pepper salad with guacamole (a well-flavoured avocado pulp).

Flat breads, such as pitta and ciabatta, can also be used with various fillings (for example, chicken tikka).

18 Bagels

Bagels are ring, doughnut-shaped rolls of leavened bread that are boiled before being baked, giving them a shiny finish and a soft middle (see page 483). They are traditionally filled with smoked salmon and cream cheese (a Jewish speciality) but other fillings can also be used.

Cut horizontally, bagels make a good base for open sandwiches.

Buns

19 Bun dough

Ingredient	12 buns	24 buns
Strong flour	500 g	1 kg
Yeast	25 g	50 g
Milk (scalded and cooled to 40 °C)	250 ml	500 ml
Butter	60 g	120 g
Eggs	2	4
Salt	5 g	10 g
Sugar	60 g	120 g

1. Sieve the flour.
2. Dissolve the yeast in half the milk and add enough of the flour to make a thick batter, cover with cling film and place in the prover to ferment.
3. Rub the butter into the rest of the flour.
4. Beat the eggs and add the salt and sugar.
5. When the batter has fermented, add to the flour together with the liquid.
6. Mix slowly for 5 minutes to form a soft dough.
7. Place in a lightly oiled bowl, cover with cling film and prove for 1 hour at 26 °C.
8. Knock back the dough and knead on the table, rest for 10 minutes before processing.

Bun wash

Bun wash is used for most bun recipes, including Bath and Chelsea buns, after baking.

Milk	250 ml
Caster sugar	100 g

1. Bring both ingredients to the boil and brush over liberally as soon the buns are removed from the oven. The heat from the buns will set the glaze and prevent it from soaking in, giving a characteristic sticky coat.

Practical Cookery 14th edition

1. Sift the flour.

2. Rub in the fat.

3. Make a well in the flour and pour in the beaten egg.

4. Pour in the liquid.

5. Fold the ingredients together.

6. Knead the dough.

7. Before and after proving: the same amount of dough is twice the size after it has been left to prove.

20 Bath buns

Ingredient	12–14 buns
Basic bun dough (recipe 19)	1 kg
Bun spice	20 ml
Sultanas	200 g
Sugar nibs	360 g
Egg yolks	8

Energy	Cals	Fat	Sat fat	Carb	Sugar	Protein	Fibre	Sodium
827 kJ	196 kcal	6.5 g	3.6 g	31.9 g	13.4 g	4.5 g	1.4 g	0.1 g

Hot cross buns and Bath buns

1. Mix the bun spice into the basic dough and knead.
2. Add the sultanas, two-thirds of the sugar nibs and all the egg yolks.
3. Using a plastic scraper, cut in the ingredients (it is usual for the ingredients not to be fully mixed in).
4. Scale into 60 g pieces.
5. Place on a paper-lined baking sheet in rough shapes.
6. Sprinkle liberally with the rest of the nibbed sugar.
7. Allow to prove until double in size.
8. Bake at 200 °C for 15–20 minutes.
9. Brush with bun wash as soon as they come out of the oven.

21 Hot cross buns

Ingredient	12–14 buns	24 buns
Basic bun dough (recipe 19)	1 kg	2 kg
Currants	75 g	150 g
Sultanas	75 g	150 g
Mixed spice	5 g	10 g
Crossing paste		
Strong flour	125 g	250 g
Water	250 ml	500 ml
Oil	25 ml	50 ml

Energy	Cals	Fat	Sat fat	Carb	Sugar	Protein	Fibre	Sodium
744 kJ	177 kcal	6.7 g	3.6 g	26.8 g	8.3 g	4.6 g	1.2 g	0.1 g

1. Add the dried fruit and spice to the basic dough, mix well.
2. Scale into 60 g pieces and roll.
3. Place on a baking sheet lined with silicone paper in neat rows opposite each other and egg wash.
4. Mix together the ingredients for the crossing paste. Pipe it in continuous lines across the buns.
5. Allow to prove.
6. Bake at 220 °C for 15–20 minutes.
7. Brush with bun wash as soon as they come out of the oven.

Variation

To make fruit buns, proceed as for hot cross buns without the crosses.

22 Swiss buns

Ingredient	12–14 buns
Basic bun dough (recipe 19)	1 kg
Fondant	500 g
Lemon oil	5 ml

Energy	Cals	Fat	Sat fat	Carb	Sugar	Protein	Fibre	Sodium
697 kJ	165 kcal	5.6g	3.4g	27.0g	8.4g	3.4g	1.0g	0.0g

1 Scale the dough into 60 g pieces.
2 Roll into balls then elongate to form oval shapes.
3 Place on a baking sheet lined with silicone paper, egg wash.
4 Allow to prove.
5 Bake at 220 °C for 15–20 minutes.
6 Allow to cool then dip each bun in lemon-flavoured or plain white fondant.

23 Doughnuts

Ingredient	12 doughnuts
Basic bun dough (recipe 19)	1 kg
Caster sugar	500 g
Raspberry jam	250 g

Energy	Cals	Fat	Sat fat	Carb	Sugar	Protein	Fibre
918 kJ	218 kcal	13.3g	4.0g	22.6g	4.0g	3.6g	1.2g

Using hard margarine and peanut oil.

1 Scale the dough into 60 g pieces.
2 Roll into balls and make a hole in the dough using a rolling pin.
3 Prove on an oiled paper-lined tray.
4 When proved, carefully place in a deep fat fryer at 180 °C.
5 Turn over when coloured on one side and fully cook.
6 Drain well on absorbent paper.
7 Toss in caster sugar.
8 Make a small hole in one side and pipe in the jam.

Variation

The caster sugar can be mixed with ground cinnamon.

Health and safety

As a fryer is not a regular piece of equipment found in a patisserie, a portable fryer is often used. Always make sure it is on a very secure surface in a suitable position. Never attempt to move it until it has completely cooled down. In addition, extreme care must be taken to avoid serious burns.
- Only use a deep fat fryer after proper training.
- Make sure the oil is clean and the fryer is filled to the correct level.
- Preheat before using but never leave unattended.
- Always carefully place the products into the fryer – never drop them in. Use a basket if appropriate.
- Never place wet products into the fryer.

Bread and dough products

Savarin doughs

24 Savarin dough

Ingredient	35 items
Strong flour	450 g
Yeast	1 g
Water at 40 °C	125 ml
Eggs	5
Caster sugar	60 g
Salt	Pinch
Melted butter	150 g

1 Sieve the flour and place in a bowl. Make a well.
2 Make a ferment by dissolving the yeast in the water and pour into the well.
3 Gradually mix the flour into the liquid, forming a thin batter. Sprinkle over a little of the flour to cover, then leave to ferment.
4 Whisk the eggs, sugar and salt.
5 When the ferment has erupted through the flour, add the eggs and mix to a smooth batter. Cover and leave to prove until double in size.
6 Add the melted butter and beat in.
7 Pipe the batter into prepared (buttered and floured) moulds one-third full.
8 Prove until the mixture reaches the top of the mould and bake at 220 °C for 12–20 minutes, depending on the size of the mould.
9 Unmould and leave to cool.

Professional tip

Savarin and savarin-based products are never served without first soaking in a flavoured syrup. They are literally dry sponges and should be:
- golden brown in colour with an even surface
- smooth, with no cracks, breaks or tears
- evenly soaked without any hard or dry areas
- sealed by brushing with apricot glaze after soaking.

Cooked products can be stored in the fridge overnight, but if left for too long they will dry out and cracks will appear. They are best wrapped in cling film, labelled and stored in the freezer.

Savarin syrup

Ingredient	3 litres
Oranges	2
Lemons	2
Water	2 litres
Sugar	1 kg
Bay leaf	2
Cloves	2
Cinnamon sticks	2

1 Peel the oranges and lemons and squeeze the juice.
2 Add all the ingredients into a large pan and bring to the boil, simmer for 2–3 minutes and pass through a conical strainer.
3 Allow to cool and measure the density (it should read 22° Baumé). Adjust if necessary. (More liquid will lower the density, more sugar will increase it.)
4 Reboil then dip the baked savarins into the hot syrup until they swell slightly. Check they are properly soaked before carefully removing and placing on to a wire rack with a tray underneath to drain.
5 When cooled, brush with boiling apricot glaze.

Note

It is important that savarin syrup is at the correct density. It should measure 22° Baumé on the saccharometer. If the syrup is too thin, the products are likely to disintegrate. If it is too dense it will not fully penetrate the product and leave a dry centre.

Practical Cookery 14th edition

1 Cream the yeast in milk to make a ferment.

2 Add the dispersed yeast to the flour and sprinkle a little flour over it.

3 The mixture after fermentation.

4 Add beaten eggs, sugar and salt.

5 The dough after proving.

6 Add the butter.

7 After proving, pipe into moulds.

8 After proving for the final time.

Bread and dough products 13

25 Savarin with fruit

A savarin is baked in a ring mould, either large or individual.
Before glazing, sprinkle with kirsch and fill the centre with prepared fruit. Serve with a crème anglaise or raspberry coulis.

Energy	Cals	Fat	Sat fat	Carb	Sugar	Protein	Fibre	Sodium
1021 kJ	241 kcal	4.6g	2.5g	49.0g	40.0g	2.7g	0.7g	0.1g

Using 40g of fruit, 1 tsp of glaze and ¼ tsp of spirit per portion.

26 Marignans chantilly

A marignan is savarin dough baked in an individual boat-shaped mould or barquette.
Split the glazed marignans and fill with Chantilly cream. Once split, and before filling, they can be sprinkled with rum or orange-flavoured liqueur.

Energy	Cals	Fat	Sat fat	Carb	Sugar	Protein	Fibre	Sodium
1407 kJ	335 kcal	14.4g	8.7g	51.0g	41.0g	2.9g	0.5g	0.1g

Using 30g of Chantilly cream, 1 tsp of glaze and ¼ tsp of spirit per portion.

> **Professional tip**
>
> Savarin paste is notorious for sticking in the mould. Always butter moulds carefully and flour. After use do not wash the moulds but wipe clean with kitchen paper.

27 Blueberry baba

For a baba, currants are usually added to the basic savarin dough before baking.
As for marignans, split the glazed baba and fill with crème diplomate and blueberries or Chantilly cream.

Energy	Cals	Fat	Sat fat	Carb	Sugar	Protein	Fibre	Sodium
1439 kJ	342 kcal	14.4g	8.7g	54.0g	45.0g	3.0g	1.2g	0.1g

Using 15g blueberries, 30g of Chantilly cream, 1 tsp of glaze and ¼ tsp of spirit per portion.

14 Basic pastry products

Recipes included in this chapter

No.	Recipe	Page
	Short pastry	
1	Short paste (*pâte à foncer*)	507
2	Quiche lorraine (cheese and ham savoury flan)	508
3	Treacle tart	509
4	Fruit pie	510
	Sweet pastry	
5	Sugar paste (sweet paste, *pâte à sucre*)	511
6	Flan cases	512
7	Fruit tart, tartlets or barquettes	514
8	Egg custard tart	514
9	Apple flan	515
10	Lemon meringue pie	516
11	Pear and almond tart	516
12	Lemon tart	517
13	Bakewell tart	518
14	Mince pies	519
	Choux pastry	
15	Choux paste (*pâte à choux*)	520
16	Cream buns (*choux à la crème*)	521
17	Profiteroles and chocolate sauce	522
18	Chocolate éclairs	522
19	Gâteau Paris-Brest	523
20	Choux paste fritters (*beignets soufflés*)	524
	Suet pastry	
21	Suet paste	525
22	Steamed fruit puddings	525

No.	Recipe	Page
	Puff pastry	
23	Puff paste (French method)	526
24	Inverted or reverse puff pastry	528
25	Rough puff paste	529
26	Puff pastry cases (*bouchées, vol-au-vents*)	530
27	Cheese straws (*paillettes au fromage*)	531
28	Sausage rolls	531
29	*Gâteau pithiviers*	532
30	Palmiers	533
31	Pear jalousie	534
32	Puff pastry slice (*mille-feuilles*)	534
33	Fruit slice (*bande aux fruits*)	535
34	Cream horns	536
35	Eccles cakes	537
36	Apple turnovers (*chausson aux pommes*)	537
	Fillings	
37	Pastry cream (*crème pâtissière*)	538
38	Chantilly cream	539
39	Buttercream	539
40	Boiled buttercream	540
41	Frangipane (almond cream)	541
42	Ganache	542
43	Italian meringue	543
44	Swiss meringue	544
45	Apple purée	544
46	Stock syrup	545

In addition to being one of the most important sections of the kitchen, pastry work can also be particularly enjoyable and rewarding. Although it is called 'pastry work', it actually includes making breads, desserts, sweets, and much more, not just goods made from pastry. Bakery products and desserts are explored in greater detail in Chapters 13, 15 and 16.

There is a range of pastes, all vital components of pastry work. Each type of paste is included in this chapter, along with several recipes that use it.

Ingredients for pastry work

This section provides information about the most commonly used ingredients in the production of pastry and bakery items.

Basic pastry products 14

The principal ingredients of pastry products are flour, fat, sugar, raising agents, eggs and cream. These ingredients form the basis of the various types of pastry products that are produced in this chapter. The type of pastry produced depends on the characteristics required. For example, **short pastry** is crisp and savoury, whereas **puff pastry** is made from light layers of fine paste, separated by butter or a pastry fat that produces steam to push the layers apart during the baking process. The other types of pastry covered are forms of **sweet paste**, containing the crisp characteristics of short pastry but with a richer and sweeter flavour. **Choux paste** is used in the production of éclairs, profiteroles and choux buns, whereas **suet paste** is used to produce steamed puddings, rolls and dumplings that can be either sweet or savoury.

Flour

Flour is probably the most common commodity in daily use. It forms the foundation of bread, pastry and cakes, and is one of the most important ingredients in patisserie, if not *the* most important.

There is a great variety of high-quality flours made from cereals, nuts or legumes, such as chestnut flour, cornflour, and so on. They have been used in patisserie, baking, dessert cuisine and savoury cuisine in all countries throughout history. The most commonly used and most versatile flour, particularly in Western cuisine, is wheat flour.

Wheat flour

Wheat flour is composed of starch, gluten, sugar, fats, water and minerals.
- Starch is the main component.
- Gluten is also a significant element. Elastic and impermeable, it is the gluten that makes wheat flour the most common flour used in bread making.
- The quantity of sugar in wheat is very small but it plays a very important role in fermentation.
- Wheat contains a maximum of only 16 per cent water, but its presence is important.
- The mineral matter (ash), which is found mainly in the husk of the wheat grain and not in the kernel, determines the purity and quality of the flour.

Wheat goes through several distinct processes from the ear to the final product, flour. These are usually carried out in modern industrial plants, where wheat is subjected to the various treatments and phases necessary for the production of different types of flour. These arrive in perfect condition at our workplaces to be made into items such as sponge cakes, yeast dough, puff pastries, biscuits, pastries and much more.

The production of flour

White flour is made up almost entirely of the part of the wheat grain known as the endosperm, which contains starch and protein. When flour is mixed with water it is converted into a sticky dough. This characteristic is due to the gluten, which becomes sticky when moistened. The relative proportion of starch and gluten varies in different wheats; those with a low percentage of gluten (soft flour) are not suitable for bread making. For this reason, wheat is blended.

In milling, the whole grain is broken up, the parts separated, and then sifted, blended and ground into flour. Some of the outer coating of bran is removed, as is the wheatgerm, which contains oil and is therefore likely to become rancid and spoil the flour. For this reason wholemeal flour should not be stored for more than 14 days.

Types of flour

- White flour contains 72–85 per cent of the whole grain (the endosperm only).
- Wholemeal flour contains 100 per cent of the whole grain.
- Wheatmeal flour contains 85–95 per cent of the whole grain.
- High-ratio or patent flour contains 40 per cent of the whole grain.
- Self-raising flour is white flour that has had baking powder (usually bicarbonate of soda and tartaric acid) added to it.
- Semolina is granulated hard flour prepared from the central part of the wheat grain. White or wholemeal semolina is available.

Storing flour

Flour is a particularly delicate living material so it must be used and stored carefully. It must always be in the best condition, which is why storing large quantities is not recommended.

It must be kept in a clean, well-organised, disinfected and aerated storeroom. It must never be stored in warm and humid places.

499

Fats

Pastry goods may be made from various types of fat, either a single named fat or a combination. Examples of fats are butter, margarine, shortening and lard.

Butter

Butter brings smoothness, rich perfumes and aromas, and impeccable textures to pastry items. Butter is an emulsion – the perfect interaction of water and fat. It is composed of a minimum of 82 per cent fat, a maximum of 16 per cent water and 2 per cent dry extracts.

Here are some important facts about butter:
- Butter is the most complete fat.
- It is a very delicate ingredient that can quickly spoil if a series of basic rules are not followed in its use.
- It absorbs odours very easily, so it should be kept well covered and should always be stored far from anything that produces strong odours.
- When kept at 15 °C, butter is stable and retains all its properties: finesse, aroma and creaminess.
- It should not be kept too long: it is always better to work with fresh butter.
- Good-quality butter has a stable texture, pleasing taste, fresh odour, homogenous (even) colour and, most importantly, it melts perfectly in the mouth.
- It softens preparations such as cookies and petits fours, and keeps products like sponge cakes soft and moist.
- Butter enhances flavour – as in brioches, for example.
- The melting point of butter is between 30 °C and 35 °C.

Margarine

Margarine is often made from a blend of oils that have been hardened or hydrogenated (with the addition of hydrogen gas). Margarine may contain up to 10 per cent butterfat.

Cake margarine is a blend of hydrogenated oils to which an emulsifying agent is added that helps combine water and fat. Cake margarine may contain up to 10 per cent butterfat.

Pastry margarine is used for puff pastry. It is a hard plastic or waxy fat that is suitable for layering.

Shortening

Shortening is the term for some other fats used in pastry making. It is made from oils and is 100 per cent fat. Examples of shortening include hydrogenated lard and rendered pork fat.

Sugar

Sugar (or sucrose) is extracted from sugar beet or sugar cane. The juice is crystallised by a complicated manufacturing process and then refined and sieved into several grades, such as granulated, caster or icing sugars. Syrup and treacle are also produced as by-products during the production of refined sugar.

Loaf or cube sugar is obtained by pressing the crystals together while they are slightly wet, drying them in blocks, and then cutting the blocks into squares.

Fondant is a cooked mixture of sugar and glucose which, when heated, can be coloured and flavoured, and used for decorating cakes, buns, gâteaux and petits fours. Fondant is generally bought ready-made.

Inverted sugar

When sucrose is broken down with water, in a chemical process called hydrolysis, it separates into the two types of sugar that make it: fructose and glucose. Sugar that has been treated in this way is called inverted sugar and is, after sucrose, one of the most commonly used sugars in the catering profession, thanks to its sweetening properties.

Inverted sugar is used because:
- It improves the aroma of products.
- It improves the texture of doughs.
- It prevents the dehydration of frozen products.
- It reduces or stops crystallisation in ice cream making, improves smoothness and lowers its freezing point.

Glucose

Glucose takes on various forms:
- the characteristics of a viscous syrup, called crystal glucose
- its natural state, in fruit and honey
- a dehydrated white paste (used mainly in the commercial food industry, but also used in catering).

Glucose syrup:
- is a transparent, viscous paste
- prevents the crystallisation of boiled sugars, jams and preserves
- delays the drying of a product
- aids consistency and creaminess in ice cream and the fillings of chocolate bonbons
- prevents the crystallisation of ice cream.

Honey

Honey is the oldest known form of sugar. It is a very sweet, viscous syrup produced when bees extract nectar from flowers. It is 30 per cent sweeter than sucrose and generally has is light golden-brown appearance, although the colour varies depending on the species of bee, the flower from which the nectar is collected and the type of honey this produces.

Honey lowers the freezing point of ice cream. It can also be used like inverted sugar, but it is important to take into account that, unlike inverted sugar, honey will give its flavour to the preparation. Also, it is inadequate for preparations that require long storage, since honey recrystallises over time.

Isomalt

Isomalt is a sweetener that has been used by the food manufacturing industry for many years in the production of confectionery (sweets and gums). It has properties distinct from those of the sweeteners already mentioned. It is produced through the hydrolysis of sugar followed by hydrogenation (the addition of hydrogen). Produced through these industrial processes, this sugar is perfect for confectionery and chewing gum production, but it is now being used far more widely in the professional kitchen.

One of its most notable characteristics is that it can melt without the addition of water or another liquid. This is a very interesting property for making artistic decorations in cooked sugar. Its appearance is like that of confectioners' sugar: a glossy powder. Its sweetening strength is half that of sucrose and it is much less soluble than sugar, which means that it melts less easily in the mouth.

Isomalt's main advance in professional patisserie work over the past few years has been as a replacement for normal sugar or sucrose when making sugar decorations, blown sugar, pulled sugar or spun sugar. Isomalt is not affected by air humidity, so sugar pieces will keep for longer.

Raising agents

Raising agents are added to cake and bread mixtures to give lightness to the product, because they produce gases that expand when heated. The gases produced are air, carbon dioxide or water vapour. These gases are introduced before baking or are produced by substances added to the mixture before baking. When the product is cooked, the gases expand. These gases are trapped in the gluten of the wheat flour. The product rises and sets on further heating and cooking because of the pressure of the gluten.

Baking powder

Chemical raising agents cause a reaction between certain acidic and alkaline compounds, which produce carbon dioxide. The alkaline component is almost always sodium bicarbonate or sodium acid carbonate, commonly known as baking soda. It is ideal because it is cheap to produce, easily purified, non-toxic and naturally tasteless. Potassium bicarbonate is available for those on low-sodium diets, but this compound tends to absorb moisture, react prematurely and give a bitter flavour.

Baking powder may be used without the addition of acid if the dough or batter is already acidic enough to react with it to produce carbon dioxide. Yoghurt and sour milk contain lactic acid and often are used in place of water or milk in products such as scones, for example. Sour milk can also be added along with the baking soda as a separate 'natural' component of the leavening.

Baking powder contains baking soda and an acid in the form of salt crystals that dissolve in water. Ground dry starch is also added to prevent premature reactions in humid air by absorbing moisture, and to dilute the powder.

Most baking powders are 'double acting' – that is, they produce an initial set of gas bubbles when the powder is mixed into the batter and then a second set during the baking process. The first and smaller reaction is necessary to form many small gas bubbles in the batter or dough; the second is necessary to expand these bubbles to form the final light texture. This second reaction must happen late enough in the baking for the surrounding materials to have set, preventing the bubbles from escaping and the product from collapsing.

Baking powder is made from alkali (bicarbonate of soda) plus acid (cream of tartar – potassium hydrogen tartrate). Commercial baking powders differ mainly in their proportions of the acid salts. Cream of tartar is not normally used due to its high cost, so calcium phosphate and glucono delta-lactone are now commonly used in its place.

Water vapour

Water vapour is produced during the baking process from the liquid content used in the mixing. Water vapour has approximately 1,600 times the volume of the original water, but its raising power is slower than that of a gas. This method is used in the production of choux pastry, puff pastry, rough puff and flaky pastry, as well as batter products.

Using raising agents

- Always buy a reliable brand of baking powder.
- Store in a dry place in an airtight tin.
- Do not store for long periods of time: baking powder loses some of its residual carbon dioxide over time and therefore will not be as effective.
- Check the recipe carefully, making sure that the correct preparation for the type of mixture is used, otherwise, under- or over-rising may result.
- Sieve the raising agent with the flour and/or dry ingredients to give an even mix, and thus an even reaction.
- Distribute moisture evenly into the mixture to ensure even action of the raising agent.
- If a large proportion of raising agent has been added to a mixture, and is not to be cooked immediately, keep it in a cool place to avoid too much reaction before baking.

Too much raising agent causes:
- over-risen products that may collapse, giving a sunken effect
- a coarse texture
- poor colour and flavour
- fruit sinking to the bottom of the cake
- a bitter taste.

Insufficient raising agent causes:
- lack of volume
- insufficient lift
- close texture
- shrinkage.

Eggs

Eggs are an important and versatile ingredient in pastry work. Hens' eggs are graded in four sizes – small, medium, large and very large (see Chapter 6). For the recipes in this chapter, use medium-sized eggs (approximately 50 g), unless otherwise stated.

Eggs are used in pastry work because of their binding, emulsifying and coating properties. Eggs also add both protein and fat, thus improving the nutritional value and flavour of the product.

Milk

Full-cream, skimmed or semi-skimmed milk can be used for the desserts in this chapter.

Milk comes in many forms and is a basic element of the diet for many people throughout the world. Milk from cows is most commonly used in the production of patisserie products, although other types of milk are being used more frequently due to their nutritional properties and reduced allergenic risk (goat's milk ice cream, for example).

Milk consists of water, sugar and fat (with a minimum fat content of 3.5 per cent). It is essential in many products, from creams, ice creams, yeast doughs, mousses and custards to ganaches, cookies, tuiles and muffins. A yeast dough will change considerably in texture, taste and colour if it is made with milk instead of water.

Milk has a slightly sweet taste and little odour. Two distinct processes are used to conserve it:
- **Pasteurisation** – the milk is heated to between 73 °C and 85 °C for a few seconds, then cooled quickly to 4 °C.
- **Sterilisation (UHT)** – the milk is heated to between 140 °C and 150 °C for two seconds, then cooled quickly.

Milk is homogenised to disperse the fat evenly, since the fat has a tendency to rise to the surface (see 'Cream', below).

Here are some useful facts about milk.
- Pasteurised milk has a better taste and aroma than UHT milk.
- Milk is useful for developing flavour in sauces and creams, due to its lactic fermentation.
- Milk contributes to colour as well as to the development of texture and aroma in doughs.
- Because of its lactic ferments, it helps in the maturation of doughs and creams.
- Milk is much more fragile than cream. In recipes, adding it in certain proportions is advisable for a much more subtle and delicate final product.
- Other types of milk, such as sheep and goat's milk, can be very interesting to use in desserts.

Cream

Cream is the concentrated milk fat that is skimmed off the top of the milk when it has been left to sit. A film forms on the surface because of the difference in density between fat and liquid. This process is speeded up mechanically in large industries by heating and using centrifuges. Cream is used in many recipes because of its great versatility and capabilities.

Cream should contain at least 18 per cent butterfat. Cream for whipping must contain more than 30 per cent butterfat. Commercially frozen cream is available in slabs, typically ranging from 2 kg to 10 kg. Types, packaging, storage and uses of cream are listed in Table 14.1.

Whipping and double cream may be whipped to make them lighter and to increase volume. Cream will whip more easily if it is kept at refrigeration temperature. Indeed, all cream products must be kept in the refrigerator for health and safety reasons. They should be handled with care and, as they will absorb odour, they should never be stored near onions or other strong-smelling foods.

As with milk, there are two main methods for conserving cream:

- **Pasteurisation** – the cream is heated to between 85 °C and 90 °C for a few seconds then cooled quickly; this cream retains all its flavour properties.
- **Sterilisation (UHT)** – this consists of heating the cream to between 140 °C and 150 °C for two seconds; cream treated this way loses some of its flavour properties, but it keeps for longer.

Always use pasteurised cream when possible, for example in the restaurant when desserts are made for immediate consumption.

Here are some useful facts about cream.

- Cream whips with the addition of air, thanks to its fat content. This retains the air bubbles formed during beating.
- Understand how to use fresh cream; remember that it is easily over-whipped.
- Cream adds texture.
- Once cream is boiled and mixed or infused with other ingredients to add flavour, it will whip again if first left to cool completely (when preparing a chocolate Chantilly, for example).
- To whip cream well, it must be cold (around 4 °C).
- Cream can be infused with other flavours when it is hot or cold. The flavour of cream will develop if left to infuse prior to preparation.

Table 14.1 Types of cream

Type of cream	Legal minimum fat (%)	Processing and packaging	Storage	Characteristics and uses
Half cream	12	Homogenised; may be pasteurised or ultra-heat treated	2–3 days	Does not whip; used for pouring; suitable for low-fat diets
Cream (single cream)	18	Homogenised; pasteurised and packaged in bottles and cartons, sealed with foil caps; may be available in bulk	2–3 days in summer; 3–4 days in winter under refrigeration	A pouring cream suitable for coffee, cereals, soup or fruit; added to cooked dishes and sauces; does not whip
Whipping cream	35	Not homogenised; pasteurised and packaged like single cream	2–3 days in summer; 3–4 days in winter under refrigeration	Ideal for whipping; suitable for piping, cake and dessert decoration; used in ice cream, cake and pastry fillings
Double cream	48	Slightly homogenised; pasteurised and packaged like single cream	2–3 days in summer; 3–4 days in winter under refrigeration	A rich pouring cream; will whip; floats on coffee or soup

Type of cream	Legal minimum fat (%)	Processing and packaging	Storage	Characteristics and uses
'Thick' double cream	48	Heavily homogenised; pasteurised and packaged like single cream; usually only sold in domestic quantities	2–3 days in summer; 3–4 days in winter under refrigeration	A rich, spoonable cream; cannot be poured
Clotted cream	55	Heated to 82 °C then cooled for 4½ hours; the cream crust is then skinned off; packed in cartons, usually by hand; may be available in bulk	2–3 days in summer; 3–4 days in winter under refrigeration	Very thick; has its own special flavour and colour; used with scones, fruit and fruit pies
Ultra-heat treated (UHT) cream	12 (half), 18 (single) or 35 (whipping)	Homogenised; heated to 132 °C for 1 second, then cooled immediately; aseptically packaged in polythene and foil-lined containers; available in catering-size packs	6 weeks if unopened; does not need refrigeration; usually date stamped	A pouring cream

Convenience products

Convenience mixes, such as short pastry, sponge mixes and choux pastry mixes, are increasingly used in a variety of establishments. These products have improved enormously over the last few years and give the chef the opportunity to save on time and labour; with skill, imagination and creativity, the finished products are not impaired.

Not surprisingly many caterers, including some luxury establishments, have turned to using frozen puff pastry. It is available in squares and rectangles, ready rolled, thereby avoiding the possibility of uneven thickness and the waste that can occur when rolling out yourself. The large food manufacturers dominate the frozen puff pastry market.

Manufactured puff pastry is available in three types, defined often by their fat content. The cheapest is made with the white hydrogenated fat, which gives the product a pale colour and a waxy taste. Puff pastry made with bakery margarine has a better colour and, often, a better flavour. The best-quality puff pastry is made with butter, giving a richer texture, colour and flavour.

Pastry bought in blocks is cheaper than pre-rolled separate sheets, but has to be rolled evenly to give an even bake. The sizes of sheets do vary with manufacturers and all are interleaved with greaseproof paper.

Filo pastry and *feuille de brick* are further examples of convenient pastry products. They are available in frozen sheets of various sizes. No rolling out is required and, once thawed, they can be used as required and moulded if necessary.

As well as convenience pastry mixes, there is a whole range of frozen products suitable to serve as sweets and afternoon tea pastries. These include fruit pies, flans, gâteaux and charlottes. The vast majority are ready to serve once defrosted, but very often they require a little more decorative finish. The availability of such products gives the caterer the advantage of further labour cost reductions, permitting the chef to concentrate on other areas of the menu.

Storage and food safety

- Store all goods according to the Food Safety and Hygiene Regulations 2013. Eggs should be stored in a refrigerator, flour in a bin with a tight-fitting lid, sugar and other dry ingredients in air-tight storage containers.
- Check all storage temperatures are correct.
- Make sure that storage containers are kept clean and returned ready for reuse. On their return they should be hygienically washed and stored.
- Handle all equipment carefully to avoid cross-contamination.

Basic pastry products

- Always work in a clean, tidy and organised way; clean all equipment after use.
- Take special care when using cream, and ensure that products containing cream are stored under refrigerated conditions.
- All piping bags must be sterilised after each use. Many kitchens use disposable plastic piping bags to avoid contamination and maximise freshness.
- Keep all small moulds clean and dry to prevent rusting.

Preparation and cooking techniques in pastry work

When handling ingredients for pastry work:
- check all weighing scales for accuracy
- follow recipes carefully.

Adding fat to flour

Fats act as a shortening agent. The fat has the effect of shortening the gluten strands in flour, which are easily broken when eaten, making the texture of the product more crumbly. However, the development of gluten in puff pastry is very important as long strands are needed to trap the expanding gases, and this is what makes the paste rise.

Fat can be added to flour by:
- **Rubbing in** by machine or by hand, for example, short pastry. When rubbing in it is much easier to produce a fine crumb if the fat is cold.
- **Creaming** by machine or by hand, for example, sweet pastry. This is easiest to do if the fat is 'plastic' (i.e. at room temperature). Always cream the fat and sugar well before adding the liquid.
- **The flour batter method**: for example, slab cakes.
- **Lamination**: for example, puff pastry.
- **Boiling**: for example, choux pastry.

Blending

Blending means mixing all the ingredients carefully by weight.

Handling pastry

Techniques used to work pastry include:
- **Folding**: for example, folding puff pastry to create its layers, as in *vol-au-vents* or *gâteau pithiviers*.
- **Kneading**: using a mixing machine or your hands to work dough or puff pastry in the first stage of making.
- **Relaxing**: keeping pastry covered with a damp cloth, cling film or plastic to prevent a skin forming on its surface. A period of resting allows the gluten in the pastry to relax and lose some of its resistance to rolling. It will also help to prevent the pastry from shrinking during the cooking process.
- **Shaping**: producing flans, tartlets, barquettes and other such goods with pastry. Shaping also refers to crimping with the back of a small knife using the thumb technique.
- **Docking**: piercing raw pastry with small holes to prevent it from rising during baking, as when cooking tartlets blind (without a filling).

Rolling

- Roll the pastry on a lightly floured surface; turn the pastry regularly to prevent it sticking. Keep the rolling pin lightly floured and free from the pastry.
- Always roll with care, treating the pastry lightly – never apply too much pressure.
- Always apply even pressure when using a rolling pin.

Cutting

- Always cut with a sharp, clean, damp knife.
- When using cutters, always flour them before use by dipping in flour. This will give a sharp, neat cut.
- Only use a lattice cutter on firm pastry; if the pastry is too soft, you will have difficulty lifting the lattice.

Glazing

A glaze is something that gives a product a smooth, shiny surface. Examples of glazes used for pastry dishes are as follows:
- A hot clear gel produced from a pectin source, obtainable commercially, for finishing flans and tartlets; always use while still hot. A cold gel is exactly the same except that it is used cold. The gel keeps a sheen on the goods and keeps out oxygen, which might otherwise cause discoloration.
- Apricot glaze, produced from apricot jam, acts in the same way as hot gels.
- Egg wash, applied prior to baking, produces a rich glaze during the cooking process.
- Icing sugar dusted on the surface of the product caramelises in the oven or under the grill.

- Fondant gives a rich sugar glaze, which may be flavoured and/or coloured.
- Water icing gives a transparent glaze, which may also be flavoured and/or coloured.

Cooking methods

The main cooking method used in the production of pastry products is baking. The time and temperature depend on the type of product being made. Pastry can also be steamed to make products such as fruit pudding or rolls, however, and certain pastes can also be deep fried (samosa and filo pastes, for example).

Other considerations when preparing pastry items

- Ensure all cooked products are cooled before finishing.
- Always plan your time carefully.
- Understand why pastry products must be rested or relaxed and docked. This will prevent excessive shrinkage in the oven, while docking allows air to escape through the product, preventing any unevenness.
- Use silicone paper for baking in preference to greaseproof.

Finishing and presentation

It is essential that all products are finished according to the recipe requirements. Finishing and presentation is often a key stage in the process as failure at this point can affect the final appearance of the product. The way that goods are presented is an important part of the sales technique. Each product of the same type must be of the same shape, size, colour and finish. The decoration should be attractive, delicate and in keeping with the product range. All piping should be neat, clean and tidy.

Some methods of finishing and presentation are as follows:

- **Dusting**: a light sprinkling of icing sugar on a product using a fine sugar dredger or sieve.
- **Piping**: using fresh cream, chocolate or fondant, for example.
- **Filling**: with fruit, cream, pastry cream, etc. Avoid overfilling as this can give the product a clumsy appearance.

Piping fresh cream

- Piping fresh cream is a skill and, like all other skills, it takes practice to become proficient. The finished item should look attractive, simple, clean and tidy.
- All piping bags should be sterilised after each use, as these may well be a source of contamination; alternatively use a disposable piping bag.
- Make sure that all the equipment you need for piping is hygienically cleaned before and after use to avoid cross-contamination.

Test yourself

1. What is the ratio of fat to flour for:
    a short pastry
    b puff pastry
    c sugar pastry?
2. How is the fat added to the flour in the production of choux pastry?
3. What type of fat is required for the production of suet paste?
4. What is meant by the term 'lamination'?
5. Name five examples of products that can be produced using puff pastry.
6. Other than éclairs and profiteroles, name three products that are made using choux paste.
7. Name one pastry product, eaten as a dessert, which would be unsuitable for a vegetarian customer.
8. Name the faults associated with the production of short pastry.
9. What is the classic filling for a *gâteau pithiviers*?
10. Name three fillings that can be used in the production of sweet tarts.

Basic pastry products 14

Short pastry

1 Short paste (*pâte à foncer*)

Short pastry is used in fruit pies, Cornish pasties, etc.

Ingredient	400 g	850 g
Flour (soft)	250 g	500 g
Salt	Pinch	Large pinch
Butter or block/cake margarine	125 g	250 g
Water	40–50 ml	80–100 ml

1 Sieve the flour and salt. Add the butter in small pieces.

2 Start to rub the fat into the flour.

3 Continue to rub in.

4 Stop rubbing in once the mixture is crumbly and the lumps of butter are gone.

5 Make a well in the centre. Add water and start to mix it in.

6 Work into a firm dough.

7 Knead into a ball. Handle as little and as lightly as possible. Refrigerate until firm before rolling.

8 Roll out the paste for use.

Practical Cookery 14th edition

Professional tip

The amount of water used varies according to:
- the type of flour (a very fine soft flour is more absorbent)
- the degree of heat (for example, prolonged contact with hot hands, or warm weather conditions).

Different fats have different shortening properties. For example, paste made with a high ratio of butter to other fat will be harder to handle.

Variation

For wholemeal short pastry, use wholemeal flour in place of half to three-quarters of the white flour.

Short pastry for sweet dishes such as baked jam roll may be made with self-raising flour.

Lard can be used in place of some or all of the fat (the butter or cake margarine). Lard has excellent shortening properties and would lend itself, in terms of flavour, to savoury products, particularly meat-based ones. However, many people view lard as an unhealthy product as it is very high in saturated fat. It is also unsuitable for anyone following a vegan or vegetarian diet as it is an animal product.

Faults

Possible reasons for faults in short pastry are detailed below.

Hard:
- too much water
- too little fat
- fat rubbed in insufficiently
- too much handling and rolling
- over-baking.

Soft–crumbly:
- too little water
- too much fat.

Blistered:
- too little water
- water added unevenly
- fat not rubbed in evenly.

Soggy:
- too much water
- too cool an oven
- baked for insufficient time.

Shrunken:
- too much handling and rolling
- pastry stretched while handling.

From left to right: correct, blistered and shrunken short paste

2 Quiche lorraine (cheese and ham savoury flan)

Ingredient	4 portions	10 portions
Short paste	100 g	250 g
Ham, chopped	75 g	150 g
Cheese, grated	50 g	125 g
Egg	1	2½
Milk	125 ml	300 ml
Cayenne pepper		
Sea-salt (e.g. Maldon)		

Energy	Cals	Fat	Sat fat	Carb	Sugar	Protein	Fibre
2,955 kJ	704 kcal	48.4g	22.6g	38.1g	6.5g	31.6g	1.8g

1. Lightly grease an appropriately sized flan ring or barquette, or tartlet moulds if making individual portions. Line thinly with pastry.
2. Prick the bottom of the pastry two or three times with a fork to dock.
3. Cook in a hot oven at 200 °C for 3–4 minutes or until the pastry is lightly set. Reduce the oven temperature to 160 °C.
4. Remove from the oven; press the pastry down if it has tended to rise.
5. Add the chopped ham and grated cheese.
6. Mix the egg, milk, salt and cayenne thoroughly. Strain over the ham and cheese.
7. Return to the oven at 160 °C and bake gently for approximately 20 minutes or until nicely browned and the egg custard mix has set.

Variation

The filling can be varied by using lightly fried lardons of bacon (in place of the ham), chopped cooked onions and chopped parsley.

A variety of savoury flans can be made by using imagination and experimenting with different combinations (for example, stilton and onion; salmon and dill; sliced sausage and tomato).

3 Treacle tart

Ingredient	4 portions	10 portions
Short paste	125 g	300 g
Treacle	100 g	250 g
Water	1 tbsp	2½ tbsp
Lemon juice	3–4 drops	8–10 drops
Fresh white bread or cake crumbs	15 g	50 g

Energy	Cals	Fat	Sat fat	Carb	Sugar	Protein	Fibre
1,100 kJ	262 kcal	10.7 g	5.8 g	41.1 g	20.3 g	2.8 g	0.8 g

1. Lightly grease an appropriately sized flan ring, or barquette or tartlet moulds if making individual portions.
2. Line with pastry.
3. Warm the treacle, water and lemon juice; add the crumbs.
4. Place into the pastry ring and bake at 170 °C for about 20 minutes.

Variation

This tart can also be made in a shallow flan ring. Any pastry debris can be rolled and cut into 0.5 cm strips and used to decorate the top of the tart before baking.

Try sprinkling with vanilla salt as a garnish.

4 Fruit pie

Ingredient	4–6 portions	10–15 portions
Fruit (see note)	400 g	1.5 kg
Sugar	100 g	250 g
Water	2 tbsp	5 tbsp
Short paste	200 g	500 g
Egg wash		

Energy	Cals	Fat	Sat fat	Carb	Sugar	Protein	Fibre
6,808 kJ	1,621 kcal	65.0 g	26.6 g	260.0 g	144.1 g	15.3 g	15.0 g

For an apple pie.

1. Prepare the fruit, wash and place in a bowl.
2. Add the sugar and water, and mix gently. (Place a clove in an apple pie.)
3. Line an appropriately sized flan ring with two-thirds of the pastry, leaving a third for the top.
4. Fill the lined ring with the fruit mixture.
5. Dampen the edge of the pastry with a little water.
6. Roll out the reserved piece of pastry to cover the fruit.
7. Carefully lay the pastry on top of the fruit and firmly seal to the edge of the lined pastry. Cut off any surplus pastry. (This can be used to create a lattice effect by running strips of pastry in diagonal lines across the pie – see picture.)
8. Brush the top of the pie with egg wash and sprinkle with caster sugar.
9. Place the pie on a baking sheet and bake at 200 °C for 10 minutes; reduce the oven to 180 °C and continue to bake for another 25–30 minutes. If the pastry colours too quickly, cover it with a sheet of paper.
10. Once cooked, allow to cool slightly before removing the flan ring. Serve with custard, fresh cream or ice cream.

Preparation of fruit for pies

The pie may be filled with a single fruit or a combination such as blackberry and apple or damson and apple.
- apples – peeled, quartered, cored, washed, cut in slices
- cherries – stalks removed, stoned, washed
- blackberries – stalks removed, washed
- gooseberries – stalks and tails removed, washed
- damsons – picked, stoned and washed
- rhubarb – leaves and root removed, tough strings removed, cut into 2 cm pieces, washed.

Basic pastry products

Sweet pastry

5 Sugar paste (sweet paste, *pâte à sucre*)

Sugar pastry is used for products such as flans, fruit tarts and tartlets.

Ingredient	400 g	1 kg
Sugar	50 g	125 g
Butter or block/cake margarine	125 g	300 g
Eggs	1	2–3
Flour (soft)	200 g	500 g
Salt	Pinch	Large pinch

Method 1 – sweet lining paste (rubbing in)

1 Sieve the flour and salt. Lightly rub in the margarine or butter to achieve a sandy texture.
2 Mix the sugar and egg until dissolved.
3 Make a well in the centre of the flour. Add the sugar and beaten egg.
4 Gradually incorporate the flour and margarine or butter and lightly mix to a smooth paste. Allow to rest before using.

Method 2 – traditional French sugar paste (creaming)

1 Taking care not to over-soften, cream the butter and sugar.
2 Add the beaten egg gradually and mix for a few seconds.
3 Gradually incorporate the sieved flour and salt. Mix lightly until smooth.
4 Allow to rest in a cool place before using.

1 Measure out the sugar and cut the butter into small chunks.
2 Cream the butter and sugar together. 
3 Add the beaten egg in stages, thoroughly mixing each time. 
4 Incorporate the flour and salt. 
5 Press into a tray and leave to chill. 
6 The paste will need to be rolled out before use in any recipe.

Practical Cookery 14th edition

> **Professional tip**
>
> The higher the percentage of butter, the shorter and richer the paste will become. However, as the butter will soften and melt during handling, the paste will become softer and more difficult to work with. Therefore chilling and light, quick handling are required when using a sweet paste with a high butter content.
>
> This also applies to the working environment. For example, in a particularly warm kitchen, it will be more difficult to work with a paste of this structure than in a cooler kitchen.
>
> The butter in this recipe could be reduced from 125 g to 100 g to make handling easier.

From left to right: short paste (recipe 1), rough puff paste (recipe 25) and sweet paste (recipe 5)

6 Flan cases

1. Allow 25 g flour per portion and prepare sugar pastry as per recipe 5.
2. Grease a flan ring and baking sheet.
3. Roll the pastry out so that the circumference is 2 cm larger than the flan ring. The pastry may be rolled between cling film or greaseproof or silicone paper.
4. Place the flan ring on the baking sheet.
5. Carefully place the pastry on the flan ring by rolling it loosely over the rolling pin, picking it up and unrolling it over the flan ring.
6. Press the pastry into shape without stretching it, being careful to exclude any air.
7. Allow a 0.5 cm ridge of pastry on top of the flan ring.
8. Cut off the surplus paste by rolling the rolling pin firmly across the top of the flan ring.
9. The rim can be left straight or moulded. Mould the edge with thumb and forefinger. Decorate either with pastry tweezers or with thumbs and forefingers, squeezing the pastry neatly to form a corrugated pattern.

> **Baking blind**
>
> Some recipes call for the flan case to be baked blind, which means that it is baked before the filling is added. Line the pastry case with cling film and fill with baking beans (ceramic pie weights) or dried beans. Bake at 190 °C.

Place the pastry into the flan ring

Firm the pastry into the bottom of the ring

Bake blind, filled with beans, if the recipe requires

Basic pastry products 14

7 Fruit tart, tartlets or barquettes

Fruit tart

Ingredient	4 portions
Sweet paste	250 g
Fruit (e.g. strawberries, raspberries, grapes, blueberries)	500 g
Pastry cream	
Glaze	5 tbsp

1. Line a flan ring with paste and cook blind at 190 °C. Allow to cool.
2. Pick and wash the fruit, then drain well. Wash and slice/segment, etc. any larger fruit being used.
3. Pipe pastry cream into the flan case, filling it to the rim. Dress the fruit neatly over the top.
4. Coat with the glaze. Use a glaze suitable for the fruit chosen, for example, with a strawberry tart, use a red glaze.

Energy	Cals	Fat	Sat fat	Carb	Sugar	Protein	Fibre	Sodium
1907 kJ	454 kcal	18.7 g	10.7 g	68.0 g	39.0 g	6.8 g	3.6 g	0.3 g

Faults

Although this strawberry tart may appear to be fine at first glance, the husks of the strawberries are visible. It would be better to present the strawberries with their tops pointing upwards or sliced and overlapping.

There is also quite a wide gap between the rows of strawberries, showing the crème pâtissière underneath. This should be avoided.

The second photo shows the importance of ensuring that fillings are prepared and/or cooked properly. In this case, the crème pâtissière has not been cooked sufficiently or prepared accurately as the filling is not structured sufficiently to support the fruit once the tart has been cut.

Professional tip

Brush the inside of the pastry case with melted couverture before filling. This forms a barrier between the pastry and the moisture in the filling.

Practical Cookery 14th edition

Tartlets

1. Roll out pastry 3 mm thick.
2. Cut out rounds with a fluted cutter and place them neatly in greased tartlet moulds. If soft fruit (such as strawberries or raspberries) is being used, the pastry should be cooked blind first.
3. After baking and filling (or filling and baking) with pastry cream, dress neatly with fruit and glaze the top.

Certain fruits (such as strawberries and raspberries) are sometimes served in boat-shaped moulds (barquettes). The preparation is the same as for tartlets. Tartlets and barquettes should be glazed and served allowing one large or two small per portion.

Energy	Cals	Fat	Sat fat	Carb	Sugar	Protein	Fibre	Sodium
690 kJ	165 kcal	8.7g	2.7g	21.1g	6.3g	2.0g	1.2g	0.1g

8 Egg custard tart

Ingredient	8 portions
Sweet paste	250 g
Egg yolks	9
Caster sugar	75 g
Whipping cream, gently warmed and infused with 2 sticks of cinnamon	500 ml
Nutmeg, freshly grated	

1. Roll out the pastry on a lightly floured surface, to 2 mm thickness. Use it to line a 20 cm flan ring, placed on a baking sheet.
2. Line the pastry with food-safe cling film or greaseproof paper and fill with baking beans. Bake blind in a preheated oven at 190 °C for about 10 minutes or until the pastry is turning golden brown. Remove the paper and beans, and allow to cool. Turn the oven down to 130 °C.
3. To make the custard filling, whisk together the egg yolks and sugar. Add the cream and mix well.
4. Pass the mixture through a fine sieve into a saucepan. Heat to 37 °C.
5. Fill the pastry case with the custard to 0.5 cm below the top. Place it carefully into the middle of the oven and bake for 30–40 minutes or until the custard appears to be set but not too firm.
6. Remove from the oven and cover liberally with grated nutmeg. Allow to cool to room temperature.

Energy	Cals	Fat	Sat fat	Carb	Sugar	Protein	Fibre	Sodium
1998 kJ	482 kcal	39.0g	22.0g	27.0g	15.8g	6.4g	0.6g	0.2g

Basic pastry products — 14

9 Apple flan

Ingredient	4 portions	10 portions
Sweet paste	100 g	250 g
Pastry cream (crème pâtissière) (see recipe 37)	250 ml	625 ml
Cooking apples	400 g	1 kg
Sugar	50 g	125 g
Apricot glaze	2 tbsp	6 tbsp

Energy	Cals	Fat	Sat fat	Carb	Sugar	Protein	Fibre
1,428 kJ	340 kcal	13.8 g	5.8 g	53.8 g	36 g	3.5 g	2.9 g

1. Line a flan ring with sweet paste. Pierce the bottom several times with a fork.
2. Pipe a layer of pastry cream into the bottom of the flan.
3. Peel, quarter and wash the selected apple.
4. Cut into neat thin slices and lay carefully on the pastry cream, overlapping each slice. Ensure that each slice points to the centre of the flan then no difficulty should be encountered in joining up the pattern neatly.
5. Sprinkle a little sugar on the apple slices and bake the flan at 200–220 °C for 30–40 minutes.
6. When the flan is almost cooked, remove the flan ring carefully, return to the oven to complete the cooking. Mask with hot apricot glaze or flan jelly.

Pipe the filling neatly into the flan case

Slice the apple very thinly for decoration

Arrange the apple slices on top of the flan

10 Lemon meringue pie

Ingredient	2 × 20 cm flan rings (16 portions)
Sweet paste flan cases	2
Granulated sugar	450 g
Lemons, grated zest	2
Fresh lemon juice	240 ml
Eggs, large	8
Large egg yolks	2
Unsalted butter, cut into small pieces	350 g
Meringue	
Egg whites	6
Caster sugar	600 g

Energy	Cals	Fat	Sat fat	Carb	Sugar	Protein	Fibre
12,138 kJ	2,895 kcal	147.4g	84.8g	379.4g	305.0g	36.4g	4.2g

1 Place the sugar into a bowl and grate the zest of lemon into it, rubbing together.
2 Strain the lemon juice into a non-reactive pan. Add the eggs, egg yolks, butter and zested sugar. Whisk to combine.
3 Place over a medium heat and whisk continuously for 3–5 minutes, until the mixture begins to thicken.
4 At the first sign of boiling, remove from the heat. Strain into a bowl and cool before filling the pastry cases.
5 Make the meringue (see page 591). Pipe it on top of the filled pie.
6 Colour in a hot oven at 220 °C.

11 Pear and almond tart

Ingredient	8 portions
Sweet paste	200 g
Apricot jam	25 g
Almond cream	350 g
Poached pears	4
Apricot glaze	
Flaked almonds	
Icing sugar	

Energy	Cals	Fat	Sat fat	Carb	Sugar	Protein	Fibre	Sodium
1500 kJ	359 kcal	23.0g	10.3g	34.0g	24.0g	5.7g	3.6g	0.3g

1. Line a buttered 20 cm flan ring with sweet paste. Trim and dock.
2. Using the back of a spoon, spread a little apricot jam over the base.
3. Pipe in almond cream until the flan case is two-thirds full.
4. Dry the poached pears. Cut them in half and remove the cores and string.
5. Score across the pears and arrange on top of the flan.
6. Bake in the oven at 200 °C for 25–30 minutes.
7. Allow to cool, then brush with apricot glaze.
8. Sprinkle flaked almonds around the edge and dust with icing sugar.

12 Lemon tart

1. Prepare 200 g of sweet paste, adding the zest of one lemon to the sugar.
2. Line a 20 cm flan ring with the paste.
3. Bake blind at 190 °C for approximately 15 minutes.
4. Prepare the filling: mix the eggs and sugar together until smooth, add the cream, lemon juice and zest. Whisk well.
5. Seal the pastry, so that the filling will not leak out. Pour the filling into the flan case and bake for 30–40 minutes at 150 °C until just set. (Take care when almost cooked as overcooking will cause the filling to rise and possibly crack.)
6. Remove from the oven and allow to cool.
7. Dust with icing sugar and glaze under the grill or with a blowtorch. Portion and serve.

Ingredient	8 portions
Sweet paste	200 g
Lemons	Juice of 3, zest from 4
Eggs	8
Caster sugar	300 g
Double cream	250 ml

Energy	Cals	Fat	Sat fat	Carb	Sugar	Protein	Fibre	Sodium
1907 kJ	456 kcal	25.0 g	13.4 g	53.0 g	44.0 g	8.5 g	0.5 g	0.2 g

Professional tip
If possible, make the filling one day in advance. The flavour will develop as the mixture matures.

Note
The mixture will fill one 16 × 4 cm or two 16 × 2 cm flan rings. If using two flan rings, double the amount of pastry and reduce the baking time when the filling is added.

Variation
Limes may be used in place of lemons. If so, use the zest and juice of five limes or use a mixture of lemons and limes.

13 Bakewell tart

Ingredient	8 portions
Sweet paste	200 g
Raspberry jam	50 g
Egg wash	1 egg
Apricot glaze	50 g
Icing sugar	35 g
Frangipane (almond cream)	250 g

Energy	Cals	Fat	Sat fat	Carb	Sugar	Protein	Fibre	Sodium
1308 kJ	313 kcal	18.5g	8.6g	34.0g	24.0g	5.0g	1.5g	0.2g

1 Line a 20 cm flan ring using three-quarters of the paste, 2 mm thick.
2 Pierce the bottom with a fork.
3 Spread with jam and the frangipane.
4 Roll the remaining paste, cut into neat 0.5 cm strips and arrange neatly criss-crossed (lattice) on the frangipane; trim off surplus paste. Brush with egg wash.
5 Bake in a moderately hot oven at 200–210 °C for 30–40 minutes. Brush with hot apricot glaze.
6 When cooled, brush over with very thin water icing. Sprinkle with flaked almonds.

14 Mince pies

Ingredient	12 small pies
Sweet paste	200 g
Mincemeat (see below)	200 g
Egg wash	1 egg
Icing sugar	

Energy	Cals	Fat	Sat fat	Carb	Sugar	Protein	Fibre	Sodium
2,009 kJ	479 kcal	23.4g	0.0g	66.6g	32.0g	4.6g	2.8g	0.3g

For a portion of two small pies.

1. Roll out the pastry 3 mm thick.
2. Cut half the pastry into fluted rounds 6 cm in diameter.
3. Place on a greased, dampened baking sheet. (Tartlet moulds may also be used.)
4. Moisten the edges. Place a little mincemeat in the centre of each.
5. Cut the remainder of the pastry into fluted rounds, 8 cm in diameter.
6. Cover the mincemeat with pastry and seal the edges. Brush with egg wash.
7. Bake at 210 °C for approximately 20 minutes.
8. Sprinkle with icing sugar and serve warm.

Accompany with a suitable sauce, such as custard, brandy sauce or brandy cream.

Mincemeat

Ingredient	
Suet, chopped	100 g
Mixed peel, chopped	100 g
Currants	100 g
Sultanas	100 g
Raisins	100 g
Apples, chopped	100 g
Barbados sugar	100 g
Mixed spice	5 g
Lemon, grated zest and juice of	1
Orange, grated zest and juice of	1
Rum	60 ml
Brandy	60 ml

1. Mix the ingredients together.
2. Seal in jars and use as required.

Variation

Short or puff pastry may also be used. Various toppings can also be added, such as crumble mixture or flaked almonds and an apricot glaze.

Choux pastry

15 Choux paste (*pâte à choux*)

Choux paste is used to make products such as éclairs, profiteroles and gâteau Paris-Brest.

Ingredient	750 g	1.5 kg
Water	250 ml	500 ml
Sugar	Pinch	Large pinch
Salt	Pinch	Large pinch
Butter or block/cake margarine	100 g	200 g
Flour (strong)	150 g	300 g
Eggs	4–5	8–10

1. Bring the water, sugar, salt and fat to the boil in a saucepan. Remove from the heat.
2. Add the sieved flour and mix in with a wooden spoon.
3. Return to a moderate heat and stir continuously until the mixture leaves the sides of the pan. (This is known as a panada.)
4. Remove from the heat and allow to cool.
5. Gradually add the beaten eggs, beating well. Do not add all the eggs at once – check the consistency as you go. The mixture should just flow back when moved in one direction (it may not take all the egg).

Variation

Wholemeal flour – 50 per cent, 70 per cent or 100 per cent – may be used to make choux paste.

Faults

Greasy and heavy paste:
- the basic mixture was over-cooked.

Soft paste, not aerated:
- flour insufficiently cooked
- eggs insufficiently beaten in the mixture
- oven too cool
- under-baked.

Split or separated mixture:
- egg added too quickly.

The choux buns on the left are light and well risen; those on the right are poorly aerated.

1. Cut the butter into cubes and melt them in the water.
2. Add the flour. 
3. When the panada is ready, it will start to come away from the sides.

Basic pastry products 14

4 Add egg until the mixture is the right consistency – it should drop from a spoon under its own weight.

5 Pipe the paste into the shape required – these rings could be used for Paris-Brest (recipe 19).

6 A selection of shapes in raw choux paste.

16 Cream buns (*choux à la crème*)

Ingredient	Makes 10 buns
Choux paste	150 ml
Egg wash	
Chopped almonds and/or nib sugar	35 g
Whipped cream/Chantilly cream	300 ml
Icing sugar, to serve	

Energy	Cals	Fat	Sat fat	Carb	Sugar	Protein	Fibre	Sodium
752 kJ	182 kcal	16.4g	8.5g	6.7g	3.6g	2.2g	0.2g	0.0g

1 Place the choux paste into a piping bag with a 1 cm plain tube.
2 Pipe pieces the size of a walnut on to a lightly greased, dampened baking sheet.
3 Using a wet finger, gently press down any spikes or peaks of paste to make round bulbs of paste, then egg wash.
4 Bake at 200–220 °C for about 30 minutes.
5 Allow to cool. Make a hole in the base of each bun.
6 Fill with sweetened, vanilla-flavoured whipped cream (Chantilly cream) using a piping bag and small tube.
7 Sprinkle with icing sugar and serve with cream and fresh fruit such as strawberries or raspberries.

Practical Cookery 14th edition

17 Profiteroles and chocolate sauce

Ingredient	10 portions
Choux paste	200 ml
Chocolate sauce (see page 622)	250 ml
Chantilly cream	250 ml
Icing sugar, to serve	

Energy	Cals	Fat	Sat fat	Carb	Sugar	Protein	Fibre
919 kJ	219 kcal	16.2g	9.7g	16.4g	12.8g	2.9g	0.2g

1 Spoon the choux paste into a piping bag with a plain nozzle (approx. 1.5 cm diameter).
2 Pipe walnut-sized balls of paste on to the greased baking sheet, spaced well apart. Level the peaked tops with the tip of a wet finger.
3 Bake for 18–20 minutes at 200 °C, until well risen and golden brown. Remove from the oven, transfer to a wire rack and allow to cool completely.
4 Make a hole in each and fill with Chantilly cream.
5 Dredge with icing sugar and serve with a sauceboat of cold chocolate sauce or coat the profiteroles with the sauce.

Variation

Coffee sauce may be served and the profiteroles filled with non-dairy cream. Profiteroles may also be filled with chocolate-, coffee- or rum-flavoured pastry cream.

18 Chocolate éclairs

Ingredient	12 portions
Choux paste	200 ml
Whipped cream/Chantilly cream	250 ml
Fondant	100 g
Chocolate couverture	25 g

Energy	Cals	Fat	Sat fat	Carb	Sugar	Protein	Fibre
516 kJ	123 kcal	9.5g	5.7g	8.8g	7.3g	1.1g	0.1g

Variations

For coffee éclairs (éclairs au café) add a few drops of coffee extract to the fondant instead of chocolate; coffee éclairs may also be filled with pastry cream (see page 538) flavoured with coffee.

522

Basic pastry products 14

1. Place the choux paste into a piping bag with a 1 cm plain tube.
2. Pipe into 8 cm lengths on to a lightly greased, dampened baking sheet.
3. Bake at 200–220 °C for about 30 minutes.
4. Allow to cool. Slit down one side, with a sharp knife.
5. Fill with Chantilly cream (or whipped cream) using a piping bag and small tube. The continental fashion is to fill with pastry cream.
6. Warm the fondant, add the finely cut chocolate, allow to melt slowly, adjusting the consistency with a little sugar and water syrup if necessary. Do not overheat or the fondant will lose its shine.
7. Glaze the éclairs by dipping them in the fondant; remove the surplus with the finger. Allow to set.

Traditionally, chocolate éclairs were filled with chocolate pastry cream.

Pierce the éclair

Pipe in the filling

Dip the éclair in fondant; wipe the edges to give a neat finish

19 Gâteau Paris-Brest

Praline

1. Place the nuts on a baking sheet and toast until evenly coloured.
2. Place the sugar in a large, heavy, stainless steel saucepan. Set the pan over a low heat and allow the sugar to caramelise. Do not over-stir, but do not allow the sugar to burn.
3. When the sugar is lightly caramelised and reaches a temperature of 170 °C, remove from the heat and stir in the nuts.
4. Immediately deposit the mixture on a non-stick silicone mat. Place another mat over the top and roll as thin as possible.
5. Allow to cool completely. Break up and store in an airtight container.

Paris-Brest

1. Pipe choux paste (recipe 15) into rings and bake.
2. Slice each ring in half. Fill with a mixture of crème diplomate or pastry cream and praline.

Ingredient	8 portions
Choux paste	
Crème diplomate (see page 538)	800 ml
For the praline	
Flaked almonds, hazelnuts and pecans (any combination)	375 g
Granulated sugar	500 g

Energy	Cals	Fat	Sat fat	Carb	Sugar	Protein	Fibre
3,180 kJ	761 kcal	47.4 g	14.7 g	74.1 g	69.9 g	14.1 g	0.2 g

523

20 Choux paste fritters (*beignets soufflés*)

Ingredient	Makes 8 portions
Choux paste	125 ml
Icing sugar or caster sugar, to serve	
Apricot sauce, to serve	125 ml

Energy	Cals	Fat	Sat fat	Carb	Sugar	Protein	Fibre
344 kJ	82 kcal	3.9g	1.3g	11.5g	8.8g	0.9g	0.2g

1 Using two spoons of the same size, shape the paste into quenelles.
2 Place on to strips of lightly greased, greaseproof paper.
3 Lower the pieces into moderately hot deep fat at 170 °C. Allow to cook gently for 10–15 minutes.
4 Drain well and roll in the caster sugar. The sugar can be flavoured at this point (ground cinnamon is often used at this stage).
5 Serve with a sauceboat of hot fruit-based sauce.

Shape the fritter with two spoons

Lower the fritters into hot oil on a strip of greaseproof paper

Lift them out with a spider

Basic pastry products

Suet pastry

21 Suet paste

Suet paste is used for steamed fruit puddings, steamed jam rolls, steamed meat puddings and dumplings.

1 Sieve the flour, baking powder and salt.
2 Mix in the suet. Make a well. Add the water.
3 Mix lightly to a fairly stiff paste.

> **Professional tip**
>
> Self-raising flour already contains baking powder so this element could be reduced in the recipe if using self-raising flour.
>
> Vegetarian suet is also available to enable products to be meat-free.

Ingredient	400 g	1 kg
Flour (soft) or self-raising flour	200 g	500 g
Baking powder	10 g	25 g
Salt	Pinch	Large pinch
Prepared beef or vegetarian suet	100 g	250 g
Water	125 ml	300 ml

> **Faults**
>
> **Heavy and soggy paste**:
> - cooking temperature may have been too low.
>
> **Tough paste**:
> - handled too much or over-cooked.

22 Steamed fruit puddings

Ingredient	10 individual puddings or 1 large pudding
Suet paste (see recipe 21)	300 g
Fruit	1 kg
Sugar	200 g
Water	60 ml

Energy	Cals	Fat	Sat fat	Carb	Sugar	Protein	Fibre	Sodium
975 kJ	231 kcal	6.3 g	3.1 g	44.0 g	33.0 g	1.8 g	2.6 g	0.1 g

1. Grease a basin or individual moulds.
2. Line the moulds, using three-quarters of the paste.
3. Add the prepared and washed fruit and the sugar. (Add between one and two cloves in an apple pudding.)
5. Add water. Moisten the edge of the paste.
6. Cover with the remaining quarter of the paste and seal firmly.
7. Cover with greased greaseproof paper, a pudding cloth or foil.
8. Steam for about 1½ hours (large basin) or 40 minutes (individual moulds).

Serve with custard.

> **Variation**
> Steamed fruit puddings can be made with apple, apple and blackberry, rhubarb, rhubarb and apple, and so on.

Puff pastry

23 Puff paste (French method)

Ingredient	Makes approx. 1.5 kg
Flour (strong)	560 g
Salt	12 g
Pastry butter or pastry margarine	60 g
Water, ice-cold	325 ml
Lemon juice, ascorbic or tartaric acid, or white vinegar	A few drops
Pastry butter or pastry margarine	500 g

1. Sieve the flour and salt together.
2. Rub in the 60 g of pastry butter/pastry margarine.
3. Make a well in the centre.
4. Add the cold water and lemon juice or acid (to make the gluten more elastic), and knead well into a smooth dough in the shape of a ball.
5. Relax the dough in a cool place for 30 minutes.
6. Cut a cross halfway through the dough and pull out the corners to form a star shape.
7. Roll out the points of the star square, leaving the centre thick.
8. Knead the remaining butter/margarine to the same texture as the dough. This is most important – if the fat is too soft it will melt and ooze out, if it is too hard it will break through the paste when being rolled.
9. Place the butter or margarine on the centre square, which is four times thicker than the flaps.
10. Fold over the flaps.
11. Roll out to 30 cm × 15 cm, cover with a cloth or plastic and rest for 5–10 minutes in a cool place.
12. Roll out to 60 cm × 20 cm, fold both the ends to the centre, and fold in half again to form a square. This is one double turn.
13. Allow to rest in a cool place for 20 minutes.
14. Half-turn the paste to the right or the left.
15. Give one more double turn and allow to rest for 20 minutes.
16. Give two more double turns, allowing to rest between each.
17. Allow to rest before using.

Basic pastry products 14

Rub the first batch of butter into the flour

Mix in the water and lemon juice

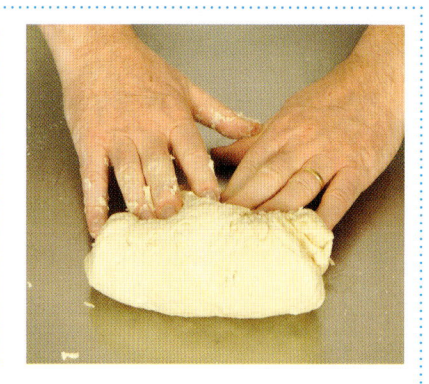

Knead into a smooth dough

Roll the dough out into a cross shape

Knead the remaining butter in a plastic bag, then place it on the centre of the dough

Fold over each flap

Roll into a neat rectangle, then take each end and fold to meet in the centre

Fold again from the top end of the paste to the bottom

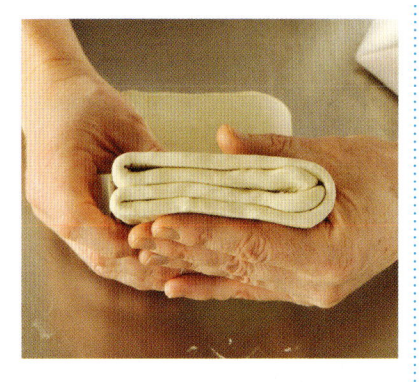

These photos have shown one double turn. When resting the turned and folded paste, leave an indented finger mark on the surface to show the number of turns completed

527

Practical Cookery 14th edition

> **Professional tip**
> - Care must be taken when rolling out the paste to keep the ends and sides square.
> - When rolling between each turn, always roll with the folded edge to the left.
> - The addition of lemon juice (or other acid) helps to strengthen the gluten in the flour, thus helping to make a stronger dough, so that there is less likelihood of the fat oozing out.
> - The rise is caused by the fat separating layers of paste and air during rolling. When heat is applied by the oven, steam is produced, causing the layers to rise and give the characteristic flaky formation. This is aeration by lamination.

> **Faults**
>
> The pastry on the left is unevenly laminated. Possible reasons for this:
> - The paste was not folded equally.
> - The paste was rolled too thinly.
> - Reused scraps of paste were used, instead of making up a virgin paste.

24 Inverted or reverse puff pastry

For standard puff pastry, the butter or pastry margarine is wrapped inside a detrempe, then rolled out and folded various times to create layers. With inverted puff pastry, butter or pastry margarine mixed with some flour is the outer layer, and the detrempe is folded inside.

This pastry can be made with strong flour or spelt flour.

Ingredient	Makes approximately 500 g
Unsalted butter or pastry margarine	513 g
Strong flour or white spelt flour	525 g
Salt	5 g
Water	150 ml approx.
White vinegar	5 ml

Energy	Cals	Fat	Sat fat	Carb	Sugar	Protein	Fibre	Sodium
23,420 kJ	5,637 kcal	429.0g	269.0g	382.0g	5.5g	63.0g	17.4g	2.0g

Using unsalted butter.

1. Combine 400 g of the butter and 175 g flour in a suitable bowl, and rub together until smooth but not aerated.
2. Spread out onto a lined tray of parchment or silpat mat. Form into a rectangle approximately 15 cm × 20 cm. Chill in the refrigerator.
3. In a large bowl combine the remaining 350 g flour and salt. Add the remaining 113 g of butter, water and vinegar, and combine the ingredients together. Knead the dough until the mix is homogenous (well mixed/one smooth dough).
4. Form the dough into a rectangle approximately the size of the butter block. Wrap in cling film and allow to chill in the refrigerator until cool and pliable.
5. Unwrap and place on a lightly floured work surface. Roll out until it is twice as long and twice as wide, approximately 40 cm × 30 cm.
6. Place the chilled dough in the centre of the butter rectangle. Fold the butter around the dough, encasing it as evenly as possible.
7. Using a little flour, roll the packet to a rectangle approximately 20 cm × 60 cm. The size and shape of the rectangle does not matter but the thickness is important – this should be approximately 6 mm. Dust off all excess flour.
8. Now produce a book fold (also referred to as a double fold). Bring the short edges of the rectangle into the centre, then fold the dough in half, resembling a book. Wrap in cling film and chill well.
9. When well chilled, remove the cling film and place back on the work surface. Roll to the same dimensions. This time, produce a letter fold (also referred to as a single turn). Taking the short sides, fold the rectangle in thirds, like a letter. Wrap in cling film and chill again.
10. After chilling, remove the cling film and repeat, doing a book fold.
11. Repeat this stage three more times, chilling between each fold.

Basic pastry products 14

Ingredients for inverted or reverse puff pastry

Combine the butter and flour in a bowl and rub together until smooth

Fold the butter around the dough, encasing it as evenly as possible

Roll the packet to a 20 cm × 60 cm rectangle, with a 6 mm thickness

Taking the short sides, fold the rectangle in thirds to produce a letter fold

Repeat three more times, chilling between each fold

Note

Depending on the intended use and how light you want the pastry, you could give the paste one double and four single turns (972 layers) as in the recipe above, or the classic five single folds (929 layers)

25 Rough puff paste

Ingredient	475 g	1.2 kg
Flour (strong)	200 g	500 g
Salt	1 large pinch	2 large pinches
Butter or block/cake margarine (lightly chilled)	150 g	375 g
Water, ice-cold	125 ml	300 ml
Lemon juice, ascorbic or tartaric acid	10 ml	25 ml

1 Sieve the flour and salt.
2 Cut the fat into small pieces and lightly mix them into the flour without rubbing in.
3 Make a well in the centre.
4 Add the liquid and mix to a dough. The dough should be fairly tight at this stage.
5 Turn on to a floured table and roll into an oblong strip, about 30 × 10 cm, keeping the sides square.
6 Give one double turn (as for puff pastry).
7 Allow to rest in a cool place, covered with cloth or plastic for 30 minutes.
8 Give three more double turns, resting between each. (Alternatively, give six single turns.) Allow to rest before using.

Professional tip

Each time you leave the paste to rest, gently make finger indentations, one for each turn you have made.

529

Practical Cookery 14th edition

Make a well in the centre of the flour and butter and add the liquid

Mix to a fairly stiff dough

Roll out and fold the ends to the middle

Keep rolling, folding and turning

The finished paste, ready to rest and then use

26 Puff pastry cases (*bouchées, vol-au-vents*)

Ingredient	Makes 12 bouchées/6 vol-au-vents
Puff paste	200 g
Egg wash	

1 Roll out the pastry to approximately 5 mm thick.
2 Cut out with a round, fluted cutter of the size required.
3 Place on a greased, dampened baking sheet; egg wash.
4 Dip a plain cutter of a slightly smaller diameter into hot fat or oil and make an incision 3 mm deep in the centre of each.
5 Allow to rest in a cool place.
6 Bake at 220 °C for about 20 minutes.
7 When cool, remove the caps or lids carefully and remove all the raw pastry from inside the cases.

Professional tip

Bouchées are filled with a variety of savoury fillings and are served hot or cold. They may also be filled with creams or curds as a pastry.

Larger versions are known as **vol-au-vents**. They may be produced in one-, two-, four- or six-portion sizes; a single-sized vol-au-vent would be approximately twice the size of a bouchée. When preparing one- and two-portion sized vol-au-vents, the method for bouchées may be followed. When preparing larger vol-au-vents, it is advisable to have two layers of puff pastry, each 5 mm thick, sealed together with egg wash. One layer should be a plain round, and the other of the same diameter with a circle cut out of the centre.

Basic pastry products 14

27 Cheese straws (paillettes au fromage)

Ingredient	8–10 portions	16–20 portions
Puff paste or rough puff paste	100 g	250 g
Cheese, grated	50 g	125 g
Cayenne pepper		

Energy	Cals	Fat	Sat fat	Carb	Sugar	Protein	Fibre
2,562 kJ	610 kcal	48.1 g	24.1 g	28.7 g	0.6 g	17.4 g	1.4 g

1 Roll out the pastry to 60 × 15 cm, 3 mm thick.
2 Sprinkle with the cheese and cayenne pepper.
3 Roll out lightly to embed the cheese.
4 Cut the paste into thin strips by length.
5 Twist each strip to form rolls in the strip.
6 Place on a silicone mat.
7 Bake in a hot oven at 230–250 °C for 10 minutes or until a golden brown. Cut into lengths as required.

28 Sausage rolls

Ingredient	Makes 12 × 8 cm rolls
Puff paste	200 g
Sausage meat	400 g
Egg wash	

Energy	Cals	Fat	Sat fat	Carb	Sugar	Protein	Fibre
799 kJ	190 kcal	15.9 g	5.8 g	7.9 g	0.2 g	4.3 g	0.4 g

1 Roll out the pastry to 3 mm thick into a strip 10 cm wide.
2 Shape the sausage meat into a roll 2 cm in diameter.
3 Place the sausage meat on to the pastry. Moisten the edges of the pastry.
4 Fold over and seal. Cut into 8 cm lengths.
5 Mark the edge with the back of a knife. Brush with egg wash.
6 Place on to a greased, dampened baking sheet.
7 Bake at 220 °C for approximately 20 minutes.

Practical Cookery 14th edition

29 Gâteau pithiviers

Ingredient	2 × 22cm gâteaux
Puff paste	1 kg
Pastry cream	60 g
Frangipane	600 g
Egg wash (yolks only)	
Granulated sugar	

Energy	Cals	Fat	Sat fat	Carb	Sugar	Protein	Fibre	Sodium
1453 kJ	349 kcal	25.8g	9.4g	25.6g	10.4g	5.3g	1.7g	0.4g

For 1/10 of one gâteau.

1. Divide the paste into four equal pieces. Roll out each piece in a circle with a 22 cm diameter, 4 mm thick.
2. Rest in the fridge between sheets of cling film, preferably overnight.
3. Lightly butter two baking trays and splash with water. Lay one circle of paste on to each tray and dock them.
4. Mark a 16 cm diameter circle in the centre of each.
5. Beat the pastry cream, if desired, and mix it with the frangipane.
6. Using a plain nozzle, pipe the cream over the inner circles, making them slightly domed.
7. Egg wash the outer edges of the paste. Lay one of the remaining pieces over the top of each one, smooth over and press down hard.
8. Mark the edges with a round cutter. Cut out a scallop pattern with a knife or use a cut piping nozzle as shown in the photo sequence.
9. Egg wash twice. Mark the top of both with a spiral pattern.
10. Bake at 220 °C for 10 minutes. Remove from the oven and sprinkle with granulated sugar. Turn the oven down to 190 °C and bake for a further 20 to 25 minutes.
11. Glaze under a salamander.

Adding the filling to the rolled base

Trimming the edge

Marking the top

Basic pastry products 14

30 Palmiers

Ingredient	
Puff paste (see page 526)	
Caster sugar	
Egg wash	

1. Roll out puff pastry into a square 3 mm thick.
2. Sprinkle liberally with caster sugar on both sides and roll into the pastry.
3. Fold into three from each end so as to meet in the middle; brush with egg wash and fold in two.
4. Cut into strips approximately 2 cm thick; dip one side in caster sugar.
5. Place on a greased baking sheet, sugared side down, leaving a space of at least 2 cm between each.
6. Bake in a very hot oven for about 10 minutes.
7. Turn with a palette knife, cook on the other side until brown and the sugar is caramelised.

Note
Palmiers are usually made from leftover or off-cuts of puff pastry. As a more biscuit-like property is sought, previously rolled pastry can be utilised because the rise required is not as much as in products such as bouchées and vol-au-vents.

Variation
Puff pastry trimmings are suitable for this recipe. Palmiers may be made in a wide variety of sizes. Two joined together with a little whipped cream may be served as a pastry or small ones for petits fours. They may be sandwiched together with soft fruit, whipped cream and/or ice cream and served as a sweet.

31 Pear jalousie

1. Roll out two-thirds of the pastry 3 mm thick into a strip 25 × 10 cm and place on a greased, dampened baking sheet.
2. Pierce with a docker. Moisten the edges.
3. Pipe on the frangipane, leaving 2 cm free all the way round. Place the pears on top.
4. Roll out the remaining one-third of the pastry to the same size. Chill before cutting.
5. Cut the dough with a trellis cutter to make a lattice.
6. Carefully open out this strip and neatly place on to the first strip.
7. Trim off any excess. Neaten and decorate the edge. Brush with egg wash.
8. Bake at 220 °C for 25–30 minutes.
9. Glaze with apricot glaze. Dust the edges with icing sugar and return to a very hot oven to glaze.

Ingredient	8–10 portions
Puff paste	200 g
Frangipane	200 g
Pears, poached or tinned (cored and cut in half lengthways)	5

Energy	Cals	Fat	Sat fat	Carb	Sugar	Protein	Fibre
1,178 kJ	282 kcal	17.8 g	5.1 g	27.2 g	17.5 g	3.8 g	0.8 g

32 Puff pastry slice (*mille-feuilles*)

1. Roll out the pastry 2 mm thick into an even-sided square.
2. Roll up carefully on a rolling pin and unroll on to a greased, dampened baking sheet.
3. Dock well.
4. Bake in a hot oven at 220 °C for 15–20 minutes; turn over after 10 minutes. Allow to cool.
5. Using a large knife, cut into three even-sized rectangles.
6. Keeping the best strip for the top, pipe the pastry cream on one strip.
7. Place the second strip on top and pipe with pastry cream.
8. Place the last strip on top, flat side up. Press gently. Brush with boiling apricot glaze to form a key.

Ingredient	10 portions
Puff pastry trimmings	600 g
Pastry cream	400 ml
Apricot glaze	
Fondant	350 g
Chocolate	100 g

Energy	Cals	Fat	Sat fat	Carb	Sugar	Protein	Fibre	Sodium
2013 kJ	479 kcal	22.0 g	8.2 g	69.0 g	49.0 g	5.8 g	1.1 g	0.4 g

Basic pastry products 14

Decorate by feather icing:
1. Warm the fondant to 37 °C (warm to the touch) and correct the consistency with sugar syrup if necessary.
2. Pour the fondant over the mille-feuilles in an even coat.
3. Immediately pipe the melted chocolate over the fondant in strips, 0.5 cm apart.
4. With the back of a small knife, wiping after each stroke, mark down the slice at 2 cm intervals.
5. Quickly turn the slice around and repeat in the same direction with strokes in between the previous ones.

6. Allow to set and trim the edges neatly.
7. Cut into even portions with a sharp, thin-bladed knife; dip into hot water and wipe clean after each cut.
8. For a traditional finish, crush the pastry trimmings and use them to coat the sides.

Variation

Whipped fresh cream may be used as an alternative to pastry cream.

The pastry cream or whipped cream may also be flavoured with an orange liqueur if desired.

Pipe cream between layers of pastry

Ice the top with fondant

Decorate with chocolate

33 Fruit slice (*bande aux fruits*)

Ingredient	8–10 portions
Puff paste	250 g
Fruit (see note)	400 g
Pastry cream	250 ml (approximately)
Apricot glaze	2 tbsp

1. Roll out the pastry 2 mm thick in a strip 12 cm wide.
2. Place on a greased, dampened baking sheet.
3. Moisten two edges with egg wash; lay two 1.5 cm-wide strips along each edge.
4. Seal firmly and mark with the back of a knife. Prick the bottom of the slice.
5. Depending on the fruit used, either put the fruit (such as apple) on the slice and cook together, or cook the slice blind and afterwards place the pastry cream and fruit (such as tinned peaches) on the pastry. Glaze and serve as for flans.

Fruit slices may be prepared from any fruit suitable for flans/tarts.

Energy	Cals	Fat	Sat fat	Carb	Sugar	Protein	Fibre	Sodium
847 kJ	202 kcal	10.3 g	3.5 g	26.0 g	14.3 g	3.2 g	1.6 g	0.2 g

Variation

Alternative methods are to use:
- short or sweet pastry for the base and puff pastry for the two side strips
- sweet pastry in a slice mould.

535

34 Cream horns

Ingredient	Makes 16
Puff paste	250 g
Egg wash	
Icing sugar, to sprinkle	
Jam	50 g
Caster sugar	50 g
Vanilla pod/vanilla extract	Seeds from 1 pod/a few drops
Cream	500 ml

Energy	Cals	Fat	Sat fat	Carb	Sugar	Protein	Fibre
735 kJ	176 kcal	14.9g	8.6g	9.8g	6.3g	1.2g	0.2g

1 Roll out the pastry to 2 mm thick, 30 cm long.
2 Cut into 1.5 cm-wide strips. Moisten on one side.
3 Wind the strips carefully round lightly greased cream horn moulds, starting at the point and carefully overlapping each round slightly.
4 Brush with egg wash on one side and place on a greased baking sheet.
5 Bake at 220 °C for about 20 minutes.
6 Sprinkle with icing sugar and return to a hot oven for a few seconds to glaze.
7 Remove carefully from the moulds and allow to cool.
8 Place a little jam in the bottom of each.
9 Add the sugar and vanilla to the cream and whip until firm peaks form.
10 Place in a piping bag with a star tube and pipe a neat rose into each horn.

Variation

These may also be partially filled with pastry cream, to which various flavourings or fruit may be added. For example:
- praline
- chocolate
- coffee
- lemon
- raspberries
- strawberries
- mango
- orange segments.

Basic pastry products 14

35 Eccles cakes

Ingredient	12 cakes
Puff paste or rough puff paste	300 g
Egg white, to brush	
Caster sugar, to coat	
Filling	
Butter	50 g
Raisins	50 g
Demerara sugar	50 g
Currants	200 g
Mixed spice (optional)	pinch

Energy	Cals	Fat	Sat fat	Carb	Sugar	Protein	Fibre	Sodium
887 kJ	212 kcal	10.7 g	4.6 g	28.0 g	21.0 g	2.3 g	1.6 g	0.2 g

1 Roll out the pastry 2 mm thick.
2 Cut into rounds 10–12 cm diameter. Damp the edges.
3 Mix together all the ingredients for the filling and place 1 tbsp of the mixture in the centre of each round.
4 Fold the edges over to the centre and completely seal in the mixture.
5 Brush the top with egg white and dip into caster sugar.
6 Place on a greased baking sheet.
7 Cut two or three incisions with a knife so as to show the filling.
8 Bake at 220 °C for 15–20 minutes.

36 Apple turnovers (*chausson aux pommes*)

Ingredient	Makes 12
Puff paste	300 g
Dry, sweetened apple purée	250 g
Egg white, to brush	
Caster sugar, to coat	

Energy	Cals	Fat	Sat fat	Carb	Sugar	Protein	Fibre	Sodium
353 kJ	84 kcal	4.4 g	2.0 g	10.4 g	4.4 g	1.5 g	0.1 g	0.0 g

1 Roll out the pastry to 2 mm thick.
2 Cut into 8 cm diameter rounds.
3 Roll out slightly oval, to 12 × 10 cm.
4 Moisten the edges and place a little apple purée in the centre of each.
5 Fold over and seal firmly.
6 Brush with egg white and dip in caster sugar.
7 Place sugar-side up on a dampened baking sheet.
8 Bake in a hot oven, 220 °C, for 15–20 minutes.

Variation

Other types of fruit may be included in the turnovers, such as apple and mango; apple and blackberry; apple and passion fruit; and apple, pear and cinnamon.

Fillings

37 Pastry cream (crème pâtissière)

Left to right: pastry cream, crème diplomate and crème chiboust

Ingredient	Makes approximately 750 ml
Milk	500 ml
Vanilla pod	1
Egg yolks	4
Caster sugar	125 g
Soft flour	75 g
Custard powder	10 g

1 Heat the milk with the cut vanilla pod and leave to infuse.
2 Beat the sugar and egg yolks together until creamy white. Add the flour and custard powder.
3 Strain the hot milk, gradually blending it into the egg mixture.
4 Strain into a clean pan and bring back to the boil, stirring constantly.
5 When the mixture has boiled and thickened, pour into a plastic bowl, sprinkle with caster sugar and cover with cling film.
6 Chill over ice and refrigerate as soon as possible. Ideally, blast chill.
7 When required, knock back on a mixing machine with a little kirsch.

Variation

The recipes below are based on the recipe for pastry cream, with additional ingredients:
- **Crème mousseline**: beat in 100 g of soft butter. The butter content is usually about 20 per cent of the volume but this can be raised to 50 per cent depending on its intended use.
- **Crème diplomate**: when the pastry cream is chilled, fold in an equal quantity of whipped double cream.
- **Crème chiboust**: when the pastry cream mixture has cooled slightly, fold in an equal quantity of Italian meringue (recipe 43).

Additional flavourings can also be added to pastry cream, crème diplomat or crème chiboust.

Professional tip

At step 4, the microwave may be used effectively. Pour the mixture into a plastic bowl and cook in the microwave for 30-second periods, stirring in between, until the mixture boils and thickens.

Basic pastry products | **14**

38 Chantilly cream

Ingredient	Makes 500 ml
Whipping cream	500 ml
Caster sugar	100 g
Vanilla essence/fresh vanilla pod	A few drops to taste/seeds from 1 vanilla pod

1. Place all ingredients in a bowl. Whisk over ice until the mixture forms soft peaks. If using a mechanical mixer, stand and watch until the mixture is ready – do not leave it unattended as the mix will over-whip quickly, curdling the cream.
2. Cover and place in the fridge immediately.

39 Buttercream

Ingredient	350 g
Icing sugar	150 g
Butter	200 g

1. Sieve the icing sugar.
2. Cream the butter and icing sugar until light and creamy.
3. Flavour and colour as required.

Variation

- Rum buttercream – add rum to flavour and blend in.
- Chocolate buttercream – add melted chocolate, sweetened or unsweetened according to taste.

40 Boiled buttercream

Ingredient	750 ml
Eggs	2
Icing sugar	50 g
Granulated sugar or cube sugar	300 g
Water	100 g
Glucose	50 g
Unsalted butter	400 g

1. Beat the eggs and icing sugar until at ribbon stage (sponge).
2. Boil the granulated or cube sugar with water and glucose to 118 °C.
3. Gradually add the sugar at 118 °C to the eggs and icing sugar at ribbon stage, whisk continuously and allow to cool to 26 °C.
4. Gradually add the unsalted butter while continuing to whisk until a smooth cream is obtained.

Variation

Buttercream may be flavoured with numerous flavours and combinations of flavours, for example:
- chocolate and rum
- whisky and orange
- strawberry and vanilla
- lemon and lime
- apricot and passion fruit
- brandy and praline
- coffee and hazelnut.

1 Whisk the eggs.
2 Add the boiling sugar and water. 
3 Add the butter.

Basic pastry products 14

41 Frangipane (almond cream)

Ingredient	8 portions
Butter	100 g
Caster sugar	100 g
Eggs	2
Ground almonds	100 g
Flour	10 g

Energy	Cals	Fat	Sat fat	Carb	Sugar	Protein	Fibre	Sodium
997 kJ	240 kcal	18.5g	7.4g	15.0g	13.7g	4.4g	1.7g	0.2g

1 Cream the butter and sugar until aerated.
2 Gradually beat in the eggs.
3 Mix in the almonds and flour (mix lightly).
4 Use as required.

Variation

Try adding lemon zest or vanilla seeds to the recipe.

Cut the butter into small pieces and add to the sugar

Cream the butter and sugar together

Beat in the eggs before adding to the flour

541

42 Ganache

Ingredient	Makes 750 g to 1 kg
Version 1 (for decoration)	
Double cream	300 ml
Couverture, cut into small pieces	350 g
Unsalted butter	85 g
Spirit or liqueur	20 ml
Version 2 (for a filling)	
Double cream	300 ml
Vanilla pod	½
Couverture, cut into small pieces	600 g
Unsalted butter	120 g

1. Boil the cream (and the vanilla for Version 2) in a heavy saucepan.
2. Pour the cream over the couverture. Whisk with a fine whisk until the chocolate has melted.
3. Whisk in the butter (and the liqueur for Version 1).
4. Stir over ice until the mixture has the required consistency.

The two versions have different textures. Version 1 is ideal for truffles; version 2 for tortes or fillings.

Basic pastry products 14

43 Italian meringue

Ingredient	Makes 250 g	Makes 625 g
Granulated or cube sugar	200 g	500 g
Water	60 ml	140 g
Cream of tartar	Pinch	Large pinch
Egg whites	4	10

1 Boil the sugar, water and cream of tartar to hard-ball stage of 121 °C. (To ensure the sugar is not heated beyond this point, it is advisable to remove from the heat at 115 °C as the sugar will continue to rise in temperature, and this will provide a little time to ensure the egg whites are whipped to the correct point.)
2 While the sugar is cooking, beat the egg whites to full peak and, while stiff, beating slowly, pour on the boiling sugar.
3 Use as required.

Boil the sugar

Combine with the beaten egg whites

The mixture will stand up in stiff peaks when it is ready

543

44 Swiss meringue

Ingredient	10 portions	15 portions
Egg whites, pasteurised	190 ml	300 ml
Caster sugar	230 ml	340 ml

Energy	Cals	Fat	Sat fat	Carb	Sugar	Protein	Fibre	Sodium
426 kJ	100 kcal	0.0g	0.0g	24.0g	24.0g	2.1g	0.0g	0.0g

1 Whisk the pasteurised egg whites and sugar over a bain-marie of simmering water until a light and aerated meringue is achieved.

45 Apple purée

Ingredient	400g	1kg
Cooking apples	400g	1kg
Butter or margarine	10g	25g
Sugar	50g	125g

1 Peel, core and slice the apples.
2 Place the butter or margarine in a thick-bottomed pan; heat until melted.
3 Add the apples and sugar, cover with a lid and cook gently until soft.
4 Drain off any excess liquid and pass through a sieve or liquidise.

Basic pastry products 14

46 Stock syrup

Ingredient	750 ml	1.5 litres
Water	500 ml	1.25 litres
Granulated sugar	250 g	625 g
Glucose	50 g	125 g

1 Boil the water, sugar and glucose together.
2 Strain and cool.

Professional tip
The glucose helps to prevent crystallising.

545

15 Cakes, sponges, biscuits and scones

Recipes included in this chapter

No.	Recipe	Page
	Cakes and sponges	
1	Victoria sandwich	553
2	Genoise sponge	554
3	Fresh cream and strawberry gâteau	555
4	Coffee gâteau	556
5	Chocolate genoise sponge	557
6	Chocolate gâteau	557
7	Roulade sponge	558
8	Swiss roll	559
9	Cup cakes	559
10	Scones	560
11	Rock cakes	561
12	Madeleines	561
13	Rich fruit cake	562
14	Lemon drizzle cake	563
	Décor	
15	Apricot glaze	564
16	Water icing (glacé icing)	564
17	Royal icing	565
18	Marzipan	565
19	Praline	566
	Biscuits	
20	Sponge fingers (*biscuits à la cuillère*)	566
21	Tuiles	567
22	Cats' tongues (*langues de chat*)	568
23	Cigarette paste cornets	569
24	Brandy snaps	570
25	Piped biscuits (*sablés à la poche*)	571
26	Shortbread biscuits	572

The base ingredients for making cakes, biscuits and scones are principally the same as those discussed in Chapter 14: flour, fat, sugar, raising agents, eggs and cream. However, there is an endless list of possibilities in terms of additional ingredients that could form part of the finished product, from chocolate, fondants, fruits and fruit products, through to nuts and pralines.

Cakes

Preparation methods for cakes

There are three basic methods of making cake mixtures, also known as cake batters. The working temperature of cake batter should ideally be around 21 °C.

Sugar batter method

For the sugar batter method, the fat (cake margarine, butter or shortening) is blended in a machine with caster sugar. This is the basic or principal stage; the other ingredients are usually then added in the order shown in the chart.

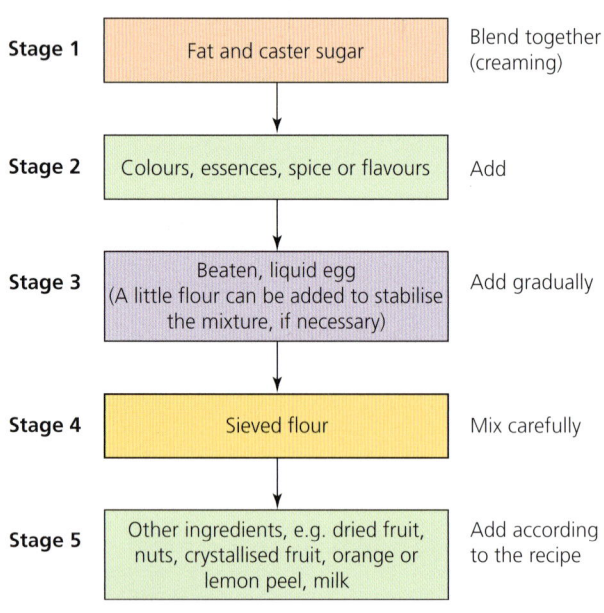

Stage	Ingredient	Action
Stage 1	Fat and caster sugar	Blend together (creaming)
Stage 2	Colours, essences, spice or flavours	Add
Stage 3	Beaten, liquid egg (A little flour can be added to stabilise the mixture, if necessary)	Add gradually
Stage 4	Sieved flour	Mix carefully
Stage 5	Other ingredients, e.g. dried fruit, nuts, crystallised fruit, orange or lemon peel, milk	Add according to the recipe

▲ The sugar batter method

Flour batter method

For the flour batter method, the eggs and sugar are whisked to a half sponge; this is the basic or principal stage, which aims to foam the two ingredients together until half the maximum volume is achieved. Other ingredients are then added as shown in the chart.

A humectant, something which helps the product to stay moist, may also be added (for example, glycerine); if so, this is added at stage 2.

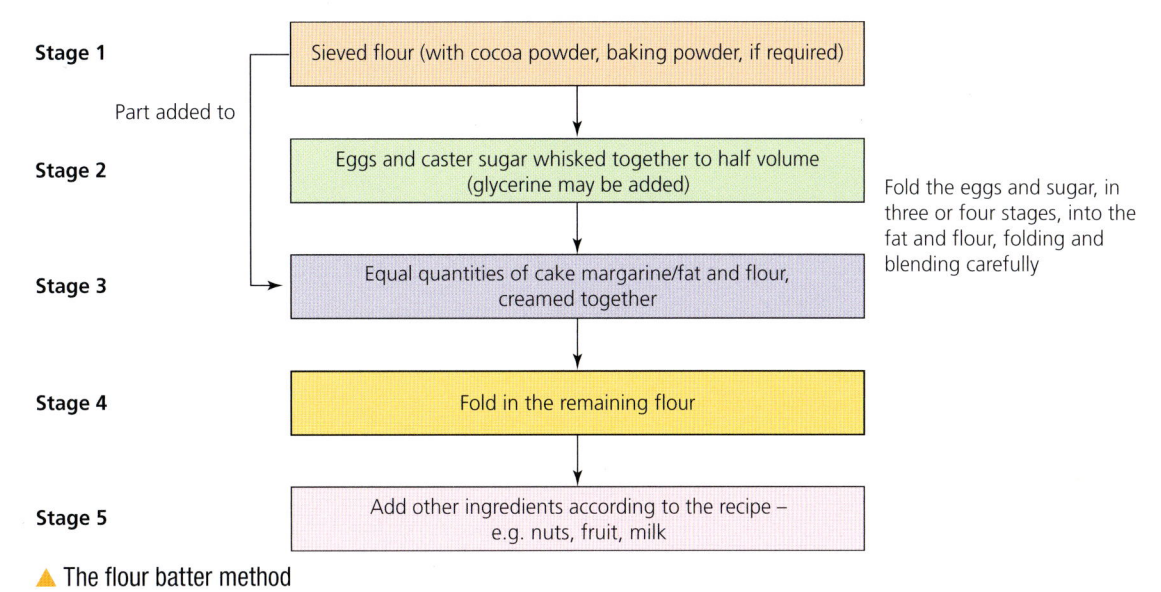

Stage 1: Sieved flour (with cocoa powder, baking powder, if required)

Part added to

Stage 2: Eggs and caster sugar whisked together to half volume (glycerine may be added)

Fold the eggs and sugar, in three or four stages, into the fat and flour, folding and blending carefully

Stage 3: Equal quantities of cake margarine/fat and flour, creamed together

Stage 4: Fold in the remaining flour

Stage 5: Add other ingredients according to the recipe – e.g. nuts, fruit, milk

▲ The flour batter method

Blending method

The blending method is used for high-ratio cake mixtures. It uses high-ratio flour, specially produced so that it will absorb more liquid. It also uses a high-ratio fat, made from oil to which a quantity of emulsifying agent has been added, enabling the fat to take up a greater quantity of liquid.

High-ratio cakes contain more liquid and sugar, resulting in a fine, stable crumb, extended shelf life, good eating and excellent freezing qualities. The principal or basic stage is the mixing of the fat and flour to a crumbling texture. It is essential that each stage of the batter is blended into the next to produce a smooth batter, free from lumps. When using mixing machines, it is important to remember to:

- blend initially on a slow speed
- beat on a medium speed, using a paddle attachment.

When blending, always clear the mix from the bottom of the bowl to ensure that any first- or second-stage batter does not remain in the bowl.

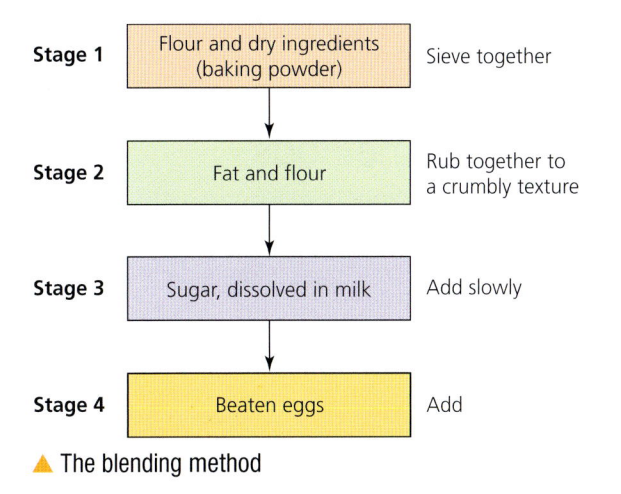

Baking powder in cakes

Baking powder may be made from one part sodium bicarbonate to two parts cream of tartar. In commercial baking the powdered cream of tartar may be replaced by another acid product, such as acidulated calcium phosphate.

When used under the right conditions, with the addition of liquid and heat, it produces carbon dioxide gas. As the acid has a delayed action, only a small amount of gas is given off when the liquid is added, and the majority is released when the mixture is heated. Therefore, when cakes are mixed they do not lose the property of the baking powder if they are not cooked right away.

Stage 1: Flour and dry ingredients (baking powder) — Sieve together

Stage 2: Fat and flour — Rub together to a crumbly texture

Stage 3: Sugar, dissolved in milk — Add slowly

Stage 4: Beaten eggs — Add

▲ The blending method

Possible reasons for faults in cakes

If your cake has an uneven texture, this may be because:
- the fat was insufficiently rubbed in
- there was too little liquid
- there was too much liquid.

If your cake has a close texture, this may be because:
- there was too much fat
- your hands were too hot when rubbing in
- the fat to flour ratio was incorrect.

If your cake is dry, this may be because:
- there was too little liquid
- the oven was too hot.

If your cake has a bad shape, this may be because:
- there was too much liquid
- the oven was too cool
- there was too much baking powder.

If the fruit in the cake has sunk, this may be because:
- the fruit was wet
- there was too much liquid
- the oven was too cool.

If the cake has cracked, this may be because:
- there was too little liquid
- there was too much baking powder.

Batters and whisked sponges

Batters and sponges allow the production of a large assortment of desserts and cakes. Basically, they are a mix of eggs, sugar, flour and the air incorporated when these are beaten. Certain other raw materials can be combined – for example, almonds, hazelnuts, walnuts, chocolate, butter, fruit, ginger, anise, coffee and vanilla.

Sponge mixtures are produced from a foam of eggs and sugar. The eggs may be whole or separated. Examples of sponge products include gâteaux, sponge fingers and sponge cakes.

The egg white traps the air bubbles. When eggs and sugar are whisked together, they thicken until a maximum volume is reached; then flour is carefully folded in by a method known as cutting in. This is the most difficult operation, as the flour must not be allowed to sink to the bottom of the bowl, otherwise it becomes lumpy and difficult to clear. However, the mixture must not be stirred too much as this will disturb the aeration and cause the air to escape, resulting in a much heavier sponge. If butter, margarine or oil is added, it is important that this is added at about 36 °C, otherwise overheating will cause the fat or oil to act on the flour and create lumps, which are difficult – often impossible – to get rid of.

Stabilisers are often added to sponges to prevent them from collapsing. The most common are ethyl methyl cellulose and glycerol monostearate; these are added to the eggs and sugar at the beginning of the mixing.

Making sponge cakes

- You should never add flour or ground dry ingredients to a batter until the end because they impede the air absorption in the first beating stage.
- When making sponge cakes, always sift the dry ingredients (flour, cocoa powder, ground nuts, and so on) to avoid clumping.
- Mix the flour in as quickly and delicately as possible – rough addition of dry ingredients acts like a weight on the primary batter and can remove part of the air already absorbed.
- Flours used in sponge cakes are low in gluten content. In certain sponge cakes a proportion of the flour can be left out and substituted with cornstarch. This yields a softer and more aerated batter.
- The eggs used in sponge cake batters should be fresh and at room temperature so that they take in air faster.
- Adding separately beaten egg whites produces a lighter, fluffier sponge cake.
- Once sponge cake batters are beaten and poured into moulds or baking trays, they should be baked as soon as possible. Delays will cause the batter to lose volume.

Preparation methods

There are several methods of making sponge cake:
- **Foaming method** – whisking eggs and sugar together to the ribbon stage; folding in/cutting flour.
- **Melting method** – as with foaming, but adding melted butter, margarine or oil to the mixture at the final stage. The fat content enriches the sponge, improves the flavour, texture and crumb structure, and will extend shelf life.

Cakes, sponges, biscuits and scones

- **Boiling method** – sponges made by this method have a stable crumb texture that is easier to handle and crumbles less when cut than the standard basic sponge containing fat (known as Genoise sponge). This method will produce a sponge that is suitable for dipping in fondant. The stages are shown in the chart.
- **Blending method** – this is used for high-ratio sponges, which follow the same principles as high-ratio cakes. As with cakes, high-ratio goods produce a fine, stable crumb, an even texture, excellent shelf life and good freezing qualities.
- **Creaming method** – this is the traditional method and is still used today for Victoria sandwich and light fruitcakes. The fat and sugar are creamed together, then beaten egg is added and, finally, the sieved flour is added with other dry ingredients as desired.
- **Separate yolk and white method** – this method is used for sponge fingers (recipe 20).

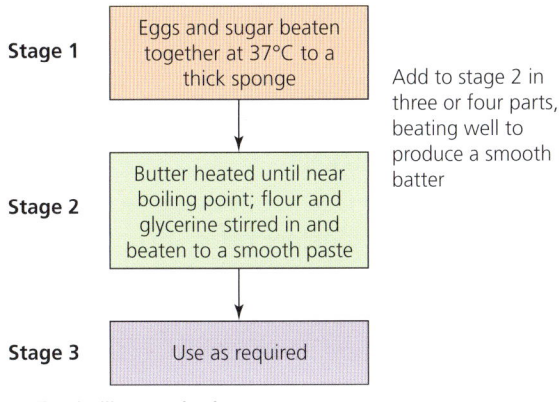

Stage 1: Eggs and sugar beaten together at 37°C to a thick sponge

Stage 2: Butter heated until near boiling point; flour and glycerine stirred in and beaten to a smooth paste

Add to stage 2 in three or four parts, beating well to produce a smooth batter

Stage 3: Use as required

▲ The boiling method

Possible reasons for faults in sponges

If your sponge has a close texture, this may be because:
- it was not beaten enough
- there was too much flour
- the oven was too cool or too hot.

If your sponge has a 'holey' texture, this may be because:
- the flour was insufficiently folded in
- the tin was unevenly filled.

If the sponge has a cracked crust, this may be because the oven was too hot.

If the sponge is sunken, this may be because:
- the oven was too hot
- the tin was removed during cooking.

White spots on the surface may indicate that it was not beaten enough.

Possible reasons for faults in Genoise sponges

If the sponge has a close texture, this may be because:
- the eggs and sugar were overheated
- the eggs and sugar were under-beaten
- there was too much flour
- the flour was insufficiently folded in
- the oven was too hot.

If the sponge is sunken, this may be because:
- there was too much sugar
- the oven was too hot
- the tin was removed during cooking.

If the sponge is heavy, this may be because:
- the butter was too hot
- the butter was insufficiently mixed in
- the flour was over-mixed.

The introduction of steam or moisture

Some cakes require an injection of steam, otherwise they become too dry while baking due to the dry atmosphere in the oven. Combination ovens are ideally suited for this purpose. The steam delays the formation of the crust until the cake batter has become fully aerated and the proteins have set. Alternatively, add a tray of water to the oven while baking. If the oven is too hot, the cake crust will form early and the cake batter will rise into a peak.

Points to remember when baking cakes and sponges

- Check all ingredients carefully.
- Make sure scales are accurate; weigh all ingredients carefully.
- Check ovens are at the right temperature and that the shelves are in the correct position.
- Check that all work surfaces and equipment are clean.
- Check that all other equipment required, such as cooling wires, is within easy reach.
- Always sieve flour to remove lumps and any foreign material.
- Make sure that eggs and fats are at room temperature.

549

- Check dried fruits carefully; wash, drain and dry if necessary.
- Always follow the recipe carefully.
- Always scrape down the sides of the mixing bowl when creaming mixtures.
- Always seek help if you are unsure.
- Try to fill the oven space when baking by planning production carefully; this saves time, labour and money.
- Never guess quantities. Time and temperature are important factors; they too should not be guessed.
- The shape and size of goods will determine the baking time and temperature: the wider and deeper the cake, the longer and more slowly it will need to bake.
- Where cake recipes contain a high proportion of sugar, this will caramelise the surface quickly before the centre is cooked. Therefore cover the cake with sheets of silicone or dampened greaseproof paper and continue to bake.
- When cake tops are sprinkled with almonds or sugar, the baking temperature needs to be lowered slightly to prevent over-colouring of the cake crust.
- When glycerine, glucose and inverted sugar, honey or treacle is added to cake mixtures, the oven temperature should be lowered as these caramelise at a lower temperature than sugar.
- Always work in a clean and hygienic way; remember the hygiene and safety rules, in particular the Food Safety and Hygiene Regulations 2013.
- All cakes and sponges benefit from being allowed to cool in their tins as this makes handling easier. If sponges need to be cooled quickly, place a wire rack over the top of the tin and invert, then remove the lining paper and cool on a wire rack.

Biscuits

Preparation methods

Biscuits and cookies may be produced by the following methods:

Rubbing in

Rubbing in is probably the best-known method and is used to produce some of the most famous types of biscuits, such as shortbread. The method is exactly the same as that for producing short pastry.

- Rub the fat into the flour by hand or by machine. Dissolve the liquid and the sugar and mix into the flour to produce a smooth biscuit paste.
- Do not overwork the paste when mixing to combine. The consequence of overworking the paste at this stage is that the gluten in the flour will strengthen and result in the tightening of the paste. If this happens the paste will become very difficult to roll and is likely to shrink during the baking process.

Foaming

This is where a foam is produced from egg whites, egg yolks or both. Sponge fingers are an example of a two-foam mixture. Meringue is an example of a single-foam mixture using egg whites. Great care must be taken not to over-mix the product.

Sugar batter method

Fat and sugar are mixed together to produce a light, aerated cream. Beaten egg is added gradually. The dry ingredients are then carefully folded in. Cats' tongues and sablé biscuits are made in this way.

Flour batter method

Half the sieved flour is creamed with the fat. The eggs and sugar are beaten together before they are added to the fat and flour mixture. Finally, the remainder of the flour is folded in, together with any other dry ingredients. Some types of cookies are made using this method.

Blending method

This method requires the blending of all the ingredients together to produce a smooth paste. It is used to make almond biscuits using a basic commercial mixture.

Convenience cake, biscuit and sponge mixes

There is now a vast range of prepared mixes and frozen goods available on the market. Premixes enable the caterer to calculate costs more effectively, reduce labour costs (with less demand for highly skilled labour) and limit the range of stock items that need to be held.

Every year, more and more convenience products are introduced on to the market by food manufacturers. The caterer should be encouraged to investigate these products and to experiment in order to assess their quality.

Decorating and finishing for presentation

Fillings

Cakes, sponges and biscuits may be filled or sandwiched together with a variety of different types of filling. Some examples are presented below.
- Creams – buttercream (plain, flavoured and/or coloured), pastry cream (flavoured and/or coloured), whipped cream, clotted cream.
- Fruit – fresh fruit purée, jams, fruit mousses, preserves, fruit gels.
- Pastes and spreads – chocolate, praline, nut, curds.

Spreading and coating

The top and sides of smaller cakes and gâteaux are commonly covered with any of the following:
- fresh whipped cream
- fondant
- chocolate
- royal icing
- buttercream
- water icing
- meringue (French, Italian or Swiss)
- commercially manufactured preparations.

Piping

Piping is a skill that takes practice and there are many different types (plain or fluted) and sizes of piping tube available, producing a variety of presentations. The following may be used:
- royal icing
- meringue
- chocolate
- boiled sugar
- fondant
- fresh cream.

Dusting, dredging and sprinkling

These techniques are used to give products a final design or glaze during cooking, using sugar. Light dusting is usually performed with icing sugar or neige décor, an icing sugar product resistant to humidity but used in the same way, using a very fine sieve.
- **Dusting**: a light dusting, giving an even finish.
- **Dredging**: heavier dusting with sugar.
- **Sprinkling**: a very light sprinkle of sugar.

Caster or granulated white sugar, Demerara, Barbados or dark brown sugar can also be used, particularly if the product is returned to the oven for glazing, glazed under a salamander or glazed using a blow torch.

Other decorative media

Remember that decorating is an art form and there is a range of equipment and materials available to assist you in this work. Some examples of decorative media are as follows:
- Glacé and crystallised fruits – cherries, lemons, oranges, pineapple, figs.
- Crystallised flowers – rose petals, violets, mimosa, lilac.
- Crystallised stems such as angelica.
- Nuts – almonds (nibbed, flaked), coconut (fresh slices, desiccated), hazelnuts, brazil nuts, pistachio.
- Chocolate – rolls, vermicelli, flakes, piping chocolate, chips.

Piped biscuit pastes

Piped biscuits can be used for decoration. For example:
- cats' tongues (recipe 22)
- piped biscuits (recipe 25).

Storing cakes, sponges, biscuits and scones

Cakes, sponges, biscuits and scones are best eaten as fresh as possible to enjoy them at their prime. However, if storage is required, care must be taken to ensure that the commodities making up the product are taken into consideration. For example, a product containing a high-risk or fragile ingredient such as fresh cream must be kept chilled or frozen to prevent spoilage.

Other products, such as biscuits, will lose their short, crisp properties if not stored appropriately. Moisture in the atmosphere will become absorbed by such products and this will start to break down the structure of the biscuit.

Sponges, particularly low-fat or fatless sponges, will tend to dry out very quickly if they are left out in open air. Once a sponge is cut, the exposed sponge is extremely prone to drying, which is one reason why sponge products are often soaked with a flavoured syrup to prevent drying as well as adding flavour.

Steps to take when storing cakes, sponges, biscuits and scones to extend their shelf life are as follows:

- Store dry products such as biscuits and scones for short-term consumption in clean, air-tight plastic containers. Store the containers in a cool, dry, well-ventilated area that has been designated for such products.
- Store products such as fresh fruit and/or cream cakes or sponges for short-term consumption in refrigerators, ensuring that they are covered with cling film or stored in air-tight containers. This will help to prevent the products from drying during storage. It is important to note that sugars dissolve over time when stored and this can lead to sogginess in products and weeping of fruits.
- Cakes, sponges, biscuits and scones can be frozen very effectively. It is important that the product is cool before freezing. The product should be sealed to prevent contact with air, removing as much air as possible in the packaging itself. The product should then be labelled, dated and frozen, ensuring that stock is easily identifiable and stock rotation procedures are followed. A blast-freezer can be used to freeze rapidly before placing into a holding freezer. This can help to retain many of the quality points of such products, for example, moisture retention.

Test yourself

1. How much flour is required to produce a four-egg Genoise sponge?
2. Describe what is meant by the 'creaming' method.
3. Describe the production of sponge fingers (*biscuit à la cuillère*).
4. What is the ratio of fat to flour for shortbread biscuits?
5. Describe tuile biscuits and what they are used for.
6. Describe the preparation and baking of:
    a madeleines
    b *sablés à la poche* (piped biscuits).
7. List the ingredients and method for a traditional Victoria sandwich.
8. Give three possible reasons why a sponge might have a tight, close texture.
9. List the two components, and their ratios, that make up baking powder.
10. What is the benefit of the presence of steam when baking cakes and sponges?

Cakes and sponges

1 Victoria sandwich

Ingredient	2 × 18 cm cakes
Butter	250 g
Caster sugar	250 g
Soft flour	250 g
Baking powder	10 g
Eggs	5
Vanilla extract	½ tsp
Jam to fill	

Energy	Cals	Fat	Sat fat	Carb	Sugar	Protein	Fibre
6,866 kJ	1,635 kcal	94.3 g	39.3 g	184.7 g	106.6 g	23.3 g	3.6 g

Using hard margarine in place of butter.

This is a classic afternoon tea cake named after Queen Victoria. Although traditionally made in two halves, a slimmer version can be made by using a single sponge and splitting it.

1. Cream the butter and sugar until soft and light.
2. Sieve the flour and baking powder twice.
3. Mix together the eggs and vanilla extract.
4. Beat the eggs gradually into the butter and sugar mixture.
5. Fold in the flour.
6. Deposit into buttered and floured cake tins and level.
7. Bake at 180 °C for approximately 15–20 minutes.
8. Turn out on to a wire rack to cool.
9. Spread the bottom half with softened jam.
10. Place on the top sponge and dust with icing sugar.

1 Beat the sugar and butter together.

2 Place the mixture into buttered cake tins.

3 Flatten the top before baking.

Variation

In addition to jam, the sponge can be filled with either butter icing or Chantilly cream.

The official Women's Institute version specifies the cake is filled with jam only and dusted with caster not icing sugar.

2 Genoise sponge

Ingredient	Single sponge	Double sponge
Eggs	4	10
Caster sugar	100 g	250 g
Flour (soft)	100 g	250 g
Butter, margarine or oil	50 g	125 g

Energy	Cals	Fat	Sat fat	Carb	Sugar	Protein	Fibre
5,978 kJ	1,423 kcal	65.8 g	25.6 g	182.8 g	106.6 g	36.5 g	3.6 g

Using hard margarine (4 portions).

1. Whisk the eggs and sugar with a balloon whisk in a bowl over a pan of hot water.
2. Continue until the mixture is light and creamy and has doubled in bulk.
3. Remove from the heat and whisk until cold and thick (ribbon stage). Fold in the flour very gently.
4. Take a small amount of the mixture and combine it with the melted butter. Then return this to the rest of the mixture and fold through.
5. Place in a greased, floured genoise mould.
6. Bake in a moderately hot oven, at 200–220 °C, for about 30 minutes.

1 Ingredients for Genoise sponge and boiling water ready for use.

2 Add the sugar to the eggs.

3 Whisk them together over boiling water.

4 Carry on whisking as the mixture warms up.

5 When the mixture is ready, it will form ribbons and you can draw a figure eight with it.

6 Fold in the flour.

7 Add part of the flour mixture to the butter.

8 Place the mixture into greased cake tins.

9 After baking, turn the sponges out to cool on a rack.

3 Fresh cream and strawberry gâteau

Ingredient	8 portions
Genoise sponge made with vanilla	1
Stock syrup (see page 563)	100 ml
Raspberry jam	50 ml
Whipping or double cream	500 ml
Icing sugar	75 g
Strawberries, sliced	1 punnet

Energy	Cals	Fat	Sat fat	Carb	Sugar	Protein	Fibre
1,975 kJ	473 kcal	28.4 g	11.1 g	53.0 g	39.7 g	4.5 g	0.9 g

Based on 60 g of sponge per portion.

1. Carefully slice the sponge cake into three equal discs. Brush each with syrup.
2. Slowly whip the cream with the icing sugar to achieve the correct consistency.
3. Place the first piece of sponge on a cake board. Soak with syrup. Spread with a layer of jam, then a layer of cream. Scatter sliced strawberries on top.
4. Place the next piece of sponge on top. Repeat the layers of syrup, cream and strawberries. Top with additional cream.
5. Place the final piece of sponge on top.
6. Coat the top and sides with cream. Chill.
7. Comb scrape the sides of the gâteau. Pipe 12 rosettes on top. Decorate with strawberries and rounds of white chocolate.

4 Coffee gâteau

Ingredient	1 × 16 cm gâteau
Plain genoise sponge (recipe 2)	1 × 16 cm
Stock syrup flavoured with rum	50 ml
Coffee buttercream	750 g
Coffee marzipan	100 g
Fondant	500 g
Crystallised violets	
Chocolate squares	

Energy	Cals	Fat	Sat fat	Carb	Sugar	Protein	Fibre	Sodium
7881 kJ	1873 kcal	75.5g	41.3g	303.0g	282.0g	12.3g	1.8g	0.6g

For ¼ of the sponge.

1. Carefully split the sponge into three and line up the three pieces.
2. Place the sponge base on a cake card and moisten with rum syrup.
3. Pipe on an even layer of buttercream, no thicker than that of the sponge.
4. Place on the next layer of sponge, moisten with the syrup and repeat to give three layers of sponge and two of buttercream. Moisten the top with syrup.
5. Put in the fridge for 1–2 hours to firm up.
6. Work some coffee essence into the marzipan, roll out to 2 mm thick and lay over the gâteau, working the sides to prevent any creases.
7. Warm the fondant to blood heat, flavour with coffee essence and adjust the consistency with syrup.
8. Place the gâteau on a wire rack with a tray underneath to catch the fondant.
9. Starting in the centre and moving outwards, pour over the fondant to completely cover. Draw a palette knife across the top to remove the excess.
10. Add some melted chocolate to some of the fondant, adjust the consistency and squeeze through muslin. Decorate the gâteau by piping on a fine line design.
11. Finish the sides with squares of chocolate and the top with crystallised violets.

Professional tip

Mark the sponge by cutting a 'v' on the side before splitting horizontally; when reassembling, line up the marks so it goes back together exactly as it came apart.

Turn the sponge upside down before splitting so the base becomes the top; this is the flattest surface and will give the best finish.

It is best practice to use a genoise that was made the day before – fresh sponges do not cut well and are susceptible to falling apart.

Fondant should never be heated above 30 °C, as the shine will be lost.

Note

A good-quality coffee gâteau should have a moist sponge and a good balance between sponge and filling (as a guide, the thickness of the sponge and the depth of the buttercream should be equal). The coffee flavour should not be in question, and the decoration should reflect and complement the coffee theme. (It is sometimes easy to get carried away, so it is good to remember when decorating, 'less is definitely more'.)

Variation

Instead of enrobing with fondant, the top and sides can be covered with buttercream, the sides can be either comb-scraped or masked with toasted nibbed/flaked almonds or grated chocolate. The top can be piped with buttercream and/or decorated with coffee marzipan cut-out shapes.

To add another texture, place a disc of meringue or dacquoise on the bottom layer. Dacquoise is an Italian meringue with the addition of toasted ground hazelnuts, spread or piped on to a silicone mat and baked at 180 °C for 15–20 minutes. Cut out the desired shape half way through cooking.

Cakes, sponges, biscuits and scones

5 Chocolate genoise sponge

Ingredient	2 × 16 cm sponges
Eggs	8
Caster sugar	225 g
Flour	175 g
Cocoa powder	50 g
Butter, melted	65 g

Energy	Cals	Fat	Sat fat	Carb	Sugar	Protein	Fibre	Sodium
1428 kJ	340 kcal	13.9g	6.6g	47.0g	30.0g	9.5g	1.6g	0.2g

For ¼ of a sponge.

1. Whisk the eggs and sugar together to form a sabayon.
2. Slowly fold in the flour and cocoa powder.
3. Take a small amount of the mixture and combine it with the melted butter. Then return this to the rest of the mixture and fold through.
4. Place in a lined mould and bake at 180 °C for 15–20 minutes.

Make sure you have prepared all the equipment before you start.

Variation

For a lighter sponge, use 100 g of soft flour and 75 g of cornflour.

6 Chocolate gâteau

Ingredient	Single gâteau	Double gâteau
Chocolate genoise sponge (recipe 5)		
Eggs	4	10
Chocolate pieces	50 g	125 g
Stock syrup (see page 563), as required		
Chocolate glaze		
Buttercream		
Unsalted butter	200 g	500 g
Icing sugar	150 g	375 g
Block chocolate (melted in a basin in a bain-marie)	50 g	125 g

Energy	Cals	Fat	Sat fat	Carb	Sugar	Protein	Fibre
20,113 kJ	4,789 kcal	260.9g	148.7g	606.0g	533.2g	41.6g	4.8g

Using hard margarine and butter (4 portions).

1. Cut the genoise into three slices crosswise.
2. Prepare the buttercream and mix in the melted chocolate.
3. Lightly moisten each slice of genoise with stock syrup, which may be flavoured with kirsch, rum, etc.
4. Lightly spread each slice of genoise with buttercream and sandwich together.
5. Lightly coat the top and sides with chocolate glaze, then decorate with chocolate pieces.

7 Roulade sponge

You should be able to bend a roulade sponge

Ingredient	2 sheets	4 sheets
Eggs	8	16
Egg yolk	2	4
Caster sugar	260 g	520 g
Soft flour	170 g	340 g

1. Make sure the mixing bowl is clean, dry and free from grease.
2. Line the baking sheets with silicone paper cut to fit.
3. Set the oven at 230 °C.
4. Place the eggs and sugar in a mixing bowl, and stir over hot water until warm.
5. Whisk to the 'ribbon' stage and sieve the flour on to greaseproof paper.
6. Carefully fold in the flour.
7. Divide equally between the baking sheets and spread evenly with a drop blade palette knife. Place immediately in the oven for between 5 and 7 minutes.
8. As soon as the sponge is cooked, turn it out on to sugared paper, place a damp, clean cloth over it and lay the hot baking sheet back on top, then leave to cool. (This will help keep the sponge moist and flexible as it cools.)

Professional tip
Each sheet should be left on the paper on which it is cooked, individually wrapped, labelled, kept flat and stored in the freezer to stop it from drying out and losing flexibility.

Faults

There are two reasons why a roulade sponge might become hard and crisp, instead of being pliable:
- baked at too low a temperature for too long
- mixture spread too thin.

Variation
A chocolate version can be made by substituting 30–40 per cent of the flour for cocoa powder. For a coffee sponge, add coffee extract to the eggs after whisking.

A roulade sponge may also be made using a 'split-egg' method, separating the eggs.

8 Swiss roll

Ingredient	4 portions	10 portions
Eggs	4	10
Caster sugar	100 g	250 g
Self-raising flour	100 g	250 g
Jam, as required		

Energy	Cals	Fat	Sat fat	Carb	Sugar	Protein	Fibre
4,445 kJ	1,058 kcal	25.3 g	8.0 g	182.7 g	106.5 g	36.5 g	3.6 g

1. Whisk the eggs and sugar with a balloon whisk in a bowl over a pan of hot water.
2. Continue until the mixture is light, creamy and double in bulk.
3. Remove from the heat and whisk until cold and thick (ribbon stage).
4. Fold in the flour very gently.
5. Grease a Swiss roll tin and line with greased greaseproof or silicone paper.
6. Pour in the mixture and bake at 220 °C for about 6 minutes.
7. Turn out on to a sheet of paper sprinkled with additional caster sugar.
8. Remove the paper from the Swiss roll, spread with warm jam.
9. Immediately roll up as tight as possible and leave to cool completely.

9 Cup cakes

Ingredient	20 portions
Flour (soft) or self-raising	200 g
Baking powder (if using plain flour)	1 level tsp
Salt (optional)	pinch
Margarine or butter	125 g
Caster sugar	125 g
Eggs	2–3

Energy	Cals	Fat	Sat fat	Carb	Sugar	Protein	Fibre
947 kJ	225 kcal	11.6 g	4.8 g	28.8 g	13.4 g	3.3 g	0.7 g

Using hard margarine.

Method 1: rubbing in

1. Sieve the flour, baking powder and salt (if using).
2. Rub in the butter or margarine to achieve a sandy texture. Add the sugar.
3. Gradually add the well-beaten eggs and mix as lightly as possible until combined.

Method 2: creaming

1. Cream the margarine and sugar in a bowl until soft and fluffy.
2. Slowly add the well-beaten eggs, mixing continuously and beating really well between each addition.
3. Lightly mix in the sieved flour, baking powder and salt (if using).

Practical Cookery 14th edition

In both cases the consistency should be a light dropping one and, if necessary, it may be adjusted with the addition of a few drops of milk.

> **Variation**
>
> **Cherry cakes**: add 50g glacé cherries cut in quarters and 3–4 drops vanilla essence to the basic mixture (method 2) and divide into 8–12 lightly greased cake tins or paper cases. Bake in a hot oven at 220°C for 15–20 minutes.
>
> **Coconut cakes**: in place of 50g flour, use 50g desiccated coconut and 3–4 drops vanilla essence to the basic mixture (method 2) and cook as for cherry cakes.
>
> **Raspberry buns**: divide basic mixture (method 1) into 8 pieces. Roll into balls, flatten slightly, dip tops into milk then caster sugar. Place on a greased baking sheet, make a hole in the centre of each and add a little raspberry jam. Bake in a hot oven at 200°C for 15–20 minutes.
>
> **Queen cakes**: to the basic mixture (method 2) add 100g washed and dried mixed fruit and cook as for cherry cakes.

10 Scones

Ingredient	16 scones
Plain flour	450g
Baking powder	25g
Salt	pinch
Butter	225g
Caster sugar	170g
Sour cream	300ml

Energy	Cals	Fat	Sat fat	Carb	Sugar	Protein	Fibre	Sodium
1196 kJ	291 kcal	16.6g	10.2g	34.0g	12.3g	3.2g	1.1g	0.4g

Per scone.

1. Sieve the flour, baking powder and salt.
2. Cut the butter into small pieces and rub into the flour to achieve a sandy texture.
3. Dissolve the sugar in the cream.
4. Add the liquid to the dry ingredients and cut in with a plastic scraper, mix lightly and do not overwork. Wrap in cling film and chill for 1 hour.
5. Set the oven at 180°C and line a baking sheet with silicone paper.
6. Roll out 2cm thick on a floured surface, cut out with a plain or fluted cutter.
7. Brush with milk or egg wash and bake at 180°C for approximately 15–20 minutes.
8. After 15 minutes, pull one apart to test if they are cooked.
9. Allow to cool and dust with icing sugar before serving.

Scones are traditionally served at afternoon tea with jam and butter or clotted cream, and are best served on the day they are made.

> **Variation**
>
> **Fruit scones**: add 50g sultanas to the basic mix, or try adding dried cranberries or apricots as alternatives.

> **Professional tip**
>
> After cutting out the scones, turn upside down on the baking sheet. This will help them rise with straight sides.

560

Cakes, sponges, biscuits and scones

11 Rock cakes

Ingredient	Makes 16
Medium flour (50% soft and 50% strong flour)	500 g
Baking powder	30 g
Salt	3 g
Caster sugar	125 g
Egg	60 g
Butter	120 g
Currants	90 g
Citrus peel	30 g
Milk	180 g
Egg wash	
Caster sugar, to sprinkle	

Energy	Cals	Fat	Sat fat	Carb	Sugar	Protein	Fibre
913 kJ	217 kcal	8.7 g	3.6 g	33.6 g	14.3 g	3.4 g	1.3 g

Using hard margarine.

1 Sieve the flour, baking powder and salt through a fine sieve.
2 Dissolve the sugar in the liquid egg.
3 Rub the butter into the flour to form a crumb mix.
4 Add the currants and citrus peel.
5 Blend in the milk to achieve a smooth mix.
6 Divide the mixture into small portions, approximately 70 g each, and place evenly on to a baking tray.
7 Egg wash and sprinkle with caster sugar.
8 Bake at 210 °C for 15–20 minutes, until light golden brown.

Variation
Add a small pinch of mixed spice.

12 Madeleines

Ingredient	Makes 45
Caster sugar	125 g
Eggs	3
Vanilla pod, seeds from	1
Flour	150 g
Baking powder	1 tsp
Beurre noisette	125 g

Energy	Cals	Fat	Sat fat	Carb	Sugar	Protein	Fibre	Sodium
392 kJ	94 kcal	5.2 g	3.0 g	10.8 g	5.8 g	0.7 g	0.2 g	0.1 g

For two madeleines.

1 Whisk the sugar, eggs and vanilla seeds to a hot sabayon.
2 Fold in the flour and the baking powder.
3 Fold in the *beurre noisette* and chill for up to 2 hours.
4 Pipe into well-buttered madeleine moulds and bake in a moderate oven.
5 Turn out and allow to cool.

13 Rich fruit cake

Ingredient	16 cm diameter, 8 cm deep	21 cm diameter, 8 cm deep	26 cm diameter, 8 cm deep
Butter	150 g	200 g	300 g
Soft brown sugar	150 g	200 g	300 g
Eggs	4	6	8
Black treacle	2 tsp	3 tsp	1 tbsp
Soft flour	125 g	175 g	275 g
Salt	6 g	8 g	10 g
Nutmeg	3 g	4 g	5 g
Mixed spice	3 g	4 g	5 g
Ground cinnamon	3 g	4 g	5 g
Ground almonds	75 g	100 g	125 g
Currants	150 g	200 g	300 g
Sultanas	150 g	200 g	300 g
Raisins	125 g	150 g	225 g
Mixed peel	75 g	100 g	125 g
Glacé cherries	75 g	100 g	125 g
Lemons, grated zest of	½	¾	1
Oven temperatures			
	150 °C	140 °C	130 °C
Approximate cooking times			
	2 hours	3 hours	4½ hours

Energy	Cals	Fat	Sat fat	Carb	Sugar	Protein	Fibre	Sodium
2,367 kJ	563 kcal	24.8 g	11.3 g	81.9 g	69.4 g	8.8 g	2.8 g	0.6 g

1. Cream the butter and sugar until soft and light.
2. Break up the eggs and beat in gradually.
3. Add the black treacle.
4. Sieve all the dry ingredients together and fold in.
5. Finally fold in the dried fruit and lemon zest.
6. Deposit into buttered cake tins lined with silicone paper.
7. Level the mix and make a well in the centre.
8. Check the cakes during baking, turn to make sure they are being cooked evenly.
9. Test to see if cooked with a metal skewer or needle.
10. Allow to cool completely before wrapping and storing in an airtight container.

In the UK fruit cakes are traditionally used as a base for celebration cakes such as Simnel and Christmas cakes, and for weddings.

Professional tip

This is a dense mixture. To prevent the outside becoming overcooked insulate the cake tins by standing on newspaper and tying several layers of newspaper around the sides.

The dried fruit can be pre-soaked in brandy or rum the day before, or, as the cake matures it can be given a 'drink' every so often.

Take a spoon and make a well in the centre of the mixture, this will help stop the cake doming as it bakes.

Unless filling the oven with cakes it is advisable to place a tray of water in the oven when baking. This will create steam and allow the cake to expand before the crust sets.

To test, insert a needle in the centre, when the cake is cooked the needle should come out clean and hot.

After cooling wrap in paper or foil and place in an airtight container and leave to mature for 3–4 weeks before covering with marzipan and decorating with icing.

Variations

If using square cake tins, increase the quantities by a quarter.

This cake can be made less rich by cutting down on the fruit and spices – these are all 'carried' ingredients and will not affect the cake as long as the basic ingredients (butter, sugar, eggs, flour) are not tampered with.

Cakes, sponges, biscuits and scones

Faults

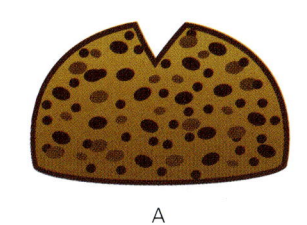

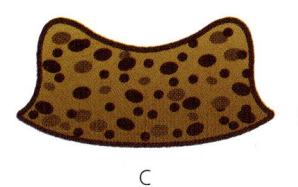

A B C D

Cake A is domed ('cauliflower top'). This occurs if:
- the flour used is too strong
- the oven is too hot and/or too dry
- there is not enough fat
- the ingredients are over-mixed after adding flour.

Cake B has a sunken top ('M' fault). This is caused by adding too much baking powder and/or too much sugar.

Cake C has a sunken top and sides ('X' fault). This occurs if the mixture is too wet.

Cake D has a low volume. This occurs if:
- too much fat is added
- the mixture is too dry
- there is not enough aeration.

A good-quality fruit cake will:
- have straight sides, a flat top and good height
- have an even distribution of fruit
- be moist and dark.

14 Lemon drizzle cake

Ingredient	2 × 16 cm cakes
Butter	250 g
Caster sugar	400 g
Lemons, grated zest of	3
Soft flour	380 g
Baking powder	10 g
Eggs	4
Vanilla extract	½ tsp
Milk	25 ml
Syrup	
Lemons, juice of	3
Caster sugar	100 g

Energy	Cals	Fat	Sat fat	Carb	Sugar	Protein	Fibre	Sodium
1437 kJ	342 kcal	14.6 g	8.6 g	51.8 g	67.0 g	4.0 g	0.9 g	0.3 g

For ⅛ of a cake, excluding icing.

1. Cream the butter, sugar and zest until soft and light.
2. Sieve the flour and baking powder twice.
3. Mix together the eggs and vanilla extract.
4. Beat the eggs into the butter and sugar mixture.
5. Fold in the flour.
6. Add milk to achieve a dropping consistency.
7. Deposit into buttered and floured cake tins.
8. Bake at 165 °C for approximately 45 minutes.
9. Boil the lemon juice and sugar.
10. When the cake is cooked, stab with a skewer and pour over the syrup.
11. Leave to cool in the tin.

This cake can be finished with lemon icing and decorated with strips of crystallised lemon peel.

Décor

15 Apricot glaze

Ingredient	Makes 150 ml
Apricot jam	100 g
Stock syrup (see page 563) or water	50 ml

1. Boil the apricot jam with a little syrup or water.
2. Pass through a strainer. The glaze should be used hot.

Professional tip

A flan jelly (commercial pectin glaze) may be used as an alternative to apricot glaze. This is usually a clear glaze to which food colour may be added.

16 Water icing (glacé icing)

Ingredient	Makes 400 g
Icing sugar	400 g
Water, warm	60 ml

1. Sieve the icing sugar and start to add the warm water; add the water until the icing is thick enough to coat the back of a spoon.
2. If necessary, add more water or icing sugar to adjust the consistency.

Variation

Water may be replaced with other liquids to add flavour to the icing – for example, orange juice, mango juice, lemon juice, apple juice, lime juice, grape juice, passion fruit juice – or use a combination of juices with orange liqueur, kirsch, rum, calvados, etc.

Cakes, sponges, biscuits and scones

17 Royal icing

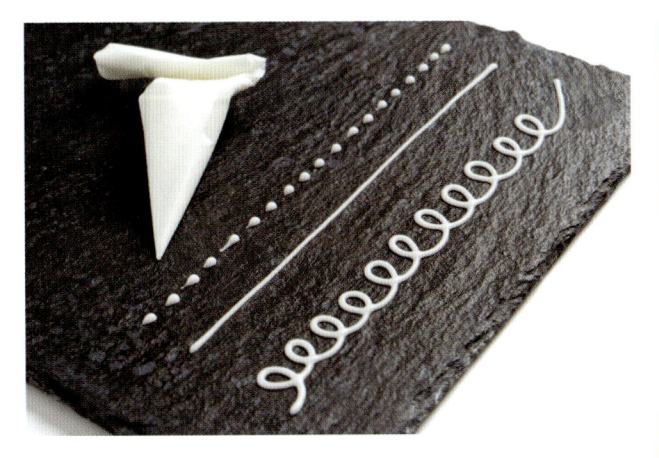

Ingredient	Makes 400 g
Icing sugar	400 g
Pasteurised egg whites	3
Lemon, juice of	1
Glycerine	2 tsp

1 Sift the icing sugar. Mix it well with the egg whites in a basin, using a wooden spoon.
2 Add a few drops of lemon juice and glycerine and beat until stiff.

Professional tip
Modern practice is to use egg white substitute or dried egg whites. Always follow the manufacturer's instructions for quantities.

Note
This amount of royal icing (400 g) is enough to cover a small (18 cm) cake.

18 Marzipan

1 Place the water and sugar in a pan and boil. Skim as necessary.
2 When the sugar reaches 116 °C, draw aside and mix in the ground almonds, then add the egg yolks and almond essence, and mix in quickly to avoid scrambling.
3 Knead well until smooth.

Ingredient	Makes 400 g
Water	250 ml
Caster sugar	1 kg
Ground almonds	400 g
Egg yolks	3
Almond essence	2–3 drops

Marzipan may be shaped into fruits, figures, etc.

19 Praline

Ingredient	Makes 1 kg
Granulated sugar	500 g
Water	200 ml
Glucose	100 g
Whole almonds	150 g
Hazelnuts	150 g

1. Boil the sugar, water and glucose to a light caramel.
2. Remove from the heat and immediately stir in the nuts.
3. Pour the mixture on a non-stick mat and cool until solid.
4. Break down to a fine powder using a food processor.

Biscuits

20 Sponge fingers (*biscuits à la cuillère*)

Ingredient	Approximately 60 × 8 cm fingers
Egg yolks	180 g
Caster sugar	125 g
Vanilla essence	Few drops
Soft flour	125 g
Cornflour	125 g
Egg whites	270 g
Caster sugar	125 g

Energy	Cals	Fat	Sat fat	Carb	Sugar	Protein	Fibre	Sodium
372 kJ	88 kcal	2.0 g	0.6 g	16.0 g	8.8 g	1.3 g	0.2 g	0.0 g

For two biscuits.

1. Prepare a baking sheet by lining with silicone paper cut to fit and set the oven at 160 °C. Have ready a piping bag fitted with a medium plain tube. Scald two mixing bowls to ensure they are clean and free of grease.
2. Whisk the yolks, sugar and vanilla over a bain-marie until warm, then continue whisking off the heat until a thick, sabayon-like consistency is reached.
3. Sieve the flours on to paper.
4. In a second mixing bowl, whisk the whites with the sugar to a soft meringue.
5. Add the whisked yolks to the meringue and start folding in. Add the flour in 2 or 3 portions, working quickly but taking care not to overwork the mixture.
6. Using a plain piping tube, immediately pipe on to the prepared baking sheet in neat rows.
7. Dust evenly with icing sugar and immediately place in the oven for approximately 25 minutes.
8. When cooked, slide the paper (and biscuits) on to a cooling rack.
9. When cool, remove from the paper and store in an airtight container at room temperature, or leave on the paper and store in a dry cabinet.

Cakes, sponges, biscuits and scones

Note
The literal translation of this is 'spoon biscuits', which comes from a time when the mixture would have been shaped between two spoons instead of being piped. They are traditionally used to line the mould for a Charlotte Russe, although the 'spooned' version would not lend itself to that.

Variation
Chocolate: instead of 125 g each of soft flour and cornflour, use 120 g soft flour, 60 g cornflour and 70 g cocoa powder.

Othellos: use the above recipe to make small, domed sponges. Hollow them out and fill with crème mousseline (see page 557). Sandwich pairs together and coat with coloured fondant.

Professional tip
It is easier to pipe the fingers all the same length if a template marked with parallel lines is placed under the silicone paper.

A common problem with this recipe is over-mixing and/or not working fast enough or being disorganised, which results in biscuits that collapse.

Sponge fingers should be pale in colour, very light in texture, be dusted with icing sugar and have a rounded shape. They should also be identical in length and width.

21 Tuiles

Ingredient	15–20 portions
Butter	100 g
Icing sugar	100 g
Flour	100 g
Egg whites	2

1 Mix all ingredients; allow to rest for 1 hour.
2 Spread to the required shape and size.
3 Bake at approx. 200–210 °C.
4 While hot, mould the biscuits to the required shape and leave to cool.

Energy	Cals	Fat	Sat fat	Carb	Sugar	Protein	Fibre	Sodium
417 kJ	100 kcal	5.5 g	3.4 g	12.1 g	7.0 g	1.1 g	0.3 g	0.1 g

22 Cats' tongues (*langues de chat*)

Pipe cats' tongues into their distinctive shape, thicker at the ends

Ingredient	Approximately 40
Icing sugar	125 g
Butter	100 g
Vanilla essence	3–4 drops
Egg whites	3–4
Flour (soft)	100 g

Energy	Cals	Fat	Sat fat	Carb	Sugar	Protein	Fibre	Sodium
676 kJ	161 kcal	8.3 g	5.2 g	20.7 g	13.2 g	2.1 g	0.4 g	0.1 g

Based on a portion of 4 biscuits.

1. Lightly cream the sugar and butter, add the vanilla essence.
2. Add the egg whites one by one, continually mixing and being careful not to allow the mixture to curdle.
3. Gently fold in the sifted flour and mix lightly.
4. Pipe on to a lightly greased baking sheet using a 3 mm plain tube, 2.5 cm apart.
5. Bake at 230–250 °C, for a few minutes.
6. The outside edges should be light brown and the centres yellow.
7. When cooked, remove on to a cooling rack using a palette knife.

23 Cigarette paste cornets

Ingredient	Approximately 30
Icing sugar	125 g
Butter, melted	100 g
Vanilla essence	3–4 drops
Egg whites	3–4
Soft flour	100 g

Energy	Cals	Fat	Sat fat	Carb	Sugar	Protein	Fibre	Sodium
444 kJ	106 kcal	5.6 g	3.6 g	14.0 g	8.8 g	0.3 g	0.2 g	0.1 g

For two biscuits.

1 Proceed as for steps 1–3 of recipe 22 (cats' tongues).
2 Using a plain tube, pipe out the mixture on to a lightly greased baking sheet into bulbs, spaced well apart. Place a template over each bulb and spread it with a palette knife.
3 Bake at 150 °C, until evenly coloured.
4 Remove the tray from the oven. Turn the cornets over but keep them on the hot tray.
5 Work quickly while the cornets are hot and twist them into a cornet shape using the point of a cream horn mould. (For a tight cornet shape it is best to set the pieces tightly inside the cream horn moulds and leave them until set.) If the cornets set hard before you have shaped them all, warm them in the oven until they become flexible.
6 The same paste may also be used for cigarettes russes, coupeaux and other shapes.

24 Brandy snaps

Ingredient	Approximately 20 snaps
Strong flour	225 g
Ground ginger	10 g
Golden syrup	225 g
Butter	250 g
Caster sugar	450 g

Energy	Cals	Fat	Sat fat	Carb	Sugar	Protein	Fibre	Sodium
2146 kJ	510 kcal	21.0 g	13.1 g	82.0 g	66.0 g	1.5 g	1.0 g	0.4 g

For two snaps.

1. Combine the flour and ginger in a bowl on the scales. Make a well.
2. Pour in golden syrup until the correct weight is reached.
3. Cut the butter into small pieces. Add the butter and sugar.
4. Mix together at a slow speed.
5. Divide into 4 even pieces. Roll into sausage shapes, wrap each in cling film and chill, preferably overnight.
6. Slice each roll into rounds. Place on a baking tray, spaced well apart.
7. Flatten each round using a fork dipped in cold water, keeping a round shape.
8. Bake in a preheated oven at 200 °C until evenly coloured and bubbly.
9. Remove from oven. Allow to cool slightly, then lift off and shape over a dariole mould.
10. Stack the snaps, no more than 4 together, on a stainless steel tray and store.

Cakes, sponges, biscuits and scones

25 Piped biscuits (*sablés à la poche*)

Ingredient	20–30 biscuits
Caster or unrefined sugar	75 g
Butter or margarine	150 g
Egg	1
Vanilla essence *or* Grated zest of one lemon	3–4 drops
Soft flour, white or wholemeal	200 g
Ground almonds	35 g

Energy	Cals	Fat	Sat fat	Carb	Sugar	Protein	Fibre	Sodium
993 kJ	237 kcal	15.2g	8.2g	23.3g	8.4g	3.4g	0.8g	0.2g

Based on 2 biscuits.

1 Cream the sugar and butter until light in colour and texture.
2 Add the egg gradually, beating continuously, add the vanilla essence or lemon zest.
3 Gently fold in the sifted flour and almonds, mix well until suitable for piping. If too stiff, add a little beaten egg.
4 Pipe on to a lightly greased and floured baking sheet using a medium-sized star tube (a variety of shapes can be used).
5 Some biscuits can be left plain, some decorated with half or whole almonds or neatly cut pieces of angelica and glacé cherries.
6 Bake in a moderate oven at 190 °C for about 10 minutes.
7 When cooked, remove on to a cooling rack using a palette knife.

26 Shortbread biscuits

Energy	Cals	Fat	Sat fat	Carb	Sugar	Protein	Fibre
507 kJ	121 kcal	7.0g	4.4g	14.1g	4.6g	1.2g	0.5g

Using butter.

Method 1

Ingredient	12 portions
Flour (soft)	150 g
Salt	pinch
Butter or margarine	100 g
Caster sugar	50 g

1. Sift the flour and salt.
2. Mix in the butter or margarine and sugar with the flour.
3. Combine all the ingredients to a smooth paste.
4. Roll carefully on a floured table or board to the shape of a rectangle or round, 0.5 cm thick. Place on a lightly greased baking sheet.
5. Mark into the desired size and shape. Prick with a fork.
6. Bake in a moderate oven at 180–200 °C for 15–20 minutes.

Method 2

Ingredient	12 portions
Flour (soft), white or wholemeal	100 g
Rice flour	100 g
Butter or margarine	100 g
Caster or unrefined sugar	100 g
Egg, beaten	1

1. Sieve the flour and rice flour into a basin.
2. Rub in the butter until the texture of fine breadcrumbs. Mix in the sugar.
3. Bind the mixture to a stiff paste using the beaten egg.
4. Roll out to 3 mm using caster sugar, prick well with a fork and cut into fancy shapes. Place the biscuits on a lightly greased baking sheet.
5. Bake in a moderate oven at 180–200 °C for 15 minutes or until golden brown.
6. Remove with a palette knife on to a cooling rack.

Method 3

Ingredient	12 portions
Butter or margarine	100 g
Icing sugar	100 g
Egg	1
Flour (soft)	150 g

1. Cream the butter or margarine and sugar thoroughly.
2. Add the egg and mix in. Mix in the flour.
3. Pipe on to lightly greased and floured baking sheets using a large star tube.
4. Bake at 200–220 °C, for approximately 15 minutes.

16 Cold and hot desserts

Recipes included in this chapter

No.	Recipe	Page
	Cold desserts	
1	Fresh fruit salad	581
2	Poached fruits or fruit compote	582
3	Crème brûlée	583
4	Zabaglione (sabayon with Marsala)	584
5	Lime and mascarpone cheesecake	584
6	Crème caramel	585
7	Fruit mousse	586
8	Bavarois	587
9	Chocolate mousse	588
10	Vanilla panna cotta served with stewed rhubarb	589
11	Meringue	590
12	Vacherin with strawberries and cream	590
13	Baked blueberry cheesecake	591
14	Fruit fool	592
15	Lime soufflé frappe	593
16	Trifle	594
	Iced desserts	
17	Apple sorbet	595
18	Chocolate sorbet	595
19	Vanilla ice cream	596
20	Lemon curd ice cream	597
21	Peach Melba	598
22	Pear belle Hélène	598
23	Raspberry parfait	599
	Hot desserts	
24	Apple charlotte	600
25	Apple fritters (*beignets aux pommes*)	601
26	Pancakes with apple	602
27	Baked apples (*pommes bonne femme*)	602
28	Griottines clafoutis	603
29	Baked rice pudding (*pouding de riz*)	604
30	Sticky toffee pudding	604
31	Cabinet pudding	605
32	Soufflé pudding	606
33	Chocolate fondant	607
34	Rice pudding	608
35	Bread and butter pudding	609
36	Apple crumble tartlets	610
37	Tarte tatin	611
38	Steamed sponge pudding	612
39	Golden syrup pudding	613
40	Christmas pudding	614
41	Baked Alaska	615
42	Vanilla soufflé	616
43	Lemon curd flourless soufflé	618
	Sweet sauces	
44	Sabyon sauce	619
45	Fresh egg custard sauce (*sauce à l'anglaise*)	620
46	Custard sauce	621
47	Fruit coulis	621
48	Strawberry sauce	622
49	Chocolate sauce	622
50	Butterscotch sauce	623
51	Caramel sauce	624
52	Rum or brandy cream or butter	624

Ingredients commonly used in desserts

There are many important ingredients used in the production of desserts. Sugar provides the sweetness that is associated with desserts, but it also plays other roles that affect texture, aroma and, depending on its form, it can also help to reduce the risk of crystallisation in products such as ice cream and dehydration of frozen products such as sponges. Eggs and other dairy products, such as milk and cream, are also regular commodities found in desserts, as is salt, perhaps surprisingly, all of which are discussed below.

Sugar

For a detailed breakdown of the various forms of sugar and its uses, refer to the section 'Ingredients for pastry work' in Chapter 14.

Specific details on the way that sugar is used in the production of ice creams and sorbets is given later in this chapter.

Eggs

Eggs are one of the principal ingredients in cooking and essential for many desserts. Their great versatility and extraordinary properties as a thickener, emulsifier and stabiliser make their presence important in various creations in patisserie, including sauces, creams, sponge cakes, custards and ice creams. Although it is often not the main ingredient, it plays specific and determining roles in terms of texture, taste and aroma. Eggs are fundamental in products such as brioches, crème anglaise, sponge cakes and pastry cream. The extent to which eggs are used (or not) makes an enormous difference to the quality of the product.

A good custard cannot be made without eggs, as they cause the required coagulation and give it the desired consistency and finesse.

Eggs are also an important ingredient in ice cream where, due to the lecithin they contain, their yolks aid the emulsion of fats.

Eggs are used for several reasons:
- They act as a texture agent in, for example, pastry cream and ice cream.
- They intensify the aroma of pastries such as brioche.
- They enhance flavours.
- They give volume to whisked sponges and batters.
- They strengthen the structure of products such as sponge cakes.
- They act as a thickening agent, for example in crème anglaise.
- They act as an emulsifier in products such as mayonnaise and ice cream.

Quality and nutritional value

Important facts about eggs:
- A fresh egg (in shell) should have a small, shallow air pocket inside it.
- The yolk of a fresh egg should be bulbous, firm and bright.
- The fresher the egg, the more viscous (thick and not runny) the egg white.
- Eggs should be stored away from strong odours as their shells are porous and smells are easily absorbed.
- In a whole 60 g egg, the yolk weighs about 20 g, the white 30 g and the shell 10 g.

Egg yolk is high in saturated fat. The yolk is a good source of protein and also contains vitamins and iron. The egg white is made up of protein (albumen) and water. The egg yolk also contains lecithin, which acts as an emulsifier in dishes such as mayonnaise – it helps to keep the ingredients mixed, so that the oils and water do not separate.

Working with egg whites

- To avoid the danger of salmonella, if the egg white is not going to be cooked or will not reach a temperature of 70 °C, use pasteurised egg whites. Egg white is available chilled, frozen or dried.
- Equipment must be thoroughly clean and free from any traces of fat, as this prevents the whites from whipping; fat or grease prevents the albumen strands from bonding and trapping the air bubbles.
- Take care that there are no traces of yolk in the white, as yolk contains fat.
- A little acid (cream of tartar or lemon juice) strengthens the egg white, extends the foam and produces more meringue. The acid also has the effect of stabilising the meringue.
- If the foam is over-whipped the albumen strands, which hold the water molecules with the sugar

suspended on the outside of the bubble, are overstretched. The water and sugar make contact and the sugar dissolves, making the meringue heavy and wet. This can sometimes be rescued by further whisking until it foams up, but very often the mixture has to be discarded and a new one produced.

Beaten egg white forms a foam that is used for aerating sweets and many other desserts, including meringues (see recipe 11). It is advisable to use Italian meringue in desserts that are not going to be cooked, such as bavarois.

Salt

Salt (chemical name 'sodium chloride') is a very important ingredient in all areas of cookery, including patisserie. Salt is a necessary part of the human diet and is present in small or large proportions in many natural foods. Salt considerably enhances many products, sweet or savoury. We generally associate it with seasoning foods to improve their flavour, but it is also necessary in the making of many sweet dishes.

It is a good idea to add a pinch of salt to all sweet preparations, nougats, chocolate bonbons and cakes to intensify flavours. Salt also softens sugar and butter, activates the taste buds and enhances all aromas. Salted caramel is an excellent example of how salt can benefit a sweet product.

What you need to know about salt
- Salt gives us the possibility of many combinations. At times these may seem normal (such as a terrine of foie gras and coarse salt), and, at others, surprising (such as praline with coarse salt).
- The addition of salt enhances the flavour of foods when its quantity is well adjusted; but if added in greater quantity than we are used to, it produces a very interesting, completely unknown result. Care needs to be taken when adding salt. There is a fine line between the enhancement of food with salt and spoiling it by adding too much.
- Excessive salt can cause high blood pressure, which could lead to strokes or heart attacks, so it should be used in moderation. For this reason, many chefs are looking for ways to reduce the amount of salt they use in their products and dishes.

Egg custard-based desserts

The essential ingredients for an egg custard are eggs and milk. Cream is often added to egg custard desserts to enrich them and to improve the feel in the mouth (mouth-feel) of the final product.

Egg custard mixture provides the chef with a versatile basic set of ingredients that covers a wide range of sweets. The mixture is often referred to as crème renversée. Some examples of sweets produced using this mixture are:
- crème caramel (recipe 6)
- bread and butter pudding (recipe 35)
- diplomat pudding
- cabinet pudding (recipe 31)
- queen of puddings
- baked egg custard.

Savoury egg custard is used to make:
- quiches
- tartlets
- flans.

When a starch, such as flour, is added to the ingredients for an egg custard mix, it changes the characteristic of the end product, as in pastry cream, for example.
- **Pastry cream** (also known as confectioner's custard or crème pâtissière) is a filling used for many sweets, gâteaux, flans and tartlets, and as a basis for soufflé mixes.
- **Sauce à l'anglaise** (crème anglaise) is used as a base for some ice creams. It is also used in its own right as a sauce to accompany a range of sweets.

Basic egg custard sets by coagulation of the egg protein. Egg white coagulates at approximately 60 °C, egg yolk at 70 °C. Whites and yolks mixed together will coagulate at 66 °C. If the egg protein is overheated or overcooked, it will shrink and water will be lost from the mixture, causing undesirable bubbles in the custard. This loss of water is called syneresis, commonly referred to as scrambling or curdling. This will occur at temperatures higher than 85 °C. Therefore, a sauce anglaise should be ideally cooked between 70 °C and 85 °C. The sauce will become thicker as it becomes closer to 85 °C, but is at risk of curdling beyond this temperature.

Traditional custard made from custard powder

Custard powder can be used to make custard sauce. It is made from vanilla-flavoured cornflour with yellow colouring added, and is a substitute for eggs. Sweetness is adjusted by adding sugar before mixing with milk and heating. The fat content can be reduced by making it with semi-skimmed milk rather than full-fat milk.

Points to remember when making egg custards

- Always work in a clean and tidy way, complying with food hygiene regulations.
- Check the temperature of refrigerators and freezers to ensure that they comply with the current regulations.
- Check all weighing scales for accuracy.
- Check all raw materials for correct use-by dates.
- Always wash your hands when handling fresh eggs or dairy products and other pastry ingredients.
- Prevent cross-contamination by not allowing any potentially harmful substances to come into contact with the mixture.
- Follow the recipe carefully.
- Always heat the egg yolks or eggs to 70°C, or use pasteurised egg yolks or eggs.
- Ensure that all heating and cooling temperatures are followed.
- Always store the end product carefully at the right temperature.
- Never use cream to decorate a product that is still warm.

Ice creams and sorbets

Ice cream

Traditional ice cream is made from a basic egg custard sauce (sauce anglaise). The sauce is cooled and mixed with fresh cream. It is then frozen using a rotating machine (churn) where the water content forms ice crystals.

Ice cream should be served at around −13°C; any colder and it will be too hard, any warmer and it will be too soft. Long-term storage should be at between −18°C and −20°C.

The traditional method of making ice cream uses only egg yolks, sugar and milk/cream in the form of a sauce anglaise base. Modern approaches to making ice cream use stabilisers (see page 578) and different sugars, and egg whites.

Ice cream regulations

The Dairy Products (Hygiene) Regulations 1995 apply to the handling of milk-based ice cream, while the Ice Cream (Heat Treatment) Regulations 1959 and 1963 apply to non-milk-based ice cream in any catering business or shop premises. The production process must also take into consideration the Food Hygiene Regulations 2006.

The regulations state that:
- Ice cream must be obtained from a mixture which has been heated to any of the temperatures in Table 16.1 for the times specified.
- The mix must be reduced to a temperature of not more than 7.2°C within one and a half hours. This temperature must not be exceeded until freezing begins.
- If the ice cream becomes warm (above −2.2°C) it cannot be sold/used until it has been heated again as described above.
- A complete cold mix that is reconstituted with water does not need to be pasteurised first to comply with these regulations.
- A complete cold mix reconstituted with water must be kept below −2.2°C once it has been frozen.

Table 16.1 Time and temperature combinations set out by the Ice Cream (Heat Treatment) Regulations 1959

Temperature	Time (not less than)
65.5°C	30 minutes
71.1°C	10 minutes
79.4°C	15 seconds

Ice cream needs this treatment to kill harmful bacteria. Freezing without the correct heat treatment does not kill bacteria; it allows them to remain dormant. The storage temperature for ice cream should not exceed −20 °C ideally, although standard freezers usually operate between −18 °C and −22 °C.

The rules for sterilised (UHT) ice cream are the same except that:
- The temperature for the heat treatment must not be less than 149.9 °C for at least two seconds.
- If the sterilised mix is kept in unopened, sterile and air-tight containers, there no requirement to refrigerate the mixture before it is frozen.
- In the case of non-milk based products, the temperature of opened containers must not exceed 7.2 °C, except where food mixtures are added that have a pH of 4.5 or less to make water ice or similar products and the combined product is frozen within one hour of combination.

Any ice cream sold must comply with the following compositional standards:
- It must contain not less than 5 per cent fat and not less than 2.5 per cent milk protein (not necessary in natural proportions).
- It must conform to the Dairy Products (Hygiene) Regulations 1995.

For further information contact the Ice Cream Alliance (see www.ice-cream.org).

Ice cream making process

1. **Weighing**: ingredients should be weighed precisely in order to ensure the best results and regularity and consistency.
2. **Pasteurisation**: this is a vital stage in making ice cream. Its primary function is to minimise bacterial contamination by heating the mixture of ingredients to 85 °C, then quickly cooling it to 4 °C.
3. **Homogenisation**: high pressure is applied to cause the explosion of fats, which makes ice cream more homogenous, creamier, smoother and much lighter. It is not usually done for homemade ice cream.
4. **Ripening**: this basic but optional stage refines flavour, further develops aromas and improves texture. This occurs during a rest period (4 to 24 hours), which gives the stabilisers and proteins time to act, improving the overall structure of the ice cream. This has the same effect on a crème anglaise, which is much better the day after it is made than it is on the same day.
5. **Churning**: the mixture is frozen while air is incorporated at the same time. The ice cream is removed from the machine at about −10 °C.

Use of sugars

- **Sucrose** (common sugar) not only sweetens ice cream but also gives it body. An ice cream that contains only sucrose (not recommended) has a higher freezing point.
- The optimum sugar percentage of ice cream is between 15 and 20 per cent.
- Ice cream that contains **dextrose** (another type of sugar) has a lower freezing point, and better taste and texture.
- As much as 50 per cent of the sucrose can be substituted with other sweeteners, but the recommended amount is 25 per cent.
- **Glucose** (another type of sugar) improves smoothness and prevents the crystallisation of sucrose.
- The quantity of glucose used should be between 25 and 30 per cent of the sucrose by weight.
- **Atomised glucose** (glucose powder) is more water absorbent, so helps to reduce the formation of ice crystals.
- The quantity of dextrose used should be between 6 and 25 per cent of the substituted sucrose (by weight).
- **Inverted sugar** is a paste or liquid obtained from heating sucrose with water and an acid (for example, lemon juice). Using inverted sugar in ice cream lowers the freezing point.
- Inverted sugar also improves the texture of ice cream and delays crystallisation.
- The quantity of inverted sugar used should be a maximum of 33 per cent of the sucrose by weight. It is very efficient at sweetening and gives ice cream a low freezing point.
- **Honey** has very similar properties as those of inverted sugar.

Use of cream and egg yolks

- The purpose of **cream** in ice cream is to improve creaminess and taste.
- **Egg yolks** act as stabilisers in ice cream due to the lecithin they contain – they help to prevent the fats and water in the ice cream from separating.
- Egg yolks improve the texture and viscosity of ice cream.
- The purpose of stabilisers (for example, gum arabic, gelatine, pectin) is to prevent crystal formation by absorbing the water contained in ice cream and making a stable gel.

Use of stabilisers

Gelling substances, thickeners and emulsifiers are all stabilisers. They are products we use regularly, each with its own specific function, but their main purpose is to retain water to make a gel. The case of ice cream is the most obvious, in which they are used to prevent ice crystal formation. They are also used to stabilise the emulsion, increase the viscosity of the mix and give a smoother product that is more resistant to melting. There are many stabilising substances, both natural and artificial.

- The quantity of stabilisers in ice cream should be between 3 g and 5 g per kg of mix, with a maximum of 10 g.
- Stabilisers promote air absorption, making products lighter to eat and also less costly to produce, as air increases the volume of the product.

What you need to know about ice cream

- Hygienic conditions are essential while making ice cream – personal hygiene and high levels of cleanliness in the equipment and the kitchen environment must be maintained.
- An excess of stabilisers in ice cream will make it sticky.
- Stabilisers should always be mixed with sugar before adding, to avoid lumps.
- Stabilisers should be added at 45 °C, which is when they begin to act.
- Cold stabilisers have no effect on the mixture, so the temperature must be raised to 85 °C.
- Ice cream should be allowed to 'ripen' for 4 to 24 hours. This helps to improve its flavour properties.
- Ice cream should be cooled quickly to 4 °C, because micro-organisms reproduce rapidly, particularly between 20 °C and 55 °C.

Sorbets

Sorbets belong to the ice cream family; they are a mixture of water, sucrose, atomised glucose, stabiliser, fruit juice, fruit pulp and, sometimes, liqueurs.

- Sorbet is generally more refreshing and easier to digest than ice cream.
- Fruit for sorbets must always be of a high quality and ripe.
- The percentage of fruit used in sorbet varies according to the type of fruit, its acidity and the properties desired.
- The percentage of sugar will depend on the type of fruit used.
- The minimum sugar content in sorbet is about 13 per cent.
- As far as ripening is concerned, the syrup should be left to rest for 4 to 24 hours and never mixed with the fruit because its acidity would damage the stabiliser.
- Stabiliser is added in the same way as for ice cream.
- Sorbets are not to be confused with granitas, which are semi-solid.

Stabilisers and setting agents

Edible gelatine

Edible gelatine is extracted from animals' bones (for example, pork and veal) and, more recently, fish skin. Sold in sheets of 2 g, it is easy to precisely control the amount used and to manipulate it. Gelatine sheets must always be washed thoroughly with lots of cold water to remove impurities and any remaining odours. They must then be drained before use.

Gelatine sheets melt at 40 °C; they should be melted in a little of the liquid from the recipe before being added to the base preparation.

Pectin

Pectin is another commonly used gelling substance because of its great absorption capacity. It comes from citrus peel (for example, oranges, lemons), though all fruits contain some pectin in their peel.

It is a good idea to mix pectin with sugar before adding it to the rest of the ingredients.

Agar-agar

Agar-agar is a gelatinous marine algae found in Asia. It is sold in whole or powdered form and has a great absorption capacity. It dissolves very easily and, in addition to gelling, adds elasticity and resists heat (this is classified as a non-reversible gel). It is a vegetarian alternative to gelatine.

Carob gum

Carob gum comes from the seeds of the carob tree; it makes sorbets creamier and improves heat resistance.

Guar gum and carrageenan

Guar gum and carrageenan are natural products. Both of these gelling substances have similar properties to agar-agar, but they are not as commonly used.

Fruit-based and other desserts

Fruit is used as an ingredient in many desserts. It can be the main feature of a dessert, as in the case of a baked apple (*bonne femme*), peach Melba or pear belle Hélène, or in conjunction with other dessert bases and ingredients. Fruit can also form the main component of batter-based desserts, such as fritters and clafoutis, for example.

Fruit is used to contribute to sponge-based desserts, such as baked Alaska with cherries or caramelised banana (see recipe 41), as a platform to support fruit mousses and/or bavarois, or as a component in steamed sponge puddings. Fruit is also regularly used in a variety of pastry-based desserts, such as tarte tatin, fruit tarts and barquettes.

Other dessert mediums include meringue (vacherins), egg custards (*crème renversée*) and purées (to flavour ice creams and sorbets). This provides just a few examples of the versatility of fruit and how it can be used alongside other mediums to produce an endless variety of desserts.

Quality and purchasing

Fresh fruit should be:
- whole and fresh looking (for maximum flavour the fruit must be ripe but not overripe)
- firm, according to type and variety
- clean, and free from traces of pesticides and fungicides
- free from external moisture
- free from any unpleasant foreign smell or taste
- free from pests or disease
- sufficiently mature; it must be capable of being handled and travelling without being damaged
- free from any defects characteristic of the variety in terms of their shape, size and colour
- free of bruising and any other damage.

Soft fruits deteriorate quickly, especially if they are not sound. Take care to see that they are not damaged or overripe when purchased. Soft fruits should look fresh; there should be no signs of wilting, shrinking or mould. The colour of certain soft fruits is an indication of their ripeness (for example, strawberries or dessert gooseberries).

Storing fruit

Hard fruits, such as apples, should be left in boxes and kept in a cool store. Soft fruits, such as raspberries and strawberries, should be left in their punnets or baskets in a cold room. Stone fruits, such as apricots and plums, are best placed in trays so that any damaged fruit can be seen and discarded. Peaches and citrus fruits are left in their delivery trays or boxes. Bananas should not be stored in chilled conditions because their skins will turn black.

Finishing and presentation

The finishing and presentation of desserts can lead to elaborate creations. With the use of ever-changing techniques, products and equipment, desserts offer chefs the opportunity to create mouth-watering dishes that are also also eye catching, impressive and imaginative.

Classically, some dessert products are finished by being filled, such as profiteroles and crêpes. Other desserts might include a chocolate cup filled with a mousse or cream, whereas others are glazed or gratinated, such as crème brûlée or bread and butter pudding.

Garnishing desserts offers endless opportunities and can be as simple as using some fresh fruit such as raspberries or other berries. Piping can also be used to enhance desserts: a cream or buttercream, for example, or a chocolate motif.

Other garnishes include items such as dried fruits and purées, fruit carpaccios and crisps, and even items such as popping 'space dust', intended to add the element of surprise by popping when it comes in contact with saliva in the mouth.

Healthy eating and desserts

Desserts and puddings remain popular with consumers today, but there is now a demand for products with reduced fat and sugar content, as many people are keen to eat a healthy diet. Chefs continue to respond to this demand by modifying recipes to reduce the fat and sugar content; they may also use alternative ingredients, such as low-calorie sweeteners where possible and unsaturated fats. Although salt is an essential part of our diet, too much of it can be unhealthy, and this is something else that chefs should take into consideration.

Test yourself

1. Name three types of setting agent.
2. Describe what would happen to a crème caramel if it was cooked at 180 °C.
3. Name the three main types of meringues, and describe their production and use.
4. Describe the conditions that promote the foam of egg whites when making meringues.
5. Name two desserts that are finished with a glaze.
6. What is the difference between a cabinet and diplomat pudding?
7. Name five fruits suitable for stewing.
8. Describe the differences between the production of a 'pudding soufflé' and a 'fruit soufflé'.
9. Name four types of sugar, giving an example of their use in a dessert.
10. Explain why salt is sometimes used in the production of desserts.

Cold desserts

1 Fresh fruit salad

1. For the syrup, boil the sugar with the water and place in a bowl.
2. Allow to cool, then add the lemon juice.
3. Peel and cut the orange into segments.
4. Peel, quarter and core the apple and pear, then cut each quarter into two or three slices, place in the bowl with the syrup and mix in the orange segments.
5. Stone the cherries but leave them whole.
6. Cut the grapes in half, peel if required, and remove any pips. Add the cherries and grapes to the fruit and syrup mix.
7. Mix the fruit salad carefully and place in a glass bowl in the refrigerator to chill.
8. Just before serving, peel and slice the banana and mix in.

Variation

- Any of the following fruits may be used: dessert apples, pears, pineapple, oranges, grapes, melon, strawberries, peaches, raspberries, apricots, bananas, cherries, kiwi fruit, plums, mangoes, paw paws and lychees. Allow about 150g unprepared fruit per portion. All fruit must be ripe.
- Kirsch or an orange liqueur could be added to the syrup.
- Fruit juice (such as apple, orange, grape or passion fruit) can be used instead of syrup.

Ingredient	4 portions	10 portions
Stock syrup		
Caster sugar	50g	125g
Water	125ml	310ml
Lemon, juice of	½	1¼
Fruit		
Orange	1	2½
Dessert apple	1	2½
Dessert pear	1	2½
Cherries	50g	125g
Grapes	50g	125g
Banana	1	2½

Energy	Cals	Fat	Sat fat	Carb	Sugar	Protein	Fibre
493 kJ	117 kcal	0.0g	0.0g	30.3g	29.5g	0.9g	3.0g

2 Poached fruits or fruit compote

Poached rhubarb and pear

Ingredient	4 portions	10 portions
Stock syrup (see page 545)	250 ml	625 ml
Fruit	400 g	1 kg
Sugar	100 g	250 g
Lemon, juice of	½	1

Energy	Cals	Fat	Sat fat	Carb	Sugar	Protein	Fibre
531 kJ	126 kcal	0.0 g	0.0 g	33.5 g	33.5 g	0.2 g	2.2 g

Using pears.

Apples, pears

1. Boil the water and sugar.
2. Quarter the fruit, remove the core and peel.
3. Place in a shallow pan in sugar syrup.
4. Add a few drops of lemon juice.
5. Cover with greaseproof paper.
6. Allow to simmer slowly, preferably in the oven, cool and serve.

Soft fruits (raspberries, strawberries)

1. Pick and wash the fruit. Place in a glass bowl.
2. Pour on the hot syrup. Allow to cool and serve.

Stone fruits (plums, damsons, greengages, cherries)

1. Wash the fruit, barely cover with sugar syrup and cover with greaseproof paper or a lid.
2. Cook gently in a moderate oven until tender.

Rhubarb

1. Trim off the stalk and leaf and wash.
2. Cut into 5 cm lengths and cook as above, adding extra sugar if necessary. A little ground ginger may also be added.

Gooseberries, blackcurrants, redcurrants

1. Top and tail the gooseberries, wash and cook as for stone fruit, adding extra sugar if necessary.
2. The currants should be carefully removed from the stalks, washed and cooked as for stone fruits.

Dried fruits (prunes, apricots, apples, pears)

1. Dried fruits should be washed and soaked in cold water overnight.
2. Gently cook in the liquor with sufficient sugar to taste.

Variation

A piece of cinnamon stick and a few slices of lemon may be added to the prunes or pears, one or two cloves to the dried or fresh apples.

Any compote may be flavoured with lavender and/or mint.

Healthy eating tips

- Use fruit juice instead of stock syrup.
- If dried fruits are used, no added sugar is needed.

Cold and hot desserts 16

3 Crème brûlée

Ingredient	4 portions	10 portions
Milk	125 ml	310 ml
Double cream	125 ml	310 ml
Natural vanilla, essence or pod	3–4 drops	7–10 drops
Eggs	2	5
Egg yolk	1	2–3
Caster sugar	25 g	60 g
Demerara sugar		

Energy	Cals	Fat	Sat fat	Carb	Sugar	Protein	Fibre
1154 kJ	278 kcal	21.9g	12.1g	14.8g	14.8g	6.2g	0.0g

1 Warm the milk, cream and vanilla essence in a pan.
2 Mix the eggs, egg yolk and caster sugar in a basin and add the warm milk. Stir well and pass through a fine strainer.
3 Pour the cream into individual dishes and place them into a tray half-filled with warm water.
4 Place in the oven at approximately 160°C for about 30–40 minutes, until set.
5 Sprinkle the tops with Demerara sugar and glaze under the salamander or by blowtorch to a golden brown.
6 Clean the dishes and serve.

Variation

Sliced strawberries, raspberries or other fruits (e.g. peaches, apricots) may be placed in the bottom of the dish before adding the cream mixture, or placed on top after the creams are caramelised.

Use a blowtorch carefully to glaze the top

583

4 Zabaglione (sabayon with Marsala)

1. Whisk the egg yolks and sugar in a bowl until almost white.
2. Mix in the Marsala.
3. Place the bowl and its contents in a bain-marie of warm water.
4. Whisk the mixture continuously until it increases to four times its bulk and is firm and frothy.
5. Pour the mixture into glass goblets.
6. Accompany with a suitable biscuit (for example, sponge fingers).

Note
This is a traditional Italian dessert, which is sometimes prepared in the restaurant in a special zabaglione pan.

Variation
Use sherry, whisky or brandy instead of Marsala.

Ingredient	4 portions	10 portions
Egg yolks, pasteurised	8	20
Caster or unrefined sugar	200 g	500 g
Marsala	150 ml	375 ml

Energy	Cals	Fat	Sat fat	Carb	Sugar	Protein	Fibre
746 kJ	177 kcal	5.5g	1.6g	27.4g	27.4g	2.9g	0.0g

5 Lime and mascarpone cheesecake

Energy	Cals	Fat	Sat fat	Carb	Sugar	Protein	Fibre	Sodium
2,624 kJ	633 kcal	54.0g	32.3g	31.5g	24.3g	7.1g	0.0g	0.3g

Using cream cheese in place of mascarpone.

Ingredient	1 cheesecake
Ginger biscuits	200 g
Butter, melted	200 g
Egg yolks, pasteurised	125 g
Caster sugar	75 g
Cream cheese	250 g
Mascarpone	250 g
Gelatine, softened in cold water	15 g
Limes, juice and grated zest of	2
Semi-whipped cream	275 ml
White chocolate, melted	225 g

Cold and hot desserts 16

1. Blitz the biscuits in a food processor. Mix in the melted butter. Line the cake ring with this mixture and chill until required.
2. Make a sabayon by whisking the egg yolks and sugar together over a pan of simmering water.
3. Stir the cream cheese and mascarpone into the sabayon until soft.
4. Meanwhile, warm the gelatine in the lime juice, and pass through a fine chinois. Whip the cream.
5. Pour the gelatine and melted white chocolate into the cheese mixture.
6. Remove from the food mixer and fold in the whipped cream with a spatula. Finally, whisk in the lime zest.
7. Pour over the prepared base. Chill for 4 hours.

6 Crème caramel

1. Prepare the caramel by placing three-quarters of the water in a thick-based pan, adding the sugar and allowing to boil gently, without shaking or stirring the pan.
2. When the sugar has cooked to a golden-brown caramel colour, add the remaining quarter of the water, reboil until the sugar and water mix, then pour into the bottom of dariole moulds.
3. Prepare the cream by warming the milk and whisking on to the beaten eggs, sugar and essence (or vanilla pod).
4. Strain and pour into the prepared moulds.
5. Place in a roasting tin half full of water.
6. Cook in a moderate oven at 150–160 °C for 30–40 minutes.
7. When thoroughly cold, loosen the edges of the crème caramel with the fingers, shake firmly to loosen and turn out on to a flat dish or plates.
8. Pour any caramel remaining in the mould around the creams.

Crème caramels may be served with whipped cream or a fruit sauce such as passion fruit, and accompanied by a sweet biscuit (e.g. shortbread, palmiers).

Ingredient	4–6 portions	10–12 portions
Caramel		
Sugar, granulated or cube	100 g	200 g
Water	125 ml	250 ml
Cream		
Milk, whole or skimmed	0.5 litres	1 litre
Eggs	4	8
Sugar, caster or unrefined	50 g	100 g
Vanilla essence or a vanilla pod	3–4 drops	6–8 drops

Energy	Cals	Fat	Sat fat	Carb	Sugar	Protein	Fibre
868 kJ	207 kcal	7.2 g	3.3 g	30.2 g	30.2 g	7.3 g	0.0 g

Using whole milk.

Professional tip

Adding a squeeze of lemon juice to the caramel will invert the sugar, thus preventing recrystallisation.

585

7 Fruit mousse

Ingredient	10 portions
Egg yolks	4
Sugar	50g
Fruit purée	250g
Gelatine	4 leaves
Lemon juice	
Lightly whipped cream	250g
Italian meringue	
Sugar	112g
Egg whites	2
Cream of tartar	pinch
Glaze topping	
Stock syrup	150ml
Fruit purée	150ml
Gelatine	3 leaves, soaked in cold water

Energy	Cals	Fat	Sat fat	Carb	Sugar	Protein	Fibre	Sodium
950 kJ	227 kcal	12.4g	7.0g	26.0g	26.0g	4.0g	2.0g	0.0g

1. Mix the egg yolks and sugar together and slowly add the boiled fruit purée which has been flavoured with a squeeze of lemon juice.
2. Return to the stove and cook to 80 °C until slightly thickened. Do not boil.
3. Add the previously softened gelatine to the warm purée and mix until fully dissolved. Chill down.
4. Prepare the Italian meringue by placing the sugar in a pan and saturating in water.
5. Boil the sugar to 115 °C, then whisk the egg whites with a pinch of cream of tartar.
6. Once the egg whites are at full peak, gradually add the boiled sugar which now should have reached the temperature of 121 °C. Whisk until cold.
7. Once the purée is cold, but not set, incorporate the Italian meringue and whipped cream.
8. Place into piping bag and pipe into the desired ring mould, normally lined with a suitable sponge such as a jaconde.
9. Level the surface using a palette knife and refrigerate.
10. Once set, glace the surface, refrigerate.
11. To remove from the mould, warm the outside of the mould with a blow torch and remove the ring mould.

Glaze

1. Warm the syrup. Add the gelatine and stir until dissolved, then add the desired fruit purée.
2. Apply to the surface of the chilled mousse whilst in a liquid state, but not hot.

Cold and hot desserts 16

8 Bavarois

Ingredient	6–8 portions
Gelatine	10 g
Eggs, pasteurised, separated	2
Caster sugar	50 g
Milk (whole, semi-skimmed or skimmed)	250 ml
Whipping or double cream (or non-dairy cream)	125 ml

Energy	Cals	Fat	Sat fat	Carb	Sugar	Protein	Fibre
970 kJ	231 kcal	18.2g	10.9g	11.8g	11.8g	5.8g	0.0g

Using whole milk and whipping cream.

1. If using leaf gelatine, soak in cold water.
2. Cream the egg yolks and sugar in a bowl until almost white.
3. Bring the milk to the boil in a thick-based saucepan then whisk it into the egg yolk and sugar mixture; mix well.
4. Clean the milk saucepan and return the mixture to it.
5. Return to a low heat and stir continuously with a wooden spoon until the mixture coats the back of the spoon. The mixture must not boil.
6. Remove from the heat; add the gelatine and stir until dissolved.
7. Pass through a fine strainer into a clean bowl. Leave in a cool place, stirring occasionally until almost at setting point.
8. Fold in the lightly beaten cream.
9. Fold in the stiffly beaten whites.
10. Pour the mixture into a mould or individual moulds (which may be very lightly greased with almond oil).
11. Allow to set in the refrigerator.
12. Shake and turn out on to a flat dish or plates.

Bavarois may be decorated with sweetened, flavoured whipped cream (crème Chantilly).

Flavours for bavarois

- **Raspberry or strawberry bavarois** (as shown): when the custard is almost cool, add 200g of picked, washed and sieved (puréed) raspberries or strawberries. Decorate with whole fruit and whipped cream.
- **Chocolate bavarois**: melt 50g chocolate couverture in the milk. Decorate with whipped cream and grated chocolate.
- **Coffee bavarois**: add coffee essence to the basic bavarois mixture, to taste.
- **Orange bavarois**: add the grated zest and juice of two oranges and one or two drops of orange colour to the mixture, and increase the gelatine by two leaves. Decorate with blanched, fine julienne of orange zest, orange segments and whipped cream.
- **Lemon or lime bavarois**: as for orange bavarois, but using lemons or limes in place of oranges.
- **Vanilla bavarois**: add a vanilla pod or a few drops of vanilla extract to the milk. Decorate with vanilla-flavoured sweetened cream (crème Chantilly).

Food safety

It is advisable to use pasteurised egg yolks and whites.

Healthy eating tips

Use semi-skimmed milk and whipping cream to reduce the overall fat content.

9 Chocolate mousse

Ingredient	8 portions	16 portions
Stock syrup at 30° Baumé (equal quantities of sugar and water will give 30° Baumé)	125 ml	250 ml
Pasteurised egg yolks	80 ml	160 ml
Bitter couverture, melted	250 g	500 g
Gelatine (soaked)	2 leaves	4 leaves
Whipping cream, whipped	500 ml	1 litre

Energy	Cals	Fat	Sat fat	Carb	Sugar	Protein	Fibre	Sodium
1760 kJ	419 kcal	37.0g	22.0g	13.7g	12.8g	5.1g	2.6g	0.0g

1 Boil the syrup.
2 Place the yolks into the bowl of a food mixer. Pour over the boiling syrup and whisk until thick (this is a *pâte à bombe*). Remove from the mixer.
3 Add all the melted couverture at once and fold it in quickly.
4 Drain the gelatine, melt it in the microwave and fold it into the chocolate sabayon mixture.
5 Add all the whipped cream at once and fold it in carefully.
6 Place the mixture into prepared moulds. Refrigerate or freeze immediately.

Faults

Possible causes of a heavy texture in chocolate mousse:
- The *pâte à bombe* is under-aerated.
- The cream is insufficiently whipped.
- The mix has been over-worked when folding in the cream and Italian meringue.

10 Vanilla panna cotta with stewed rhubarb

Ingredient	6 portions
Milk	125 ml
Double cream	375 ml
Aniseeds	2
Vanilla pod	½
Gelatine (soaked)	2 leaves
Caster sugar	50 g
Stewed rhubarb	
Rhubarb	500 g
Vanilla pod	1
Stock syrup	250 ml
Orange	1
Blueberries	75 g
Raspberries	50 g

Energy	Cals	Fat	Sat fat	Carb	Sugar	Protein	Fibre	Sodium
1808 kJ	436 kcal	34.0g	21.0g	31.0g	31.0g	3.0g	2.9g	0.0g

1 Prepare the rhubarb by finely peeling it.
2 Split the vanilla pod lengthways and scrape the seeds into a saucepan with the stock syrup and the zest and juice of the orange.
3 Bring the syrup to a gentle simmer and add the rhubarb. Stew until the rhubarb is cooked through but still holding its shape. Use a spider to remove the rhubarb and cut diagonally into strips.
4 For the panna cotta, boil the milk and cream, add aniseeds, infuse with the vanilla pod and remove after infusion.
5 Heat again and add the soaked gelatine and caster sugar. Strain through a fine strainer.
6 Place in a bowl set over ice and stir until it thickens slightly; this will allow the vanilla seeds to suspend throughout the mix instead of sinking to the bottom.
7 Fill individual dariole moulds.
8 Turn out the panna cotta and serve with the rhubarb. Decorate with a split, dried vanilla pod, a shortbread biscuit or a tuile.

Practical Cookery 14th edition

11 Meringue

Ingredient	4 portions	10 portions
Lemon juice or cream of tartar		
Egg whites, pasteurised	4	10
Caster sugar	200 g	500 g

Energy	Cals	Fat	Sat fat	Carb	Sugar	Protein	Fibre	Sodium
913 kJ	214 kcal	0.1 g	0.0 g	52.0 g	52.0 g	4.0 g	0.0 g	0.1 g

1 Whip the egg whites stiffly with a squeeze of lemon juice or cream of tartar.
2 Sprinkle on the sugar and carefully mix in.
3 Place in a piping bag with a large plain tube and pipe on to silicone paper on a baking sheet.
4 Bake in the slowest oven possible or in a hot plate (110 °C). The aim is to dry out the meringues without any colour whatsoever.

Whipping egg whites

The reason egg whites increase in volume when whipped is because they contain so much protein (11 per cent). The protein forms tiny filaments, which stretch on beating, incorporate air in minute bubbles then set to form a fairly stable puffed-up structure expanding to seven times its bulk. To gain maximum efficiency when whipping egg whites, the following points should be observed.

Because of possible weakness in the egg-white protein, it is advisable to strengthen it by adding a pinch of cream of tartar and a pinch of dried egg-white powder. If all dried egg-white powder is used no additions are necessary.

Other points to note:
- Eggs should be fresh.
- When separating yolks from whites no speck of egg yolk must be allowed to remain in the white; egg yolk contains fat, the presence of which can prevent the white being correctly whipped.
- The bowl and whisk must be scrupulously clean, dry and free from any grease.
- When egg whites are whipped, the addition of a little sugar (15 g to 4 egg whites) will assist efficient beating and reduce the chances of over-beating.

12 Vacherin with strawberries and cream

Ingredient	4 portions	10 portions
Egg whites	4	10
Caster sugar	200 g	500 g
Cream (whipped and sweetened) or non-dairy cream	125 ml	300 ml
Strawberries, picked and washed)	100–300 g	250–750 g

Energy	Cals	Fat	Sat fat	Carb	Sugar	Protein	Fibre
1,436 kJ	341 kcal	12.6 g	7.9 g	56.3 g	56.3 g	3.9 g	0.6 g

590

1 Stiffly whip the egg whites. (Refer to the notes in recipe 11 for more guidance.)
2 Carefully fold in the sugar.
3 Place the mixture into a piping bag with a 1 cm plain tube.
4 Pipe on to silicone paper on a baking sheet.
5 Start from the centre and pipe round in a circular fashion to form a base of 16 cm then pipe around the edge 2–3 cm high.
6 Bake in a cool oven at 100 °C until the meringue case is completely dry. Do not allow to colour.
7 Allow the meringue case to cool then remove from the paper.
8 Spread a thin layer of cream on the base. Add the strawberries.
9 Decorate with the remainder of the cream.

Note

A vacherin is a round meringue shell piped into a suitable shape so that the centre may be filled with sufficient fruit (such as strawberries, stoned cherries, peaches and apricots) and whipped cream to form a rich sweet. The vacherin may be prepared in one-, two- or four-portion sizes, or larger.

Variation

Melba sauce may be used to coat the strawberries before decorating with cream.

Raspberries can be used instead of strawberries.

Healthy eating tips

- Try 'diluting' the fat in the cream with some low-fat fromage frais.

13 Baked blueberry cheesecake

Ingredient	8–12 portions
Base	
Digestive biscuits	150 g
Butter, melted	50 g
Filling	
Full-fat cream cheese	350 g
Caster sugar	150 g
Eggs	4
Lemon, zest and juice of	1
Vanilla essence	1 tsp
Blueberries	125 g
Soured cream	350 ml

Energy	Cals	Fat	Sat fat	Carb	Sugar	Protein	Fibre
1,791 kJ	431 kcal	33.5 g	19.5 g	28.0 g	19.7 g	6.4 g	0.4 g

1 Blitz the biscuits in a food processor. Stir in the melted butter. Press the mixture into the bottom of a lightly greased cake tin with a removable collar.
2 Whisk together the cheese, sugar, eggs, vanilla and lemon zest and juice until smooth.
3 Stir in the blueberries, then pour the mixture over the biscuit base.
4 Bake at 160 °C for approximately 30 minutes.
5 Remove from the oven and leave to cool slightly for 10–15 minutes.
6 Spread soured cream over the top and return to the oven for 10 minutes.
7 Remove and allow to cool and set. Chill.

14 Fruit fool

Method 1

Ingredient	4 portions	10 portions
Fruit (apple, gooseberry, rhubarb, etc.)	400 g	1 kg
Water	60 ml	150 ml
Granulated or unrefined sugar	100 g	250 g
Cornflour	25 g	60 g
Milk, whole or semi-skimmed	250 ml	625 ml
Caster or unrefined sugar	25 g	60 g

Energy	Cals	Fat	Sat fat	Carb	Sugar	Protein	Fibre
942 kJ	222 kcal	2.6 g	1.6 g	50.3 g	4.5 g	2.4 g	1.6 g

For an apple fool made with whole milk.

1. Cook the fruit to a purée in the water with the granulated sugar. Pass through a sieve.
2. Dilute the cornflour in a little of the milk and add the caster sugar.
3. Boil the remainder of the milk.
4. Pour on to the diluted cornflour and stir well.
5. Return to the pan on a low heat and stir to the boil.
6. Mix with the fruit purée. The quantity of mixture should not be less than 0.5 litres (for four portions).
7. Pour into glass coupes or suitable dishes and allow to set.
8. Decorate with sweetened whipped cream or non-dairy cream. The colour may need to be adjusted slightly with food colour.

Method 2

Ingredient	4 portions	10 portions
Fruit purée (raspberry, strawberry, etc.)	400 g	1 kg
Caster sugar	100 g	250 g
Fresh whipped cream	250 ml	625 ml

Energy	Cals	Fat	Sat fat	Carb	Sugar	Protein	Fibre
1,540 kJ	370 kcal	25.3 g	15.8 g	35.7 g	35.7 g	2.0 g	1.2 g

For a strawberry fool.

Mix the ingredients and serve in coupes.

Method 3

Ingredient	4 portions	10 portions
Cornflour	35 g	85 g
Water	375 ml	940 ml
Sugar	100 g	250 g
Fruit purée (raspberry, strawberry, etc.)	400 g	1 kg
Cream	185 ml	460 ml

Energy	Cals	Fat	Sat fat	Carb	Sugar	Protein	Fibre
1,606 kJ	385 kcal	25.2 g	15.6 g	40.0 g	31.9 g	2.0 g	2.7 g

For a raspberry fool made with double cream.

1. Dilute the cornflour in a little of the water.
2. Boil the remainder of the water with the sugar and prepared fruit until soft.
3. Pass through a fine sieve.
4. Return to a clean pan and reboil.
5. Stir in the diluted cornflour and reboil. Allow to cool.
6. Lightly whisk the cream and fold into the mixture.
7. Serve as for method 1.

> **Professional tip**
>
> In methods 2 and 3 the fat content may be reduced by using equal quantities of cream and natural Greek-style yoghurt.

15 Lime soufflé frappe

Ingredient	10 portions	15 portions
Couverture	150 g	200 g
Sponge, thin slices, cut into rounds	10	15
Lime syrup	100 ml	150 ml
Swiss meringue		
Sabayon		
Whipping cream	600 ml	900 ml
Lime zest, finely grated and blanched, and juice	8	12
Egg yolks	10	15
Caster sugar	170 g	250 g
Leaf gelatine, soaked in iced water	9½	14
To decorate		
Confit of lime segments		
Moulded chocolate		

Energy	Cals	Fat	Sat fat	Carb	Sugar	Protein	Fibre	Sodium
2,734 kJ	655 kcal	40.8 g	20.7 g	66.9 g	61.2 g	9.2 g	0.8 g	0.2 g

1. Use individual stainless steel ring moulds. Cut a strip of acetate, 8 cm wide, to fit inside each ring. Cut a 6 cm strip to fit inside the first, spread it with tempered couverture and place inside the first strip, in the mould.
2. Place a round of sponge in the base of each mould and moisten with lime syrup.
3. Make the Swiss meringue (see page 544).
4. Whisk the cream until it is three-quarters whipped, then chill.
5. Whisk together the egg yolks, sugar and blanched lime zest. Boil the juice and pour it over the mixture to make the sabayon. Whisk over a bain-marie until it reaches 75 °C, then continue whisking away from the heat until it is cold.
6. Drain and melt the gelatine. Fold it into the sabayon.
7. Fold in the Swiss meringue, and then the chilled whipped cream.
8. Fill the prepared moulds. Level the tops and chill until set.
9. To serve, carefully remove the mould, peel away the acetate, plate and decorate.

16 Trifle

Ingredient	6–8 portions
Sponge (made with 3 eggs)	1
Jam	25 g
Tinned fruit (pears, peaches, pineapple) in syrup	1
Sherry (optional)	
Custard	
Custard powder	35 g
Milk, whole or skimmed	375 ml
Caster sugar	50 g
Cream (¾ whipped) or non-dairy cream	125 ml
Whipped sweetened cream or non-dairy cream	250 ml
Angelica	25 g
Glacé cherries	25 g

Energy	Cals	Fat	Sat fat	Carb	Sugar	Protein	Fibre
2,280 kJ	543 kcal	29.1 g	17.1 g	66.2 g	51.3 g	8.2 g	1.9 g

1. Cut the sponge in half, sideways, and spread with jam.
2. Place in a glass bowl or individual dishes and soak with fruit syrup drained from the tinned fruit; a few drops of sherry may be added.
3. Cut the fruit into small pieces and add to the sponge.
4. Dilute the custard powder in a basin with some of the milk and add the sugar.
5. Boil the remainder of the milk, pour a little on the custard powder, mix well, return to the saucepan and over a low heat stir to the boil. Allow to cool, stirring occasionally to prevent a skin forming; fold in the three-quarters whipped cream.
6. Pour on to the sponge. Leave to cool.
7. Decorate with the whipped cream, angelica and cherries.

Variation

Other flavourings or liqueurs may be used in place of sherry (such as whisky, rum, brandy, coffee liqueur).

For raspberry or strawberry trifle use fully ripe fresh fruit in place of tinned and decorate with fresh fruit in place of angelica and glacé cherries.

A fresh egg custard may be used with fresh egg yolks (see page 620).

Cold and hot desserts | 16

Iced desserts

17 Apple sorbet

Energy	Cals	Fat	Sat fat	Carb	Sugar	Protein	Fibre
673 kJ	158 kcal	0.1 g	0.0 g	41.5 g	38.7 g	0.4 g	2.4 g

1. Cut the apples into 1 cm pieces and place into lemon juice.
2. Bring the water, sugar and glucose to the boil, then allow to cool.
3. Pour the water over the apples. Freeze overnight. Blitz in a food processor.
4. Pass through a conical strainer, then churn in an ice cream machine.

> **Professional tip**
>
> For best results, after freezing, process in a Pacojet.

Ingredient	8–10 portions
Granny Smith apples, washed and cored	4
Lemon, juice of	1
Water	400 ml
Sugar	200 g
Glucose	50 g

> **Variation**
>
> **Fruits of the forest sorbet**: use a mixture of forest fruits instead of apples.

18 Chocolate sorbet

Ingredient	8 portions
Water	400 ml
Skimmed milk	100 ml
Sugar	150 g
Ice cream stabiliser	40 g
Cocoa powder	30 g
Dark couverture	60 g

1. Combine the water, milk, sugar, stabiliser and cocoa powder. Bring to the boil slowly. Simmer for 5 minutes.
2. Add the couverture and allow to cool.
3. Pass and churn.

Energy	Cals	Fat	Sat fat	Carb	Sugar	Protein	Fibre
544 kJ	129 kcal	3.0 g	1.8 g	25.4 g	24.9 g	1.6 g	6.3 g

19 Vanilla ice cream

1. Whisk the yolks and sugar in a bowl until almost white.
2. Boil the milk with the vanilla pod or essence in a thick-based pan.
3. Whisk on to the eggs and sugar; mix well.
4. Return to the cleaned saucepan, place on a low heat.
5. Stir continuously with a wooden spoon until the mixture coats the back of the spoon.
6. Pass through a fine strainer into a bowl.
7. Freeze in an ice cream machine, gradually adding the cream.

Ingredient	8–10 portions
Egg yolks	4
Caster or unrefined sugar	100 g
Milk, whole or skimmed	375 ml
Vanilla pod or essence	
Cream or non-dairy cream	125 ml

Energy	Cals	Fat	Sat fat	Carb	Sugar	Protein	Fibre
616 kJ	147 kcal	8.1 g	4.2 g	15.8 g	15.8 g	3.5 g	0.0 g

Using whole milk and single cream.

Variation

Coffee ice cream: add coffee essence, to taste, to the custard after it is cooked.

Chocolate ice cream: add 50–100 g of chopped couverture to the milk before boiling.

Strawberry ice cream: add 125 ml of strawberry pulp in place of 125 ml of milk. The pulp is added after the custard is cooked.

Rum and raisin ice cream: soak 50 g raisins in 2 tbsp rum for 3–4 hours. Add to mixture before freezing.

1. Whisk boiling milk into the egg yolks and sugar
2. Return the mixture to the hot pan used for the milk 
3. Test the consistency on the back of a spoon

Cold and hot desserts | **16**

4 Pass through a fine strainer into a cold pot

5 The mixture will cool down; if it was left in the hot pan it would continue to cook

6 Gradually add cream to the mixture in the ice cream machine

20 Lemon curd ice cream

Ingredient	6–8 portions
Lemon curd	250 g
Crème fraîche	125 g
Greek yoghurt	250 g

Energy	Cals	Fat	Sat fat	Carb	Sugar	Protein	Fibre
774 kJ	185 kcal	8.9g	5.2g	24.8g	16.7g	2.8g	0.0g

1 Mix all ingredients together.
2 Churn in the ice cream machine.

597

Practical Cookery 14th edition

21 Peach Melba

1. Poach the peaches. Allow to cool, then peel, halve and remove the stones.
2. Dress the fruit on a ball of the ice cream in an ice cream coupe or in a tuile basket.
3. Finish with the sauce.

The traditional presentation is to coat the peach in Melba sauce or coulis and decorate with whipped cream.

Professional tip
If using fresh peaches, dip them in boiling water for a few seconds, cool them by placing into cold water, then peel and halve.

Variation
Fruit Melba can also be made using pear or banana instead of peach. Fresh pears should be peeled, halved and poached. Bananas should be peeled at the last moment.

Ingredient	4 portions	10 portions
Peaches	2	5
Vanilla ice cream	125 ml	300 ml
Raspberry coulis	125 ml	300 ml

Energy	Cals	Fat	Sat fat	Carb	Sugar	Protein	Fibre
607 kJ	145 kcal	2.6g	1.3g	30.5g	30.2g	1.6g	1.3g

22 Pear belle Hélène

Traditional presentation
1. Serve a poached pear on a ball of vanilla ice cream in a coupe.
2. Decorate with whipped cream. Serve with a sauceboat of hot chocolate sauce.

Modern presentation
1. Coat a poached pear with chocolate sauce.
2. Dress on a plate with vanilla ice cream, more sauce and a tuile.

Energy	Cals	Fat	Sat fat	Carb	Sugar	Protein	Fibre	Sodium
1,888 kJ	453 kcal	29.7g	18.2g	44.5g	43.6g	4.5g	5.3g	0.0g

23 Raspberry parfait

Ingredient	6–8 portions
Italian meringue	
Caster sugar	150 g
Glucose	20 g
Water	80 ml
Egg whites	200 g
Additional ingredients	
Egg yolks, pasteurised	80 g
Caster sugar	60 g
Gelatine, soaked	1½ leaves
Raspberry liqueur	10 ml
Lemon juice	10 ml
Raspberry purée	120 g
Whipped cream	150 ml
Sponge	

Energy	Cals	Fat	Sat fat	Carb	Sugar	Protein	Fibre
981 kJ	234 kcal	10.7 g	5.6 g	31.3 g	30.2 g	4.7 g	0.5 g

1. Make up the Italian meringue (see page 543).
2. Combine the egg yolks and caster sugar in a stainless steel bowl. Whisk over a bain-marie to make a sabayon.
3. Drain the gelatine and dissolve it in the liqueur and lemon juice.
4. Fold the gelatine mixture into the sabayon, then fold in the raspberry purée.
5. Fold in the Italian meringue, then fold in the whipped cream.
6. Place into prepared moulds lined with sponge and freeze.
7. Once set, remove from the moulds.
8. In this presentation, the parfait has been lined with sponge only on the base. It is served with a raspberry coulis and fresh and dried raspberry garnishes.

Practical Cookery 14th edition

Hot desserts

24 Apple charlotte

Ingredient	8 individual or 2 small charlotte moulds
Dessert apples (Cox's)	1 kg
Butter	30 g
Caster sugar	100 g
Lemon, zest of	1
Breadcrumbs	
Large, thin-sliced loaf of bread	1
Clarified butter	250 g

Energy	Cals	Fat	Sat fat	Carb	Sugar	Protein	Fibre
2,163 kJ	515 kcal	22.3 g	9.3 g	74.5 g	23.4 g	9.4 g	6.1 g

Using hard margarine instead of butter.

1. Peel, core and cut the apples into thick slices.
2. Melt the butter in a pan, add the sugar and finely grated lemon zest.
3. Add the apples and simmer until barely cooked, stir in some breadcrumbs to absorb any liquid.
4. Cut out circles of bread for the top and base of the moulds.
5. Cut the crusts and the rest of the bread into fingers 2–3 cm wide, depending on whether you are making individual or larger charlottes.
6. Butter the moulds, dip half the circles in the clarified butter and place them butter-side down in the base of each mould.
7. Next, dip the bread fingers and line them around the outside of the moulds, slightly overlapping.
8. Fill the centre with the apple filling, pressing in carefully.
9. Dip the rest of the circles in the butter and place on top, pressing firmly.
10. Bake at 230 °C for 30–40 minutes until the bread is coloured and crisp.
11. Allow to cool slightly before unmoulding; serve with hot apricot sauce or crème anglaise.

Professional tip

As this dessert will most likely be plated and sent from the kitchen, it will more often than not be made in individual portions. Larger versions (such as that in the photograph) would be suitable for family or silver service, but could not be cut and made to look presentable if served from the kitchen.

Variation

Replace the apples with pears, or use a mixture of both.

Cold and hot desserts | 16

Faults

A common fault is that the charlotte collapses when unmoulded (the larger versions are more prone to this). The main reasons for this are:

- The filling is too wet. To avoid this, ensure that cooking apples are never used, and do not overcook.
- The bread is not baked crisp enough to withstand the pressure of supporting the filling.

If making individual charlottes, make sure that the ratio of bread to filling is not compromised by using bread that is cut too thick or overlapping too much.

25 Apple fritters (*beignets aux pommes*)

Mixed fruit fritters

Ingredient	4 portions	10 portions
Cooking apples	400 g	1 kg
Flour, as needed		
Frying batter	150 g	375 g
Apricot sauce	125 ml	300 ml

Energy	Cals	Fat	Sat fat	Carb	Sugar	Protein	Fibre
1,034 kJ	246 kcal	10.2 g	1.9 g	38.9 g	25.0 g	2.1 g	3.0 g

Fried in peanut oil.

1. Peel and core the apples and cut into 0.5 cm rings.
2. Pass through flour, shake off the surplus.
3. Dip into the frying batter (see page 230).
4. Lift out with the fingers, into fairly hot deep fat: 185 °C.
5. Cook for about 5 minutes on each side.
6. Drain well on kitchen paper, dust with icing sugar and glaze under the salamander.

Serve with hot apricot sauce.

601

26 Pancakes with apple

Ingredient	4 portions	10 portions
Cooked apple, thinly sliced	150 g	375 g
Flour, white or wholemeal	100 g	250 g
Salt	pinch	large pinch
Egg	1	2–3
Milk, whole, semi-skimmed or skimmed	250 ml	625 ml
Melted butter, margarine or oil	10 g	25 g
Oil for frying		
Caster sugar to serve		

1 Place a little cooked apple in a pan, add the pancake mixture and cook on both sides.
2 Turn out, sprinkle with caster sugar and roll up.

Energy	Cals	Fat	Sat fat	Carb	Sugar	Protein	Fibre
1,178 kJ	280 kcal	8.2 g	2.9 g	47.7 g	28.7 g	6.6 g	2.8 g

27 Baked apples (*pommes bonne femme*)

Ingredient	4 portions	10 portions
Medium-sized cooking apples	4	10
Sugar, white or unrefined	50 g	125 g
Cloves	4	10
Butter	20 g	50 g
Water	60 ml	150 ml

Energy	Cals	Fat	Sat fat	Carb	Sugar	Protein	Fibre
663 kJ	156 kcal	5.1 g	2.2 g	29.7 g	29.5 g	0.4 g	2.7 g

Using hard margarine.

> **Professional tip**
>
> To protect the peeled apple, wrap it in lightly oiled greaseproof or silicone paper before putting it in the oven.
>
> Cooking apples requires careful temperature control: some varieties will turn into purée very quickly. Check carefully at the end of step 5: some apples, baked without the skin, may be fully cooked by this point, in which case, skip steps 6 and 7.

1 Core the apples and make a 2 mm-deep incision round the centre of each. Wash well. Peel the apples for a modern presentation.
2 Place in a roasting tray or ovenproof dish.
3 Fill the centre with sugar and add a clove to each.
4 Place 5 g butter on each apple. Add the water.
5 Bake in a hot oven, at 200–220 °C, for 15–20 minutes.
6 Turn the apples over carefully.
7 Return to the oven until cooked, about 40 minutes in all.
8 Serve with a little cooking liquor and custard, cream or ice cream.

Variation
- Traditional baked apples are cooked with the skin on.
- For stuffed baked apples, fill the centre of each apple with washed sultanas, raisins or chopped dates, or a combination of these.

28 Griottines clafoutis

Ingredient	4 portions	10 portions
Eggs	2	5
Caster sugar	40 g	100 g
Flour	40 g	100 g
Milk	175 ml	440 ml
Kirsch	1 tsp	1 tbsp
Griottine cherries	28	70
Neige décor to dust		

Energy	Cals	Fat	Sat fat	Carb	Sugar	Protein	Fibre
790 kJ	187 kcal	4.3 g	1.5 g	28.8 g	21.4 g	6.7 g	1.3 g

This dish originates from the Limousin region of France and is traditionally made with black cherries.

1 Whisk the eggs and sugar together.
2 Add the flour and whisk until smooth.
3 Add the milk and kirsch; mix well and pass through a conical strainer.
4 Brush four (or ten) sur le plat dishes with soft butter.
5 Add seven cherries to each dish and pour over the batter.
6 Bake at 200 °C for 12–15 minutes until the batter has risen and set.
7 Serve warm, dusted with neige décor or icing sugar, and a kirsch sabayon.

Variation

- Griottines work particularly well in this dish but could be substituted for any other hard or fleshy fruit.
- Substitute 25 per cent of the flour with ground almonds or hazelnuts.
- To make a richer mixture, substitute up to half the milk with cream.

Professional tip

- Good-quality clafoutis should be golden brown and will rise around the edges but stay flatter in the centre. Check to make sure they are set; if not, bake for a little longer.
- Like most batters, this one benefits from resting before cooking and can be made the day before.
- Clafoutis can also be made in Yorkshire pudding tins and served unmoulded.

Practical Cookery 14th edition

29 Baked rice pudding (*pouding de riz*)

Ingredient	4 portions	10 portions
Rice, short or whole grain	50 g	125 g
Sugar, caster or unrefined	50 g	125 g
Milk (whole, semi-skimmed or skimmed)	0.5 litres	1.25 litres
Butter or margarine	10 g	25 g
Vanilla essence	2–3 drops	6–8 drops
Grated nutmeg		

Energy	Cals	Fat	Sat fat	Carb	Sugar	Protein	Fibre
1,006 kJ	239 kcal	7.0 g	3.9 g	40.7 g	19.0 g	5.8 g	0.6 g

Using whole milk and hard margarine.

1. Wash the rice and place it in a pie dish or individual dishes.
2. Add the sugar and milk, and mix well.
3. Add the butter, vanilla essence and nutmeg.
4. Place on a baking sheet; clean the rim of the pie dish.
5. Bake at 180–200 °C, until the milk starts simmering.
6. Reduce the heat and allow the pudding to cook slowly, allowing 1½–2 hours in all (less time for individual dishes).

The pudding may be garnished with nuts, as shown.

30 Sticky toffee pudding

Ingredient	10 puddings
Dates	375 g
Water	625 ml
Butter	125 g
Caster sugar	375 g
Eggs	5
Soft flour	375 g
Baking powder	10 g
Vanilla compound	1 tsp

Energy	Cals	Fat	Sat fat	Carb	Sugar	Protein	Fibre
4,104 kJ	980 kcal	60.4 g	36.7 g	106.7 g	78.9 g	9.1 g	1.8 g

1. Remove stones and chop the dates, place in the water and simmer for about 5 minutes until soft, set aside to cool.
2. Butter and sugar individual dariole moulds.
3. Cream the butter and sugar until light in colour and aerated.
4. Gradually add the beaten eggs, beating continuously.
5. Sieve the flour and baking powder twice and fold in.
6. Finally add the dates and water and vanilla compound.
7. Fill the moulds three-quarters full and bake at 180°C for 30–35 minutes.

> **Professional tip**
>
> Sticky toffee pudding can be steamed instead of baked. If steaming, remember to cover with a disc of silicone paper and seal with a pleated square of foil, as for steamed puddings (recipe 38).

Sticky toffee sauce

Granulated sugar	600 g
Unsalted butter	300 g
Double cream	450 g
Brandy	30 ml

1. Make a dry caramel by carefully melting the sugar until a deep golden colour is achieved.
2. Cut the butter into small cubes, add to the cream and heat.
3. Gradually add the hot cream and butter to the caramel a little at a time.
4. Finally stir in the brandy.

To serve, coat the pudding with the sauce and serve with vanilla or milk ice cream.

31 Cabinet pudding

Ingredient	4 portions	10 portions
Plain sponge cake	100 g	250 g
Zest of unwaxed lemons, grated		
Currants and sultanas	25 g	60 g
Milk, whole or skimmed	0.5 litres	1.25 litres
Eggs	3–4	8–10
Caster or unrefined sugar	50 g	125 g
Vanilla essence or a vanilla pod	2–3 drops (1 pod)	7 drops (2 pods)

Energy	Cals	Fat	Sat fat	Carb	Sugar	Protein	Fibre
1,512 kJ	360 kcal	17.3 g	7.7 g	40.9 g	35.5 g	12.7 g	0.7 g

Using whole milk and 4 eggs.

1. Cut the cake into 0.5 cm dice.
2. Mix with the lemon zest and fruits (which can be soaked in rum).
3. Place in a greased, sugared charlotte mould or 4 dariole moulds. Do not fill more than halfway.
4. Warm the milk and whisk on to the eggs, sugar and essence (or vanilla pod).
5. Strain on to the mould.
6. Place in a roasting tin, half full of water; allow to stand for 5–10 minutes.
7. Cook in a moderate oven at 150–160°C for 30–45 minutes.
8. Leave to set for a few minutes before turning out.

Serve a fresh egg custard (page 620) or hot apricot sauce separately.

> **Variation**
>
> Diplomat pudding is made as for cabinet pudding, but served cold with either redcurrant, raspberry, apricot or vanilla sauce.

Practical Cookery 14th edition

32 Soufflé pudding

1. Boil the milk in a sauteuse.
2. Combine the flour, butter and sugar.
3. Whisk into the milk and reboil.
4. Remove from heat, add the egg yolks one at a time, whisking continuously.
5. Stiffly beat the whites and carefully fold into the mixture.
6. Three-quarters fill buttered and sugared dariole moulds.
7. Place in a roasting tin, half full of water.
8. Bring to the boil and place in a hot oven at 230–250 °C for 12–15 minutes.
9. Turn out on to a flat dish.

Serve with a suitable hot sauce, such as custard or sabayon sauce.

Ingredient	5 portions	10 portions
Milk, whole or skimmed	185 ml	375 ml
Flour, white or wholemeal	25 g	50 g
Butter or margarine	25 g	50 g
Caster or unrefined sugar	25 g	50 g
Eggs, separated	3	6

Variation

Orange or lemon soufflé pudding is made by flavouring the basic mixture with the grated zest of an orange or lemon and a little appropriate sauce. Use the juice in the accompanying sauce.

Energy	Cals	Fat	Sat fat	Carb	Sugar	Protein	Fibre
510 kJ	122 kcal	7.6 g	3.2 g	5.9 g	4.8 g	0.2 g	0.0 g

Using white flour and hard margarine.

33 Chocolate fondant

Ingredient	10 portions
Unsalted butter	260 g
Dark couverture	260 g
Eggs, pasteurised	120 g
Egg yolks, pasteurised	40 g
Caster sugar	150 g
Instant coffee	5 g
Plain flour	110 g
Baking powder	5 g
Cocoa powder	75 g
Salt	Pinch

Energy	Cals	Fat	Sat fat	Carb	Sugar	Protein	Fibre
2,830 kJ	675 kcal	46.8 g	29.6 g	55.9 g	40.9 g	11.0 g	0.6 g

Cold and hot desserts

1. Melt the butter and couverture together.
2. Warm the eggs, egg yolks, sugar and coffee and whisk to the ribbon stage.
3. Sieve all the dry ingredients twice.
4. Fold the chocolate and butter into the eggs.
5. Fold in the dry ingredients.
6. Pipe into individual stainless steel rings lined with silicone paper and placed on a silicone paper-lined baking sheet.
7. Bake at 190 °C for 5 minutes.
8. Carefully slide off the rings and serve with vanilla ice cream.

1 Melt the chocolate and butter in small pieces.

2 Fold the melted chocolate into the egg mixture.

3 Add the dry ingredients.

4 To make a contrasting centre, add white chocolate pieces on a base of the chocolate mixture.

5 Pipe in more of the chocolate mixture until the mould is full.

Professional tip

These fondants can be kept in the refrigerator and cooked to order. If they are chilled, then extend the cooking time by 2 minutes.

Chocolate fondant should have a liquid centre with a rich, buttery, chocolate taste. Because of the liquid centre, they are very delicate; if piped inside a ring they are much easier and quicker to serve, rather than trying to turn them out of a mould.

Precise timing is essential or the centre of the fondant will not be liquid.

Like most recipes, the quality of the finished product relies on the quality of the ingredients. Always use good-quality chocolate (couverture) which contains a high percentage of cocoa butter and solids.

Variation

Try adding salted caramel to the centre by making and freezing it in ice cube trays.

Serve with malt ice cream (just add malt powder instead of vanilla and mix in some crushed chocolates) or replace the cream with crème fraiche to give a less rich ice cream.

Prepare fondants in moulds lined with melted butter and roasted sesame seeds.

34 Rice pudding

Ingredient	10 portions
Milk	650 ml
Vanilla pod	1
Short grain rice	60 g
Liaison	
Pasteurised egg	60 g
Caster sugar	60 g
Butter (diced)	30 g

Energy	Cals	Fat	Sat fat	Carb	Sugar	Protein	Fibre	Sodium
455 kJ	108 kcal	4.5 g	2.5 g	14.5 g	9.4 g	3.5 g	0.1 g	0.1 g

1. Rinse a heavy pan with cold water and add the milk.
2. Split the vanilla pod, scrape out the seeds and add along with the pod.
3. Slowly bring to the boil.
4. Wash the rice and sprinkle into the boiling milk, stir, cover with a lid and allow to simmer until the rice is tender.
5. In a bowl whisk the eggs and sugar and drop in the butter.
6. Ladle a quarter of the boiling milk and rice on to the liaison, mix well and return all to the pan, carefully cook out until the mixture thickens, before removing from the heat (it must not be allowed to boil).
7. Place into suitable individual or large (usually china) dishes.
8. Grate with nutmeg and glaze under the salamander.

Serve with a warm seasonal fruit compote.

Variation

Place some good-quality jam in the base of the dish.

Place in a serving dish before piping meringue on top and baking in a hot oven until coloured.

Leftover rice pudding can be used as an alternative to crème pâtissière or frangipane as a filling for a baked flan.

Food safety

As this recipe requires some ingredients that are not boiled, ensure all work surfaces and equipment are kept scrupulously clean.

It is recommended that pasteurised eggs are used.

Rice pudding can be held over service at a temperature of no less than 75 °C for 2 hours.

Any leftover rice pudding must be cooled to below 5 °C within 20 minutes, labelled and stored in a refrigerator.

Professional tip

Rinsing out the saucepan with cold water and adding the milk to the wet pan will help prevent the milk from catching on the bottom.

35 Bread and butter pudding

Ingredient	10 portions
Washed sultanas	100 g
Thin slices of white bread	Approximately 5
Butter, melted	200 g
Custard	
Vanilla pod	1
Milk	300 ml
Cream	300 ml
Eggs	5
Caster sugar	100 g
Nutmeg	
To finish	
Apricot jam	100 g

Energy	Cals	Fat	Sat fat	Carb	Sugar	Protein	Fibre	Sodium
1463 kJ	350 kcal	23.0 g	14.4 g	34.0 g	27.0 g	3.7 g	0.3 g	0.4 g

1. Butter an earthenware or other suitable dish and sprinkle with some of the sultanas.
2. Cut the crusts off the bread, dip in melted butter on both sides and cut in half diagonally.
3. Arrange overlapping bread slices neatly in the dish.
4. Sprinkle with more sultanas and cover with another layer of bread.
5. To make the custard, split the vanilla pod, add to the milk and cream and slowly bring to the boil.
6. Whisk the eggs and sugar together and add the boiling liquid, leave to infuse for 5 minutes before passing through a conical strainer.
7. Pour the custard over the bread and grate on some fresh nutmeg.
8. Place in a bain-marie and place in a moderate oven at 160 °C, pour hot water into the bain-marie until it comes half way up the dish.
9. Bake for around 45 minutes until the custard is just set.
10. Once removed from the oven sprinkle with sugar and place under the salamander to crisp up and colour the top.
11. Finally, brush with boiled apricot glaze and serve with pouring cream or crème fraiche.

Professional tip
Add the custard in two or three lots, allowing it to soak in before adding the next. This will prevent the bread floating to the top.

Variation
This pudding can be made in individual dishes or baked in a tray and cut and plated.

Try using alternatives to bread such as fruit loaf, brioche, baguette slices or panettone.

Soak the sultanas in rum the day before.

Try adding a layer of caramelised apple slices.

A chocolate version can be made by adding couverture (good-quality chocolate) to the custard.

Healthy eating tips
- Reduce the sugar content and add more dried fruit, apricots or cranberries.
- Try using milk only, semi-skimmed or skimmed.
- Dip the bread in the butter on just one side to reduce the fat content.

36 Apple crumble tartlets

Ingredient	10 tarts
Sweet paste	500 g
Dessert apples	5
Filling	
Soured cream	500 ml
Caster sugar	70 g
Plain flour	75 g
Egg	1
Vanilla extract	
Crumble	
Plain flour	80 g
Walnuts, chopped	60 g
Brown sugar	65 g
Ground cinnamon	Pinch
Salt	Pinch
Unsalted butter, melted	65 g
Icing sugar, to decorate	

Energy	Cals	Fat	Sat fat	Carb	Sugar	Protein	Fibre	Sodium
2200 kJ	541 kcal	36.0g	19.3g	51.0g	20.0g	7.3g	2.6g	0.3g

1 Line individual tartlet moulds with the sweet paste.
2 Peel, core and finely slice the apples and divide between the tartlets.
3 Whisk together the soured cream, sugar, flour, egg and a few drops of vanilla, and pass through a conical strainer.
4 Pour over the apples and bake at 190 °C for 10 minutes.
5 Combine the dry crumble ingredients and mix with the melted butter.
6 Divide the crumble mixture between the tartlets and bake for a further 10 minutes.
7 Allow to cool slightly before unmoulding. Dust with icing sugar and serve with *sauce à l'anglaise*.

Variation

This dish could be made with pears or plums instead of apples.

Cold and hot desserts | **16**

37 Tarte tatin

Ingredient	10 portions
Granulated sugar	500 g
Soft butter	120 g
Caster sugar	120 g
Dessert apples	5
Caramel, crushed	120 g
Puff paste	150 g

Energy	Cals	Fat	Sat fat	Carb	Sugar	Protein	Fibre	Sodium
1946 kJ	462 kcal	15.2 g	7.2 g	85.2 g	79.9 g	1.0 g	1.3 g	0.2 g

Note

This is the name given to an apple tart that is cooked under a lid of pastry, but then served with the pastry underneath the fruit. This is a delicious dessert in which the taste of caramel is combined with the flavour of the fruit and finished with a crisp pastry base. It was the creation of the Tatin sisters, who ran a hotel-restaurant in Lamotte-Beuvron at the beginning of the last century. Having been made famous by the Tatin sisters the dish was first served at Maxim's in Paris as a house speciality. It is still served there to this day.

1. Make a dry caramel by placing the granulated sugar in a hot heavy-based saucepan. When the sugar reaches a deep amber colour, pour it out onto a silicone mat and leave to cool completely.
2. When cold, crush the caramel into small pieces.
3. Take a medium-sized sauteuse and spread the butter thickly around the base and sides. Sprinkle over the caster sugar and then sprinkle over the caramel. (Any spare caramel can be stored in an airtight container for later use.)
4. Peel, core and halve the apples (if large, cut into quarters) and pack into the sauteuse core-side up and with the cores running horizontally, not facing outside.
5. Roll out the pastry 2 mm thick and leave to rest.
6. Place the pan on a medium heat for 10–12 minutes to allow the caramel to melt and infuse.
7. Quickly lay over the pastry and trim, tucking the edges down the side of the pan.
8. Bake at 220 °C for 15 minutes until the pastry is crisp and the apples cooked through.
9. Invert onto a hot plate – please be aware this procedure can be tricky and requires two dry cloths and very careful handling.
10. Serve with cream, crème fraiche or ice cream.

38 Steamed sponge pudding

Ingredient	10 individual puddings
Butter	250 g
Caster sugar	250 g
Self-raising flour	250 g
Baking powder	15 g
Eggs	6
Milk	20–40 g

Energy	Cals	Fat	Sat fat	Carb	Sugar	Protein	Fibre	Sodium
1755 kJ	418 kcal	24.0 g	14.1 g	46.0 g	27.0 g	6.3 g	0.9 g	0.6 g

1. Cream the butter and sugar until lighter in colour and an increase in volume of approximately 30 per cent is achieved.
2. Sieve the flour and baking powder twice to ensure even dispersion.
3. Beat the eggs and gradually add to the butter and sugar, beating in each addition before adding the next.
4. Finally, fold in the dry ingredients.
5. Add enough milk to achieve a dropping consistency.
6. Fill buttered dariole moulds three-quarters full.
7. Place a disc of silicone paper on top and cover with foil; create a pleat to allow for expansion and crimp the edges around the lip of the mould to seal.
8. Steam for 45–50 minutes.

Flavours for sponge puddings

- **Vanilla**: scrape the seeds from a vanilla pod into the mixture at the creaming stage. Use the pod to flavour the accompanying crème anglaise.
- **Chocolate**: replace 50 g of the flour in the basic recipe with an equal amount of cocoa powder, and add 150 g ground almonds, a pinch of sea salt, a splash of coffee essence and two more eggs. Add extra butter to the base of the mould and cover with muscovado sugar before filling. Serve with hot chocolate sauce.
- **Lemon or orange**: add the grated zest of a large lemon or an orange to the mixture at the creaming stage. Serve with lemon or orange sauce as appropriate.
- **Sultana**: add 100 g of washed sultanas and a few drops of vanilla compound. Serve with crème anglaise. The sultanas may be replaced by any dried fruit.
- **Ginger**: add 10 g of ground ginger (sieved in with the dry ingredients) and 50 g of finely diced stem ginger folded in at the end. Serve with crème anglaise.
- **Golden syrup**: after buttering the mould pour a generous layer of warmed golden syrup into the base before adding the sponge mixture. Serve with crème anglaise sweetened with golden syrup.
- **Chocolate and fig/date**: add six diced figs or dates to the chocolate recipe above.

Note

A good-quality steamed sponge pudding will be light, moist and slightly spongy in texture. As steaming at 100 °C imparts no colour, it should be as light in colour as the ingredients allow.

39 Golden syrup pudding

Ingredient	5 portions	12 portions
Flour	150 g	300 g
Salt	pinch	large pinch
Baking powder	10 g	20 g
Suet, chopped	75 g	150 g
Caster or unrefined sugar	50 g	100 g
Lemon, zest of	1	2
Egg, beaten	1	2
Milk, whole or skimmed	125 ml	250 ml
Golden syrup	125 ml	250 ml

Energy	Cals	Fat	Sat fat	Carb	Sugar	Protein	Fibre
1315 kJ	313 kcal	13.0 g	5.9 g	47.8 g	26.6 g	4.3 g	0.9 g

1. Sieve the flour, salt and baking powder (or replace the flour and baking powder with self-raising flour) into a bowl.
2. Mix the suet, sugar and zest.
3. Add the beaten egg and milk and mix to a medium dough.
4. Pour the syrup in a well-greased basin or individual moulds (1 hour cooking time). Place the pudding mixture on top.
5. Cover securely; steam for 1½–2 hours.

Serve with a sauceboat of warm syrup containing the lemon juice, or with sauce anglaise or ice cream.

Variation

To make a treacle pudding, use a light treacle in place of the golden syrup. Vegetarian suet is available.

40 Christmas pudding

Ingredient	2 × 1 kg puddings
Currants	175 g
Sultanas	175 g
Raisins	350 g
Guinness	500 ml
Cognac	50 ml
Strong flour	175 g
Mixed spice	4 g
Nutmeg	4 g
Cinnamon	4 g
Breadcrumbs	175 g
Suet	350 g
Mixed peel	80 g
Ground almonds	80 g
Eggs	4
Soft dark brown sugar	175 g
Salt	3 g
Lemon, juice and zest of	1

Energy	Cals	Fat	Sat fat	Carb	Sugar	Protein	Fibre	Sodium
2077 kJ	495 kcal	23.9g	11.6g	64.9g	45.8g	6.3g	3.6g	0.2g

For 1/8 of a pudding.

1 Place all the dried fruit in a bowl, pour over the Guinness and cognac and leave to soak overnight.
2 Sieve the flour with the mixed spice, grate over the nutmeg and cinnamon and place in a large bowl.
3 Add the breadcrumbs, suet, peel and ground almonds and mix well.
4 Make a well in the centre.
5 Whisk the eggs, sugar and salt, add the lemon juice and zest.
6 Pour the wet ingredients into the well and add the soaked fruit.
7 Mix well.
8 Place mixture into two buttered pudding basins, cover with a disc of silicone paper and seal with foil, crimping around the edges.
9 Steam for 7 hours, cool and store in the fridge.
10 Reheat in the steamer for a couple of hours. Serve with brandy or rum sauce and/or brandy butter.

Professional tip

Like a Christmas fruit cake, Christmas pudding is best made in September and allowed to mature.

Cold and hot desserts — 16

41 Baked Alaska

1. Sit the ice cream or parfait on a base of sponge.
2. Cut more sponge to fit and completely cover.
3. Brush all over with the syrup.
4. Set on squares of silicone paper, coat with the meringue and decorate by piping on a design with a small plain tube.
5. Dust with icing sugar and place in a very hot oven at 230 °C for 2–3 minutes until the meringue is coloured.

Serve immediately with crème anglaise or a fruit coulis.

Ingredient	10 portions
Vanilla ice cream or parfait	10 × 5 cm diameter rings (500 g approx.)
Roulade sponge (see page 558)	1 sheet
Stock syrup flavoured with rum or kirsch	50 ml
Italian meringue	500 g

Energy	Cals	Fat	Sat fat	Carb	Sugar	Protein	Fibre
290 kJ	521 kcal	16.4 g	7.3 g	91.3 g	81.2 g	7.7 g	0.6 g

Variation

Classic variations are omelette soufflé milady, which contains poached sliced peaches with vanilla or raspberry ice cream, and omelette soufflé milord, which contains poached sliced pear with vanilla ice cream.

Professional tip

Baked Alaska is best made in advance and held in the freezer, then flashed through the oven just before serving. It is now common practice to colour the meringue with a blowtorch, but the meringue will have a much better texture and more even colouring if it is finished in the oven.

If making individual baked Alaskas, as in the photographs, take care not to upset the balance between filling and meringue – when scaled down it is easy to pipe on too much meringue.

Food safety

Under no circumstances should this dessert be re-frozen once it has been removed from the freezer and baked. Ice cream is highly susceptible to contamination by bacteria, which can cause food poisoning.

Brush the sponge with syrup

Pipe meringue to cover

Pipe swirls of meringue to decorate

615

42 Vanilla soufflé

Ingredient	10 individual soufflés
Base mixture	
Milk	500 ml
Vanilla pods	2
Butter	75 g
Strong flour	60 g
Egg yolks	10
Caster sugar	50 g
Additional ingredients for every 400 g of base mixture	
Egg whites	150 g
Caster sugar	60 g
Cornflour	12 g
Lemon juice	2–3 drops

Energy	Cals	Fat	Sat fat	Carb	Sugar	Protein	Fibre
932 kJ	223 kcal	13.7 g	6.7 g	19.5 g	13.9 g	6.6 g	0.2 g

1. Rinse a heavy saucepan with cold water and add the milk. Split the vanilla pod, scrape out the seeds, and add both to the milk. Put on the heat to boil.
2. Melt the butter in another heavy pan. Add the flour and cook out to form a white roux. Gradually add the boiling milk, mixing in each addition before adding the next.
3. When all the milk has been added, allow to simmer for a few minutes.
4. Whisk the egg yolks and sugar. Add to the mixture in the saucepan and keep stirring over the heat until the mixture starts to bubble around the edges. This forms the panada.
5. Pour on to a clean tray and cover with cling film to prevent a skin forming. Allow to cool. (This can be kept in the fridge until needed, as soufflés must be cooked to order.)
6. Take 400 g of the base and beat in a clean bowl until smooth.
7. Whisk the egg whites, sugar, cornflour and lemon juice to form firm peaks.
8. Add one-third of the whites to the base and mix in, then very carefully fold in the remaining whites.
9. Carefully fill prepared individual china ramekins (see below). Level the top and run your thumb around the edge, moving the mixture away from the lip of the mould.
10. Space well apart on a solid baking sheet (if they are close together they will not rise evenly and will bake stuck together).
11. Place immediately in the oven at 215 °C for 12–14 minutes.
12. The soufflés should rise out of the moulds by around 5–6 cm and have a flat top with no cracks.
13. Dust with icing sugar and serve immediately with fruit coulis and/or ice cream (chocolate or vanilla).

Preparing a soufflé mould

Mould preparation is very important. The rule is to butter the sides twice and the bottom once. Always use soft, not melted, butter, so that it stays where you put it. Give the moulds one coat all over to start with, then place in the fridge to set before giving a second coat only to the sides. (Giving the base two coats results in a puddle of butter in the bottom.)

After giving the sides a second coat of butter, the mould is usually coated with sugar.

Cold and hot desserts 16

Prepare the mould

Knock one-third of the meringue into the panada

Fold in the remaining meringue

Thumb the edge

Faults

Soufflé does not rise:
- under- or over-beaten whites
- wrong proportion of whites to base
- mixture left to stand before cooking
- moulds not buttered correctly.

Soufflé rises but drops back:
- too much egg white used.

Soufflé does not rise evenly:
- moulds not prepared correctly (mixture has stuck to the mould on one side)
- uneven heat in the oven.

Soufflé has a cracked top:
- too much egg white used
- egg white is overbeaten.

Professional tips

- Be organised with your timings. Make sure you have the moulds fully prepared and that the oven is up to heat well before the egg whites are whisked.
- Before whisking the egg whites, scald the bowl to remove any trace of fat.
- When the egg whites are whisked with the sugar, lemon juice and cornflour, they should be firm but creamy. Over-whisking will ruin them.
- The recipe uses more egg white than is needed – always take from the centre and leave behind the egg white on the edge of the bowl, which is never good.
- A soufflé should have flavour as well as an impressive 'rise'. Too much egg white can dilute the flavour.

Variation

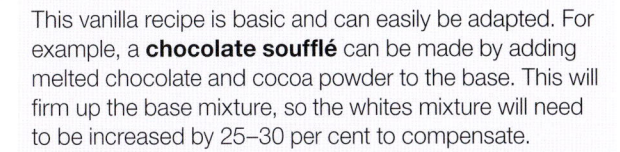

This vanilla recipe is basic and can easily be adapted. For example, a **chocolate soufflé** can be made by adding melted chocolate and cocoa powder to the base. This will firm up the base mixture, so the whites mixture will need to be increased by 25–30 per cent to compensate.

Soufflés can be made in many different flavours and combinations. Recipes can vary considerably. For example, **fruit soufflés** can be made using a sabayon or a boiled sugar base.

As an alternative to coating the moulds with sugar, if compatible, dust them with cocoa powder, grated chocolate or try adding some cinnamon to the sugar.

Practical Cookery 14th edition

43 Lemon curd flourless soufflé

To make the lemon curd:

1. Prepare by whisking all the ingredients over a pan of simmering water until the mixture thickens.
2. After preparing the soufflé moulds as described in recipe 42, divide the lemon curd mixture between them.

To make the soufflés:

1. Separate the eggs. Place together the yolks, sugar, lemon zest and juice, and whisk together well.
2. In a separate bowl, whisk the whites with the cream of tartar and egg-white powder until soft but in strong peaks.
3. Carefully fold the two mixtures together.
4. Fill the prepared moulds, level the top and run your thumb around the edge, moving the mixture away from the lip of the mould.
5. Place well apart on a heavy baking sheet and bake at 200 °C for 16–18 minutes.
6. Dust with icing sugar and serve immediately.

Note

As this dessert is gluten-free it would be suitable for coeliacs or those with a wheat intolerance.

Ingredient	10 individual soufflés
Lemon curd	
Eggs	2
Caster sugar	100 g
Lemons, juice of	5
Unsalted butter	60 g
Cornflour	15 g
Soufflés	
Eggs	9
Caster sugar	190 g
Lemons, zest and juice of	5
Cream of tartar	Pinch
Egg-white powder	Pinch

Energy	Cals	Fat	Sat fat	Carb	Sugar	Protein	Fibre
1,179 kJ	280 kcal	13.3 g	5.7 g	31.7 g	30.4 g	10.1 g	0.1 g

Sweet sauces

44 Sabayon sauce

Ingredient	8 portions (450–500 ml)
Egg yolks, pasteurised	6
Caster or unrefined sugar	100 g
Dry white wine	250 ml

1 Whisk the egg yolks and sugar in a 1-litre pan or basin until white.
2 Dilute with the wine.
3 Place the pan or basin in a bain-marie of boiling water.
4 Whisk the mixture continuously until it increases its bulk by four times and is firm and frothy.

Note
Sauce sabayon may be offered as an accompaniment to any suitable hot sweet (for example, soufflés or pudding soufflé).

Variation
A sauce sabayon may also be made using milk in place of wine, which can be flavoured according to taste (for example, with vanilla, nutmeg or cinnamon).

Energy	Cals	Fat	Sat fat	Carb	Sugar	Protein	Fibre
454 kJ	108 kcal	3.4 g	1.0 g	13.3 g	13.3 g	1.8 g	0.0 g

Using 5 egg yolks.

45 Fresh egg custard sauce (*sauce à l'anglaise*)

1. Mix the yolks, sugar and vanilla in a bowl.
2. Whisk in the boiled milk and return to a thick-bottomed pan.
3. Place on a low heat and stir with a wooden spoon until it coats the back of the spoon. Do not allow the mix to boil or the egg will scramble. A probe can be used to ensure the temperature does not go any higher than 85 °C.
4. Put through a fine sieve into a clean bowl. Set on ice to seize the cooking process and to chill rapidly.

Variation

Other flavours may be used in place of vanilla, for example:
- brandy
- cardamom seeds
- chocolate
- coffee or coffee liqueur
- kirsch
- orange flower water
- orange liqueur
- rum
- star anise
- whisky.

Ingredient	300 ml	700 ml
Egg yolks, pasteurised	40 ml	100 ml
Caster or unrefined sugar	25 g	60 g
Vanilla extract or vanilla pod (seeds)	2–3 drops/ ½ pod	5–7 drops/ 1 pod
Milk, whole or skimmed, boiled	250 ml	625 ml

Energy	Cals	Fat	Sat fat	Carb	Sugar	Protein	Fibre	Sodium
281 kJ	67 kcal	3.7 g	1.6 g	6.3 g	6.3 g	2.5 g	0.0 g	0.0 g

For 50 ml of sauce, using whole milk.

Cold and hot desserts | **16**

46 Custard sauce

Ingredient	Makes 250 ml
Custard powder	10 g
Milk, whole or semi-skimmed	250 ml
Caster or unrefined sugar	25 g

Energy	Cals	Fat	Sat fat	Carb	Sugar	Protein	Fibre
1,245 kJ	296 kcal	9.6g	6.0g	47.2g	38.0g	8.3g	0.3g

Using whole milk.

1 Dilute the custard powder with a little of the milk.
2 Boil the remainder of the milk.
3 Pour a little of the boiled milk on to the diluted custard powder.
4 Return to the saucepan.
5 Stir to the boil and mix in the sugar.

47 Fruit coulis

Ingredient	1.4 litres
Fruit purée	1 litre
Caster sugar	500 g
Lemon juice	10 g

1 Warm the purée.
2 Boil the sugar with a little water to soft-ball stage (121 °C).
3 Pour the soft-ball sugar into the warm fruit purée while whisking vigorously. Add the lemon juice. Bring back to the boil.
4 This will then be ready to store.

> **Professional tip**
>
> The reason the soft-ball stage needs to be achieved when the sugar is mixed with the purée is that this stabilises the fruit and prevents separation once the coulis is presented on the plate.
>
> Adding lemon juice brings out the flavour of the fruit.

621

48 Strawberry sauce

Ingredient	Makes 225 ml	Makes 600 ml
Strawberries (fresh or puréed)	200 g	500 g
Icing sugar	50 g	125 g
Lemon juice	10 ml	25 ml

Blend all the ingredients together (using a liquidiser if using fresh fruit) and strain through a fine sieve.

Variation

Alternative fruits or purées that can be used include: peach, apricot, mango, paw paw, blackberry and raspberry. For peach sauce, for example, proceed as above, substituting peach purée for the strawberries.

49 Chocolate sauce

Method 1

Ingredient	300 ml	750 ml
Double cream	150 ml	375 ml
Butter	25 g	60 g
Milk or plain couverture callets	180 g	420 g

Energy	Cals	Fat	Sat fat	Carb	Sugar	Protein	Fibre	Sodium
1287 kJ	310 kcal	26.0 g	16.0 g	17.5 g	17.5 g	2.7 g	0.2 g	0.1 g

For 50 ml of sauce, using milk chocolate.

1. Place the cream and butter in a saucepan and gently bring to a simmer.
2. Add the chocolate and stir well until the chocolate has melted and the sauce is smooth.

Cold and hot desserts 16

Method 2

Ingredient	300 ml	750 ml
Caster sugar	40 g	100 g
Water	120 ml	300 ml
Dark chocolate couverture (75 per cent cocoa solids)	160 g	400 g
Unsalted butter	25 g	65 g
Single cream	80 ml	200 ml

1 Dissolve the sugar in the water over a low heat.
2 Remove from the heat. Stir in the chocolate and butter.
3 When everything has melted, stir in the cream and gently bring to the boil.

Energy	Cals	Fat	Sat fat	Carb	Sugar	Protein	Fibre	Sodium
1012 kJ	244 kcal	18.7 g	11.5 g	13.9 g	13.0 g	2.9 g	2.6 g	0.0 g

For 50 ml of sauce.

50 Butterscotch sauce

Ingredient	300 ml	750 ml
Double cream	250 ml	625 ml
Butter	62 g	155 g
Demerara sugar	100 g	250 g

Energy	Cals	Fat	Sat fat	Carb	Sugar	Protein	Fibre	Sodium
1454 kJ	351 kcal	31.0 g	19.4 g	18.3 g	18.3 g	0.8 g	0.0 g	0.2 g

For 50 ml of sauce.

1 Boil the cream, then whisk in the butter and sugar.
2 Simmer for 3 minutes.

51 Caramel sauce

1. In a large saucepan, dissolve the sugar with the water over a low heating and bring to boiling point.
2. Wash down the inside of the pan with a pastry brush dipped in cold water to prevent crystals from forming.
3. Cook until the sugar turns to a deep amber colour. Immediately turn off the heat and whisk in the cream.
4. Set the pan back over a high heat and stir the sauce with the whisk. Let it bubble for 2 minutes, then turn off the heat.
5. You can now strain the sauce and use it when cooled, or, for a richer, smoother sauce, pour a little caramel on to the egg yolks, then return the mixture to the pan and heat to 80 °C, taking care that it does not boil.
6. Pass the sauce through a conical strainer and keep in a cool place, stirring occasionally to prevent a skin from forming.

Ingredient	750 ml
Caster sugar	100 g
Water	80 ml
Double cream	500 ml
Egg yolks, lightly beaten (optional)	2

Energy	Cals	Fat	Sat fat	Carb	Sugar	Protein	Fibre	Sodium
883 kJ	213 kcal	19.9 g	12.1 g	8.1 g	8.1 g	1.0 g	0.0 g	0.0 g

For 50 ml of sauce.

52 Rum or brandy cream or butter

To make rum/brandy cream, flavour whipped, sweetened cream with rum or brandy to taste.

To make rum/brandy butter, cream equal quantities of butter and sieved icing sugar together and add rum or brandy to taste.

Glossary

à la   In the style of

à la française   In the French style

à la minute   Cooked to order

à la carte   Dishes prepared to order and priced individually

Abatis de volaille   Poultry offal, giblets, etc.

Abats   Offal: heads, hearts, liver, kidney, etc.

Accompaniments   Items offered separately with a dish of food

Agar-agar   A vegetable gelling agent obtained from seaweed, used as a substitute for gelatine

Aile   A wing (of poultry or game birds)

Aloyau de boeuf   Sirloin of beef

Ambient   Room temperature, surrounding atmosphere

Amino acid   Organic acids found in proteins

Antibiotic   A drug used to destroy disease-producing germs within human or animal bodies

Antiseptic   A substance that prevents the growth of bacteria and moulds, specifically on or in the human body

Aromats   Fragrant herbs and spices

Arroser   To baste, for example during roasting

Ascorbic acid   Known as Vitamin C; found in citrus fruits and blackcurrants; necessary for growth and the maintenance of health

Aspic   A savoury jelly mainly used for decorative larder work

Assorti   An assortment

Au bleu   When applied to meat, this means very underdone

Au beurre   With butter

Au four   Baked in the oven

Au gratin   Sprinkled with cheese or breadcrumbs and then browned

Au vin blanc   With white wine

Bactericide   A substance that destroys bacteria

Bacterium (plural: bacteria)   Single-celled micro-organisms: some are harmful and cause food poisoning; others are useful, such as those used in cheese making

Bain-marie
- A container of water to keep foods hot without burning them
- A container of water for cooking foods without burning them
- A deep, narrow container for storing hot sauces, soups and gravies

Barding   Covering the breasts of birds with thin slices of bacon

Barquette   A boat-shaped pastry case

Basting   Spooning melted fat over food during cooking to keep it moist

Bat out   To flatten slices of raw meat with a cutlet bat

Bean curd   Also known as tofu (see below); a curdled, soft, cheese-like preparation made from soybean milk; a good source of protein

Beansprouts   Young shoots of dried beans, e.g. mung beans, alfalfa or soybeans

Beurre manié   Equal quantities of flour and butter used for thickening sauces

Blanc   A cooking liquor of water, lemon juice, flour and salt; also used to describe the white of chicken (breast and wings)

Blanch
- To make something white (referring to bones and meat)
- To cook but retain colour (referring to certain vegetables)
- To skin (referring to tomatoes)
- To make limp (referring to certain braised vegetables)
- To cook without colour, e.g. the first frying of fried potatoes (chips)

Blanquette   A white stew cooked in stock from which the sauce is made

Blitz   To rapidly purée or foam a light sauce, generally using an electric hand blender at the last moment before service

Bombay duck   Small, dried, salted fish; fried, it is used as an accompaniment to curry dishes

Bombe   An ice cream speciality of different flavours in a bomb shape

Bone out   To remove the bones

Botulism   A rare form of food poisoning

Bouchée   A small puff paste case, literally 'a mouthful'

Bouillon   Unclarified stock

Bouquet garni   A bundle of herbs (e.g. parsley stalks, thyme and bay leaf), tied in pieces of celery and leek

Brine   A preserving solution of water, salt, saltpetre and aromats, used for meats (e.g. silverside, brisket, tongue)

Brunoise   Small dice

Buttermilk   Liquid remaining from the churning of butter

Calcium   A mineral required for building bones and teeth, obtained from cheese and milk

Calorie   A unit of heat or energy, known as a kilocalorie

Canapé   Traditionally, a cushion of bread on which are served various foods, hot or cold; also used to describe small, attractive, well-flavoured dishes offered before a meal or at a drinks reception

Carbohydrate   A nutrient; there are three types of carbohydrate – sugar and starch, which provide the body with energy, and cellulose, which provides roughage (dietary fibre)

Carbon dioxide   A gas produced by all raising agents

Carbon footprint The amount of carbon emissions produced in the growing, processing, production and disposal of food

Carbon offsetting Planting trees to offset carbon dioxide

Carrier A person who harbours and may transmit pathogenic organisms without showing signs of illness

Carte du jour Menu for the day

Casserole An earthenware, fireproof dish with a lid

Cellulose The coarse structure of fruit, vegetables and cereals that is not digested but is used as roughage (dietary fibre)

Châteaubriand The head of the fillet of beef

Chaud-froid A demi-glace or creamed velouté with gelatine or aspic added, used for masking cold dishes

Chiffonade Fine shreds, e.g. of spinach, lettuce

Chinois A conical strainer

Chlorophyll The green colour in vegetables

Ciseler To make slight incisions in the surface of a thick fillet of fish, on or off the bone, to allow even cooking

Civet A brown stew of game, usually hare

Clarification/to clarify To make something clear, such as stock, jelly or butter

Clostridium perfringens Food-poisoning bacterium found in the soil, vegetables and meat

Coagulation The solidification of protein; it is irreversible; examples occur when frying an egg or cooking meat

Cocotte Porcelain or earthenware fireproof dish

Collagen/elastin Proteins in connective tissue (e.g. gristle)

Compote Stewed (e.g. stewed fruit)

Concassé Coarsely chopped (e.g. parsley, tomatoes)

Confit Meat, poultry or game gently cooked in flavoured fat or oil

Consommé A simple, clear soup

Contamination The occurrence of any objectionable matter in food

Contrefilet Boned-out sirloin of beef

Cook out The process of cooking flour in a roux, soup or sauce

Cordon A thread or thin line of sauce

Correcting Adjusting the seasoning, consistency and colour

Côte A rib or chop

Côtelette A cutlet

Coulis Sauce made of fruit or vegetable puree (e.g. raspberry, tomato)

Coupe An individual serving bowl

Couper To cut

Court bouillon A well-flavoured cooking liquor for fish

Crème fraiche A light cream soured with a culture

Crêpes Pancakes

Credit note Issued when an invoice contains incorrect details; credit is therefore given

Croquettes Cooked foods moulded into a cylinder shape, coated in flour and egg, crumbed and deep fried

Cross-contamination The transfer of micro-organisms from contaminated to uncontaminated hands, utensils or equipment

Croutons Cubes of fried or toasted bread served with soup; also triangular pieces served with spinach, and heart-shaped pieces with certain dishes

Crudités Small, neat pieces of raw vegetables served with a dip as an appetiser

Cuisse de poulet Chicken leg

Danger zone of bacterial growth The temperature range within which pathogenic bacteria are able to multiply; between 5 and 63 °C

Dariole A small mould, as used for crème caramel

Darne A slice of round fish (e.g. salmon) on the bone

Déglacer (to deglaze) To swill out a pan in which food has been roasted or fried, with wine, stock or water, in order to use the sediment for the accompanying sauce or gravy

Dégraisser To skim fat off liquid

Delivery note A form sent by a supplier with the delivery of goods

Demi-glace A brown stock reduced to a light consistency

Désosser To bone out meat

Detergent A substance that dissolves grease

Dilute To mix a powder (e.g. cornflour) with a liquid

Disinfectant A substance that destroys bacteria

Doily A fancy dish paper

Drain To place food in a colander, allowing liquid to seep out

Duxelle Finely chopped mushrooms cooked with chopped shallots

Eco footprint Measurement of our actions in the environment

Eggwash Beaten egg with a little milk or water

Emulsion A mixture of liquid (e.g. vinegar) and oil, which does not separate when left to stand (e.g. mayonnaise, hollandaise)

Entrecôte A steak cut from a boned sirloin

Enzymes Chemical substances produced from living cells

Escalope A thin slice such as escalope of veal

Farce Stuffing

Fecule Fine potato flour

Feuilletage Puff pastry

Fines herbes Chopped fresh herbs (e.g. parsley, tarragon, chervil)

First aid materials Suitable and sufficient bandages and dressings, including waterproof dressings and antiseptic; all dressings must be individually wrapped

Glossary

Fixed costs   Regular charges, such as labour and overheads, that do not vary according to the volume of business

Flake   To break something into natural segments (e.g. fish)

Flan   An open tart

Fleurons   Small, crescent-shaped pieces of puff pastry

Flute   A 20 cm diameter French bread used for soup garnishes

Food-borne   Bacteria carried on food

Food handling   Any operation in the storage, preparation, production, processing, packaging, transportation, distribution and sale of food

Food miles   The distance food travels from farm to plate

Frappé   Chilled (e.g. melon frappé)

Freezer burn   Affects frozen items, which are spoiled due to being left unprotected for too long

Friandises   Sweetmeats, petits fours

Fricassée   A white stew in which the meat, poultry or fish is cooked in the sauce

Friture   A pan that contains deep fat

Fumé   Smoked (e.g. *saumon fumé* is smoked salmon)

Garam masala   A combination of spices

Garnish   Served as part of the main item; trimmings

Gastroenteritis   Inflammation of the stomach and intestinal tract that normally results in diarrhoea

Gâteau   A cake of more than one portion

Ghee   The Indian name for clarified butter; ghee is pure butter fat

Gibier   Game

Glace   Ice or ice cream from which all milk solids have been removed

Glaze
- To colour a dish under the salamander (e.g. fillets of sole *bonne femme*)
- To finish a flan or tartlet (e.g. with apricot jam)
- To finish certain vegetables (e.g. glazed carrots)

Gluten   This is formed from the protein in flour when mixed with water

Gratin   A thin coating of grated cheese and/or breadcrumbs on certain dishes, which is then browned under the grill or in an oven

Gross profit   The difference between the cost of an item and the price at which it is sold

Haché   Finely chopped or minced

Hazard   Something that could cause injury, ill health or harm

Hors d'oeuvre   Appetising first course dishes, hot or cold

Humidity   The amount of moisture in the air

Incubation period   The time between infection and the first signs of illness

Infestations   Pests breeding on the premises

Insecticide   A chemical used to kill insects

Invoice   A bill listing items delivered, with the costs of the items

Jardinière   Cut into batons

Julienne   Cut into fine strips

Jus-lié   Thickened gravy

Larding   Inserting strips of fat bacon into meat

Lardons   Batons of thick streaky bacon

Liaison   A thickening or binding

Macédoine
- A mixture of fruit or vegetables
- Cut into 0.5 cm dice

Magnetron   A device that generates microwaves in a microwave oven

Marinade   A richly spiced pickling liquid used to give flavour and assist in tenderising meats

Marmite   A stock pot

Mascarpone   An Italian cheese resembling clotted cream

Menu   A list of the dishes available

Micro-organisms   Very small living plants or animals (bacteria, yeasts, moulds)

Mignonette   Coarsely ground pepper

Mildew   A type of fungus, similar to mould

Mineral salts   Mineral elements, small quantities of which are essential for health

Mirepoix   Roughly cut vegetables (e.g. onions, leeks, celery and carrots), often with a sprig of thyme and a bay leaf, used as flavouring elements

Mise-en-place   Basic preparation before serving

Miso   Seasoning made from fermented soybeans

Monosodium glutamate (MSG)   A substance added to food products to increase flavour

Moulds   Microscopic plants (fungi) that may appear as woolly patches on food

Mousse   A dish of light consistency, hot or cold

Napper   To coat or mask with sauce

Natives   A menu term for English oysters

Navarin   Brown stew of lamb

Net profit   The difference between the selling price of an item and the total cost of the product (this includes food, labour and overheads)

Niacin   Part of Vitamin B; found in liver, kidney, meat extract, bacon

Noisette (nut)   A cut from a boned-out loin of lamb

Nutrients   The components of food required for health: protein, fats, carbohydrates, vitamins, mineral salts, water

Optimum   Best, most favourable

Palatable   Pleasant to taste

Pané Floured, dipped in egg and crumbed

Panettone A very light, traditional Italian Christmas cake

Parsley butter Butter containing lemon juice and chopped parsley

Pass To put through a sieve or strainer

Pathogen A disease-producing organism

Paupiette A stuffed and rolled strip of fish or meat

Paysanne Cut in even, thin, triangular, round or square pieces

Persillé Finished with chopped parsley

Pesticide A chemical used to kill pests

Pests Unwanted creatures that may enter food premises, e.g. cockroaches, flies, silverfish

Petits fours Very small pastries, biscuits, sweets, sweetmeats

pH value A scale indicating the acidity or alkalinity in food

Phosphorus A mineral element found in fish; required for building bones and teeth

Piquant Sharply flavoured

Piqué Studded clove in an onion

Plat du jour Special dish of the day

Poppadoms Dried, thin, large, round wafers made from lentil flour, used as an accompaniment to Indian dishes

Printanier A garnish of spring vegetables

Protein The nutrient needed for growth and repair

Prove To allow a yeast dough to rest in a warm place so that it can expand

Pulses Vegetables grown in pods (peas and beans) and dried; a source of protein and roughage

Quark A salt-free soft cheese made from semi-skimmed milk

Ragout A stew, for example *ragout de boeuf* is brown beef stew

Rare When applied to meat, it means underdone

Réchauffer To reheat

Reduce To concentrate a liquid by boiling

Refresh To make cold under running cold water

Residual insecticide An insecticide that remains active for a considerable period of time

Riboflavin Vitamin B2; found in yeast, liver, eggs, cheese

Risk The likelihood that a hazard will cause injury, ill health or harm

Rissoler To fry to a golden brown

Rodents Rats and mice

Roux A thickening of cooked flour and fat

Sabayon Egg yolks and a little water or wine, cooked until creamy

Saccharometer An instrument for measuring the density of sugar

Salamander A type of grill, heated from above

Salmonella A food-poisoning bacterium found in meat and poultry

Sanitiser A chemical agent used for cleaning and disinfecting surfaces and equipment

Sauté
- Toss in fat (e.g. *pommes sautées*)
- Cook quickly in a sauté pan or frying pan
- A brown stew of a specific type (e.g. veal sauté)

Seal To place meat in a hot oven or pan to colour the surface and retain the juices

Seared Cooked quickly on both sides in a little hot fat or oil

Seasoned flour Flour seasoned with salt and pepper

Set
- To seal the outside surface
- To allow to become firm or firmer (e.g. jelly)

Shredded Cut in fine strips (e.g. lettuce, onion)

Silicone paper Non-stick paper (e.g. siliconised paper)

Singe To brown or colour

Smetana A low-fat product; a cross between soured cream and yoghurt

Sodium Mineral element in the form of salt (sodium chloride); found in cheese, bacon, fish, meat

Soufflé A very light dish, sweet or savoury, hot or cold

Soy sauce Made from soybeans; used extensively in Chinese cookery

Spores The resistant resting phase of bacteria, protecting them against adverse conditions such as high temperatures

Staphylococcus A food-poisoning bacterium found in the human nose and throat, and also in septic cuts

Starch A carbohydrate found in cereals, certain vegetables and farinaceous foods

Sterile Free from all living organisms

Sterilisation A process that destroys living organisms

Steriliser A chemical used to destroy all living organisms

Stock rotation The sequence of issuing goods, so that the first into store are the first to be issued

Strain To separate the liquid from the solids by passing through a strainer

Sustainable resources Resources that will not run out

Sweat To cook in fat under a lid without colour

Syneresis The squeezing out of liquid from an overcooked protein and liquid mixture (e.g. scrambled egg, egg custard)

Table d'hôte A meal at a fixed price; a set menu

Tahini A strong-flavoured sesame seed paste

Tartlet A small, round pastry case

Terrine An earthenware dish used for cooking and serving pâté; also used as a name for certain products

Thiamine Vitamin B1; it assists the nervous system; found in yeast, bacon, wholemeal bread

Glossary

Timbale A double serving dish

Tofu Low-fat bean curd made from soybeans

Tourné Turned, shaped in barrels or large olive shapes

Tranche A slice

Trichinosis A disease caused by hair-like worms in the muscles of meat (e.g. pork)

Tronçon A slice of flat fish on the bone (e.g. turbot)

TVP Texturised vegetable protein, derived from soybeans

Variable costs Costs that vary according to the volume of business; includes food and materials costs

Vegan A person who does not eat fish, meat, poultry, game, dairy products, honey and eggs, and who does not use any animal products (e.g. leather)

Vegetarian A person who does not eat meat, poultry or game

Velouté
- A basic sauce
- A soup of velvety or smooth consistency

Viruses Microscopic pathogens that multiply in the living cells of their host

Vitamins Chemical substances that assist the regulation of body processes

Vol-au-vent A large puff pastry case

Wok A round-bottomed pan used extensively in Chinese cooking

Yeast extract A mixture of brewer's yeast and salt, high in flavour and protein

Yield The number of portions obtained from a recipe. It is essential to get the exact number of portions in order to achieve the desired income and the gross profit from the recipe

Yoghurt An easily digested fermented milk product

Index of recipes

alcohol, red wine jus 124
apples, apple sauce 127
artichokes
    bottoms 434–5
    in cream sauce 430
    globe 436
asparagus
    poached duck egg, asparagus, cured ham, grain mustard dressing 148
    soup 99
    tips 437
    wrapped in puff pastry with Gruyère 438
aubergine
    fried 443
    stuffed 443
aurora sauce 116–17
avocado, and bacon salad 471
bacon
    boiled 326
    roasted 329
    terrine of bacon, spinach and mushrooms 339
beans *see* pulses
béarnaise sauce 130
béchamel sauce 112
beef
    bourguignon 302–3
    braised 304–5
    carbonnade 301
    Cornish pasties 309
    goulash 308
    grilled 296
    hamburger, American style 296–7
    Hamburg/Vienna steak 300
    jus 122–3
    roast wing of 312
    silverside, boiled, carrots and dumplings 305
    sirloin, slow-cooked, lyonnaise onions and carrot purée 314
    sirloin steak with red wine 298–9
    steak pie 310–11
    steak pudding 306–7
    stock, brown 86–7
    stroganoff 299
beetroot 399–400
    goats' cheese and beetroot tarts with watercress salad 400
    salad 465
biscuits
    brandy snaps 570
    cats' tongues 568
    cigarette paste cornets 569
    piped 571
    shortbread 572
    sponge fingers 566–7
    tuiles 567
bisques, prawn 111
bread
    bagels 483, 490
    bath buns 493
    blueberry baba 497
    bun dough 491–2
    cholla 484
    club sandwich 489
    doughnuts 494
    focaccia 484–5
    hot cross buns 493
    marignans chantilly 497
    naan 485
    olive 480–1
    parmesan rolls 478
    pitta 487
    pitta, without yeast 488

pizza 486
red onion and sage rolls 478
rye 482
sandwiches 489
savarin dough 495–6
savarin with fruit 497
Scandinavian smorgasbord 489
seeded rolls 477
soda 481
with sundried tomato 479
Swiss buns 494
toasted sandwiches 489
wholemeal 476
wraps 490
broad beans 409
broccoli 406
butter, melted butter sauce 131
butternut squash
    roasted 447
    roasted with cinnamon and ginger 448
    soup 103
cabbage 432
    braised, red 433
cakes
    chocolate gâteau 557
    chocolate genoise sponge 557
    coffee gâteau 556
    cup cakes 559–60
    fresh cream and strawberry gâteau 555
    genoise sponge 554
    lemon drizzle cake 563
    medeleines 561
    rich fruit cake 562–3
    rock cakes 561
    roulade sponge 558
    scones 560
    Swiss roll 559
    Victoria sandwich 553
    see also glazes and decor
carrots
    buttered 398
    in cream sauce 398–9
    purée of 399
cauliflower
    au gratin 407
    boiled 407
celeriac
    buttered 401
    purée of 402
celery, spinach and celery cream soup 100
Chasseur sauce 117
cheese
    cheese (mornay) sauce 113
    fritters 459
    goats' cheese and beetroot tarts with watercress salad 400
    lentil and goats' cheese salad 169
    macaroni cheese 183
    soufflé 460
    straws 531
chicken
    à la king 364
    braised leg forestière 361
    confit leg with leeks and artichokes 366
    crumbed breast with asparagus 355
    deep-fried 358
    fricassée of 363
    fried, with spinach and spices 357
    grilled 360
    Kiev 358–9
    paella 356–7
    pie 369–70

poached suprême, Madeira and mushroom café cream sauce 365
    in red wine 368
    roast, with dressing 367
    roast chicken jus 123
    salad 336
    sauté chasseur 354–5
    soup 98
    spatchcock 359
    steamed ballotine with herb stuffing and red wine jus 362
    stock, white 87
    tandoori 370
    terrine, with vegetables 376
chicory
    braised 439
    shallow-fried 439
chocolate
    ganache 542
    mousse 588
    sauce 622–3
    sorbet 595
clear soup 110–11
cold meat
    chicken salad 336
    raised pork pie 337
    terrine of bacon, spinach and mushrooms 339
    veal and ham pie 338
coleslaw 466
consommé 110–11
corn on the cob 411
courgettes
    deep-fried 445
    fettuccine with chopped basil and balsamic vinegar 446
    flowers 446–7
    shallow-fried 445
couscous
    fritters with feta 171
    with meat and vegetables 170
    salad, roasted vegetables and mixed herbs 172
cranberry sauce 128
croutons 97
cucumber 463
curry
    biryani 454
    gravy 127
    sauce 455
    Thai-style Quorn and vegetable curry 458
desserts
    cold
        baked blueberry cheesecake 591
        bavarois 587
        chocolate mousse 588
        crème brûlée 583
        crème caramel 585
        fruit fool 592
        fruit mousse 586
        lime and mascarpone cheesecake 584–5
        lime soufflé frappe 593
        meringue 590
        trifle 594
        vacherin with strawberries and cream 590–1
        vanilla panna cotta with stewed rhubarb 589
        zabaglione (sabayon with Marsala) 584
    hot
        apple charlotte 600–1
        apple crumble tartlets 610
        apple fritters 601
        baked Alaska 615

Index of recipes

baked apples 602
baked rice pudding 604
bread and butter pudding 609
cabinet pudding 605
chocolate fondant 606–7
Christmas pudding 614
golden syrup pudding 613
griottines clafoutis 603
lemon curd flourless soufflé 618
pancakes with apple 602
rice pudding 608
soufflé pudding 606
steamed sponge pudding 612
sticky toffee pudding 604–5
tart tatin 611
vanilla soufflé 616–17
iced
   apple sorbet 595
   chocolate sorbet 595
   lemon curd ice cream 596–7
   peach melba 598
   pear belle Hélène 598
   raspberry parfait 599
   vanilla ice cream 596–7
see also cakes
desserts (cold)
   fruit salad 581
   poached fruits 582
devilled sauce 118
dough, pasta 178
dressings
   cranberry and orange 375
   mustard 148
   sage and onion 328, 375
duck
   breast steaks with cherries 372
   confit leg with red cabbage and green beans 373
   eggs 147–8
   roast 374
dumplings 305
eggs
   Benedict 140
   duck 147–8
   en cocotte 139
   feta, mint, lentil and pistachio omelette 146
   fried 139
   frittata with sweetcorn and beans 147
   hard boiled 138
   omelette 144
   poached duck egg, asparagus, cured ham, grain mustard dressing 148
   poached quail eggs, smoked haddock chowder 149
   quail 141
   Scotch 142–3
   scrambled 138
   soft boiled 137
   Spanish omelette 145
   sur le plat 142
fennel, braised, with black olives and cardamom 404
fish
   barramundi, with garlic, ginger, lemon butter and pak choi 240
   brill, poached 216
   cod
      baked, herb crust 222
      boulangère 224
      poached 216
   deep-fried 231
      coated with breadcrumbs 231
      frying batters 230
   fillets
      grilled 212
      mornay 219

      Véronique 220
      in white wine sauce 218
   fishcakes
      salmon 232–3
      Thai 241
   flat, white, délice of flat white fish Dugléré 217
   haddock 212
      chowder 149
      poached, smoked 215
   hake, baked, tomatoes and olives 223
   halibut
      poached 216
      steamed, with lime and fennel 228
   herring, soused 252
   kedgeree 221
   mackerel
      grilled, tomatoes, basil and shaved fennel 212–13
      soused 252
   meunière 236
   oysters 248–9
   pie 225
   plaice 212
      goujons 232
   poached 215–16
   red mullet, with baby leeks 239
   salad 250
   salmon
      cold 249–50
      en papillote, with crushed new potatoes 226–7
      fishcakes 232–3
      poached 215
      smoked 248
   sardines, with tapenade 214
   sea bass, ceviche 251
   shallow-fried 234
   skate, pan-fried, capers and *beurre noir* 238
   sole 212
      grilled, with traditional accompaniments 213
      pan-fried, rocket and broad beans 237
      shrimp and caper dressing 235
      steamed, with garlic, spring onions and ginger 227
   stock 88
   Thai fishcakes 241
   tuna, grilled, rocket and fennel salad 211
   turbot, poached 216
   see also shellfish
forcemeat, gratin 294
French bean, salad 468
French beans 410
frittata with sweetcorn and beans 147
fruit
   fool 592
   mousse 586
   poached 582
   puddings, steamed 525–6
   salad 581
   tart 513–14
   see also pastry
game
   grouse, roast 380
   hare, German-style saddle 384
   partridge, roast 379
   pigeon, pot au feu 378–9
   quail
      pot-roasted, roast carrots and mashed potato 381
      stuffed, roasted 382
   rabbit, braised baron with olives and tomatoes 383
   venison
      medallions, with buttered cabbage and haricots blancs 385
      medallions, with celeriac purée and braised red cabbage 386

gazpacho 105
glazes and decor
   apricot glaze 564
   marzipan 565
   praline 566
   royal icing 565
   water icing 564
gnocchi
   Parmesan gnocchi with tomato sauce 191
   potato gnocchi 190
goose, roast 377
grains
   couscous, meat and vegetables 170
   couscous, roasted vegetables 172
   couscous fritters with feta 171
   crisp polenta and roasted Mediterranean vegetables 167
   polenta and lentil cakes, roasted vegetables, cucumber and yoghurt sauce 168
gravy
   roast gravy 125
   thickened 126
gribiche sauce 133
grouse, roast 380
guinea fowl, suprême, with pepper and basil coulis 377
ham hocks 325
hare, German-style saddle 384
hollandaise sauce 129
horseradish sauce 132
Italian sauce 121
ivory sauce 116
Jerusalem artichokes see artichokes
kohlrabi 440
lamb
   best end with breadcrumbs and parsley 292
   braised chump chop 286
   braised shanks 287
   grilled cutlets 280
   grilled loin chops 282
   hot pot 288
   Irish stew 290
   jus 89–90
   kebabs 281
   noisettes with baby ratatouille 283
   pot-roast shoulder with gratin forcemeat 294
   roast leg with mint, lemon and cumin 291
   roast saddle with rosemary mash 292
   rosettes with thyme and blueberries 282
   samosas 284–5
   satay 279
   shepherd's pie 295
   slow-cooked shoulder with potatoes boulangère 293
   stew, brown 289
   valentine steaks with hummus 283
leeks
   braised, with garlic and olives 404–5
   chilled leek and potato soup 104–5
lentils, lentil and goats' cheese salad 169
liver, pâté 335
Madeira sauce 120
mangetout 409
marrow 444
   provençale 444
meat
   mixed grill 280–1
   see also cold meat; meats by name
mincemeat 519
minestrone soup 92
mushrooms
   braised rice with mushrooms 160
   Greek-style 469
   grilled 408

631

sauce 115
soup 96
stuffed 408
terrine of bacon, spinach and mushrooms 339
mustard dressing 148
mutton
   hot pot 288
   stew, brown 289
offal
   beef's cheek in red wine 333
   calf's cheeks with vegetables 332
   calf's liver and bacon 330
   lamb's kidneys, devilled 331
   lamb's kidneys, grilled 331
   lamb's sweetbreads, shallow-fried 334
okra
   in cream sauce 412
   curry 412–13
omelettes 144–6
onions
   button, caramelised 403
   French-fried 405–6
   fried 403
   soup, brown 91
paella 356–7
parsley sauce 113
parsnips 401
   purée of 402
partridge, roast 379
pasta
   dough 178
   lasagne 186–7
   lasagne, vegetarian 188
   macaroni cheese 183
   penne arrabiata 181
   ravioli 182–3
   ravioli, squash and spinach, wild mushroom sauce 185
   ricotta and spinach cannelloni, tomato and basil sauce 189
   spaghetti bolognaise 180–1
   spaghetti with tomato sauce 179
   spinach fettuccine, ham and cream cheese 184
   tagliatelle carbonara 184
pastry
   apple flan 515
   apple turnovers 537
   Bakewell tart 518
   cheese straws 531
   chocolate éclairs 522–3
   choux paste 520–1
   choux paste fritters 524
   cream buns 521
   cream horns 536
   Eccles cakes 537
   egg custard tart 514
   fillings
      apple purée 544
      boiled buttercream 540
      buttercream 539
      chantilly cream 539
      cream 538
      frangipane 541
      ganache 542
      Italian meringue 543
      stock syrup 545
      Swiss meringue 544
   flan cases 512
   fruit pie 510
   fruit slice 535
   fruit tart 513–14
   gâteau Paris-Brest 523
   gâteau pithiviers 532
   inverted puff pastry 528–9

lemon meringue pie 516
lemon tart 517
mince pies 519
palmiers 533
pear and almond tart 516–17
pear jalousie 534
profiteroles and chocolate sauce 522
puff cases 530
puff paste 526–8
puff pastry slice 534–5
quiche lorraine 508–9
rough puff paste 529–30
sausage rolls 531
short paste 507–8
steamed fruit puddings 525–6
suet paste 525
sugar paste 511–12
treacle tart 509
pâté, liver 335
peas
   French-style 410–11
   green pea, cream soup 94
pepper sauce 122
peppers, stuffed 449
pies
   chicken 369–70
   fruit 509
   pork 337
   steak 310–11
   veal and ham 338
   see also pastry
pigeon, pot au feu 378–9
piquant sauce 119
pizza, bread 486
polenta
   crisp polenta and roasted Mediterranean vegetables 167
   and lentil cakes with roasted vegetables, cucumber and yoghurt sauce 168
pork
   bacon, boiled 326
   bacon, roasted 329
   belly, roasted with shallots and champ potatoes 328
   belly, slow-roasted 328
   escalope with calvados sauce 321
   fillet, stir-fried 323
   leg, roasted 326
   pie 337
   sauerkraut, ham hocks and lentils 323–5
   spare ribs in barbeque sauce 329
   sweet and sour 322
potatoes
   with bacon and onions 429
   baked, in jackets 417
   boiled 413
   boulangère 293
   Byron 427
   chateau 418
   cocotte 423
   cooked in milk with cheese 428
   croquette 427
   delmonico 430
   duchess 416
   fondant 424
   fried or chipped 419
   Macaire (potato cakes) 426
   mashed 415
   new 414
   new potato rissoles 422
   noisette 423
   parmentier 422
   parsley 413
   potato and watercress soup 104

roast 418
salad 466–7
sauté 420
sauté with onions 421
savoury 425
steamed, in jackets 417
Swiss cakes 428
potatoes, soup 102–3
poultry *see* birds by name
prawns, bisque 111
pulses
   bean goulash 165
   butter beans, carrot and butter bean soup 108
   haricot bean salad 469
   lentil and goats' cheese salad 169
   Mexican bean pot 166
   red lentil soup 102
   soup with croutons 97
   three-bean salad 470
pumpkin
   roasted with cinnamon and ginger 448
   velouté 109
quail
   poached quail eggs, smoked haddock chowder 149
   pot-roasted, roast carrots and mashed potato 381
   Scotch eggs 141
   stuffed, roasted 382
Quorn, Thai-style Quorn and vegetable curry 458
rabbit, braised baron with olives and tomatoes 383
radishes 463
red wine jus 124
reduced-fat recipes, béchamel sauce 112
rice
   Asian rice salad 164
   boiled 158
   braised with mushrooms 160
   brown 162
   brown rice salad 163
   Indian-style (pilau) 161
   pilaff 159, 455
   risotto with Parmesan 160–1
   salad 162
   steamed 158
Robert sauce 118–19
salads
   Asian rice salad 164
   avocado and bacon 471
   beetroot 465
   brown rice salad 163
   Caesar 470
   chicken 336
   coleslaw 466
   couscous, roasted vegetables 172
   cucumber 463
   French 462
   French bean 468
   green 462
   haricot bean 469
   leaves 461
   lentil and goats' cheese salad 169
   mixed 461
   Niçoise 471
   potato 466–7
   radishes 463
   Russian 468
   three-bean 470
   tomato and cucumber 465
   tomato 464
   Waldorf 467
salsa verde 131
salsify 402
samosas 284–5
sauces (savoury)

Index of recipes

apple 127
aurora 116–17
béarnaise 130
béchamel 112
beef jus 122–3
bread 380
brown onion 120
Chasseur 117
cheese (mornay) 113
cranberry 128
curry 455
curry gravy 127
devilled 118
gribiche 133
hollandaise 129
horseradish 132
Italian 121
ivory 116
Madeira 120
melted butter 131
mushroom 115
parsley 113
pepper 122
piquant 119
red wine jus 124
reduced-fat béchamel 112
roast chicken jus 123
roast gravy 125
Robert sauce 118–19
salsa verde 131
soubise 114
suprême 114–5
sweet and sour 132
thickened gravy 126
tomato 128
white 112
sauces (sweet)
  butterscotch 623
  caramel 624
  chocolate 622–3
  custard 621
  egg custard 620
  fruit coulis 621
  rum or brandy cream 624
  sabayon 619
  strawberry 622
sauerkraut, ham hocks and lentils 323–5
savarin
  dough 495–6
  with fruit 497
  marignans chantilly 497
  syrup 495
Scotch broth 93
Scotch eggs 142–3
seafood
  paella 356–7
  prawn bisque 111
shellfish
  clams
    chowder 243

    steamed, saffron and spring green broth 229
  cocktail 252
  crab
    crabcakes, chilli lime dipping sauce 244
    dressed 247
  fruits de mer 254
  mussels, in white wine sauce 242
  prawns, with chilli and garlic 245
  scallops, and bacon 246
  shrimps, potted 253
soubise 114
soups
  asparagus 99
  brown onion 91
  carrot and butter bean 108
  chicken 98
  chilled leek and potato 104–5
  clear 110–11
  cream of green pea 94
  cream of spinach and celery 100
  cream of tomato 95
  cream of vegetables 100–1
  gazpacho 105
  minestrone 92
  mushroom 96
  pea velouté 109
  potato 102–3
  potato and watercress soup 104
  pulse, with croutons 97
  pumpkin velouté 109
  red lentil 102
  roasted butternut squash 103
  roasted red pepper and tomato 107
  Scotch broth 93
  vegetable purée 101
soya products, papaya and soya bean salad 457
Spanish omelette 145
spinach 431
  and celery cream soup 100
  fettuccine, ham and cream cheese 184
  purée 432
  ricotta and spinach cannelloni, tomato and basil sauce 189
spring greens 431
sprouts, Brussels 434
stocks
  brown 86–7
  brown vegetable 89
  fish 88
  lamb jus 89–90
  reduced veal 90
  white 86
  white chicken 87
  white vegetable 88
suprême sauce 114–15
swede
  buttered 401
  purée of 402
sweet and sour sauce 132
sweetbreads, shallow-fried lamb's sweetbreads 334

sweetcorn, corn on the cob 411
tapenade 214
tofu, crispy deep-fried tofu 456
tomatoes
  concassé 440–1
  cream soup 95
  and cucumber salad 465
  roasted red pepper and tomato soup 107
  salad 464
  stuffed 442
  tomato sauce 128
turkey
  escalopes 372
  roast 371
turnips
  buttered 401
  purée of 402
veal
  braised shin 320
  breadcrumbed escalope with ham and cheese 316
  escalope 315
  escalope with Parma ham and mozzarella cheese 317
  fricassée of 318–19
  reduced stock 90
  veal and ham pie 338
vegetables
  biryani 454
  cream soup 100–1
  curry, with rice pilaff 455
  mixed 450
  purée soup 101
  ratatouille 450–1
  ratatouille pancakes with cheese sauce 451
  roasted 452
  Russian salad 468
  stock
    brown 86–7
    white 86
  tempura 452–3
  see also salads; vegetables by name
vegetarian recipes
  cheese fritters 459
  cheese soufflé 460
  Chinese vegetables and seitan stir-fry 456–7
  crispy deep-fried tofu 456
  lasagne 188
  papaya and soya bean salad 457
  potato samosas 284–5
  Thai-style Quorn and vegetable curry 458
venison
  with buttered cabbage and haricots blancs 385
  with celeriac purée and braised red cabbage 386
vichyssoise 104–5
watercress and potato soup 104
Yorkshire pudding 313

Index

accidents 71, 73
    reporting 76
    see also health and safety
accompaniments, for soups 82
acid foods, and bacteria 45
aduki beans 152
aerobes 45
agar-agar 578
agnolini 174
alcohol, in sauces 84
alkaline foods, and bacteria 45
allergies
    allergen information 7, 36–7
    allergic reaction 35–6
    anaphylactic shock 36
    bread 475
    nuts 9
    safeguards 9
American aromatic rice 151
amuse-bouche 82
anaerobes 45
anaphylactic shock 36
ants 40
appraisals 61
apprentice 54
aprons 30
arborio rice 150
aromatic rice 151
aromats 81
arrowroot 85
Asian cuisine 3
atmospheric steamer 21
Bacillus cereus 34
bacteria
    danger zone 44, 47
    high-risk foods 44
    oxygen requirements 45
    pathogenic 34
    spores 35
    and temperature 44–5, 47–8
    time factors 45
    toxins 35
    unsafe behaviour 32
    see also handling food; health and safety
bains-marie 22
baking powder 501, 547
baking sheet 16
baking tin 16
barley 154
basmati 151
beef 264
    butchery 264–5
    cooking 268
    cuts of 265–8
    grilled 268–9
    hearts 276
    liver 275
    preparing 265–6
best-before dates 43
beurre fondu 84
beurre manié 85
beurre noisette 83
biological contamination 34
birds 40

biscuits 550–2
bisque 81
bitter taste 3
black beans 152
black-eyed beans 152
blanching 393
blenders 18
blending, soups 82
blinis 473
blond roux 84
blow torch 17
blue peas 153
blue warning signs 72
boiling pans 21
bone marrow 277
boning 14
    lamb 261
    pork 273
    poultry 348
    veal 271
boning knife 10
borlotti beans 152
'botulinum cook' 45
bouillabaisse 81
bouillon 79
bowls 17
braising 394
bran 154
brasserie, kitchen organisation 55
bratt pans 21
bread 472
    allergies 475
    bulk fermentation 474–5
    presentation 475
    yeast 472–3
    see also dough
brioche 473
brisket 264–5
British winkles 209
broad beans 152
broiler chickens 341
broth 80
brown (espagnole) sauce 83
brown rice 150
brown roux 84
brunoise vegetables 392
buckwheat 154
bulgar wheat 156
burns 32, 73, 76
business
    fixed costs 63–4
    gross profit 64
    labour costs 63–4
    menu costing 63–6
    net profit 64
    overheads 63
    selling price 65
    variable costs 63–4
butcher's saw 10–11
butchery
    beef 264–5
    lamb 260
    pork 272
butter 500

beurre fondu 84
beurre noisette 83
    as a sauce 83–4
butter as, clarified 83
butter beans 152
cake margarine 500
cakes
    blending method 547
    decoration 551
    faults in 548–9
    fillings 551
    flour batter method 547
    preparation methods 546–8
    sponges 548–50
    storing 551–2
    sugar batter method 546
calf's
    hearts 276
    liver 275
calibrating probes 47
calories *see* kilocalories (kcals)
Campylobacter 35
can opener 17
cancer, and obesity 4
candling eggs 135
canned products 42–3
cannellini beans 152
cannelloni 174
canning
    fish 195
    meat 257
capons 341
cappelletti 174
carbohydrates 4
    and healthy diet 4–5
    starchy foods 5
    sugars 5
carbon offsetting 66
carob gum 578
carrageenan 579
carving 14
    lamb 263
carving knife and fork 10
ceilings 37
cereals
    cooking 156
    grains 154–5
    millet 155–6
    oats 155
    quinoa 156
    rye 156
    spelt 156
    storing 157
    wheat 156
challenges, in the workplace 59
chapatti 473
Chateaubriand 266, 267
chef de partie 54
chef jacket 30
chemical contamination 35
chewing gum 32
chicken 341–2
    ballotine 346
    cutting 343–4

634

Index

spatchcock 344
stock 79
suprêmes 345
trussing 342–3
chickpeas 153
children, and obesity 5
chill rooms 23
Chinese cuisine 3
chinois 17
chopping 14
chopping boards *see* cutting: surfaces
chopping knife 10
chops, lamb 262
chowder 81
clarified butter 83
cleaning
    bains-marie 22
    cloths 38–9
    deep fat fryers 22
    and food safety 38
    freezers 24
    grills 22
    hobs 20
    knives 13
    ovens 20
    products 38
    refrigerators 23, 42
    steamers 21
    surfaces 39
    work areas 33
Clostridium botulinum 34
Clostridium perfringens 34
cockles 208
cockroaches 40
colander 17
collagen 258–9
colour, of food 3
colour-coded chopping boards 46
    see also cutting: surfaces
combination oven 20
commis chef 54
communication 55, 58–9
composting waste 68
compound butter sauces 84
concassé 393
condiments 8
consommé 111
contaminated food 29, 34
    see also food: safety
contamination
    biological 34
    chemical 35
    physical 35
continental roux 84
Control of Substances Hazardous to Health (COSHH) Regulations (2002) 72–3
convection oven 20
convenience stocks 80
cooked foods
    cooling/chilling 47
    storing 43
cooking
    to control bacteria 47
    eggs 136
    fish 200–3
    game 350

for healthy diet 6–7
    meat 258–9, 268
    pasta 174–6
    pasty 506
    potatoes 394
    poultry 341
    shellfish 204–9
    vegetables 393–4
    see also equipment; recipe index
cooling rack 17
corical strainer 17
coring 14
corn 154–5
cornflour 85
cornmeal 154
costing menu items 63–6
couscous 156
crab 207–8
crawfish 207
crayfish 205
cream 80, 503–4, 577
    piping 506
creaming 505
crème anglaise 575
crème St Germain 80
crépinettes 278
croissants 473
cross-contamination 13, 46
croutons 81
crushing 14
crustaceans 204
cuisine
    Asian 3
    Chinese 3
customer feedback 26
cutlet bats 17
cutlets 263
cuts 32, 73
cutting
    equipment 10–11
    surfaces 12, 19, 46
dairy
    and healthy diet 5
    storage of 42
dairy free diet 8
damaged equipment 37–8
Danish pastries 473
deep fat fryers 22
defrosting food 42, 44, 47
demersal fish 193
demi-glace 83
desserts
    egg custard-based 575–9
    fruit-based 579
    and healthy eating 579–80
    ice cream 576–8
    ingredients 574–6
    presentation 579
    sorbets 576–8
    stabilisers 578–9
detergent 38
dextrinisation 84
dhal 153
diabetes 4
    diabetic diet 8
diarrhoea 76

dicing 14
diet *see* healthy diet; medical diets; religious diets; special diets
discrimination 58
dishwashing
    automatic 39
    by hand 39
disinfectant 38
disposable gloves 31
diversity 58
dolcelatte 176
domestic pets 40
doors 37
dough
    fermentation 472–3
    laminated 473
    quality points 473–4
    speciality 473
    storing 474
    types of 473
    see also bread
Dover sole, preparing 199
drainage 37
dressings 8
dry goods, storage 41, 42
dual steamer 21
Dublin Bay prawns 205
duck 348
due diligence 50
Dutch brown beans 152
E. coli 0157 35
easy-cook rice 151
Eatwell Guide 5
eggs 502, 574–5
    candling 135
    cooking 136
    egg custard 575–6
    'Lion' quality mark 135
    purchasing 135
    quality grading 135
    sabayon 85
    Salmonella 135
    sizes 135
    storing 42, 136
    structure 134
    temperatures for 136
    as thickening agent 85
    types of 135
    whites 134
    yolks 85, 134, 577
electric shock 72
electricity 72
Electricity at Work Regulations 1989 72
electronic fly killer (EFK) 40–1
electronic systems 59
emergencies 73
energy 4
energy audits 70
entrecôte 267
environment 37
Environmental Health Officers (EHOs) 48, 50–1
equality 58
equipment
    bains-marie 22
    damaged 37–8
    deep fat fryers 22

freezers 24
grills 22
hot cupboards 23
knives 10–11
large 19–20
lifting and handling 74
ovens and hobs 19–20
pans 21
proving cabinets 23
refrigerators 23, 41–2
small 16–19
steamers 21
vacuum packaging machine 23
water baths 23–4
EU Food Information for Consumers (EU FIC) 2014 7
executive head chef 54
Facebook 2
facultative anaerobes 45
fat 4
   and healthy diet 4–5
   and pastry work 500
fax messaging 59
feather steaks 268
feedback
   from customers 26
   evaluating performance 60–1
   via social media 2
fillet
   beef 264–6
   steak 267
fillet mignon 266, 268
filleting 14
   fish 197–9
filleting knife 10
fingernails 31
fire safety 74–5
first aid 73
fish
   canning 195
   coating 197
   cooking 200–3
   cuts of 199–200
   demersal 193
   filleting 197–9
   fillets 193
   frozen 193, 195
   gutting 196
   healthy options 5, 204
   marinating 197
   oily 193
   overfishing 193
   pickling 195
   portion control 200
   preparation 196
   preservation 195
   quality points 193–4
   salting 195
   seasonality 193–4
   skinning 197
   smoked 193
   smoking 195–6
   storing 42, 194–5
   types of 192–3
   white 193
   whole 193
fish slice 17

fixed costs 63–4
flageolet beans 152
flan rings 17
flank, beef 264–5
flavour profile 3
flies 40–1
floors 37, 71
flour
   adding fat to 505
   buckwheat 154
   millet 156
   refined corn starch 155
   storing 157, 499
   types of 499
   wheat 156, 499
food
   allergy *see* allergies
   colour of 3
   contaminated 29, 34
   costing 63–6
   defrosting 42, 44, 47
   frozen *see* frozen foods
   handling 30, 37, 45–6
   holding for service 47
   intolerance 36
   labels 2, 7, 43
   leftovers 68
   poisoning 29, 34, 44
   portion control 25, 68
   preservation 43, 44
   provenance 1
   purchasing 24, 66–7
   regional 1
   reheating 47
   safety 3, 29–51
     see also health and safety
   seasonal calendar 1
   spoilage 43
   stock control 24–5
   storage *see* storage
   suppliers 67
   supply chain 66
   sustainability 66, 69–70
   temperature *see* temperature
   see also cooking
Food Hygiene (England/Wales/Scotland/Northern Ireland, as applicable) Regulations 2006 29
food miles 66
food mixers 17
food processors 17
food production control 24
Food Safety Act 1990 29
Food Standards Agency 48, 50, 51
food-borne illness 35
footwear 30
fowl 340–1
   see also poultry
Freedom Foods 1
freezers 24
   and bacteria 44
   defrosting food 42, 44, 47
frozen foods
   defrosting 42
   fish 193, 195
fruit
   conserving 23

   and healthy diet 5
   storing 42, 579
fruitarian 8
frying pan 16
   see also deep fat fryers
ful mesdames 152
game 348
   birds 350–1
   cooking 350
   hare and rabbits 351
   seasonality 349
   storing and hanging 350
   venison 351–3
   wild boar 353
gammon 274–5
gas 72
gastronome tray 16
gazpacho 81, 83
geese 348
gelatine 578
genetically modified (GM) foods 1
glazes 80
glazing, pastry 505–6
gloves 31
glucose 500
gluten 475, 499
gluten-free diet 8
gorgonzola 176
grains
   barley 154
   bran 154
   buckwheat 154
   cooking 156
   corn 154–5
graters 18
gravies 83
gravity-fed slicers 18
grazes 32
green lentils 153
green safety signs 72
griddle pan 16
griddling 259
grilling, beef 268–9
grills 22
gross profit 64
grouse 350
guar gum 579
hair 31
halal meat 257
hand washing 31
handling food 30, 37, 45–6
hanger steak 268
hare 351
haricot beans 152
hats 30
Hazard Analysis Critical Control Points (HACCP) 49–50
hazardous substances 72–3
hazards 34, 45, 48–50, 70–6
   warning signs 71–2
head chef 54
health and safety
   accidents 71, 72, 76
   cross-contamination 13, 46
   due diligence 50
   emergencies 73
   fire safety 74–5

Index

food safety 3, 13, 29–51
  handling food 30, 37, 45–6
  hazards 34, 45, 48–50, 70–6
  inspections 50–1
  knives 12
  legislation 29, 70–6
  manual handling 74
  non-compliance notices 51
  protective clothing 30–1
  risk assessment 49–50
  risks 45, 71
  security 75–6
  slips, trips and falls 71
Health and Safety at Work Act 1974 70–1
Health and Safety Executive (HSE) 70
Health and Safety (First Aid) Regulations 1981 73
Health and Safety Information for Employees Regulations 1989 71
healthy diet 6
  carbohydrates 4
  cooking techniques 6–7
  Eatwell Guide 5
  fat 4
  fruit and vegetables 5
  importance of 4–5
  protein 4
  salt 4
  soups 82–3
  vitamins and minerals 4
heart disease 4
hearts 276
heavy lifting 74
herbs 3, 81
high blood pressure 4
Hindu diet 8
hobs 20
holding for service 47
honey 501
hot cupboards 23
hotel kitchen 55
hygiene
  personal 30–2
  work areas 33
Hygiene Emergency Prohibition Notice 51
Hygiene Improvement Notice 51
Hygiene Prohibition Order 51
ice cream 576–8
illness
  food-borne 35
  reporting 76
  see also food: poisoning
Indian brown lentils 153
induction hobs 20
infections 32, 76
ingredients
  costing 63–6
  local 1
  measuring 81
  pastry work 498–504
  quality of 81
insects 40–1
instructions, types of 56
inverted sugar 500
irradiated foods 1
isomalt 501
japonica rice 151
jasmine rice 151

jewellery 31
Jewish diet 8
job roles 54–5
jointing 14
julienne vegetables 392
jumbo oat flakes 155
jus rôti 83
jus-lié 83
kidneys 276
kilocalories (kcals) 4
kilojoules (kj) 4
king prawns 205
kitchen
  efficiency 1–2
  hotel 55
  job roles 54–5
  layout 33
  management 2, 54–5
  operations 54–5, 63–6
  staffing structure 55
  workflow 33
Kitchen CUT 2
kitchen scissors 11
knives 9
  cleaning 13
  materials for 11
  parts of 10
  safety 12
  sharpening 12–13
  skills and techniques 14–15
  types of 10
  using 11–12
kosher meat 257
labelling
  allergen information 7
  best-before dates 43
  calorie information 7
  reading and interpreting 7
  software 2
  use-by dates 43
lacto-vegetarian 8
ladles 18
lamb 260–3
  hearts 276
  kidneys 276
  liver 275
leftovers 68
lifting 74
lighting 37
liquidisers 18
listeria 35
Listeria monocytogenes 45
liver 275
lobster 206–7
local ingredients 1
long-grain rice 150
low cholesterol diet 9
low fat diet 9
low residue diet 9
low salt diet 9
Maillard reaction 259
maize 154–5
Management of Health and Safety at Work Regulations 1999 75
mandolins 18
Manual Handling Operations Regulations 1992 74
margarine 500

market trends 26
marking and scoring 15
marrowfat peas 153
mashers 18
mashing potatoes 394
measuring, ingredients 81
measuring jugs 18
meat
  bacon 274
  barbecuing 268
  beef 264–9
  bone marrow 277
  bones 277
  butchery 264
  canning 257
  carving 263
  connective tissue 259
  cooking 258–9, 268
  crépinettes 278
  cuts of 256–7
  forcemeats 277–8
  freezing 257
  gammon 274–5
  griddling 259
  halal 257
  and healthy diet 5
  kosher 257
  lamb 260–3
  Maillard reaction 259
  marbling 256
  mutton 260
  offal 275–7
  pork 271–3
  preparing 257
  preserving 257
  quality points 256–7, 264
  salting 257
  seasoning 268
  storing 42, 257
  structure of 256
  tenderising 258
  veal 269–71
meat cleaver 10–11
medical diets 8–9
menu, costing 63–6
messages, recording 59
mice 40
milk 502
  and healthy diet 5
millet 155–6
mincers 18
minerals, and healthy diet 4
minute steaks 266
mirepoix 81
mise-en-place 2–3
mobile app ordering service 1
moisture, and bacteria 44
molluscs 204
moulds
  equipment 18
  poisonous 35
mouth, and taste 3
mozzarella 176
mung beans 152
mushrooms, equipment 18
Muslim diet 8
mussels 208

mutton 260
mycoprotein 396–7
mycotoxins 35
naan bread 473
nage 79
negative behaviour 58
negative feedback 26
net profit 64
non-stick frying pan 16
non-verbal gestures 59
noodles 177
norovirus 35
nose, and taste 3
nut allergy 9
nutrients
    carbohydrates 4
    fat 4
    minerals 4
    protein 4
    salt 4
    vitamins 4
nutrition *see* healthy diet; nutrients
oatmeal 155
oats 155
obesity 4
offal 275–7
orange lentils 153
osteoporosis 4
ovens 19–20
overfishing 193
overheads 63
ovo-vegetarian 8
ox kidney 276
oxtail 277
oysters 209
packaging, vacuum packaging machine 1
palette knife 10
pans 16, 21
paring knife 10
Parmesan 176
partridge 350
pasta 173
    cooking 174–6
    making 175
    sauces 176
    stuffed 173–4, 176
    types of 173–4
pasteurisation 502, 503
pastry
    brushes 18
    choux 499
    convenience products 504
    cooking 506
    cutting 505
    glazing 505
    handling 505
    ingredients 498–504
    piping cream 506
    puff 499
    rolling 505
    short 499
    suet 499
    sweet 499
    techniques 505
pastry cream 575
pathogenic bacteria 34
pearl barley 154

pecorino 176
pectin 578
peeling 15
personal development 59–60
personal hygiene 30–2
Personal Protective Equipment (PPE) at Work Regulations 1992 30
pests 40–1
pets, domestic 40
pH scale 45
pharynx 3
pheasant 350
pickling, fish 195
pictorial communication 59
pigeon 350–1
pig's
    kidneys 276
    liver 275
    trotters 277
pinto beans 152–3
piping 551
    fresh cream 506
piping bags 18
pitta bread 473
pizza dough 473
poaching, fish 201
poisoning *see* food: poisoning
poisonous foods 35
pokers 19
polenta 154–5
pork
    bacon 274
    belly 273
    butchery 272
    joints and cuts 272–3
Porterhouse steaks 266, 267
portion control 25, 68, 200
pot barley 154
potage 81
potassium bicarbonate 501
potatoes 389
    cooking 394
    mashing 394
    ready-prepared 393
    roasting 395
    storing 390–1
    varieties of 395
    yield 395
poultry 340
    chicken 341–6
    cooking 341
    cutting 343–4
    duck 348
    fowl 340–1
    game birds 350–1
    geese 348
    grouse 350
    partridge 350
    pheasant 350
    pigeon 350–1
    preparing 341, 344–5, 347
    quail 351
    storing 42, 341
    stuffing and tying 346
    trussing 342–3
    tunnel boning 348
    turkey 346–8

poussin 341
prawns 205
preparation, *mise-en-place* 2–3
pressure steamer 21
professional development 26
prohibition signs 72
protective clothing 30–1
protein 4
    coagulation 258
    and healthy diet 4–5
provenance 1, 389
proving cabinets 23
pulses
    beans 152–3
    cooking 153
    lentils 153
    peas 153
    storing 154
    types of 152–3
puree 80, 82
puree-based sauces 83
puy lentils 153
quail 351
quails' eggs 135
quality control 25
quinoa 156
Quorn 397
rabbit 351
rack of lamb 262–3
raising agents 501–2
Rastafarian diet 8
rats 40
ravioli 174
ravolini 174
recycling 70
    see also sustainability
red kidney beans 153
red lentils 153
Red Tractor 1
red warning signs 72
reducing, stock 80
refined corn starch 155
refrigerators 23
    and bacteria 44
    cooling cooked food 47
    multi-use 41–2
    temperature 23, 47
regional food 1
Regulatory Reform (Fire Safety) Order 2005 74–5
reheating food 47
religious diets 8
restaurant
    design 26
    marketing 2
    trends 26
rib
    beef 264–5, 266–7
    pork 273
rib-eye steak 267
rice 150
    cakes 151
    cooking 151–2
    noodles 151
    paper 151
    risotto 152
    storing 152
    structure 150

Index

varieties 150–1
wine 151
ricers 18
ricotta 176
RIDDOR (Reporting of Injuries, Diseases and Dangerous Occurrences Regulations) 2013 76
risk assessment 49–50, 71
see also health and safety
roast gravy 83
roasting tray 16
rolled oats 155
rolling pins 19
round rice 150
roux 84
RSPCA Assured 1
rubbing in 505, 550
rump steak 264–5, 267
rye 156
saddle of lamb 261, 263
salamander 22
salmon, filleting 197
Salmonella 34, 135
salsa 83
salt 575
and healthy diet 4
low salt diet 9
seasoning 3
taste 3
salting
fish 195
meat 257
sanitiser 38
saucepan 16
sauces 8
alcohol in 84
beurre manié 85
brown (espagnole) 83
butter as 83
demi-glace 83
finishing 85
flour 85
gravies 83
roux 84
salsa 83
spice-based 83
thickening 84–5
types of 83–4
velouté 83
white (béchamel) 83
saute pan 16
sauteuse 16
savarin 473
scales 19
scallops 208–9
scampi 205
scissors 11
'Scores on the Doors' 51
scrag-end 261
seasonality 1
fish 193–4
game 349
vegetables 389–90
seasoning 3
secateurs 11
security 75–6
segmenting 15
seitan 397

semolina 156
serrated knives 10
service, efficiency 1–2
sheep's hearts 276
sheep's kidneys 276
shellfish
British winkles 209
cockles 208
cooking 204–9
crab 207–8
crawfish 207
lobster 206–7
mussels 208
oysters 209
ready prepared 209
scallops 208–9
shrimps/prawns 205
storing 204
types of 204
whelks 209
shortening 500
short-grain rice 150
shoulder, pork 273
shredding 15
shrimps 205
sieves 19
signage 71–2
Sikh diet 8
silverside 264–5
simmering 79
sirloin 264–6, 267
skimming, stock 79
skimming spoon 19
skin infections 76
skinning 15
skirt, beef 264–5
slicers 18
slicing 15
smart meters 1
smoked fish 193
smoking 32
fish 195–6
social media 2, 59
sodium chloride 4
see also salt
soissons 153
sorbets 576–8
soups 80–3
accompaniments 82
bisque 81
blending 82
bouillabaisse 81
broth 80
chowder 81
cooking 81
cream 80
finishing 81, 82
gazpacho 81, 83
potage 81
puree 80, 82
straining 82
velouté 81
vichyssoise 81
sour taste 3
sous chef 54
sous-vide 23, 201
soya products 396

soybeans 153
spatchcock chicken 344
spatulas 19
special diets 8
vegan 8
vegetarian 8
spelt 156
spices 3, 83
spider 19
split green peas 153
split yellow peas 153
spoilage 43
spoons 19
spores 35, 47
spring chickens 341
squid 207
stabilisers 578–9
staff
costs 63–4
structure 55
see also job roles
stainless steel tray 16
standard operating procedures (SOPs) 2, 25
Staphylococcus aureus 34
star rating 51
starch 85, 575
starchy foods 5
steamers 21
steaming, vegetables 393
sterilisation (UHT) 502, 503
stewing 261, 393
stir-frying 393
stock
control 2, 24–5
inventory 68
rotation 43, 67
see also storage
stocks 79–80
bouillon 79
consommé 111
convenience 80
glazes 80
ingredients for 79
jus-lié 83
nage 79
reducing 80
storing 80
straining 80
storage
area 41
cakes 551–2
canned products 42–3
cereals 157
cooked foods 43
dairy products 42
dough 474
dry goods 41, 42
eggs 136
fish 42, 194–5
flour 499
food 41
fruit and vegetables 42, 390–1, 579
game 350
meat 257
potatoes 390–1
poultry 341
pulses 154

639

raw meat and poultry 42
rice 152
shellfish 204
stock rotation 67
waste management 67
straight-bladed knives 10
strainers 17
straining
    soups 82
    stock 80
streaky bacon 274
stuffed pasta 173–4, 176
stuffing and tying, poultry 346
suet 277
sugar 500
    and desserts 574
    and healthy diet 5
supply chain 66
surfaces 37–8
    cleaning 39
sustainability 1, 66, 69–70
sweet taste 3
sweetbreads 276–7
tail of fillet 266
taste
    flavour profile 3
    sensation 3
T-bone steaks 266
tea towel 39
teamwork 55, 57–8
technology
    kitchen management 2
    labelling software 2
    mobile app ordering 1
    smart meters 1
    social media 2
telephone 59
temperature
    and bacteria 34–5, 44–5, 47
    cooked foods 43
    dairy products 42
    dishwashing 39
    food held for service 47
    food storage 41–3
    frozen foods 42
    Maillard reaction 259
    probes 19, 47, 268
    proving cabinets 23
    refrigerators 23, 47
    and taste 3
    vacuum packaging machine 23
    water 44
    see also storage
tenderising meat 258
textured vegetable protein (TVP) 396
thawing *see* defrosting food
thickening, sauces 84–5

time management 56
timing, defrosting food 47
tofu 396
tongues 277
tooth decay 4
toppings 8
topside, beef 264–5
tortellini 174
tortelloni 174
tournedos 266, 268
toxins 35, 47
Trade Descriptions Act 1968 7
training
    requirements for 50
    role of technology 2
trays 16
trends 26
trimming 15
tripe 277
trussing, poultry 342–3
trussing needles 19
tunnel boning 348
turbot, filleting 198
turkey 346–8
turning 15
turning knife 10
umami 3
use-by dates 43
vacuum packaging machine 1, 23
variable costs 63–4
veal 269–71
vegan diet 8
vegetable peeler 10
vegetable protein 396
    mycoprotein 396–7
    Quorn 397
    seitan 397
    soya products 396
    textured vegetable protein (TVP) 396
    tofu 396
vegetables 388
    brunoise 392
    bulb 388
    concassé 393
    cooking 393–4
    cutting 391–2
    finishing dishes 395
    flower 388
    fruits of 389
    green 389
    and healthy diet 5
    julienne 392
    leaf 389
    parts of 388–9
    paysanne 393
    pod 389
    preparing 391–2

purchasing 389
quality points 389
root 388, 389
seasonality 389–90
seed 389
serving 396
stem 388
storing 42, 390–1
tuber 389
see also potatoes
vegetarian diet 8
velouté 81, 83
venison 351–3
ventilation 37
vichyssoise 81
vitamins, and healthy diet 4
vomiting 76
walls 37
warning signs 71–2
washing hands 31
wasps 40
waste
    bins 39–40
    calculating wastage 69
    composting 68
    disposal 39–40
    management 67–8
    tracking systems 1
water, and bacteria 44
water baths 23–4
Water Industry Act 1991 39
water vapour 502
weevils 40
weighing, ingredients 81
wheat 156
    flour 499
whelks 209
whisks 19
white (béchamel) sauce 83
white coats 30
white roux 84
wholegrain cereals 154
wholegrain rice 151
wild boar 353
wild rice 151
windows 37
wing rib 266–7
wok 16
workflow 33
working relationships 58–9
    see also communication; teamwork
written communication 59
xanthan gum 155
yeast 472–3, 474
yellow lentils 153
yellow warning signs 71–2
yolks *see* eggs: yolks